Database Mana
Oracle SQL and PL/SQL

Second Edition

Pranab Kumar Das Gupta
Scientist 'F'
Additional Director
Proof & Experimental Establishment
Defence Research & Development Organization

P. Radha Krishna
Principal Research Scientist
Infosys Labs
Infosys Limited

PHI Learning Private Limited
Delhi-110092
2015

₹ 525.00

DATABASE MANAGEMENT SYSTEM, ORACLE SQL AND PL/SQL, Second Edition
Pranab Kumar Das Gupta and P. Radha Krishna

ISBN-978-81-203-4842-4

The export rights of this book are vested solely with the publisher.

Fourth Printing (Second Edition) ... ... **January, 2015**

Published by Asoke K. Ghosh, PHI Learning Private Limited, Rimjhim House, 111, Patparganj Industrial Estate, Delhi-110092 and Printed by Rajkamal Electric Press, Plot No. 2, Phase IV, HSIDC, Kundli-131028, Sonepat, Haryana.

To
our family members
Wife Esha and children Anumita and Aastik
Wife Gayatri and children Niharika and Pranav

To

our family members

Wife Esha and children Anumita and Aastik

Wife Gayatri and children Niharika and Pranav

Contents

Part II
Database Management System: Application Using Oracle PL/SQL

Part III
Database Management System: Advanced Concepts and Technologies

Preface

Database Management System (DBMS) and Oracle need no formal introduction. A majority of the computer-based applications use DBMS and Oracle in some form or the other. DBMS is essentially a part of the curriculum for undergraduate and postgraduate courses in computer science, computer applications, computer science and engineering, information technology and several other branches of engineering. Oracle, on the other hand, has become the de-facto standard in the field of relational database server.

The apparent questions that may arise on the arrival of yet another book on database management system are:

Why one more book on DBMS?

Why should one buy this book?

Database-related books can be classified based on volume, precision, theory and applications. Most of the books written on database are very voluminous and focus only on theory, while other similar books primarily concentrate on programming. Other books on the subject are too precise and target specific readers. This edition presents a balanced approach on the subject in terms of volume, precision, theory and programming concepts. It caters to the need of all categories of readers. The uniqueness of the book lies in the fact that it gradually develops the subject without demanding prior knowledge of DBMS and Oracle. This book will serve the purpose of a textbook on DBMS and Oracle at the undergraduate and postgraduate levels related to computer science, information technology and management (BCA, MCA, BBA, MBA, BE, B.Tech, M.Tech, etc). Practicing professionals will be able to use this book as a ready reference. The unique feature of this book lies in the fact that both groups will get a feeling that it is specially written for them.

In this book, equal importance has been given to the theoretical and practical aspects related to DBMS, so that students can take on both written exams and viva voce/campus interview with confidence. Difficult to understand topics such as normalization, relational algebra, query processing, index file organization, hashing, distributed architecture, concurrency control, triggers, cursors, Oracle architecture, data warehousing, OLAP, data mining and so on are explained lucidly using real-life examples. A large number of examples, objective questions and exercises (with sufficient hints and solutions) are included in the book. Simple illustrations, precision and to-the-point approach to elaborate various intricate topics are the key features of the book.

The first edition of this book contained 10 chapters. The wide acceptance and feedbacks from readers encouraged us to write the second edition of the book. The second edition of the book contains additional eight chapters. Most of the universities and engineering colleges have included data warehousing and data mining as part of their DBMS syllabus. In this edition, four new chapters on these topics are incorporated. Based on the desire of students to include advanced concepts related to PL/SQL programming, four new chapters are included in the book. The second edition of the book contains about 800 examples, practice questions and workouts, which are almost double compared to the first edition. The book is organized into three parts for better understanding of DBMS and programming concepts.

Part I consists of Chapter 1–4. Chapter 1 starts with the basics related to database management system, software development life cycle, data flow diagram and entity relationship model. Chapter 2 discusses relational database and concepts related to various normal forms. Theoretical concepts learnt in Chapters 1 and 2 are put into practice in Chapters 3 and 4. SQL basics, group functions and subquery are explained in Chapter 3, whereas data manipulation language, views, sequence, synonym, index, constraints, privileges, roles, profile and password–related topics are covered in Chapter 4.

Part II comprises Chapter 5–12. In this part, basic and advanced concepts of Oracle PL/SQL programming are explained. Chapters 5 and 6 elaborate PL/SQL basics, functions, procedures and packages. Concepts related to PL/SQL such as exception handler, database trigger, implicit, explicit and advanced cursors are explained in Chapters 7–9. Chapters 10–12 exclusively deal with advanced concepts related to PL/SQL.In Chapter 10, associative arrays, nested tables and collection methods are explained using suitable examples. In Chapter 11, objects in PL/SQL and dynamic SQL are elaborated. PL/SQL performance tuning, Oracle optimization parameter and cost-based optimizer are discussed in Chapter 12, which are essentially required to ensure fast execution of PL/SQL centric software.

Part III includes Chapters 13–18 and elaborates advanced database concepts. Chapter 13 delves into query optimization, index file organization, hashing and distributed architecture. Chapter 14 is devoted to explain Codd's rule, transaction processing, concurrency control, backup and recovery and Oracle architecture. Chapter 15 is related to data warehousing. In this chapter, architecture components of a data warehouse and ETL processes are discussed. OLAP and materialized view related concepts are illustrated in Chapter 16. Chapter 17 gives an overview of data mining. In this chapter, key processes related to knowledge discovery, predictive and descriptive data mining tasks, association rules, classification and clustering are explained using suitable examples. Data mining techniques are discussed in Chapter 18. In this chapter, Apriori algorithm, *k*-NN, Naïve Bayes classification, decision trees, K-means algorithm, agglomerative hierarchical clustering and practical use of data mining techniques through case studies are discussed.

All the chapters contain a large number of examples. To further enforce the concepts, numerous objective type questions and workouts are provided at the end of each chapter. Appendix A presents recent advances in the field of databases and Appendix B provides solutions to the practice questions and workouts.

DBMS–based applications using Oracle find wide use and industry is consistently looking for competent professionals. There exists a gap between software industry demand and skill set of available workforce. This book will work as ready reckoner for the aspirants who want to gain expertise in both DBMS and Oracle in a short span of time.

Teaching Aid Material for all the 18 chapters is provided in the website of PHI Learning, which can be used by faculties/teachers for delivering lectures. Visit www.phindia.com/gupta to refer the contents.

Author invites your valuable feedback and suggestions on the book: pkdasgupta@gmail.com pisipati.radhakrishna@gmail.com.

Pranab Kumar Das Gupta
P. Radha Krishna

Acknowledgements

In the course of publication we have received help from friends, colleagues and PHI Learning. We express sincere gratitude to all of them.

We are indebted to Mr. Avinash Chander, SA to RM, Mr. S. Sundaresh, CC (ACE & SI) and Mr. R. Appavuraj, Director PXE for their kind support. Their encouragement was the greatest motivational factor for us to complete this tough assignment. We are thankful to Ms. Bagmi Mohapatra and Mr. Rajesh for their valuable inputs.

We express our heartfelt gratitude to editorial and production teams of PHI Learning for their dynamism towards publishing the book in such a short span of time.

Last but not least, we express sincere thanks to our family members whose moral support encouraged us to complete the book.

Pranab Kumar Das Gupta
P. Radha Krishna

Part I

Database Management System

Basic Concepts and Oracle SQL

Database Basics, Software Analysis and Design, Data Flow Diagram and ER Model

Learning Objectives

You will learn following key concepts after completion of the chapter:

- ✓ Advantages, disadvantages and characteristics of database management system
- ✓ Architecture and models of database management system
- ✓ System development life cycle and its phases
- ✓ Data flow diagram and entity relationship model

1.1 INTRODUCTION

A database is a collection of interrelated data stored together without harmful or unnecessary redundancy. Its main objective is to provide convenient and efficient way to storage and retrieval of database information. Additionally it must ensure safety of data. A Database Management System (DBMS) is a software package used to create and manage databases. System analysis and design deals with the software development activities. This is an organized way of dealing with a problem. System development life cycle is a systematic process of developing and maintaining systems. Data flow diagrams and ER model are the most popular techniques for documenting the process of system design.

1.2 DATABASE SYSTEM

Database systems and development of applications to process the stored data have evolved over the years. In early 1960's magnetic tapes were used for storage and processing of data. They were sequential in nature and data processing related applications were very limited. In the late 1960's, emergence of hard disks changed the scenario of data processing greatly. With hard disks data could be accessed directly and limitation of sequential access was over. Database related applications improved with the invention of hard disks. Network and hierarchical data models were also developed in this era. These data models were quite popular till late 1970s. Hardware gradually improved and the process is continuing. In late 1980's the hard disk space that was thought to be sufficient is now available in main memory. At present servers with 1 GB to 8 GB main memory is quite common. Hard disk space in servers are of the order of 1000 GBs. Relational Database Management Software (RDBMS) also evolved and dominated the market. Lots of Graphics User Interface (GUI) based software are available for the development of very sophisticated database applications. Current trend is object oriented relational database system. It is still in the process of refinement and may be used in future database management systems.

1.2.1 Advantages of Database Management System

In the current era, use of DBMS is inevitable. The power of DBMS is because of its systematic and revolutionary development over few decades.

Centralized management and control over the data

All controls related to the database are done from a central place. The role of a Database Administrator (DBA) is very important. The DBA creates users and assign privileges to them. The DBA is also responsible for creation, deletion, modification and fine-tuning of the database and all other database maintenance related jobs.

Sharing of database and elimination of redundant operation

The data stored in database are shared among different applications. Consider a scenario of an automated office where all applications are developed based on some database. All applications related to the automation essentially require sharing of common data of each employee. If the data is available in some tables, it should be available to all other applications. The applications related to database should be developed so that redundancy in data storage and redundancy in data entry is totally eliminated.

Security

Security of data is of prime importance. All database management software incorporate security features in some form or other. Security of data ensures that only the authorized user is allowed to access relevant data. Security of data also addresses the problems related to virus attack and safety of data during transmission from one place to other.

1.2.2 Disadvantages of Database Management System

The database management system like any other technology is not free from the negative aspects. Few disadvantages because of which small organizations are reluctant to implement DBMS are implementation and maintenance cost.

Implementation cost

The first time implementation cost of database related application is very high. The major implementation costs are related to software, hardware and application development. It ranges right from few lakhs to crores of rupees and depends on the target requirements and type of application.

Maintenance cost

Even after implementation of database application, its maintenance cost is quite high. Maintenance cost is mainly due to day-to-day data entry, modification of application, creation of database, backup, recovery and fine-tuning of the databases.

1.3 CHARACTERISTIC OF DATABASE MANAGEMENT SYSTEM

The most desirable characteristics of a database system are as under.

1.3.1 Data Representation

Data representation is divided into two parts: high-level details and low-level details. The high-level view of data represents information related to the table, number of records in the table and attributes that form the record. The low-level details deal with the physical storage of data.

1.3.2 Performance

The performance of a DBMS is determined by its response time. The type of physical storage and memory do effect response time. In any database, data should be stored in such a manner that they can be accessed quickly and conveniently.

1.3.3 Integrity

When large number of users concurrently uses a database, the data items and associations between them must not be destroyed. A unit of activity must be either completed or appear to never have started. Storage, insertion, updation and deletion of data have to be performed in such a fashion that the system can recover from hardware failure, if any.

1.3.4 Minimal Redundancy

The redundant data consume a lot of memory space. They also lead to problems related to insertion, updation, deletion and inconsistency. DBMS should therefore, eliminate redundancy wherever possible.

1.3.5 Privacy

The privacy of DBMS implies that individuals and corporation, as a whole should have a due right to determine themselves when, how and to what extent information available with them is to be transmitted to others.

1.3.6 Security

The security of data means protecting data against accidental or intentional disclosure to unauthorized persons. It also implies unauthorized modification or destruction. The DBMS should include mechanism to authenticate users to access data as per their authorization.

1.4 DATABASE MANAGEMENT SYSTEM ARCHITECTURE

The architecture of database management system is based on three-schema architecture, which is based on different levels of abstraction. The three levels of database architecture are internal, conceptual and external.

1.4.1 Internal Level

The internal level is also known as **physical level** database architecture. It is mainly concerned with the methodology through which the data is stored physically. It describes the complete details related to physical data storage and access paths.

1.4.2 Conceptual Level

The conceptual level is also known as **logical level** database architecture. It hides the details of physical storage from the developer and user of the database. It mainly describes entities, data types, relationships, constraints and other details.

1.4.3 External Level

The external level is also known as **view level** database architecture. It is concerned with the way data will be viewed by a user.

1.5 DATABASE MODELS

The three types of database models are: record based database model, object based database model and physical data model.

1.5.1 Record Based Database Models

Record based database models are: network model, hierarchical model and relational model. In the present scenario use of relational model is dominant over the other two.

Network model

In network model data is represented by collection of records. Relationships among data are established by links, a concept similar to pointers.

Hierarchical model

Hierarchical model is similar to network model. The difference between the two is that hierarchical model organizes records as the collection of trees rather than records and link-like graph representation.

Relational model

This model uses concept of a table, a rectangular structure with rows and columns, to represent data and relationship among data. Table has a number of columns with unique names. In this chapter relational model will be discussed in detail. All the popular and most used DBMS like ORACLE, DB2, Informix, Sybase and SQL Server are based on relational model.

1.5.2 Object Based Database Models

Object Based Database Model is realized to be based on the concept of objects of several types. In this type of model, data is described at the conceptual and view levels of abstraction. The widely used models of this category are ER model and object oriented data model. The ER model is based on entity and relationship. The object oriented data model is based on the concept of object oriented programming language, where data and methods form the class.

1.5.3 Physical Data Model

It is the lowest level of data model for database related implementations. In this model concepts related to the record formats, record ordering and access paths, etc. are of prime importance. The frame memory model and unifying model are the examples of physical data model.

1.6 SYSTEM ANALYSIS AND DESIGN

System Analysis and Design (SAD) deals with the software development activities. This is an organized way of dealing with a problem. The major components of SAD comprises of understanding a system, its phases and system designing. SAD primarily comprise system definition and system development life cycle.

1.7 SYSTEM DEFINITION

The three major components in any system are input, processing and output. These components are connected with each other, however they are interdependent. For example, application software represents a complete system. It is dependent on some operating systems with an assumption that an output is produced as a result of processing the suitable inputs.

1.8 SYSTEM DEVELOPMENT LIFE CYCLE

The System Development Life Cycle (SDLC) is a systematic methodology of developing and maintaining systems. SDLC means combination of various phases of software development cycle as shown below:

- Feasibility study
- System analysis
- System design
- Coding
- Testing
- Implementation
- Maintenance

The Popular SDLC models are waterfall, iterative waterfall, prototype and evolutionary models. Waterfall is the first classical and theoretical model to introduce the various development phases as shown above. Other models are derivatives of waterfall model. Waterfall model resembles a cascade of waterfall as all the phases flow in sequential manner starting from feasibility study to system analysis ... to maintenance. Iterative waterfall model as its name suggests, allows feedback from various phases. In the prototype model, working model is demonstrated to the user before developing the actual software. In the evolutionary model a software is improved with successive versions. Iterative waterfall, prototype and evolutionary models are commonly used in to develop software. Iterative waterfall is less customer friendly as the software product is demonstrated on completion. The prototype and evolutionary models on the other hand are more customer friendly as developers share the overall flow of the system and their experience with customers during the course of actual software development. The SDLC commonly followed in software development is shown in Figure 1.1. It is basically the combination of iterative waterfall, prototype and evolutionary models. The seven phases mentioned above are common in all the models and will be briefly discussed.

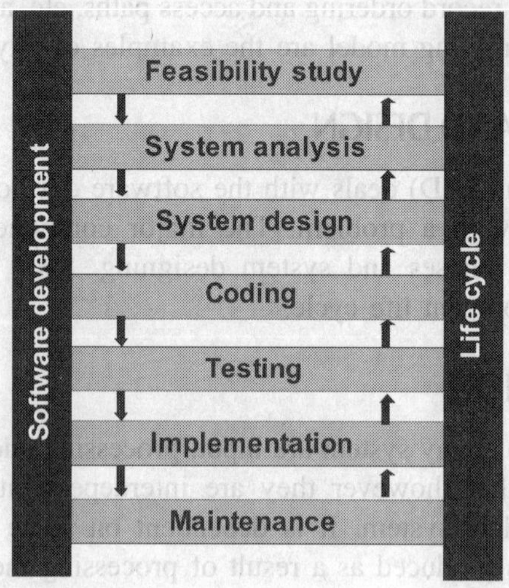

FIGURE 1.1 The System Development Life Cycle (SDLC).

Different phases of SDLC and the related activity of system development life cycle is described below.

1.8.1 Feasibility Study

Feasibility study is the first stage of SDLC and it gives a clear picture of the physical system. The initial survey of the system is done to identify the scope of the system. The proposed system contains the details of the present system and suggestions to overcome the limitations of the present system with respect to the user's requirements. On the basis of the outcome of the initial survey, feasibility study takes place. The major components of the feasibility study are meeting the user's requirements and effective use of resources. The main goal of feasibility study is not to solve the problem rather to achieve the scope. In the process of feasibility study, the cost-benefits are done with greater accuracy.

1.8.2 System Analysis

The system analysis is a detailed study of the current system, leading to specifications of the new system. System analysis is a detailed study of various operations performed by a system and their relationships within and outside the system. During system analysis, data are collected from the existing resources, decision points and various transactions handled by the present system. Interviews, on-site observation and questionnaire are the tools used for system analysis. Following are the two points of system analysis:

- Specification of the new system to be accomplished based on the user requirements.
- Functional hierarchy of the functions to be performed by the new system and their relationship with each other.

1.8.3 System Design

System designing is a most crucial phase in the development of a system. Normally, the design comprises two stages. They are preliminary design and detailed design. In the preliminary design, the features of the new system are specified. Requirements are analyzed and documented in the form of detailed data flow diagrams, entity relationship model, data dictionary, logical data structures and miniature specifications. In this stage, the operating system, programming language and the hardware in which the new system will be developed and execute are also decided. The system analysis also includes sub-dividing complex process involving the entire system. In the detailed design stage, computer oriented work begins. At this stage, the design of the system becomes more structured. Structure design is a blue print of the solution to a given problem having the same components and inter-relationship as the original problem. Algorithm, input, output and processing specifications are elaborated in detail in the phase.

1.8.4 Coding

The whole system is essentially required to be converted into coding after the design of the new system. Coding is an important stage where the defined algorithms are programmed into control specifications with the help of a computer language. The programs coordinate the data movements and control the entire process in a system.

1.8.5 Testing

A test run of the system is done to remove all the bugs before actual implementation of the new system into operations. It is an important phase of a successful system. After codification a test plan should be developed and run on a given set of test data. The output of the test run should match the expected results. Testing is done at unit and system level.

The unit test is carried out at the program level. All the programs must be individually tested. The white box testing, black box testing, boundary level testing and stress testing are commonly used in unit level testing. The white box testing ensures testing of all the logics and execution paths in the programs. The black box testing is done with random input data whose output is known. In boundary value testing (as its name suggests) programs are tested with extreme limits of input values. Whereas in stress testing robustness of the program is tested by giving spurious values. Any undesirable happening with the testing process must be noted and debugged.

The system test (or validation) is done after carrying out the unit test for each of the programs of the system. At this stage the test is done on realistic data. The complete system is executed on the actual data. At each stage of the execution, the results or output of the system is analyzed. During the system testing if the outputs are not matching with the expected output; in such cases the errors in the particular programs are identified and are fixed and further tested for the expected output. System testing commonly consists of three kinds of testing: alpha level testing, beta level testing and acceptance level testing. The developer performs alpha level testing. The potential customers perform beta level testing. Whereas acceptance level testing is performed by the customer to accept or reject the product.

1.8.6 Implementation

The implementation phase begins after the user acceptance of the new system. Implementation is the stage of a project during which the system is put into practice in realistic environment. During this phase, all the programs of the system are loaded onto the server and client machines. The user and software maintenance level starts in this phase.

After the users are trained on the computerized system, manual working has to shift from manual to computerized working. Commonly the strategies followed for running the newly developed system are: parallel run and pilot run. In case of parallel run computerized as well as manual systems are executed in parallel. This strategy is helpful because manual results can be compared with the results of the computerized system. Also failure of the computerized system at the early stage does not affect the working of the organization. In case of pilot run, the new system is installed in parts. Some parts of the new system is installed first and executed for a considerable time period. When the results are found satisfactory then only other parts are implemented. This strategy builds the confidence and the errors are traced easily.

1.8.7 Maintenance

The maintenance of software is the most important phase of SDLC. This phase generates maximum revenue in software industries. Maintenance is necessary to eliminate errors in the system during its lifetime and tune the system to the changing working environment. It has been observed that there are always some errors found in the system, which must be addressed. It also implies the review of the system from time to time. The review of the system is done for knowing the full capabilities of the system, knowing the required changes, identifying the additional requirements and studying the performance. In case of a major change to a system, usually a new project may have to be taken up to carry out the change. The new project will then proceed through all the above life cycle phases.

1.9 DATA FLOW DIAGRAM

The Data Flow Diagrams (DFD) are the most commonly used way of documenting the process of system design. They are a pictorial way of showing the flow of data into, around and out of a system. DFDs do not give detailed descriptions of modules, but graphically describe a system's data and how the data interact with the system. DFDs are constructed using four major components viz. process, data flow, external entity and data stores as depicted in Figure 1.2.

The DFD is also known as **bubble chart**. It comprises only four types of components and is simple to use. It is used to provide the end user with a physical idea of flow of data.

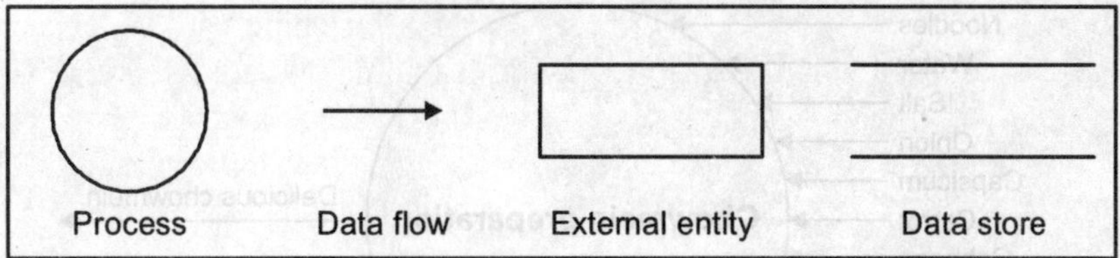

FIGURE 1.2 The data flow diagram.

1.9.1 Process

The first component of the DFD is known as a **process**. It is also known as a **bubble**, a **function**, or a **transformation**. Process represent activity transforms the input data into output data, i.e. it shows how one or more inputs are changed into outputs. The process is represented graphically as a circle. Some systems analysts prefer to use an oval to represent a process. A good process name usually consists of a verb and an object, i.e. an active verb and an object to form a descriptive phrase of the process. Examples of process names are VALIDATE DATA, COMPUTE INCOME TAX, CALCULATE TRAJECTORY and similar to that. Diagrammatically a process is shown in Figure 1.2.

1.9.2 Data Flow

The data flow is used to describe the movement of information from one part of the system to another part. Thus, the flows represent data in motion. The data flow shows direction using an arrowhead at either ends of the flow. It indicates whether the data are moving into or out of a process or doing both. A flow is represented graphically by an arrow as shown in Figure 1.2.

1.9.3 External Entities

The external entities represent the source of data as input to the system. They are also the destination of system data. These are represented by rectangle as shown in Figure 1.2.

1.9.4 Data Stores

The data stores represent stores of data within the system. The store is used to model a collection of data at rest. The notation for a store is two parallel lines as shown in Figure 1.2.

Example: In this example preparation of chowmein with the help of DFD is demonstrated. This example is chosen because majority of people more or less know the steps involved in preparation of chowmein. It is therefore, comparatively easy to understand the process involved in the design of DFD. Three levels of DFD are shown in Figures 1.3 to 1.5. Note that the inputs and output remain same in all the levels of DFD. Figure 1.3 represents the context diagram (or DFD level 0), which has got 11 inputs and 1 output.

Figure 1.4 represents DFD level 1. In this level there are three processes viz. 'boil noodles', 'prepare vegetables' and 'prepare chowmein'. Note that no new inputs are included in this level of DFD. The input 'Oil' is used in 'boil noodles' as well as in 'prepare vegetables'.

The process 'prepare vegetables' in DFD level 1 is broken into 'chop the vegetables' and 'saute chopped vegetables' in DFD level 2 (Figure 1.5).

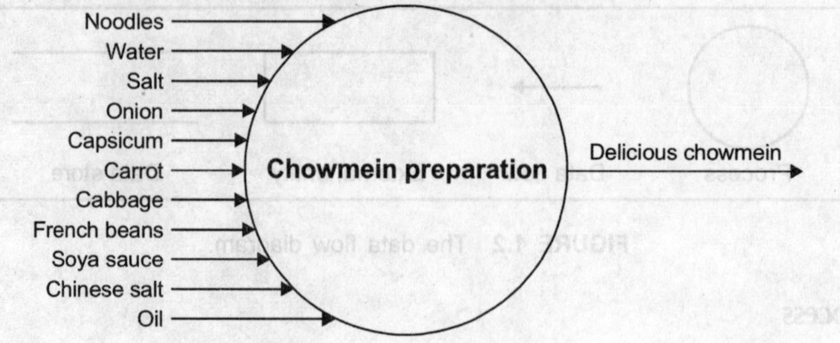

FIGURE 1.3 Context diagram.

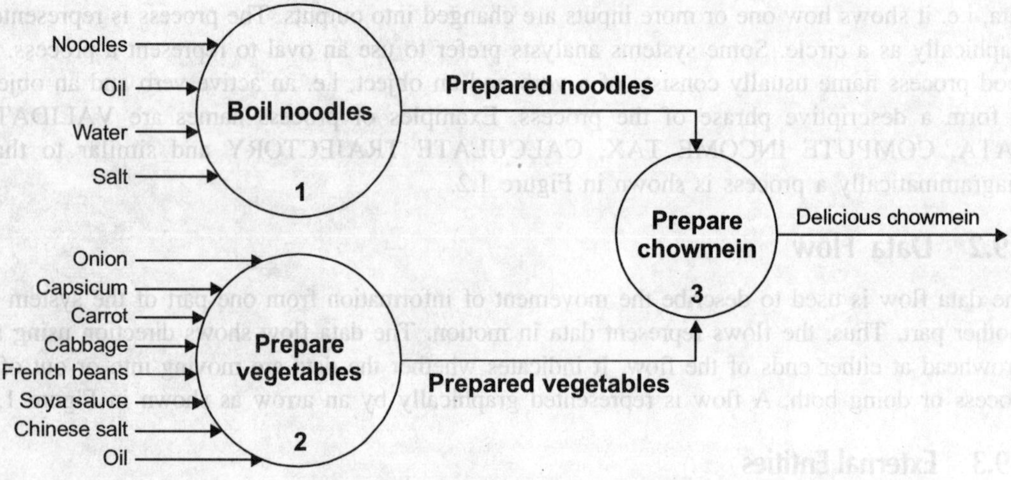

FIGURE 1.4 Data flow diagram level 1.

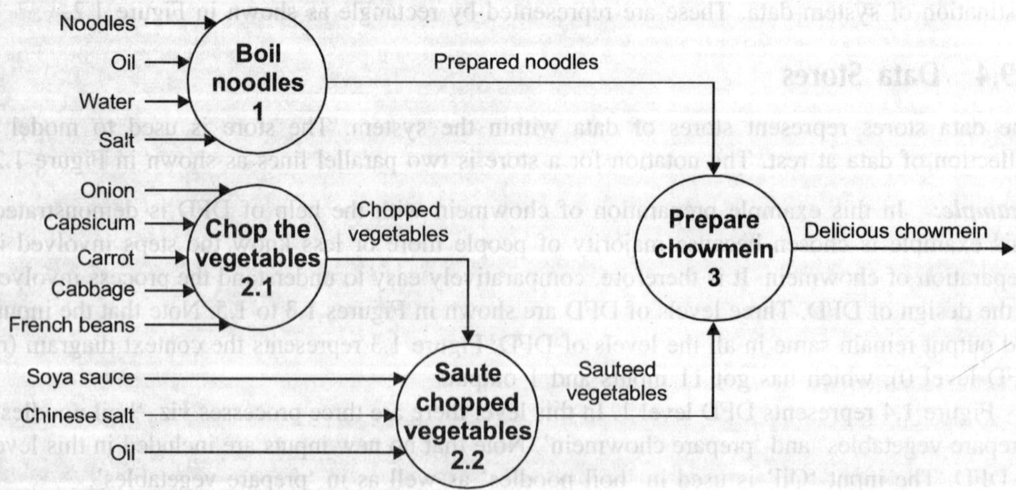

FIGURE 1.5 Data flow diagram level 2.

1.10 ENTITY RELATIONSHIP MODEL (ER MODEL)

Data requirements of an application are represented in an implementation independent way using a data model. The data model use a set of construct and rules to provide a precise representation of the data content, structure, and constraints required by an application. In database related applications, Entity-relationship model (ER Model) is the most popular and the commonly used technique. It is a high-level database design model. An entity is an object in the real world, which is distinguishable from other objects. In a database entities are described by a set of attributes.

1.10.1 ER Model Components

Components that are essentially required to design an ER Model are entity, attribute, line to link entities and relationships among entities. Table 1.1 shows the above mentioned components along with its symbols and examples.

TABLE 1.1 The ER Model Components

Component	Symbol	Example
Entity	Rectangle	CUST
Attribute	Ellipse	CNAME
Linking entity with attribute	Line	CNAME CUST
Relationship among entities	Diamond	CUST SALE_DETAIL PROD

Other components along with its symbols and examples related to ER model, which are used in design of ER model are shown in Table 1.2. Illustration related to the components and their examples are shown in Table 1.3.

TABLE 1.2 Entity Relationship Advance Components

S. No.	Component	Symbol	Example
1	Weak entity	Double rectangle	ACCOUNT
2	Weak relationship	Double diamond	ACC_TRANS TRANSACTION
3	Multi-valued attributes	Double ellipse	ADDRESS
4	Composite attribute	Combination one ellipse along with multiple ellipses	FNAME LNAME NAME
5	Derived attribute	Dotted ellipse	BIRTH_DT AGE EMPLOYEE
6	Generaliz-ation and specialization	Triangle	Generalization ACCOUNT ISA CURRENT SAVINGS Specialization

TABLE 1.3 Entity Relationship Component Description

S. No.	Description
1 and 2	Weak entity and weak relationship usually depends on some entity. They do not exist in isolation. In the example TRANSACTION is dependent on ACCOUNT, but the opposite does not hold. In such type of cases weak entity is collapsed with the associated entity.
3	Multi-valued attribute is used to represent fields, which comprises multiple sub-fields. In the example ADDRESS, multiple sub-fields like house number, street number, city, etc. form the address.
4	Composite attribute contains fixed sub-values. The example NAME contains two sub-values FNAME and LNAME to represent first name and last name, respectively.
5	Derived attribute derive values based on some calculations. In the example AGE is derived from BIRTH_DT.
6	Generalization basically imply entity which are generic in nature, whereas specialization are entities, which are specific and specialized. In the example ACCOUNT is generalized, whereas CURRENT and SAVINGS are specialized accounts.

1.10.2 Aggregation

Aggregation in ER model is used to represent relationships among relationship. Aggregation is basically treating a relationship and all its participating entities, relations and attributes as a single entity, so that to link with some other entity. An example is shown in Figure 1.6. The aggregated ER model comprising of entities EMPLOYEE, PROJECT and relation ASSIGNED is linked with SOFTWARE entity. The employee use software for the purpose of development of project. It is therefore, linked with an entity SOFTWARE.

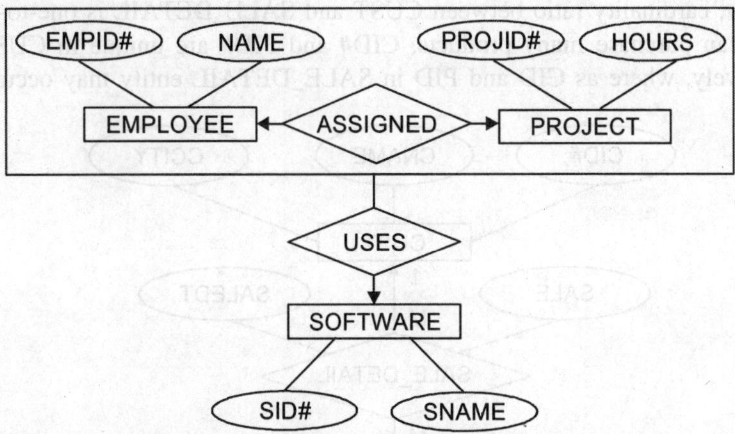

FIGURE 1.6 Entity relationship aggregation.

1.10.3 Degree of Relationship

The degree of relationship is based on the numbers of entities to form the relation. A relationship between two entity types is called a **binary type** relationship. Similarly, relationship among three entity type is ternary type and so on. Figure 1.7 shows an example of binary relationship.

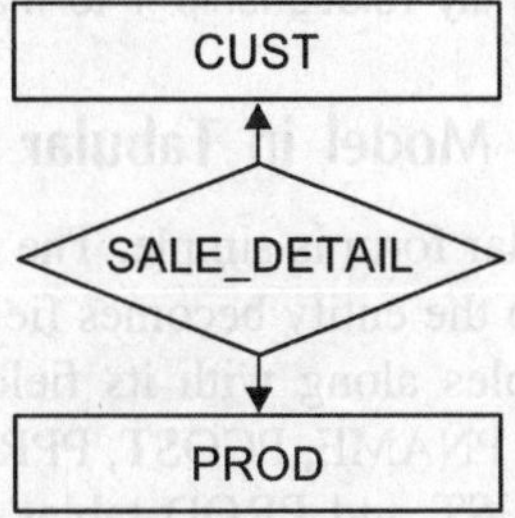

FIGURE 1.7 Entity relationship binary type relationship.

1.10.4 Cardinality Ratio

Three types of cardinality ratios are possible in ER Model, they are as follows:

One-to-many (1 : M) or many-to-one (M : 1): Relation between state and city of that state is an example of one-to-many cardinality ratio.

One-to-one (1 : 1): Relation between country and its capital is an example of one-to-one cardinality ratio. One country will have only one capital.

Many-to-many (M : M): Relation between parents and their children is an example of many-to-many. Many-to-many cardinality ratio should be broken into many-to-one and one-to-many. Figure 1.8 shows an example where many-to-many (CUST vs PROD) is broken into two by introducing SALE_DETAIL. CID#, CNAME and CCITY are attributes of CUST entity. Similarly PID#, PNAME, PCOST, PPROFIT are attributes of PROD entity. Cardinality ratio between PROD and SALE_DETAIL is one-to-many because one product can be sold multiple times. Similarly, cardinality ratio between CUST and SALE_DETAIL is one-to-many because one customer can purchase many products. CID# and PID# are unique in CUST and PROD entity, respectively, where as CID and PID in SALE_DETAIL entity may occur many times.

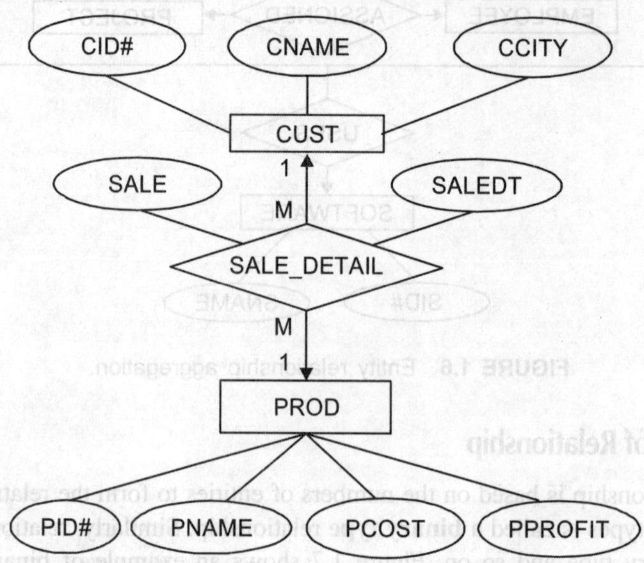

FIGURE 1.8 Entity relationship 1 to many relationship.

1.10.5 Representation of ER Model in Tabular Form

Representing an ER model in a tabular form is simple. The name of entity is named as the table name and attributes corresponding to the entity becomes fields of the table. For example in case of the entity CUST and PROD, tables along with its fields are represented by CUST(CID#, CNAME, CCITY) and PROD(PID#, PNAME, PCOST, PPROFIT), respectively. Note that CID# and PID# ensures uniqueness in CUST and PROD tables, respectively. In case of a relation, attributes along with unique attribute corresponding to the associated entities becomes the fields of the table. For example, the relation SALE_DETAIL will be represented as SALE_DETAIL(CID#, PID#, SALE, SALEDT#). Tabular structure with sample data corresponding to CUST, PROD and SALE_DETAIL are shown in Figure 1.9.

CUST

CID#	CNAME	CCITY
C1	PRADIP	MYSORE
C2	TUSHAR	PUNE
C3	AASTIK	KOLKATA
C4	ARPAN	CHENNAI
C5	ANUMITA	INDORE

SALE_DETAIL

CID#	PID#	SALE	SALEDT#
C1	P3	2	14-JUL-13
C3	P2	10	15-JUL-13
C2	P3	1	14-JUL-13
C1	P1	5	14-JUL-13
C1	P3	3	20-AUG-13
C4	P3	3	14-NOV-13
C5	P2	2	18-SEP-13

PROD

PID#	PNAME	PCOST	PPROFIT
P3	PEN	20.5	20
P2	FLOPPY	30	12
P1	PENCIL	5.25	

FIGURE 1.9 Tables with records-running example.

1.11 SUMMARY

A database is a collection of interrelated data with minimal or no redundancy. A database management system is software used to create and manage databases. Relational and object-relational database management system is most used due to its scalability and ease of management. Software analysis and design, and software development life cycle are essentially required in any RDBMS intrinsic software development. Data flow diagram is used to represent flow of data. Entity relationship provides a means to establish relationship between entities.

SHORT/OBJECTIVE TYPE QUESTIONS

1. What is the role of 'security' in DBMS?
2. What do you mean by 'maintenance' of a database?
3. Briefly describe various types of database models.
4. Mention the names of two customer friendly SDLC models.
5. Which phase of SDLC generates maximum revenue in the software industry?
6. Describe black box, white box, alpha and beta level test strategies.
7. Describe four major components of data flow diagram.

8. Elaborate the terms aggregation, generalization and specializations in ER model.
9. How ER module is represented in the tabular form?
10. The DFD of an application mainly shows
    (a) Processing requirements and the flow of data
    (b) Decision and control information
    (c) Communication network structure
    (d) Entity relationship model
11. In an ER diagram ellipse represent
    (a) Entity set
    (b) Attributes
    (c) Generalization
    (d) Specialization
12. ER modelling technique is a
    (a) Bottom-up approach
    (b) Black-box approach
    (c) Top-down approach
    (d) White-box approach
13. Primary job of database administration is/are
    (a) Backup
    (b) Recovery
    (c) Fine-tuning
    (d) None of the above
14. Low-level data representation deals with
    (a) Number of records
    (b) Physical storage of data
    (c) Logical representation of data
    (d) None of the above
15. Match the following w.r.t. DBMS

(a) Internal level	(a) View level
(b) External level	(b) Physical level
(c) Conceptual level	(c) Logical level

16. Record based model(s) is/are
    (a) ER model
    (b) Network model
    (c) Hierarchical model
    (d) Physical data model
17. Number of phases in SDLC is
    (a) 5
    (b) 6
    (c) 7
    (d) 8

18. In SDLC, DFD and ER model are part of
   (a) Feasibility study
   (b) System analysis
   (c) System design
   (d) System study

19. In ER model, derived attribute is represented by
   (a) Double rectangle
   (b) Double diamond
   (c) Dotted ellipse
   (d) Dotted rectangle

20. In ER model, degree of relationship is based on
   (a) Number of attributes
   (b) Number of entities
   (c) Number of relations
   (d) None of the above

WORKOUT SECTION

W1_1 This workout comprises of four entities viz. PERSON, STUDENT, FACULTY and PROJECT. The entity PERSON is generalization of entities STUDENT and FACULTY. ASSIGNED_TO is a relation between STUDENT and PROJECT. Details of attributes along with its brief description are given in Table 1.4.

TABLE 1.4 List of Attributes

Attribute	Description
PID#	Person's identification number
NAME	Name of the person
FNAME	First name
LNAME	Last name
DT_BIRTH	Person's date of birth
SEX	Person's sex
ADDRESS	Multi-valued attribute
AGE	Derived attribute
COURSE	Student registered for the course
GRADE	Student's grade
DESIGNATION	Faculty's designation
SPECIALIZATION	Faculty's specialization
ORGN	Assigned to the organization
PROJID#	Project's identification number
ST_DATE	Project's start date
DAYS	Project duration

Skeleton of ER model is shown in Figure 1.10. Fill up the entities along with relevant attributes based on the description given above. Also represent all the entities and relations along with relevant attributes in tabular form.

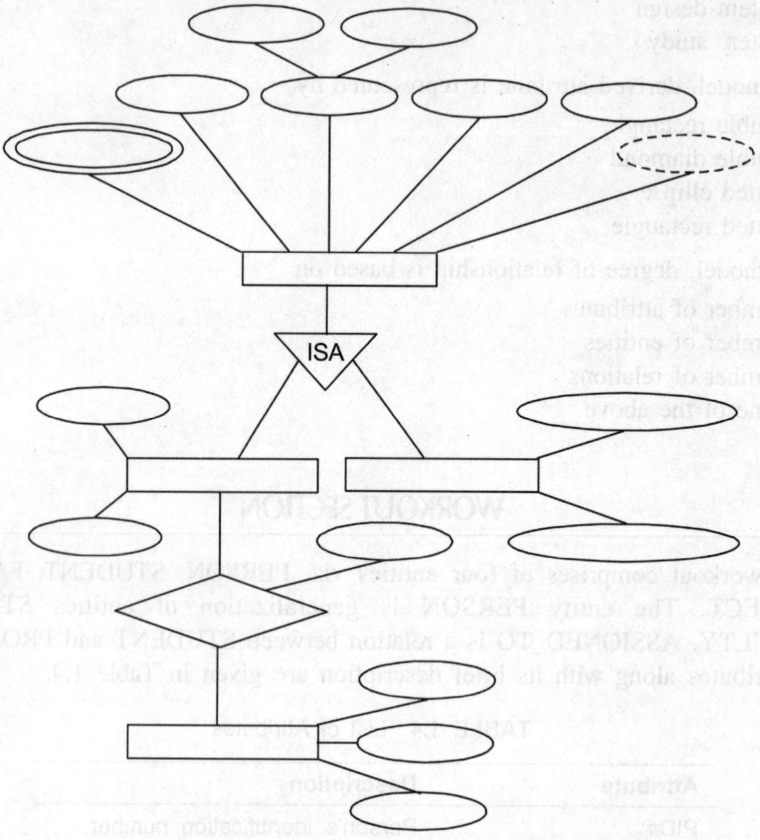

FIGURE 1.10 Skeleton of entity relationship model.

W1_2 TEACHING LOAD ALLOCATION SYSTEM

The objective of the Teaching Load Allocation System (TLAS) is to allocate the teaching workload of theory classes among faculty members. This is done so that each faculty member gets the course of his preference as far as possible. At the same time care is taken that all the courses are fully covered during the allocation, i.e. no course is left uncovered. The allocation must meet the following goals:

- Every faculty member should normally get 6 periods per week. This is the maximum working load capacity for each member. In other words, no faculty member can be given more than 6 periods per week (6 days a week) to teach. This quantity is liable to be changed under special conditions.
- There are exactly 3 periods per week in each course.

Special conditions

Under normal circumstances the number of faculty members and number of courses should be such that an allocation is feasible with maximum working load capacity of 6 periods per week per teacher, as there are 3 periods per week per course so the "feasibility criterion" is as follows.

$6 \times m > 3 \times n$, Where m is the number of teachers and n is the number of courses.

In case the feasibility criterion is not met then the exception handler computes the maximum workload (say load) which satisfy the following feasibility criterion:

$$\text{Load} \times m > 3 \times n$$

However, the new maximum workload is kept below an acceptable value so that it does not shoot up to a value, which is unrealistic. In case of violation of the above condition the system should give an appropriate error message.

Further the system should take care of "invalid choice". There are two criteria for valid choice. They are:

- Every teacher should enter the specified minimum number of choices. This has been kept 4 in our case.
- Every course should occur at least twice in the overall preference matrix.

These two conditions must hold true and so proper check should be made to ensure that both of these hold good. In case either of them or both of them fail then an appropriate error message should be printed. The user should be given a fair chance to correct his mistakes according to the error messages. Even then if the user responds with the same faulty input then the exception handler should take over.

This system is designed using triple redundancy for satisfying the acceptance tests and should normally produce an acceptable allocation. The three allocation methodologies incorporated are as follows:

- Linear Programming Model (LP Model)
- Transportation model
- Heuristic models
  - Course major order
  - Teacher major order

In rare circumstances if all the allocation strategies fail a suitable error message should be printed and the system should be terminated.

The allocation should aim at maximizing the total satisfaction of the entire faculty, subject to the constraints mentioned in 'special conditions' given above.

Inputs

- The number and name of faculty members.
- The number and names of courses to be allocated.
- The course preferences along with respective weightage of all teachers, with at least 4 from every teacher.

Outputs

- Load allocation.
- Satisfaction report, which has the satisfaction values of each faculty member, total satisfaction of entire faculty, average workload, maximum and minimum workloads.
- Error messages, if any.

Context diagram along with portions of DFD of level 1 and DFD of level 2 are shown in Figure 1.11. to Figure 1.14. Minutely observe the data flow and process and corelate with the information provided above.

Draw data flow diagram (Level 1 and Level 2) corresponding to TLAS.

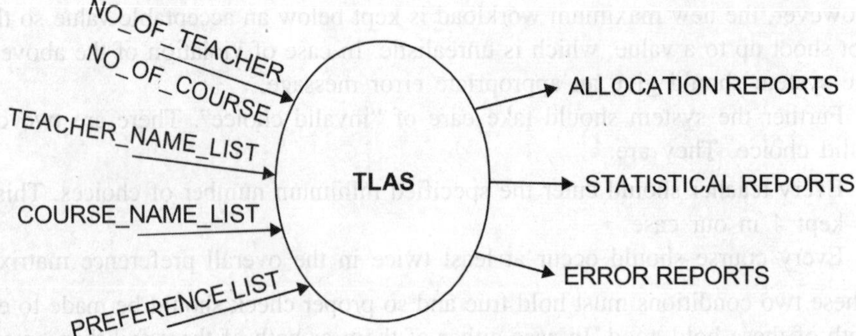

FIGURE 1.11 Context diagram.

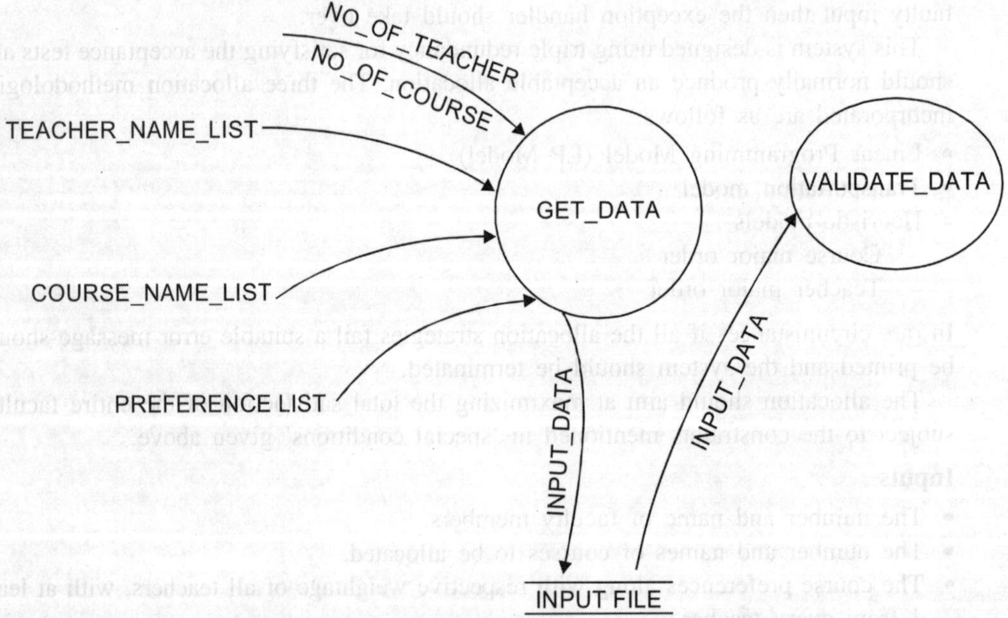

FIGURE 1.12 Part of data flow diagram—level 1.

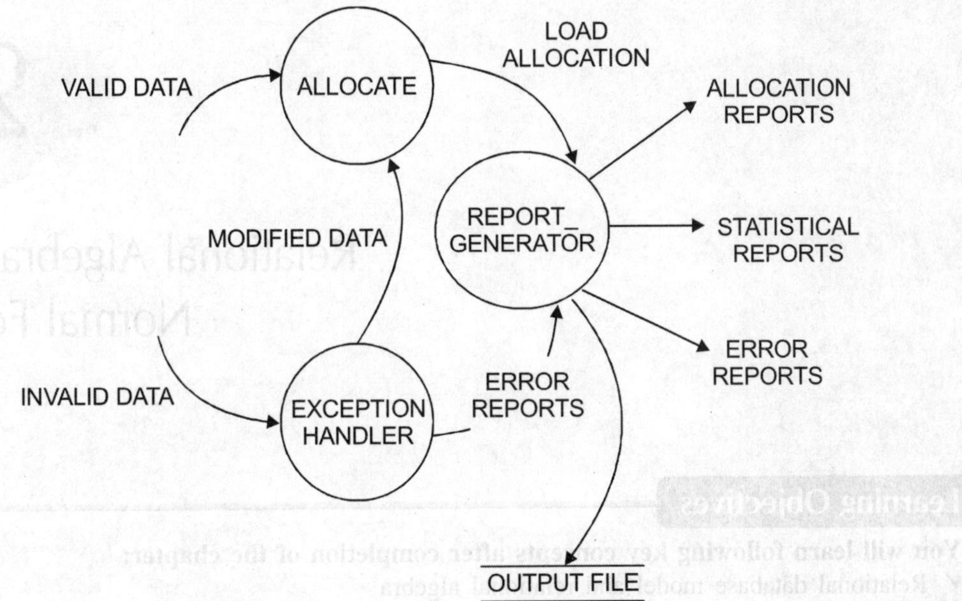

FIGURE 1.13 Part of data flow diagram—level 2.

COURSE_ MAJOR_ ORDER
HIEURIS- TICALLY_ ALLOCATE
LOAD ALLOCATION
OPTION
TEACHER_ MAJOR_ ORDER
ALLOCATE
OPTION
LOAD ALLOCATION
TRANSPO- RTATION MODEL
LOAD ALLOCATION
OPTION
L.P. MODEL
LOAD ALLOCATION

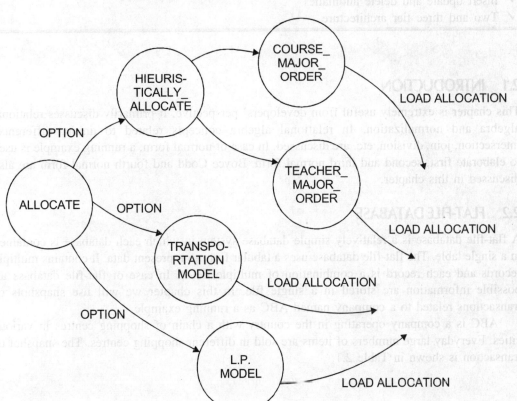

FIGURE 1.14 Part of data flow diagram—level 2.

Relational Algebra and Normal Forms

Learning Objectives

You will learn following key concepts after completion of the chapter:

- ✓ Relational database model and relational algebra
- ✓ Functional dependency and normalization techniques
- ✓ Insert update and delete anomalies
- ✓ Two and three tier architecture

2.1 INTRODUCTION

This chapter is extremely useful from developers' perspective. It primarily discusses relational algebra and normalization. In relational algebra concepts related to union, difference, intersection, join, division, etc. are discussed. In case of normal form, a running example is used to elaborate first, second and third normal form. Boyce Codd and fourth normal form are also discussed in this chapter.

2.2 FLAT-FILE DATABASE

A flat-file database is a relatively simple database system in which each database is contained in a single table. The flat-file database uses a tabular form to represent data. It contains multiple records and each record is a combination of multiple fields. In case of flat-file database all possible information are stored in a single file. In this chapter we will use snapshots of transactions related to a company named ABC as a running example.

ABC is a company operating in the country with a chain of shopping centres in various cities. Everyday large numbers of items are sold in different shopping centres. The snapshot of transaction is shown in Table 2.1.

TABLE 2.1 Snapshot of Transaction Details

CUST_PROD

CID	CNAME	CCITY	STATE	PID	PNAME	PCOST	PPROFIT	SALE	SALEDT
C1	PRADIP	MYSORE	KARNATAKA	P1	PENCIL	5.25		5	14-JUL-13
C1	PRADIP	MYSORE	KARNATAKA	P3	PEN	20.5	20	2	14-JUL-13
C1	PRADIP	MYSORE	KARNATAKA	P3	PEN	20.5	20	3	20-AUG-13
C2	TUSHAR	PUNE	MAHARASTRA	P3	PEN	20.5	20	1	14-JUL-13
C3	AASTIK	KOLKATA	WEST BENGAL	P2	FLOPPY	30	12	10	15-JUL-13
C4	ARPAN	CHENNAI	TAMILNADU	P3	PEN	20.5	20	3	14-NOV-13
C5	ANUMITA	INDORE	MADHYA PRADESH	P2	FLOPPY	30	12	2	18-SEP-13

CUST_PROD is represented in flat-file database format. Flat-file database representation is effective to track the transactions and to answer different type of queries. Brief description of fields of CUST_PROD are as follows.

CID	Customer Identification Number. Its first character is 'C' followed by a number
CNAME	Customer Name
CCITY	Customer City
STATE	State of CCITY
PID	Product Identification Number. Its first character is 'P' followed by a number
PNAME	Product Name
PCOST	Product Cost. It is a number of decimal type
PPROFIT	Profit on PNAME in percentage. It is a number of integer type
SALE	Number of product sold
SALEDT	Date on which product was sold

CUST_PROD consists of 07 rows/records and 10 columns/fields. First record corresponding to (CID, CNAME, CCITY, STATE, PID, PNAME, PCOST, PPROFIT, SALE, SALEDT) is shown in Table 2.2.

TABLE 2.2 First Record of the Transaction

CID	CNAME	CCITY	STATE	PID	PNAME	PCOST	PPROFIT	SALE	SALEDT
C1	PRADIP	MYSORE	KARNATAKA	P1	PENCIL	5.25		5	14-JUL-13

Second row is shown in Table 2.3.

TABLE 2.3 Second Record of the Transaction

CID	CNAME	CCITY	STATE	PID	PNAME	PCOST	PPROFIT	SALE	SALEDT
C1	PRADIP	MYSORE	KARNATAKA	P3	PEN	20.5	20	2	14-JUL-13

Similarly all the remaining five records can be shown. There may be large number of queries that can be answered easily by referring to Table 2.1. Some of them may be as under.

Customers visited the store on 14-JUL-2013

Information related to this query can be easily extracted by referring to CNAME and SALEDT field. The result is shown in Table 2.4.

TABLE 2.4 Records Based on the Query

CNAME
PRADIP
TUSHAR

Name of products available in the store

PNAME field can be referred to retrieve the name of the products. Note that out of 7 only 3 are unique. The result is shown in Table 2.5.

TABLE 2.5 Records Based on the Query

PNAME
PEN
FLOPPY
PENCIL

The details of customer and product

Customer details are available in CID, CNAME and CCITY columns. The result is shown in Table 2.6.

TABLE 2.6 Records Based on the Query

CID	CNAME	CCITY
C1	PRADIP	MYSORE
C3	AASTIK	KOLKATA
C2	TUSHAR	PUNE
C4	ARPAN	CHENNAI
C5	ANUMITA	INDORE

Similarly product details is shown in Table 2.7.

TABLE 2.7 Records Based on the Query

PID	PNAME	PCOST	PPROFIT
P3	PEN	20.5	20
P1	PENCIL	5.25	
P2	FLOPPY	30	12

The sale details of a product sold between 01-AUG-13 and 01-OCT-2013

Only two records fulfil the condition in CUST_PROD table. The result is shown in Table 2.8.

TABLE 2.8 Records Based on the Query

CID	CNAME	CCITY	STATE	PID	PNAME	PCOST	PPROFIT	SALE	SALEDT
C1	PRADIP	MYSORE	KARNATAKA	P3	PEN	20.5	20	3	20-AUG-13
C5	ANUMITA	INDORE	MADHYA PRADESH	P2	FLOPPY	30	12	2	18-SEP-13

The flat-file database is useful for very small applications. It is not suitable for large applications. Redundancy is a major problem with flat-file database. In CUST_PROD C1, PRADIP, MYSORE and KARNATAKA are present in the 1st, 2nd and 3rd records respectively. Similarly, P3, PEN, 20.5 and 20 are in the 2nd, 3rd, 4th and 6th records. Problems related to insertion, deletion and updation are common in the flat-file database representation. Relational database is used to overcome the problems associated to flat-file database.

2.3 RELATIONAL DATABASE MODEL

The relational database management system separates the program from the physical implementation of the database. This makes the program less sensitive to changes of the physical representation of the data. Relational database model is powerful yet conceptually simple as it is based on the relational algebra.

2.3.1 Sets and Domains

A domain is a finite or infinite set from which values can be chosen. Set of all integers is an example of infinite domain. States of India is an example of finite domain.

2.3.2 Cartesian Product

For the two domains D1 and D2, the Cartesian product, denoted by D1 × D2, is defined as the set of all ordered pairs such that the first element is a member of D1 and second element is a member of D2. If there are n values in D1 and m values in D2, there will be $n \times m$ combinations in D1 × D2. For example if D1 is {1, 2} and D2 is {a, b} then D1 × D2 will be {(1, a), (1, b), (2, a), (2, b)}.

EX2_1 Refer to Table 2.1. Domain related to CID (say D1) is {C1, C2, C3, C4, C5} and domain related to PNAME (say D2) is {PENCIL, PEN, FLOPPY}. D1 × D2 will be {(C1, PENCIL), (C1, PEN), (C1, FLOPPY), (C2, PENCIL), (C2, PEN), (C2, FLOPPY), (C3, PENCIL), (C3, PEN), (C3, FLOPPY), (C4, PENCIL), (C4, PEN), (C4, FLOPPY), (C5, PENCIL), (C5, PEN), (C5, FLOPPY)}. There are 5 values in D1 and 3 values in D2. Clearly there is 5 × 3, i.e. 15 sets of values in D1 × D2.

2.3.3 Relations

A relation is defined as any subset of the cartesian product of the domains. For example if D1 is {1, 2} and D2 is {a, b} then D1 × D2 will be {(1, a), (1, b), (2, a), (2, b)}. A relation may be the subset of D1 × D2 and can be defined as R = {(1, a), (2, a)}, which is a subset of D1 × D2.

EX2_2 Let D1 = {C1, C2, C3, C4, C5} and D2 = {PENCIL, PEN, FLOPPY}. Relation R is defined by the following rule:
R = {(d1, d2) such that d1 belongs to D1 and d2 belongs to D2, and d2 = PENCIL} then R = {(C1, PENCIL), (C2, PENCIL), (C3, PENCIL), (C4, PENCIL), (C5, PENCIL)}.

2.4 STRUCTURE OF RELATIONAL MODEL

In the theoretical model, data are represented by relations, and the relations are physically implemented as tables. The columns/fields of the table stands for data attributes. Each row of the table represents a record that is a collection of related data values for the attributes. Mapping of terms between theoretical model and implementation model is shown in Table 2.9. These terms are interchangeably used in RDBMS.

TABLE 2.9 Mapping between Theoretical and Implementation Models

Theoretical Model	Implementation Model
Relation	Table
Attribute	Column or field
Tuple	Row or record

2.4.1 Attributes

In the relational model attribute is essentially same as entity relationship model and are data items of interest.

2.4.2 Tables

Relations are physically represented by two-dimensional table. Column/fields represents attributes, and rows/records represents tuples. Table 2.1 shows a table with columns and rows.

2.4.3 Domains

Domains are the sets from which values of attributes are chosen. For some attributes, the value for a particular entity may be unknown or not applicable. In that case the table is permitted to have a null value for that attribute.

EX2_3 Domain of all fields in CUST_PROD are shown in Table 2.10.

TABLE 2.10 Domain Corresponding to CUST_PROD Table

Field	Domain	Example
CID	C+ Positive Integer	{C1, C2, C3, C4, C5}
CNAME	Customer name	{PRADIP, TUSHAR, AASTIK, ARPAN, ANUMITA}
CCITY	Cites of India	{MYSORE, PUNE, KOLKATA, CHENNAI, INDORE}
STATE	States of India	{KARNATAKA, MAHARASHTRA, WEST BENGAL, ...}
PID	P + Positive Integer	{P1, P2, P3}
PNAME	Item name	{PENCIL, PEN, FLOPPY}
PCOST	Item cost	{5.25, 20.5, 30}
PPROFIT	Profit percentage	{NULL, 12, 20}
SALE	Integer	{5, 2, 3, 1, 10, 3, 2}
SALEDT	Date	{14-JUL-13, 20-AUG-13, 15-JUL-13, 14-NOV-13,...}

2.5 KEYS

A key is a combination of one or more attributes that are used to identify one or more records in a table. Different types of keys are defined in relational model.

2.5.1 Primary Key

Primary Key is a minimal combination of field(s) that uniquely identifies the corresponding values of other field in a table. The field(s) of a primary key is known as **prime attribute(s)**. The values of prime attributes can never be NULL.

EX2_4 In the CUST_PROD table the primary key is a combination of field names (CID+PID+SALEDT), which uniquely identifies the corresponding field names of the table. For example (CID, PID, SALEDT) with the value (C1, P3, 14-JUL-13) will uniquely retrieve record as per Table 2.11.

TABLE 2.11 Records Based on the Query

CID	CNAME	CCITY	STATE	PID	PNAME	PCOST	PPROFIT	SALE	SALEDT
C1	PRADIP	MYSORE	KARNATAKA	P3	PEN	20.5	20	2	14-JUL-13

Similarly, (CID,PID,SALEDT) with value (C4, P3, 14-NOV-13) will uniquely retrieve record as shown in Table 2.12.

TABLE 2.12 Records Based on the Query

CID	CNAME	CCITY	STATE	PID	PNAME	PCOST	PPROFIT	SALE	SALEDT
C4	ARPAN	CHENNAI	TAMILNADU	P3	PEN	20.5	20	3	14-NOV-13

2.5.2 Foreign Key

A foreign key is an attribute or set of attributes that is the primary key of another table. It is used to link two tables.

EX2_5 In Table 2.10 primary key of CUST table is CID#, which is a foreign key of SALE_DETAIL table. CID is used to link both the tables. Similarly PID# is the primary key of PROD table and foreign key of SALE_DETAIL table.

2.5.3 Super Key

A super key is a combination of prime attribute(s) and one or more nonprime key attribute(s). Super key also uniquely identifies a record in a table. Primary key can be defined as super key with minimal attributes.

EX2_6 In Table 2.10 CID+CNAME+CCITY of CUST table is an example of super key as it contains prime attribute (CID) and nonprime attributes (CNAME and CCITY).

2.5.4 Candidate Key and Alternate Key

Candidate key is a minimal set of attributes that uniquely identifies a record in a table. There can be one or more candidate keys in a table. Any one out of the candidate keys can be chosen as a primary key. The remaining keys are called alternate keys.

EX2_7 In CUST_PROD table (CID+PID+SALEDT) and (CNAME+PNAME+SALEDT) are candidate keys. Both can uniquely identify record of CUST_PROD. Out of these two (CID+PID+SALEDT) is selected as a primary key. The remaining (CNAME+PNAME+SALEDT) becomes alternate key as it is not chosen as the primary key.

2.6 RELATIONAL ALGEBRA

Relational algebra is a collection of operations to manipulate relations. The basic operations are union, difference and intersection.

2.6.1 Union

Two relations P and Q are said to be union compatible if both P and Q are of same degree n and the domain of the corresponding n attributes are identical. Union is represented by $\cup$.

2.6.2 Difference

The difference operation removes common tuples from the first relation. Difference is represented by –.

2.6.3 Intersection

The intersection operation selects the common tuples from the two relations. Intersection is represented by $\cap$.

EX2_8 Let P and Q be defined by

P:

CID	CNAME
C1	PRADIP
C3	AASTIK
C4	ARPAN
C5	ANUMITA

Q:

CID	CNAME
C2	TUSHAR
C4	ARPAN

Based on the definition of union, intersection and difference, P $\cup$ Q, P – Q and P $\cap$ Q will be as follows:

P $\cup$ Q:

CID	CNAME
C1	PRADIP
C2	TUSHAR
C3	AASTIK
C4	ARPAN
C5	ANUMITA

P – Q

CID	CNAME
C1	PRADIP
C3	AASTIK
C5	ANUMITA

P $\cap$ Q:

CID	CNAME
C4	ARPAN

2.6.4 Projection

The projection operation yields a vertical subset of a relation. Projection is represented by Π.

2.6.5 Selection

The selection operation yields a horizontal subset of a relation. Selection is represented by σ.

EX2_9 This example demonstrates projection based on CUST table.

CUST TABLE

CID#	CNAME	CCITY
C1	PRADIP	MYSORE
C2	TUSHAR	PUNE
C3	AASTIK	KOLKATA
C4	ARPAN	CHENNAI
C5	ANUMITA	INDORE

Π_{CNAME} **(CUST)**

CNAME
PRADIP
TUSHAR
AASTIK
ARPAN
ANUMITA

EX2_10 This example demonstrates selection based on PROD table.

PROD TABLE

PID#	PNAME	PCOST	PROFIT
P1	PENCIL	5.25	
P2	FLOPPY	30	12
P3	PEN	20.5	20

$\sigma_{PCOST< 10}$ (PROD)

PID#	PNAME	PCOST	PROFIT
P1	PENCIL	5.25	

EX2_11 This example demonstrates projection and selection based on PROD table. It displays PNAME and PCOST whose PCOST is greater than 10.

$\Pi_{PNAME,PCOST}$ ($\sigma_{PCOST>10}$ (PROD))

PNAME	PCOST
FLOPPY	30
PEN	20.5

2.6.6 Join

The Join operation allows combining of two relations to form a single row relation. It is represented by ⋈.

EX2_12 This example demonstrates use of join operation with the help of two relations viz. CUST and SALE_DETAIL.

CUST

CID#	CNAME	CCITY
C1	PRADIP	MYSORE
C2	TUSHAR	PUNE
C3	AASTIK	KOLKATA
C4	ARPAN	CHENNAI
C5	ANUMITA	INDORE

SALE_DETAIL

CID#	PID#	SALE	SALEDT#
C1	P3	2	14-JUL-13
C3	P2	10	15-JUL-13
C2	P3	1	14-JUL-13
C1	P1	5	14-JUL-13
C1	P3	3	20-AUG-13
C4	P3	2	14-NOV-13
C5	P2	2	18-SEP-13

(a) Find CNAME and SALE whose SALE < 5.

$\Pi_{\text{CUST.CNAME, SALE\_DETAIL.SALE}}$
$(\sigma_{\text{CUST.CID=SALE\_DETAIL.CID}\wedge\text{SALE\_DETAIL.SALE}<5}(\text{CUST} \bowtie \text{SALE\_DETAIL}))$

CNAME	SALE
PRADIP	2
TUSHAR	1
PRADIP	3
ARPAN	2
ANUMITA	2

(b) Find all the columns of CUST relation, who have purchased product P2.

$\text{CUST} \bowtie \Pi_{\text{CID\#}}(\sigma_{\text{PID\#='P2'}}(\text{SALE\_DETAIL}))$

CUST⋈('C3', 'C5')

CID#	CNAME	CCITY
C3	AASTIK	KOLKATA
C5	ANUMITA	INDORE

This is an example of implicit join and implicit projection of all columns of a relation. Note that there is neither any join condition (like CUST.CID=SALE_DETAIL.CID) nor any project symbol to display CID#, CNAME and CCITY.

(c) Find CNAME and CCITY of CUST relation, who have purchased product P2.

$\Pi_{\text{CNAME,CCITY}}$ $(\text{CUST} \bowtie \Pi_{\text{CID\#}}(\sigma_{\text{PID\#='P2'}}(\text{SALE\_DETAIL})))$

CNAME	CCITY
AASTIK	KOLKATA
ANUMITA	INDORE

2.6.7 Division

The division operation is precisely "for all objects having all the specified properties". It is represented by ÷.

EX2_13 In the example relation P is constant and division is performed with Qs.

P

X	Y
x1	y1
x1	y2
x2	y1
x3	y1
x4	y2
x5	y1
x5	y2
x6	y1
x6	y2

(a) Find P ÷ Q1.

Q1

Y
y1
y2

In this case all x1, x5 and x6 are common to (y1, y2). Once again note the quoted sentence in the definition "for all objects having all the specified properties".

P ÷ Q1

X
x1
x5
x6

(b) Find P ÷ Q2

Q2

Y
y2

In this case x1, x4, x5 and x6 correspond to (y2).

P ÷ Q2

X
x1
x4
x5
x6

EX2_14 Find CID who has purchased pencil and pen both.

$\Pi_{PID,CID}$(SALE_DETAIL) will return the set of values corresponding to (PID, CID).

PID	CID
P3	C1
P2	C3
P3	C2
P1	C1
P3	C1
P3	C4
P2	C5

Π_{PID} ($\sigma_{PNAME= \text{'PENCIL'} \wedge PNAME \text{ 'PEN'}}$(PROD)) will return PID who have purchased PENCIL or PEN.

PID
P1
P3

Hence,

$\Pi_{PID,CID}$(SALE_DETAIL) ÷ Π_{PID} ($\sigma_{PNAME = PENCIL' \wedge PNAME = \text{'PEN'}}$(PROD)) = ('C1')

EX2_15 This example demonstrates use of various operators in relation algebra.

EMPLOYEE

EMP#	ENAME
1	DEVASIA
3	MINI
4	SUDARSHAN
6	DARSHAN
7	JAWAHAR
8	PANKAJ
9	MINI

ALLOTTED

PRJ#	EMP#
P1	1
P2	3
P2	4
P4	6
P5	6
P6	6
P2	6
P1	6
P4	7
P6	7
P5	8
P6	9
P2	9

PROJECT

PRJ#	PRJ_NAME	PRJ_LEADER
P1	RDBMS	1
P2	OS	4
P4	JAVA	7
P5	OBJECT	8
P6	RDBMS	7

FIGURE 2.1 Tables with records.

(a) Find details of employees (both EMP# and ENAME) working on Project P6.
EMPLOYEE ⋈ $\Pi_{EMP\#}$($\sigma_{PRJ\# = \text{'P6'}}$(ALLOTTED))

EMP#	ENAME
6	DARSHAN
7	JAWAHAR
9	MINI

(b) Find the EMP# who works on at least all of the projects that employee 7 works on.
(ALLOTTED) ÷ ($\Pi_{PRJ\#}$($\sigma_{EMP\#=7}$(ALLOTTED))) – 7

EMP#
6

(c) Find the EMP# who do not works on project P1.
$\Pi_{EMP\#}$(ALLOTTED) – $\Pi_{EMP\#}$($\sigma_{PRJ\# = \text{'P1'}}$ (ALLOTTED))

EMP#
4
7
8
9

2.7 NORMALIZATION

Normalization is a process for assignment of attributes to entities. It involves identification of the required attributes and their subsequent decomposition based on related attributes. Normalization ensures that the relations derived from the data model are free from data redundancy. There are several normal forms each with its own restrictions. The normalization process uses a series of tests to determine whether it satisfies the requirements of each normal form. In case it does not conform to the normal form, it may be possible to decompose the relation into two or more equivalent relations that satisfy the requirements of the form. Decomposition of relation is done to eliminate insertion, updation and deletion anomalies. The insertion anomaly arises due to failure to place information about a new entry in a table. The updation anomaly arises due to non synchronization of data while updating certain columns. Failure to remove information of an existing record from a table causes deletion anomaly. All these three types of anomalies are highly undesirable and must be eliminated. The highest level of normalization is fifth normal form in practical implementations. However, it is not always desirable as it requires additional processing to join the decomposed tables. We usually stop at third normal form. Flat-file database shown in Table 2.1 is used as an example for normalization from first normal form to third normal form.

2.8 FUNCTIONAL DEPENDENCY

Given is a relation R, A and B are attributes or a set of attributes of relation R. B is said to be functionally dependent on A if each values of A in R is associated with exactly one value of B.

EX2_16 In Figure 2.4 the following functional dependency exists.

CID → CNAME, CCITY, STATE

PID → PNAME, PCOST, PPROFIT

CID, PID, SALEDT → SALE

This means CNAME, CCITY and STATE depends on CID. Similarly, PNAME, PCOST and PPROFIT depends on PID. CID and PID act as primary keys for the respective groups. SALE is uniquely identified by composite primary key comprising of CID, PID and SALEDT.

An attribute or set of attributes B is fully functionally dependent on an attribute or set of attributes A if it is functionally dependent on A, but not on any proper subset of A. That is, all of the attributes of A (say A1, A2, A3, ..., A*n*) are needed to functionally determine B.

EX2_17 In Figure 2.4 the following are fully functional dependent.

PID → PNAME, PCOST, PPROFIT

CID, PID, SALEDT → SALE

2.9 FIRST NORMAL FORM

A relation is in first Normal Form (1NF) if the domains of all its attributes are atomic, and the value of any attribute in a tuple is a single value from its domain. Multiple values for an attribute are strictly not allowed in 1NF. In CUST_PROD (Table 2.1) C1 is listed thrice, once for each product he has purchased. We could have put all the three in the same record as shown in Table 2.13 to make it non-atomic. A table is in 1NF, if it is free from any non-atomic values. Formally a relation is in 1NF if and only if all underlying domains contain atomic values only.

TABLE 2.13 An Example of Non-atomicity

CID#	CNAME	CCITY	STATE	PID#	PNAME	PCOST	PPROFIT	SALE	SALEDT#
C1	PRADIP	MYSORE	KARNATAKA	P1	PENCIL	5.25		5	14-JUL-13
				P3	PEN	20.5	20	2	14-JUL-13
				P3	PEN	20.5	20	3	20-AUG-13

Table 2.13 can be made atomic by inserting the values corresponding to CID, CNAME, CCITY and STATE for C1 as shown in Table 2.14. Atomiticity is an essential requirement for any relational database management system.

TABLE 2.14 An Example of Atomicity

CID#	CNAME	CCITY	STATE	PID#	PNAME	PCOST	PPROFIT	SALE	SALEDT#
C1	PRADIP	MYSORE	KARNATAKA	P1	PENCIL	5.25		5	14-JUL-13
C1	PRADIP	MYSORE	KARNATAKA	P3	PEN	20.5	20	2	14-JUL-13
C1	PRADIP	MYSORE	KARNATAKA	P3	PEN	20.5	20	3	20-AUG-13

CUST_PROD as shown in Table 2.15 is in 1NF.

TABLE 2.15 First Normal Form

CUST_PROD

CID#	CNAME	CCITY	STATE	PID#	PNAME	PCOST	PPROFIT	SALE	SALEDT#
C1	PRADIP	MYSORE	KARNATAKA	P1	PENCIL	5.25		5	14-JUL-13
C1	PRADIP	MYSORE	KARNATAKA	P3	PEN	20.5	20	2	14-JUL-13
C1	PRADIP	MYSORE	KARNATAKA	P3	PEN	20.5	20	3	20-AUG-13
C2	TUSHAR	PUNE	MAHARASTRA	P3	PEN	20.5	20	1	14-JUL-13
C3	AASTIK	KOLKATA	WEST BENGAL	P2	FLOPPY	30	12	10	15-JUL-13
C4	ARPAN	CHENNAI	TAMILNADU	P3	PEN	20.5	20	3	14-NOV-13
C5	ANUMITA	INDORE	MADHYA PRADESH	P2	FLOPPY	30	12	2	18-SEP-13

Representing CUST_PROD in 1NF is the basic requirement, but it is only the first step towards systematic way of storage and retrieval of data. 1NF is not free from insertion, updation and deletion anomalies.

2.9.1 Insert Anomaly Related to 1NF

EX2_18 A new customer (C6, PRANAB, ALLAHABAD, UP) wants to register but does not want to purchase any product.

In this case the customer related information can not be inserted. This is because PID, PNAME, PCOST, PPROFIT, SALE and SALEDT will be NULL. In these fields PID and SALEDT are present which are prime attributes and as per the definition of primary key it cannot be NULL (Table 2.16).

TABLE 2.16 Insert Anomaly in First Normal Form

CUST_PROD

CID#	CNAME	CCITY	STATE	PID#	PNAME	PCOST	PPROFIT	SALE	SALEDT#
C1	PRADIP	MYSORE	KARNATAKA	P1	PENCIL	5.25		5	14-JUL-13
C1	PRADIP	MYSORE	KARNATAKA	P3	PEN	20.5	20	2	14-JUL-13
C1	PRADIP	MYSORE	KARNATAKA	P3	PEN	20.5	20	3	20-AUG-13
C2	TUSHAR	PUNE	MAHARASTRA	P3	PEN	20.5	20	1	14-JUL-13
C3	AASTIK	KOLKATA	WEST BENGAL	P2	FLOPPY	30	12	10	15-JUL-13
C4	ARPAN	CHENNAI	TAMILNADU	P3	PEN	20.5	20	3	14-NOV-13
C5	ANUMITA	INDORE	MADHYA PRADESH	P2	FLOPPY	30	12	2	18-SEP-13
C6	PRANAB	ALLAHABAD	UP	???					???

EX2_19 Insert a new product's information (P4, RUBBER, 2, 10) that is not purchased by any customer.

It cannot be inserted because the prime attribute CID and SALEDT will be NULL (Table 2.17).

TABLE 2.17 Insert Anomaly in First Normal Form

CUST_PROD

CID#	CNAME	CCITY	STATE	PID#	PNAME	PCOST	PPROFIT	SALE	SALEDT#
C1	PRADIP	MYSORE	KARNATAKA	P1	PENCIL	5.25		5	14-JUL-13
C1	PRADIP	MYSORE	KARNATAKA	P3	PEN	20.5	20	2	14-JUL-13
C1	PRADIP	MYSORE	KARNATAKA	P3	PEN	20.5	20	3	20-AUG-13
C2	TUSHAR	PUNE	MAHARASTRA	P3	PEN	20.5	20	1	14-JUL-13
C3	AASTIK	KOLKATA	WEST BENGAL	P2	FLOPPY	30	12	10	15-JUL-13
C4	ARPAN	CHENNAI	TAMILNADU	P3	PEN	20.5	20	3	14-NOV-13
C5	ANUMITA	INDORE	MADHYA PRADESH	P2	FLOPPY	30	12	2	18-SEP-13
???				P4	RUBBER	2	10		???

The problems related to insertion of data mentioned above is called **insertion anomaly.**

2.9.2 Update Anomaly Related to 1NF

EX2_20 Update PEN with product code P3 to PAPER. What will happen if it is correctly updated in 3 places and not updated in 1 place.

In this case P3 refers to PAPER as well as PEN, which is ambiguous. This is known as non-synchronization in a table (Table 2.18).

TABLE 2.18 Update Anomaly in First Normal Form

CUST_PROD

CID#	CNAME	CCITY	STATE	PID#	PNAME	PCOST	PPROFIT	SALE	SALEDT#
C1	PRADIP	MYSORE	KARNATAKA	P3	PAPER	20.5	20	2	14-JUL-13
C3	AASTIK	KOLKATA	WEST BENGAL	P2	FLOPPY	30	12	10	15-JUL-13
C2	TUSHAR	PUNE	MAHARASTRA	P3	PAPER	20.5	20	1	14-JUL-13
C1	PRADIP	MYSORE	KARNATAKA	P1	PENCIL	5.25		5	14-JUL-13
C1	PRADIP	MYSORE	KARNATAKA	P3	PEN	20.5	20	3	20-AUG-13
C4	ARPAN	CHENNAI	TAMILNADU	P3	PAPER	20.5	20	3	14-NOV-13
C5	ANUMITA	INDORE	MADHYA PRADESH	P2	FLOPPY	30	12	2	18-SEP-13

EX2_21 PRADIP is transferred from MYSORE to ANANTAPUR. While updating 2 values are modified correctly, whereas in one place instead of typing ANANTPUR, ANANTRUR is typed.

This will also lead to non-synchronization of data. These types of updation problems which lead to non-synchronization of data are known as **updation anomaly**.

2.9.3 Delete Anomaly Related to 1NF

EX2_22 TUSHAR is going to New Jersey and wants to delete his name from CUST_PROD. Record related to TUSHAR is shown in Table 2.19.

TABLE 2.19 Delete Anomaly in First Normal Form

CID#	CNAME	CCITY	STATE	PID#	PNAME	PCOST	PPROFIT	SALE	SALEDT#
C2	TUSHAR	PUNE	MAHARASTRA	P3	PEN	20.5	20	1	14-JUL-13

In this case PEN is purchased only by TUSHAR and if his record is deleted then all information related to PEN will be lost.

EX2_23 M/s ABC has decided to stop selling FLOPPY.
Records related to FLOPPY is shown in Table 2.20.

TABLE 2.20 Delete Anomaly In First Normal Form

CID#	CNAME	CCITY	STATE	PID#	PNAME	PCOST	PPROFIT	SALE	SALEDT#
C3	AASTIK	KOLKATA	WEST BENGAL	P2	FLOPPY	30	12	10	15-JUL-13
C5	ANUMITA	INDORE	MADHYA PRADESH	P2	FLOPPY	30	12	2	18-SEP-13

In this case if FLOPPY related information are deleted, all information related to AASTIK and ANUMITA will also be deleted which is not desired.
These types of problems are called as **deletion anomaly**.

In case of 1NF, insertion, updation and deletion anomaly are common in nature. Data redundancy is also an issue in 1NF. Anomalies encountered in 1NF can be avoided in higher normal form.

2.10 SECOND NORMAL FORM

The insertion, updation and deletion anomalies encountered in 1NF are due to partial functional dependencies. The primary key of CUST_PROD is {CID, PID, SALEDT}. However, some of the nonkey attributes are functionally dependent on only one of the attributes in the key. For example, CID $\rightarrow$ CNAME, without PID or SALEDT. This is an example of partial dependency, which second normal form (2NF) does not allow. To eliminate the problem, the relation should be decomposed into three relations, each of which is in 2NF. Formally a relation is in 2NF if and only if it is in 1NF and every non key attribute is functionally dependent on the primary key.

In CUST_PROD non key attributes are CNAME, CCITY, STATE, PNAME, PCOST, PPROFIT and SALE fields. CNAME, CCITY and STATE are functionally dependent on CID. PCOST, PPROFIT and STATE are functionally dependent on PID. And SALE is functionally dependent on CID+PID+SALEDT fields. Diagrammatically it is shown in Figure 2.2.

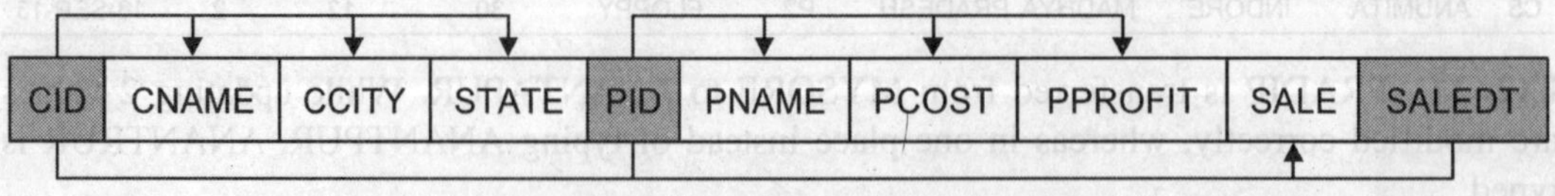

FIGURE 2.2 Functional dependency.

CUST_PROD columns can be grouped into CUST, PROD and SALE_DETAIL tables. CUST table contains customer related information. PROD contains product related information and SALE_DETAIL is related to sales details. CID is primary key of CUST tables and is represented by CID#, similarly PID# is primary key of PROD table and CID#+PID#+SALEDT# is a primary key of SALE_DETAIL table. Common fields CID and PID connect CUST and PROD tables with SALE DETAIL table. Diagrammatically it is shown in Figure 2.3.

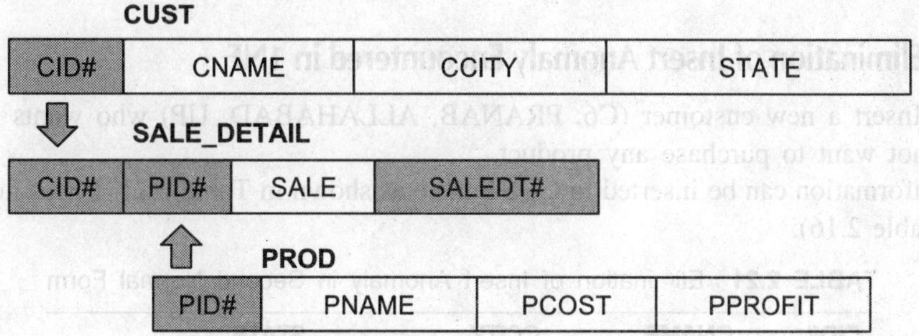

FIGURE 2.3 Relationship among tables.

The CUST, PROD and SALE_DETAIL tables with respective records are shown in Figure 2.4.

CUST

CID#	CNAME	CCITY	STATE
C1	PRADIP	MYSORE	KARNATAKA
C3	AASTIK	KOLKATA	WEST BENGAL
C2	TUSHAR	PUNE	MAHARASTRA
C4	ARPAN	CHENNAI	TAMILNADU
C5	ANUMITA	INDORE	MADHYA PRADESH

SALE_DETAIL

CID#	PID#	SALE	SALEDT#
C1	P3	2	14-JUL-13
C3	P2	10	15-JUL-13
C2	P3	1	14-JUL-13
C1	P1	5	14-JUL-13
C1	P3	3	20-AUG-13
C4	P3	3	14-NOV-13
C5	P2	2	18-SEP-13

PROD

PID#	PNAME	PCOST	PPROFIT
P3	PEN	20.5	20
P2	FLOPPY	30	12
P1	PENCIL	5.25	

FIGURE 2.4 Tables with records.

The CUST and SALE_DETAIL tables can be joined using CID column available in both the tables. In CUST table CID is primary key, whereas in SALE_DETAIL CID is foreign key. Similarly, in case of PROD, PID is primary key, whereas in SALE_DETAIL it is foreign key. If a foreign key is defined in one table, any value in it should exist as a primary key in another table. Note that redundant rows of CUST and PROD table are eliminated; at the same time no information is lost. All the three tables can be joined using common columns. This is called **loss less join**.

2.10.1 Elimination of Insert Anomaly Encountered in 1NF

EX2_24 Insert a new customer (C6, PRANAB, ALLAHABAD, UP) who wants to register and does not want to purchase any product.

This information can be inserted in CUST table as shown in Table 2.21. It was not possible in 1NF (Table 2.16).

TABLE 2.21 Elimination of Insert Anomaly in Second Normal Form

CID#	CNAME	CCITY	STATE
C1	PRADIP	MYSORE	KARNATAKA
C3	AASTIK	KOLKATA	WEST BENGAL
C2	TUSHAR	PUNE	MAHARASTRA
C4	ARPAN	CHENNAI	TAMILNADU
C5	ANUMITA	INDORE	MADHYA PRADESH
C6	PRANAB	ALLAHABAD	UP

EX2_25 Insert a new product's information (P4, RUBBER, 2, 10), which is yet not purchased by any customer.

This information can be entered in PROD table as shown in Table 2.22. It was not possible in 1NF (Table 2.17).

TABLE 2.22 Elimination of Insert Anomaly in Second Normal Form

PID#	PNAME	PCOST	PPROFIT
P3	PEN	20.5	20
P2	FLOPPY	30	12
P1	PENCIL	5.25	
P4	RUBBER	2	10

2.10.2 Elimination of Update Anomaly Encountered in 1NF

EX2_26 Update PEN with product code P3 to PAPER. What will happen if it is correctly updated in 3 places and not updated in 1 place.

Updation anomaly is eliminated as only one record P3 is updated in PROD table. It is shown in Table 2.23. In SALE_DETAIL table P3 in all four places will be the same, i.e. (PAPER, 20.5, 20). It was also not possible in 1NF (Table 2.18).

TABLE 2.23 Elimination of Update Anomaly in Second Normal Form

PROD

PID#	PNAME	PCOST	PPROFIT
P3	PAPER	20.5	20
P2	FLOPPY	30	12
P1	PENCIL	5.25	

EX2_27 PRADIP is transferred from MYSORE to ANANTPUR, while updation 2 is modified correctly, whereas in one place instead of typing ANANTPUR, ANANTRUR (RUR in place of PUR) is typed.

There is no updation anomaly as one record corresponding to PRADIP is updated. It is shown in Table 2.24. In SALE_DETAIL table C1 in all the three places will be the same, i.e. (PRADIP, ANANTAPUR, KARNATAKA).

TABLE 2.24 Elimination of Update Anomaly in the Second Normal Form

CUST

CID#	CNAME	CCITY	STATE
C1	PRADIP	ANANTAPUR	KARNATAKA
C3	AASTIK	KOLKATA	WEST BENGAL
C2	TUSHAR	PUNE	MAHARASTRA
C4	ARPAN	CHENNAI	TAMILNADU
C5	ANUMITA	INDORE	MADHYA PRADESH

2.10.3 Elimination of Delete Anomaly Encountered in 1NF

EX2_28 TUSHAR is going to New Jersey and wants to delete his name.
Record related to TUSHAR can be deleted in CUST table. PROD table records are intact and not effected by deletion operation in CUST table. It is shown in Figure 2.5. However, CCITY and STATE related information will be lost.

CUST

CID#	CNAME	CCITY	STATE
C1	PRADIP	MYSORE	KARNATAKA
C3	AASTIK	KOLKATA	WEST BENGAL
C4	ARPAN	CHENNAI	TAMILNADU
C5	ANUMITA	INDORE	MADHYA PRADESH

PROD

PID	PNAME	PCOST	PPROFIT
P3	PEN	20.5	20
P2	FLOPPY	30	12
P1	PENCIL	5.25	

FIGURE 2.5 Elimination of delete anomaly in second normal form

EX2_29 ABC has decided to stop selling FLOPPY.
Record related to FLOPPY in PROD table can be deleted without effecting records of CUST table. It is shown in Figure 2.6.

PROD

PID#	PNAME	PCOST	PPROFIT
P3	PEN	20.5	20
P1	PENCIL	5.25	

CUST

CID#	CNAME	CCITY	STATE
C1	PRADIP	MYSORE	KARNATAKA
C3	AASTIK	KOLKATA	WEST BENGAL
C2	TUSHAR	PUNE	MAHARASTRA
C4	ARPAN	CHENNAI	TAMILNADU
C5	ANUMITA	INDORE	MADHYA PRADESH

FIGURE 2.6 Elimination of delete anomaly in second normal form.

All anomalies related to 1NF are eliminated in 2NF by decomposing CUST_PROD into three tables. 2NF is also not fully free from all anomalies. Anomalies occurring in 2NF are due to transitive dependency. Transitive dependency is $A \rightarrow B$ and $B \rightarrow C \Rightarrow A \rightarrow C$.

2.10.4 Insert Anomaly in 2NF

EX2_30 Insert a record (HYDERABAD, AP) in CUST table.
It can not be inserted because no customer belongs to HYDERABAD. Prime attribute CID# of CUST table will be empty, which is not allowed. It is shown in Table 2.25.

TABLE 2.25 Insert Anomaly in Second Normal Form

CUST

CID#	CNAME	CCITY	STATE
C1	PRADIP	MYSORE	KARNATAKA
C3	AASTIK	KOLKATA	WEST BENGAL
C4	ARPAN	CHENNAI	TAMILNADU
C5	ANUMITA	INDORE	MADHYA PRADESH
???		HYDERABAD	AP

2.10.5 Delete Anomaly in 2NF

EX2_31 TUSHAR is going to New Jersey and wants to delete his name.
CCITY and STATE related information will be lost if TUSHAR related information is deleted. It is shown in Table 2.26.

TABLE 2.26 Delete Anomaly in Second Normal Form

CUST

CID#	CNAME	CCITY	STATE
C1	PRADIP	MYSORE	KARNATAKA
C3	AASTIK	KOLKATA	WEST BENGAL
C2	TUSHAR	PUNE	MAHARASTRA
C4	ARPAN	CHENNAI	TAMILNADU
C5	ANUMITA	INDORE	MADHYA PRADESH

Anomalies encountered in 2NF are eliminated in third normal form.

2.11 THIRD NORMAL FORM

A transitive dependency exists when a nonprime attribute determines another nonprime attribute. In CUST table CID -> CCITY and CCITY -> STATE => CID->STATE. Diagrammatically it is shown in Figure 2.7. In third normal form transitive dependency is not allowed.

CID# | CNAME | CCITY | STATE

FIGURE 2.7 Transitive relationship.

To avoid transitive dependency CUST table is further partitioned in two tables. CUST and STATE_NAME tables as shown in Figure 2.8.

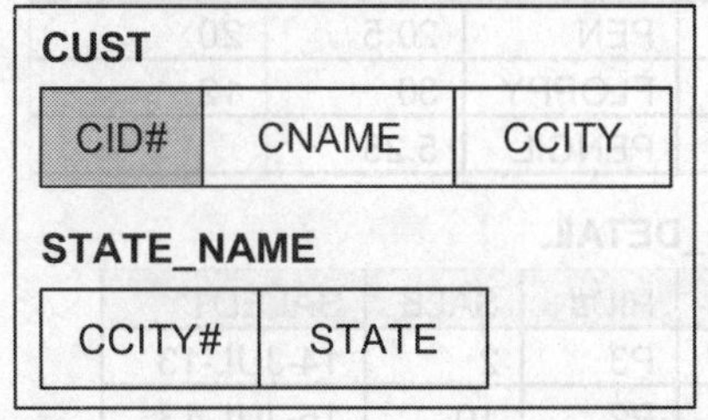

FIGURE 2.8 Tables free from transitive dependency.

Formally a relation is in third normal form (3NF) if and only if it is in 2NF which is free from transitive dependency. After 3NF, there will be four tables and the relations are shown in Figure 2.9.

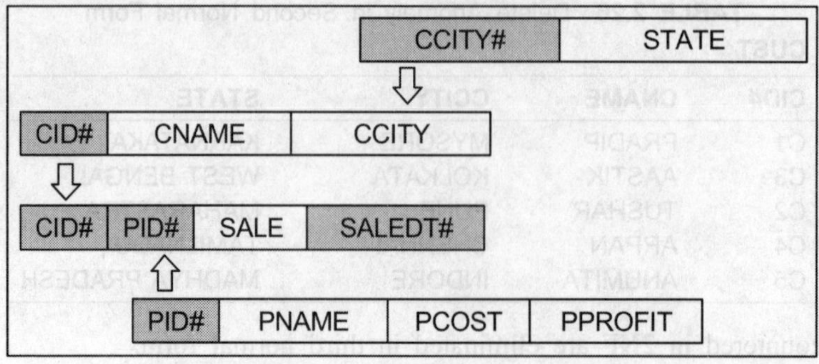

FIGURE 2.9 Relationship of tables.

All the four tables along with its records are shown in CUST, PROD, SALE_DETAIL and STATE_NAME tables. It is shown in Figure 2.10

CUST

CID#	CNAME	CCITY
C1	PRADIP	MYSORE
C3	AASTIK	KOLKATA
C2	TUSHAR	PUNE
C4	ARPAN	CHENNAI
C5	ANUMITA	INDORE

PROD

PID#	PNAME	PCOST	PPROFIT
P3	PEN	20.5	20
P2	FLOPPY	30	12
P1	PENCIL	5.25	

SALE_DETAIL

CID#	PID#	SALE	SALEDT
C1	P3	2	14-JUL-13
C3	P2	10	15-JUL-13
C2	P3	1	14-JUL-13
C1	P1	5	14-JUL-13
C1	P3	3	20-AUG-13
C4	P3	3	14-NOV-13
C5	P2	2	18-SEP-13

STATE_NAME

CCITY#	STATE
MYSORE	KARNATAKA
KOLKATA	WEST BENGAL
PUNE	MAHARASTRA
CHENNAI	TAMILNADU
INDORE	MADHYA PRADESH

FIGURE 2.10 Tables with records after third normal form.

2.11.1 Elimination of Insert Anomaly Encountered in 2NF

EX2_32 Insert a record (HYDERABAD, AP) in CUST table.
It can be inserted without any problem, as STATE_NAME is a separate table. It is shown in Table 2.27. It was not possible in 2NF (Table 2.25).

TABLE 2.27 Elimination of Insert Anomaly in Third Normal Form

STATE_NAME

CCITY#	STATE
MYSORE	KARNATAKA
KOLKATA	WEST BENGAL
PUNE	MAHARASTRA
CHENNAI	TAMILNADU
INDORE	MADHYA PRADESH
HYDERABAD	AP

2.11.2 Elimination of Delete Anomaly Encountered in 2NF

EX2_33 TUSHAR is going to New Jersey and wants to delete his name. Even after deleting TUSHAR related information from CUST table, CCITY and STATE related information is not lost as they are stored in STATE_NAME table. It is shown in Figure 2.11. It was not possible in 2NF (Table 2.26).

CUST

CID#	CNAME	CCITY
C1	PRADIP	MYSORE
C3	AASTIK	KOLKATA
C4	ARPAN	CHENNAI
C5	ANUMITA	INDORE

STATE_NAME

CCITY#	STATE
MYSORE	KARNATAKA
KOLKATA	WEST BENGAL
PUNE	MAHARASTRA
CHENNAI	TAMILNADU
INDORE	MADHYA PRADESH

FIGURE 2.11 Elimination of delete anomaly in third normal form.

2.12 BOYCE–CODD NORMAL FORM

A relation is in Boyce Codd Normal Form (BCNF) if and only if every determinant is a candidate key. Recall that determinant, If A → B is a functional dependency, and if B is not functionally dependent upon any subset of A, then A is said to be the determinant of B. This definition states that a determinant is a column on which some of the columns are fully functional dependent. In most cases 3NF is also BCNF. 3NF is not BCNF only when a relation has composite candidate keys that have atleast one attribute in common.

The BCNF is implemented in cases where the table has

(a) Multiple candidate keys
(b) Composite candidate keys
(c) Candidate keys that overlap

EX2_34 The following relation is in BCNF (and also in 3NF)

SUPPLIERS (SUP_NO, SUP_NAME, CITY, ZIP)

We assume that each supplier has a unique supplier SUP_NO, so that SUP_NO and SUP_NAME are both candidate keys. Note that city have multiple 'zips'.

Functional dependencies are as follows.

SUP_NO → CITY
SUP_NO → ZIP
SUP_NO → SUP_NAME
SUP_NAME → CITY
SUP_NAME → ZIP
SUP_NAME → SUP_NO

The relation is in BCNF since both determinants (SUP_NO and SUP_NAME) are unique (i.e. are candidate keys).

2.12.1 Insert Anomaly in BCNF

We cannot record the city for a supplier _no without also knowing the SUP_NAME.

2.12.2 Delete Anomaly in BCNF

If we delete the row for a given SUP_NAME, we lose the information that the SUP_NO is associated with a given city.

The SUPPLIERS relation can be decomposed to address BCNF.

SUP_INFO (SUP_NO, CITY, ZIP)
SUP_NAME (SUP_NO, SUP_NAME)

2.13 FOURTH NORMAL FORM

A relation is in fourth normal form if it is in BCNF and has no nontrivial multivalue dependencies. Multivalued dependency may arise out of the process of normalization to achieve 1NF. It is because 1NF forbids multiple values in a cell of a table. A multivalued dependency exists when there are three attributes A, B, and C in a relation R such that for each value of A the set of B values associated with the A value are independent of the set of C values associated with the A value. Multivalued dependency is eliminated by decomposing the 3NF relation so that multiple values in a cell of a table are removed.

A table is in fifth normal form if it is in fourth normal form and if every join dependency in the table is a consequence of the candidate key of the table. In practical implementations normalization up to 3NF is sufficient. BCNF, 4NF, 5NF and higher normal forms are of academic interest.

EX2_35 This is an example related to 4NF.

COURSE_DETAIL

COURSE_ID	INSTRUCTOR	TEXT_BOOK
C107	PKDG	EOP
C107	PKDG	OPLSQL
C107	SP	EOP
C107	SP	OPLSQL

By placing the multivalued attributes in tables by themselves, we can convert the above to 4NF.

COURSE_INST (COURCE_ID, INSTRUCTOR)

COURSE_TEXT (COURSE_ID,TEXT_BOOK)

2.14 ORACLE DATABASE SERVER

Oracle database server is a true Relational Database Management System (RDBMS). The tools provided by Oracle are very user friendly. A person may use it with minimal skill in the field of computer science. At present Oracle is the most popular, most used and most trusted RDBMS. It can be used both in two-tier as well as in three-tier architecture. In a two-tier architecture, a client communicates directly with a server. This is also known as Client–Server Architecture. Diagrammatically it is shown in Figure 2.12.

BACK END : Oracle 10g Database Server
FRONT END : Oracle 10g Clients/Oracle Developer 2000

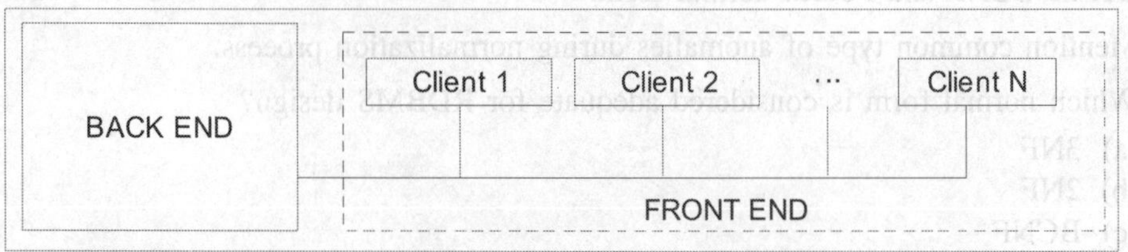

FIGURE 2.12 Client/server architecture.

In a three-tier architecture, the role of middle-tier is to provide business logic, acting as a bridge between back-end and front-end, monitor to balance the load of servers placed in middle tier, and mapping a request to the right server. Diagrammatically it is shown in Figure 2.13.

BACK END : Oracle 10g database server
MIDDLE TIER : Oracle 10g application server/web server/e-mail server/proxy server
FRONT END : Internet explorer 6 or mozila, etc.

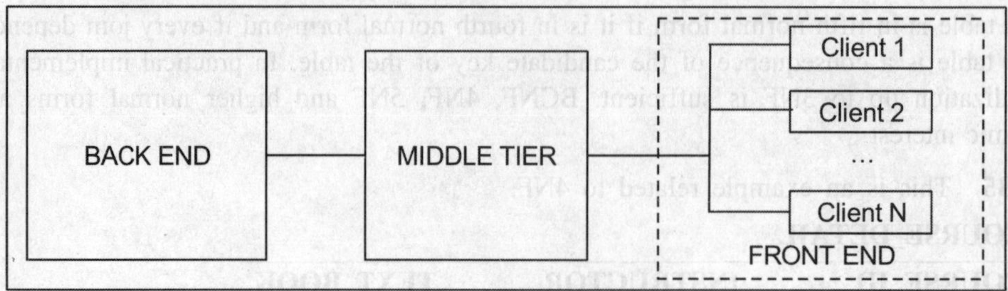

FIGURE 2.13 Three tier architecture.

2.15 SUMMARY

Normalization is a process for assignment of attributes to entities in such a way that they become free from any anomalies and redundancy. Oracle database server is a true object-relational database management system. It is dominating the market because of its robust architecture and ease of usage.

SHORT/OBJECTIVE TYPE QUESTIONS

1. What are the disadvantages of flat file database?
2. How 'Cartesian product' and 'relations' are associated with each other?
3. What is the difference between primary key and unique key?
4. Define candidate key.
5. Define division operation.
6. Describe fully functional dependency with the help of an example.
7. Define BCNF and Fourth normal form.
8. Mention common type of anomalies during normalization process.
9. Which normal form is considered adequate for RDBMS design?
   (a) 3NF
   (b) 2NF
   (c) BCNF
   (d) 4NF
10. If every non-key attribute is functionally dependent on the primary key, the relation will be in
    (a) 1NF
    (b) 2NF
    (c) 3NF
    (d) 4NF

11. The column of a table is referred to as the
(a) Tuple
(b) Entity
(c) Degree
(d) Attribute

12. Relation produced from an ER model will always be in
(a) 1NF
(b) 2NF
(c) 3NF
(d) 4NF

13. Select true/false statement
(a) An alternate key is a primary key that is not a candidate key
(b) An alternate key is a candidate key that is not a primary key
(c) An alternate key is a candidate key that is also a primary key

14. An attribute of one table matching the primary key of another table, is called as
(a) Primary key
(b) Unique key
(c) Composite key
(d) Foreign key

15. Oracle database server supports
(a) Client/server architecture
(b) Three-tier architecture
(c) None of the above

16. Join correctly the following

(a) Projection	(a) yields a horizontal subset of a relation
(b) Selection	(b) selects a vertical subset of a relation
(c) Join	(c) allows combining two relations

17. A domain is/are
(a) Finite set from which values can be chosen
(b) Infinite set from which values can be chosen
(c) None of the above

18. Primary key can also be defined as
(a) Super key with minimal attributes
(b) Any one candidate key
(c) Combination of prime attributes
(d) Alternate key

19. Disadvantage of normalization is/are
(a) Elimination of anomalies
(b) Increase in execution time because of join
(c) Overall reduction of space
(d) Minimal redundancy

20. Transitive dependency is related to
(a) 1NF
(b) 2NF
(c) 3NF
(d) 4NF

WORKOUT SECTION

W2_1 In the example relation P is constant and division is performed with Qs.

P

X	Y
x1	y1
x1	y2
x2	y1
x3	y1
x4	y2
x5	y1
x5	y2
x6	y1
x6	y2

(i) Find **P ÷ Q1** if

Q1

Y
y1

(ii) Find **P ÷ Q2** if

Q2

Y

W2_2 Write query using relational operators based on EMPLOYEE, ALLOTTED and PROJECT tables (as shown in Figure 2.1).

(i) Find EMP# working on Project P6.
(ii) Find details of employees (both EMP# and ENAME) working on the RDBMS Project.
(iii) Find details of employees (both EMP# and ENAME) working on both P6 and P2.
(iv) Find the EMP# who work on all projects.
(v) Find the EMP# other than employee 7 who work on at least one project that employee 7 works on.

W2_3 Snapshot of flat-file database DAILY_ALLOWANCE is shown in Table 2.28. It is required to determine the amount to be paid to the employee who is going to a different city for some office related work. The payable amount is calculated based on CCODE, PCODE and mode of stay, i.e. HOTELRATE if stayed in a hotel or ORDYRATE if stayed in his own arrangement. The following rules are applicable to calculate the payable amount.

- CNAME is based on CCODE.
- LOSAL and HISAL is the range of pay and is defined by PCODE.
- Daily allowance (HOTELRATE or ORDYRATE) is based on CCODE and PCODE.

For example a person goes to MUMBAI, his pay is 15,000 and stays in hotel. In this case CCODE = A1, PCODE = P2 (because his pay is 15,000 and range of P2 is from 8000 to 16,399) and he stays in hotel. Clearly the payable amount will be ₹ 505.

Answer the following with respect to DAILY_ALLOWANCE table shown in Table 2.28.

(i) What is the primary key in DAILY_ALLOWANCE table?
(ii) Is it possible to insert city related data like CCODE, CNAME, etc. whose PCODE, LOSAL, etc. are not known? If no, why?
(iii) Explain Update anomaly with respect to DAILY_ALLOWANCE.
(iv) What are the functional dependencies in DAILY_ALLOWANCE?
(v) Draw ER model corresponding to DAILY_ALLOWANCE.
(vi) Decompose DAILY_ALLOWANCE into 2NF with relevant data.
(vii) Does any transitive dependency occur in 2NF?

TABLE 2.28 Tables and Records

DAILY_ALLOWANCE

CCODE	CNAME	PCODE	LOSAL	HISAL	HOTELRATE	ORDYRATE
A1	MUMBAI	P1	16,400	99,999	650	260
A1	MUMBAI	P2	8000	16,399	505	230
A1	MUMBAI	P3	6500	7999	380	200
A1	MUMBAI	P4	4100	6499	245	170
A1	MUMBAI	P5	0	4099	125	105
A	HYDERABAD	P1	16,400	99,999	525	210
A	HYDERABAD	P2	8000	16,399	405	185
A	HYDERABAD	P3	6500	7999	305	160
A	HYDERABAD	P4	4100	6499	195	135
A	HYDERABAD	P5	0	4099	100	85
B1	BHOPAL	P1	16,400	99,999	425	170
B1	BHOPAL	P2	8000	16,399	330	150
B1	BHOPAL	P3	6500	7999	250	130
B1	BHOPAL	P4	4100	6499	160	110
B1	BHOPAL	P5	0	4099	85	70

W2_4 Table 2.29 shows PROJECT table that is already in 1NF.

TABLE 2.29 Tables and Records

PROJECT

EMPNO	ENAME	DESG	HRRATE	PROJNO	PROJNAME	HRWORKED
E1	ANUP	ANALYST	800	P2	CODING	15
E2	ARUP	DBA	1000	P3	DATA RECOVERY	10
E2	ARUP	DBA	1000	P1	DATABASE SW	40
E2	ARUP	DBA	1000	P2	CODING	10
E3	KAUSHIK	ANALYST	800	P1	DATABASE SW	20
E4	AMIT	PROGRAMMER	500	P2	CODING	40
E5	CHANDRA	PROGRAMMER	500	P1	DATABASE SW	30

Answer the following with respect to PROJECT table.

(i) What is the primary key in PROJECT table?

(ii) Is it possible to insert employee related data like EMPNO, ENAME, DESG, etc. who is yet not assigned to any project? If no, why?

(iii) Is it possible to insert project related data like PROJNO, PROJNAME, etc. to which no employee is associated? If no, why?

(iv) If ARUP leaves the company and all records relevant to him are deleted, what is the side effect?

(v) What are the functional dependencies in PROJECT?

(vi) Draw ER model corresponding to PROJECT.

(vii) Decompose PROJECT into 2NF with relevant data.

(viii) In 2NF, find the transitive dependency.

(ix) Decompose required relations to 3NF.

3

SQL Basics, Functions, Sub Query and Joins

Learning Objectives

You will learn following key concepts after completion of the chapter:

✓ Data control language, data definition language and data manipulation language
✓ Transaction control language and data retrieval
✓ Single and group functions
✓ Equi, non-equi, outer and self joins

3.1 INTRODUCTION

Structured Query Language is the standard language for creation and maintenance of relational database management system. The language allows users to create and modify the objects of a relational database. User can insert, update, delete the data and perform queries on the data using Structured Query Language (SQL). SQL is not a case sensitive language. It can be described as a declarative language because data can be retrieved without specifying the procedures for retrieving it. Oracle was one of the first commercial relational databases to use SQL as its language. SQL provides specialized functions to perform operations using data manipulation commands. A function is a module that takes one or more arguments and returns a single value. Functions are very powerful feature of SQL. It can be used to perform calculations on data, modify individual data, manipulate output for groups of rows, convert column datatypes and format dates and numbers. Subquery is an advance feature of Oracle. It is also used in complex type of query. Subqueries are written in the WHERE clause of another SQL statement to obtain values based on an unknown conditional value. Use of a subquery is equivalent to performing two or more sequential queries. The result of the inner query is fed to the outer query to display the values. A join condition is used when data from more than one table in the database is required to be displayed. Rows in one table can be joined to rows of another table according to common values existing in the corresponding columns, that are usually primary key and foreign key columns.

3.1.1 Operators in SQL

Arithmetic and comparison operators are extensively used in SQL. Arithmetic operators in SQL are +, –, * and /. Comparison operators are =, like, >, >=, <, <=, != and <>. The logical connectives are AND, OR and NOT. The standard order of operations is also used in evaluating complex expressions. However, small brackets should be used in complex expression for clarity. An attribute cannot be tested for null values by using the standard equality or inequality operators. Instead, IS NULL or IS NOT NULL is used.

3.1.2 Data Control Language

Date Control Language (DCL) is used to create a user, drop a user, grant permission to a user and revoking permission from a user. CREATE USER command is used to create a user. An existing user can be dropped using DROP USER command. User must be granted privilege after its creation to use and access data.

Syntax:

CREATE USER <user_name> IDENTIFIED BY <password>;
DROP USER <user_name>;
GRANT <resource or role> TO <user_name>;

Default Oracle users

Users with passwords are created at the time of installation of Oracle database.

User	Password
SYSTEM	MANAGER/ Password Defined at the time of installation
SYS	CHANGE_ON_INSTALL/ Password Defined at the time of installation
INTERNAL	ORACLE/ Password Defined at the time of installation
SCOTT	TIGER

Invoking SQL prompt from operating system

SQL prompt can be invoked from personal Oracle and Oracle database server.

Oracle database server

User Name: SYSTEM/MANAGER@HOSTSTRING
SYSTEM is user with default password MANAGER. In Oracle 11g and 10g, password has to be assigned at the time of installation. HOSTSTRING determines the machine where the target Oracle database server is installed and running. In general DBA changes the default password for security reasons.

Personal Oracle

C:/> SQLPLUS
Enter user-name: SYSTEM/MANAGER (or password defined at the time of installation)
HOSTSTRING is blank in personal Oracle in most cases. DCL will be elaborated in detail in subsequent chapter.

3.1.3 Data Definition Language

Data Definition Language (DDL) is used to create and change the structure of a table in a database. It is also used to drop a table from a database. Alter table command is used to change the structure of the table, i.e. to modify column type and its length. TRUNCATE TABLE or DROP TABLE commands are used to delete the table along with records. DESC command is used to view the structure of the table.

Syntax:

CREATE TABLE <table_name>
(column_name 1 datatype,
column_name 2 datatype,
....
....
column_name n datatype,
CONSTRAINTS <constraint_name> <CONSTRAINT_TYPE> <constraint_field(s)>);

DROP TABLE <table_name>;

The following guidelines should be followed at the time of creation of tables:

- First character of table should be an alphabet.
- Two different tables should not have the same name.
- Underscore, numerals, alphabets are allowed in table name.

Frequently used data types are VARCHAR2, NUMBER and DATE. VARCHAR2 is used if the column is character type. CNAME VARCHAR2(10) implies that CNAME is character type and its maximum length can be 10 characters. NUMBER is used to represent integer as well as floating point number. For example in case of PCOST NUMBER(4, 2), PCOST range is from 00.00 to 99.99. Similarly, PPROFIT NUMBER(3) implies that it is an integer type data and can range from 0 to 999. DATE is used to represent date type data. Its default format is DD-MON-YYYY. DDL will be elaborated in detail in subsequent chapter.

3.1.4 Data Manipulation Language

Newly created table remains in a skeleton structure unless it is populated with records or rows. Data Manipulation Language (DML) is used to populate records in the newly created table. It is used to insert, update and delete records from a table in a database. It is also used to retrieve data from one or more tables.

Syntax:

INSERT into <table_name> VALUES <val1,val2, … ,valn>;
UPDATE <table_name> SET <column_name> = <new_val> WHERE <condition>;
DELETE FROM <table_name> WHERE <condition>;
SELECT <col_name(s)> FROM <table_name(s)>;
SELECT <col_name(s)> FROM <table_name(s)> [WHERE <cond>];

SELECT <col_name(s)> FROM <table_name(s)> [WHERE <cond>][ORDER BY <col_name(s)>];

'*' may be used in place of <col_name(s)> to display all columns of a table. SELECT and FROM clause are mandatory. In SELECT statement ';' is the terminating symbol and statements are executed only when ';' symbol is encountered. WHERE and ORDER BY clause are optional. In case no tables are used in the query, DUAL may be used. ORDER BY clause sorts and displays records as per the field. By default it sorts records in ascending order.

3.1.5 Transaction Control Language

Transaction Control Language (TCL) is used in conjunction with DML to save or forego the transaction made on table(s) permanently. COMMIT is used to save the transactions whereas ROLLBACK is used to recall the DMLs performed after the last COMMIT.

EX3_1 This example creates CUST, PROD, SALE_DETAIL and STATE_NAME tables and inserts records in the relevant tables. Entity relationship model is shown in Figure 3.1. All the chapters of this book use these tables as a running example. In all the examples and exercises text shown in *italics* is message from Oracle. It is assumed that password of SYSTEM user is MANAGER and connect string (or host string) name is ORA11G.

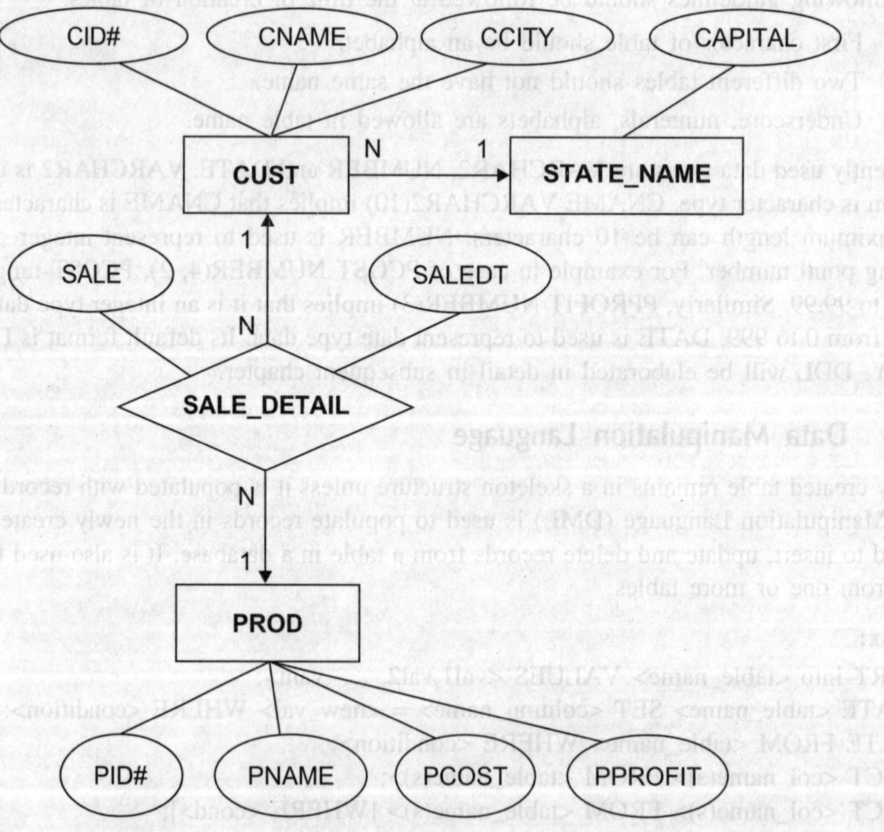

FIGURE 3.1 Entity relationship diagram—running example.

i. Connect to SYSTEM/MANAGER@ORA11G

SQL prompt can be invoked both from command line and graphics user interface.

Invoking SQL prompt from DOS

C:/> SQLPLUS

SQL>Enter user-name: SYSTEM/MANAGER@ORA11G

SQL>

Invoking SQL using Graphics User Interface

In most case the path is

Start -> Program ->Oracle … ->SQL Plus …

User Name - SYSTEM

Password - MANAGER

Host String - ORA11G

In Personal Oracle Host String is usually empty.

ii. Create a user named TTP with password TTP123, grant RESOURCE & CONNECT privilege to TTP. Connect to the newly created user.

SQL> CREATE USER TTP IDENTIFIED BY TTP123;

User created.

SQL> GRANT RESOURCE, CONNECT TO TTP;

Grant succeeded.

SQL> CONNECT TTP/TTP123@ORA11G;

Connected.

iii. Drop CUST, PROD, SALE_DETAIL and STATE_NAME tables before creating them. This is required because due to DMLs, records in the tables may be altered. Ignore the errors generated by SQL. These errors are generated in case tables do not exists.

SQL> DROP TABLE SALE_DETAIL;

SQL> DROP TABLE CUST;

SQL> DROP TABLE PROD;

SQL> DROP TABLE STATE_NAME;

iv. Create CUST based on following details.

Name	Type	Remark
CID	VARCHAR2(6)	Primary Key
CNAME	VARCHAR2(10)	
CCITY	VARCHAR2(8)	

SQL> CREATE TABLE CUST

(CID VARCHAR2(6),

CNAME VARCHAR2(10),

CCITY VARCHAR2(8),

CONSTRAINT CUST_PK PRIMARY KEY (CID));

Table created.

v. Insert and save records in CUST table. Note that VARCHAR2 data type related entries must be in single quotes.

CID	CNAME	CCITY
C1	PRADIP	MYSORE
C3	AASTIK	KOLKATA
C2	TUSHAR	PUNE
C4	ARPAN	CHENNAI
C5	ANUMITA	INDORE

```
SQL> INSERT INTO CUST VALUES ('C1','PRADIP','MYSORE');
SQL> INSERT INTO CUST VALUES ('C3','AASTIK','KOLKATA');
SQL> INSERT INTO CUST VALUES ('C2','TUSHAR','PUNE');
SQL> INSERT INTO CUST VALUES ('C4','ARPAN','CHENNAI');
SQL> INSERT INTO CUST VALUES ('C5','ANUMITA','INDORE');
SQL> COMMIT;
Commit complete.
```

vi. Create PROD based on following details.

Name	Type	Remark
PID	VARCHAR2(6)	Primary Key
PNAME	VARCHAR2(6)	
PCOST	NUMBER(4,2)	
PPROFIT	NUMBER(3)	

```
SQL> CREATE TABLE PROD
(PID        VARCHAR2(6),
PNAME       VARCHAR2(6),
PCOST       NUMBER(4,2),
PPROFIT     NUMBER(3),
CONSTRAINT PROD_PK PRIMARY KEY (PID));
Table created.
```

vii. Insert and save records in PROD table.

PID	PNAME	PCOST	PPROFIT
P3	PEN	20.5	20
P2	FLOPPY	30	12
P1	PENCIL	5.25	

```
SQL> INSERT INTO PROD VALUES ('P3','PEN',20.50,20);
SQL> INSERT INTO PROD VALUES ('P2','FLOPPY',30,12.00);
SQL> INSERT INTO PROD VALUES ('P1','PENCIL',5.25,NULL);
SQL> COMMIT;
Commit complete.
```

viii. Create SALE_DETAIL based on following details:

Name	Type	Remark
CID	VARCHAR2(6)	Composite Primary Key
PID	VARCHAR2(6)	Composite Primary Key
SALE	NUMBER(3)	
SALEDT	DATE	Composite Primary Key

```
SQL> CREATE TABLE SALE_DETAIL
(CID      VARCHAR2(6) REFERENCES CUST(CID),
PID       VARCHAR2(6) REFERENCES PROD(PID),
SALE      NUMBER(3),
SALEDT DATE,
CONSTRAINT SALE_DETAIL_PK PRIMARY KEY (CID, PID, SALEDT));
```

Table created.

ix. Insert and save records in SALE_DETAIL table.

CID	PID	SALE	SALEDT
C1	P3	2	14-JUL-13
C3	P2	10	15-JUL-13
C2	P3	1	14-JUL-13
C1	P1	5	14-JUL-13
C1	P3	3	20-AUG-13
C4	P3	2	14-NOV-13
C5	P2	2	18-SEP-13

```
SQL> INSERT INTO SALE_DETAIL VALUES ('C1','P3',2,'14-JUL-2013');
SQL> INSERT INTO SALE_DETAIL VALUES ('C3','P2',10,'15-JUL-2013')
SQL> INSERT INTO SALE_DETAIL VALUES ('C2','P3',1,'14-JUL-2013');
SQL> INSERT INTO SALE_DETAIL VALUES ('C1','P1',5,'14-JUL-2013');
SQL> INSERT INTO SALE_DETAIL VALUES ('C1','P3',3,'20-AUG-2013');
SQL> INSERT INTO SALE_DETAIL VALUES ('C4','P3',2,'14-NOV-2013');
SQL> INSERT INTO SALE_DETAIL VALUES ('C5','P2',2,'18-SEP-2013');
SQL> COMMIT;
```

Commit complete.

x. Create STATE_NAME based on following details:

Name	Type	Remarks
CCITY	VARCHAR2(8)	Primary Key
STATE	VARCHAR2(15)	

```
SQL> CREATE TABLE STATE_NAME
(CCITY    VARCHAR2(8),
STATE     VARCHAR2(15),
CONSTRAINT STATE_NAME_PK PRIMARY KEY (CCITY));
```

Table created.

xi. Insert and save records in STATE_NAME table.

CCITY	STATE
MYSORE	KARNATAKA
KOLKATA	WEST BENGAL
PUNE	MAHARASHTRA
CHENNAI	TAMILNADU
INDORE	MADHYA PRADESH

```
SQL> INSERT INTO STATE_NAME VALUES ('MYSORE','KARNATAKA');
SQL> INSERT INTO STATE_NAME VALUES ('KOLKATA','WEST BENGAL');
SQL> INSERT INTO STATE_NAME VALUES ('PUNE','MAHARASHTRA');
SQL> INSERT INTO STATE_NAME VALUES ('CHENNAI','TAMILNADU');
SQL> INSERT INTO STATE_NAME VALUES ('INDORE','MADHYA PRADESH');
SQL> COMMIT;
```

Commit complete.

As an alternative (and more preferred) SQL script can be typed and saved in CUST_PROD.SQL (Figure 3.2) to create and populate records in CUST, PROD, SALE_DETAIL & STATE_NAME tables automatically. This is preferred because at times due to DMLs or DDLs values of tuples or structure of the table is altered. Executing the script (i.e. CUST_PROD.SQL) will re-create relevant tables with default records without going through the process as mentioned in EX3_1.In this case also it is assumed that the tables will be created in TTP/TTP123@ORA11G and CUST_PROD.SQL is saved in C:/TTP/ directory.

```
C:/> SQLPLUS
SQL> CONNECT TTP/TTP123@ORA11G;
```

Connected.

Execute CUST_PROD.SQL using @ symbol to create all tables and insert records.

```
SQL> @ C:\TTP\CUST_PROD.SQL
```

```
DROP TABLE SALE_DETAIL;
DROP TABLE STATE_NAME;
DROP TABLE CUST;
DROP TABLE PROD;
CREATE TABLE CUST
(CID VARCHAR2(6),
CNAME VARCHAR2(10),
CCITY VARCHAR2(8),
CONSTRAINT CUST_PK PRIMARY KEY (CID));
CREATE TABLE PROD
(PID VARCHAR2(6),
PNAME VARCHAR2(6),
PCOST NUMBER(4,2),
PPROFIT NUMBER(3),
CONSTRAINT PROD_PK PRIMARY KEY (PID));
CREATE TABLE SALE_DETAIL
(CID VARCHAR2(6) REFERENCES CUST(CID),
PID VARCHAR2(6) REFERENCES PROD(PID),
SALE NUMBER(3),
SALEDT DATE,
CONSTRAINT SALE_DETAIL_PK PRIMARY KEY (CID,PID,SALEDT));
CREATE TABLE STATE_NAME
(CCITY VARCHAR2(8),
STATE VARCHAR2(15),
CONSTRAINT STATE_NAME_PK PRIMARY KEY (CCITY));
INSERT INTO CUST VALUES ('C1','PRADIP','MYSORE');
INSERT INTO CUST VALUES ('C3','AASTIK','KOLKATA');
INSERT INTO CUST VALUES ('C2','TUSHAR','PUNE');
INSERT INTO CUST VALUES ('C4','ARPAN','CHENNAI');
INSERT INTO CUST VALUES ('C5','ANUMITA','INDORE');
INSERT INTO PROD VALUES ('P3','PEN',20.50,20);
INSERT INTO PROD VALUES ('P2','FLOPPY',30,12.00);
INSERT INTO PROD VALUES ('P1','PENCIL',5.25,NULL);
INSERT INTO SALE_DETAIL VALUES ('C1','P3',2,'14-JUL-2013');
INSERT INTO SALE_DETAIL VALUES ('C3','P2',10,'15-JUL-2013');
INSERT INTO SALE_DETAIL VALUES ('C2','P3',1,'14-JUL-2013');
INSERT INTO SALE_DETAIL VALUES ('C1','P1',5,'14-JUL-2013');
INSERT INTO SALE_DETAIL VALUES ('C1','P3',3,'20-AUG-2013');
INSERT INTO SALE_DETAIL VALUES ('C4','P3',2,'14-NOV-2013');
INSERT INTO SALE_DETAIL VALUES ('C5','P2',2,'18-SEP-2013');
INSERT INTO STATE_NAME VALUES ('MYSORE','KARNATAKA');
INSERT INTO STATE_NAME VALUES ('KOLKATA','WEST BENGAL');
INSERT INTO STATE_NAME VALUES ('PUNE','MAHARASHTRA');
INSERT INTO STATE_NAME VALUES ('CHENNAI','TAMILNADU');
INSERT INTO STATE_NAME VALUES ('INDORE','MADYA PRADESH');
COMMIT;
SELECT * FROM TAB;
DESC CUST;
DESC PROD;
DESC SALE_DETAIL;
DESC STATE_NAME;
```

FIGURE 3.2 Tables with records—running example.

EX3_2 In this example dependency among different tables are demonstrated. This dependency is due to declaration of foreign key using REFERENCES parameter in SALE_DETAIL table.

i. Is it possible to insert ('C6','P3',2,'18-JAN-2014') in SALE_DETAIL?

It is not possible because 'C6' related details are not available in CUST table..

SQL> INSERT INTO SALE_DETAIL VALUES ('C6','P3',2,'18-JAN-2014');

INSERT INTO SALE_DETAIL VALUES ('C6','P3',2,'18-JAN-2014')

*

ERROR at line 1:

ORA-02291: integrity constraint (TTP.SYS_C001210) violated—parent key not found

ii. Is it possible to delete records with CID='C1' in CUST table?

No, because 'C1' is present SALE_DETAIL.CID. Parent (CUST.CID) cannot be deleted before the children (SALE_DETAIL.CID).

SQL> DELETE FROM CUST WHERE CID='C1';

DELETE FROM CUST WHERE CID='C1'

*

ERROR at line 1:

ORA-02292: integrity constraint (TTP.SYS_C001210) violated—child record found

iii. Insert ('C6','PANKAJ','BALASORE') in CUST table so that ('C6','I3',2,'18-JAN-2014') can be inserted in SALE_DETAIL table.

SQL> INSERT INTO CUST VALUES ('C6','PANKAJ','BALASORE');

SQL> COMMIT;

Commit complete.

iv. Is it now possible to insert ('C6','P3',2,'18-JAN-2014') in SALE_DETAIL table?

Yes, now it is possible because 'C6' related information is available in CUST table.

SQL> INSERT INTO SALE_DETAIL VALUES ('C6','P3',2,'18-JAN-2014');

SQL> COMMIT;

Commit complete.

v. Is it possible to drop PROD or CUST tables?

No, it cannot be dropped because primary key of CUST is referred in SALE_DETAIL table.

SQL> DROP TABLE PROD;

DROP TABLE PROD

*

ERROR at line 1:

ORA-02449: unique/primary keys in table referenced by foreign keys

SQL> DROP TABLE CUST;

DROP TABLE CUST

*

ERROR at line 1:

ORA-02449: unique/primary keys in table referenced by foreign keys

vi. Is it possible to drop STATE_NAME table?

Yes, it can be dropped as it is not referenced by any other table.

SQL> DROP TABLE STATE_NAME;

Table dropped.

vii. Is it possible to drop PROD and CUST tables after dropping SALE_DETAIL table?

Yes it is possible to drop PROD and CUST tables after dropping SALE_DETAIL table.

SQL> DROP TABLE SALE_DETAIL;

Table dropped.

SQL> DROP TABLE PROD;

Table dropped.

SQL> DROP TABLE CUST;

Table dropped.

viii. Re-execute CUST_PROD.SQL to re-create CUST, PROD, SALE_DETAIL and STATE_NAME with records.

SQL>@ C:\TTP\CUST_PROD.SQL

ix. Drop SALE_DETAIL & STATE_NAME tables and re-create without REFERENCE parameter. Insert all records. Use the script as shown below.

```
CREATE TABLE SALE_DETAIL
(CID VARCHAR2(6),
PID VARCHAR2(6),
SALE NUMBER(3),
SALEDT DATE,
CONSTRAINT SALE_DETAIL_PK PRIMARY KEY (CID,PID,SALEDT));
INSERT INTO SALE_DETAIL VALUES ('C1','P3',2,'14-JUL-2013');
INSERT INTO SALE_DETAIL VALUES ('C3','P2',10,'15-JUL-2013');
INSERT INTO SALE_DETAIL VALUES ('C2','P3',1,'14-JUL-2013');
INSERT INTO SALE_DETAIL VALUES ('C1','P1',5,'14-JUL-2013');
INSERT INTO SALE_DETAIL VALUES ('C1','P3',3,'20-AUG-2013');
INSERT INTO SALE_DETAIL VALUES ('C4','P3',2,'14-NOV-2013');
INSERT INTO SALE_DETAIL VALUES ('C5','P2',2,'18-SEP-2013');
COMMIT;
SQL> CREATE TABLE STATE_NAME
(CCITY VARCHAR2(8),
STATE   VARCHAR2(15),
CONSTRAINT STATE_NAME_PK PRIMARY KEY (CCITY));
SQL> INSERT INTO STATE_NAME VALUES ('MYSORE','KARNATAKA');
SQL> INSERT INTO STATE_NAME VALUES ('KOLKATA','WEST BENGAL');
SQL> INSERT INTO STATE_NAME VALUES ('PUNE','MAHARASHTRA');
SQL> INSERT INTO STATE_NAME VALUES ('CHENNAI','TAMILNADU');
SQL> INSERT INTO STATE_NAME VALUES ('INDORE','MADHYA PRADESH');
SQL> COMMIT;
```

Commit complete

Note that SALE_DETAIL table is created without REFERENCES parameter. In other words foreign key is not exclusively defined. Due to this no restrictions are imposed on the DMLs.

x. Is it now possible to insert ('C6','P3',2,'18-JAN-2014') in SALE_DETAIL?

Yes, it is possible to insert 'C6'. Note that 'C6' does not exist in CUST table. In most cases such type of insertion is not desired.

SQL> INSERT INTO SALE_DETAIL VALUES ('C6','P3',2,'18-JAN-2014');

xi. Is it now possible to delete records with CID='C1'?

Yes, it is possible. Such type of deletion results into dangling tupples (children without parent) not desired in most cases.

SQL> DELETE FROM CUST *WHERE CID='C1';*

1 row deleted.

xii. Is it now possible to drop PROD or CUST tables?

This is also possible after re-creation of SALE_DETAIL & STATE_NAME tables. However, such types of requirements are rare.

SQL> DROP TABLE PROD;

Table dropped.

SQL> DROP TABLE CUST;

Table dropped.

Note:

It is not mandatory to define foreign key using REFERENCES parameter. However, to avoid accidental deletion of parent it is recommended to use foreign key.

Do not forget to re-execute CUST_PROD.SQL script as shown in Figure 3.2 to create CUST, PROD, SALE_DETAIL and STATE_NAME Tables again.

3.2 DATA RETRIEVAL

General form of SELECT statement is:

```
SELECT [DISTINCT] COLUMN_NAME [AS NEWNAME],[,COLUMN_NAME...]...
FROM TABLE_NAME [ALIAS][,TABLE_NAME]...
[WHERE PREDICATE]
[GROUP BY COLUMN_NAME [,COLUMN_NAME]
[HAVING PREDICATE]
[ORDER BY COLUMN_NAME [,COLUMN_NAME]...];
```

In the SELECT statement, SELECT and FROM are mandatory. If tables are not required then DUAL is used. Other clauses are optional and it must follow the same order, if used. In all the examples, CUST, PROD, SALE_DETAIL and STATE_NAME tables are used. Ensure that each and every records are same (Figure 3.2) to reconcile with the examples and workout.

3.2.1 Use of '*' to Denote 'All Columns'

EX3_3 Write a query to display all columns of CUST table.
SQL> SELECT * FROM CUST;

CID	CNAME	CCITY
C1	*PRADIP*	*MYSORE*
C3	*AASTIK*	*KOLKATA*
C2	*TUSHAR*	*PUNE*
C4	*ARPAN*	*CHENNAI*
C5	*ANUMITA*	*INDORE*

SELECT, FROM and ';' are part of Oracle SQL syntax and are essentially required in any query. In this example, table name used is CUST where all data is stored. This query displays all the 5 rows of CUST table.

3.2.2 Using 'ORDER BY' Clause

EX3_4 Write a query to display PNAME of all records. Sort all records by PNAME.
SQL> SELECT PNAME FROM PROD ORDER BY PNAME;

PNAME
FLOPPY
PEN
PENCIL

EX3_5 Write a query to display CNAME and CCITY of all records. Sort by CCITY in descending order.
SQL> SELECT CNAME,CCITY FROM CUST ORDER BY CCITY DESC;

CNAME	*CCITY*
TUSHAR	*PUNE*
PRADIP	*MYSORE*
AASTIK	*KOLKATA*
ANUMITA	*INDORE*
ARPAN	*CHENNAI*

Increasing order, i.e. ASC is default. For decreasing order DESC has to be used. A second column for minor order may be used in the event of a tie in values of the first column.

3.2.3 Retrieval with a Condition

EX3_6 Write a query to display CNAME and CCITY who lives in MYSORE.
SQL> SELECT CUST.CNAME, CUST.CCITY FROM CUST WHERE CCITY='MYSORE';

CNAME	*CCITY*
PRADIP	*MYSORE*

In this query CNAME and CCITY are displayed who are staying in MYSORE. Note that optionally the tables name before the column name using dot notation can be used.

3.2.4 Natural Join

Queries often involve choosing columns from two or more tables that have matching values on a common column.

EX3_7 Write a query to display CNAME, PNAME, SALE, SALEDT for all customers.

```
SQL> SELECT CUST.CNAME, PROD.PNAME, SALE_DETAIL.SALE, SALE_DETAIL
.SALEDT FROM CUST,PROD,SALE_DETAIL
WHERE CUST.CID=SALE_DETAIL.CID AND PROD.PID=SALE_DETAIL.PID;
```

CNAME	*PNAME*	*SALE*	*SALEDT*
PRADIP	*PEN*	*2*	*14-JUL-13*
AASTIK	*FLOPPY*	*10*	*15-JUL-13*
TUSHAR	*PEN*	*1*	*14-JUL-13*
PRADIP	*PENCIL*	*5*	*14-JUL-13*
PRADIP	*PEN*	*3*	*20-AUG-13*
ARPAN	*PEN*	*2*	*14-NOV-13*
ANUMITA	*FLOPPY*	*2*	*18-SEP-13*

In this query CNAME, PNAME, SALE and SALEDT are displayed. CNAME is column of CUST table, PNAME is column of PROD table and SALE and SALEDT is of SALE_DETAIL table. Three tables are used in the FROM clause and all the tables are joined using common column of SALE_DETAIL, CUST and PROD.

CUST.CID=SALE_DETAIL.CID is used to join CUST and SALE_DETAIL tables and PROD.PID=SALE_DETAIL.PID is used to join PROD and SALE_DETAIL tables.

As a rule of thumb, if there are N tables essentially there will be N–1 joins. In this case there are 3 tables hence, the number of joins are 2. Note that these joins only connect the tables used in the SQL. Check out, what will be the output if WHERE clause is not used?

3.2.5 Using Complex Conditions

EX3_8 Write a query to display CNAME who has purchased PEN.

```
SQL> SELECT CUST.CNAME
FROM CUST, PROD, SALE_DETAIL
WHERE CUST.CID=SALE_DETAIL.CID AND PROD.PID=SALE_DETAIL.PID
AND PROD.PNAME='PEN';
```

CNAME
PRADIP
TUSHAR
PRADIP
ARPAN

In this query note that only one column is displayed, but 3 tables are used. This is because there is a condition to display CNAME who has purchased PEN. CNAME is in CUST, PNAME is in PROD and details of purchase are in SALE_DETAIL. Obviously to display the name of CNAME who has purchased PEN, 3 tables and 3 conditional statements (2 to join 3 tables + 1 for PNAME='PEN') are required.

3.2.6 Using 'Relational Operator' in 'Date' Type Column

EX3_9 Write a query to display SALEDT and total SALE on the date labeled as SALE of all items sold after 01-Sep-2013.

SQL> SELECT S.SALEDT, P.PCOST*S.SALE AMOUNT
FROM SALE_DETAIL S,PROD P
WHERE S.PID=P.PID AND SALEDT > '01-SEP-2013';

SALEDT	*AMOUNT*
14-NOV-13	*41*
18-SEP-13	*60*

In previous queries table_name, column_name were used to represent columns if more than one table were involved. It can be shortened using alias on column name. In this query S is used to represent SALE_DETAIL and P is used to represent PROD tables. This query also shows that relational operator can be used for DATE type.

3.2.7 Using 'Aliases' and 'Arithmetic Operators'

EX3_10 Write a query to display SALEDT and total SALE on the date labelled as SALE of all items other than FLOPPY.

SQL> SELECT S.SALEDT,P.PNAME,P.PCOST*S.SALE AMOUNT
FROM SALE_DETAIL S,PROD P
WHERE S.PID=P.PID AND P.PNAME != 'FLOPPY';

SALEDT	*PNAME*	*AMOUNT*
14-JUL-13	*PEN*	*41*
14-JUL-13	*PEN*	*20.5*
14-JUL-13	*PENCIL*	*26.25*
20-AUG-13	*PEN*	*61.5*
14-NOV-13	*PEN*	*41*

PCOST belongs to PROD table and SALE belongs to SALE_DETAIL. Product of PCOST and SALE is computed and named as AMOUNT. This query also demonstrate '!=' operator.

3.2.8 Use of 'Distinct', 'Between' and 'In' Clause

EX3_11 Find the Product Ids in SALE_DETAIL table.

SQL> SELECT PID FROM SALE_DETAIL;

PID
P3
P2
P3
P1
P3
P3
P2

Notice that duplicates values are displayed in the result. To prevent duplicate rows, DISTINCT in SELECT clause is used.

SQL> SELECT DISTINCT PID FROM SALE_DETAIL;

PID
P1
P2
P3

EX3_12 Write a query to display CNAME and CCITY of all the customers who live in 'KOLKATA' or 'CHENNAI'.

SQL> SELECT CNAME,CCITY FROM CUST WHERE CCITY IN ('KOLKATA', 'CHENNAI');

CNAME	*CCITY*
AASTIK	*KOLKATA*
ARPAN	*CHENNAI*

EX3_13 Write a query to display the PNAME and PCOST of all the customers where PCOST lies between 5 and 25.

SQL> SELECT PNAME,PCOST FROM PROD WHERE PCOST BETWEEN 5 AND 25;

PNAME	*PCOST*
PEN	*20.5*
PENCIL	*5.25*

EX3_14 Write a query to display distinct Customer ID where Product ID is P3 or Sale date is '18-SEP-2013'.

SQL> SELECT DISTINCT CID FROM SALE_DETAIL WHERE PID='P3' OR SALEDT=TO_DATE('18-SEP-2013');

CID
C1
C2
C4
C5

EX3_15 Write a query to display CNAME, PID and SALEDT of those customers whose CID is in C1 or C2 or C4 or C5.

SQL> SELECT C.CNAME, S.PID, S.SALEDT FROM CUST C,SALE_DETAIL S WHERE C.CID=S.CID AND C.CID IN ('C1','C2','C4','C5');

CNAME	*PID*	*SALEDT*
ANUMITA	*P2*	*18-SEP-13*
ARPAN	*P3*	*14-NOV-13*
TUSHAR	*P3*	*14-JUL-13*
PRADIP	*P1*	*14-JUL-13*
PRADIP	*P3*	*14-JUL-13*
PRADIP	*P3*	*20-AUG-13*

EX3_16 Write a query to display CNAME, PID, SALEDT of those customers whose PID is 'P3' or sale date is '18-SEP-2013'.
SQL> SELECT C.CNAME,S.PID,S.SALEDT FROM CUST C,SALE_DETAIL S WHERE C.CID=S.CID AND (S.PID='P3' OR S.SALEDT=TO_DATE('18-SEP-2013'));

CNAME	*PID*	*SALEDT*
PRADIP	*P3*	*14-JUL-13*
TUSHAR	*P3*	*14-JUL-13*
PRADIP	*P3*	*20-AUG-13*
ARPAN	*P3*	*14-NOV-13*
ANUMITA	*P2*	*18-SEP-13*

3.2.9 Use of 'Dual'

DUAL is used when the data is not related to any table.

EX3_17 Write a query to display system date.
SQL> SELECT SYSDATE FROM DUAL;

SYSDATE
08-NOV-13

EX3_18 Write a query to sum two numbers. Numbers are 3 and 5. Label the heading Sum3_5.
SQL> SELECT 3+5 SUM3_5 FROM DUAL;

SUM3_5
8

3.2.10 Use of 'Like' Operator

LIKE is similar to '=' operator. The only difference is that it allows wildcard characters. '_' character is used for any one alphabet, whereas '%' character is used to represent any alphabet string.

EX3_19 Write a query to display all records of PROD table in which first and third character of PNAME is any character and second character is 'E'.
SQL> SELECT * FROM PROD WHERE PNAME LIKE '_E_';

PID	*PNAME*	*PCOST*	*PPROFIT*
P3	*PEN*	*20.5*	*20*

EX3_20 Write a query to display all CNAME which includes two 'A' in the name.
SQL> SELECT CNAME FROM CUST WHERE CNAME LIKE '%A%A%';

CNAME
AASTIK
ARPAN
ANUMITA

3.3 SQL*PLUS

SQL*Plus is a command line SQL language interface. It comes with the Oracle database Client and Server and can be used interactively or from scripts. SQL*Plus is frequently used by Programmers, Data Base Administrators and Developers to interact with Oracle database. Almost all SQL statements can be executed in the default setting of SQL*Plus.

AFIEDT.BUF is the SQL*Plus default edit save file. When the command "ed" or "edit" without arguments is issued, the last SQL command will be saved to a file called AFIEDT.BUF and opened in the default editor.

EX3_21 SQL> SELECT SYSDATE FROM DUAL;

SYSDATE

28-OCT-13

SQL> ED

Wrote file afiedt.buf (Figure 3.3)

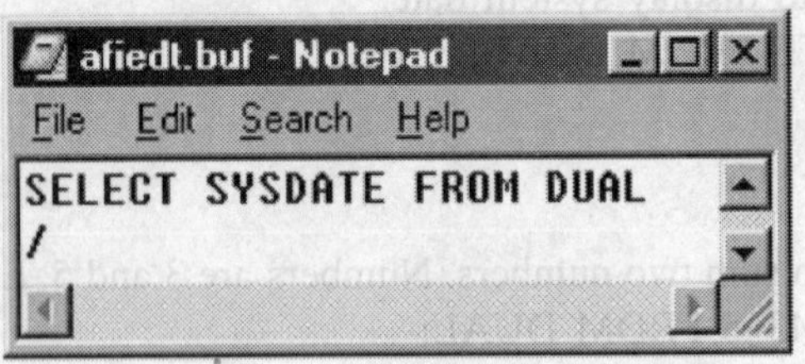

FIGURE 3.3 SQL* Plus editor.

SQL> SAVE SQLP1

Created file SQLP1

SQL> @ SQLP1

SYSDATE

28-OCT-13

Frequently used SQL*PLUS Commands

ACCEPT	Get input from the user
CLEAR SCREEN	Clear the text on the screen
DESCRIBE	List the attributes of tables and other objects (short: DESC)
EDIT	Invokes external editor to edit the contents of a file (short: ED)
EXIT or QUIT	Disconnect from the database and terminate SQL*Plus
HOST	Issue an operating system (short: !)
PASSWORD	Used to change Oracle password
PAUSE	It prompts the user to press the ENTER key.
PROMPT	Display a text string on the screen.
RUN	List and Run the command stored in SQL buffer (short: /)
SAVE	Saves command in the SQL buffer to a file.
SET ECHO OFF	Used to stop echo in SQL * Plus
SHUT DOWN	Shutdown the database
START	Run a SQL script file (short: @)
& and &&	Substitution variables to temporarily store values.

EX3_22 This example demonstrates usage of '&'.
SQL> SELECT * FROM PROD WHERE PID='&PID';
Enter value for pid: P1
*old 1: SELECT * FROM PROD WHERE PID='&PID'*
*new 1: SELECT * FROM PROD WHERE PID='P1'*

PID	*PNAME*	*PCOST*	*PPROFIT*
P1	*PENCIL*	*5.25*	

EX3_23 This example demonstrates usage of '&' and '&&'. SET VERIFY OFF suppresses the confirmation of substitution variables.

SQL> SET VERIFY OFF
SQL> SELECT &&PROD_COL_NAME FROM &TABLE_NAME ORDER BY &COL_ORDER;
Enter value for prod_col_name: CNAME
Enter value for table_name: CUST
Enter value for col_order: CNAME

CNAME
AASTIK
ANUMITA
ARPAN
PRADIP
TUSHAR

EX3_24 Create a file EX3_24 with default extension '.SQL' using the SQL*Plus editor. It should perform following actions:

- Display the objective of the script
- Accept a user name followed by a password
- Connect to the user
- Accept table name
- Describe definition of the table
- Prompt to disconnect followed by exit

SQL> EDIT EX3_24
Press 'Yes' to create a new file. Type the script shown in Figure 3.4.
Invoke File → Save to save the script in EX3_24. SQL followed by File → Exit to exit.
SQL>@ EX3_24.

This script will first connect to the desired user, then it will prompt for the table name to describe the structure of the table.
USER NAME > TTP
PASSWORD > TTP123
Connected.
ENTER THE TABLE NAME > PROD
PROD DEFINITION

Name	*Null?*	*Type*
PID	*NOT NULL*	*VARCHAR2(6)*
PNAME		*VARCHAR2(6)*
PCOST		*NUMBER(4,2)*
PPROFIT		*NUMBER(3)*

Press any key to disconnect
Disconnected
Press any key to quit

This example assume that Personal Oracle is used and connection string is not required.

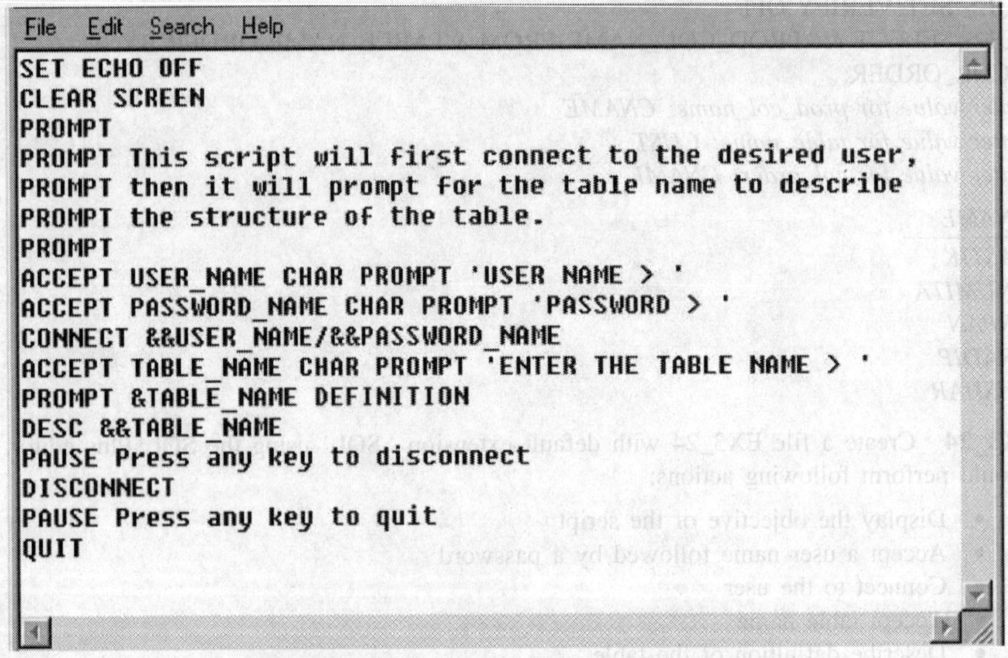

FIGURE 3.4 Working with SQL*Plus editor.

3.4 SINGLE ROW FUNCTIONS

A single row function or scalar function returns only one value for every row queried in the table. Single row functions can be broadly classified as: Date function, Numeric function, Character function, Conversion function and Miscellaneous function. All these functions are elaborated in succeeding sections.

3.4.1 Date Function

Date functions operate on the date values producing output which also belongs to date datatype. Date functions commonly used in SQL are shown in Table 3.1.

TABLE 3.1 Date Functions

Function	Purpose
ADD_MONTHS(d,n) where d is date and n is integer	Add calendar months to date
LAST_DAY(d) where d is date	Last day of the month
NEXT_DAY(d,day) where d is date	Next day of the date specified
MONTHS_BETWEEN(d1,d2) where d1 and d2 are dates	Number of months between two dates
ROUND(d,[format]) where d is date	Rounded to the unit specified by the format which may be MONTH or YEAR
TRUNC(d,[format]) where d is date	Truncated to the unit specified by the format
GREATEST(d1,d2,d3....) where d1,d2,d3,... are dates	Returns the greatest date present in the argument
LEAST(d1,d2,d3...)where d1,d2,d3,... are dates	Returns the least date present in the argument

All the examples are based on CUST, PROD, SALE_DETAIL and STATE_NAME tables with default values. Output may differ whereever SYSDATE is used.

EX3_25 Write a query to display the system date by rounding it to next month.
SQL> SELECT SYSDATE, ROUND(SYSDATE,'MONTH') FROM DUAL;

SYSDATE ROUND(SYS

05-OCT-13 01-OCT-13

EX3_26 Write a query to display the system date by rounding it to the next year.
SQL> SELECT SYSDATE, ROUND(SYSDATE,'YEAR') FROM DUAL;

SYSDATE ROUND(SYS

05-OCT-13 01-JAN-14

EX3_27 Write a query to display the last date of the system date.
SQL> SELECT SYSDATE, LAST_DAY(SYSDATE) FROM DUAL;

SYSDATE LAST_DAY

05-OCT-13 31-OCT-13

EX3_28 Write a query to display the next date of system date which is FRIDAY.
SQL> SELECT SYSDATE, NEXT_DAY(SYSDATE,'FRIDAY') FROM DUAL;

SYSDATE NEXT_DAY

05-OCT-1310-OCT-13

EX3_29 Write a query to display the system date along with the truncated value of sale date to the next month.
SQL> SELECT SYSDATE, TRUNC(SALEDT,'MONTH') FROM SALE_DETAIL;

SYSDATE	*TRUNC(SAL*
05-OCT-13	*01-JUL-13*
05-OCT-13	*01-JUL-13*
05-OCT-13	*01-AUG-13*
05-OCT-13	*01-JUL-13*
05-OCT-13	*01-JUL-13*
05-OCT-13	*01-NOV-13*
05-OCT-13	*01-SEP-13*

EX3_30 Write a query to display the sale date along with the truncated value of sale date to the next month.

SQL> SELECT SALEDT, TRUNC(SALEDT,'MONTH') FROM SALE_DETAIL;

SALEDT	*TRUNC(SAL*
14-JUL-13	*01-JUL-13*
14-JUL-13	*01-JUL-13*
20-AUG-13	*01-AUG-13*
14-JUL-13	*01-JUL-13*
15-JUL-13	*01-JUL-13*
14-NOV-13	*01-NOV-13*
18-SEP-13	*01-SEP-13*

EX3_31 Write a query to display sale date and date after 02 months from sale date.

SQL>SELECT SALEDT,ADD_MONTHS(SALEDT,2) FROM SALE_DETAIL;

SALEDT	*ADD_MONTH*
14-JUL-13	*14-SEP-13*
14-JUL-13	*14-SEP-13*
20-AUG-13	*20-OCT-13*
14-JUL-13	*14-SEP-13*
15-JUL-13	*15-SEP-13*
14-NOV-13	*14-JAN-14*
18-SEP-13	*18-NOV-13*

EX3_32 Write a query to display system date, sale date and months between two dates.

SQL>SELECT SYSDATE, SALEDT, MONTHS_BETWEEN (SALEDT, SYSDATE) AS DIFF FROM SALE_DETAIL WHERE SALEDT>SYSDATE;

SYSDATE	*SALEDT*	*DIFF*
05-OCT-13	*14-NOV-13*	*1.2893739*

EX3_33 Write a query to display the greatest date between sale date and system date, name it as BIG, also display sale date and SYSDATE.

SQL> SELECT GREATEST(SYSDATE, SALEDT) AS BIG,SALEDT,SYSDATE
FROM SALE_DETAIL;

BIG	*SALEDT*	*SYSDATE*
05-OCT-13	*14-JUL-13*	*05-OCT-13*
05-OCT-13	*14-JUL-13*	*05-OCT-13*
05-OCT-13	*20-AUG-13*	*05-OCT-13*
05-OCT-13	*14-JUL-13*	*05-OCT-13*
05-OCT-13	*15-JUL-13*	*05-OCT-13*
14-NOV-13	*14-NOV-13*	*05-OCT-13*
05-OCT-13	*18-SEP-13*	*05-OCT-13*

EX3_34 Write a query to display the least date between sale date and system date name it as SMALL, also display sale date and SYSDATE.

SQL>SELECT LEAST(SYSDATE, SALEDT) AS SMALL,SALEDT,SYSDATE FROM SALE_DETAIL;

SMALL	*SALEDT*	*SYSDATE*
14-JUL-13	*14-JUL-13*	*05-OCT-13*
14-JUL-13	*14-JUL-13*	*05-OCT-13*
20-AUG-13	*20-AUG-13*	*05-OCT-13*
14-JUL-13	*14-JUL-13*	*05-OCT-13*
15-JUL-13	*15-JUL-13*	*05-OCT-13*
05-OCT-13	*14-NOV-13*	*05-OCT-13*
18-SEP-13	*18-SEP-13*	*05-OCT-13*

3.4.2 Numeric Function

Numeric functions along with their purposes are shown in Table 3.2.

TABLE 3.2 Numeric Functions

Functions	Purposes
ROUND(column/expression, n)	Rounds the column, expression, or value to n decimal places
TRUNC(column/expression, n)	Truncates the column, expression or value to n decimal places
MOD(m, n)	Returns the remainder of m/n

EX3_35 Write a query to display the product name along with the rounded value of product cost for product name is "PENCIL".

SQL> SELECT PNAME, ROUND(PCOST,0) FROM PROD WHERE PNAME='PENCIL';

PNAME	*ROUND(PCOST,0)*
PENCIL	*5*

EX3_36 Write a query to display the product name along with the rounded value of product cost to –1 decimal places where product name is "PENCIL".

SQL> SELECT PNAME, ROUND(PCOST,1) FROM PROD WHERE PNAME='PENCIL';

PNAME	*ROUND(PCOST,1)*
PENCIL	*5.3*

EX3_37 Write a query to display the product name along with the rounded value of product cost to –1 decimal places where product name is "PENCIL".
SQL> SELECT PNAME, ROUND(PCOST,-1) FROM PROD WHERE PNAME='PENCIL';

PNAME	*ROUND(PCOST,-1)*
PENCIL	*10*

EX3_38 Write a query to display product name along with truncated value of product cost to 0, 1, –1 decimal places for PEN.
SQL>SELECT PNAME, TRUNC(PCOST,0),TRUNC(PCOST,1),TRUNC(PCOST,–1) FROM PROD WHERE PNAME='PEN';

PNAME	*TRUNC(PCOST,0)*	*TRUNC(PCOST,1)*	*TRUNC(PCOST,–1)*
PEN	*20*	*20.5*	*20*

EX3_39 Write a query to display product cost along with MOD value if divided by 5.
SQL>SELECT PCOST, MOD(PCOST,5) FROM PROD;

PCOST	*MOD(PCOST,5)*
20.5	.5
30	0
5.25	.25

3.4.3 Character Function

Character functions accept data as input and can return both character and number values. Character functions along with their purposes are shown in Table 3.3.

TABLE 3.3 Character Functions

Functions	**Purposes**
LOWER	Converts alpha character values to lowercase
UPPER	Converts alpha character values to uppercase
INITCAP	Converts first character of alpha character values to uppercase
CONCAT(COL 1, COL 2, … COL N)	Concatenates the characters (equivalent to || operator)
SUBSTR(COL, M,[N])	Returns specified character from character value starting at character position m, n characters long. If m is negative, the count starts from the end of the character value. If n is omitted, all the characters to the end of string are returned)
LENGTH(COL)	Returns the number of characters in value
INSTR(COL, M)	Returns the numeric position of a named character
LPAD(COL, N, 'STRING')	Pads the character value right-justified to a total width of n character positions
RPAD(COL,N)	Pads the character value left justified to a total width of n character positions
TRIM	Trims leading/trailing character from a string

EX3_40 Write a query to display cname in uppercase, lowercase, titlecase from CUST table where customer name is "PRADIP".
SQL>SELECT CNAME,LOWER(CNAME),UPPER(CNAME),INITCAP(CNAME) FROM CUST WHERE CNAME='PRADIP';

CNAME	*LOWER(CNAME)*	*UPPER(CNAME)*	*INITCAP(CNAME)*
PRADIP	*pradip*	*PRADIP*	*Pradip*

EX3_41 Write a query to display all concatenated value of CNAME, CCITY by converting CNAME into titlecase and CCITY into uppercase.
SQL> SELECT CONCAT(INITCAP(CNAME), UPPER(CCITY)) CUSTCITY FROM CUST;

CUSTCITY
PradipMYSORE
AastikKOLKATA
TusharPUNE
ArpanCHENNAI
AnumitaINDORE

EX3_42 Write a query to display the first three characters of CNAME.
SQL> SELECT SUBSTR(CNAME,1,3) FROM CUST;

SUB
PRA
AAS
TUS
ARP
ANU

EX3_43 Write a query to display the position of character 'M' in the CNAME of the customer whose name is "ANUMITA".
SQL> SELECT INSTR(CNAME,'M') FROM CUST WHERE CNAME='ANUMITA';

INSTR(CNAME,'M')
4

EX3_44 Write a query to display the length of all customer names.
SQL> SELECT 'Length of' || CNAME || 'is' || LENGTH(CNAME) FROM C

LENGTHOF CNAME IS	*LENGTH(CNAME)*
Length of PRADIP is	*6*
Length of AASTIK is	*6*
Length of TUSHAR is	*6*
Length of ARPAN is	*5*
Length of ANUMITA is	*7*

EX3_45 PAD # character in left of product cost to a total width of 5 character positions.
SQL> SELECT PNAME, LPAD(PCOST,5,'#') FROM PROD;

PNAME	*LPAD(PCOST)*
PEN	*#20.5*
FLOPPY	*###30*
PENCIL	*#5.25*

EX3_46 PAD # character in right of product cost to a total width of 5 character positions. Write a query to display along with PNAME.

SQL> SELECT PNAME, RPAD(PCOST,5,'#') FROM PROD

PNAME	*RPAD(PCOST)*
PEN	*20.5#*
FLOPPY	*30###*
PENCIL	*5.25#*

EX3_47 Write a query to display PNAME by trimming 'P' if it is first character in PNAME.

SQL> SELECT PNAME, TRIM('P' FROM PNAME) WO_P FROM PROD;

PNAME	*WO_P*
PEN	*EN*
FLOPPY	*FLOPPY*
PENCIL	*ENCIL*

EX3_48 Write a query to display the customer name, product name and sale details from CUST, PROD and SALE_DETAIL table using '||' operator.

SQL> SELECT C.CNAME || 'PURCHASED' || P.PNAME || 'ON' || S.SALEDT "PURCHASE DETAILS" FROM CUST C, PROD P, SALE_DETAIL S WHERE S.CID=C.CID AND S.PID=P.PID;

PURCHASE DETAILS
PRADIP PURCHASED PEN ON 14-JUL-13
PRADIP PURCHASED PEN ON 20-AUG-13
PRADIP PURCHASED PENCIL ON 14-JUL-13
AASTIK PURCHASED FLOPPY ON 15-JUL-13
TUSHAR PURCHASED PEN ON 14-JUL-13
ARPAN PURCHASED PEN ON 14-NOV-13
ANUMITA PURCHASED FLOPPY ON 18-SEP-13

3.4.4 Conversion Function

Conversion functions along with their purposes are shown in Table 3.4.

TABLE 3.4 Conversion Functions

Functions	**Purposes**
TO_CHAR(number/date,[fmt])	Converts a number or date value to a VARCHAR2 character string with format model fmt.
TO_DATE(char,[fmt])	Converts a character string representing date to a date value to the fmt specified. If fmt is omitted, the format is DD-MON-YY.
TO_NUMBER(char,[fmt])	Converts a character string containing a number in the format specified by the optional format model fmt.

Date related format is shown in Table 3.5.

TABLE 3.5 Date Related Formats

Format	Function
mm	Number of month i.e. 12
rm	Roman Numeral of month i.e. XII
mon	Three letter abbreviation of month i.e. AUG
month	Month fully spelt out i.e. AUGUST
dd	Number of days in a month
d	Number of days in a week
dy	Three letter abbreviation of a day i.e. FRI
day	Day fully spelled out i.e. FRIDAY
yyyy	Year (Four digit)
yy	Year (Two digit)
q	Number of quarter
ww	Number of weeks in a year
w	Number of weeks in a month
hh	Hours of day (12 Hr. format)
hh24	Hours of day (24 Hr. format)
mi	Minutes of hour
ss	Seconds of hour
am/pm	Displays A.M. or P.M.
BC/AD	Displays B.C. or A.D.

EX3_49 Write a query to display sale date in character format DD-MM-YY from SALE_DETAIL.

SQL> SELECT TO_CHAR(SALEDT,'DD-MM-YY') DT_DESC FROM SALE_DETAIL;

DT_DESC

14-07-13
14-07-13
20-08-13
14-07-13
15-07-13
14-11-13
18-09-13

EX3_50 Write a query to display sale date in character format DD-MONTH-YYYY HH:MI from SALE_DETAIL.

SQL> SELECT TO_CHAR(SALEDT,'DD-Month YYYY HH:MI') DT_DESC FROM SALE_DETAIL;

DT_DESC

14-July 2013 12:00
14-July 2013 12:00
20-August 2013 12:00
14-July 2013 12:00
15-July 2013 12:00
14-November 2013 12:00
18-September 2013 12:00

EX3_51 Write a query to display sale detail in character format MONTH YEAR from SALE_DETAIL.

SQL> SELECT CID || 'sold on' || INITCAP(TO_CHAR(SALEDT,'MONTH YEAR')) DT_DESC FROM SALE_DETAIL;

DT_DESC
C1 sold on July Two Thousand Eight
C1 sold on July Two Thousand Eight
C1 sold on August Two Thousand Eight
C2 sold on July Two Thousand Eight
C3 sold on July Two Thousand Eight
C4 sold on November Two Thousand Eight
C5 sold on September Two Thousand Eight

EX3_52 Write a query to display PNAME with difference between 31-Dec-2013 and Sale Date.

SQL> SELECT P.PNAME,'31-DEC-2013' LAST_DAY,TO_DATE('31-DEC-2013')-S.SALEDT DIFF FROM PROD P, SALE_DETAIL S WHERE P.PID=S.PID;

PNAME	LAST_DAY	DIFF
PENCIL	31-DEC-2013	170
FLOPPY	31-DEC-2013	169
FLOPPY	31-DEC-2013	104
PEN	31-DEC-2013	47
PEN	31-DEC-2013	133
PEN	31-DEC-2013	170
PEN	31-DEC-2013	170

EX3_53 Write a query to display the numeric value of string "13th" by adding 10 to it using TO_NUMBER and SUBSTR function.

SQL> SELECT TO_NUMBER(SUBSTR('13th',1,2))+10 NUM_DESC FROM DUAL;

NUM_DESC
23

EX3_54 Write a query to display distinct customer ID whose product ID is P3.

SQL> SELECT DISTINCT CID FROM SALE_DETAIL WHERE PID='P3';

CID
C1
C2
C4

EX3_55 Write a query to display distinct sale date having product ID P3.

SQL> SELECT DISTINCT SALEDT FROM SALE_DETAIL WHERE PID='P3';

SALEDT
14-JUL-13
14-NOV-13
20-AUG-13

3.4.5 Miscellaneous Function

NVL

NVL is used to convert a NULL value to an actual value. With this function date, character and number data types can be used.

NVL (exp 1, exp 2), where exp 1 is the source value and exp 2 is the target value for converting NULL.

DECODE

The DECODE function decodes an expression in a way similar to the IF-THEN-ELSE logic. The DECODE function decodes expression after comparing it to each search value. If the expression is the same as search, result is returned. If the default value is omitted, a NULL value is returned where a search value does not match any of the result values.

ROWNUM

The ROWNUM function generates number starting from 1 to the number of rows display.

ROWID

ROWID represents the physical location of the record in the database. One of the important use of ROWID is to differentiate between duplicate rows, as no two rows within the same table will have the same ROWID.

EX3_56 Example comparing NVL and without NVL is shown in Figure 3.5.

SQL Statement Without Using NVL

```
SQL> SELECT PNAME, PCOST,
PPROFIT FROM PROD;
```

PNAME	*PCOST*	*PPROFIT*
PEN	*20.5*	*20*
FLOPPY	*30*	*12*
PENCIL	*5.25*	

```
SQL> SELECT PNAME, PCOST,
PCOST*PPROFIT/100 FROM PROD;
```

PNAME	*PCOST*	*PCOST*PPROFIT/100*
PEN	*20.5*	*4.1*
FLOPPY	*30*	*3.6*
PENCIL	*5.25*	

SQL Statement Using NVL

```
SQL> SELECT PNAME, PCOST,
NVL(PPROFIT,0) FROM PROD;
```

PNAME	*PCOST*	*NVL(PPROFIT,0)*
PEN	*20.5*	*20*
FLOPPY	*30*	*12*
PENCIL	*5.25*	*0*

```
SQL> SELECT PNAME, PCOST,
PCOST*NVL(PPROFIT,0)/100 FROM PROD;
```

PNAME	*PCOST*	*PCOST*NVL(PPROFIT,0)/100*
PEN	*20.5*	*4.1*
FLOPPY	*30*	*3.6*
PENCIL	*5.25*	*0*

FIGURE 3.5 Working with NVL.

EX3_57 Write a query to display the name and cost of a product as per the following logic. If product name is 'PEN' then revised cost = cost*1.1 else if product name is 'PENCIL' then revised cost =cost*1.15.

```
SQL> SELECT PNAME, PCOST,
DECODE(PNAME, 'PEN', PCOST*1.1, 'PENCIL', PCOST *1.15)
REVISED_PCOST      FROM PROD;
```

PNAME	*PCOST*	*REVISED_PCOST*
PEN	*20.5*	*22.55*
FLOPPY	*30*	
PENCIL	*5.25*	*6.0375*

EX3_58 Write a query to display the name and cost of a product as per the following logic. If product name is 'PEN' then revised cost = cost*1.1 else if product name is 'PENCIL' then revised cost = cost*1.15 else revised cost = pcost.

```
SQL> SELECT NAME, PCOST, DECODE (PNAME, 'PEN', PCOST*1.1, 'PENCIL',
PCOST*1.15, PCOST) REVISED_PCOST FROM PROD;
```

PNAME	*PCOST*	*REVISED_PCOST*
PEN	*20.5*	*22.55*
FLOPPY	*30*	*30*
PENCIL	*5.25*	*6.0375*

EX3_59 This example demonstrates usage of ROWNUM.

```
SQL> SELECT ROWNUM,CNAME,CCITY FROM CUST;
```

ROWNUM	*CNAME*	*CCITY*
1	*PRADIP*	*MYSORE*
2	*AASTIK*	*KOLKATA*
3	*TUSHAR*	*PUNE*
4	*ARPAN*	*CHENNAI*
5	*ANUMITA*	*INDORE*

EX3_60 This example demonstrates usage of ROWID.

```
SQL>SELECT ROWID,CID FROM SALE_DETAIL;
```

ROW ID	CID
AAARVAAAEAAAAG2AAD	C1
AAARVAAAEAAAAG2AAA	C1
AAARVAAAEAAAAG2AAE	C1
AAARVAAAEAAAAG2AAC	C2
AAARVAAAEAAAAG2AAB	C3
AAARVAAAEAAAAG2AAF	C4
AAARVAAAEAAAAG2AAG	C5

3.5 GROUP FUNCTIONS

Group functions operate on sets of rows to give one result per group. Group functions along with their purposes are shown in Table 3.6.

TABLE 3.6 Group Functions

Functions	Purposes
AVG(DISTINCT/ ALL/n)	Average value of n, ignoring null values
COUNT(*/DISTINCT/ALL)	Number of rows, where exp evaluates to something other than NULL (count all selected rows using *; including duplicates and rows with NULLS)
MAX(DISTINCT/ALL)	Maximum value of exp, ignoring NULL values
MIN(DISTINCT/ALL)	Minimum value of exp, ignoring NULL values
STDDEV(DISTINCT/ALL)	Standard deviation of n, ignoring NULL values
SUM(DISTINCT/ ALL)	Sum of values of n, ignoring NULL values
VARIANCE (DISTINCT/ALL)	Variance of n, ignoring NULL values

EX3_61 Write a query to display the total count of customer.
SQL> SELECT COUNT(*) T_CUST FROM CUST;

T_CUST
5

EX3_62 Write a query to display minimum cost of product.
SQL> SELECT MIN(PCOST), MAX(PCOST) FROM PROD;

MIN(PCOST)	*MAX(PCOST)*
5.25	*301*

EX3_63 Write a query to display average value of product cost rounded to 2nd decimal places.
SQL> SELECT ROUND(AVG(PCOST),2) FROM PROD;

ROUND(AVG(PCOST),2)
18.58

EX3_64 Write a query to display product name with total sale detail in descending order.
SQL> SELECT P.PNAME,SUM(S.SALE) FROM PROD P,SALE_DETAIL S WHERE P.PID=S.PID GROUP BY P.PNAME ORDER BY P.PNAME DESC;

PNAME	*SUM(S.SALE)*
PENCIL	*5*
PEN	*8*
FLOPPY	*12*

EX3_65 Write a query to display product name, sale date and total amount collected for the product.
SQL> SELECT P.PNAME, S.SALEDT, SUM(S.SALE*P.PCOST) FROM PROD P,SALE_DETAIL S WHERE P.PID=S.PID GROUP BY P.PNAME,S.SALEDT;

PNAME	SALEDT	SUM(S.SALE*P.PCOST)
PEN	14-NOV-13	41
PEN	14-JUL-13	61.5
FLOPPY	18-SEP-13	60
FLOPPY	15-JUL-13	300
PENCIL	14-JUL-13	26.25
PEN	20-AUG-13	61.5

EX3_66 Write a query to display product name, sale date and total amount collected in date wise sale of Pen and Pencil.

SQL> SELECT P.PNAME, S.SALEDT, SUM(S.SALE*P.PCOST) FROM PROD P,SALE_DETAIL S WHERE P.PID=S.PID GROUP BY P.PNAME,S.SALEDT HAVING P.PNAME IN ('PEN','PENCIL');

PNAME	SALEDT	SUM(S.SALE*P.PCOST)
PEN	14-NOV-13	41
PEN	14-JUL-13	61.5
PENCIL	14-JUL-13	26.25
PEN	20-AUG-13	61.5

EX3_67 Write a query to display product name, sale date and total amount collected date wise for Pen and Pencil. Arrange them in ascending order of total collected amount.

SQL> SELECT P.PNAME, S.SALEDT, SUM(S.SALE*P.PCOST) FROM PROD P,SALE_DETAIL S WHERE P.PID=S.PID GROUP BY P.PNAME,S.SALEDT HAVING P.PNAME IN ('PEN','PENCIL') ORDER BY SUM(S.SALE*P.PCOST);

PNAME	SALEDT	SUM(S.SALE*P.PCOST)
PENCIL	14-JUL-13	26.25
PEN	14-NOV-13	41
PEN	20-AUG-13	61.5
PEN	14-JUL-13	61.5

EX3_68 Write a query to display sale date and total sale date wise which was sold after "14-JUL-13".

SQL>SELECT SALEDT, SUM(SALE) FROM SALE_DETAIL GROUP BY SALEDT HAVING SALEDT>'14-JUL-13';

SALEDT	SUM(SALE)
18-SEP-13	2
14-NOV-13	2
15-JUL-13	10
20-AUG-13	3

3.6 SET FUNCTIONS

There are three set operators used in SQL, Union, Intersect and Minus.

3.6.1 Union

The UNION operator returns all distinct rows selected by both the queries. It eliminates the duplicate rows.

EX3_69 Write a query to display the customer name who belongs to those places whose name is having character I or P. Using UNION operator.

```
SQL> SELECT CNAME FROM CUST WHERE CCITY LIKE 'I%'
UNION
SELECT CNAME FROM CUST WHERE CCITY LIKE 'P%';
```

CNAME
ANUMITA
TUSHAR

3.6.2 Intersect

The 'INTERSECT' operator returns only rows that are common to both the queries.

EX3_70 Write a query to display customer name who belongs to a city whose name contains character 'C' and whose name contains character 'A'.

```
SQL> SELECT CNAME FROM CUST WHERE CNAME LIKE 'A%'
INTERSECT
SELECT CNAME FROM CUST WHERE CCITY LIKE 'C%';
```

CNAME
ARPAN

3.6.3 Minus

The 'MINUS' operator returns all distinct rows selected only by the first query and not by the second.

EX3_71 Write a query to display the customer name who does not belong to PUNE.

```
SQL> SELECT CNAME FROM CUST
MINUS
SELECT CNAME FROM CUST WHERE CCITY LIKE 'P%';
```

CNAME
AASTIK
ANUMITA
ARPAN
PRADIP

3.7 SUBQUERY

A subquery is a SELECT statement that is embedded in a clause of another SELECT statement. Subqueries are useful when rows need to be selected from a table with condition that depends on the data in the table itself. Subquery can be placed in WHERE and HAVING clause.

EX3_72 Write a query to display distinct CNAME who have purchased items according to the following details:

- same as customers purchased item P3 and
- same as SALEDT on which item P3 was sold
- order by CNAME.

```
SQL> SELECT DISTINCT C.CNAME FROM CUST C,SALE_DETAIL S
WHERE C.CID=S.CID AND S.CID IN (SELECT DISTINCT CID FROM SALE_DETAIL
WHERE PID='P3') AND S.SALEDT IN (SELECT DISTINCT SALEDT FROM
SALE_DETAIL WHERE PID='P3') ORDER BY C.CNAME;
```

CNAME
ARPAN
PRADIP
TUSHAR

EX3_73 Write a query to display the PID with lowest average SALE.

```
SQL> SELECT PID,AVG(SALE) FROM SALE_DETAIL
GROUP BY PID
HAVING AVG(SALE)=(SELECT MIN(AVG(SALE))
FROM SALE_DETAIL GROUP BY PID);
```

PID	*AVG(SALE)*
P3	*2*

EX3_74 Write a query to display PID, PNAME, PCOST and REVISED_PCOST. REVISED_PCOST for P1 is cost increased by 10%, for P2 cost is increased by 20% and for P3 no increase in cost.

```
SQL> SELECT PID,PNAME,PCOST,
DECODE(PID,   'P1', PCOST*1.10,
              'P2', PCOST*1.20,
              PCOST) REVISED_PCOST
FROM PROD
ORDER BY PID;
```

PID	*PNAME*	*PCOST*	*REVISED_PCOST*
P1	*PENCIL*	*5.25*	*5.775*
P2	*FLOPPY*	*30*	*36*
P3	*PEN*	*20.5*	*20.5*

3.8 JOINS

A join condition in a WHERE clause is required to combine all rows from all tables. If a join condition is omitted, the result is a cartesian product in which all combinations of rows will be displayed, which is undesirable in most conditions. The four types of join in SQL are equi join, non-equi join, outer join and self join. Each is with a different purpose.

3.8.1 Equi Join

Equi join as its name suggests is based on equalities. The equi join combines rows that have equivalent values for the specified columns. This is also called **simple join** or **inner join**. This is the most used join among all.

In this section, all the examples related to joins are based on SCOTT/TIGER, which by default is available with Oracle database. Tables with records are shown as under.

TABLES:

EMP

EMPNO	ENAME	JOB	MGR	HIREDATE	SAL	COMM	DEPTNO
7876	ADAMS	CLERK	7788	23-MAY-87	1100		20
7499	ALLEN	SALESMAN	7698	20-FEB-81	1600	300	30
7698	BLAKE	MANAGER	7839	01-MAY-81	2850		30
7782	CLARK	MANAGER	7839	09-JUN-81	2450		10
7902	FORD	ANALYST	7566	03-DEC-81	3000		20
7900	JAMES	CLERK	7698	03-DEC-81	9500		30
7566	JONES	MANAGER	7839	02-APR-81	2975		20
7839	KING	PRESIDENT		17-NOV-81	5000		10
7654	MARTIN	SALESMAN	7698	28-SEP-81	1250	1400	30
7934	MILLER	CLERK	7782	23-JAN-82	1300		10
7788	SCOTT	ANALYST	7566	19-APR-87	3000		20
7369	SMITH	CLERK	7902	17-DEC-80	800		20
7844	TURNER	SALESMAN	7698	08-SEP-81	1500	0	30
7521	WARD	SALESMAN	7698	22-FEB-81	1250	500	35

DEPT

DEPTNO	DNAME	LOC
10	ACCOUNTING	NEW YORK
20	RESEARCH	DALLAS
30	SALES	CHICAGO
40	OPERATIONS	BOSTON

SALGRADE

GRADE	LOSAL	HISAL
1	700	1200
2	1201	1400
3	1401	2000
4	2001	3000
5	3001	9999

EX3_75 Write a query to display the name and department name of those employees who work in department No. 10.

```
SQL> SLELECT E.ENAME, D.DNAME FROM EMP E,DEPT D
WHERE E.DEPTNO=D.DEPTNO AND D.DEPTNO=10;
```

ENAME	*DNAME*
CLARK	*ACCOUNTING*
KING	*ACCOUNTING*
MILLER	*ACCOUNTING*

3.8.2 Non-equi Join

In case of non-equi join, column from one table does not directly corresponds to column of second table. Non-equi join is best used with BETWEEN clauses. This join specifies the relationship between columns belonging to different tables. In this type of join >, >=, <, <= and != operators can also be used.

EX3_76 Write a query to display the name, salary and grade of those employees whose salary is greater than 1300 and less than 3000.

SQL> SELECT E.ENAME,E.SAL,G.GRADE FROM EMP E,SALGRADE G WHERE E.SAL>1300 AND E.SAL<3000 AND E.SAL BETWEEN G.LOSAL AND G.HISAL;

ENAME	*SAL*	*GRADE*
ALLEN	*1600*	*3*
TURNER	*1500*	*3*
BLAKE	*2850*	*4*
CLARK	*2450*	*4*
JONES	*2975*	*4*

3.8.3 Outer Join

An outer join returns all the rows returned by simple join, equi join as well as those from one table that do not match any row from the other table. This type of join is rarely used in practical implementations.

EX3_77 Write a query to display the name of the subordinate who reports to the boss along with the nameof the boss. Include name of employees, who does not report to any one.

SQL> SELECT SUBORDINATE.ENAME || 'REPORTS TO' || BOSS.ENAME REPORTS_TO
FROM EMP SUBORDINATE,EMP BOSS
WHERE SUBORDINATE.MGR=BOSS.EMPNO(+);

SUBORDINATE	*REPORTS_TO*	*BOSS*
FORD	*REPORTS TO*	*JONES*
SCOTT	*REPORTS TO*	*JONES*
ALLEN	*REPORTS TO*	*BLAKE*
JAMES	*REPORTS TO*	*BLAKE*
WARD	*REPORTS TO*	*BLAKE*
TURNER	*REPORTS TO*	*BLAKE*
MARTIN	*REPORTS TO*	*BLAKE*
MILLER	*REPORTS TO*	*CLARK*
ADAMS	*REPORTS TO*	*SCOTT*
BLAKE	*REPORTS TO*	*KING*
CLARK	*REPORTS TO*	*KING*
JONES	*REPORTS TO*	*KING*
SMITH	*REPORTS TO*	*FORD*
KING	*REPORTS TO*	--------

3.8.4 Self Join

Joining a table to itself is known as self join. In this type of join different alias is used for the same table. This join is used only in very specific cases.

EX3_78 Write a query to display the name of the subordinate who reports to the boss along with the name of the boss.

```
SQL> SELECT SUBORDINATE.ENAME || 'REPORTS TO' || BOSS.ENAME REPORTS_TO
FROM EMP SUBORDINATE,EMP BOSS
WHERE SUBORDINATE.MGR=BOSS.EMPNO;
```

SUBORDINATE	*REPORTS_TO*	*BOSS*
FORD	*REPORTS TO*	*JONES*
SCOTT	*REPORTS TO*	*JONES*
ALLEN	*REPORTS TO*	*BLAKE*
JAMES	*REPORTS TO*	*BLAKE*
WARD	*REPORTS TO*	*BLAKE*
TURNER	*REPORTS TO*	*BLAKE*
MARTIN	*REPORTS TO*	*BLAKE*
MILLER	*REPORTS TO*	*CLARK*
ADAMS	*REPORTS TO*	*SCOTT*
BLAKE	*REPORTS TO*	*KING*
CLARK	*REPORTS TO*	*KING*
JONES	*REPORTS TO*	*KING*
SMITH	*REPORTS TO*	*FORD*

EX3_79 Write a query to display ENAME, SAL and DEPTNO of those employees who are getting SAL more than the average salary of the DEPTNO in which they are posted. For example average salary of DEPTNO=30 is 1567. Only ALLEN and BLAKE of that department is getting more than 1567.

```
SQL> SELECT ENAME,SAL,DEPTNO FROM EMP E
WHERE SAL > (SELECT AVG(SAL) FROM EMP WHERE DEPTNO=E.DEPTNO);
```

ENAME	*SAL*	*DEPTNO*
ALLEN	*1600*	*30*
JONES	*2975*	*20*
BLAKE	*2850*	*30*
CLARK	*2450*	*10*
SCOTT	*3000*	*20*
KING	*5000*	*10*
FORD	*3000*	*20*

EX3_80 Write a query to display the ENAME and SAL of employees getting lowest three salaries.

```
SQL> SELECT ENAME,SAL FROM EMP E
WHERE 3 > (SELECT COUNT(*) FROM EMP WHERE SAL<E.SAL);
```

ENAME	*SAL*
SMITH	*800*
ADAMS	*1100*
JAMES	*950*

3.9 SUMMARY

In this chapter Oracle SQL is introduced. Concepts related to DCL, DDL, DML and TCL are explained with the help of examples. Important and most required commands of SQL * Plus are also discussed. In this chapter we have also learnt SQL functions, subqueries and joins. All these features are explained using examples. These features are not only extensively used in SQL but also in PL/SQL—Programming language of Oracle.

SHORT/OBJECTIVE TYPE QUESTIONS

1. Describe DCL, DDL, DML and TCL.

2. Briefly explain all the group function of SQL.

3. Elaborate all the join clauses with the help of suitable example.

4. Match the following.

DDL	Grant, Revoke
DML	Select
DCL	Commit
Transaction	15.35
Data Retrieval	Create Table
VARCHAR2(10)	Insert, Update, Delete
NUMBER(4)	+, –, *
Arithmetic Operators	>, like, =
Relational Operator	'Allahabad'
NUMBER(4,2)	1947

Answer questions from 5–10 based on following DCL and DDL.

- Connect to SQL from DOS prompt. Assume the details as under.

  User Name : SYSTEM
  Password : MANAGER
  Connection String : MKGCONNECT
  SYSTEM is having all privileges to perform any action.

- Create a user from SQL prompt as per following details.
  User Name : EMP
  Password : MKG
- Grant CONNECT and RESOURCE privilege to EMP.
- Connect to newly created EMP user.
- Create a table with the following details.

Name	Type	Remarks
NAME	VARCHAR2(10)	Primary Key
AGE		NUMBER(3)
JOB	VARCHAR2(10)	

- Insert records as per following details.

Name	Age	Job
PRANAB	30	DBA
PANKAJ	39	DBA
RAVI	24	PROGRAMMER
ABHYUDAY	32	OPERATOR

5. Is it possible to insert a record ('RAVI', 45, 'ANALYST')? If no, Why?

6. Insert a record ('RAVI1', 45, 'ANALYST'), List all the records to confirm that the record is inserted. What will happen if ROLLBACK command is issued?

7. DROP the EMPLOYEE table. What will happen if DESC EMPLOYEE command is issued?

8. At present EMP is connected to Oracle database server. What will happen if we try to drop it?

9. Connect to SYSTEM and then drop EMP user.

10. What will happen if we try to connect EMP user?

WORKOUT SECTION

W3_1 All questions are based on CUST, PROD, SALE_DETAIL and STATE_NAME tables.

i. Write a query to display CNAME & STATE of all records and sort it based on CNAME.

CNAME	*STATE*
AASTIK	*WEST BENGAL*
ANUMITA	*MADHYA PRADESH*
ARPAN	*TAMIL NADU*
PRADIP	*KARNATAKA*
TUSHAR	*MAHARASHTRA*

ii. Write a query to display CID & SALEDT of all records.

CID	*SALEDT*
C1	*14-JUL-13*
C3	*15-JUL-13*
C2	*14-JUL-13*
C1	*14-JUL-13*
C1	*20-AUG-13*
C4	*14-NOV-13*
C5	*18-SEP-13*

iii. Write a query to display CID and SALE*PCOST of all records whose PNAME starts with 'F'.

CID	*PNAME*	*S.SALE*P.PCOST*
C3	*FLOPPY*	*300*
C5	*FLOPPY*	*60*

iv. Write a query to display distinct CNAME who have purchased PEN and lives in KARNATAKA.
Hint: Closely observe the tables used in SELECT and WHERE clause. Total number of tables which will be used are 3 or 4?

CNAME
PRADIP

v. Insert ('RAMESH','ROORKEE') corresponding to (CNAME, CCITY) of CUST table. Is it possible to insert records with NULL prime attribute?

W3_2 CITY, PAY and DARATE tables are required to compute the applicable DARATE of an employee who has performed duty at some city. ER Model and tables are shown in Figures 3.6 and 3.7, respectively. The following rules are applicable to calculate the payable amount.

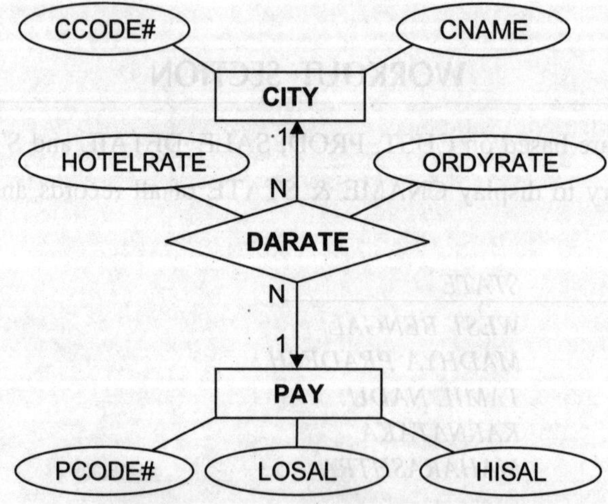

FIGURE 3.6 Entity relationship model.

CITY(CCODE#, CNAME)

CCODE#	CNAME
A1	MUMBAI
A	HYDERABAD
B1	BHOPAL

PAY(PCODE#, LOSAL, HISAL)

PCODE#	LOSAL	HISAL
P1	16400	99999
P2	8000	16399
P3	6500	7999
P4	4100	6499
P5	0	4099

DARATE(CCODE#, PCODE#, HOTELRATE, ORDYRATE)

CCODE#	PCODE#	HOTELRATE	ORDYRATE
A1	P1	650	260
A1	P2	505	230
A1	P3	380	200
A1	P4	245	170
A1	P5	125	105
A	P1	525	210
A	P2	405	185
A	P3	305	160
A	P4	195	135
A	P5	100	85
B1	P1	425	170
B1	P2	330	150
B1	P3	250	130
B1	P4	160	110
B1	P5	85	70

FIGURE 3.7 Tables with records.

- CNAME is based on CCODE.
- LOSAL and HISAL is the range of pay and is defined by PCODE.
- Daily allowance applicable (HOTELRATE or ORDYRATE) is based on CCODE & PCODE.

i. Create tables related to CITY, PAY and DARATE.

ii. Write a query to find HOTELRATE and ORDYRATE of A1 class city.

HOTELRATE	*ORDYRATE*
650	*260*
505	*230*
380	*200*
245	*170*
125	*105*

iii. Write a query to find the PCODE who is getting Rs. 10,000 salary.

PCODE

P2

iv. Write a query to find the CNAME with CCODE A1.

CNAME
MUMBAI

v. Find the payable DARATE (ORDYRATE or HOTELRATE) if an employee has gone to HYDERABAD, his salary is Rs. 20,000 and stayed in Hotel.

HOTELRATE
525

W3_3 Project related ER Model and tables are shown in Figures 3.8 and 3.9 respectively. PROJNO is primary key of PROJ and EMPNO is primary key of EMP table. EMPNO+PROJNO is foreign key of PROJ_DETAIL table.

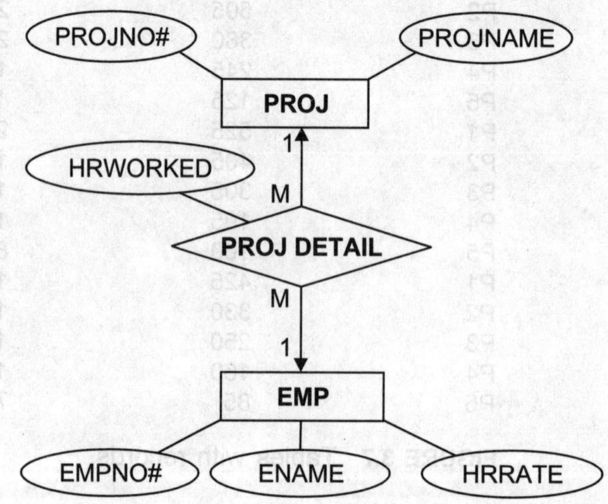

FIGURE 3.8 Entity relationship model.

i. Create PROJ, EMP and PROJ_DETAIL tables and insert records.

ii. Write a query to display ENAME, DESG, HRRATE, PROJNAME and HRRATE of all records.

ENAME	*DESG*	*HRRATE*	*PROJNAME*	*HRWORKED*
ANUP	*ANALYST*	*800*	*CODING*	*15*
KAUSHIK	*ANALYST*	*800*	*DATABASE SW*	*20*
ARUP	*DBA*	*1000*	*DATABASE SW*	*40*
ARUP	*DBA*	*1000*	*DATA RECOVERY*	*10*
ARUP	*DBA*	*1000*	*CODING*	*10*
AMIT	*PROGRAMMER*	*500*	*CODING*	*40*
CHANDRA	*PROGRAMMER*	*500*	*DATABASE SW*	*30*

PROJ(PROJNO#, PROJNAME)

PROJNO#	PROJNAME
P2	CODING
P3	DATA RECOVERY
P1	DATABASE SW

EMP(EMPNO#, ENAME, DESG)

EMPNO#	ENAME	DESG
E1	ANUP	ANALYST
E2	ARUP	DBA
E3	KAUSHIK	ANALYST
E4	AMIT	PROGRAMMER
E5	CHANDRA	PROGRAMMER

DESGRATE(DESG#, HRRATE)

DESG#	HRRATE
DBA	1000
ANALYST	800
PROGRAMMER	500

PROJ_DETAIL(EMPNO#, PROJNO#, HRWORKED)

EMPNO#	PROJNO#	HRWORKED
E1	P2	15
E2	P3	10
E2	P1	40
E2	P2	10
E3	P1	20
E4	P2	40
E5	P1	30

FIGURE 3.9 Tables with records.

iii. Write a query to display ENAME and HRWORKED of all employees who are DBA and they are working on project CODING.

ENAME	*HRWORKED*
ARUP	*10*

iv. Write a query to display ENAME and PROJNAME, Order on ENAME in descending order followed by PROJNAME in ascending order.

ENAME	*PROJNAME*
KAUSHIK	*DATABASE SW*
CHANDRA	*DATABASE SW*
ARUP	*CODING*
ARUP	*DATA RECOVERY*
ARUP	*DATABASE SW*
ANUP	*CODING*
AMIT	*CODING*

v. What will be the output of the following SQL script?
SQL> SELECT E.EMPNO, E.ENAME, E.DESG, D.HRRATE, P.PROJNO, P.PROJNAME, PD.HRWORKED
FROM EMP E, DESGRATE D, PROJ P, PROJ_DETAIL PD
WHERE E.EMPNO=PD.EMPNO AND P.PROJNO=PD.PROJNO AND E.DESG= D.DESG;

vi. What will be the output of the following SQL script?
SQL> COLUMN EMPNO HEADING 'Emp |No' FORMAT A6
SQL> COLUMN ENAME HEADING 'Name' FORMAT A8
SQL> COLUMN DESG HEADING 'Designation' FORMAT A12
SQL> COLUMN HRRATE HEADING 'HR |Rate' FORMAT 9999
SQL> COLUMN PROJNO HEADING 'Proj |No' FORMAT A8
SQL> COLUMN PROJNAME HEADING 'Project' FORMAT A8
SQL> COLUMN HRWORKED HEADING 'HR |Worked'
SQL> SELECT E.EMPNO, E.ENAME, E.DESG, D.HRRATE, P.PROJNO, P.PROJNAME, PD.HRWORKED FROM EMP E, DESGRATE D, PROJ P, PROJ_ DETAIL PD
WHERE E.EMPNO=PD.EMPNO AND P.PROJNO=PD.PROJNO AND E.DESG= D.DESG;

vii. What will be the output of the following SQL script?
SQL> COLUMN ENAME HEADING 'Name' FORMAT A8
SQL> COLUMN PROJNAME HEADING 'Project' FORMAT A8 WORD_WRAPPED
SQL> SELECT E.ENAME, P.PROJNAME
FROM EMP E, PROJ P, PROJ_DETAIL PD
WHERE E.EMPNO=PD.EMPNO AND P.PROJNO=PD.PROJNO;

W3_4 All questions are based on CUST, PROD, SALE_DETAIL and STATE_NAME tables.

i. Write a query to display sale date, product ID and total sale date wise and product wise.

SALEDT	*PID*	*SUM(SALE)*
15-JUL-13	*P2*	*10*
14-JUL-13	*P1*	*5*
14-JUL-13	*P3*	*3*
20-AUG-13	*P3*	*3*
14-NOV-13	*P3*	*2*
18-SEP-13	*P2*	*2*

ii. Write a query to display maximum and minimum cost of product.

Max and Min	*Cost Product*
30	*5.25*

iii. Write a query to display date wise the name of the customers along with the product purchased

Name has purchased product at the cost of on date

PRADIP HAS PURCHASED PEN AT THE COST OF 20.5 ON 14-JUL-13
PRADIP HAS PURCHASED PEN AT THE COST OF 20.5 ON 20-AUG-13
PRADIP HAS PURCHASED PENCIL AT THE COST OF 5.25 ON 14-JUL-13
AASTIK HAS PURCHASED FLOPPY AT THE COST OF 30 ON 15-JUL-13
TUSHAR HAS PURCHASED PEN AT THE COST OF 20.5 ON 14-JUL-13
ARPAN HAS PURCHASED PEN AT THE COST OF 20.5 ON 14-NOV-13
ANUMITA HAS PURCHASED FLOPPY AT THE COST OF 30 ON 18-SEP-13

iv. Write a query to display the product name and its actual cost.

PNAME	*ACTUAL COST*
PEN	*16*
FLOPPY	*21*
PENCIL	*5*

v. Write a query to display customer name, city and state (upto 5 character from the beginning).

CNAME	*CCITY*	*STATE*
PRADIP	*MYSORE*	*KARNA*
AASTIK	*KOLKATA*	*WEST*
TUSHAR	*PUNE*	*MAHAR*
ARPAN	*CHENNAI*	*TAMIL*
ANUMITA	*INDORE*	*MADHYA*

5. All questions are based on CUST, PROD, SALE_DETAIL and STATE_NAME tables.

i. Write a query to display name, city of the customer where 'first character of name' < 'first character of city'.

CNAME	*CCITY*
AASTIK	*KOLKATA*
ANUMITA	*INDORE*
ARPAN	*CHENNAI*

ii. Write a query to display customer name, product name who has purchased the product which was purchased by 'ANUMITA'.

CNAME	*PNAME*
AASTIK	*FLOPPY*
ANUMITA	*FLOPPY*

iii. Write a query to display following output. Note that records of CUST and PROD are displayed and they are not linked with each other.

CID	CNAME	CCITY	PID	PNAME	PCOST	PPROFIT
C1	PRADIP	MYSORE	P3	PEN	20.5	20
C3	AASTIK	KOLKATA	P3	PEN	20.5	20
C2	TUSHAR	PUNE	P3	PEN	20.5	20
C4	ARPAN	CHENNAI	P3	PEN	20.5	20
C5	ANUMITA	INDORE	P3	PEN	20.5	20
C1	PRADIP	MYSORE	P2	FLOPPY	30	12
C3	AASTIK	KOLKATA	P2	FLOPPY	30	12
C2	TUSHAR	PUNE	P2	FLOPPY	30	12
C4	ARPAN	CHENNAI	P2	FLOPPY	30	12
C5	ANUMITA	INDORE	P2	FLOPPY	30	12
C1	PRADIP	MYSORE	P1	PENCIL		5.25
C3	AASTIK	KOLKATA	P1	PENCIL		5.25
C2	TUSHAR	PUNE	P1	PENCIL		5.25
C4	ARPAN	CHENNAI	P1	PENCIL		5.25
C5	ANUMITA	INDORE	P1	PENCIL		5.25

iv. Write a query to display customer name, product name and sale of those products whose name contains character 'F'.

CNAME	PNAME	SALE
AASTIK	FLOPPY	10
ANUMITA	FLOPPY	2

v. Write a query to display customer name along with product name for those customers name which contains character 'A'.

CNAME	PNAME
PRADIP	PEN
PRADIP	PENCIL
TUSHAR	PEN

vi. SQL query along with the output is given. Explain the output of the query with reasoning.

```
SQL> SELECT PID, SALE FROM SALE_DETAIL S
WHERE SALE<(SELECT AVG(SALE) FROM SALE_DETAIL WHERE
PID=S.PID);
```

PID	SALE
P3	1
P2	2

W3_6 All questions are based on PROJ, EMP, DESGRATE and PROJ_DETAIL tables. Figure 3.10 shows records in all the tables.

PROJ(PROJNO#, PROJNAME)

PROJNO#	PROJNAME
P2	CODING
P3	DATA RECOVERY
P1	DATABASE SW

EMP(EMPNO#, ENAME, DESG)

EMPNO#	ENAME	DESG
E1	ANUP	ANALYST
E2	ARUP	DBA
E3	KAUSHIK	ANALYST
E4	AMIT	PROGRAMMER
E5	CHANDRA	PROGRAMMER

DESGRATE(DESG#, HRRATE)

DESG#	HRRATE
DBA	1000
ANALYST	800
PROGRAMMER	500

PROJ_DETAIL(EMPNO#, PROJNO#, HRWORKED)

EMPNO#	PROJNO#	HRWORKED
E1	P2	15
E2	P3	10
E2	P1	40
E2	P2	10
E3	P1	20
E4	P2	40
E5	P1	30

FIGURE 3.10 Tables with records.

i. What will be the output of this SQL?
SQL> SELECT COUNT(*) FROM PROJ,EMP,DESGRATE,PROJ_DETAIL WHERE PROJ_DETAIL.PROJNO=PROJ.PROJNO AND EMP.EMPNO=PROJ_DETAIL.EMPNO;

ii. Write a query to display ENAME and PROJNAME of those ENAMEs which starts with 'A' and ends with 'P'.

ENAME	*PROJNAME*
ANUP	*CODING*
ARUP	*DATABASE SW*
ARUP	*DATA RECOVERY*
ARUP	*CODING*

iii. Write a query to display PROJNAME and profit earned on each project. Profit earned in a project is computed by 20% of summation of HRWORKED x HRRATE.

PROJNAME	*PROFIT*
CODING	*8400*
DATA RECOVERY	*2000*
DATABASE SW	*14,200*

iv. Write a query to display DESG and HRRATE which are other than maximum or minimum HRRATE.

DESG	*HRRATE*
ANALYST	*800*

v. Write a query to display ENAME along with total earning of those employees who have earned less than the average of HRRATE × HRWORKED. Order the output by ENAME.

ENAME	*EARNED*
ANUP	*12,000*
CHANDRA	*15,000*
KAUSHIK	*16,000*

4

Data Manipulation Language, Objects, Constraints and Security in Oracle

Learning Objectives

You will learn following key concepts after completion of the chapter:

- ✓ Working with views
- ✓ Working with sequence, synonym and index
- ✓ Table and column level constraints
- ✓ Oracle privileges, roles and profiles

4.1 INTRODUCTION

The data manipulation language is used to add, modify and delete records in a table. Tables are interdependent due to the declaration of foreign key at the time of its creation. Transaction control language acts on the transaction due to DMLs. It plays a vital role to ensure consistency of data in tables. Views are created to ensure data security and minimize data redundancy. Sequences are used to generate numeric value, which may be used to represent primary key of a table. It is an independent object that can be used with any table that requires its output. A synonym is a database object used as an alias for a table, view or sequence. Indexing a table is way to sort and search records in the table. Security maintenance and integrity of a database is the most important factor in judging the success of a system. This integrity can be applied to different levels. An integrity constraint is a mechanism to prevent invalid data entry into the table. Oracle database security covers access and use of database, database objects and the actions that users can have on objects. Privileges are the right to execute particular SQL statements. Around 150 privileges are available to the user or role. A role is a named group of related privileges that can be granted to the user. The password is used to authenticate a user before he can perform any action. A profile is a named set of password, which is used to fine tune the password.

4.2 THE INSERT STATEMENT

A new row in a table can be inserted using INSERT statement. At a time only one row can be inserted. Syntax of INSERT statement is:

INSERT INTO TABLE_NAME [COLUMN_LIST]
VALUES (DATA_VALUE_LIST);

All examples related to INSERT statement are based on CUST, PROD, SALE_DETAIL and STATE_NAME tables (CUST_PROD.SQL) as described in Chapter 3.

4.2.1 Inserting New Rows in a Table

New rows can be inserted without mentioning column name only if the values are listed according to the default order of the columns in the table.

EX4_1 This example demonstrates insertion of row without mentioning the column names.

SQL> DESC STATE_NAME

Name	*Null?*	*Type*
CCITY	*NOT NULL*	*VARCHAR2(8)*
STATE		*VARCHAR2(15)*

SQL> INSERT INTO STATE_NAME VALUES ('BALASORE', 'ORISSA');
SQL> INSERT INTO STATE_NAME VALUES ('DELHI', 'NEW DELHI');
SQL> INSERT INTO STATE_NAME VALUES ('LUCKNOW', 'UTTAR PRADESH');
SQL>INSERT INTO STATE_NAME VALUES ('AGRA', 'UTTAR PRADESH');

This example demonstrates that columns can be inserted in a record in any order.

SQL> INSERT INTO CUST (CNAME,CID,CCITY) VALUES ('ABHYUDAY','C7', 'BALASORE');
SQL> COMMIT;
Commit complete.

4.2.2 Integrity Constraint Error in INSERT Statement

If we attempt to insert a record with a value that is tied to an integrity constraint, it will result into an error.

EX4_2 This example demonstrates violation of integrity constraint. ('C6', 'RAKESH', 'MUMBAI') can be inserted only after inserting ('MUMBAI', 'MAHARASHTRA') in STATE_NAME table.

SQL> INSERT INTO CUST VALUES ('C6', 'RAKESH', 'MUMBAI');
INSERT INTO CUST VALUES ('C6', 'RAKESH', 'MUMBAI')
ERROR at line 1:
ORA-02291: integrity constraint (TTP.SYS_C001034) violated - parent key not found
SQL> INSERT INTO STATE_NAME VALUES ('MUMBAI', 'MAHARASHTRA');
SQL> INSERT INTO CUST VALUES ('C6', 'RAKESH', 'MUMBAI');
SQL> COMMIT;
Commit complete.

4.2.3 Inserting Rows Using Substitution Variables

Rows can be inserted interactively using SQL*Plus substitution variable.

EX4_3 This example shows insertion of rows in CUST table using substitution variable '&'. It prompts the user for the CID, CNAME and CCITY. Note that VARCHAR2 type of values are enclosed in single quotation marks.

SET VERIFY OFF
SQL> INSERT INTO CUST VALUES (&CID, &CNAME, &CCITY);
Enter value for cid: 'C8'
Enter value for cname: 'PRAKASH'
Enter value for ccity: 'INDORE'
1 row created.

For VARCHAR2 values, the ampersand and the variable name are enclosed in single quotation marks in the INSERT statement itself. This facilitates users to insert values interactively without single quotation marks.

SQL> INSERT INTO CUST VALUES ('&CID','&CNAME','&CCITY');
Enter value for cid: C9
Enter value for cname: ANIL
Enter value for ccity: DELHI
1 row created.

4.2.4 Inserting Rows with NULL Values

NULL values in a row can be inserted if it is not a key. It can be implicit or explicit. In case of implicit insertion omit the column from the column list, whereas in case of explicit insertion, specify the empty string (' ') in the VALUES list.

EX4_4 This example shows insertion of NULL value corresponding to the column explicitly.
SQL> INSERT INTO CUST VALUES ('C10','','AGRA');

This example shows insertion of NULL value corresponding to column implicitly.
SQL> INSERT INTO CUST (CID,CCITY) VALUES ('C11','LUCKNOW');

4.2.5 Inserting SYSDATE in a New Row

The format DD-MON-YYYY is usually used to insert a date value. If a date is required to be inserted other than the default format, TO_DATE function must be used.

EX4_5 In this example date is inserted in SALE_DETAIL table in default format.
SQL> INSERT INTO SALE_DETAIL VALUES ('C7','P2', 4, SYSDATE);
SQL>COMMIT;
Commit complete.

4.2.6 Copying Rows from Another Table

INSERT statement can be used to add rows to a table where the values are derived from existing table(s). In place of the VALUES clause, subquery is used. Syntax to copy rows from another table(s) is as follows:

```
INSERT INTO TABLE_NAME [COLUMN (, COLUMN)]
SUBQUERY;
```

EX4_6 Create a table CUST_A. Copy all rows whose CNAME starts with 'A'. Note that the number of columns and their datatypes in the column list of the INSERT clause must match the number of values and their datatypes in the subquery.

```
SQL> CREATE TABLE CUST_A
(CID VARCHAR2(6) PRIMARY KEY,
CNAME VARCHAR2(10),
CCITY VARCHAR2(8));
Table created.
SQL> SELECT * FROM CUST_A;
no rows selected
SQL> INSERT INTO CUST_A (CID, CNAME, CCITY)
SELECT CID, CNAME, CCITY
FROM CUST
WHERE CNAME LIKE 'A%';
5 rows created.
SQL> SELECT * FROM CUST_A;
```

CID	*CNAME*	*CCITY*
C3	*AASTIK*	*KOLKATA*
C4	*ARPAN*	*CHENNAI*
C5	*ANUMITA*	*INDORE*
C7	*ABHYUDAY*	*BALASORE*
C9	*ANIL*	*DELHI*

4.3 THE UPDATE STATEMENT

UPDATE statement is used to modify existing rows in a table. Syntax of UPDATE statement is as follows:

```
UPDATE TABLE_NAME
SET COLUMN=VALUE [, COLUMN = VALUE, ...]
[WHERE CONDITION];
```

Depending on the condition, zero, one, many, or all records of the table can be updated by a single UPDATE command. Update can be confirmed by querying the table to display the updated rows.

4.3.1 Updating Rows Based on WHERE Clause

Specific row(s) are modified when WHERE clause is specified.

EX4_7 This example demonstrates usage of WHERE clause in UPDATE statement. In this example 'ANIL' is transferred to 'AGRA'.

SQL> UPDATE CUST SET CCITY='AGRA'
WHERE CNAME='ANIL';
1 row updated.
SQL> COMMIT;
Commit complete.

4.3.2 Updating Rows without WHERE Clause

All rows in a table are modified if WHERE clause is omitted.

EX4_8 In this example all the rows are modified. CCITY of all rows will be modified to 'CHENNAI'.

SQL> UPDATE CUST SET CCITY='CHENNAI';
11 rows updated.

This type of requirement is very rare and not desired in most cases. Use ROLLBACK command to recall all rows.

SQL> ROLLBACK;
Rollback complete.

4.3.3 Update with Multiple Column Subquery

Multiple column subqueries can be implemented in the SET clause of an UPDATE statement. Syntax to execute update multiple column subquery is as under.

UPDATE TABLE_NAME
SET (COLUMN, COLUMN, …) =
(SELECT COLUMN, COLUMN, … FROM TABLE WHERE CONDITION)
WHERE CONDITION;

EX4_9 This example updates CNAME with 'NONAME' where CNAME is NULL and CCITY is 'AGRA'.

SQL> UPDATE CUST SET CNAME='NONAME'
WHERE (CID, CCITY) IN (SELECT CID, CCITY FROM CUST WHERE CNAME IS NULL AND CCITY='AGRA');
1 row updated

4.3.4 Integrity Constraint Error in UPDATE Statement

If we attempt to update a record with a value that is tied to an integrity constraint, it will result into an error.

EX4_10 In this example PID with 'P4' does not exist in parent table, PROD. If we try to update value of PID it leads to an error.

SQL> UPDATE SALE_DETAIL SET PID='P4'
WHERE PID='P3';
UPDATE SALE_DETAIL SET PID='P4'
ERROR at line 1:
ORA-02291: integrity constraint (TTP.SYS_C001037) violated - parent key not found

This type of error can be avoided if 'P4' related row is inserted in the parent table, PROD.

SQL> INSERT INTO PROD VALUES ('P4','CD',15, 20);
SQL> UPDATE SALE_DETAIL SET PID='P4'
WHERE PID='P3';
4 rows updated.
SQL> COMMIT;
Commit complete.

Note that 'P4' is now inserted in PROD and 'P3' is updated to 'P4' in SALE_DETAIL table.

4.4 THE DELETE STATEMENT

DELETE statement is used to delete row(s) from a table. Syntax of DELETE statement is as under.

DELETE FROM TABLE_NAME
[WHERE CONDITION];

The statement can target zero, one, many, or all records.

4.4.1 Deletion of Rows Based on WHERE Clause

Specific row(s) are deleted when WHERE clause is specified.

EX4_11 This example demonstrates usage of WHERE clause in a DELETE statement. All records of CUST table with CID = 'C1' are deleted. It can be saved using COMMIT statement and can be verified using SELECT statement.

SQL> DELETE FROM CUST WHERE CID='C11';
1 row deleted.

4.4.2 Deletion of Rows without WHERE Clause

All rows in the table are deleted if WHERE clause is omitted.

EX4_12 This example demonstrates DELETE statement without WHERE clause. It is not desired in most cases. ROLLBACK command is used to recall all rows.

SQL> DELETE FROM SALE_DETAIL;
7 rows deleted.
SQL> ROLLBACK;
Rollback complete.

4.4.3 Integrity Constraint Error in DELETE Statement

It is not possible to delete a row that contains a primary key that is used as a foreign key in another table.

EX4_13 This example demonstrates integrity constraint error.

SQL> DELETE FROM CUST WHERE CID='C7';

DELETE FROM CUST

*

ERROR at line 1:

ORA-02292: integrity constraint (TTP.SYS_C001036) violated-child record found

This type of error can be avoided by deleting related row in child table where CID is foreign key.

SQL> DELETE FROM SALE_DETAIL WHERE CID='C7';

1 row deleted.

SQL> DELETE FROM CUST WHERE CID='C7';

1 row deleted.

SQL> COMMIT;

Commit complete.

4.4.4 Deleting Rows Based on Another Table

Subqueries can be used in DELETE statements to remove rows from a table based on values from another table.

EX4_14 This example demonstrates usage of subquery in DELETE statement. In this example all CNAME which contains two 'A's are deleted.

SQL> DELETE FROM SALE_DETAIL
WHERE CID IN (SELECT CID FROM CUST WHERE CNAME LIKE '%A%A%');

3 rows deleted.

SQL> COMMIT;

Commit complete.

4.5 TRANSACTION CONTROL LANGUAGE

Transactions consist of DML statements that make up one consistent change to the data. Oracle server ensures data consistency based on transactions. It ensures data consistency in the event of user process failure or system failure. Database transactions consist of one or more DMLs, one DDL or one DCL statement. Database transactions begin with the DMLs and ends with COMMIT, ROLLBACK, DDL or DCL statement. It also terminates when user exits or system crashes.

All examples related to TCL statement are based on CUST, PROD, SALE_DETAIL and STATE_NAME tables (CUST_PROD.SQL) as described in Chapter 3.

4.5.1 COMMIT, ROLLBACK and SAVEPOINT Statements

A COMMIT or ROLLBACK statement ensures data consistency. It allows grouping of logically related operation. Changes can be previewed before making the changes permanent. Transactions can be controlled using COMMIT, SAVEPOINT and ROLLBACK statements. COMMIT ends the transaction by making all pending data changes permanent. SAVEPOINT marks a savepoint within the current transaction and ROLLBACK ends the current transaction by discarding all pending data changes. ROLLBACK TO SAVEPOINT rolls back the current transaction to the specified savepoint, thereby discarding the savepoint and any subsequent changes. If the SAVEPOINT clause is omitted the ROLLBACK statement rolls back the entire transactions.

EX4_15 This example demonstrates usage of SAVEPOINT command. Insert few records in SALE_DETAIL table.

```
SQL> SELECT * FROM SALE_DETAIL;
```

CID	*PID*	*SALE*	*SALEDT*
C3	*P2*	*10*	*15-JUL-13*
C1	*P1*	*5*	*14-JUL-13*
C5	*P2*	*2*	*18-SEP-13*

```
SQL> INSERT INTO SALE_DETAIL VALUES ('C2','P2',2,SYSDATE);
SQL> INSERT INTO SALE_DETAIL VALUES ('C2','P3',2,SYSDATE);
SQL> SELECT * FROM SALE_DETAIL;
```

CID	*PID*	*SALE*	*SALEDT*
C2	*P3*	*2*	*06-NOV-13*
C3	*P2*	*10*	*15-JUL-13*
C1	*P1*	*5*	*14-JUL-13*
C5	*P2*	*2*	*18-SEP-13*
C2	*P2*	*2*	*06-NOV-13*

```
SQL> INSERT INTO SALE_DETAIL VALUES ('C1','P2',4, SYSDATE);
```

Create a SAVEPOINT and name it 'A'.

```
SQL> SAVEPOINT A;
```

Savepoint created.

Issue DELETE command.

```
SQL> DELETE FROM SALE_DETAIL
WHERE PID='P2';
```

4 rows deleted.

ROLLBACK TO A will ignore the alteration after the SAVEPOINT 'A'.

```
SQL> ROLLBACK TO A;
```

Rollback complete.

Delete some rows based on condition.

```
SQL> DELETE FROM SALE_DETAIL
WHERE PID='P2' AND CID<>'C1';
```

3 rows deleted.

Issue a COMMIT statement and write a query to display the saved transactions.

```
SQL> COMMIT;
```

Commit complete.

SQL> SELECT * FROM SALE_DETAIL;

CID	*PID*	*SALE*	*SALEDT*
C2	*P3*	*2*	*06-NOV-13*
C1	*P2*	*4*	*06-NOV-13*
C1	*P1*	*5*	*14-JUL-13*

4.5.2 Automatic COMMIT and ROLLBACK

An automatic COMMIT occurs either due to a DDL or DCL statement. Normal exit from SQL* Plus, without explicit COMMIT or ROLLBACK also save the transactions automatically. An automatic rollback occurs under an abnormal termination of SQL*Plus or system failure.

EX4_16 SQL>@ C:\TTP\CUST_PROD.SQL

SQL> SELECT * FROM SALE_DETAIL;

CID	*PID*	*SALE*	*SALEDT*
C1	*P3*	*2*	*14-JUL-13*
C3	*P2*	*10*	*15-JUL-13*
C2	*P3*	*1*	*14-JUL-13*
C1	*P1*	*5*	*14-JUL-13*
C1	*P3*	*3*	*20-AUG-13*
C4	*P3*	*2*	*14-NOV-13*
C5	*P2*	*2*	*18-SEP-13*

7 rows selected.

SQL> DELETE FROM SALE_DETAIL WHERE PID='P3';

4 rows deleted.

SQL> DROP TABLE CUST_A;

Table dropped.

SQL> ROLLBACK;

Rollback complete.

SQL> SELECT * FROM SALE_DETAIL;

CID	*PID*	*SALE*	*SALEDT*
C3	*P2*	*10*	*15-JUL-13*
C1	*P1*	*5*	*14-JUL-13*
C5	*P2*	*2*	*18-SEP-13*

Note that inspite of issuing ROLLBACK statement, 4 records are deleted. This has happened because of implicit COMMIT due to the DDL statement 'DROP TABLE CUST_A;'.

4.5.3 Locking Due to TCL Statements

Locking in Oracle is fully automatic and requires no user action. The Oracle default locking mechanism automatically uses the lowest applicable level of restriction, thus, providing the highest degree and maximum data integrity. Oracle also allows the user to lock data manually though it is rarely required in practical implementations.

State of transactions before COMMIT or ROLLBACK statements

In a multi-user environment, the current user can review the results of the DML operations using SELECT statement. Other users cannot view the results of the DML statements by the current user. The affected rows are locked; other users cannot change the data within the affected rows.

State of transactions after COMMIT or ROLLBACK statements

Data changes are made permanent in the tables after executing COMMIT statement or ROLLBACK statement. The previous state of data is lost and all rows users can view the result. Locks on the affected rows are also released and savepoints are erased after issuing COMMIT or ROLLBACK statement.

EX4_17 This example demonstrates the effect of DMLs and TCLs when same user and table is used by two users as shown in Table 4.1 and Figure 4.1. Transaction of first user is shown in 'Session 1' and transaction of second user is shown in 'Session 2'.

TABLE 4.1 Concurrent Use of a Table by Two Users

SQL statement number	Session 1	Session 2
1	Displays all rows of PROD table.	–
2	–	Displays all rows of PROD table.
3	Rows inserted, but not saved.	–
4	–	COMMIT issued from Session 2 to check whether the insertion made in Session 1 is saved or not.
5	–	On confirmation it is found that the insertion made in Session 1 cannot be saved in Session 2.
6	–	One row modified in Session 2.
7	–	Updated record is displayed correctly in Session 2.
8	No effect of update statement executed in Session 2.	–
9	–	Save the updated record.
10	Changes carried out in Session 2 is reflected in Session 1. This is because commit statement executed in Session 2 has made the changes permanent.	–
11	Save the inserted record in Session 1.	–
12	–	Rows inserted in Session 2 is saved and reflected in Session 2.

Session 1

SQL> SELECT * FROM PROD; **1**

PID	PNAME	PCOST	PPROFIT
P3	PEN	20.5	20
P2	FLOPPY	30	12
P1	PENCIL	5.25	

SQL> INSERT INTO PROD **3**
VALUES ('P4','CD',15,20);
1 row created.

SQL> SELECT * FROM PROD; **8**

PID	PNAME	PCOST	PPROFIT
P3	PEN	20.5	20
P2	FLOPPY	30	12
P1	PENCIL	5.25	
P4	CD	15	20

SQL> SELECT * FROM PROD; **10**

PID	PNAME	PCOST	PPROFIT
P3	PEN	20.5	10
P2	FLOPPY	30	12
P1	PENCIL	5.25	
P4	CD	15	20

SQL> COMMIT; **11**
Commit complete.

Session 2

SQL> SELECT * FROM PROD; **2**

PID	PNAME	PCOST	PPROFIT
P3	PEN	20.5	20
P2	FLOPPY	30	12
P1	PENCIL	5.25	

SQL> COMMIT; **4**
Commit complete.

SQL> SELECT * FROM PROD; **5**

PID	PNAME	PCOST	PPROFIT
P3	PEN	20.5	20
P2	FLOPPY	30	12
P1	PENCIL	5.25	

SQL> UPDATE PROD **6**
SET PPROFIT=10 WHERE PID='P3';
1 row updated.

SQL> SELECT * FROM PROD; **7**

PID	PNAME	PCOST	PPROFIT
P3	PEN	20.5	10
P2	FLOPPY	30	12
P1	PENCIL	5.25	

SQL> COMMIT; **9**
Commit complete.

SQL> SELECT * FROM PROD; **12**

PID	PNAME	PCOST	PPROFIT
P3	PEN	20.5	10
P2	FLOPPY	30	12
P1	PENCIL	5.25	
P4	CD	15	20

FIGURE 4.1 Concurrent sessions with TTP/TTP123@ORA11G.

4.6 VIEW

An SQL view is a virtual table, dynamically constructed for a user by extracting data from actual base tables. A view is a tailored presentation of the data contained in one or more tables (or other views). A view takes the output of a query and treats it as a table; therefore, a view can be thought of as a "stored query" or a "virtual table". The tables using with a view is created are called base tables. Joining of tables is also possible in a view. A table is key preserved if every key of the table can also be a key of the result of the join. Single row functions comprising number, character, date, group functions and expressions can also be used in views. There are several advantages of views.

- It provides an additional level of table security by restricting access to a predetermined set of rows and/or columns of a table.
- It hides data complexity. For example a single view might be defined with a join, which is a collection of related columns or rows in multiple tables.

- It simplifies commands for the user because they allow them to select information from multiple tables without actually knowing how to perform a join.
- It isolates applications from changes in definitions of base tables. For example, if a view's defining query references three columns of a four column table and a fifth column is added to the table, the view's definition is not affected and all applications using the view are not affected.
- It provides data in a different perspective than that of a base table by renaming columns without affecting the base table.

Syntax:

CREATE[OR REPLACE][[NO][FORCE]] VIEW <VIEW NAME> [COLUMN ALIAS NAME…] AS <QUERY>;

EX4_18 Execute CUST_PROD.SQL to create fresh PROD, STATE_NAME, CUST and SALE_DETAIL tables all with default rows.

SQL> @ C:\TTP\CUST_PROD.SQL

Create a simple view PROD_VU based on PROD table and display all the rows using PROD_VU.

SQL> CREATE VIEW PROD_VU AS
SELECT * FROM PROD;

View created.

SQL> SELECT * FROM PROD_VU;

PID	*PNAME*	*PCOST*	*PPROFIT*
P3	*PEN*	*20.5*	*20*
P2	*FLOPPY*	*30*	*12*
P1	*PENCIL*	*5.25*	

Insert a row ('P4', 'CD', 15, 20) using PROD_VU. Check that the row is inserted in the base table and can be retrieved using the view.

SQL> INSERT INTO PROD_VU VALUES ('P4','CD',15,20);
SQL> COMMIT;

Commit complete.

SQL> SELECT * FROM PROD;

PID	*PNAME*	*PCOST*	*PPROFIT*
P3	*PEN*	*20.5*	*20*
P2	*FLOPPY*	*30*	*12*
P1	*PENCIL*	*5.25*	
P4	*CD*	*15*	*20*

SQL> SELECT* FROM PROD_VU;

PID	*PNAME*	*PCOST*	*PPROFIT*
P3	*PEN*	*20.5*	*20*
P2	*FLOPPY*	*30*	*12*
P1	*PENCIL*	*5.25*	
P4	*CD*	*15*	*20*

Create a complex view named PROD_SALE_VU comprising PID, PNAME, PCOST, PPROFIT, CID, SALE and SALEDT columns.

```
SQL>CREATE VIEW PROD_SALE_VU AS
SELECT P.PID, P.PNAME, P.PCOST, P.PPROFIT, C.CID, SD.SALE, SD.SALEDT
FROM PROD P, CUST C, SALE_DETAIL SD
WHERE P.PID=SD.PID AND C.CID=SD.CID;
SQL> SELECT * FROM PROD_SALE_DETAIL_VU;
```

PID	*PNAME*	*PCOST*	*PPROFIT*	*CID*	*SALE*	*SALEDT*
P3	*PEN*	*20.5*	*20*	*C1*	*2*	*14-JUL-13*
P2	*FLOPPY*	*30*	*12*	*C3*	*10*	*15-JUL-13*
P3	*PEN*	*20.5*	*20*	*C2*	*1*	*14-JUL-13*
P1	*PENCIL*	*5.25*		*C1*	*5*	*14-JUL-13*
P3	*PEN*	*20.5*	*20*	*C1*	*3*	*20-AUG-13*
P3	*PEN*	*20.5*	*20*	*C4*	*2*	*14-NOV-13*
P2	*FLOPPY*	*30*	*12*	*C5*	*2*	*18-SEP-13*

7 rows selected.

Check whether it is possible to insert ('P4','CD',15,20,'C1',4,SYSDATE) in the complex view. Drop PROD_SALE_VU.

```
SQL> INSERT INTO PROD_SALE_DETAIL_VU VALUES
('P4','CD',15,20,'C1',4,SYSDATE);
```

INSERT INTO PROD_SALE_DETAIL_VU VALUES
***

ERROR at line 1:
ORA-01779: cannot modify a column which maps to a non key-preserved table

Drop CUST_PROD_VU.

```
SQL> DROP VIEW CUST_PROD_VU;
```

View dropped.

EX4_19 PROD_SALE_VU is recreated from TTP user. DICT_COLUMNS table can be accessed from SYSTEM user. It is an extremely useful table and it keeps information of other useful tables, its column names and comments. In this example, it is shown how to find the table which keeps VIEW information related to different users. View name and its text created in TTP user is displayed by a SQL statement.

```
SQL>CONNECT TTP/TTP123;
SQL>CREATE VIEW PROD_SALE_VU AS
SELECT P.PID, P.PNAME, P.PCOST, P.PPROFIT, C.CID, SD.SALE, SD.SALEDT
FROM PROD P, CUST C, SALE_DETAIL SD
WHERE P.PID=SD.PID AND C.CID=SD.CID;
```

View created.

Check number of rows in DICT_COLUMNS table.

SQL> DESC DICT_COLUMNS

Name	*Null?*	*Type*
TABLE_NAME		*VARCHAR2(30)*
COLUMN_NAME		*VARCHAR2(30)*
COMMENTS		*VARCHAR2(4000)*

SQL> SELECT COUNT(*) FROM DICT_COLUMNS;

COUNT(*)
8285

Write a SQL query to find tables related to VIEW.

SQL> SELECT DISTINCT TABLE_NAME FROM DICT_COLUMNS WHERE TABLE_NAME LIKE '%VIEWS';

TABLE_NAME
ALL_MVIEWS
ALL_VIEWS
DBA_MVIEWS
DBA_VIEWS
USER_MVIEWS
USER_VIEWS

6 rows selected.

Check the columns of ALL_VIEW table.

SQL> DESC ALL_VIEWS;

Name	*Null?*	*Type*
OWNER	*NOT NULL*	*VARCHAR2(30)*
VIEW_NAME	*NOT NULL*	*VARCHAR2(30)*
TEXT_LENGTH		*NUMBER*
TEXT		*LONG*
TYPE_TEXT_LENGTH		*NUMBER*
TYPE_TEXT		*VARCHAR2(4000)*
OID_TEXT_LENGTH		*NUMBER*
OID_TEXT		*VARCHAR2(4000)*
VIEW_TYPE_OWNER		*VARCHAR2(30)*
VIEW_TYPE		*VARCHAR2(30)*

Execute SQL to display all VIEW_NAME and associated TEXT created in TTP user.

SQL> SELECT VIEW_NAME,TEXT
FROM ALL_VIEWS
WHERE OWNER LIKE '%TTP%';

VIEW_NAME	*TEXT*
PROD_SALE_VU	*SELECT P.PID, P.PNAME, P.PCOST, P.PPROFIT, C.CID, SD.SALE, SD.SALEDT FROM PROD P*

4.7 SEQUENCE

A sequence is a database object, which can generate unique, sequential integer values. It can be used to automatically generate primary key or unique key values.

Syntax:

CREATE SEQUENCE <SEQUENCE NAME> [INCREMENT BY N] [START WITH N] [MAX VALUE N] [MIN VALUE N] [CYCLE / NO CYCLE] [CACHE/ NO CACHE];

INCREMENT BY N

'N' is an integer which specifies the interval between sequence numbers. The default is 1.

START WITH N

It specifies the first sequence numbers to be generated.

MAX VALUE N

It specifies the maximum value that the sequence can generate.

MIN VALUE N

It specifies the minimum value that the sequence can generate.

CYCLE

It specifies that the sequence continues to generate values from the beginning after reaching either its max or min value.

NO CYCLE

It specifies that the sequence cannot generate more values after reaching either its max value or min value. The default value is NO CYCLE.

CACHE

This option pre-allocates a set of sequence numbers and retains them in memory so that sequence numbers can be accessed faster. When the last sequence numbers in the cache has been used, ORACLE reads another set of numbers into the cache.

NO CACHE

The default value in NO CACHE does not pre-allocates sequence numbers for faster access.

After creating a sequence its value can be accessed with the help of pseudocolumns like currval and nextval. A pseudocolumn behaves like a table column, but it is not actually stored in the table.

NEXTVAL

It returns initial value of the sequence, when referred to, for the first time. Later references to nextval will increment the sequence using the INCREMENTBY clause and return the new value.

CURRVAL

It returns the current value of the sequence that is the value returned by the last reference to NEXTVAL.

EX4_20 Connect to TTP/TTP123 and create EMPLOYEE table.

```
SQL> CONNECT TTP/TTP123;
Connected.
SQL> CREATE TABLE EMPLOYEE
(ID NUMBER(4) PRIMARY KEY,
NAME VARCHAR2(20),
AGE NUMBER(3));
Table created.
```

Create a sequence named EMPLOYEE_SEQ.

```
SQL> CREATE SEQUENCE EMPLOYEE_SEQ
INCREMENT BY 1
START WITH 1
MAXVALUE 5
NOCACHE
NOCYCLE;
Sequence created.
```

Insert and save rows in EMPLOYEE table using EMPLOYEE_SEQ.NEXTVAL.

```
SQL> INSERT INTO EMPLOYEE(ID,NAME,AGE)
VALUES (EMPLOYEE_SEQ.NEXTVAL,'RICK',18);
SQL> INSERT INTO EMPLOYEE(ID,NAME,AGE)
VALUES (EMPLOYEE_SEQ.NEXTVAL,'ESHA',29);
SQL> COMMIT;
Commit complete.
SQL> SELECT * FROM EMPLOYEE;
```

ID	*NAME*	*AGE*
1	*RICK*	*18*
2	*ESHA*	*29*

Check the value corresponding to EMPLOYEE_SEQ.CURRVAL.

```
SQL> SELECT EMPLOYEE_SEQ.CURRVAL FROM DUAL;
CURRVAL
-------
2
```

Insert a syntactically wrong row using EMPLOYEE_SEQ.NEXTVAL to ensure that sequence number '3' is generated and wasted.

```
SQL> INSERT INTO EMPLOYEE(ID, NAME, AGE)
VALUES (EMPLOYEE_SEQ.NEXTVAL,BOSE,40);
VALUES (EMPLOYEE_SEQ.NEXTVAL,BOSE,40)
 *
ERROR at line 2:
ORA-00984: column not allowed here
```

Insert two more rows to ensure loss of previous sequence.

SQL> INSERT INTO EMPLOYEE (ID, NAME, AGE)
VALUES (EMPLOYEE_SEQ.NEXTVAL,'BOSE',40);
SQL> SELECT EMPLOYEE_SEQ.CURRVAL FROM DUAL;

CURRVAL
4

SQL> INSERT INTO EMPLOYEE (ID,NAME,AGE)
VALUES (EMPLOYEE_SEQ.NEXTVAL,'NEEL',20);
1 row created.

Maximum range of sequence, i.e. 5 is already reached. Check what happens if we try to insert one more row.

SQL> INSERT INTO EMPLOYEE(ID,NAME,AGE)
VALUES (EMPLOYEE_SEQ.NEXTVAL,'RASHI',21);
INSERT INTO EMPLOYEE(ID,NAME,AGE)
*

ERROR at line 1:
ORA-08004: sequence EMPLOYEE_SEQ.NEXTVAL exceeds MAXVALUE and cannot be instantiated

SQL> COMMIT;
Commit complete.

Check different parameters of EMPLOYEE_SEQ by executing a SQL statement.

SQL> SELECT SEQUENCE_NAME, MIN_VALUE, MAX_VALUE, INCREMENT_BY, LAST_NUMBER
FROM USER_SEQUENCES
WHERE SEQUENCE_NAME LIKE 'EMP%';

SEQUENCE_NAME	*MIN_VALUE*	*MAX_VALUE*	*INCREMENT_BY*	*LAST_NUMBER*
EMPLOYEE_SEQ	*1*	*5*	*1*	*6*

Modify EMPLOYEE_SEQ to increase the maximum value and then try to insert a new row.

SQL> ALTER SEQUENCE EMPLOYEE_SEQ
MAXVALUE 10;
Sequence altered.
SQL> INSERT INTO EMPLOYEE(ID,NAME,AGE)
VALUES (EMPLOYEE_SEQ.NEXTVAL,'RASHI',21);
SQL> COMMIT;
Commit complete.
SQL> SELECT * FROM EMPLOYEE;

ID	*NAME*	*AGE*
1	*RICK*	*18*
2	*ESHA*	*29*
4	*BOSE*	*40*
5	*NEEL*	*20*
6	*RASHI*	*21*

Check MAX_VALUE of the sequence to ensure that it has increased to 10.

```
SQL> SELECT SEQUENCE_NAME, MAX_VALUE
FROM USER_SEQUENCES
WHERE SEQUENCE_NAME LIKE 'EMP%';
```

SEQUENCE_NAME	*MAX_VALUE*
EMPLOYEE_SEQ	*10*

Drop the sequence and try to insert row using the dropped sequence.

```
SQL> DROP SEQUENCE EMPLOYEE_SEQ;
Sequence dropped.
SQL> INSERT INTO EMPLOYEE(ID,NAME,AGE)
VALUES (EMPLOYEE_SEQ.NEXTVAL,'SHAW',20);
VALUES (EMPLOYEE_SEQ.NEXTVAL,'SHAW',20)
 *
ERROR at line 2:
ORA-02289: sequence does not exist
```

EX4_21 Recreate EMPLOYEE_SEQ from TTP user. Locate the table from DICT_COLUMNS which stores SEQUENCE related information of different users. Write a query to extract information related to sequence created in TTP user.

```
SQL>CONNECT TTP/TTP123;
SQL>CREATE SEQUENCE EMPLOYEE_SEQ
INCREMENT BY 1
START WITH 1
MAXVALUE 5
NOCACHE
NOCYCLE;
Sequence created.
SQL>CONNECT SYSTEM/MANAGER
SQL> DESC DICT_COLUMNS
```

Name	*Null?*	*Type*
TABLE_NAME		*VARCHAR2(30)*
COLUMN_NAME		*VARCHAR2(30)*
COMMENTS		*VARCHAR2(4000)*

```
SQL>SELECT TABLE_NAME,COLUMN_NAME FROM DICT_COLUMNS WHERE
TABLE_NAME LIKE 'ALL_SEQUENCE%';
```

TABLE_NAME	*COLUMN_NAME*
ALL_SEQUENCES	*SEQUENCE_OWNER*
ALL_SEQUENCES	*SEQUENCE_NAME*
ALL_SEQUENCES	*MIN_VALUE*
ALL_SEQUENCES	*MAX_VALUE*
ALL_SEQUENCES	*INCREMENT_BY*
ALL_SEQUENCES	*CYCLE_FLAG*
ALL_SEQUENCES	*ORDER_FLAG*
ALL_SEQUENCES	*CACHE_SIZE*
ALL_SEQUENCES	*LAST_NUMBER*

9 rows selected.

SQL> CONNECT SYSTEM/ODRD$EXP@PXEDATA;
Connected.
SQL> SELECT SEQUENCE_NAME FROM ALL_SEQUENCES WHERE SEQUENCE _OWNER='TTP';

SEQUENCE_NAME
EMPLOYEE_SEQ

4.8 SYNONYM

A synonym is a database object, which is used as an alias for a table, view or sequence. Synonyms are used in many cases.

- Simplify SQL statements
- Hide the name and owner of an object
- Provide location transparency for remote objects of a distributed database
- Provide public access to an object.

Synonyms can either be private or public. The former is created by normal user, which is available only to that person, whereas the latter is created by the DBA, which can be availed by any database user.

Syntax:
CREATE [PUBLIC] SYNONYM <SYNONYM NAME> FOR <TABLE NAME>;
Public synonyms are created by a database administrator to hide the identity of a base table and reduce the complexity of SQL statements. TAB is an example of public synonym that is used for selecting the tables owned by the user. User group PUBLIC owns these public synonyms.

EX4_22 Connect to TTP/TTP123.
SQL> CONNECT TTP/TTP123;
Connected.

Create a synonym EMP_SYN based on EMPLOYEE table.
SQL> CREATE SYNONYM EMP_SYN
FOR EMPLOYEE;
Synonym created.

Execute a query to display all rows using the synonym.
SQL> SELECT * FROM EMP_SYN;

ID	*NAME*	*AGE*
1	*RICK*	*18*
2	*ESHA*	*29*
4	*BOSE*	*40*
5	*NEEL*	*20*
6	*RASHI*	*21*

Perform DMLs on the EMP_SYN. Ensure that the transactions can be retrieved from the synonym as well as from the base table.

SQL> INSERT INTO EMP_SYN
VALUES (7,'SHAW',30);
1 row created.
SQL> DELETE FROM EMP_SYN
WHERE AGE>20;
4 rows deleted.
SQL> COMMIT;
Commit complete.
SQL> SELECT * FROM EMP_SYN;

ID	*NAME*	*AGE*
1	*RICK*	*18*
5	*NEEL*	*20*

SQL> SELECT * FROM EMPLOYEE;

ID	*NAME*	*AGE*
1	*RICK*	*18*
5	*NEEL*	*20*

Drop base table EMPLOYEE to ensure that synonym is automatically dropped.

SQL> DROP TABLE EMPLOYEE;
Table dropped.
SQL> SELECT * FROM EMP_SYN;
*SELECT * FROM EMP_SYN*
*
ERROR at line 1:
ORA-00980: synonym translation is no longer valid
SQL> DROP SEQUENCE EMP_SYN;
DROP SEQUENCE EMP_SYN
*
ERROR at line 1:
ORA-02289: sequence does not exist

EX4_23 This example displays SYNONYMs related details created in TTP user

SQL> CONNECT TTP/TTP123
SQL> CREATE SYNONYM EMP_SYN
FOR EMPLOYEE;
Synonym created.
SQL> CONNECT SYSTEM/MANAGER;
SQL> SELECT TABLE_NAME, COLUMN_NAME FROM DICT_COLUMNS
WHERE TABLE_NAME LIKE 'ALL_SYN%';

TABLE_NAME	*COLUMN_NAME*
ALL_SYNONYMS	*OWNER*
ALL_SYNONYMS	*SYNONYM_NAME*
ALL_SYNONYMS	*TABLE_OWNER*
ALL_SYNONYMS	*TABLE_NAME*
ALL_SYNONYMS	*DB_LINK*

SQL> SELECT OWNER,SYNONYM_NAME,TABLE_NAME FROM ALL_SYNONYMS WHERE OWNER='TTP';

OWNER	*SYNONYM_NAME*	*TABLE_NAME*
TTP	*EMP_SYN*	*EMPLOYEE*

4.9 INDEX

Indexes are optional structures associated with tables. Indexes can be created explicitly to speed up SQL statement execution on a table. Similar to the indexes in books that helps us to locate information faster, an Oracle index provides a faster access path to table data.

The index points directly to the location of the rows containing the value. Indexes are the primary means of reducing disk I/O when properly used. The absence or presence of an index does not require a change in wording of any SQL statement. An index is merely a fast access path to the data; it affects only the speed of execution.

Syntax:

CREATE INDEX <INDEX NAME> ON <TABLE NAME>(COLUMN NAME ASC/DESC);

If no order is specified, ASC is default. When we create an index, Oracle fetches and sorts the columns to be indexed, and stores the ROWID along with the index value for each row. Then Oracle loads the index from the bottom up. Oracle sorts the table on the field name. It then loads the index with the item code and corresponding ROWID values to locate the rows having the sought field value.

Indexes are logically and physically independent of the data in the associated table. The indexes can be dropped or created at any time without affecting the base tables or other indexes. If we drop an index, all applications continue to work; however access to previously indexed data might be slower. Indexes, as independent structures, require storage space.

Oracle automatically maintains and uses indexes once they are created. Oracle automatically reflects changes to data, such as addition of new rows, updating rows, or deleting rows.

Retrieval performance for indexed data remains almost constant, even as new rows are inserted. However, the presence of more number of indexes on a table decreases the performance of updates, deletes, and inserts.

4.9.1 Unique Indexes

Indexes can be unique or non-unique. Unique indexes guarantee that no two rows of a table have duplicate values in the columns that define the index. Non-unique indexes do not impose this restriction on the column values. Oracle enforces unique integrity constraints by automatically defining a unique index on the unique key.

Syntax:

CREATE UNIQUE INDEX <INDEX NAME> ON <TABLE NAME>(COLUMN NAME);

4.9.2 Composite Indexes

A composite index (also called a concatenated index) is an index created on multiple columns of a table. Columns in a composite index can appear in any order and need not be adjacent columns of the table.

Syntax:

CREATE INDEX <INDEX NAME> ON <TABLE NAME>(COLUMN NAME1, COLUMN NAME 2);

EX4_24 Create a table EMPLOYEE and insert few rows. Note that '/' is used to re-execute the previous SQL statement.

```
SQL> CREATE TABLE EMPLOYEE
(ID NUMBER(4) PRIMARY KEY,
NAME VARCHAR2(20),
AGE NUMBER(3));
Table created.
SET VERIFY OFF
SQL> INSERT INTO EMPLOYEE VALUES (&ID,'&NAME',&AGE);
Enter value for id: 1
Enter value for name: PK
Enter value for age: 20
1 row created.
SQL> /
Enter value for id: 2
Enter value for name: SK
Enter value for age: 21
1 row created.
SQL> /
Enter value for id: 3
Enter value for name: RK
Enter value for age: 35
1 row created.
SQL> /
Enter value for id: 4
Enter value for name: MC
Enter value for age: 20
1 row created.
SQL> COMMIT;
Commit complete.
```

Create an index EMPLOYEE_IND based on EMPLOYEE.NAME.

```
SQL> CREATE INDEX EMPLOYEE_IND
ON EMPLOYEE(NAME);
```

Index created.

Perform SQL to ensure that index is created.

```
SQL> SELECT INDEX_NAME,COLUMN_NAME
FROM USER_IND_COLUMNS
WHERE TABLE_NAME='EMPLOYEE';
```

INDEX_NAME	*COLUMN_NAME*
SYS_C001052	*ID*
EMPLOYEE_IND	*NAME*

Drop the index and confirm the dropping through a SQL.

```
SQL> DROP INDEX EMPLOYEE_IND;
```

Index dropped.

```
SQL> SELECT INDEX_NAME,COLUMN_NAME
FROM USER_IND_COLUMNS
WHERE TABLE_NAME='EMPLOYEE';
```

INDEX_NAME	*COLUMN_NAME*
SYS_C001052	*ID*

EX4_25 This example displays indexes created in TTP user.

```
SQL> SELECT DISTINCT TABLE_NAME FROM DICT_COLUMNS
WHERE TABLE_NAME LIKE 'ALL_INDEXES';
```

TABLE_NAME
ALL_INDEXES

```
SQL> SELECT INDEX_NAME,TABLE_NAME FROM ALL_INDEXES
WHERE OWNER='TTP';
```

INDEX_NAME	*TABLE_NAME*
CITY_PK	*CITY*
CUST_PK	*CUST*
CUST_PROD_PK	*CUST_PROD*
PROD_PK	*PROD*
SALE_DETAIL_PK	*SALE_DETAIL*
STATE_NAME_PK	*STATE_NAME*

6 rows selected.

4.10 DEFINING CONSTRAINTS

Oracle uses constraints to prevent invalid data entry into tables. Constraints are used to enforce rules at the table level whenever a DML is executed. It prevents deletion of table accidentally from the database. Different types of constraints are shown in Table 4.2.

TABLE 4.2 Constraints Types

Constraint	Characteristics
NOT NULL	Specifies that a column cannot contain NULL values.
UNIQUE	Requires that every value in a column or set of columns be unique.
PRIMARY KEY	Designates a column or group of columns to uniquely identify rows of a table.
FOREIGN KEY	A column or set of columns as a foreign key in a referential integrity constraint.
CHECK	Specifies a condition that each row of the table must satisfy.

4.10.1 Table Level and Column Level Constraints

The table level constraint is part of the table definition. An integrity constraint defined at the table level can impose rules on any columns in the table whereas column level constraint being a part of the column definition can be imposed only on the column on which it is defined.

Syntax:

```
CREATE TABLE TABLE_NAME
(COLUMN DATATYPE [DEFAULT EXPR] [COLUMN_CONSTRAINT],
…
[TABLE_CONSTRAINT][, …]);
```

4.10.2 Entity Integrity Constraints

UNIQUE constraint

This constraint is used to prevent the duplication of values within the rows of a specified column or a set of columns in a table. Columns defined with this constraint can also allow NULL values. If unique constraint is defined in more than one column, it is said to be composite unique key. Maximum combination of columns that a composite key can contain is 16.

EX4_26 This example ensure uniqueness in CID column. UNIQUE constraints can be defined in column level as well as in table level, if it corresponds to the column. If UNIQUE constraint is composite it must be declared in table level constraint.

```
CREATE TABLE CUST
(CID VARCHAR2(6) UNIQUE,
CNAME VARCHAR2(10),
CCITY VARCHAR2(8));
```

or

```
CREATE TABLE CUST
(CID VARCHAR2(6),
CNAME VARCHAR2(10),
CCITY VARCHAR2(8)
CONSTRAINT CUST_UK UNIQUE(CID));
```

PRIMARY KEY constraint

This constraint avoids duplication of rows and does not allow NULL values, when enforced in a column or set of columns. If a primary key constraint is assigned to a combination of columns it is said to be a composite primary key.

EX4_27 This example declares primary key of CUST table.

```
CREATE TABLE CUST
(CID VARCHAR2(6) PRIMARY KEY,
CNAME VARCHAR2(10) UNIQUE,
CCITY VARCHAR2(8));
```

or

```
CREATE TABLE CUST
(CID VARCHAR2(6),
CNAME VARCHAR2(10) UNIQUE,
CCITY VARCHAR2(8),
CONSTRAINT CUST_PK PRIMARY KEY (CID));
```

4.10.3 Domain Integrity Constraints

These constraints set a range, and any violations that take place will prevent the user from performing the manipulation that caused the breach. There are basically two types of domain integrity constraint:

NOT NULL constraint

By default all columns in a table allow NULL values. When a NOT NULL constraint is enforced, either on a column or a set of columns in a table, it will not allow NULL values. The user has to provide a value for the column. NOT NULL constraint can be given only at column level and not at table level. If the records present in the table have null values in the column on which the constraint is to be defined then not null constraint cannot be implemented.

EX4_28 This example demonstrates NOT NULL constraint. It must be declared only in column level.

```
CREATE TABLE STATE_NAME
(CCITY VARCHAR2(8),
STATE VARCHAR2(15) NOT NULL,
CONSTRAINT STATE_NAME_PK PRIMARY KEY (CCITY));
```

CHECK constraint

This constraint checks the condition enforced on a column before entering the data in it. References to ROWNUM, SYSDATE, etc. and queries that refer to other values in other rows are not permitted in CHECK constraint.

EX4_29 This example restricts PPROFIT between 0 to 30% using CHECK constraint. It can be assigned in column level or table level.

```
CREATE TABLE PROD
(PID VARCHAR2(6),
PNAME VARCHAR2(6),
PCOST NUMBER(4,2) NOT NULL,
PPROFIT NUMBER(3) CHECK (PPROFIT BETWEEN 0 AND 30),
CONSTRAINT PROD_PK PRIMARY KEY (PID));
```

or

```
CREATE TABLE PROD
(PID VARCHAR2(6),
PNAME VARCHAR2(6),
PCOST NUMBER(4,2) NOT NULL,
PPROFIT NUMBER(3),
CONSTRAINT PROD_PK PRIMARY KEY (PID),
CONSTRAINT PROD_CHK CHECK (PPROFIT BETWEEN 0 AND 30));
```

4.10.4 Referential Integrity Constraint

The referential integrity constraint enforces relationship between tables. It designates a column or combination of columns as a foreign key. The foreign key establishes a relationship with a specified primary key or unique key in another table, called the **referenced key**. In this relationship, the table containing the foreign key is called the **child table** and the table containing the referenced key is called the **parent table**. This constraint is used to establish a 'parent-child' or a 'master-detail' relationship between two tables having a common column. To implement this, the common column should be defined in the parent table as a primary key and in the child table as foreign key. The referential integrity constraint does not use foreign key keyword to identify the columns that make up the foreign key. This is because the constraint is defined at column level. The foreign key is automatically enforced on the columns.

EX4_30 This example demonstrates referential integrity constraint. CUST.CCITY is foreign key, which references STATE_NAME.CCITY primary key of STATE_NAME table. Similarly SALE_DETAIL.CID & SALE_DETAIL.PID are foreign key that references to CUST.CID and PROD.PID columns, respectively. Drop CUST, PROD, SALE_DETAIL and STATE_NAME tables before creating the modified tables.

```
CREATE TABLE PROD
(PID VARCHAR2(6),
PNAME VARCHAR2(6) UNIQUE,
PCOST NUMBER(4,2) NOT NULL,
PPROFIT NUMBER(3) CHECK (PPROFIT BETWEEN 0 AND 30),
CONSTRAINT PROD_PK PRIMARY KEY (PID));
CREATE TABLE STATE_NAME
(CCITY VARCHAR2(8),
STATE VARCHAR2(15) NOT NULL,
CONSTRAINT STATE_NAME_PK PRIMARY KEY (CCITY));
CREATE TABLE CUST
(CID VARCHAR2(6),
CNAME VARCHAR2(10) UNIQUE,
CCITY VARCHAR2(8) REFERENCES STATE_NAME(CCITY),
CONSTRAINT CUST_PK PRIMARY KEY (CID));
CREATE TABLE SALE_DETAIL
(CID VARCHAR2(6) REFERENCES CUST(CID),
```

```
PID VARCHAR2(6) REFERENCES PROD(PID),
SALE NUMBER(3),
SALEDT DATE,
CONSTRAINT SALE_DETAIL_PK PRIMARY KEY (CID,PID,SALEDT));
```

Use the INSERT script given in CUST_PROD.SQL to create records corresponding to the tables.

EX4_31 This example is based on modified STATE_NAME, CUST, PROD and SALE _DETAIL tables as shown in Figure 3.2. Message from Oracle is shown in italics.

i. Check the rows in PROD table and try to insert ('P4','PEN', 22,10) row in the table.

SQL> SELECT * FROM PROD;

PID	*PNAME*	*PCOST*	*PPROFIT*
P3	*PEN*	*20.5*	*20*
P2	*FLOPPY*	*30*	*12*
P1	*PENCIL*	*5.25*	

SQL> INSERT INTO PROD VALUES ('P4','PEN',22,10);
INSERT INTO PROD
ERROR at line 1:
ORA-00001: unique constraint (TTP.SYS_C001093) violated

Insertion is not allowed because PNAME is unique and PEN exists in the table.

ii. Check whether it is possible to insert NULL values corresponding to PNAME.

SQL> INSERT INTO PROD
VALUES ('P4','',22,10);
1 row created.
SQL> SELECT * FROM PROD;

PID	*PNAME*	*PCOST*	*PPROFIT*
P3	*PEN*	*20.5*	*20*
P2	*FLOPPY*	*30*	*12*
P1	*PENCIL*	*5.25*	
P4		*22*	*10*

Insertion is possible because NULL is allowed in UNIQUE constraint.

iii. Is it possible to update PROD.PNAME with PEN? If not, can we update the value with some other UNIQUE PNAME?

SQL> UPDATE PROD SET PNAME='PEN'
WHERE PID='P4';
UPDATE PROD SET PNAME='PEN'
ERROR at line 1:
ORA-00001: unique constraint (TTP.SYS_C001093) violated
SQL> UPDATE PROD SET PNAME='PEN1'
WHERE PID='P4';
1 row updated.
SQL> COMMIT;
Commit complete.

iv. Check records of STATE_NAME table and try to insert ('MUMBAI','') in the table. If it is not possible insert ('MUMBAI','MAHARASHTRA') and save the record.

SQL> SELECT * FROM STATE_NAME;

CCITY	*STATE*
MYSORE	*KARNATAKA*
KOLKATA	*WEST BENGAL*
PUNE	*MAHARASHTRA*
CHENNAI	*TAMILNADU*
INDORE	*MADYA PRADESH*

SQL> INSERT INTO STATE_NAME
VALUES ('MUMBAI','');
INSERT INTO STATE_NAME
ERROR at line 1:
ORA-01400: cannot insert NULL into ("TTP"."STATE_NAME"."STATE")
SQL> INSERT INTO STATE_NAME
VALUES ('MUMBAI','MAHARASHTRA');
1 row created.
SQL> COMMIT;
Commit complete.
SQL> SELECT * FROM STATE_NAME;

CCITY	*STATE*
MYSORE	*KARNATAKA*
KOLKATA	*WEST BENGAL*
PUNE	*MAHARASHTRA*
CHENNAI	*TAMILNADU*
INDORE	*MADYA PRADESH*
MUMBAI	*MAHARASHTRA*

6 rows selected.

v. Is it possible to update PROD with PPROFIT = 50? What about updating PROD with PPROFIT = 30 for PNAME = 'PEN'? Save the transaction and confirm the update.

SQL> SELECT * FROM PROD;

PID	*PNAME*	*PCOST*	*PPROFIT*
P3	*PEN*	*20.5*	*20*
P2	*FLOPPY*	*30*	*12*
P1	*PENCIL*	*5.25*	
P4	*PEN1*	*22*	*10*

SQL> UPDATE PROD
SET PPROFIT=50
WHERE PNAME LIKE 'PEN%';
UPDATE PROD
ERROR at line 1:
ORA-02290: check constraint (TTP.SYS_C001091) violated

```
SQL> UPDATE PROD
SET PPROFIT=30
WHERE PNAME LIKE 'PEN%';
3 rows updated.
SQL> COMMIT;
Commit complete.
SQL> SELECT * FROM PROD;
```

PID	PNAME	PCOST	PPROFIT
P3	PEN	20.5	30
P2	FLOPPY	30	12
P1	PENCIL	5.25	30
P4	PEN1	22	30

4.10.5 Constraints Related Query

Information related to constraint can be obtained using the DBA_CONSTRAINTS and DBA_CONS_COLUMNS views.

EX4_32 In this example constraints associated with CUST, PROD, SALE_DETAIL and STATE_NAME tables are displayed. In this 'P' refers to primary key, 'U' is unique key, 'R' is for reference and C represents check constraint.

```
SQL> CONNECT TTP/TTP123
SQL> COLUMN SEARCH_CONDITION FORMAT A30
SQL> COLUMN TABLE_NAME FORMAT A15
SQL> SELECT TABLE_NAME, CONSTRAINT_NAME, CONSTRAINT_TYPE,
SEARCH_CONDITION FROM USER_CONSTRAINTS
WHERE TABLE_NAME IN ('PROD', 'CUST', 'STATE_NAME', 'SALE_DETAIL')
ORDER BY TABLE_NAME;
```

TABLE_NAME	CONSTRAINT_NAME	C	SEARCH_CONDITION
CUST	CUST_PK	P	
CUST	SYS_C001289	U	
CUST	SYS_C001290	R	
PROD	SYS_C001282	C	"PCOST" IS NOT NULL
PROD	SYS_C001283	C	PPROFIT BETWEEN 0 AND 30
PROD	PROD_PK	P	
PROD	SYS_C001285	U	
SALE_DETAIL	SALE_DETAIL_PK	P	
SALE_DETAIL	SYS_C001292	R	
SALE_DETAIL	SYS_C001293	R	
STATE_NAME	SYS_C001286	C	"STATE" IS NOT NULL
STATE_NAME	STATE_NAME_PK	P	

```
12 rows selected.
SQL>CONNECT TTP/TTP123
SQL> COLUMN COLUMN_NAME FORMAT A15
```

```
SQL> SELECT TABLE_NAME,CONSTRAINT_NAME,COLUMN_NAME
FROM USER_CONS_COLUMNS
WHERE TABLE_NAME IN ('PROD','CUST','STATE_NAME','SALE_DETAIL')
ORDER BY TABLE_NAME;
```

TABLE_NAME	*CONSTRAINT_NAME*	*COLUMN_NAME*
CUST	*CUST_PK*	*CID*
CUST	*SYS_C001289*	*CNAME*
CUST	*SYS_C001290*	*CCITY*
PROD	*PROD_PK*	*PID*
PROD	*SYS_C001283*	*PPROFIT*
PROD	*SYS_C001285*	*PNAME*
PROD	*SYS_C001282*	*PCOST*
SALE_DETAIL	*SALE_DETAIL_PK*	*CID*
SALE_DETAIL	*SALE_DETAIL_PK*	*PID*
SALE_DETAIL	*SALE_DETAIL_PK*	*SALEDT*
SALE_DETAIL	*SYS_C001292*	*CID*
SALE_DETAIL	*SYS_C001293*	*PID*
STATE_NAME	*STATE_NAME_PK*	*CCITY*
STATE_NAME	*SYS_C001286*	*STATE*

14 rows selected.

In this example both the views mentioned above are joined to display more meaningful outputs.

```
SQL> COLUMN COL_NAME FORMAT A20
SQL> SELECT UCOL.TABLE_NAME|| '.' ||UCOL.COLUMN_NAME COL_NAME,
UCONS .CONSTRAINT_TYPE C_TYPE,UCONS.SEARCH_CONDITION
FROM USER_CONS_COLUMNS UCOL, USER_CONSTRAINTS UCONS
WHERE UCOL.TABLE_NAME=UCONS.TABLE_NAME AND
UCOL.CONSTRAINT _NAME = UCONS.CONSTRAINT_NAME AND
UCOL.TABLE_NAME IN ('PROD','CUST','STATE_NAME','SALE_DETAIL')
ORDER BY UCOL.TABLE_NAME;
```

COL_NAME	*C*	*SEARCH_CONDITION*
CUST.CID	*P*	
CUST.CNAME	*U*	
CUST.CCITY	*R*	
PROD.PCOST	*C*	*"PCOST" IS NOT NULL*
PROD.PPROFIT	*C*	*PPROFIT BETWEEN 0 AND 30*
PROD.PID	*P*	
PROD.PNAME	*U*	
SALE_DETAIL.CID	*P*	
SALE_DETAIL.PID	*P*	
SALE_DETAIL.SALEDT	*P*	
SALE_DETAIL.CID	*R*	
SALE_DETAIL.PID	*R*	
STATE_NAME.STATE	*C*	*"STATE" IS NOT NULL*
STATE_NAME.CCITY	*P*	

14 rows selected.

4.10.6 Adding a CONSTRAINT

Constraint can be added to an existing table using ALTER TABLE statement with the ADD CONSTRAINT clause.

Syntax:

ALTER TABLE TABLE_NAME
ADD [CONSTRAINT CONSTRAINT_NAME] TYPE (COLUMN_NAME);
To add a NOT NULL constraint, use MODIFY clause.

EX4_33 This example demonstrates use of ADD CONSTRAINT.
SQL> ALTER TABLE PROD ADD CONSTRAINT PROD_CHK CHECK (PCOST>0);
Table altered.
SQL> INSERT INTO PROD VALUES ('P4','RUBBER',–10,10);
INSERT INTO PROD VALUES ('P4','RUBBER',–10,10)
ERROR at line 1:
ORA-02290: check constraint (TTP.PROD_CHK) violated

4.10.7 Dropping a CONSTRAINT

To drop a constraint, use ALTER TABLE statement with the DROP clause. CASCADE option can be used to drop any dependent constraint.

Syntax:

ALTER TABLE TABLE_NAME
DROP PRIMARY KEY | UNIQUE (COLUMN_NAME) | CONSTRAINT
CONSTRAINT _NAME [CASCADE];

EX4_34 This example demonstrates use of DRO CONSTRAINT.
SQL> ALTER TABLE PROD DROP CONSTRAINT PROD_CHK;
Table altered.
SQL> INSERT INTO PROD VALUES ('P4','RUBBER',-10,10);
1 row created.
SQL> ROLLBACK;
Rollback complete.

4.10.8 Disabling or Enabling CONSTRAINT

A constraint can be disabled or enabled using ALTER TABLE with the DISABLE/ ENABLE clause.

Syntax:

ALTER TABLE TABLE_NAME DISABLE | ENABLE CONSTRAINT
CONSTRAINT _NAME [CASCADE];
It is used to insert values, which are restricted due to some constraint, or copy table, which is linked with some other table.

EX4_35 This example demonstrates use of DISABLE CONSTRAINT.

```
SQL> SELECT TABLE_NAME, CONSTRAINT_NAME, CONSTRAINT_TYPE
FROM USER_CONSTRAINTS
WHERE TABLE_NAME='STATE_NAME';
TABLE_NAME      CONSTRAINT_NAME      C
--------------------------------------
STATE_NAME      SYS_C001286          C
STATE_NAME      STATE_NAME_PK        P
SQL> ALTER TABLE STATE_NAME
DISABLE CONSTRAINT SYS_C001286;
Table altered.
SQL> INSERT INTO STATE_NAME VALUES ('PATNA','');
1 row created.
SQL> ROLLBACK;
Rollback complete.
SQL> ALTER TABLE STATE_NAME
ENABLE CONSTRAINT SYS_C001286;
Table altered.
```

4.11 ORACLE PRIVILEGES AND ROLES

Privileges allow the user to log on to the system and create or manipulate objects. It also allows the user to access data within an object, or allows the user to execute a stored program. The number of privileges varies on the version of the Oracle database server. SYSTEM_PRIVILEGE_MAP table may be accessed to list all the privileges. The most used privileges along with its characteristics are listed in Table 4.3.

TABLE 4.3 Oracle Privileges

Privilege	Characteristics
ALTER	Structure of the table or sequence may be altered.
CREATE	Allows the user to create a table.
DELETE	Allows rows to be removed from the table.
EXECUTE	Apply only to stored procedure and functions.
GRANT	Allows the user receiving the grant option to grant privileges to other users.
INDEX	Allows the user to create an index only on table.
INSERT	Allows new rows to be created in the table.
LOCK	Allows the user to lock an object.
RENAME	The table can be renamed.
SELECT	All data may be selected for viewing from the table.
UPDATE	The data in the columns may be modified. Only privilege that can be restricted to specific columns.
READ	Allows the user to read from a directory.
REFERENCES	Allows the user to define foreign key integrity constraint only on the table.
WRITE	Allows the user to write to a directory.

A role is a named collection of privileges. A user cannot be assigned to a role, but a role can be assigned to a user. Important default roles along with their characteristics (or privileges) are listed in Table 4.4. DBA_SYS_PRIVS can be queried to determine the privileges assigned to a role.

TABLE 4.4 Oracle Roles

Role	Characteristics
CONNECT	Allows login and ability to create tables, views, synonyms, and database links.
DBA	Complete authority to manage database and users.
RESOURCE	Adds clusters, procedure, and trigger privileges.
SYSOPER	Ability to start up and shutdown the database.
SYSDBA	Similar to DBA with the ability to create, start up, shutdown, and recover a database.

EX4_36 This example shows privileges associated with RESOURCE and GRANT roles.

```
SQL> SELECT GRANTEE, PRIVILEGE
FROM DBA_SYS_PRIVS
WHERE GRANTEE='RESOURCE';
GRANTEE                    PRIVILEGE
---------------------------------------
RESOURCE                   CREATE CLUSTER
RESOURCE                   CREATE INDEXTYPE
RESOURCE                   CREATE OPERATOR
RESOURCE                   CREATE PROCEDURE
RESOURCE                   CREATE SEQUENCE
RESOURCE                   CREATE TABLE
RESOURCE                   CREATE TRIGGER
RESOURCE                   CREATE TYPE
8 rows selected.

SQL> SELECT GRANTEE,PRIVILEGE
FROM DBA_SYS_PRIVS
WHERE GRANTEE='CONNECT';
GRANTEE                    PRIVILEGE
---------------------------------------
CONNECT                    ALTER SESSION
CONNECT                    CREATE CLUSTER
CONNECT                    CREATE DATABASE LINK
CONNECT                    CREATE SEQUENCE
CONNECT                    CREATE SESSION
CONNECT                    CREATE SYNONYM
CONNECT                    CREATE TABLE
CONNECT                    CREATE VIEW
8 rows selected.
```

EX4_37 This example demonstrates grant of privilege and role to users.

```
SQL> CONNECT SYSTEM/MANAGER
Connected.
SQL> CREATE USER TTP1 IDENTIFIED BY TTP123;
User created.
SQL> CONNECT TTP1
WITH ADMIN OPTION;
Grant succeeded.
SQL> CONNECT TTP1/TTP123;
Connected.
```

i. Execute CUST_PROD.SQL script as shown in Figure 3.2.

```
SQL> @ C:\TTPCUST_PROD.SQL
```

ii. Connect to SYSTEM user and create a user MKG1 with password MKG123.

```
SQL> CONNECT SYSTEM/MANAGER
Connected.
SQL> CREATE USER MKG1 IDENTIFIED BY MKG123;
User created.
```

iii. Connect to TTP1 user and grant SELECT privilege to MKG1 user.

```
SQL> CONNECT TTP1/TTP123
Connected.
SQL> GRANT SELECT
ON PROD
TO MKG1;
Grant succeeded.
```

iv. Try to connect MKG1 user. It will fail because CREATE SESSION privilege is not assigned to the user.

```
SQL> CONNECT MKG1/MKG123
ERROR:
ORA-01045: user MKG1 lacks CREATE SESSION privilege; lo
Warning: You are no longer connected to ORACLE.
```

v. Connect to SYSTEM user and grant CREATE SESSION privilege, so that MKG1 can connect.

```
SQL> CONNECT SYSTEM/MANAGER
Connected.
SQL> GRANT CREATE SESSION TO MKG1;
Grant succeeded.
```

vi. Connect MKG1 to Oracle and write few queries to display rows of TTP1.PROD.

```
SQL> CONNECT MKG1/MKG123
Connected.
SQL> SELECT * FROM TTP1.PROD;
```

PID	*PNAME*	*PCOST*	*PPROFIT*
P3	*PEN*	*20.5*	*20*
P2	*FLOPPY*	*30*	*12*
P1	*PENCIL*	*5.25*	

SQL> SELECT PNAME, PCOST, PCOST*PPROFIT/100 PROFIT
FROM TTP1.PROD;

PNAME	*PCOST*	*PROFIT*
PEN	*20.5*	*4.1*
FLOPPY	*30*	*3.6*
PENCIL	*5.25*	

vii. Perform some queries, DMLs and DDLs on the table on which MKG does not have any privilege.

SQL> SELECT * FROM TTP1.CUST;
*SELECT * FROM TTP1.CUST*
ERROR at line 1:
ORA-00942: table or view does not exist
SQL> DELETE FROM TTP1.PROD;
DELETE FROM TTP1.PROD
ERROR at line 1:
ORA-01031: insufficient privileges
SQL> DROP USER TTP1;
DROP USER TTP1
ERROR at line 1:
ORA-01031: insufficient privileges
Connect

viii. Connect to SYSTEM user and drop TTP1 user using cascade.

SQL> CONNECT SYSTEM/MANAGER
Connected.
SQL> DROP USER TTP1;
DROP USER TTP1
ERROR at line 1:
ORA-01922: CASCADE must be specified to drop 'TTP1'
SQL> DROP USER TTP1 CASCADE;
User dropped.

ix. Connect to MKG1 user. No query is possible because its parent user is dropped.

SQL> CONNECT MKG1/MKG123
Connected.
SQL> SELECT * FROM TTP1.PROD;
*SELECT * FROM TTP1.PROD*
ERROR at line 1:
ORA-00942: table or view does not exist

x. Finally drop MKG1 user.
SQL> CONNECT SYSTEM/MANAGER
Connected.
SQL> DROP USER MKG1;
User dropped.

4.12 PROFILES

A profile is a named set of password and resource limit. Profiles are assigned to user by the CREATE USER or ALTER USER command. After a profile is created, the database administrator can assign it to any user. Oracle server limits the database usage and resources as defined in the associated profile. Table 4.5 shows important parameters along with its characteristics.

TABLE 4.5 Oracle Profile Parameters

Parameter	Characteristics
FAILED_LOGIN_ATTEMPTS	Number of failed attempts before the account is locked.
PASSWORD_LOCK_TIME	Number of days an account will be locked after the specified number of failed login attempts.
PASSWORD_LIFE_TIME	Lifetime of the password in days.
PASSWORD_GRACE_TIME	Number of days after the grace period has begun during which a warning will be given that the password is going to expire.
PASSWORD_REUSE_TIME	Number of days before a password can be reused.
PASSWORD_REUSE_MAX	An integer value for the number of password changes before a password can be reused.
PASSWORD_VERIFY_FUNCTION	Complexity of a password defined in the script.

EX4_38 This example demonstrates creation of a profile, assigning to a user and displaying the parameter of the profile by a SQL query.

i. Connect to SYSTEM/MANAGER@[CONNECT_STRING]
SQL>CONNECT SYSTEM/MANAGER
Connected.

ii. Create a profile named as DEFAULT_PROFILE. This profile locks for 2 min after 3 invalid logins. Note that 2 min = 1/(24*30) = 1/720.
SQL> CREATE PROFILE DEFAULT_PROFILE LIMIT
FAILED_LOGIN_ATTEMPTS 3
PASSWORD_LOCK_TIME 1/720;
Profile created.

iii. Create a user named TEST_PROFILE with DEFAULT_PROFILE. Grant CREATE SESSION privilege so that the user can connect to Oracle database. Confirm the connection of newly created user with Oracle database.
SQL> CREATE USER TEST_PROFILE IDENTIFIED BY TEST_PROFILE
PROFILE DEFAULT_PROFILE;
User created.

SQL> GRANT CREATE SESSION TO TEST_PROFILE
Grant succeeded.
SQL> CONNECT TEST_PROFILE/TEST_PROFILE
Connected.

iv. **Perform three invalid logins to confirm working of FAILED_LOGIN_ATTEMPTS profile parameter.**

SQL> CONNECT TEST_PROFILE/TEST
ERROR:
ORA-01017: invalid username/password; logon denied
Warning: You are no longer connected to ORACLE.
SQL> CONNECT TEST_PROFILE/PROFILE
ERROR:
ORA-01017: invalid username/password; logon denied
SQL> CONNECT TEST_PROFILE/TEST_PROF
ERROR:
ORA-01017: invalid username/password; logon denied

v. **Confirm that the account is locked for 2 minutes due to the profile parameter PASSWORD_LOCK_TIME.**

SQL> CONNECT TEST_PROFILE/TEST_PROFILE
ERROR:
ORA-28000: the account is locked

vi. **Login is allowed after 2 minutes.**

SQL> CONNECT TEST_PROFILE/TEST_PROFILE
Connected.

vii. **Connect to SYSTEM/MANAGER@[CONNECT_STRING] to see columns of DBA_PROFILES which keeps information of all profiles.**

SQL> CONNECT SYSTEM/MANAGER
Connected.
SQL> DESC DBA_PROFILES

Name	*Null?*	*Type*
PROFILE	*NOT NULL*	*VARCHAR2(30)*
RESOURCE_NAME	*NOT NULL*	*VARCHAR2(32)*
RESOURCE_TYPE		*VARCHAR2(8)*
LIMIT		*VARCHAR2(40)*

viii. **Write a query to display information of profiles. Observe the changed values of profile parameter created by us.**

SQL> COLUMN PROFILE FORMAT A20
SQL> COLUMN LIMIT FORMAT A10
SQL> SELECT PROFILE,RESOURCE_NAME NAME, LIMIT
FROM DBA_PROFILES
WHERE RESOURCE_TYPE='PASSWORD'
ORDER BY PROFILE;

PROFILE	*NAME*	*LIMIT*
DEFAULT	*FAILED_LOGIN_ATTEMPTS*	*UNLIMITED*
DEFAULT	*PASSWORD_LIFE_TIME*	*UNLIMITED*
DEFAULT	*PASSWORD_REUSE_MAX*	*UNLIMITED*
DEFAULT	*PASSWORD_LOCK_TIME*	*UNLIMITED*
DEFAULT	*PASSWORD_GRACE_TIME*	*UNLIMITED*
DEFAULT	*PASSWORD_VERIFY_FUNCTION*	*UNLIMITED*
DEFAULT	*PASSWORD_REUSE_TIME*	*UNLIMITED*
DEFAULT_PROFILE	*FAILED_LOGIN_ATTEMPTS*	*3*
DEFAULT_PROFILE	*PASSWORD_LIFE_TIME*	*DEFAULT*
DEFAULT_PROFILE	*PASSWORD_REUSE_MAX*	*DEFAULT*
DEFAULT_PROFILE	*PASSWORD_LOCK_TIME*	*.0013*
DEFAULT_PROFILE	*PASSWORD_GRACE_TIME*	*DEFAULT*
DEFAULT_PROFILE	*PASSWORD_VERIFY_FUNCTION*	*DEFAULT*
DEFAULT_PROFILE	*PASSWORD_REUSE_TIME*	*DEFAULT*

14 rows selected.

ix. Drop the DEFAULT_PROFILE. Note that it can be dropped with CASCADE parameter. This is because TEST_PROF user is associated with DEFAULT _PARAMETER. Once the parameter is dropped user is automatically assigned to DEFAULT profile created by system.

SQL> DROP PROFILE DEFAULT_PROFILE;
DROP PROFILE DEFAULT_PROFILE
ERROR at line 1:
ORA-02382: profile DEFAULT_PROFILE has users assigned cannot drop without CASCADE
SQL> DROP PROFILE DEFAULT_PROFILE CASCADE;
Profile dropped.
SQL> CONNECT TEST_PROFILE/TEST_PROFILE
Connected.

4.13 PASSWORD

There is a SQL* Plus command, PASSWORD, which can be used to change the password. With DBA privilege on database one can use this command to change another user's password.

EX4_39 This example demonstrates changing password from the user as well as from SYSTEM. For security reasons, '*' is echoed. Note that in case of SYSTEM user old password is not asked.

i. Connect to TEST_PROFILE/TEST_PROFILE@[CONNECT_STRING]

SQL> CONNECT TEST_PROFILE/TEST_PROFILE
Connected.

ii. Invoke PASSWORD command and confirm the change of password.

SQL> PASSWORD
Changing password for TEST_PROFILE
Old password: ************
New password: ************
Retype new password: ************
Password changed

SQL> CONNECT TEST_PROFILE/BEST_PROFILE
Connected.

EX4_40 This example demonstrates change of password from SYSTEM/MANAGER@[CONNECT_STRING].

SQL> CONNECT SYSTEM/MANAGER
Connected.
SQL> PASSWORD TEST_PROFILE
Changing password for TEST_PROFILE
New password: ****
Retype new password: ****
Password changed
SQL> CONNECT TEST_PROFILE/TEST
Connected.

4.14 SUMMARY

In this chapter, data manipulation language, which includes INSERT, UPDATE and DELETE statements, is explained in detail. Transaction control language related commands and locking due to concurrent session is discussed. Objects of Oracle viz. VIEW, SEQUENCE, SYNONYM and INDEX are elaborated using examples. Accessing objects related information using DICT_COLUMNS, security concepts like privileges, roles, profile and password required in practical implementations are discussed in this chapter.

SHORT/OBJECTIVE TYPE QUESTIONS

1. What is the advantage of using views?
2. Briefly explain use of synonym.
3. Describe some scenario where use of sequence is essentially required.
4. What is the basic purpose of using index?
5. Describe various types of constraints.
6. Describe characteristics related to Oracle privileges, role and profiles.

7. All SQL statements are based on EMP, DESGRATE and PROJ_DETAIL tables as shown in Figure 4.2. What will be the output corresponding to each SQL statement.

```
SQL> INSERT INTO EMP VALUES ('E6','PRANAB','MANAGER');
SQL> INSERT INTO DESGRATE (HRRATE, DESG) VALUES (500,'MANAGER');
SQL> INSERT INTO EMP VALUES ('E6','PRANAB','MANAGER');
SQL> INSERT INTO PROJ_DETAIL VALUES ('E6','P1',50);
SQL> COMMIT;
SQL> SELECT * FROM DESGRATE;
SQL> SELECT * FROM EMP;
SQL> SELECT * FROM PROJ_DETAIL;
```

```
DROP TABLE PROJ_DETAIL;
DROP TABLE PROJ;
DROP TABLE EMP;
DROP TABLE DESGRATE;
CREATE TABLE PROJ
(PROJNO       VARCHAR2(5) PRIMARY KEY,
PROJNAME      VARCHAR2(15));
CREATE TABLE DESGRATE
(DESG         VARCHAR2(15) PRIMARY KEY,
HRRATE        NUMBER(5));
CREATE TABLE EMP
(EMPNO        VARCHAR2(5) PRIMARY KEY,
ENAME         VARCHAR2(15),
DESG          VARCHAR2(15) REFERENCES DESGRATE(DESG));
CREATE TABLE PROJ_DETAIL
(EMPNO        VARCHAR2(5) REFERENCES EMP(EMPNO),
PROJNO        VARCHAR2(5) REFERENCES PROJ(PROJNO),
HRWORKED NUMBER(3));
INSERT INTO PROJ VALUES ('P2','CODING');
INSERT INTO PROJ VALUES ('P3','DATA RECOVERY');
INSERT INTO PROJ VALUES ('P1','DATABASE SW');
INSERT INTO DESGRATE VALUES ('ANALYST',800);
INSERT INTO DESGRATE VALUES ('DBA',1000);
INSERT INTO DESGRATE VALUES ('PROGRAMMER',500);
INSERT INTO EMP VALUES ('E1','ANUP','ANALYST');
INSERT INTO EMP VALUES ('E2','ARUP','DBA');
INSERT INTO EMP VALUES ('E3','KAUSHIK','ANALYST');
INSERT INTO EMP VALUES ('E4','AMIT','PROGRAMMER');
INSERT INTO EMP VALUES ('E5','CHANDRA','PROGRAMMER');
INSERT INTO PROJ_DETAIL VALUES ('E1','P2',15);
INSERT INTO PROJ_DETAIL VALUES ('E2','P3',10);
INSERT INTO PROJ_DETAIL VALUES ('E2','P1',40);
INSERT INTO PROJ_DETAIL VALUES ('E2','P2',10);
INSERT INTO PROJ_DETAIL VALUES ('E3','P1',20);
INSERT INTO PROJ_DETAIL VALUES ('E4','P2',40);
INSERT INTO PROJ_DETAIL VALUES ('E5','P1',30);
COMMIT;
```

FIGURE 4.2 Tables and records—workout.

8. All questions are based on the tables and rows shown in Figure 6.7. What will be the final output after the transaction shown here.

SQL> INSERT INTO PROJ VALUES ('&PROJNO','&PROJNAME');
Enter value for projno: P4
Enter value for projname: CRYPTOGRAPHY
SQL> SAVEPOINT ONE;
SQL> DELETE FROM PROJ_DETAIL;
SQL> ROLLBACK TO ONE;
SQL> DELETE FROM PROJ_DETAIL
WHERE PROJNO='P1' AND EMPNO='E2';
SQL> SAVEPOINT TWO;
SQL> UPDATE FROM EMP SET DESG='DBA';
SQL> UPDATE EMP SET DESG='DBA';
SQL> ROLLBACK TO TWO;
SQL> COMMIT;
SQL> SELECT * FROM PROJ_DETAIL;
SQL> SELECT * FROM EMP;

9. Is it possible to drop table by the following sequence of DDL statements. What is the correct sequence to drop each table.

SQL> DROP TABLE PROJ;
SQL> DROP TABLE EMP;
SQL> DROP TABLE DESGRATE;
SQL> DROP TABLE PROJ_DETAIL;

10. This question is based on PROD, STATE_NAME, CUST and SALE_DETAIL tables with default rows.

i. Create a view CUST_PROD_VIEW1 comprising CNAME, CCITY, STATE, PNAME, SPENT (PCOST × SALE) and SALEDT using relevant tables.

ii. Write a query to display all columns of CUST_PROD_VIEW1 who have purchased PEN.

WORKOUT SECTION

W4_1 Create a sequence which starts with 10, goes upto 5 and then again becomes 10. This process is repeated for infinite times. Write a SQL statement to display sequence name, minimum value, maximum value and increment step.

W4_2 All the questions are primarily based on constraints.

i. Connect to TTP/TTP123@[CONNECT_STRING]

ii. Drop PROJ_DETAIL, PROJ, EMP and DESGRATE tables.

iii. Create DESGRATE table

Column Name	Type	Constraint
DESG	VARCHAR2(15)	Primary Key
HRRATE	NUMBER(5)	Values between 500 & 5000

iv. Insert rows in DESGRATE table

DESG	HRRATE
ANALYST	800
DBA	1000
PROGRAMMER	500

v. Create EMP table

Column Name	Type	Constraint
EMPNO	VARCHAR2(5)	Primary Key
ENAME	VARCHAR2(15)	Unique
DESG	VARCHAR2(15)	Foreign key refers to DESGRATE.DESG

vi. Insert rows in EMP table

EMPNO	ENAME	DESG
E1	ANUP	ANALYST
E2	ARUP	DBA
E3	KAUSHIK	ANALYST
E4	AMIT	PROGRAMMER
E5	CHANDRA	PROGRAMMER

vii. Create PROJ table

Column Name	Type	Constraint
PROJNO	VARCHAR2(5)	Primary Key
PROJNAME	VARCHAR2(15)	Unique

viii. Insert rows in PROJ table

PROJN	PROJNAME
P2	CODING
P3	DATA RECOVERY
P1	DATABASE SW

ix. Create PROJ_DETAIL table

Column Name	Type	Constraint
EMPNO	VARCHAR2(5)	Foreign key refers to EMP.EMPNO
PROJNO	VARCHAR2(5)	Foreign key refers to PROJ.PROJNO
HRWORKED	NUMBER(3)	NOT NULL and values between 10 & 100

Composite primary key is EMPNO+PROJNO.

x. Insert rows in PROJ_DETAIL table

EMPNO	PROJN	HRWORKED
E1	P2	15
E2	P3	10
E2	P1	40
E2	P2	10
E3	P1	20
E4	P2	40
E5	P1	30

xi. Save all the insertions.

xii. Verify insertion of rows in DESGRATE table. Try to insert HRRATE=400 in DESGRATE table.

xiii. Verify updation of rows in EMP table. Is it possible to update EMP with ENAME=AMIT where EMPNO=E5?

xiv. Verify insertion of rows in PROJ table. Is it possible to insert ('P4','') in PROJ table? Save the transaction if it is possible.

xv. Is it possible to update PROJNAME=CODING where PROJNO=P4?

xvi. Update PROJNAME=CODING_NEW where PROJNO=P4 and save the changes.

xvii. Verify insertion of rows in PROJ_DETAIL table. Is it possible to insert ('E1', 'P1',NULL) in the table? What about inserting ('E1', 'P1',5) or ('E1', 'P1',50)?

W4_3 This question is based on constraints.

i. Connect to SYSTEM/MANAGER@[CONNECT_STRING].

ii. Create user MYUSER with password USER123.

iii. Grant CONNECT and RESOURCE role with ADMIN OPTION to MYUSER, and connect to the user.

iv. Connect to SYSTEM/MANAGER@[CONNECT_STRING], and create USER1 with password USER1. Grant CONNECT, RESOURCE to USER1.

v. Connect to MYUSER and grant SELECT, INSERT and UPDATE privilege on STATE_NAME table

vi. Connect to SYSTEM/MANAGER@[CONNECT_STRING], and write a query to display granted role to MYUSER and USER1.

vii. Connect to USER1/USER1@[CONNECT_STRING} and display structure of STATE_NAME and CUST table present in MYUSER.

viii. Write a query to display CNAME, CCITY and STATE columns.

CNAME	*CCITY*	*STATE*
PRADIP	*MYSORE*	*KARNATAKA*
AASTIK	*KOLKATA*	*WEST BENGAL*
TUSHAR	*PUNE*	*MAHARASHTRA*
ARPAN	*CHENNAI*	*TAMILNADU*
ANUMITA	*INDORE*	*MADHYA PRADESH*

ix. Write a query to insert ('MUMBAI', 'MAHARASHTRA') in STATE_NAME table, and ('C6', 'PRANAB', 'MUMBAI') in CUST table. Save the inserted rows.

x. Write a query to display CNAME, CCITY and STATE columns.

CNAME	*CCITY*	*STATE*
PRADIP	*MYSORE*	*KARNATAKA*
AASTIK	*KOLKATA*	*WEST BENGAL*
TUSHAR	*PUNE*	*MAHARASHTRA*
ARPAN	*CHENNAI*	*TAMILNADU*
ANUMITA	*INDORE*	*MADHYA PRADESH*
PRANAB	*MUMBAI*	*MAHARASHTRA*

6 rows selected.

xi. Try to delete all rows from STATE_NAME table. What is the message displayed by Oracle.

xii. Connect to MYUSER/USER123@[CONNECT_STRING]. Write a query to display rows of STATE_NAME and CUST table to ensure that the rows inserted from USER1 can be retrieved from MYUSER.

W4_4 Create a profile named MY_PROFILE which will lock the user account after 2 unsuccessful logins. After 12 hours, account will be unlocked automatically if it has been locked by failed attempts. The password will expire after 60 days, and there will be a 10-day grace period starting from the time at which the account is accessed after the 59th day.

Part II

Database Management System Application Using Oracle PL/SQL

Introduction to PL/SQL Programming

Learning Objectives

You will learn following key concepts after completion of the chapter:

- ✓ PL/SQL basics and its importance over SQL
- ✓ PL/SQL character sets, identifiers, literals and data types
- ✓ PL/SQL structure and its interface with Oracle
- ✓ PL/SQL conditional statements and looping constructs

5.1 INTRODUCTION

Structured Query Language (SQL) is the standard language for creation and maintenance of relational database management system. Oracle was one of the first commercial relational databases to use SQL as its language. Procedural Language/Structured Query Language (PL/SQL) is an extension of SQL with design features of programming languages. An obvious question is why to expertise PL/SQL when SQL fulfills almost all requirements related to storage and retrieval of data from a database? SQL is a fourth-generation language and it emphasizes on 'what should be done?', rather than 'how to do it?'. For example, in case of a SELECT statement, rows are retrieved and displayed based on the query. Users need not bother 'how the records were retrieved?'. Same is the case with Data Manipulation Languages (DMLs) and other SQL statements. Third-generation language C, Pascal, FORTRAN, etc are procedural language. It implements a step-by-step algorithm to solve a particular problem. Importance of third-generation language is due to its features such as conditional statements and looping constructs. These features can be used to write complex program with ease. PL/SQL combines best of both world, that is, third-generation language and SQL. This makes PL/SQL very powerful language to develop useful software. In this chapter, basics of PL/SQL are discussed. PL/SQL structure, conditional statements, looping construct and scope of variable in nested block are explained with the help of examples and workouts (with solutions). This chapter assumes Oracle database is installed, user database is in place and reader is comfortable with Oracle SQL. This chapter and succeeding chapters of this part will use the running example introduced in the previous chapters. This part is dominated with a large number of examples, workouts and short type questions and students are advised to complete all the chapters to ensure a firm grip on the programming aspect of PL/SQL.

5.2 PL/SQL BASICS

The first version of PL/SQL (Ver. 1.0) was more like a scripting language of SQL*Plus, and it was inbuilt with Oracle Database Release 6.0. The major update of PL/SQL (Ver. 2.0) was part of Oracle Database Release 7.0 and was significantly improved to support subprograms, tables and package extensions. With the launch of Oracle 8i, PL/SQL (Ver. 8.0 and 8.1) reflected effort of Oracle to synchronize its version across all its related products. In this version, object-oriented features along with support for Java were included. PL/SQL (Ver. 9.1 and 9.2) provided support for multilevel collections and XML. With the release of Oracle 10g, PL/SQL (Ver. 10.1 and 10.2) was drastically improved with several optimisation features. At present, Oracle 11g is fairly stable and extensively used. PL/SQL (Ver. 11.1 and 11.2) allow administrators to modify PL/SQL code on the fly, while the PL/SQL code is accessed by users.

The suffix ‘g’ in Oracle 10g or Oracle 11g represents ‘grid’. Grid computing is analogous to the way electric utilities work, in that one need not know where the generator is or how the electric grid is wired. You just ask for electricity and you get it. The central idea of grid computing is that computing should be available as per requirement in a reliable and transparent manner. It should not matter where your data or application resides, or what computer processes your request. You should be able to request information or computation and have it delivered —as much as you want, whenever you want and whereever you want. The goal is to make computing a utility—a ubiquitous commodity, hence the name grid.

In most cases, PL/SQL programs contains SQL statements though it is not mandatory. Oracle database server and all Oracle development tools use PL/SQL as its native language. PL/SQL also allows Data Manipulation Language (DML), which includes insertion, updating and deletion of records in a table. It is a block-structured language and program is divided into separate logical blocks. PL/SQL is the most powerful language for Oracle Server. It is used in Internet Developer Suite, Oracle Application Server, Java, Visual Studio and any language, where Oracle Database Server is used in the back-end. Programs written in PL/SQL may be transported across any Operating System or host environment.

5.2.1 PL/SQL Character Set

PL/SQL language is constructed from alphabets, digits, symbols and white space as defined in Table 5.1. Character sets can be grouped together into four lexical units: identifiers, literals, delimiters and comments.

TABLE 5.1 PL/SQL Types

<table>
<tr><th>Type</th><th>Characters</th></tr>
<tr><td>Upper and lowercase letters</td><td>A–Z, a–z</td></tr>
<tr><td>Digits</td><td>0–9</td></tr>
<tr><td>Mathematical and punctuation symbols</td><td>~ ! @ # $ % & * ( ) _ - + = | [ ] { } : ; “ ‘ < > ? /</td></tr>
<tr><td>White space</td><td>space, tab, and carriage return</td></tr>
</table>

5.2.2 Identifiers

Identifiers are used to name PL/SQL objects such as constants, variables, exceptions, procedures, cursors and reserved words. Identifiers can be up to 30 characters in length, must start with a letter and can include a dollar sign, an underscore, and a pound sign. Identifiers are not case sensitive and cannot include space, tab or carriage return. An identifier can be enclosed within double quotes.

5.2.3 Literals

Literals are specific values and are not represented by identifiers. It is a character, number or boolean value. To embed single quotes within a string literal, two single quotes next to each other may be placed.

Example: In this example, *literal* and its *displayed value* are shown.

```
Literal                            Displayed Value
'It"s nice book'                   It's nice book
'"The PL/SQL Case Study book"'     "The PL/SQL Case Study book"
'Name=''PK'''                      Name='PK'
```

5.2.4 Delimiters

Delimiters are symbols with special meaning to PL/SQL. They are used to separate identifier from each other. Table 5.2 shows the allowable delimiters in Oracle.

TABLE 5.2 PL/SQL Symbols

Delimiter	Characteristics
—	Single-line comment indicator
/*	Initial multiline comment delimiter
*/	Final multiline comment delimiter
+	Addition operator
-	Subtraction operator
*	Multiplication operator
/	Division operator
**	Exponentiation operator
||	Concatenation operator
:=	Assignment operator
=	Equality operator
<>	Inequality operators
!=	Inequality operators (equivalent to <>)
<	'Less than' operator
<=	'Less than or equal to' operator
>	'Greater than' operator
>=	'Greater than or equal to' operator
(	Initial expression or list delimiter
)	Final expression or list delimiter
<<	Begin label delimiter
>>	End label delimiter

Delimiter	Characteristics
,	Item separator
‘	Literal delimiter
“	Quoted literal delimiter
:	Host variable indicator
%	Attribute indicator
.	Component selector
@	Remote database indicator
=>	Association operator
..	Range operator
;	Statement terminator

5.2.5 Comments

Comments are sections of the code that improve readability. The compiler ignores them. A single-line comment begins with a double hyphen (–) and ends with a new line. Multiline comments begin with slash asterisk (/*) and end with asterisk slash (*/). The /* */ comment delimiters can also be used for a single-line comment.

Example

```
-- There are large numbers of examples in this book.
/* There are large numbers of examples in this book. */
/* This book not only contains large number of examples
 but problems also.
*/
```

5.2.6 Variable Declaration and Data Types

PL/SQL programs are normally used to manipulate database information. This is done by declaring variables and data structures in the programs. A variable is a named instantiation of a data structure declared in a PL/SQL program. Unless the variable is declared as a CONSTANT, its value can be changed at any time in your program. Table 5.3 shows variable types along with their purpose.

TABLE 5.3 PL/SQL Data Types

Type		Purpose and example
Scalar	Numeric type	This type of data stores a numeric value. It may be either integer or floating point. It is similar to NUMBER(P,S) database type, where ‘P’ is the precision and ‘S’ is the scale. The maximum precision is 38 digits. ***Example:*** Refer to Figure 5.1
	Character type	This type of data stores strings or character data. It is similar to VARCHAR2, CHAR and LONG database type. CHAR and VARCHAR2 are up to 32767 bytes in PL/SQL. ***Example:*** The city name represents a VARCHAR2.

(Contd.)

TABLE 5.3 PL/SQL Data Types (*Contd.*)

Type		Purpose and example
	Date type	The DATE PL/SQL type behaves exactly in the same way as the DATE database type. Range is between 01-Jan-4712 BC and 31-Dec-9999 AD ***Example:*** 15-AUG-1947 represents a DATE
	Boolean type	The only data type in the boolean is BOOLEAN. A BOOLEAN variable can hold TRUE, FALSE or NULL only. AND, OR and NOT logical operations determine the Boolean value ***Example:*** TRUE represents a Boolean value
	Raw type	This type of data is used to store binary data. RAW is similar to CHAR variables and LONG RAW is similar to LONG except that both cannot convert between character sets. LONG RAW can be up to 2 gigabytes ***Example:*** The text of a speech represents a LONG RAW
LOB	BFILE	File locators pointing to read-only large objects in operating system files. With BFILEs, the large objects are outside the database. BFILE can be up to 4 gigabytes ***Example:*** The movie represents a BFILE.
	BLOB	BLOB locators that point to large binary objects inside the database. BLOB can be up to 4 gigabytes ***Example:*** The photograph represents a BLOB
	CLOB	CLOB locators point to large "character" objects inside the database. CLOB can be up to 4 gigabytes. ***Example:*** Locator pointing to a story represents a CLOB.
	NCLOB	NCLOB locators point to large national character set objects inside the database. It can be up to 4 gigabytes ***Example:*** Locator pointing to US character set

Numeric type data can be declared in different ways. If the number is 3-digit long, then declaration NUMBER(2) will lead to an error, as it will allow the maximum value comprising of 2 digits, that is, 99. Similarly, NUMBER (4, 2) implies 4 digits (XXXX), out of which 2 (XX.XX) are reserved for decimals. Hence, the largest value that can be represented using NUMBER (4, 2) is 99.99. Similarly, NUMBER (4, –1) will replace the last digit with 0. Figure 5.1 shows few interesting examples representing numeric type.

Declaration	Assigned Values	Stored Value
NUMBER	123.456	123.456
NUMBER(2)	12	12
NUMBER(2)	123	Error – exceeds precision
NUMBER(4,2)	123.4	Error – exceeds precision
NUMBER(4,2)	12.34	12.34
NUMBER(4,2)	12.3456	12.35
NUMBER(4,-1)	1234	1230
NUMBER(4,-2)	1234	1200
NUMBER(4,-3)	1234	1000

FIGURE 5.1 PL/SQL numeric type examples.

5.2.7 NULL Value

PL/SQL represents unknown values as NULL values. NULL is never equal or not equal to anything. All functions, except NVL, CONCAT, & REPLACE, return a NULL when passed a NULL argument. 'IS NULL' or 'IS NOT NULL' clause is used to check for NULL values. A variable must be declared in the declaration section of PL/SQL block. When a variable is declared, PL/SQL allocates memory for the variable's value and names the storage location so that the value can be retrieved and changed.

5.2.8 Constants

The CONSTANT keyword in a declaration requires an initial value and does not allow that value to be changed.

5.2.9 Default Values

Whenever you declare a variable, it is assigned a default value of NULL. If the variable is required to be initialized to a value other than NULL, it can be done in the declaration with either the assignment operator (:=) or the DEFAULT keyword.

5.2.10 Statements

A PL/SQL program is composed of one or more logical statements. All PL/SQL statements are SQL or procedural statements. Procedural statements include variable declarations, conditional statements and looping constructs. A semicolon delimiter terminates a statement.

5.3 PL/SQL STRUCTURE

PL/SQL is a block-structured language and is divided into logical blocks. It consists up to three sections—DECLARE, EXECUTABLES and EXCEPTION—DECLARE and EXCEPTION sections are optional and they may or may not be present in a PL/SQL program. Basic Syntax of PL/SQL block structure and brief description are shown in Figure 5.2 and Table 5.4, respectively.

```
DECLARE
    Variables, Cursor and other Declarations
BEGIN
    Executables comprising of SQL and Procedural statements
EXCEPTION
    Statements to perform action in case of errors
END;
```

FIGURE 5.2 PL/SQL block structure.

TABLE 5.4 Block Structure Description

DECLARE	All variables, constants, cursors and user-defined exceptions used in EXECUTABLE section are declared in this section
EXECUTABLE (BEGIN ... END)	SQL DMLs, assignment statements, conditional statements, loop statements and other PL/SQL statements are written in this section
EXCEPTION	This section deals with error handling and an action is performed based on the type of error. Program is terminated after the action is taken

In this book, we will store PL/SQL programs in a systematic manner in the relevant chapters in "C:/BOOK" folder. For example, the first program of this chapter EX5_1.SQL will be stored in C:\BOOK\CHAPTER5\EX5_1.SQL. This strategy is suggested for easy access of programs in future; however, this is not mandatory and most of the programs will execute seamlessly even in any folder or drive of the machine. Few programs related to dynamic SQL are path dependent and care must be taken to modify the relevant portion of the program for successful execution.

EX5_1 This example demonstrates a simple PL/SQL program.

```
SET SERVEROUTPUT ON
BEGIN
     DBMS_OUTPUT.PUT_LINE('My first program using PL/SQL');
END;
/

SQL> @ C:/BOOK/CHAPTER5/EX5_1
My first program using PL/SQL
```

Illustration

In Windows environment, use Notepad to create 'EX5_1.SQL' PL/SQL program.
Start -> Programs -> Accessories -> Notepad

Save the file 'EX5_1.SQL 'in 'C:/ BOOK/CHAPTER5' Folder
File -> Save As... -> "EX5_1.SQL" -> SAVE
Do not forget to save the file in double quotes i.e. "EX5_1.SQL"
Connect to the desired user.
Execute EX5_1.SQL from SQL prompt.

SET SERVEROUTPUT ON is required for displaying text on the screen. It works with DBMS_OUTPUT.PUT_LINE. BEGIN ... END; is part of PL/SQL structure. DBMS_OUTPUT.PUT_LINE('My first program using PL/SQL'); displays the message. '/' is Oracle environment declaration. If it is omitted, '/' is required to be typed at the time of execution of program. The program can be executed using @<path name/plsql file name> on SQL prompt.

EX5_2 This example demonstrates usage of variable in PL/SQL program.

```
SET SERVEROUTPUT ON
SET VERIFY OFF
DECLARE
   —Variable declaration
   INPUT_NO   NUMBER(3);
   INPUT_CHAR VARCHAR2(20);
   INPUT_DATE DATE;
```

```
BEGIN
  —Accept name, age and date
  INPUT_CHAR := '&YOUR_NAME';
  INPUT_NO := &YOUR_AGE;
  INPUT_DATE := SYSDATE;
  DBMS_OUTPUT.PUT_LINE(INPUT_CHAR || ' IS ' || INPUT_NO ||
  ' YEARS OLD ' || ' ON ' || ' INPUT_DATE);
END;
/

SQL>@ C:/BOOK/CHAPTER5/EX5_2
Enter value for your_name: PK
Enter value for your_age: 36
PK IS 36 YEARS OLD ON 23-AUG-13
```

Illustration

SET VERIFY OFF sets off verification during execution. INPUT_NO is of NUMBER type, INPUT_CHAR is VARCHAR2 type andINPUT_DATE is DATE type. INPUT_CHAR: = '&YOUR_NAME'; is used to assign values to variable and '&' is used to accept valid input at run-time. System Date is assigned to INPUT_DATE.

5.3.1 Conditional Statement in PL/SQL

In PL/SQL, two types of conditional statements are allowed, IF and CASE statements.

IF Statement

The IF statement allows actions to be performed selectively based on conditions. IF statement can also be nested inside other IF statements. There are three forms of IF statement:

- IF … THEN …
- IF … THEN … ELSE …
- IF … THEN … ELSIF … ELSE ….

The first two are most commonly used and cater all conditional requirements.

EX5_3 Write a PL/SQL program to find the largest number among three.

```
SET SERVEROUTPUT ON
SET VERIFY OFF
DECLARE
   —Declare and accept values for A, B & C
   A NUMBER := &A;
   B NUMBER := &B;
   C NUMBER := &C;
BEGIN
   IF A>=B THEN
       IF A>=C THEN
          DBMS_OUTPUT.PUT_LINE('Largest Number is ' || A);
       ELSE
          DBMS_OUTPUT.PUT_LINE('Largest Number is ' || C);
       END IF;
       ELSE
```

```
        IF B>=C THEN
            DBMS_OUTPUT.PUT_LINE('Largest Number is ' ||B);
        ELSE
            DBMS_OUTPUT.PUT_LINE('Largest Number is ' || C);
        END IF;
    END IF;
END;
/
```

Execution

```
SQL>@ C:/BOOK/CHAPTER5/EX5_3
Enter value for a: 34
Enter value for b: 76
Enter value for c: 12
Largest Number is 76
```

Illustration

This is an example of two-level If Then Else statement to find and display the largest number among three.

CASE Statement

The CASE statement selects one sequence of statements to execute. The CASE statement is more readable and more efficient. It is always advisable to rewrite lengthy IF-THEN-ELSIF statements using CASE statements.

The CASE statement begins with the keyword CASE. The keyword is followed by a selector. Usually it consists of a single variable. The selector expression may be arbitrarily complex. The selector expression is evaluated only once. The value it yields can have PL/SQL data type. BLOB, BFILE, an object type, a PL/SQL record, an index-by-table, a varray or a nested table cannot be used in CASE statement. The selector is followed by one or more WHEN clauses and are checked sequentially. The value of the selector determines which clause is to be executed. If the value of the selector equals the value of a WHEN-clause expression, that WHEN clause is executed. The ELSE clause works similarly to the ELSE clause in an IF statement. If the CASE statement does not match any of the WHEN clauses and you omit the ELSE clause, PL/SQL raises the predefined exception CASE_NOT_FOUND. The keywords END CASE terminate the CASE statement. These two keywords must be separated by a space.

```
CASE selector
    WHEN exp1 THEN statements1;
    WHEN exp2 THEN statements2;
    ...
    WHEN expN THEN statementsN;
    [ELSE statementsN+1;]
END CASE;
```

EX5_4 This example demonstrates use of Case statement.

```
SET SERVEROUTPUT ON
SET VERIFY OFF
DECLARE
   VDIGIT NUMBER := &DIGIT;

BEGIN
CASE VDIGIT
   WHEN 0 THEN DBMS_OUTPUT.PUT_LINE('ZERO');
   WHEN 1 THEN DBMS_OUTPUT.PUT_LINE('ONE');
   WHEN 2 THEN DBMS_OUTPUT.PUT_LINE('TWO');
   WHEN 3 THEN DBMS_OUTPUT.PUT_LINE('THREE');
   WHEN 4 THEN DBMS_OUTPUT.PUT_LINE('FOUR');
   WHEN 5 THEN DBMS_OUTPUT.PUT_LINE('FIVE');
   WHEN 6 THEN DBMS_OUTPUT.PUT_LINE('SIX');
   WHEN 7 THEN DBMS_OUTPUT.PUT_LINE('SEVEN');
   WHEN 8 THEN DBMS_OUTPUT.PUT_LINE('EIGHT');
   WHEN 9 THEN DBMS_OUTPUT.PUT_LINE('NINE');
   ELSE DBMS_OUTPUT.PUT_LINE(VDIGIT || ' IS WRONG INPUT. VALID
   NUMBER IS 0 TO 9.');
END CASE;
END;
/
```

Execution

```
SQL> @ C:\BOOK_PLSQL\CHAPTER5\EX5_4
Enter value for digit: 6
SIX

SQL> /
Enter value for digit: 0
ZERO

SQL> /
Enter value for digit: 12
12 IS WRONG INPUT. VALID NUMBER IS 0 TO 9.
```

Illustration

This is an example of Case statement which displays the string (ZERO to NINE) based on the input variable VDIGIT. Note the use of ELSE part of CASE statement, which traps input values other than 0–9.

5.3.2 Loops in PL/SQL

Three types of loops are available in PL/SQL: Loop … End Loop, For Loop and While Loop. Loops are used for iterations.

LOOP ... END LOOP

The keyword LOOP should be placed before the first statement in the sequence and the keyword END LOOP after the last statement in the sequence. Syntax for simple loop is as follows:

```
   Loop
      PL/SQL statements
      Exit Condition
   End Loop
```

EX5_5 This example displays summing of numbers from 1 to I_NUM using LOOP ... END.

```
SET VERIFY OFF
SET SERVEROUTPUT ON
DECLARE
   I_NUM     NUMBER;
   S_NUM     NUMBER;
   SUM_NUM   NUMBER;
BEGIN
   I_NUM := &I_NUM;
   —Initialize SUM_NUM to 0
   SUM_NUM := 0;
   —Store value of I_NUM in S_NUM for future use
   S_NUM := I_NUM;
   IF I_NUM >0 AND I_NUM < 1001 THEN
      LOOP
         SUM_NUM := SUM_NUM+I_NUM;
         I_NUM := I_NUM-1;
         EXIT WHEN I_NUM=0;
      END LOOP;
      DBMS_OUTPUT.PUT_LINE('SUM OF NUMBER FROM 1 TO ' || S_NUM ||
      ' IS ' || SUM_NUM);
   ELSE
      DBMS_OUTPUT.PUT_LINE('Input Number Range is from 1 to 1000');
   END IF;
END;
/
```

Execution

```
SQL>@ C:/BOOK/CHAPTER5/EX5_5
Enter value for i_num: 10
SUM OF NUMBER FROM 1 TO 10 IS 55
```

Illustration

This example accepts a number I_NUM and displays the summation from 1 to I_NUM. Note the use of If Then Else statements to allow valid input and also the use of EXIT statement to exit from the loop.

FOR LOOP

The For Loop statement specifies a range of integers to execute the sequence of statements once for each integer. Syntax of for loop is as follows:

```
For variable IN Start..End
   PL/SQL Statements
End Loop;
```

EX5_6 This example displays summing of numbers from 1 to I_NUM using FOR LOOP.

```
SET VERIFY OFF
SET SERVEROUTPUT ON
DECLARE
   I_NUM NUMBER;
   SUM_NUM  NUMBER;
BEGIN
   I_NUM := &I_NUM;
   SUM_NUM := 0;
   IF I_NUM >0 AND I_NUM < 1001 THEN
      FOR I IN 1..I_NUM LOOP
         SUM_NUM := SUM_NUM+I;
      END LOOP;
      DBMS_OUTPUT.PUT_LINE('SUM OF NUMBER FROM 1 TO '|| I_NUM ||
      ' IS ' || SUM_NUM);
   ELSE
      DBMS_OUTPUT.PUT_LINE('Input Number Range is from 1 to 1000');
   END IF;
END;
/
```

Execution

```
SQL>@ C:/BOOK/CHAPTER5/EX5_6
Enter value for i_num: 10
SUM OF NUMBER FROM 1 TO 10 IS 55
```

Illustration

This example is similar to EX5_5. The only difference between both examples is that EX5_6 uses FOR LOOP instead of LOOP … END LOOP.

WHILE … LOOP

The while loop statement includes a condition associated with a sequence of statements. If the condition is true, the sequence of statements will be executed and again control will resume at the beginning of the loop. If the condition is false, then the loop is bypassed and control is passed to the next statement.

```
While <Condition> Loop
   PL/SQL Statements
End Loop
```

EX5_7 This example displays summing of numbers from 1 to I_NUM using WHILE … LOOP.

```
SET VERIFY OFF
SET SERVEROUTPUT ON
DECLARE
   I_NUM NUMBER;
   S_NUM NUMBER;
   SUM_NUM  NUMBER;
BEGIN
   I_NUM := &I_NUM;
   SUM_NUM := 0;
   S_NUM := I_NUM;
   IF I_NUM >0 AND I_NUM < 1001 THEN
      WHILE I_NUM >= 0 LOOP
         SUM_NUM := SUM_NUM+I_NUM;
         I_NUM := I_NUM-1;
      END LOOP;
      DBMS_OUTPUT.PUT_LINE('SUM OF NUMBER FROM 1 TO ' || S_NUM ||
      ' IS ' || SUM_NUM);
   ELSE
      DBMS_OUTPUT.PUT_LINE('Input Number Range is from 1 to
      1000');
   END IF;
END;
/
```

Execution

```
SQL>@ C:/BOOK/CHAPTER5/EX5_7
Enter value for i_num: 10
SUM OF NUMBER FROM 1 TO 10 IS 55
```

Illustration

This example is also similar to EX5_5. The only difference between both examples is that EX5_7 uses WHILE LOOP instead of LOOP … END LOOP.

5.3.3 Scope of Variable in Nested Block

PL/SQL statements can be nested wherever an executable statement is allowed. A nested block acts as a statement and executable statements can be broken into smaller blocks. Scope and visibility of a variable are demonstrated in the example.

EX5_8 This example demonstrates use of the variable scope in MAIN and NESTED blocks.

```
SET SERVEROUTPUT ON
DECLARE
   VA NUMBER(4)  := 10;
```

```
   VMSG VARCHAR2(20) := '*** MAIN ***';
   VB NUMBER(4)  := 11;
BEGIN
   DECLARE
      VA NUMBER(4)  := 1000;
      VB NUMBER(4)  := 1001;
   BEGIN
      DBMS_OUTPUT.PUT_LINE('VA IN NESTED BLOCK = '||VA);
      DBMS_OUTPUT.PUT_LINE('VMSG IN NESTED BLOCK =
      '||VMSG);
      DBMS_OUTPUT.PUT_LINE('VB IN NESTED BLOCK = '||VB);
   END;
   DBMS_OUTPUT.PUT_LINE('------------------------------');
   DBMS_OUTPUT.PUT_LINE('VA IN MAIN BLOCK = '||VA);
   DBMS_OUTPUT.PUT_LINE('VMSG IN MAIN BLOCK = '||VMSG);
   DBMS_OUTPUT.PUT_LINE('VB IN MAIN BLOCK = '||VB);
END;
/
```

Execution

```
SQL>@ C:/BOOK/CHAPTER5/EX5_8
VA IN NESTED BLOCK = 1000
VMSG IN NESTED BLOCK = *** MAIN ***
VB IN NESTED BLOCK = 1001
-------------------------------------
VA IN MAIN BLOCK = 10
VMSG IN MAIN BLOCK = *** MAIN ***
VB IN MAIN BLOCK = 11
```

Illustration

In this example, both VA and VB are declared in MAIN and NESTED blocks. Values of VA and VB in MAIN block are 10 and 11, respectively. Values of VA and VB in NESTED block are 1000 and 1001, respectively. VMSG is declared and assigned value only in MAIN block. Value of VA and VB defined in NESTED block (i.e., 1000 and 1001) and value of VMSG is *** MAIN *** as initialized in MAIN is displayed when called from NESTED block, Value of VA, VB and VMSG defined in MAIN block (i.e., 10, 11 and VMSG) is displayed when called from MAIN block.

5.4 PL/SQL AND ORACLE

All the examples given in this chapter are based on CUST, PROD, SALE_DETAIL and STATE_NAME tables. ER model is shown in Figure 5.3. SQL script to create tables and populate rows in the relevant tables are shown in Figure 5.4. Ensure that all columns and rows of each table exist (Figures 5.5 and 5.6). CUST and STATE_NAME are directly joined as it is a case of Third Normal Form.

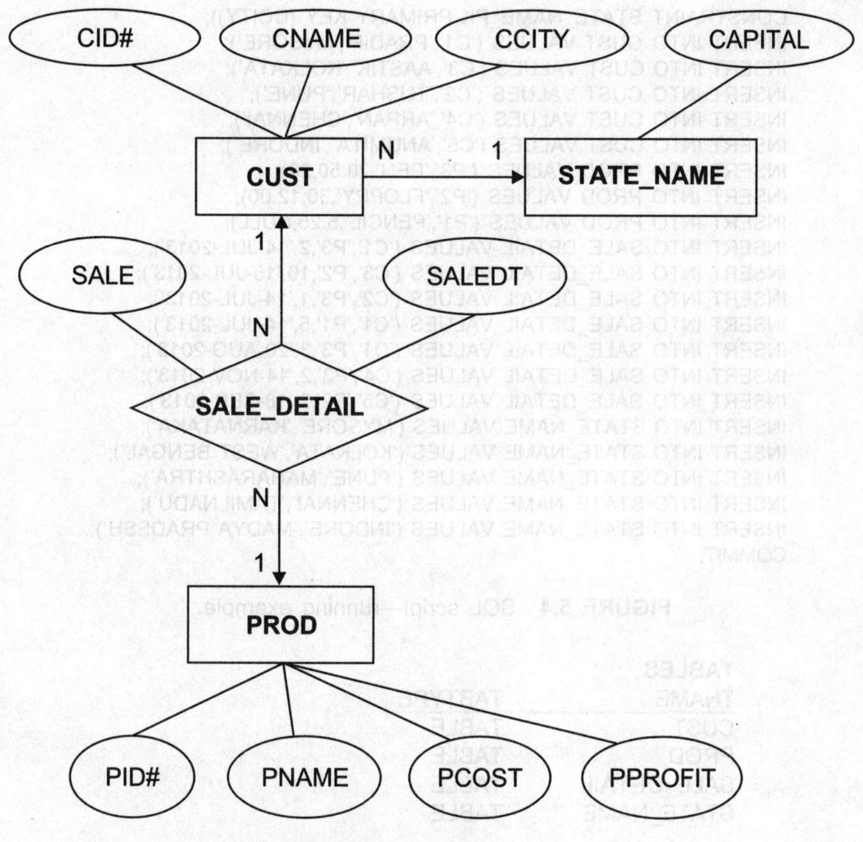

FIGURE 5.3 ER model.

```
DROP TABLE SALE_DETAIL;
DROP TABLE STATE_NAME;
DROP TABLE CUST;
DROP TABLE PROD;
CREATE TABLE CUST
(CID VARCHAR2(6),
CNAME VARCHAR2(10),
CCITY VARCHAR2(8),
CONSTRAINT CUST_PK PRIMARY KEY (CID));
CREATE TABLE PROD
(PID VARCHAR2(6),
PNAME VARCHAR2(6),
PCOST NUMBER(4,2),
PPROFIT NUMBER(3),
CONSTRAINT PROD_PK PRIMARY KEY (PID));
CREATE TABLE SALE_DETAIL
(CID VARCHAR2(6) REFERENCES CUST(CID),
PID VARCHAR2(6) REFERENCES PROD(PID),
SALE NUMBER(3),
SALEDT DATE,
CONSTRAINT SALE_DETAIL_PK PRIMARY KEY (CID,PID,SALEDT));
CREATE TABLE STATE_NAME
(CCITY VARCHAR2(8) REFERENCES CUST(CCITY),
STATE VARCHAR2(15),
```

FIGURE 5.4 *Contd.*

```
CONSTRAINT STATE_NAME_PK PRIMARY KEY (CCITY));
INSERT INTO CUST VALUES ('C1','PRADIP','MYSORE');
INSERT INTO CUST VALUES ('C3','AASTIK','KOLKATA');
INSERT INTO CUST VALUES ('C2','TUSHAR','PUNE');
INSERT INTO CUST VALUES ('C4','ARPAN','CHENNAI');
INSERT INTO CUST VALUES ('C5','ANUMITA','INDORE');
INSERT INTO PROD VALUES ('P3','PEN',20.50,20);
INSERT INTO PROD VALUES ('P2','FLOPPY',30,12.00);
INSERT INTO PROD VALUES ('P1','PENCIL',5.25,NULL);
INSERT INTO SALE_DETAIL VALUES ('C1','P3',2,'14-JUL-2013');
INSERT INTO SALE_DETAIL VALUES ('C3','P2',10,'15-JUL-2013');
INSERT INTO SALE_DETAIL VALUES ('C2','P3',1,'14-JUL-2013');
INSERT INTO SALE_DETAIL VALUES ('C1','P1',5,'14-JUL-2013');
INSERT INTO SALE_DETAIL VALUES ('C1','P3',3,'20-AUG-2013');
INSERT INTO SALE_DETAIL VALUES ('C4','P3',2,'14-NOV-2013');
INSERT INTO SALE_DETAIL VALUES ('C5','P2',2,'18-SEP-2013');
INSERT INTO STATE_NAME VALUES ('MYSORE','KARNATAKA');
INSERT INTO STATE_NAME VALUES ('KOLKATA','WEST BENGAL');
INSERT INTO STATE_NAME VALUES ('PUNE','MAHARASHTRA');
INSERT INTO STATE_NAME VALUES ('CHENNAI','TAMILNADU');
INSERT INTO STATE_NAME VALUES ('INDORE','MADYA PRADESH');
COMMIT;
```

FIGURE 5.4 SQL script—running example.

TABLES

TNAME	TABTYPE
CUST	TABLE
PROD	TABLE
SALE_DETAIL	TABLE
STATE_NAME	TABLE

CUST TABLE

Name	Null?	Type
CID	NOT NULL	VARCHAR2(6)
CNAME		VARCHAR2(10)
CCITY		VARCHAR2(8)

PROD TABLE

Name	Null?	Type
PID	NOT NULL	VARCHAR2(6)
PNAME		VARCHAR2(6)
PCOST		NUMBER(4,2)
PPROFIT		NUMBER(3)

SALE_DETAIL TABLE

Name	Null?	Type
CID	NOT NULL	VARCHAR2(6)
PID	NOT NULL	VARCHAR2(6)
SALE		NUMBER(3)
SALEDT	NOT NULL	DATE

STATE TABLE

Name	Null?	Type
CCITY	NOT NULL	VARCHAR2(8)
STATE		VARCHAR2(15)

FIGURE 5.5 Tables—running example.

All DML and transaction related commands might be used in PL/SQL. DCL and DDL related commands are not allowed in PL/SQL program. SELECT statement is used along with INTO clause for data retrieval. Syntax of SELECT statement in PL/SQL is as follows:

SELECT COL_NAMES INTO {VAR_NAME [, VAR_NAME] | REC_NAME}
FROM TABLE_NAME
[WHERE COND]
[ORDER BY VAR_NAME(S)];

EX5_9 This example demonstrates use of DMLs in PL/SQL program.

```
SET SERVEROUTPUT ON
DECLARE
   VCNT NUMBER(2);
BEGIN
DBMS_OUTPUT.PUT_LINE('______________________________');
   SELECT COUNT(*) INTO VCNT FROM CUST;
   DBMS_OUTPUT.PUT_LINE('Number of records in CUST before  INSERT');
   DBMS_OUTPUT.PUT_LINE(VCNT);
   INSERT INTO CUST VALUES ('P10','C1','KOLKATA');
   INSERT INTO CUST VALUES ('P11','C2','INDORE');
   COMMIT;
   DBMS_OUTPUT.PUT_LINE('Records inserted in CUST Table');
   DBMS_OUTPUT.PUT_LINE('P10, C1, KOLKATA');
   DBMS_OUTPUT.PUT_LINE('P11, C2, INDORE');
   SELECT COUNT(*) INTO VCNT FROM CUST;
   DBMS_OUTPUT.PUT_LINE('Number of records in CUST after INSERT and
   before DELETE');
   DBMS_OUTPUT.PUT_LINE(VCNT);
   DELETE FROM CUST WHERE CID IN ('P10','P11');
   COMMIT;
   SELECT COUNT(*) INTO VCNT FROM CUST;
   DBMS_OUTPUT.PUT_LINE('Number of records after DELETE. CID with P10
   and P11 deleted');
   DBMS_OUTPUT.PUT_LINE(VCNT);
   DBMS_OUTPUT.PUT_LINE('______________________________');
END;
/
```

Execution

```
SQL> @ C:\BOOK\CHAPTER5\EX5_9
________________________________
Number of records in CUST before INSERT
5
Records inserted in CUST Table
P10, C1, KOLKATA
P11, C2, INDORE
```

```
Number of records in CUST after INSERT before DELETE
7
Number of records after DELETE. CID with P10 and P11 deleted
5
_____________________________________________
```

Illustrations

This is an example to show effect of INSERT and DELETE statements to display a number of records after the COMMIT statements.

5.4.1 SQL Cursor

A cursor is a private SQL work area where all commands defined in the cursor are executed. There are two types of cursors implicit cursor and explicit cursor.

Implicit cursor, as its name suggests, is implied and supported by Oracle Server. It is automatically created and handled by Oracle Server. DMLs and SELECT statement that returns only one row are candidates for implicit cursor. In this chapter, we will see several examples and exercise of implicit cursors. Explicit cursor, on the other hand, needs to be declared explicitly by the programmer. It is handled using cursor-related commands. Explicit cursor will be explained in detail in subsequent chapters.

5.4.2 INTO Clause

The INTO clause is mandatory in PL/SQL and occurs between SELECT and FROM clauses. This clause is used to specify the names of variables that will be populated by the items being selected in the SELECT clause. Queries must return only one row or else it will generate error.

Example EX5_10 to EX5_14 are based on CUST, PROD and SALE_DETAIL tables as shown in Figure 5.6 and are examples of implicit cursor.

EX5_10 This example demonstrates use of INTO clause in PL/SQL program.

```
SET SERVEROUTPUT ON
DECLARE
 VPID            VARCHAR2(6) := '&PID';
 VCNT            NUMBER;
BEGIN
 SELECT COUNT(*) INTO VCNT FROM SALE_DETAIL WHERE PID=VPID;
 DBMS_OUTPUT.PUT_LINE(VPID || '- SOLD ' || VCNT || ' TIMES');
END;
/
```

Execution

```
SQL>@ C:\BOOK\CHAPTER5\EX5_10
Enter value for pid: P3
P3- SOLD 4 TIMES
```

CUST

CID	CNAME	CCITY
C1	PRADIP	MYSORE
C3	AASTIK	KOLKATA
C2	TUSHAR	PUNE
C4	ARPAN	CHENNAI
C5	ANUMITA	INDORE

PROD TABLE

PID	PNAME	PCOST	PPROFIT
P3	PEN	20.5	20
P2	FLOPPY	30	12
P1	PENCIL	5.25	

SALE_DETAIL TABLE

CID	PID	SALE	SALEDT
C1	P3	2	14-JUL-13
C3	P2	10	15-JUL-13
C2	P3	1	14-JUL-13
C1	P1	5	14-JUL-13
C1	P3	3	20-AUG-13
C4	P3	2	14-NOV-13
C5	P2	2	18-SEP-13

STATE_NAME TABLE

CCITY	STATE
MYSORE	KARNATAKA
KOLKATA	WEST BENGAL
PUNE	MAHARASHTRA
CHENNAI	TAMILNADU
INDORE	MADHYA PRADESH

FIGURE 5.6 Records—running example.

Illustrations

VPID is VARCHAR2(6) and it corresponds to PID of SALE_DETAIL table. In SELECT … INTO … FROM … WHERE, value of COUNT(*) is stored in VCNT based on the WHERE PID=VPID condition. In this, VCNT acts as a container to hold one numeric type of data.

5.4.3 %TYPE Attribute

<VARIABLE NAME> TABLENAME.COLUMN%TYPE

%TYPE attribute is used to declare variables that refer to database columns. Using this method, the data type and size of the variable are determined when the block is compiled. The %TYPE is most often used when the value stored in the variable value will be derived from a table or if the variable is to be written in the table. The major advantage of declaring variable using %TYPE changes made at the table are automatically reflected in the variable.

EX5_11 This example demonstrates use of %TYPE attribute in PL/SQL program.

```
SET SERVEROUTPUT ON
DECLARE
   VCID    CUST.CID%TYPE := '&CID';
   VCNAME    CUST.CNAME%TYPE;
   VCCITY    CUST.CCITY%TYPE;
   VCNT  NUMBER;
BEGIN
   SELECT COUNT(*) INTO VCNT FROM CUST WHERE CID=VCID;
   IF VCNT=1 THEN
      SELECT CNAME,CCITY INTO VCNAME,VCCITY FROM CUST WHERE
      CID=VCID;
      DBMS_OUTPUT.PUT_LINE(VCID || '-' || VCNAME || ' STAYS IN '
      || VCCITY);
   ELSE
      DBMS_OUTPUT.PUT_LINE(VCID || '-' || 'INVALID CID');
   END IF;
END;
/
```

Execution

```
SQL>@ C:\BOOK\CHAPTER5\EX5_11
Enter value for cid: C3
C3-AASTIK STAYS IN KOLKATA
```

Illustrations

In VCNAME CUST.CNAME%TYPE; declaration using %TYPE is demonstrated. In this VCNAME is a variable of the type CNAME of CUST table. In this case CNAME is VARCHAR2(10) and the same is VCNAME. In case CNAME is changed to VARCHAR2(15), VCNAME will also become VARCHAR2(15). Same is the case with VCID and VCCITY.

5.4.4 %ROWTYPE Attribute

%ROWTYPE attribute provides a record type that represents a row in a table. It is used to declare a record based on a collection of columns in a database table or view. The fields within the record will obtain their names and data types from the columns of table or view referenced in the record declaration. Records are declared in the DECLARE section of block, along with other types of variables.

EX5_12 This example demonstrates use of %ROWTYPE attribute in PL/SQL program.

```
SET VERIFY OFF
SET SERVEROUTPUT ON
DECLARE
   VCUST CUST%ROWTYPE;
   VCID  VARCHAR2(6);
   VCNT  NUMBER;
```

```
BEGIN
   VCID := '&CID';
   SELECT COUNT(*) INTO VCNT FROM CUST WHERE CID=VCID;
   IF VCNT=1 THEN
      SELECT * INTO VCUST FROM CUST WHERE CID=VCID;
      DBMS_OUTPUT.PUT_LINE(VCID || '-' || VCUST.CNAME || ' STAYS
      IN ' || VCUST.CCITY);
   ELSE
      DBMS_OUTPUT.PUT_LINE(VCID || '-' || 'INVALID CID');
   END IF;
END;
/
```

Execution

```
SQL>C:>@ C:\BOOK\CHAPTER5\EX5_12
Enter value for cid: C1
C1-PRADIP STAYS IN MYSORE
```

Illustrations

In VCUST CUST%ROWTYPE; all column defined in CUST table are declared. VCUST.CID corresponds to CID, VCUST.CNAME corresponds to CNAME and CUST.CCITY corresponds to CCITY of CUST table. In SELECT * INTO VCUST FROM CUST WHERE CID=VCID; all values are stored in VCUST and any values can be accessed using VCUST.<Col Name>.

EX5_13 Write a PL/SQL program to display the costliest and cheapest product in PROD table.

```
SET SERVEROUTPUT ON
DECLARE
   VPNAMEMIN    PROD.PNAME%TYPE;
   VPNAMEMAX    PROD.PNAME%TYPE;
   VPCOST       PROD.PCOST%TYPE;
BEGIN
   SELECT PNAME,PCOST INTO VPNAMEMAX,VPCOST
   FROM PROD
   WHERE PCOST=(SELECT MAX(PCOST) FROM PROD);
   DBMS_OUTPUT.PUT_LINE('COSTLIEST PRODUCT IS ' || VPNAMEMAX
   || ' AND ITS COST IS ' || VPCOST);
   SELECT PNAME,PCOST INTO VPNAMEMIN,VPCOST
   FROM PROD
   WHERE PCOST=(SELECT MIN(PCOST) FROM PROD);
   DBMS_OUTPUT.PUT_LINE('CHEAPEST PRODUCT IS ' || VPNAMEMIN || '
   AND ITS COST IS ' || VPCOST);
END;
/
```

Execution

```
SQL>@ C:\BOOK\CHAPTER5\EX5_13
```

```
COSTLIEST PRODUCT IS FLOPPY AND ITS COST IS 30
CHEAPEST PRODUCT IS PENCIL AND ITS COST IS 5.25
```

Illustration

This example demonstrates use of Group Functions (MAX and MIN) in the PL/SQL code.

EX5_14 Write a PL/SQL program which will accept PID and display PID and its total sale value, that is, sum (prod.pcost * sale_detail.sale).

```
SET SERVEROUTPUT ON
DECLARE
   VPID  SALE_DETAIL.PID%TYPE := '&PID';
   VTPCOST  NUMBER(8,2);
BEGIN
   SELECT SUM(S.SALE*P.PCOST) INTO VTPCOST
   FROM PROD P, SALE_DETAIL S
   WHERE P.PID=S.PID AND S.PID=VPID;
   DBMS_OUTPUT.PUT_LINE('PRODUCT ID:' || VPID || ' TOTAL SALE
VALUE=' || VTPCOST);
END;
/
```

Execution

```
SQL>@ C:\BOOK\CHAPTER5\EX5_14
Enter value for pid: P1
PRODUCT ID:P1 TOTAL SALE VALUE=26.25
SQL> /
Enter value for pid: P2
PRODUCT ID:P2 TOTAL SALE VALUE=360
SQL> /
Enter value for pid: P3
PRODUCT ID:P3 TOTAL SALE VALUE=164
```

Illustration

This example works based on the Product Id to display the total sale value. Note the use of SUM function in the program.

5.5 SUMMARY

PL/SQL is a combination of SQL and third-generation language. It is the native language of all Oracle back-end and front-end software. In this chapter, we have learnt basics of PL/SQL and these conceptions will be essentially required to understand the succeeding chapters. Students are requested to solve all the workouts and attempt short type questions to reinforce the topics learnt in this chapter.

SHORT/OBJECTIVE TYPE QUESTIONS

1. Write the basic structure of a procedural PL/SQL block.
2. Write five data types allowed in a PL/SQL program.
3. Write the difference between SQL and PL/SQL.
4. Write the mandatory keywords in a PL/SQL program.
5. How a variable type is associated and assigned with a table?
6. Write different forms of IF constructs.
7. What are the major advantages of PL/SQL over SQL?
8. What is the major advantage of using the %ROWTYPE?
9. What is the function of an identifier in PL/SQL program?
10. Is it possible to apply NOT NULL constraint of a database column to %TYPE variables?
11. How SQL group functions are used within a procedural statement? Explain with suitable example.
12. Is it possible to use DECODE function in PL/SQL procedural statement? What is the equivalent of DECODE function in the PL/SQL program?
13. Write short notes on an anonymous block and its execution.
14. Write short notes on bind variable.
15. How a global variable is declared within a nested block?
16. Define NVL function.
17. Write short notes on Transaction Control Language.
18. What is the difference between the CREATE ANY TABLE and the CREATE TABLE?
19. What are the advantages of using roles to grant privileges?
20. Can you access SQL session information?

WORKOUT SECTION

W5_1 Write a PL/SQL program which will accept 3 numbers and print the smallest among them.

```
SQL>@ C:/BOOK/CHAPTER5/W5_1
Enter value for a: 12
Enter value for b: 34
Enter value for c: 12
Smallest Number is 12
```

W5_2 to W5_4 Write PL/SQL program using Loop … End Loop(W5_2), For Loop(W5_3) and While Loop(W5_4), which will accept integer from 1 to 10 and print factorial. For example, Factorial of 6 is 5*4*3*2*1 = 720.

SQL>@ C:/BOOK/CHAPTER5/W5_2
Enter value for i_num: 6
FACTORIAL OF 6 IS 720

W5_5 Write a PL/SQL program which will accept a number from 1 to 20 and display following figure.

```
SQL>@ C:/BOOK/CHAPTER5/W5_3
Enter value for i_num: 10
__ *
____ *
______ *
________ *
__________ *
____________ *
______________ *
________________ *
__________________ *
____________________ *
```

Questions W5_6 to W5_10 are based on PROJ, PROJ_DETAIL, EMP and DESGRATE tables. Script to create tables is shown in Figure 5.7. Ensure that the rows inserted in tables are as shown in Figure 5.8.

W5_6 Write a PL/SQL program that accepts DESG and displays message as per the sample output shown below.

```
SQL> @ C:\BOOK\CHAPTER5\W5_6
Enter value for desg: ANALYST
THERE ARE 2 ANALYST AND THE SERVICE CHARGE IS Rs 800 PER HOUR.
SQL> /
Enter value for desg: DBA
THERE IS ONLY 1 DBA AND THE SERVICE CHARGE IS Rs 1000 PER HOUR.
SQL> /
Enter value for desg: WRITTER
WRITTER DOES NOT EXISTS, PLEASE TRY AGAIN
```

W5_7 Write a PL/SQL program that accepts PROJNO and displays message as per the sample output shown below.

```
SQL> @ C:\BOOK\CHAPTER5\W5_7
Enter value for projno: P1

TOTAL EXPENDITURE ON DATABASE SW IS 71000

PL/SQL procedure successfully completed.
SQL> /
Enter value for projno: P2
```

```
DROP TABLE PROJ_DETAIL;
DROP TABLE PROJ;
DROP TABLE EMP;
DROP TABLE DESGRATE;
CREATE TABLE PROJ
(PROJNO  VARCHAR2(5) PRIMARY KEY,
PROJNAME VARCHAR2(15));
CREATE TABLE DESGRATE
(DESG VARCHAR2(15) PRIMARY KEY,
HRRATE  NUMBER(5));
CREATE TABLE EMP
(EMPNO   VARCHAR2(5) PRIMARY KEY,
ENAME    VARCHAR2(15),
DESG  VARCHAR2(15) REFERENCES DESGRATE(DESG));
CREATE TABLE PROJ_DETAIL
(EMPNO   VARCHAR2(5) REFERENCES EMP(EMPNO),
PROJNO   VARCHAR2(5) REFERENCES PROJ(PROJNO),
HRWORKED NUMBER(3));
INSERT INTO PROJ VALUES ('P2','CODING');
INSERT INTO PROJ VALUES ('P3','DATA RECOVERY');
INSERT INTO PROJ VALUES ('P1','DATABASE SW');
INSERT INTO DESGRATE VALUES ('ANALYST',800);
INSERT INTO DESGRATE VALUES ('DBA',1000);
INSERT INTO DESGRATE VALUES ('PROGRAMMER',500);
INSERT INTO EMP VALUES ('E1','ANUP','ANALYST');
INSERT INTO EMP VALUES ('E2','ARUP','DBA');
INSERT INTO EMP VALUES ('E3','KAUSHIK','ANALYST');
INSERT INTO EMP VALUES ('E4','AMIT','PROGRAMMER');
INSERT INTO EMP VALUES ('E5','CHANDRA','PROGRAMMER');
INSERT INTO PROJ_DETAIL VALUES ('E1','P2',15);
INSERT INTO PROJ_DETAIL VALUES ('E2','P3',10);
INSERT INTO PROJ_DETAIL VALUES ('E2','P1',40);
INSERT INTO PROJ_DETAIL VALUES ('E2','P2',10);
INSERT INTO PROJ_DETAIL VALUES ('E3','P1',20);
INSERT INTO PROJ_DETAIL VALUES ('E4','P2',40);
INSERT INTO PROJ_DETAIL VALUES ('E5','P1',30);
COMMIT;
```

FIGURE 5.7 SQL script—workout.

```
TOTAL EXPENDITURE ON CODING IS 42000
SQL> /
Enter value for projno: P4
P4 PROJECT NUMBER DOES NOT EXISTS, PLEASE TRY AGAIN
```

W5_8 Write a PL/SQL program that accepts EMPNO and PROJNO and display message as per the sample output shown below.

```
SQL> @ C:\BOOK\CHAPTER5\W5_8
Enter value for empno: E1
Enter value for projno: P2

YES, ANUP WORKED ON CODING PROJECT.

SQL> /
Enter value for empno: E1
```

EMP TABLE

EMPNO	ENAME	DESG
E1	ANUP	ANALYST
E2	ARUP	DBA
E3	KAUSHIK	ANALYST
E4	AMIT	PROGRAMMER
E5	CHANDRA	PROGRAMMER

DESGRATE TABLE

DESG	HRRATE
ANALYST	800
DBA	1000
PROGRAMMER	500

PROJ TABLE

PROJNO	PROJNAME
P2	CODING
P3	DATA RECOVERY
P1	DATABASE SW

PROJ_DETAIL TABLE

EMPNO	PROJNO	HRWORKED
E1	P2	15
E2	P3	10
E2	P1	40
E2	P2	10
E3	P1	20
E4	P2	40
E5	P1	30

FIGURE 5.8 Tables and records—workout.

```
Enter value for projno: P1
NO, ANUP HAS NOT WORKED ON DATABASE SW PROJECT.

SQL> /
Enter value for empno: E6
Enter value for projno: P1
E6 IS NOT PRESENT IN EMP TABLE

SQL> /
Enter value for empno: E1
Enter value for projno: P5
P5 IS NOT PRESENT IN PROJ TABLE
SQL> /
Enter value for empno: E7
Enter value for projno: P6
E7 IS NOT PRESENT IN EMP TABLE
```

W5_9 Write a PL/SQL program that accepts ENAME and display message as per the sample output shown below.

```
SQL> @ C:\BOOK\CHAPTER5\W5_9
```

Enter value for ename: ANUP
ANUP HAS WORKED ON 1 PROJECT(S) FOR A TOTAL OF 15 HOURS

SQL> /
Enter value for ename: ARUP
ARUP HAS WORKED ON 3 PROJECT(S) FOR A TOTAL OF 60 HOURS

SQL> /
Enter value for ename: E6
E6 IS NOT PRESENT IN EMP TABLE

W5_10 Write a PL/SQL program, which accepts PROJNO and deletes rows from PROJ_TABLE based on the value of PROJNO. Sample output is shown below.

SQL> @ C:\BOOK\CHAPTER5\W5_10
Enter value for projno: P1

3 ROWS DELETED FROM PROJ_DETAIL TABLE
INVOKE COMMIT OR ROLLBACK TO MAKE THE CHANGES PERMANENT

SQL> ROLLBACK;

Rollback complete.

SQL> @ C:\BOOK\CHAPTER5\W5_10
Enter value for projno: P6

0 ROWS DELETED FROM PROJ_DETAIL TABLE

W5_11 Will the following PL/SQL program execute successfully? If no, why?

```
BEGIN
   SELECT EMPNO, ENAME, DESG
   FROM EMP
   WHERE EMPNO='E1';
END;
/
```

W5_12 Will the following PL/SQL program execute successfully? If no, why?

```
DECLARE
   VEMPREC EMP%ROWTYPE;
BEGIN
   SELECT *
   INTO VEMPREC
   FROM EMP;
END;
/
```

Oracle Function, Procedure and Package

Learning Objectives

You will learn following key concepts after completion of the chapter:

- ✓ Structure of function and procedure
- ✓ Creation and use of packages
- ✓ Use of IN and OUT parameters in procedures
- ✓ Encapsulating functions and procedures in a package

6.1 INTRODUCTION

Functions, procedures (also known as subprograms) and packages are extensively used and supported in Oracle. Subprograms are suitable for use where a particular segment of code is used again and again. Appropriate usage of subprograms ensures not only less typing but also increases consistency. Packages are used for better management of subprograms specific to an application. For instance, all functions and procedures related to matrix operations may be encapsulated in a single package. In this chapter, functions, procedures and packages are explained using a large number of examples.

6.2 SUBPROGRAMS

Subprograms are named PL/SQL blocks that can accept parameters and return processed results. A subprogram consists of declarative section, an executable section and exceptional handling section. Subprograms are frequently used because of its reusability and ease of writing code in PL/SQL. Two types of subprograms supported by Oracle are procedures and functions. Functions are used to compute a value, whereas procedures are used to perform some action. In this chapter, functions, procedures and packages are discussed in detail. Exceptional handling deals with PL/SQL run-time errors and will be dealt later in this book.

6.3 FUNCTIONS

A function is a subprogram that computes a value. Function essentially returns some value. A function has two parts: function specification and body. The syntax for creating a function is as follows:

```
CREATE [OR REPLACE] FUNCTION <FUNCTION_NAME> [ARGUMENTS]
RETURN DATATYPE IS (VARIABLE DATATYPE)
BEGIN
   (EXECUTABLE STATEMENTS)
[EXCEPTION]
   (EXCEPTION HANDLERS)
END;
```

EX6_1 Write a function that accepts two numbers A and B, sum it and store the computed value in C.

```
CREATE OR REPLACE FUNCTION FSUM(A NUMBER,B NUMBER)
RETURN NUMBER IS C NUMBER;
BEGIN
   C:=A+B;
   RETURN C;
END;
/
```

Execution

```
SQL>  @ C:\BOOK\CHAPTER6\EX6_1.SQL
Function created.
SQL> SELECT FSUM(10,15) FROM DUAL;
FSUM(10,15)
25
SQL> SELECT PNAME,PCOST,FSUM(PCOST,2) NEW_PCOST FROM PROD;
```

PNAME	PCOST	NEW_PCOST
PEN	*20.5*	*22.5*
FLOPPY	*30*	*32*
PENCIL	*5.25*	*7.25*

EX6_2 Write a function that accepts two numbers A and B, subtract the numbers and store the value in C.

```
CREATE OR REPLACE FUNCTION FMINUS(A NUMBER,B NUMBER)
RETURN NUMBER IS C NUMBER;
BEGIN
   C:=A-B;
   RETURN C;
END;
/
```

Execution

```
SQL> @ C:\BOOK\CHAPTER6\EX6_2.SQL
Function created.

SQL> SELECT FSUM(10,2)+FMINUS(20,2) FROM DUAL;
FSUM(10,2)+FMINUS(20,2)
30

SQL> SELECT PNAME,PCOST,FMINUS(PCOST,4) FROM PROD;
PNAME      PCOST      FMINUS(PCOST,4)
PEN        20.5       16.5
FLOPPY     30         26
PENCIL     5.25       1.25
```

EX6_3 Write a function which accepts A and B and divide if B > 0. If B = 0, it returns –1.

```
CREATE OR REPLACE FUNCTION FDIVIDE (A NUMBER,B NUMBER) RETURN NUMBER IS
   C NUMBER;
BEGIN
   IF B<>0 THEN
      C:=A/B;
   ELSE
      C:=-1;
   END IF;
   RETURN C;
END;
/
```

Execution

```
SQL> @ C:\BOOK\CHAPTER6\EX6_3.SQL
Function created.
SQL> SELECT ROUND(FDIVIDE(10,3),2) FROM DUAL;
ROUND(FDIVIDE(10,3),2)
3.33

SQL> SELECT FDIVIDE(10,0) FROM DUAL;
FDIVIDE(10,0)
-1
```

EX6_4 Write a function which accepts two numbers and multiply.

```
CREATE OR REPLACE FUNCTION FMULTIPLY(A NUMBER,B NUMBER)
RETURN NUMBER IS C NUMBER;
BEGIN
   C:=A*B;
   RETURN C;
END;
/
```

Execution

```
SQL> @ C:\BOOK\CHAPTER6\EX6_4.SQL
Function created.

SQL>SELECT PNAME,FMULTIPLY(PCOST,FDIVIDE(NVL(PPROFIT,0),100))
PROFIT_IN_₹ FROM PROD;
PNAME         PROFIT_IN_₹
PEN           4.1
FLOPPY        3.6
PENCIL        0
```

EX6_5 This program demonstrates use of functions in PL/SQL program.

```
SET SERVEROUTPUT ON
SET VERIFY OFF
DECLARE
   A NUMBER := &A;
   B NUMBER := &B;
   N1   NUMBER;
   N2   NUMBER;
   N3   NUMBER;
   N4   NUMBER;
BEGIN
   N1 := FSUM(A,B);
   N2 := FMINUS(A,B);
   N3 := FDIVIDE(A,B);
   N4 := FMULTIPLY(A,B);
   DBMS_OUTPUT.PUT_LINE('SUM='||N1||' MINUS='||N2||'
   DIVIDE='||N3||' MULTIPLY =
   '||N4);
END;
/
```

Execution

```
SQL>  @ C:\BOOK\CHAPTER6\EX6_5.SQL
Enter value for a: 20
Enter value for b: 4
SUM=24 MINUS=16 DIVIDE=5 MULTIPLY=80
```

EX6_6 Write a function to find the maximum PCOST in PROD Table.

```
CREATE OR REPLACE FUNCTION FORA RETURN NUMBER IS VPCOST NUMBER;
BEGIN
  SELECT MAX(PCOST) INTO VPCOST FROM PROD;
  RETURN VPCOST;
END;
/
```

Execution

```
SQL> @ C:\BOOK\\CHAPTER6\EX6_6.SQL
Function created.

SQL> SELECT FORA FROM DUAL;
FORA
30

SQL> SELECT PNAME,FORA FROM PROD WHERE PCOST=FORA;
PNAME         FORA
FLOPPY        30
```

Illustrations

Example EX6_1 to EX6_6

- Function, PL/SQL, etc can be typed using any text editor that saves the text in ASCII. Extension must be .SQL. *Most programs do not run only because the program is not saved properly.* To ensure the file is saved correctly, simply go to command line prompt and type TYPE <PATH_NAME>/FILE_NAME.SQL. For example, C:\>TYPE C:\BOOK\CHAPTER6\EX6_6.SQL should display contents of EX6_6.SQL.
- Functions must be compiled before it is used. In case of error, type SHOW ERROR at SQL prompt to see errors in the function.
- Functions can be executed from SQL prompt using SELECT … FROM … clause. Tables may or may not be used. The only requirement to execute a function properly is to provide correct arguments.
- Functions can be called from PL/SQL program. As function always returns some value, there must be some container to hold that returned value. In EX6_5, N1, N2, N3 and N4 acts as container for FSUM, FMINUS, FDIVIDE and FMULTIPLY, respectively.
- Functions can be written to access columns from table(s). EX6_6 shows how functions can be used in WHERE clause.

6.4 PROCEDURES

A procedure is a subprogram that performs a specific action. The syntax for creating a procedure is as follows:

```
CREATE OR REPLACE PROCEDURE <PROCEDURE NAME> [PARAMETER LIST] IS
(VARIABLE DATA TYPE);
BEGIN
   {EXECUTABLE STATEMENTS}
{EXCEPTION}
   {EXCEPTION HANDLERS}
END;
```

EX6_7 Write a procedure that accepts two numbers, add them and print.

```
SET SERVEROUTPUT ON
CREATE OR REPLACE PROCEDURE PSUM(A NUMBER,B NUMBER)
IS C NUMBER;
BEGIN
   C:=A+B;
   DBMS_OUTPUT.PUT_LINE('SUM OF ' || A || ' & ' || B || ' IS '|| C);
END PSUM;
/
```

Execution

```
SQL> @ C:/BOOK/CHAPTER6/EX6_7.SQL
Procedure created.

SQL> EXECUTE PSUM(10,20)
SUM OF 10 & 20 IS 30
```

6.4.1 IN Parameter

Default parameter is IN parameter. The IN parameter mode is used to pass values to the subprogram when invoked. It acts as a constant and it cannot be assigned a value.

EX6_8 This program demonstrates usage of IN parameter.

```
SET SERVEROUTPUT ON
CREATE OR REPLACE PROCEDURE PMINUS(A IN NUMBER,B IN NUMBER)
IS C NUMBER;
BEGIN
   C:=A-B;
   DBMS_OUTPUT.PUT_LINE(A || ' - ' | B || ' IS ' || C);
END PMINUS;
/
```

Execution

```
SQL> @ C:/BOOK/CHAPTER6/EX6_8.SQL
Procedure created.

SQL> EXECUTE PMINUS(78,45)
78 - 45 IS 33
```

6.4.2 IN OUT Parameter

The IN OUT parameter is used to pass initial values to the subprograms when invoked and it also returns updated values to the caller. An IN OUT parameter acts as an initialized variable and can be assigned to other variables or to itself. Procedures with IN OUT parameter cannot be executed using SQL>EXECUTE <Procedure Name>. It must be called from other PL/SQL program.

EX6_9 This program demonstrates IN OUT parameter.

```
CREATE OR REPLACE PROCEDURE PMULTIPLY(A IN OUT NUMBER,
B IN OUT NUMBER)
IS C NUMBER;
BEGIN
   C:=A*B;
   DBMS_OUTPUT.PUT_LINE(A || ' * ' || B || ' = ' || C);
END PMULTIPLY;
/
```

Execution

```
SQL> @ C:/BOOK/CHAPTER6/EX6_9
Procedure created.

SQL> EXECUTE PMULTIPLY(10,2)
BEGIN PMULTIPLY(10,2); END;
*
ERROR at line 1:
ORA-06550: line 1, column 17:
PLS-00363: expression '10' cannot be used as an assignment target
ORA-06550: line 1, column 20:
PLS-00363: expression '2' cannot be used as an assignment target
ORA-06550: line 1, column 7:
PL/SQL: Statement ignored
```

Illustrations

EXECUTE PMULTIPLY(10,2) leads to error as it contains IN OUT parameter. PCALL_MULT.SQL program calls PMULTIPLY procedure.

EX6_9_CALL This program is used to call PMULTIPLY program.

```
DECLARE
   A NUMBER := &A;
   B NUMBER := &B;
BEGIN
   PMULTIPLY(A,B);
END;
/
```

Execution

```
SQL> @ C:/BOOK/CHAPTER6/EX6_9_CALL
Enter value for a: 10
Enter value for b: 2
10 * 2 = 20
```

6.4.3 OUT Parameter

The OUT parameter is used to return values to the caller of a subprogram. Since the initial value for an OUT parameter is undefined, its value can be assigned to another variable. Procedures with OUT parameter cannot be executed with SQL>EXECUTE <Procedure Name>. It must be called from other PL/SQL program.

EX6_10 Create a procedure and call the procedure.

```
CREATE OR REPLACE PROCEDURE PDIV_OUT(A NUMBER,B NUMBER,
C OUT NUMBER) IS
BEGIN
   IF B<>0 THEN
      C:=A/B;
   ELSE
      C:=-1;
   END IF;
END PDIV_OUT;
/
```

EX6_10_CALL This program calls PDIV_OUT.

```
SET SERVEROUTPUT ON
SET VERIFY OFF
DECLARE
   A NUMBER := &A;
   B NUMBER := &B;
   C NUMBER;
BEGIN
   PDIV_OUT(A,B,C);
   DBMS_OUTPUT.PUT_LINE('DIVIDE='||C);
END;
/
```

Execution

```
SQL> @ C:/BOOK/CHAPTER6/EX6_10
Procedure created.

SQL> @ C:/BOOK/CHAPTER6/EX6_10_CALL
Enter value for a: 12
Enter value for b: 3
DIVIDE=4
```

EX6_11 Write a procedure that will accept two numbers (say A and B). After adding 1 to B, divide A by B and store it in C. Also, write a calling program.

```
CREATE OR REPLACE PROCEDURE PDIV_INOUT(A NUMBER,B IN OUT NUMBER,
C OUT NUMBER) IS
```

```
BEGIN
   B:=B+1;
   C:=A/B;
END PDIV_INOUT;
/
```

EX6_11_CALL This program calls PDIV_INOUT.

```
SET SERVEROUTPUT ON
SET VERIFY OFF
DECLARE
   A NUMBER := &A;
   B NUMBER := &B;
   C NUMBER;
BEGIN
   PDIV_INOUT(A,B,C);
   DBMS_OUTPUT.PUT_LINE('B is now ' || B);
   DBMS_OUTPUT.PUT_LINE('DIVIDE='||C);
END;
/
```

Execution

```
SQL> @ C:/BOOK/CHAPTER6/EX6_11
Procedure created.

SQL> @ C:/BOOK/CHAPTER6/EX6_11_CALL
Enter value for a: 20
Enter value for b: 1
B is now 2
DIVIDE=10
```

EX6_12 This procedure demonstrates usage of Oracle table in procedure.

```
SET SERVEROUTPUT ON
CREATE OR REPLACE PROCEDURE PORA(VCID VARCHAR2) IS
   VCNAME VARCHAR2(10);
   VCITY  VARCHAR2(10);
   VCNT   NUMBER;
BEGIN
   SELECT COUNT(*) INTO VCNT FROM CUST WHERE CID=VCID;
   IF VCNT=0 THEN
      DBMS_OUTPUT.PUT_LINE('No Customer exists with CID='||VCID);
   ELSE
      SELECT CNAME,CCITY INTO VCNAME,VCITY FROM CUST WHERE
      CID=VCID;
      DBMS_OUTPUT.PUT_LINE(VCID || ' - ' || VCNAME || ' lives in
      ' || VCITY);
   END IF;
END PORA;
/
```

Execution

```
SQL> @ C:\BOOK\CHAPTER6\EX6_12.SQL
Procedure created.

SQL> EXECUTE PORA('C1')
C1 - PRADIP lives in MYSORE

SQL> EXECUTE PORA('C9')
No Customer exists with CID=C9
```

Illustrations

EX6_10 to EX6_12

- Procedure can be typed using any text editor that saves the text in ASCII. Extension must be .SQL. Always ensure that the program is saved with .SQL extension. To confirm, simply type TYPE <PATH_NAME>/FILE_NAME.SQL. It should display contents of the procedure. For example, C:\>TYPE C:\BOOK\CHAPTER6\EX6_10.SQL should display contents of EX6_10.SQL.
- Procedures must be compiled before it is used. In case of error, type SHOW ERROR at SQL prompt to see errors in the procedure.
- Procedures can be executed from SQL prompt using EXECUTE <Procedure Name> where only IN parameters are used. Correct argument values must be supplied along with the procedure. The same procedure can also be called from any PL/SQL program.
- Procedures where OUT or IN OUT parameter are used, a separate PL/SQL is required to call the procedure. Tables may or may not be used. In both cases, correct arguments of procedure are required.

6.5 PACKAGES

Packages are created to club relevant objects such as function, procedures and cursors in one place. A package is a database object which encapsulates functions, procedures, cursors, exceptions, variables and constants. It consists of two parts: package specification and package body. A brief introduction and examples of cursors were given in the previous chapter. Cursors will be discussed in detail in the following chapters.

6.5.1 Package Specification

In the package specification, functions, procedures and cursors are specified.

```
CREATE OR REPLACE PACKAGE <PACKAGE_NAME> IS <DECLARATIONS>
BEGIN
    (EXECUTABLE STATEMENTS)
END (PACKAGE_NAME);
```

6.5.2 Package Body

In package body, detailed program corresponding to function, procedure, cursors, etc. is written.

CREATE OR REPLACE PACKAGE BODY <PACKAGE_NAME> IS <DECLARATIONS>
BEGIN
(EXECUTABLE STATEMENTS)
END (BODY_NAME);

Example

In this example, the package is encapsulated with 2 procedures and 4 functions. Name of package, functions and procedures are as under.

Package Name	Description
PACKSPN.SQL	Package specification file name
PACKBODY.SQL	Package body file name
CALCULATE	Package name

Function Name	Description
EX6_1.SQL	Accepts two numbers and returns sum
EX6_2.SQL	Accepts two numbers and returns difference
EX6_4.SQL	Accepts two numbers and returns multiplied value
EX6_3.SQL	Accepts two numbers and returns divided value

Procedure Name	Description
EX6_7.SQL	Accepts two numbers and displays sum
EX6_8.SQL	Accepts two numbers and displays difference

Package specification and package body needs to be compiled before it can be used.

6.5.3 Creating Package

Step 1

Individually test all the functions and procedures to be used in the package. Functions and procedures used in this example are EX6_1 to EX6_4, EX6_7 and EX6_8. CREATE OR REPLACE is required to be deleted when it is encapsulated in package. Compile and test all functions and procedures. It is worthwhile to mention that content of functions and procedures are embedded in a package. Package is not dependent on individual functions or procedures. It is a good practice to first write and test all functions and procedures before embedding in package. After successful execution of all the functions and procedures, simply copy and paste relevant portion in the package.

Functions and procedures can be deleted and dropped at any point of time. This will not create any problem as package contains details of functions and procedures along with its code in package specification and package body, respectively.

Step 2

Create PACKSPN.SQL. Note the name of package, it is CALCULATE, not PACKSPN. In this instead of typing again, simply copy the first line from the relevant functions and procedures. Do not paste CREATE OR REPLACE. Complete content of PACKSPN.SQL is given below.

PACKSPN.SQL

```
CREATE OR REPLACE PACKAGE CALCULATE AS
FUNCTION FSUM(A NUMBER,B NUMBER) RETURN NUMBER;
FUNCTION FMINUS(A NUMBER,B NUMBER) RETURN NUMBER;
FUNCTION FMULTIPLY(A NUMBER,B NUMBER) RETURN NUMBER;
FUNCTION FDIVIDE(A NUMBER,B NUMBER) RETURN NUMBER;
PROCEDURE PSUM(A NUMBER,B NUMBER);
PROCEDURE PMINUS(A NUMBER,B NUMBER);
END CALCULATE;
/
```

Step 3

Create PACKBODY.SQL. Note that the same name CALCULATE (defined in PACKSPN.SQL) is used here also. In this also copy the text from the relevant functions and procedures as mentioned in Step 1. Do not paste CREATE OR REPLACE. Complete content of PACKBODY.SQL is given below.

PACKBODY.SQL

```
SET SERVEROUTPUT ON
CREATE OR REPLACE PACKAGE BODY CALCULATE AS
FUNCTION FSUM(A NUMBER,B NUMBER) RETURN NUMBER IS
   C NUMBER;
BEGIN
   C:=A+B;
   RETURN C;
END;

FUNCTION FMINUS(A NUMBER,B NUMBER) RETURN NUMBER IS
   C NUMBER;
BEGIN
   C:=A-B;
   RETURN C;
END;

FUNCTION FMULTIPLY(A NUMBER,B NUMBER) RETURN NUMBER IS
   C NUMBER;
BEGIN
   C:=A*B;
   RETURN C;
END;

FUNCTION FDIVIDE(A NUMBER,B NUMBER) RETURN NUMBER IS
   C NUMBER;
BEGIN
   IF B<>0 THEN
      C:=A/B;
```

```
   ELSE
      C:=-1;
   END IF;
   RETURN C;
END;
PROCEDURE PSUM(A NUMBER,B NUMBER) IS
   C NUMBER;
BEGIN
   C:=A+B;
   DBMS_OUTPUT.PUT_LINE('SUM OF ' || A || ' & ' || B || ' IS ' ||
   C);
END PSUM;

PROCEDURE PMINUS(A IN NUMBER,B IN NUMBER) IS
   C NUMBER;
BEGIN
   C:=A-B;
   DBMS_OUTPUT.PUT_LINE(A || ' - ' || B || ' IS ' || C);
END PMINUS;
END CALCULATE;
/
```

Step 4

After creation of PACKSPN.SQL and PACKBODY.SQL, compile both from SQL prompt.

```
SQL> @ C:\BOOK\CHAPTER6\PACKSPN;
Package created.
SQL> @ C:\BOOK\CHAPTER6\PACKBODY;
Package body created.
```

Step 5

Once package-related files are compiled, functions and procedures encapsulated can be called.

```
SQL> SELECT CALCULATE.FSUM(1,2) FROM DUAL;
CALCULATE.FSUM(1,2)
3
SQL> SELECT CALCULATE.FMINUS(1,2) FROM DUAL;
CALCULATE.FMINUS(1,2)
 -1
SQL> SELECT CALCULATE.FMULTIPLY(2,4) FROM DUAL;
CALCULATE.FMULTIPLY(2,4)
8

SQL> SELECT CALCULATE.FDIVIDE(10,4) FROM DUAL;
CALCULATE.FDIVIDE(10,4)
2.5
```

```
SQL> EXECUTE CALCULATE.PSUM(10,20)
SUM OF 10 & 20 IS 30
SQL> EXECUTE CALCULATE.PMINUS(20,16)
20 - 16 IS 4
```

6.6 SUMMARY

In this chapter, we have learnt functions, procedures and packages. These are essentially required for efficient development of application software. Combination of IN and OUT parameters is of importance and the same is discussed at length. A large number of short type questions and workouts are provided in this chapter, and the students are advised to attempt all of them.

SHORT/OBJECTIVE TYPE QUESTIONS

1. What are the major advantages of a subprogram?
2. What are the different types of subprograms in PL/SQL?
3. Can we use %TYPE and %ROWTYPE within a procedure?
4. Is it possible to store functions in Oracle Forms?
5. What are the various advantages of packages?
6. Which command is used to drop the package specification and the package body?
7. Which command is used to drop the package body without dropping the package specification?
8. When should you use a procedure?
9. Is it possible to declare and define a procedure inside a PL/SQL program?
10. What are the uses of Oracle supplied packages?
11. What do you understand by signature of a procedure?
12. Where can you store a package?
13. What is the primary difference between procedure and function?
14. Can procedure be stored in a database?
15. What does the REPLACE option specifies in the procedure definition?
16. What do you understand by formal parameters in a subprogram specification?
17. What do you understand by actual parameters in a subprogram specification?
18. What are the various parameter modes in a procedure specification?
19. Is it possible to assign default value to IN OUT parameter in a procedure?
20. Is it possible to assign default value to IN parameter in a procedure?
21. What are the different ways to pass parameters to a procedure?

22. When a package is required to be recompiled?
23. Is it possible to overload stand-alone program?
24. Is it possible to assign IN parameter within a procedure?
25. Is it possible to use BOOLEAN data type in functions that are called from SQL statements?
26. Can you make a function part of the If Then Else block?
27. Is it possible to invoke a stored subprogram from the Oracle Forms?
28. Which error is displayed if the function is executed when it is in the invalid state?
29. Is it possible to write multiple RETURN statements within a function?
30. What will happen to the dependent objects when a package body is modified?
31. Is it possible to use a role to define privileges to access database objects of another schema in methods?
32. Where the compilation error of a subprogram is stored?
33. Where the text of a procedure or function specification is stored?
34. Is it possible to call a complete package?
35. Can you write a package specification without writing the package body?
36. Is it possible to implement concept of overloading in a package?
37. Does PL/SQL allows overloading subprogram names?
38. How can you debug subprograms?
39. How can you customize error messages within a procedure?
40. Is it possible to call functions as stand-alone programs like procedures?

WORKOUT SECTION

W6_1 Write a function which will accept a four-digit year and will print whether the year is leap year or not.

SQL> @ C:/BOOK/CHAPTER6/W6_1.SQL

Function created.

SQL> SELECT FLEAP(2004) FROM DUAL;

FLEAP(2004)
2004 IS A LEAP YEAR

SQL> SELECT FLEAP(2003) FROM DUAL;

FLEAP(2003)
2003 IS NOT A LEAP YEAR

W6_2 Write a function FAREA to calculate area of square or area of circle. It accepts a number and a character parameter. Character parameter is either 'C' to compute area of circle or 'S' to compute area of square.

SQL> @ C:/BOOK/CHAPTER6/W6_2.SQL

Function created.

SQL> SELECT FAREA(10,'C') FROM DUAL;

FAREA(10,'C')
AREA OF CIRCLE IS 314

SQL> SELECT FAREA(10,'S') FROM DUAL;

FAREA(10,'S')
AREA OF SQUARE IS 100

W6_3 Write a function which will accept CID and return CNAME and CCITY in the following format. For invalid CID, display appropriate message as shown below.

SQL> SELECT DISTINCT FQ23('C1') FROM CUST;
FQ23('C1')
C1 - PRADIP LIVES IN MYSORE

SQL> SELECT DISTINCT FQ23('C10') FROM CUST;

FQ23('C10')
C10 - INVALID CUSTOMER ID

W6_4 Write a procedure, which accepts two numbers and prints its sum, difference, multiplication and division.

SQL> EXECUTE PSUM(20,10)

SUM OF 20 & 10 IS 30
DIFF OF 20 & 10 IS 10
MULT OF 20 & 10 IS 200
DIV OF 20 & 10 IS 2

W6_5 Write a procedure as mentioned in W6_4 using OUT parameter to print sum, difference, multiplication and division of two numbers. Write the calling procedure also.

SQL> @ C:/BOOK/CHAPTER6/W6_5

Procedure created.

SQL> @ C:/BOOK/CHAPTER6/W6_5_CALL
Enter value for a: 30
Enter value for b: 20

SUM OF 30 & 20 IS 50
DIFF OF 30 & 20 IS 10
MULT OF 30 & 20 IS 600
DIV OF 30 & 20 IS 1.5

W6_6 Write a procedure which accepts SALEDT of SALE_DETAIL table and prints total sale on that date.

SQL> EXECUTE PQ26('14-JUL-2013')

TOTAL SALE ON 14-JUL-13 IS Rs87.75

SQL> EXECUTE PQ26('24-JUL-2013')

NO SALE ON 24-JUL-13

All workouts from W6_7 to W6_9 are based on EMP, DESGRATE, PROJ and PROJ_DETAIL tables. All the tables along with their rows are shown in Figure 5.8.

W6_7 Write a procedure that will accept EMPNO and PROJNO and will display whether the employee has worked in the given project. Also, write a program to call the procedure. Few sample outputs are shown below.

SQL> @ C:\BOOK\CHAPTER6\W6_7

Procedure created.

SQL> @ C:\BOOK\CHAPTER6\W6_7_CALL
Enter value for v1: E1
Enter value for v2: P1
NO, ANUP HAS NOT WORKED ON DATABASE SW PROJECT.
PL/SQL procedure successfully completed.

SQL> @ C:\BOOK\CHAPTER6\W6_7_CALL

Enter value for v1: *E4*
Enter value for v2: *P2*

YES, AMIT WORKED ON CODING PROJECT.
PL/SQL procedure successfully completed.

SQL> @ C:\BOOK\CHAPTER6\W6_7_CALL

Enter value for v1: E6
Enter value for v2: P1

E6 IS NOT PRESENT IN EMP TABLE
PL/SQL procedure successfully completed.

SQL> @ C:\BOOK\CHAPTER6\W6_7_CALL

Enter value for v1: *E8*
Enter value for v2: *P9*
E8 IS NOT PRESENT IN EMP TABLE P9 IS NOT PRESENT IN PROJ TABLE
PL/SQL procedure successfully completed.

W6_8 Write a function, which will accept ENAME and return whether the employee was involved to execute projects or not. Sample outputs are shown below.

SQL> @ C:\BOOK\CHAPTER6\W6_8

Function created.

SQL> SELECT DISP_INFO('ARUP') FROM DUAL;

DISP_INFO('ARUP')
ARUP HAS WORKED ON 3 PROJECT(S) FOR A TOTAL OF 60 HOURS

SQL> SELECT DISP_INFO('RAMESH') FROM DUAL;

DISP_INFO('RAMESH')
RAMESH IS NOT PRESENT IN EMP TABLE

W6_9 Create a package to include FIND_EMPPRJ procedure and DISP_INFO function created in W6_7 and W6_8, respectively. Drop the procedure and function before compiling specification and body of procedure. Also write a program to call the procedure embedded in the package. Sample output is shown below.

SQL> DROP PROCEDURE FIND_EMPPRJ;

Procedure dropped.

SQL> DROP FUNCTION DISP_INFO;

Function dropped.

SQL> @ C:\BOOK\CHAPTER6\PACKSPN_PROJECT.SQL

Package created.

SQL> @ C:\BOOK\CHAPTER6\PACKBODY_PROJECT.SQL

Package body created.

SQL> @ C:\BOOK\CHAPTER6\CALL_PACK_PROJECT
Enter value for v1: E1
Enter value for v2: P2

YES, ANUP WORKED ON CODING PROJECT.
PL/SQL procedure successfully completed.

SQL> @ C:\BOOK\CHAPTER6\CALL_PACK_PROJECT
Enter value for v1: *E7*

Enter value for v2: *P4*
E7 IS NOT PRESENT IN EMP TABLE P4 IS NOT PRESENT IN PROJ TABLE
PL/SQL procedure successfully completed.

SQL> SELECT PACK_PROJECT.DISP_INFO('ANUP') FROM DUAL;

PACK PROJECT.DISP INFO('ANUP')
ANUP HAS WORKED ON 1 PROJECT(S) FOR A TOTAL OF 15 HOURS

SQL> SELECT PACK_PROJECT.DISP_INFO('PRADEEP') FROM DUAL;

PACK PROJECT.DISP INFO('PRADEEP')
PRADEEP IS NOT PRESENT IN EMP TABLE

7 Oracle Exception Handler and Database Triggers

Learning Objectives

You will learn following key concepts after completion of the chapter:

- ✓ Predefined and user-defined exceptions
- ✓ Use of database triggers in appropriate places
- ✓ Use of PRAGMA in PL/SQL code
- ✓ Concepts related to mutating table error

7.1 INTRODUCTION

Exception Handler makes the PL/SQL code foolproof as it deals with anticipated and unanticipated problems. It is an optional PL/SQL segment and is useful to trap run-time errors. Oracle Triggers are stored procedure, which is fired when insert, update or delete statements are used. Triggers make the Oracle tables robust as far as Data Manipulation Language is concerned. In this chapter, Exception Handler and Database Triggers are discussed using a large number of examples and workouts.

7.2 EXCEPTION HANDLER

Exceptions and exception handler deal with run-time errors in PL/SQL programs. It is an aid to develop program efficiently. When an exception occurs, the control is passed to the exception handler for error handling. If exception is raised and there is no exception handler, the PL/SQL block terminates with failure and the exception is propagated to the calling environment. Good PL/SQL program traps the anticipated error using PL/SQL statements and only unanticipated errors are diverted to exception handler. Exceptions are classified into Predefined Exception and User-Defined Exception which we will discuss in following sections.

EXCEPTION HANDLER is present inside BEGIN … END block of PL/SQL program as shown below.

```
DECLARE
   Variables, Cursor and other Declarations
BEGIN
   Executables comprising of SQL and Procedural statements
EXCEPTION
   Statements to perform action in case of errors
END;
```

7.3 PREDEFINED EXCEPTION

Predefined Exception is defined as a part of Oracle Database Server. Frequently used Predefined Exception along with its error number and purpose is shown in Table 7.1.

TABLE 7.1 Predefined Exceptions

Predefined exception	Error no.	Purpose
NO_DATA_FOUND	0RA-01403	This exception is raised when SELECT ... INTO statement returns no rows
TOO_MANY_ROWS	0RA-01422	This exception is raised when SELECT ... INTO statement returns more than one row
ZERO_DIVIDE	0RA-01476	This exception is raised when zero divides a number
DUP_VAL_ON_INDEX	0RA-00001	This exception is raised when duplicate values in a database that is constraint by unique index is inserted
INVALID_NUMBER	ORA-01722	This exception is raised when conversion of character string to a number fails because the character string does not represent a valid number
INVALID_CURSOR	0RA-01001	This exception is raised when an illegal cursor operation is performed. For example, if a cursor is attempted to close that is not opened at all
CURSOR_ALREADY_OPEN	0RA-06511	This exception occurs if an already opened cursor is attempted to open. A cursor must be closed before it is reopened
LOGIN_DENIED	0RA-01017	This exception is raised on trying to log on to Oracle with an invalid username or password
PROGRAM_ERROR	0RA-06501	This exception is raised when PL/SQL has an internal problem
STORAGE_ERROR	0RA-06500	PL/SQL runs out of memory
TIMEOUT_ON_RESOURCE	0RA-00051	A timeout occurs while Oracle is waiting for a resource
VALUE_ERROR	0RA-06502	This exception occurs in case of arithmetic conversion, truncation or size constraint restriction

The best way to appreciate use of exception handler is to see it working in the form of PL/SQL program. We will discuss several examples to demonstrate how exception handler should be used. All the examples are based on PROD and SALE_DETAIL tables as mentioned.

PROD Table

PID	PNAME	PCOST	PPROFIT
P3	PEN	20.5	20
P2	FLOPPY	30	12
P1	PENCIL	5.25	

SALE_DETAIL Table

CID	PID	SALE	SALEDT
C1	P3	2	14-JUL-13
C3	P2	10	15-JUL-13
C2	P3	1	14-JUL-13
C1	P1	5	14-JUL-13
C1	P3	3	20-AUG-13
C4	P3	2	14-NOV-13
C5	P2	2	18-SEP-13

EX7_1 This example demonstrates default error handling by Oracle where exception handling is not an explicit.

```
—PL/SQL WITHOUT EXCEPTION HANDLING
SET SERVEROUTPUT ON
SET VERIFY OFF
SET ECHO OFF
DECLARE
   VCID      SALE_DETAIL.CID%TYPE:=UPPER('&VCID');
   VSALEDT   SALE_DETAIL.SALEDT%TYPE;
BEGIN
   SELECT SALEDT INTO VSALEDT FROM SALE_DETAIL WHERE CID=VCID;
   DBMS_OUTPUT.PUT_LINE(VCID || ' PURCHASED ON ' || VSALEDT);
END;
/
```

Execution

```
SQL> @ C:\BOOK\CHAPTER7\EX7_1
Enter value for vcid: C1
DECLARE
*
ERROR at line 1:
ORA-01422: exact fetch returns more than requested number of rows
ORA-06512: at line 5

SQL> /
Enter value for vcid: C2
C2 PURCHASED ON 14-JUL-13
```

Illustration

This PL/SQL code displays sale details of a customer based on the customer identification number. It works fine if one record is retrieved. In other cases it generates error. In this PL/SQL program exception handler is not used.

EX7_2 This example demonstrates use of anticipated exceptions.

```
— HANDLING EXCEPTION - NO_DATA_FOUND & TOO_MANY_ROWS
SET SERVEROUTPUT ON
SET VERIFY OFF
SET ECHO OFF
DECLARE
   VCID      SALE_DETAIL.CID%TYPE:=UPPER('&VCID');
   VSALEDT  SALE_DETAIL.SALEDT%TYPE;
BEGIN
   SELECT SALEDT INTO VSALEDT FROM SALE_DETAIL
   WHERE CID=VCID;
   DBMS_OUTPUT.PUT_LINE(VCID || ' PURCHASED ON ' || VSALEDT);

EXCEPTION
   WHEN NO_DATA_FOUND THEN
      RAISE_APPLICATION_ERROR(-20001, 'NO DATA FOUND');
   WHEN TOO_MANY_ROWS THEN
      RAISE_APPLICATION_ERROR(-20002, 'MORE THAN ONE ROW FOUND');
END;
/
```

Execution

```
SQL> @ C:\BOOK\CHAPTER7\EX7_2
Enter value for vcid: C1
DECLARE
*
ERROR at line 1:
ORA-20002: MORE THAN ONE ROW FOUND
ORA-06512: at line 12

SQL> /
Enter value for vcid: C2
C2 PURCHASED ON 14-JUL-13

SQL> /
Enter value for vcid: C9
DECLARE
*
ERROR at line 1:
ORA-20001: NO DATA FOUND
ORA-06512: at line 10
```

Illustration

This PL/SQL program is similar to EX7_1 except that in this program exception handler is used. This program works if one record is retrieved. In other cases, error will be trapped and user-defined message is displayed. Program is terminated after displaying the error message.

EX7_3 This example is a refined version of EX7_2, where COUNT function is intelligently used to avoid possible exceptions.

```
– HANDLING ERROR USING COUNT(*) WITHOUT USING EXCEPTION HANDLER
SET SERVEROUTPUT ON
SET VERIFY OFF
SET ECHO OFF
DECLARE
   VCID      SALE_DETAIL.CID%TYPE:=UPPER('&VCID');
   VSALEDT   SALE_DETAIL.SALEDT%TYPE;
   VCNT      NUMBER(2);
BEGIN
   SELECT COUNT(*) INTO VCNT FROM SALE_DETAIL
   WHERE CID=VCID;
   IF VCNT=1 THEN
      SELECT SALEDT INTO VSALEDT FROM SALE_DETAIL
      WHERE CID=VCID;
DBMS_OUTPUT.PUT_LINE(VCID || ' PURCHASED ON ' || VSALEDT);
   ELSIF VCNT=0 THEN
      DBMS_OUTPUT.PUT_LINE('NO DATA FOUND');
      DBMS_OUTPUT.PUT_LINE('Further processing cannot be done
      - Invalid CID is entered');
      DBMS_OUTPUT.PUT_LINE('Valid CID are C2, C3, C4 and C5');
   ELSIF VCNT>1 THEN
      DBMS_OUTPUT.PUT_LINE('MORE THAN ONE RECORD RETRIEVED');
      DBMS_OUTPUT.PUT_LINE('Further processing cannot be done');
   END IF;
END;
/
```

Execution

```
SQL> @ C:\BOOK\CHAPTER7\EX7_3
Enter value for vcid: C1
MORE THAN ONE RECORD RETRIEVED

Further processing cannot be done

SQL> /
Enter value for vcid: C2
C2 PURCHASED ON 14-JUL-13

SQL> /
Enter value for vcid: C9
NO DATA FOUND
```

```
Further processing cannot be done - Invalid CID is entered
Valid CID are C2, C3, C4 and C5
```

Illustration

This PL/SQL program is also similar to EX7_1 except that in this PL/SQL program, exception handler is not used. This program works in all cases. Expected error like retrieval of more than one record or no record is trapped using COUNT group function. Program can continue even after the occurrence of error. Minutely observe the difference among EX7_1, EX7_2 and EX7_3.

7.4 USER-DEFINED EXCEPTIONS

In the previous section, we have seen use of Oracle predefined exceptions through numerous examples. One important point that emerged in the previous section was to ensure that anticipated errors must be trapped using common PL/SQL code. This is not only effective in terms of execution but also helpful to avoid embarrassment caused due to the sudden exit of the program. Apart from Oracle Predefined Exceptions, programmers can explicitly define exceptions as per requirement.

User-defined exception(s) must be explicitly declared in the Declaration Section. It should also be raised in the Execution Section and finally handled by referencing its name in the Exception Section.

EX7_4 This example demonstrates User-defined Exceptions.

```
– USER DEFINED EXCEPTION
SET SERVEROUTPUT ON
SET VERIFY OFF
SET ECHO OFF
DECLARE
   VPPROFIT PROD.PPROFIT%TYPE;
   VPNAME   PROD.PNAME%TYPE:=UPPER('&PNAME');
   ZERO_PROFIT EXCEPTION;

BEGIN
   SELECT NVL(PPROFIT,0) INTO VPPROFIT FROM PROD WHERE PNAME=VPNAME;
   IF VPPROFIT=0 THEN
      RAISE ZERO_PROFIT;
   ELSE
      DBMS_OUTPUT.PUT_LINE('PROFIT ON ' || VPNAME || ' IS ' ||
      VPPROFIT ||'%');
   END IF;
EXCEPTION
   WHEN NO_DATA_FOUND THEN
      RAISE_APPLICATION_ERROR(-20001,'NO DATA FOUND');
   WHEN ZERO_PROFIT THEN
      DBMS_OUTPUT.PUT_LINE('ZERO COST EXCEPTION RAISED');
END;
/
```

Execution

```
SQL> @ C:\BOOK\CHAPTER7\EX7_4
Enter value for pname: PEN
PROFIT ON PEN IS 20%

SQL> /
Enter value for pname: PENCIL
ZERO COST EXCEPTION RAISED
```

Illustration

This program accepts PNAME and PPROFIT is extracted from table corresponding to the product. In case PPROFIT is 0, user-defined exception are invoked.

In the next example, before proceeding further ensure to execute the following script:

```
DROP TABLE SALE_DETAIL;

CREATE TABLE SALE_DETAIL
(CID VARCHAR2(6),
PID VARCHAR2(6),
SALE NUMBER(3),
SALEDT DATE,
CONSTRAINT SALE_DETAIL_PK PRIMARY KEY (CID,PID,SALEDT));

INSERT INTO SALE_DETAIL VALUES ('C1','P3',2,'14-JUL-2013');
INSERT INTO SALE_DETAIL VALUES ('C3','P2',10,'15-JUL-2013');
INSERT INTO SALE_DETAIL VALUES ('C2','P3',1,'14-JUL-2013');
INSERT INTO SALE_DETAIL VALUES ('C1','P1',5,'14-JUL-2013');
INSERT INTO SALE_DETAIL VALUES ('C1','P3',3,'20-AUG-2013');
INSERT INTO SALE_DETAIL VALUES ('C4','P3',2,'14-NOV-2013');
INSERT INTO SALE_DETAIL VALUES ('C5','P2',2,'18-SEP-2013');
COMMIT;
```

EX7_5 In this example User-defined Exception is defined.

```
SET SERVEROUTPUT ON
SET VERIFY OFF
SET ECHO OFF
DECLARE
   LARGE_QTY EXCEPTION;
   CURSOR ITEM_QTY IS
   SELECT PID, SUM(SALE) AS QTY FROM SALE_DETAIL GROUP BY PID;
   MSG VARCHAR2(100);
   VPID SALE_DETAIL.PID%TYPE;
   VQTY NUMBER(3);
   QTY_LIMIT NUMBER(3) := &QTY_LIMIT;
```

```
BEGIN
   OPEN ITEM_QTY;
   LOOP
      FETCH ITEM_QTY INTO VPID,VQTY;
      IF VQTY >= QTY_LIMIT THEN
         RAISE LARGE_QTY;
      ELSE
         MSG := 'FROM LOOP SECTION - THE NUMBER OF QUANTITY OF '
         || VPID || ' IS ' || VQTY || '. SPECIAL DISCOUNTS NOT
         ALLOWED';
      END IF;
      DBMS_OUTPUT.PUT_LINE (MSG);
      EXIT WHEN ITEM_QTY%NOTFOUND;
   END LOOP;

EXCEPTION
   WHEN LARGE_QTY THEN
   MSG := 'FROM EXCETION SECTION - THE NUMBER OF QUANTITY OF ' ||
   VPID || ' IS ' || VQTY || '. DISCOUNTS ALLOWED. EXECUTION TERMINATED.';
   DBMS_OUTPUT.PUT_LINE (MSG);
END;
/
```

Execution

```
SQL> @ C:\BOOK\CHAPTER7\EX7_5
Enter value for qty_limit: 5
FROM EXCETION SECTION - THE NUMBER OF QUANTITY OF P1 IS 5.
DISCOUNTS ALLOWED. EXECUTION TERMINATED.

SQL>
Enter value for qty_limit: 10
FROM LOOP SECTION - THE NUMBER OF QUANTITY OF P1 IS 5.
SPECIAL DISCOUNTS NOT ALLOWED
FROM EXCETION SECTION - THE NUMBER OF QUANTITY OF P2 IS 12.
DISCOUNTS ALLOWED. EXECUTION TERMINATED.

SQL> /
Enter value for qty_limit: 20
FROM LOOP SECTION - THE NUMBER OF QUANTITY OF P1 IS 5.
SPECIAL DISCOUNTS NOT ALLOWED
FROM LOOP SECTION - THE NUMBER OF QUANTITY OF P2 IS 12.
SPECIAL DISCOUNTS NOT ALLOWED
FROM LOOP SECTION - THE NUMBER OF QUANTITY OF P3 IS 8.
SPECIAL DISCOUNTS NOT ALLOWED
FROM LOOP SECTION - THE NUMBER OF QUANTITY OF P3 IS 8.
SPECIAL DISCOUNTS NOT ALLOWED
```

Illustration

In the example, note the declaration of user-defined exception LARGE_QTY. Inside the loop, whenever VQTY >= QTY_LIMIT, control is passed to the EXCEPTION Section and the program terminates after displaying the message. Observe the three inputs and the corresponding outputs for QTY_LIMIT 5, 10 and 20.

7.5 PRAGMA AND OTHERS CLAUSE

Any unanticipated exceptions is usually trapped using PRAGMA EXCEPTION_INIT or OTHERS clause. OTHERS clause is the last exception handler and it traps all exceptions not already trapped. PRAGMA is used where tables are linked by column(s) using primary key and foreign key. Its syntax is PRAGMA EXCEPTION_INIT (exception, error number). Syntax to use PRAGMA is shown as follows:

```
DECLARE
   Exception_Name Exception;
   PRAGMA
   Exception_Init (Exception_Name, Err_Code);
BEGIN
Execution Section
EXCEPTION
  When Exception_Name then handle the Exception
END;
```

EX7_6 This example demonstrates use of OTHERS exception.

```
– EXCEPTION HANDLER TO SUPPRESS ERROR MESSAGES.
– In this program intentionally VCNT=0 is not handled to show the effect
of OTHERS EXCEPTION
SET SERVEROUTPUT ON
SET VERIFY OFF
SET ECHO OFF
DECLARE
   VCID  SALE_DETAIL.CID%TYPE:=UPPER('&VCID');
   VSALEDT  SALE_DETAIL.SALEDT%TYPE;
   VCNT  NUMBER(2);
BEGIN
   SELECT COUNT(*) INTO VCNT FROM SALE_DETAIL WHERE CID=VCID;
   IF VCNT=1 THEN
      SELECT SALEDT INTO VSALEDT FROM SALE DETAIL WHERE
   CID=VCID;
      DBMS_OUTPUT.PUT_LINE(VCID || ' PURCHASED ON ' || VSALEDT);
```

```
   ELSIF VCNT>1 THEN
      DBMS_OUTPUT.PUT_LINE('MORE THAN ONE ROW FOUND');
   END IF;
EXCEPTION
   WHEN OTHERS THEN
      DBMS_OUTPUT.PUT_LINE('');
END;
/
```

Execution

```
SQL> @ C:\BOOK\CHAPTER7\EX7_6
Enter value for vcid: C1
MORE THAN ONE ROW FOUND

SQL> /
Enter value for vcid: C2
C2 PURCHASED ON 14-JUL-13

SQL> /
Enter value for vcid: C9
PL/SQL procedure successfully completed.
```

Illustration

In this PL/SQL program, exception handler is used to suppress messages in cases where unexpected errors occur. This program works in all cases. Expected error such as retrieval of more than one record or no record is trapped using COUNT group function. This example is an effective way of writing PL/SQL program as it traps expected error using COUNT and it also caters for unexpected errors using the exception handler. Minutely observe the difference between EX7_3 and EX7_6.

EX7_7 This example demonstrates use of PRAGMA in PL/SQL program. Execute the following script before typing and executing the program. Note the REFERENCES statement in CREATE TABLE SALE_DETAIL.

```
DROP TABLE SALE_DETAIL;

CREATE TABLE SALE_DETAIL
(CID VARCHAR2(6) REFERENCES CUST(CID),
PID VARCHAR2(6) REFERENCES PROD(PID),
SALE NUMBER(3),
SALEDT DATE,
CONSTRAINT SALE_DETAIL_PK PRIMARY KEY (CID,PID,SALEDT));

INSERT INTO SALE_DETAIL VALUES ('C1','P3',2,'14-JUL-2013');
INSERT INTO SALE_DETAIL VALUES ('C3','P2',10,'15-JUL-2013');
INSERT INTO SALE_DETAIL VALUES ('C2','P3',1,'14-JUL-2013');
INSERT INTO SALE_DETAIL VALUES ('C1','P1',5,'14-JUL-2013');
```

```
INSERT INTO SALE_DETAIL VALUES ('C1','P3',3,'20-AUG-2013');
INSERT INTO SALE_DETAIL VALUES ('C4','P3',2,'14-NOV-2013');
INSERT INTO SALE_DETAIL VALUES ('C5','P2',2,'18-SEP-2013');
COMMIT;

SET SERVEROUTPUT ON
DECLARE
   CHILD_RECORD_EXCEPTION EXCEPTION;
   PRAGMA
   EXCEPTION_INIT (CHILD_RECORD_EXCEPTION, -2292);
BEGIN
   DELETE FROM PROD WHERE PID= 'P3';
EXCEPTION
   WHEN CHILD_RECORD_EXCEPTION THEN DBMS_OUTPUT.PUT_LINE('CHILD
   RECORDS ARE PRESENT FOR PID = P3');
END;
/
```

Execution

```
SQL> @ C:\BOOK\CHAPTER7\EX7_7
CHILD RECORDS ARE PRESENT FOR PID = P3
```

Illustration

In this example, observe the declaration of the exception CHILD_RECORD_EXCEPTION. In the next line, PRAGMA is used to assign the Oracle default exception number 2292 to CHILD_RECORD_EXCEPTION using EXCEPTION_INIT. This is done to display user-defined message instead of handling directly through Oracle .

7.6 DATABASE TRIGGER

Oracle database trigger is a stored procedure that is fired when a DML (Insert, Delete or Update) statement is issued against an associated table. Execution of trigger is irrespective of logged user and application. Trigger is mainly used to enforce checks, security and backing up of data. Triggers should be used with care and it must not be used to duplicate or replace the built-in functionality of Oracle Server. An excessive use of triggers may lead to problems such as complex interdependencies, recursive situation and cascading effects.

Trigger comprises of trigger statement, trigger restriction and trigger body. The trigger statement specifies the DML statement related to a table and it fires the trigger body comprising of PL/SQL statement. Restriction on a trigger can be achieved in trigger statement using WHEN clause. Triggers are categorised into three types:

- **BEFORE** INSERT / UPDATE / DELETE **FOR EACH ROW / STATEMENT**
- **AFTER** INSERT / UPDATE / DELETE **FOR EACH ROW / STATEMENT**
- **INSTEAD OF** INSERT / UPDATE / DELETE **FOR EACH ROW / STATEMENT**

In case of BEFORE option, Oracle fires the trigger before executing the trigger body and vice versa for AFTER option. INSTEAD OF trigger is used with VIEWS. It provides a transparent way of modifying VIEW that cannot be modified directly through DML statements. It works in the background performing the action coded in the trigger body directly on the underlying tables. FOR EACH ROW / STATEMENT option specifies that the trigger fires once per row. By default, a database trigger fires for each statement. When a triggering DML affects multiple rows, the STATEMENT trigger fires once, whereas the ROW trigger fires only once for each row. Syntax for creating trigger is as follows:

```
CREATE [OR REPLACE] TRIGGER <TRIGGER_NAME>
[BEFORE / AFTER] [INSERT / UPDATE / DELETE] ON <TABLE_NAME>
[FOR EACH STATEMENT/ FOR EACH ROW] [WHEN ,COND.]
DECLARE
   PL/SQL declarable statements
BEGIN
   PL/SQL executable statements
END;
```

7.6.1 OLD and New Qualifiers

OLD and NEW qualifiers are related to row triggers. Value of a column before the data change is referenced by prefixing OLD, similarly value of a column after the data change is referenced by prefixing NEW qualifier. This is shown in Table 7.2.

TABLE 7.2 Old and New Trigger Qualifiers

DML	OLD Value	NEW Value
INSERT	Null	Value inserted
UPDATE	Value before update	Value after update
DELETE	Value before delete	Null

Transactional statements like COMMIT or ROLLBACK are not allowed in triggers. Trigger is removed from a database using DROP TRIGGER <trigger_name> command.

We will go through few examples to demonstrate different types of scenarios where triggers can be used. EMP_TRIG and EMP_BKUP tables are used for all examples related to triggers. Minutely observe the PL/SQL code and the associated output. Details related to the tables are given below. Before executing the examples, you must create both the tables. Detailed commands to create tables from SQL prompt are given below.

```
CREATE TABLE EMP_TRIG
(ENAME VARCHAR2(20),
SAL NUMBER(8));

CREATE TABLE EMP_BKUP
(ENAME VARCHAR2(20),
SAL NUMBER(8),
DELETEDT DATE);
```

EX7_8 This example demonstrates use of BEFORE INSERT OR UPDATE ON EACH ROW Trigger.

```
/*
CREATE TABLE EMP_TRIG (ENAME VARCHAR2(20), SAL NUMBER(8));
*/
CREATE OR REPLACE TRIGGER MIN_SAL_CHK BEFORE INSERT OR UPDATE ON EMP_TRIG
FOR EACH ROW
WHEN (NEW.SAL<500)
BEGIN
   RAISE_APPLICATION_ERROR(-20000,'SAL must be above 500');
END;
/
```

Execution

```
SQL> @ C:\BOOK\CHAPTER7\EX7_8.SQL
Trigger created.

SQL> SELECT * FROM EMP_TRIG;
no rows selected

SQL> INSERT INTO EMP_TRIG VALUES ('PK',300);
INSERT INTO EMP_TRIG VALUES ('PK',300)
  *
ERROR at line 1:
ORA-20000: SAL must be above 500
ORA-06512: at "BOOK.MIN_SAL_CHK", line 2
ORA-04088: error during execution of trigger 'BOOK.MIN_SAL_CHK'

SQL> INSERT INTO EMP_TRIG VALUES ('PK',3000);
1 row created.

SQL> COMMIT;
Commit complete.

SQL> SELECT * FROM EMP_TRIG;
ENAME    SAL
PK    3000
```

Illustration

This trigger checks the value of SAL before insert or updates statement and ensures that SAL below 500 is not inserted. It acts BEFORE insertion or updation.

EX7_9 This example demonstrates use of trigger to keep information of deleted records. This type of scenario is most suited for the purpose of audit.

```
/*
CREATE TABLE EMP_TRIG (ENAME VARCHAR2(20), SAL NUMBER(8));
```

```
CREATE TABLE EMP_BKUP (ENAME VARCHAR2(20), SAL NUMBER(8),
DELETEDT DATE);
*/
CREATE OR REPLACE TRIGGER BKUP_REC
AFTER DELETE ON EMP_TRIG FOR EACH ROW
BEGIN
  INSERT INTO EMP_BKUP VALUES (:OLD.ENAME,:OLD.SAL,SYSDATE);
END;
/
```

Execution

```
SQL> @ C:\BOOK\CHAPTER7\EX7_9.SQL
Trigger created.

SQL> SELECT * FROM EMP_TRIG;
ENAME     SAL
PK 3000

SQL> SELECT * FROM EMP_BKUP;
no rows selected

SQL> DELETE FROM EMP_TRIG;
1 row deleted.

SQL> COMMIT;
Commit complete.

SQL> SELECT * FROM EMP_TRIG;
no rows selected

SQL> SELECT * FROM EMP_BKUP;
ENAME     SAL     DELETEDT
PK        3000    13-AUG-13

SQL> INSERT INTO EMP_TRIG VALUES ('SK',6000);
1 row created.

SQL> INSERT INTO EMP_TRIG VALUES ('PG',20000);
1 row created.

SQL> INSERT INTO EMP_TRIG VALUES ('SP',25000);
1 row created.

SQL> COMMIT;
Commit complete.

SQL> SELECT * FROM EMP_TRIG;
ENAME     SAL
SK        6000
```

```
PG        20000
SP        25000

SQL> DELETE FROM EMP_TRIG WHERE SAL>15000;
2 rows deleted.
SQL> COMMIT;
Commit complete.

SQL> SELECT * FROM EMP_TRIG;
ENAME     SAL
SK        6000

SQL> SELECT * FROM EMP_BKUP;
ENAME    SAL      DELETEDT
PG       20000    13-AUG-13
SP       25000    13-AUG-13
PK       3000     13-AUG-13
```

Illustration

This trigger keeps backup of deleted records of EMP_TRIG table. Deleted records of EMP_TRIG are inserted in EMP_BKUP table.

EX7_10 This trigger checks for any duplicate value and disallows insertion.

```
/* CREATE TABLE EMP_TRIG (ENAME VARCHAR2(20), SAL NUMBER(8), DELETEDT
DATE);*/
CREATE OR REPLACE TRIGGER UNIQUE_VAL BEFORE INSERT ON EMP_TRIG FOR EACH
ROW
DECLARE
   VCNT NUMBER(2);
BEGIN
   SELECT COUNT(*) INTO VCNT FROM EMP_TRIG
   WHERE ENAME=:NEW.ENAME;
   IF VCNT=1 THEN
      RAISE_APPLICATION_ERROR(-20000,'You have entered duplicate
      ENAME');
   END IF;
END;
/
```

Execution

```
SQL> @ C:\BOOK\CHAPTER7\EX7_10.SQL
Trigger created.

SQL> SELECT * FROM EMP_TRIG;
ENAME     SAL
SK        6000
```

```
SQL> INSERT INTO EMP_TRIG VALUES ('SK',8000);
INSERT INTO EMP_TRIG VALUES ('SK',8000)
 *
ERROR at line 1:
ORA-20000: You have entered duplicate ENAME
ORA-06512: at "BOOK.UNIQUE_VAL", line 6
ORA-04088: error during execution of trigger 'BOOK.UNIQUE_VAL'

SQL> INSERT INTO EMP_TRIG VALUES ('SN',8000);
1 row created.

SQL> COMMIT;
Commit complete.

SQL> SELECT * FROM EMP_TRIG;
ENAME    SAL
SK       6000
SN       8000
```

Illustration

Single attribute-based Primary or Unique Key ensures nonduplication of record. However, to ensure nonduplication of nonprime attribute, the trigger with BEFORE INSERT can be used. Note the display of user-defined error along with system generated error.

EX7_11 This is an example of security-level trigger. This triggers disallows any DML performed after 1300 hrs.

```
/*
CREATE TABLE EMP_TRIG (ENAME VARCHAR2(20), SAL NUMBER(8));
*/
CREATE OR REPLACE TRIGGER RESTRICT_ACCESS BEFORE INSERT OR UPDATE OR
DELETE ON EMP_TRIG
BEGIN
   IF (TO_CHAR(SYSDATE,'HH24') > '12') THEN
      IF INSERTING THEN
         RAISE_APPLICATION_ERROR(-20000,'Insertion not allowed
         after 1300hrs');
      ELSIF UPDATING THEN
         RAISE_APPLICATION_ERROR(-20000,'Updation not allowed
         after 1300hrs');
      ELSIF DELETING THEN
         RAISE_APPLICATION_ERROR(-20000,'Deletion not allowed
         after 1300hrs');
      ELSE
         RAISE_APPLICATION_ERROR(-20000,'Nothing allowed after
         1300hrs');
      END IF;
   END IF;
END;
/
```

Execution

```
SQL> INSERT INTO EMP_TRIG VALUES ('XXX',3456);
1 row created.
SQL> @ C:\BOOK\CHAPTER7\EX7_11.SQL
Trigger created.

SQL> INSERT INTO EMP_TRIG VALUES ('RKT',3456);

INSERT INTO EMP_TRIG VALUES ('RKT',3456)
 *
ERROR at line 1:
ORA-20000: Insertion not allowed after 1300hrs
ORA-06512: at "BOOK.RESTRICT_ACCESS", line 4
ORA-04088: error during execution of trigger 'BOOK.RESTRICT_ACCESS

SQL> DROP TRIGGER RESTRICT_ACCESS;
Trigger dropped.

SQL> INSERT INTO EMP_TRIG VALUES ('RKT',3456);
1 row created.

SQL> COMMIT;
Commit complete.

SQL> SELECT * FROM EMP_TRIG;
ENAME     SAL
SK        6000
RND       40000
RKP       8000
SN        8000
XXX       3456
RKT       3456
6 rows selected.

SQL> DELETE FROM EMP_TRIG WHERE ENAME LIKE 'XXX';
1 row deleted.

SQL> COMMIT;
Commit complete.

SQL> SELECT * FROM EMP_TRIG;
ENAME     SAL
SK        6000
RND       40000
RKP       8000
SN        8000
RKT       3456
```

Illustration

This example shows the power of Oracle Triggers to protect data from unauthorised usage.

EX7_12 This is an example of INSTEAD OF trigger. This trigger disallows insertion and updation of SAL if the same SAL is present in any record.

```
/*
CREATE VIEW EMP_VU_LO AS SELECT * FROM EMP_TRIG WHERE SAL<10000;
*/
CREATE OR REPLACE TRIGGER MIN_SAL_CHK INSTEAD OF INSERT OR UPDATE ON
EMP_VU_LO FOR EACH ROW
DECLARE
  VCNT NUMBER(2);
BEGIN
  SELECT COUNT(*) INTO VCNT FROM EMP_VU_LO WHERE SAL=:NEW.SAL;
  IF VCNT=1 THEN
    RAISE_APPLICATION_ERROR(-20000,'Duplicate SAL not
    allowed');
  END IF;
END;
/
```

Execution

```
SQL> SELECT * FROM EMP_TRIG;
ENAME     SAL
SK        6000
RND       40000
RKP       8000
SN        8000
RKT       3456

SQL> SELECT * FROM EMP_VU_LO;
ENAME     SAL
SK        6000
RKP       8000
SN        8000
RKT       3456

SQL> @ C:\BOOK\CHAPTER7\EX7_12.SQL
Trigger created.

SQL> INSERT INTO EMP_VU_LO VALUES ('PKK',6000);
INSERT INTO EMP_VU_LO VALUES ('PKK',6000)
  *
ERROR at line 1:
ORA-20000: Duplicate SAL not allowed
ORA-06512: at "PXEPROJ.MIN_SAL_CHK", line 6
ORA-04088: error during execution of trigger 'PXEPROJ.MIN_SAL_CHK'
```

7.7 MUTATING TABLE ERROR

In a PL/SQL program, if a row-level trigger is written that invokes a SELECT statement against the same table that the trigger is defined on, it will result into a mutating table error. In this case, the trigger will compile cleanly. However, whenever a statement is executed that fires the trigger, an error will be raised, which is known as mutating table error. This error generates a message which communicates that the table is mutating and the trigger might not able to see the changes. In such type of scenario, trigger fails to execute properly.

EX7_13

```
CREATE OR REPLACE TRIGGER CHECK_BEFORE_UPDATE
BEFORE UPDATE OF SALE
ON SALE_DETAIL
FOR EACH ROW
DECLARE
   TOTAL_SALE NUMBER;
BEGIN
   SELECT SUM(SALE) INTO TOTAL_SALE
   FROM SALE_DETAIL WHERE CID=:NEW.CID;

   IF (:NEW.CID > TOTAL_SALE) THEN
      RAISE_APPLICATION_ERROR(-20001, ' SALE VALUE CAN NOT EXCEED TOTAL
      SALE VALUE.');
   END IF;
END;
/
```

Execution

```
SQL> UPDATE SALE_DETAIL
  2 SET SALE = 0
  3 WHERE CID = 'C1';
UPDATE SALE_DETAIL
  *
ERROR at line 1:
ORA-04091: table TEST.SALE_DETAIL is mutating, trigger/function may not
see it
ORA-06512: at "TEST.CHECK BEFORE_UPDATE", line 4
ORA-04088: error during execution of trigger 'TEST.CHECK_BEFORE_UPDATE'
```

7.8 SUMMARY

In this chapter, concepts related to handling run-time errors in PL/SQL is discussed. Run-time error can be efficiently handled using If…End If for anticipated errors. Exception Handles can be used for both anticipated and unanticipated errors. Example related to different aspects like taking backup, security, run-time case conversion and imposing checks at the DML level have been covered. This chapter includes a large number of short type questions to delve into intricacies on exception and triggers. Students must attempt all the questions and refer to Oracle PL/SQL documentation from their website if the need arises.

SHORT/OBJECTIVE TYPE QUESTIONS

1. What do you understand by an exception? How it is raised and handled?
2. Define OTHERS exception handler.
3. Which DML operations raise a trigger?
4. What do you understand by ALTER TRIGGER statement?
5. What do you understand by DROP TRIGGER statement?
6. Can data types LONG, LONG RAW, CLOB or BLOB be used inside a trigger?
7. Write different types of exceptions.
8. Is it possible to write a RETURN statement in the exception part of a function?
9. What do you understand by explicitly raised exceptions and implicitly raised exceptions?
10. What system privileges are required by a user to create a trigger?
11. What are the two different types of triggers?
12. Is it possible to refer other tables through a role?
13. State the difference between row-level triggers and statement-level triggers.
14. Can you combine several triggering events into one trigger?
15. How triggers are used for auditing?
16. How you can restrict row trigger action?
17. What is the advantage of using schema-level triggers?
18. When database event triggers are used?
19. When disabling a trigger is advantageous?
20. Is it possible to stop execution of DML statement using triggers?
21. Can we have transaction control statements inside a trigger?
22. Is it possible to use cursors inside a trigger body?
23. Can you write a trigger that will execute only when a specific call on a table is updated?
24. Can you include an INSERT statement on the same table to which the trigger is assigned?
25. What will happen if an unhandled exception is raised inside a procedure?
26. Is it possible to have more than one exception at a time?
27. Can you have more than one OTHERS exception handler?
28. How do you trap user-defined exceptions?
29. What do you understand by RAISE_APPLICATION_ERROR?

30. What will happen if an exception is not trapped in a subblock?

31. Is it possible to resume processing from the point of exception?

32. What do you understand by PRAGMA keyword?

33. Where INSTEAD OF triggers are used?

34. What do you understand by a mutating table?

35. Where trigger information is available?

36. Can you pass parameters to triggers?

37. Can you use SELECT statement to fire a trigger?

38. What is the use of the REFERENCING clause in a trigger?

39. Is it possible to use INSTEAD OF triggers to fire once for each statement on a view?

40. What is the use of conditional predicates in triggers?

WORKOUT SECTION

W7_1A Write a PL/SQL program without exception handler which accepts two numbers A and B, calculates C = A/B and displays the value of C. Input B = 0 and see the effect.

SQL> @ C:\BOOK\CHAPTER7\W7_1A.SQL
Enter value for a: 5
Enter value for b: 3

5/3 = 1.67

SQL> /
Enter value for a: 6
Enter value for b: 0

DECLARE
***
ERROR at line 1:
ORA-01476: divisor is equal to zero
ORA-06512: at line 6

W7_1B Write a PL/SQL program with exception handler which accepts two numbers A and B, calculates C = A/B and displays the value of C. Input B = 0 and see the effect.

SQL> @ C:\BOOK\CHAPTER7\W7_1B

DOC> A/B - EXCEPTION HANDLE ZERO_DIVIDE USED
DOC>/*

Enter value for a: 5

Enter value for b: 0
****
5/0 is invalid operation - Divide by 0

W7_1C Write a PL/SQL program without exception handler which accepts two numbers A and B, calculates C = A/B and displays the value of C. If B is 0 trap it using IF … END IF and use exception handler for any other error. Input B = 0 and see the effect.

SQL> @ C:\BOOK\CHAPTER7\W7_1C

DOC> A/B - EXCEPTION HANDLER USED EFFECTIVELY
DOC>/*

Enter value for a: 0
Enter value for b: 0

0/0 is invalid operation

W7_2 What will be the output of the following program and why? Assume that SALE_DETAIL table exists as per EX7_7.

```
SET SERVEROUTPUT ON
DECLARE
   CHILD_RECORD_EXCEPTION EXCEPTION;
   PRAGMA
      EXCEPTION_INIT (CHILD_RECORD_EXCEPTION, -2200);

BEGIN
   DELETE FROM PROD WHERE PID= 'P3';

EXCEPTION
      WHEN CHILD_RECORD_EXCEPTION THEN
      DBMS_OUTPUT.PUT_LINE('CHILD RECORDS ARE PRESENT FOR PID =
      P3');

END;
/
```

W7_3 Write a trigger which will convert ENAME to uppercase at the time of insertion of record.

```
SQL> @ C:\BOOK\CHAPTER7\W7_3.SQL

DOC>CREATE TABLE EMP_TRIG (ENAME VARCHAR2(20), SAL NUMBER(8));
DOC>*/
Trigger created.
```

```
SQL> select * from emp_trig;

ENAME      SAL
SK         6000
SN         8000
SQL> insert into emp_trig values ('rnd',40000);
1 row created.
SQL> commit;
Commit complete.
SQL> select * from emp_trig;
ENAME      SAL
SK         6000
RND        40000
SN         8000
```

W7_4 Write a trigger which will not allow to DELETE records of EMP_BKUP.

```
SQL> @ C:\BOOK\CHAPTER7\W7_4

DOC>CREATE TABLE EMP_TRIG (ENAME VARCHAR2(20), SAL NUMBER(8));
DOC>*/
Trigger created.

SQL> DELETE FROM EMP_BKUP;

DELETE FROM EMP_BKUP
*
ERROR at line 1:
ORA-20000: Delete not allowed
ORA-06512: at "BOOK.NO_DELETE", line 2
ORA-04088: error during execution of trigger 'BOOK.NO_DELETE'
```

W7_5 Write a trigger which will check on maximum value of SAL. Maximum SAL allowed is 50,000.

```
SQL> @ C:\BOOK\CHAPTER7\W7_5

DOC>CREATE TABLE EMP_TRIG (ENAME VARCHAR2(20), SAL NUMBER(8));
DOC>*/
Trigger created.

SQL> INSERT INTO EMP_TRIG VALUES ('RKP',8000);

1 row created.

SQL> INSERT INTO EMP_TRIG VALUES ('SND',90000);

INSERT INTO EMP_TRIG VALUES ('SND',90000)
            *
```

```
ERROR at line 1:
ORA-20000: SAL must be below 50000
ORA-06512: at "BOOK.MAX_SAL_CHK", line 2
ORA-04088: error during execution of trigger 'BOOK.MAX_SAL_CHK'

SQL> COMMIT;
Commit complete.
SQL> SELECT * FROM EMP_TRIG;
ENAME         SAL
SK            6000
RND           40000
RKP           8000
SN            8000
```

Implicit and Explicit Cursors

Learning Objectives

You will learn following key concepts after completion of the chapter:

- ✓ Concepts associated with implicit cursors
- ✓ Concepts associated with explicit cursors
- ✓ Different attributes of implicit and explicit cursors
- ✓ Use of various types of loops in explicit cursors

8.1 INTRODUCTION

A cursor is a private SQL work area where all commands defined in the cursor are executed. An implicit cursor is automatically created by Oracle when a PL/SQL block is used to execute a DML statement or a SELECT statement that returns only one row. When a SELECT statement returns more than one row, the explicit cursor is required. In explicit cursor, rows are accessed sequentially. Attributes of implicit and explicit cursors and different types of looping constructs to process explicit cursor is discussed. In this chapter, it is worthwhile to emphasize that concepts on implicit and explicit cursors are essentially required to expertise PL/SQL programming.

8.2 IMPLICIT CURSOR

Implicit cursor is automatically created and handled by Oracle. Oracle does the following actions internally to handle the implicit cursor.

- Reserve an area in main memory to populate the data.
- Release the memory area after the processing.

Implicit cursor handles all DMLs, that is, all insert, update and delete operations which effect multiple rows and SELECT statement which returns exactly one row.
Table 8.1 shows attributes of implicit cursor. These attributes can be used to access information about the status of last DML or single-row SELECT statement. In case of the implicit cursor, SQL is appended before the attribute.

TABLE 8.1 Implicit Cursor Attributes

Cursor Attribute	Description	Example
%ROWCOUNT	Contains the number of records processed from the cursor.	SQL%ROWCOUNT
%FOUND	Contains the value TRUE if row was fetched successfully, FALSE otherwise.	SQL%FOUND
%NOTFOUND	Contains the value TRUE if row was not fetched successfully, FALSE otherwise.	SQL%NOTFOUND
%ISOPEN	Contains the value TRUE if cursor is open, FALSE otherwise.	SQL%ISOPEN

EX8_1 In this example, the value of implicit cursor attributes on DML is demonstrated. This example is based on CUST, PROD and SALE_DETAIL tables as shown in Figure 5.6

```
—This example checks the value of CURSOR attribute of implicit cursor.
SET SERVEROUTPUT ON
SET VERIFY OFF
DECLARE
   VPCOST   PROD.PCOST%TYPE := '&PCOST';
   VCNT  NUMBER(4);
BEGIN
   —DML statement
   DBMS_OUTPUT.PUT_LINE('UPDATE PROD SET PCOST=PCOST*1.1 WHERE
   PCOST< ' || VPCOST);
   UPDATE PROD SET PCOST=PCOST*1.1 WHERE PCOST< VPCOST;
   —Check effect of %FOUND attribute
   DBMS_OUTPUT.PUT_LINE('SQL%FOUND VALUE');
   IF SQL%FOUND THEN
      DBMS_OUTPUT.PUT_LINE('TRUE');
   ELSE
      DBMS_OUTPUT.PUT_LINE('FALSE');
   END IF;
   —Check effect of %NOTFOUND attribute (It is always opposite of %FOUND)
   DBMS_OUTPUT.PUT_LINE('SQL%NOTFOUND VALUE');
   IF SQL%NOTFOUND THEN
      DBMS_OUTPUT.PUT_LINE('TRUE');
   ELSE
      DBMS_OUTPUT.PUT_LINE('FALSE');
   END IF;
   —Check effect of %ROWCOUNT attribute
   DBMS_OUTPUT.PUT_LINE('SQL%ROWCOUNT VALUE');
   VCNT := SQL%ROWCOUNT;
   IF SQL%ROWCOUNT>0 THEN
      DBMS_OUTPUT.PUT_LINE(VCNT);
   ELSE
```

```
    DBMS_OUTPUT.PUT_LINE('No Row found');
  END IF;
  —Check effect of %ISOPEN attribute (It is always FALSE in IMPLICIT
  CURSOR)
  DBMS_OUTPUT.PUT_LINE('SQL%ISOPEN VALUE');
  IF SQL%ISOPEN THEN
     DBMS_OUTPUT.PUT_LINE('TRUE');
  ELSE
     DBMS_OUTPUT.PUT_LINE('FALSE');
  END IF;
END;
/

SQL> SELECT * FROM PROD;
PID   PNAME     PCOST    PPROFIT
P3    PEN       24.81    20
P2    FLOPPY    36.3     12
P1    PENCIL    6.36
```

Execution

```
SQL> @ C:\BOOK\CHAPTER8\EX8_1
Enter value for pcost: 2
UPDATE PROD SET PCOST=PCOST*1.1 WHERE PCOST< 2
SQL%FOUND VALUE
FALSE
SQL%NOTFOUND VALUE
TRUE
SQL%ROWCOUNT VALUE
No Row found
SQL%ISOPEN VALUE
FALSE

SQL> /
Enter value for pcost: 80
UPDATE PROD SET PCOST=PCOST*1.1 WHERE PCOST< 80
SQL%FOUND VALUE
TRUE
SQL%NOTFOUND VALUE
FALSE
SQL%ROWCOUNT VALUE
3
SQL%ISOPEN VALUE
FALSE
```

EX8_2 In this example, the attribute of implicit cursor with respect to SELECT statement is demonstrated. This example is based on CUST, PROD and SALE_DETAIL tables as shown in Figure 5.6.

```
—This example checks the value of CURSOR attribute of an implicit cursor.
SET SERVEROUTPUT ON
SET VERIFY OFF
DECLARE
   VCNT  NUMBER(4);
BEGIN
   —SELECT statement which returns 1 value.
   SELECT COUNT(*) INTO VCNT FROM CUST;
   —Check effect of %FOUND attribute
   DBMS_OUTPUT.PUT_LINE('SQL%FOUND VALUE');
   IF SQL%FOUND THEN
      DBMS_OUTPUT.PUT_LINE('TRUE');
   ELSE
      DBMS_OUTPUT.PUT_LINE('FALSE');
   END IF;
   —Check effect of %ROWCOUNT attribute
   DBMS_OUTPUT.PUT_LINE('SQL%ROWCOUNT VALUE');
   VCNT := SQL%ROWCOUNT;
   IF SQL%ROWCOUNT>0 THEN
      DBMS_OUTPUT.PUT_LINE(VCNT);
   ELSE
      DBMS_OUTPUT.PUT_LINE('No Row found');
   END IF;
END;
/
```

Execution

```
SQL> SELECT * FROM CUST;
```

CID	CNAME	CCITY
C1	PRADIP	MYSORE
C3	AASTIK	KOLKATA
C2	TUSHAR	PUNE
C4	ARPAN	CHENNAI
C5	ANUMITA	INDORE

```
SQL> @ C:\BOOK\CHAPTER8\EX8_2
SQL%FOUND VALUE
TRUE
SQL%ROWCOUNT VALUE
   1
```

8.3 EXPLICIT CURSOR

When a SELECT statement returns more than one row of results, the programmer must create an explicit cursor to do data processing. The following five steps are required to handle an explicit cursor:

- Declare the cursor
- Open the cursor
- Fetching rows from the cursor
- Termination statement
- Close the cursor

Explicit cursor attributes are almost similar to implicit cursor attributes. The major difference is that cursor name is appended to the attribute name. EX8_3 demonstrates attributes of explicit cursor and is self-explanatory. Table 8.2 shows attributes of explicit cursor:

TABLE 8.2 Explicit Cursor Attributes

Cursor attribute	Description	Example
%ROWCOUNT	This numeric attribute returns the number of rows fetched by the cursor	CUST_CURSOR% ROWCOUNT
%FOUND	It is a boolean attribute. It returns TRUE if the previous FETCH returned a row, FALSE otherwise	CUST_CURSOR% FOUND
%NOTFOUND	Opposite of %FOUND. It returns TRUE if the previous FETCH does not return a row, FALSE otherwise	CUST_CURSOR% NOTFOUND
%ISOPEN	Evaluates to TRUE, if an explicit cursor is open, FALSE otherwise. Contains the value TRUE if cursor is open, FALSE otherwise.	CUST_CURSOR% ISOPEN

EX8_3 In this PL/SQL program attributes of explicit cursor are demonstrated. This example is based on CUST, PROD and SALE_DETAIL tables as shown in Figure 5.6.

```
—This example of EXPLICIT CURSOR explores cursor attributes
SET SERVEROUTPUT ON
SET VERIFY OFF
DECLARE
   VREC   CUST%ROWTYPE;
   VCNT   NUMBER(4);
   CURSOR CUST_CURSOR IS SELECT * FROM CUST ORDER BY CNAME;
BEGIN
   IF CUST_CURSOR%ISOPEN THEN
      DBMS_OUTPUT.PUT_LINE('CUST_CURSOR%ISOPEN - Before OPEN
      - TRUE');
   ELSE
      DBMS_OUTPUT.PUT_LINE('CUST_CURSOR%ISOPEN - Before OPEN
      - FALSE');
   END IF;
   OPEN CUST_CURSOR;
   IF CUST_CURSOR%ISOPEN THEN
      DBMS_OUTPUT.PUT_LINE('CUST_CURSOR%ISOPEN - After OPEN
      and Before CLOSE - TRUE');
   ELSE
      DBMS_OUTPUT.PUT_LINE('CUST_CURSOR%ISOPEN - After OPEN
```

```
        and Before CLOSE - FALSE');
    END IF;
    LOOP
        FETCH CUST_CURSOR INTO VREC;
        EXIT WHEN CUST_CURSOR%NOTFOUND;
        DBMS_OUTPUT.PUT_LINE(VREC.CNAME || ' lives in ' || VREC.CCITY);
    END LOOP;
    —Check effect of %ROWCOUNT attribute
    VCNT := CUST_CURSOR%ROWCOUNT;
    IF CUST_CURSOR%ROWCOUNT>0 THEN
        DBMS_OUTPUT.PUT_LINE('CUST_CURSOR%ROWCOUNT VALUE= '|| VCNT);
    ELSE
        DBMS_OUTPUT.PUT_LINE('No Row found');
    END IF;
    CLOSE CUST_CURSOR;
    IF CUST_CURSOR%ISOPEN THEN
        DBMS_OUTPUT.PUT_LINE('CUST_CURSOR%ISOPEN - After CLOSE - TRUE');
    ELSE
        DBMS_OUTPUT.PUT_LINE('CUST_CURSOR%ISOPEN - After CLOSE -
        FALSE');
    END IF;
END;
/
```

Execution

```
SQL>@ C:\BOOK\CHAPTER8\EX8_3
CUST_CURSOR%ISOPEN - Before OPEN - FALSE
CUST_CURSOR%ISOPEN - After OPEN and Before CLOSE - TRUE
AASTIK lives in KOLKATA
ANUMITA lives in INDORE
ARPAN lives in CHENNAI
PRADIP lives in MYSORE
TUSHAR lives in PUNE
CUST_CURSOR%ROWCOUNT VALUE= 5
CUST_CURSOR%ISOPEN - After CLOSE - FALSE
```

Illustrations

Important steps related to EX8_3 are given next

(i) **Declare the cursor:** Declare the cursor to define the name (CUST_CURSOR) and associate it with a SELECT statement (SELECT * FROM CUST ORDER BY CNAME). Syntax to declare a cursor is as follows:

CURSOR CURSOR_NAME IS SELECT_STATEMENT;

SELECT_STATEMENT does not contain INTO clause. INTO clause is part of FETCH statement.

```
CURSOR CUST_CURSOR IS SELECT * FROM CUST ORDER BY CNAME;
```

CUST_CURSOR will load rows based on the SELECT statement in main memory when the cursor is opened. This is called active set of the cursor.

(ii) Open the cursor: When a cursor is opened, the active set is determined based on the SELECT statement in the cursor declaration. The active set pointer (➡) is set to the first row as shown in Figure 8.1.

```
OPEN CUST_CURSOR
```

➡	**C3**	**AASTİK**	**KOLKATA**
	C5	ANUMITA	INDORE
	C4	ARPAN	CHENNAI
	C1	PRADIP	MYSORE
	C2	TUSHAR	PUNE

FIGURE 8.1 Position of pointer on the first record.

(iii) Fetching rows from the cursor: The FETCH statement is responsible to retrieve rows based on the pointer position. After each FETCH, the active set pointer is advanced to the next row. Each FETCH will therefore return successive rows in the active set until the entire active set is exhausted.
Diagrammatically FETCHING of rows is shown in Figure 8.2.

```
LOOP
FETCH CUST_CURSOR INTO VREC;
.......
_____
END LOOP;
```

(iv) Termination statement: Termination condition is essentially required so that the control can exit from loop. It must be placed immediately after the FETCH statement. Figure 8.2 shows the values associated with termination clause, that is, CUST_CURSOR%NOTFOUND.

```
LOOP
FETCH CUST_CURSOR INTO VREC;
EXIT WHEN CUST_CURSOR%NOTFOUND;
_____
_____
END LOOP;
```

(v) Close the cursor: A cursor should be closed when the active set has been retrieved. This will release storage resource held by the cursor.

```
CLOSE CUST_CURSOR;
```

1st Iteration (CUST_CURSOR%NOTFOUND = FALSE)

➡ C3	**AASTIK**	**KOLKATA**
C5	ANUMITA	INDORE
C4	ARPAN	CHENNAI
C1	PRADIP	MYSORE
C2	TUSHAR	PUNE

2nd Iteration (CUST_CURSOR%NOTFOUND = FALSE)

C3	AASTIK	KOLKATA
➡ C5	**ANUMITA**	**INDORE**
C4	ARPAN	CHENNAI
C1	PRADIP	MYSORE
C2	TUSHAR	PUNE

3rd Iteration (CUST_CURSOR%NOTFOUND = FALSE)

C3	AASTIK	KOLKATA
C5	ANUMITA	INDORE
➡ C4	**ARPAN**	**CHENNAI**
C1	PRADIP	MYSORE
C2	TUSHAR	PUNE

4th Iteration (CUST_CURSOR%NOTFOUND = FALSE)

C3	AASTIK	KOLKATA
C5	ANUMITA	INDORE
C4	ARPAN	CHENNAI
➡ C1	**PRADIP**	**MYSORE**
C2	TUSHAR	PUNE

5th Iteration (CUST_CURSOR%NOTFOUND = FALSE)

C3	AASTIK	KOLKATA
C5	ANUMITA	INDORE
C4	ARPAN	CHENNAI
C1	PRADIP	MYSORE
➡ C2	**TUSHAR**	**PUNE**

6th Iteration (CUST_CURSOR%NOTFOUND = TRUE)

C3	AASTIK	KOLKATA
C5	ANUMITA	INDORE
C4	ARPAN	CHENNAI
C1	PRADIP	MYSORE
➡ C2	**TUSHAR**	**PUNE**

FIGURE 8.2 Position of pointer on iterations.

8.4 LOOPS IN EXPLICIT CURSOR

In explicit cursor, the most essential operation is fetching all the rows from the active set. This is achieved using loops, which simply extract each row one by one from active set. In this section, we will take a very simple example to explain various types of fetch loops.

8.4.1 Explicit Cursor Using Simple Loop

Syntax of simple loop is
LOOP … END LOOP;

Explicit cursor attribute %NOTFOUND is used to control how many times the loop executes. There are five basic operations that are shown in Table 8.3.

This style of fetch loop is mostly used with explicit cursor due to the freedom of the fine grain control of operations. In case of parameterized cursors, which we will discuss in Chapter 10, simple loop fetch is used.

8.4.2 Explicit Cursor Using While Loop

A cursor fetch loop can also be done using the WHILE … LOOP syntax. It is illustrated in example EX8_5. In this type of loop, FETCH is used twice. One is outside the loop and the other is inside the loop. The basic operations of WHILE … LOOP are shown in Table 8.4.

EX8_4 In this PL/SQL program explicit cursor using LOOP … END LOOP command is demonstrated. This example is based on CUST, PROD and SALE_DETAIL tables as shown in Figure 5.6.

```
—This is a simple example of EXPICIT CURSOR
SET SERVEROUTPUT ON
SET VERIFY OFF
DECLARE
   VREC CUST%ROWTYPE;
   CURSOR CUST_CURSOR IS SELECT * FROM CUST ORDER BY CNAME;
BEGIN
   OPEN CUST_CURSOR;
   LOOP
      FETCH CUST_CURSOR INTO VREC;
      EXIT WHEN CUST_CURSOR%NOTFOUND;
      DBMS_OUTPUT.PUT_LINE(VREC.CNAME || ' lives in ' ||
        VREC.CCITY);
   END LOOP;
   CLOSE CUST_CURSOR;
END;
/
```

Execution

```
SQL> @ C:\BOOK\CHAPTER8\EX8_4
AASTIK lives in KOLKATA
ANUMITA lives in INDORE
ARPAN lives in CHENNAI
PRADIP lives in MYSORE
TUSHAR lives in PUNE
```

Illustrations

Detailed illustration of EX8_4 is provided in Table 8.3.

TABLE 8.3 Illustration of EX8_4

Operation	PL/SQL statement with explanation
Creating the Cursor	CURSOR CUST_CURSOR IS SELECT * FROM CUST ORDER BY CNAME; Active Set is created based on SELECT statement
Opening the Cursor	OPEN CUST_CURSOR; Active Set is opened in memory
Fetching rows	LOOP FETCH CUST_CURSOR INTO VREC; --- --- END LOOP; Each row is fetched and placed in VREC
Termination statement	LOOP FETCH CUST_CURSOR INTO VREC; EXIT WHEN CUST_CURSOR%NOTFOUND; --- --- END LOOP; EXIT statement must be placed immediately after FETCH ...VREC; statement. Check W8_3 to see the effect if EXIT statement is not put immediately after FETCH
Closing the Cursor	CLOSE CUST_CURSOR; It is a good habit to close the cursor once the job is finished. It not only releases the memory resource but also is useful if the same cursor needs to be reopened for some reason

EX8_5 In this PL/SQL program explicit cursor using WHILE … END LOOP command is demonstrated. This example is based on CUST, PROD and SALE_DETAIL tables as shown in Figure 5.6.

```
—Explicit Cursor using While Loop
SET SERVEROUTPUT ON
SET VERIFY OFF
DECLARE
   VREC CUST%ROWTYPE;
   CURSOR CUST_CURSOR IS SELECT * FROM CUST ORDER BY CNAME;
BEGIN
   OPEN CUST_CURSOR;
   FETCH CUST_CURSOR INTO VREC;
   WHILE CUST_CURSOR%FOUND LOOP
   DBMS_OUTPUT.PUT_LINE(VREC.CNAME || ' lives in ' ||VREC.CCITY);
      FETCH CUST_CURSOR INTO VREC;
   END LOOP;
   CLOSE CUST_CURSOR;
END;
/
```

Execution

```
SQL> @ C:\BOOK\CHAPTER8\EX8_5.SQL
AASTIK lives in KOLKATA
ANUMITA lives in INDORE
ARPAN lives in CHENNAI
PRADIP lives in MYSORE
TUSHAR lives in PUNE
```

Illustrations

Detailed illustration of EX8_5 is provided in Table 8.4.

TABLE 8.4 Illustration of EX8_5

Operation	PL/SQL statement with explanation
Creating the Cursor	CURSOR CUST_CURSOR IS SELECT * FROM CUST ORDER BY CNAME; Active Set is created based on SELECT statement
Opening the Cursor	OPEN CUST_CURSOR; Active Set is opened in memory
Fetching rows and Termination Statement	FETCH CUST_CURSOR INTO VREC; WHILE CUST_CURSOR%FOUND LOOP FETCH CUST_CURSOR INTO VREC; — — END LOOP; Note two FETCH statement and use of %FOUND in terminating statement
Closing the Cursor	CLOSE CUST_CURSOR; It is a good habit to close the cursor once the job is finished so that the memory resource is released

8.4.3 Explicit Cursor Using For Loop

FOR … END LOOP provides a simpler type of loop. It implicitly handles the cursor processing which includes opening of cursor, container to store fetched values, termination and closing of cursor. This type of fetch loop is popularly used in simple explicit cursors. Table 8.5 shows the basic operation of FOR … END LOOP.

EX8_6 In this PL/SQL program explicit cursor using FOR … END LOOP command is demonstrated. This example is based on CUST, PROD and SALE_DETAIL tables as shown in Figure 5.6.

```
—Explicit Cursor using For Loop
SET SERVEROUTPUT ON
SET VERIFY OFF
DECLARE
   CURSOR CUST_CURSOR IS SELECT * FROM CUST ORDER BY CNAME;
BEGIN
   FOR VREC IN CUST_CURSOR LOOP
```

```
      DBMS_OUTPUT.PUT_LINE(VREC.CNAME || ' lives in ' ||
      VREC.CCITY);
   END LOOP;
END;
/
```

Execution

```
SQL> @ C:\BOOK\CHAPTER8\EX8_6.SQL
AASTIK lives in KOLKATA
ANUMITA lives in INDORE
ARPAN lives in CHENNAI
PRADIP lives in MYSORE
TUSHAR lives in PUNE
```

Illustrations

Detailed illustration of EX8_6 is provided in Table 8.5.

TABLE 8.5 Illustration of EX8_6

Operation	PL/SQL statement with explanation
Creating the Cursor	CURSOR CUST_CURSOR IS SELECT * FROM CUST ORDER BY CNAME; Active Set is created based on SELECT statement
Implicit opening of cursor, fetching of rows from active set, terminating and closing of cursor	FOR VREC IN CUST_CURSOR LOOP — END LOOP;

8.4.4 Explicit Cursor Using Implicit For Loop

FOR … END LOOP implicit fetch loop implicitly handles the cursor processing which includes opening of cursor, container to store fetched vales, termination and closing of cursor. In this type of fetch loop, even declaration of cursor is part of FOR … END LOOP statement. Table 8.10 shows the basic operation of FOR … END LOOP implicit loop.

EX8_7 In this PL/SQL program explicit cursor using FOR … END LOOP explicit command is demonstrated. This example is based on CUST, PROD and SALE_DETAIL tables as shown in Figure 5.6.

```
—Explicit Cursor using Implicit For Loop
SET SERVEROUTPUT ON
SET VERIFY OFF
BEGIN
   FOR VREC IN (SELECT * FROM CUST ORDER BY CNAME) LOOP
      DBMS_OUTPUT.PUT_LINE(VREC.CNAME || ' lives in ' ||
         VREC.CCITY);
   END LOOP;
END;
/
```

Execution

```
SQL> @ C:\BOOK\CHAPTER8\EX8_7.SQL
AASTIK lives in KOLKATA
ANUMITA lives in INDORE
ARPAN lives in CHENNAI
PRADIP lives in MYSORE
TUSHAR lives in PUNE
```

Illustrations

Detailed illustration of EX8_7 is provided in Table 8.6.

TABLE 8.6 Illustration of EX8_7

Operation	PL/SQL statement with explanation
Implicit operation Creating of cursor Opening of cursor Fetching of rows Terminating condition Closing of cursor	FOR VREC IN (SELECT * FROM CUST ORDER BY CNAME) LOOP ... END LOOP;

EX8_8 This PL/SQL program demonstrates use of explicit and implicit cursors in one program. This program displays the number of days items are sold. This exampleis based on CUST, PROD and SALE_DETAIL tables as shown in Figure 5.6.

```
SET SERVEROUTPUT ON
DECLARE
  VPID SALE_DETAIL.PID%TYPE;
  VCNT NUMBER;
  CURSOR PROD_CURSOR IS SELECT PID FROM PROD ORDER BY PID;
BEGIN
  OPEN PROD_CURSOR;
  LOOP
    FETCH PROD_CURSOR INTO VPID;
    EXIT WHEN PROD_CURSOR%NOTFOUND;
    SELECT COUNT(*) INTO VCNT FROM SALE_DETAIL WHERE PID=VPID;
    IF VCNT=1 THEN
      DBMS_OUTPUT.PUT_LINE(VPID||' IS SOLD ONLY ON '||VCNT||'
DAY');
    END IF;
    IF VCNT>1 THEN
      DBMS_OUTPUT.PUT_LINE(VPID||' IS SOLD ONLY ON '||VCNT||' DAYS');
    END IF;
  END LOOP;
  CLOSE PROD_CURSOR;
END;
/
```

Execution

```
SQL> @ C:\BOOK\CHAPTER8\EX8_8
P1 IS SOLD ONLY ON 1 DAY
P2 IS SOLD ON 2 DAYS
P3 IS SOLD ON 4 DAYS
```

EX8_9 This example computes average SALE of products and displays status of sold products which are below and above average sale. This example is based on CUST, PROD and SALE_DETAIL tables as shown in Figure 5.6.

```
SET SERVEROUTPUT ON
DECLARE
   VAVG NUMBER;
   VPNAME PROD.PNAME%TYPE;
   VSALE SALE_DETAIL.SALE%TYPE;
   VSALEDT SALE_DETAIL.SALEDT%TYPE;
   CURSOR SALE_CURSOR IS
   SELECT P.PNAME,S.SALE,S.SALEDT
   FROM PROD P, SALE_DETAIL S
   WHERE P.PID=S.PID;

BEGIN
   —Computes average sale
   SELECT ROUND(AVG(SALE),2) INTO VAVG FROM SALE_DETAIL;
   DBMS_OUTPUT.PUT_LINE('AVERAGE SALE IS '||VAVG);
   —Sale status of items above average sale
   DBMS_OUTPUT.PUT_LINE('SALE ABOVE AVERAGE SALE(i.e. '||VAVG||')');
   OPEN SALE_CURSOR;
   LOOP
      FETCH SALE_CURSOR INTO VPNAME,VSALE,VSALEDT;
      EXIT WHEN SALE_CURSOR%NOTFOUND;
      IF VSALE>VAVG THEN
      DBMS_OUTPUT.PUT_LINE(VPNAME || ' '||VSALE||' NOS
         '||VSALEDT);
      END IF;
   END LOOP;
   CLOSE SALE_CURSOR;
   DBMS_OUTPUT.PUT_LINE('----------------------------------------');
   — Sale status of items below average sale
   DBMS_OUTPUT.PUT_LINE('SALE BELOW AVERAGE SALE(i.e. '|| VAVG ||') ');
   OPEN SALE_CURSOR;
   LOOP
      FETCH SALE_CURSOR INTO VPNAME,VSALE,VSALEDT;
      EXIT WHEN SALE_CURSOR%NOTFOUND;
      IF VSALE<VAVG THEN
         DBMS_OUTPUT.PUT_LINE(VPNAME || ' '||VSALE||' NOSc
            '||VSALEDT);
```

```
    END IF;
    END LOOP;
    CLOSE SALE_CURSOR;
END;
/
```

Execution

```
SQL> @ C:\BOOK\CHAPTER8\EX8_9
AVEARGE SALE IS 3.57
SALE ABOVE AVERAGE SALE(i.e. 3.57)
FLOPPY 10 NOS 15-JUL-13
PENCIL 5 NOS 14-JUL-13
--------------------------------------
SALE BELOW AVERAGE SALE(i.e. 3.57)
PEN 2 NOS 14-JUL-13
PEN 1 NOS 14-JUL-13
PEN 3 NOS 20-AUG-13
PEN 2 NOS 14-NOV-13
FLOPPY 2 NOS 18-SEP-13
```

EX8_10 This PL/SQL program calculates total sale of individual items and grand total of all sold items. This example is based on CUST, PROD and SALE_DETAIL tables as shown in Figure 5.6.

```
SET SERVEROUTPUT ON
DECLARE
    VSALE NUMBER;
    VTOTALSALE NUMBER;
    VPNAME PROD.PNAME%TYPE;
    CURSOR PROD_CURSOR IS SELECT PNAME FROM PROD;
BEGIN
    OPEN PROD_CURSOR;
    VTOTALSALE:=0;
    LOOP
        FETCH PROD_CURSOR INTO VPNAME;
        EXIT WHEN PROD_CURSOR%NOTFOUND;
        SELECT SUM(P.PCOST*S.SALE) INTO VSALE
        FROM PROD P, SALE_DETAIL
        WHERE P.PID=S.PID AND P.PNAME=VPNAME;
        DBMS_OUTPUT.PUT_LINE('Total sale of '||VPNAME||' is
            '||VSALE);
    VTOTALSALE:=VTOTALSALE+VSALE;
    END LOOP;
    CLOSE PROD_CURSOR;
    DBMS_OUTPUT.PUT_LINE('-----------------------------------');
    DBMS_OUTPUT.PUT_LINE('Grand total of sale is '||VTOTALSALE);
END;
/
```

Execution

```
SQL> @ C:\BOOK\CHAPTER8\EX8_10.SQL
Total sale of PEN is 164
Total sale of FLOPPY is 360
Total sale of PENCIL is 26.25
-----------------------------------
Grand total of sale is 550.25
```

8.5 SUMMARY

PL/SQL programming can be expertised only with clear concepts on implicit and explicit cursors. In this chapter, a large number of workouts are given and it is suggested to attempt all of them without referring to the solutions. Students are also requested to go through all the short type questions provided in this chapter.

SHORT/OBJECTIVE TYPE QUESTIONS

1. How you can fetch multiple rows in a PL/SQL program?
2. What do you understand by cursor? Illustrate the difference between implicit cursor and explicit cursor.
3. What are the essential commands to handle explicit cursor?
4. What is the function of cursor variables?
5. Which attribute is used to exit from a loop?
6. Is it possible to define a record type in an explicit cursor?
7. Can you use FOR loop to handle explicit cursor?
8. Define implicit record.
9. How can you determine the current status of a cursor?
10. What is the reason SQL%ISOPEN always returns the FALSE value?
11. How can it be confirmed that an UPDATE statement is successfully executed?
12. What is the sequence of events due to OPEN cursor command?
13. What is the difference between WHILE-LOOP and FOR-LOOP?
14. Is it possible to reassign counter value inside a FOR-LOOP?
15. Is it possible to force FOR-LOOP to end unconditionally?
16. Can you define a default value for a record field?
17. What is the value of SQL%FOUND attribute before an INSERT statement is executed?
18. What is the value of SQL%FOUND attribute after an INSERT statement is executed?
19. What will be the value of %NOTFOUND attribute between a Cursor OPEN and FETCH statement?
20. What will be the value of %NOTFOUND attribute after the FETCH statement?

WORKOUT SECTION

W8_1 Find the error in the following PL/SQL program:

```
SET SERVEROUTPUT ON
SET VERIFY OFF
DECLARE
   VCNAME CUST.CNAME%TYPE;
   VCNT  NUMBER(4);
BEGIN
   —SELECT statement which returns multiple value.
   SELECT CNAME INTO VCNAME FROM CUST;
   —Check effect of %FOUND attribute
   DBMS_OUTPUT.PUT_LINE('SQL%FOUND VALUE');
   IF SQL%FOUND THEN
      DBMS_OUTPUT.PUT_LINE('TRUE');
   ELSE
      DBMS_OUTPUT.PUT_LINE('FALSE');
   END IF;
   —Check effect of %ROWCOUNT attribute
   DBMS_OUTPUT.PUT_LINE('SQL%ROWCOUNT VALUE');
   VCNT := SQL%ROWCOUNT;
   IF SQL%ROWCOUNT>0 THEN
      DBMS_OUTPUT.PUT_LINE(VCNT);
   ELSE
      DBMS_OUTPUT.PUT_LINE('No Row found');
   END IF;
END;
/
```

W8_2 Write a PL/SQL program which will insert ('110','CD', 20, 10) in PROD table. After insertion, check the %ROWCOUNT attribute. Finally, roll back to undo the insertions.

```
SQL> @ C:\BOOK\CHAPTER8\W8_2

SQL%ROWCOUNT VALUE
4
```

W8_3 What will be the output of this PL/SQL code?

```
SET SERVEROUTPUT ON
DECLARE
   VCNAME CUST.CNAME%TYPE;
   CURSOR CNAME_CURSOR IS SELECT CNAME FROM CUST;
BEGIN
   OPEN CNAME_CURSOR;
   LOOP
```

```
        FETCH CNAME_CURSOR INTO VCNAME;
        DBMS_OUTPUT.PUT_LINE(VCNAME);
        EXIT WHEN CNAME_CURSOR%NOTFOUND;
    END LOOP;
    CLOSE CNAME_CURSOR;
END;
/
```

W8_4 Find error in the PL/SQL program. What will be the output of this program?

```
SET SERVEROUTPUT ON
DECLARE
    VCNAME CUST.CNAME%TYPE;
    CURSOR CNAME_CURSOR IS SELECT CNAME FROM CUST;
BEGIN
    OPEN CNAME_CURSOR;
    LOOP
        FETCH CNAME_CURSOR INTO VCNAME;
        DBMS_OUTPUT.PUT_LINE(VCNAME);
    END LOOP;
    CLOSE CNAME_CURSOR;
END;
/
```

W8_5 Find error in this PL/SQL program.

```
SET SERVEROUTPUT ON
DECLARE
    VCNAME CUST.CNAME%TYPE;
    CURSOR CNAME_CURSOR IS SELECT CNAME FROM CUST;
BEGIN
    OPEN CNAME_CURSOR;
    LOOP
        FETCH CNAME_CURSOR INTO VCNAME;
        EXIT WHEN CNAME_CURSOR%NOTFOUND;
        DBMS_OUTPUT.PUT_LINE(VCNAME);
        CLOSE CNAME_CURSOR;
    END LOOP;
END;
/
```

W8_6 Find the error in this PL/SQL program.

```
SET SERVEROUTPUT ON
DECLARE
    VCNAME CUST.CNAME%TYPE;
    CURSOR CNAME_CURSOR IS SELECT CNAME FROM CUST;
```

```
BEGIN
    LOOP
        OPEN CNAME_CURSOR;
        FETCH CNAME_CURSOR INTO VCNAME;
        EXIT WHEN CNAME_CURSOR%NOTFOUND;
        DBMS_OUTPUT.PUT_LINE(VCNAME);
        CLOSE CNAME_CURSOR;
    END LOOP;
END;
/
```

W8_7 What will be the output of this PL/SQL program?

```
SET SERVEROUTPUT ON
DECLARE
    VCNAME CUST.CNAME%TYPE;
    CURSOR CNAME_CURSOR IS SELECT CNAME FROM CUST;
BEGIN
    OPEN CNAME_CURSOR;
    LOOP
        FETCH CNAME_CURSOR INTO VCNAME;
        FETCH CNAME_CURSOR INTO VCNAME;
        EXIT WHEN CNAME_CURSOR%NOTFOUND;
        DBMS_OUTPUT.PUT_LINE(VCNAME);
    END LOOP;
    CLOSE CNAME_CURSOR;
END;
/
```

W8_8 to W8_11 are based on PROJ, EMP, PROJ_DETAIL and DESGRATE tables. Refer to Figure 5.8 for the tables along with data.

W8_8 Write a PL/SQL program to display name of all ANALYST and DBA along with their total earnings.

SQL> @C:\BOOK\CHAPTER8\W8_8.SQL

ARUP, DBA—earned—>60000
ANUP, ANALYST—earned—>12000
KAUSHIK, ANALYST—earned—>16000

W8_9 Write a PL/SQL program to display the highest and lowest value project.

SQL> @C:\BOOK\CHAPTER8\W8_9.SQL

Highest value project is DATABASE SW with a value of 71000
Lowest value project is DATA RECOVERY with a value of 10000

W8_10 Write a PL/SQL program to display total earnings of ANALYST and PROGRAMMER.

SQL> @C:\BOOK\CHAPTER8\W8_10.SQL

Total earnings of ANALYST is 28000
Total earnings of PROGRAMMER is 35000

W8_11 Write a PL/SQL program to compute and print bonus awarded to each employee. Bonus is computed as per following rule:

For ANALYST: 25% of total earnings subject to a maximum of 3000
For DBA; 10% of total earnings subject to a maximum of 5000
For PROGRAMMER: 15% of total earnings subject to a maximum of 2500

SQL> @C:\BOOK\CHAPTER8\W8_11.SQL

Bonus given to ANUP, ANALYST is 3000
Bonus given to ARUP, DBA is 5000
Bonus given to KAUSHIK, ANALYST is 3000
Bonus given to AMIT, PROGRAMMER is 2500
Bonus given to CHANDRA, PROGRAMMER is 2250

Advance Cursors

Learning Objectives

You will learn following key concepts after completion of the chapter:

- ✓ Use of cursors in subqueries
- ✓ Concepts associated with REF cursors
- ✓ Use of parameters in a cursor
- ✓ Use of iteration in an advance cursor

9.1 INTRODUCTION

Advance cursors are extensively used in PL/SQL programming. Advance cursors are also known as parameterized cursors, as parameters are passed at run-time. This is extremely useful to extract records based on values of column, which are not known in advance. In this chapter, FOR UPDATE and WHERE CURRENT clauses are discussed at length. All the concepts are explained using numerous examples, with an assumption that the reader has gone through the previous chapter and possesses clear conception on use of the implicit and explicit cursors.

9.2 PARAMETERS IN CURSORS

Parameters can be included in a cursor to pass values at run-time. Parameters in cursors are useful when a cursor is required to be opened based on a different set of parameter values. A cursor with parameter can be opened and closed several times. Each time a new active set is loaded in the memory and the pointer is placed at first record. In most cases cursors with parameters are used in a loop. Cursors with parameters can also be used in functions and procedures. Use of cursor with parameter inside a procedure is demonstrated using examples. Basic syntax of parameters in cursor is as follows:

```
CURSOR CURSOR_NAME(PARAMETER_NAME DATATYPE, ... ) IS
SELECT_STATEMENT;
```

In this syntax

CURSOR_NAME	is name of the explicit cursor
PARAMETER_NAME	is name of parameter (one or more)
DATATYPE	is data type of each parameter
SELECT_STATEMENT	is a SELECT statement, which must contain parameter name in WHERE clause

Example

```
CURSOR SALE_CURS(VCID VARCHAR2) IS
SELECT P.PNAME, P.PCOST
FROM PROD P, SALE_DETAIL S
WHERE P.PID=S.PID AND S.CID=VCID;
```

In this example,

CURSOR_NAME	is SALE_CURS
PARAMETER_NAME	is VCID
DATATYPE	is VARCHAR2
SELECT_STATEMENT	is SELECT P.PNAME, P.PCOST FROM PROD P, SALE_DETAIL S WHERE P.PID=S.PID AND S.CID=VCID;

Note that parameter name VCID is present in the SELECT statement.

All examples (EX9_1 to EX9_7) are based on CUST, PROD, SALE_DETAIL and STATE_NAME tables. Refer to Figure 5.6 for all the tables along with their rows.

EX9_1 Write a PL/SQL program to display purchase details of all customers based on SALE_DATE. This is an example of the cursor with parameter. Major steps of this program are discussed in detail.

```
SET SERVEROUTPUT ON
DECLARE
   CURSOR CURS_DATE IS SELECT DISTINCT SALEDT
   FROM SALE_DETAIL ORDER BY SALEDT;
   CURSOR CURS_DETAIL(VDATE DATE) IS
   SELECT S.SALE,P.PNAME,C.CNAME
   FROM SALE_DETAIL S,PROD P,CUST C
   WHERE (S.PID=P.PID) AND (S.CID=C.CID) AND (S.SALEDT=VDATE)
   ORDER BY P.PNAME, C.CNAME;
   R_DATE   CURS_DATE%ROWTYPE;
   R_DETAIL CURS_DETAIL%ROWTYPE;
BEGIN
   OPEN CURS_DATE;
   LOOP
      FETCH CURS_DATE INTO R_DATE;
      EXIT WHEN CURS_DATE%NOTFOUND;
      DBMS_OUTPUT.PUT_LINE('SALE DATE : '||R_DATE.SALEDT);
      OPEN CURS_DETAIL(R_DATE.SALEDT);
```

```
        LOOP
            FETCH CURS_DETAIL INTO R_DETAIL;
            EXIT WHEN CURS_DETAIL%NOTFOUND;
            DBMS_OUTPUT.PUT_LINE(R_DETAIL.CNAME||' purchased
            '||R_DETAIL.SALE || ' number of ' || R_DETAIL.PNAME);
        END LOOP;
        CLOSE CURS_DETAIL;
        DBMS_OUTPUT.PUT_LINE('——————————————');
    END LOOP;
    CLOSE CURS_DATE;
END;
/
```

Execution

```
SQL> @ C:\BOOK\CHAPTER9\EX9_1

SALE DATE : 14-JUL-13
PRADIP purchased 2 number of PEN
TUSHAR purchased 1 number of PEN
PRADIP purchased 5 number of PENCIL
--------------------------------------
SALE DATE : 15-JUL-13
AASTIK purchased 10 number of FLOPPY
--------------------------------------
SALE DATE : 20-AUG-13
PRADIP purchased 3 number of PEN
--------------------------------------
SALE DATE : 18-SEP-13
ANUMITA purchased 2 number of FLOPPY
--------------------------------------
SALE DATE : 14-NOV-13
ARPAN purchased 2 number of PEN
--------------------------------------
```

Illustrations

Major steps of the complete program are as under. Text related to the program is shown in capital letters.

i. `CURSOR CURS_DATE IS SELECT DISTINCT SALEDT`
   `FROM SALE_DETAIL ORDER BY SALEDT;`
   Declare CURS_DATE cursor to retrieve distinct SALEDT from SALE_DETAIL table. Order SALEDT in ascending order.

ii. `CURSOR CURS_DETAIL(VDATE DATE) IS`
   `SELECT S.SALE, P.PNAME, C.CNAME`
   `FROM SALE_DETAIL S,PROD P,CUST C`

```
WHERE (S.PID=P.PID) AND (S.CID=C.CID) AND (S.SALEDT=VDATE)
ORDER BY P.PNAME, C.CNAME;
```

Declare CURS_DETAIL cursor with VDATE parameter. Value of VDATE will be assigned at run-time and based on the value active set will be loaded in the memory. This cursor retrieves SALE, PNAME and CNAME values from SALE_DETAIL, PROD and CUST tables. Retrieval of rows is ordered by PNAME and CNAME.

iii.
```
R_DATE    CURS_DATE%ROWTYPE;
R_DETAIL  CURS_DETAIL%ROWTYPE;
```

Declare container to hold field values by the cursors. Note the use of cursor names (CURS_DATE and CURS_DETAIL) in the declaration.

iv.
```
BEGIN
   OPEN CURS_DATE;
   LOOP
      FETCH CURS_DATE INTO R_DATE;
      EXIT WHEN CURS_DATE%NOTFOUND;
      DBMS_OUTPUT.PUT_LINE('SALE DATE :
      '||R_DATE.SALEDT);
      OPEN CURS_DETAIL(R_DATE.SALEDT);
      ----------
      ----------
```

Open CURS_DATE cursor, fetch values (RDATE.SALEDT) corresponding to the first row from active set. Open CURS_DETAIL with the value of RDATE.SALEDT so that active set corresponding to the current value is loaded in the memory.

v.
```
OPEN CURS_DATE;
LOOP
   FETCH CURS_DATE INTO R_DATE;
   _____

   _____
   OPEN CURS_DETAIL(R_DATE.SALEDT);
      LOOP
         FETCH CURS_DETAIL INTO R_DETAIL;
         EXIT WHEN CURS_DETAIL%NOTFOUND;
         DBMS_OUTPUT.PUT_LINE(R_DETAIL.CNAME||' purchased
      '||R_DETAIL.SALE || ' number of ' || R_DETAIL.PNAME);
         END LOOP;
      CLOSE CURS_DETAIL;
   DBMS_OUTPUT.PUT_LINE('——————————————');
END LOOP;
CLOSE CURS_DATE;
```

After opening the CURS_DETAIL cursor using the current value of SALEDT, iterate inside a loop to fetch and print all rows. Close CURS_DETAIL cursor after the control comes out from the loop. Reopen CURS_DETAIL with the newly fetched value by CURS_DATE cursor and repeat the process till the time all rows related to CURS_DATE are fetched. Refer to Table 9.1 for details related to retrieval of rows by both the cursors.

TABLE 9.1 Movement of Pointer in Parameterized Cursor

Iteration		Cursor status		Active set and pointer of cursors			
Outer loop	**Inner loop**	**CURS_ DATE**	**CURS_ DETAIL**	**CURS_DATE**	**CURS_DETAIL**		
				SALE_DATE	SALE	PNAME	CNAME
Ist	Ist	Open	Open	**14-JUL-13** 15-JUL-13 20-AUG-13 18-SEP-13 14-NOV-13	**2** 1 5	**PEN** PEN PENCIL	**PRADIP** TUSHAR PRADIP
	IInd	Open	Open		2 **1** 5	PEN **PEN** PENCIL	PRADIP **TUSHAR** PRADIP
	IIIrd	Open	Open		2 1 **5**	PEN PEN **PENCIL**	PRADIP TUSHAR **PRADIP**
	IVth	Open	Exit Close		2 1 5	PEN PEN PENCIL	PRADIP TUSHAR PRADIP
IInd	Ist	Open	Open	14-JUL-13 **15-JUL-13** 20-AUG-13 18-SEP-13 14-NOV-13	**10**	**FLOPPY**	**AASTIK**
	IInd	Open	Exit Close		10	FLOPPY	AASTIK
IIIrd	Ist	Open	Open	14-JUL-13 15-JUL-13 **20-AUG-13** 18-SEP-13 14-NOV-13	**3**	**PEN**	**PRADIP**
	IInd	Open	Exit Close		3	PEN	PRADIP
IVth	Ist	Open	Open	14-JUL-13 15-JUL-13 20-AUG-13 **18-SEP-13** 14-NOV-13	**2**	**FLOPPY**	**ANUMITA**
	IInd	Open	Exit Close		2	FLOPPY	ANUMITA
Vth	Ist	Open	Open	14-JUL-13 15-JUL-13 20-AUG-13 18-SEP-13 **14-NOV-13**	**3**	**PEN**	**ARPAN**
	IInd	Open	Exit Close		3	PEN	ARPAN
VIth		Exit Close		14-JUL-13 15-JUL-13 20-AUG-13 18-SEP-13 14-NOV-13			

EX9_2 Write a PL/SQL program to display items purchased by each customer. Consolidate all purchases into one by each customer.

```
DECLARE
   CURSOR NAME_CURS IS SELECT C.CID, C.CNAME, C.CCITY, ST.STATE
   FROM CUST C,STATE_NAME ST
   WHERE C.CCITY=ST.CCITY;
   CURSOR SALE_CURS(VCID VARCHAR2) IS
   SELECT  P.PNAME, P.PCOST, P.PID, S.CID
   FROM PROD P, SALE_DETAIL S
   WHERE P.PID=S.PID AND S.CID=VCID ;
   E_NAME NAME_CURS%ROWTYPE;
   E_SALE SALE_CURS%ROWTYPE;
   VGTOTAL NUMBER:=0;
   VCTOTAL NUMBER;
   VCID CUST.CID%TYPE;
   VTOTAL NUMBER(8,2);
   VSALE SALE_DETAIL.SALE%TYPE:=0;
   AC VARCHAR2(20):='ABC';
BEGIN
   OPEN NAME_CURS;
   LOOP
      FETCH NAME_CURS INTO E_NAME;
      EXIT WHEN NAME_CURS%NOTFOUND;
      DBMS_OUTPUT.PUT_LINE(INITCAP(E_NAME.CNAME)||' of
      '||INITCAP(E_NAME.CCITY)||', '||INITCAP(E_NAME.STATE) ||
      'purchased items as per following details.');
      VCTOTAL:=0;
      OPEN SALE_CURS(E_NAME.CID);
      LOOP
         FETCH SALE_CURS INTO E_SALE;
         EXIT WHEN SALE_CURS%NOTFOUND;
         IF AC <> (E_SALE.CID||E_SALE.PID) THEN
            SELECT SUM(SALE) INTO VSALE
            FROM SALE_DETAIL WHERE CID=E_NAME.CID;
            VTOTAL:=VSALE*E_SALE.PCOST;
            DBMS_OUTPUT.PUT_LINE(E_SALE.PNAME||' at a unit
            price of Rs '||E_SALE.PCOST||', quantity '||VSALE||' at a
            total price of Rs '||VTOTAL);
            VCTOTAL:=VCTOTAL+VTOTAL;
         END IF;
         AC:=E_SALE.CID||E_SALE.PID;
      END LOOP;
      DBMS_OUTPUT.PUT_LINE('Total expenditure by the customer is Rs
      '||VCTOTAL);
      CLOSE SALE_CURS;
```

```
        VGTOTAL:=VGTOTAL+VCTOTAL;
        DBMS_OUTPUT.PUT_LINE('---------------------');
    END LOOP;
    CLOSE NAME_CURS;
    DBMS_OUTPUT.PUT_LINE('GRAND TOTAL     '||VGTOTAL);
END;
/
```

Execution

```
SQL> @ C:\BOOK\CHAPTER9\EX9_2.SQL
Pradip of Mysore, Karnataka purchased items as per following details.
PENCIL at a unit price of Rs 5.25, quantity 10 at a total price of Rs
52.5
PEN at a unit price of Rs 20.5, quantity 10 at a total price of Rs 205
Total expenditure by the customer is Rs 257.5
-----------------------------------------------------------------------
Aastik of Kolkata, West Bengal purchased items as per following details.
FLOPPY at a unit price of Rs 30, quantity 10 at a total price of Rs 300
Total expenditure by the customer is Rs 300
-----------------------------------------------------------------------
Tushar of Pune, Maharashtra purchased items as per following details.
PEN at a unit price of Rs 20.5, quantity 1 at a total price of Rs 20.5
Total expenditure by the customer is Rs 20.5
-----------------------------------------------------------------------
Arpan of Chennai, Tamilnadu purchased items as per following details.
PEN at a unit price of Rs 20.5, quantity 2 at a total price of Rs 41
Total expenditure by the customer is Rs 41
-----------------------------------------------------------------------
Anumita of Indore, Madhya Pradesh purchased items as per following
details.
FLOPPY at a unit price of Rs 30, quantity 2 at a total price of Rs 60
Total expenditure by the customer is Rs 60
-----------------------------------------------------------------------
GRAND TOTAL    679
```

Illustration

This example is similar to EX9_1. Students are encouraged to trace the program similar to Table 9.1 to understand and appreciate the concept of advance cursor.

EX9_3 Write a PL/SQL procedure to display product names using OUT parameter, which are below and above cut-off price. This is an example of using cursor with parameter in a procedure.

```
CREATE OR REPLACE PROCEDURE PROC_CUTOFF(CUTOFF IN  NUMBER,PBELOW OUT
VARCHAR2,PABOVE OUT VARCHAR2) IS
CURSOR CURS_PROD IS
SELECT PID,PNAME,PCOST FROM PROD ORDER BY PID;
```

```
CURSOR CURS_SALE(VPID PROD.PID%TYPE)  IS
SELECT SALE FROM SALE_DETAIL WHERE PID=VPID;
E_PROD CURS_PROD%ROWTYPE;
E_SALE CURS_SALE%ROWTYPE;
VSALE NUMBER;
VTOTAL NUMBER;
VPBELOW VARCHAR2(100):='';
VPABOVE VARCHAR2(100):='';

BEGIN
   OPEN CURS_PROD;
   LOOP
      FETCH CURS_PROD INTO E_PROD;
      EXIT WHEN CURS_PROD%NOTFOUND;
       VTOTAL:=0;
      OPEN CURS_SALE(E_PROD.PID);
      LOOP
         FETCH CURS_SALE INTO E_SALE;
         EXIT WHEN CURS_SALE%NOTFOUND;
         VSALE:=E_SALE.SALE*E_PROD.PCOST;
         VTOTAL:=VTOTAL+VSALE;
      END LOOP;
      CLOSE CURS_SALE;
      IF VTOTAL>CUTOFF THEN
         VPABOVE:=VPABOVE||' ['||E_PROD.PNAME||'] ';
      END IF;
      IF VTOTAL<=CUTOFF THEN
         VPBELOW:=VPBELOW||' ['||E_PROD.PNAME||'] ';
      END IF;
   END LOOP;
   CLOSE CURS_PROD;
   PBELOW:=VPBELOW;
   PABOVE:=VPABOVE;
END PROC_CUTOFF;
/
```

Execution

```
SQL> @ C:\BOOK\CHAPTER9\EX9_3.SQL
```

Procedure created.

EX9_4 Write a PL/SQL program to call PROC_CUTOFF procedure. This program simply calls a procedure.

```
SET SERVEROUTPUT ON
SET VERIFY OFF
```

```
DECLARE
    CUTOFF NUMBER;
    PBELOW VARCHAR2(100);
    PABOVE VARCHAR2(100);
BEGIN
    CUTOFF:=&CUTOFFSALE;
    PROC_CUTOFF(CUTOFF,PBELOW,PABOVE);
    DBMS_OUTPUT.PUT_LINE('PRODUCTS BELOW CUT-OFF SALE:');
    DBMS_OUTPUT.PUT_LINE(PBELOW);
    DBMS_OUTPUT.PUT_LINE('PRODUCTS ABOVE CUT-OFF SALE:');
    DBMS_OUTPUT.PUT_LINE(PABOVE);
END;
/
```

Execution

```
SQL> @ C:\BOOK\CHAPTER9\EX9_4.SQL
Enter value for cutoffsale: 200
PRODUCTS BELOW CUT-OFF SALE:
[PENCIL]   [PEN]
PRODUCTS ABOVE CUT-OFF SALE:
[FLOPPY]

SQL> @ C:\BOOK\CHAPTER9\EX9_4.SQL
Enter value for cutoffsale: 100
PRODUCTS BELOW CUT-OFF SALE:
[PENCIL]
PRODUCTS ABOVE CUT-OFF SALE:
[FLOPPY]   [PEN]
```

9.3 FOR UPDATE CLAUSE

FOR UPDATE clause is used to lock rows before updating or deleting of records. FOR UPDATE clause is added in the cursor query to lock the affected records when the cursor is opened. Oracle Server releases the lock at the end of the transaction. Transaction should not be committed across fetches if FOR UPDATE clause is used in the explicit cursor. FOR UPDATE clause is used to ensure that the record is not changed by another user before the update or delete.

Syntax of FOR UPDATE clause is as follows:

```
SELECT ….
FROM …
FOR UPDATE [OF REFERENCED_COLUMN(S)] [NOWAIT];
```

In this, REFERENCED_COLUMN(S) is/are single or list of columns in the table against which the query is performed and NOWAIT returns an error if the rows are locked by another session. It tells Oracle Server to wait if requested rows have been locked by some other user. In case NOWAIT keyword is omitted, Oracle Server will wait for the rows till the time it is released and available for use.

FOR UPDATE clause is the last clause in the select statement. In case ORDER BY clause is used in the select statement, it must be just before FOR UPDATE clause.

9.4 WHERE CURRENT OF CLAUSE

WHERE CURRENT OF clause is used for referencing the current row of the active set retrieved by the explicit cursor. WHERE CURRENT OF clause allows to apply updates and deletes to the row currently being accessed without referencing ROWID. Syntax of WHERE CURRENT OF clause is as follows:

WHERE CURRENT OF CURSOR_NAME;

Where CURSOR_NAME is the name of a declared cursor with FOR UPDATE clause.

EX9_5 This program demonstrates use of FOR UPDATE and WHERE CURRENT OF clause in a cursor.

```
SET SERVEROUTPUT ON
SET VERIFY OFF
DECLARE
   VREC PROD%ROWTYPE;
   CURSOR PROD_CURSOR IS SELECT * FROM PROD
   WHERE PID IN ('P1','P3')
   ORDER BY PID
   FOR UPDATE OF PID,PNAME,PCOST NOWAIT;
BEGIN
   OPEN PROD_CURSOR;
   LOOP
      FETCH PROD_CURSOR INTO VREC;
      EXIT WHEN PROD_CURSOR%NOTFOUND;
      UPDATE PROD
      SET PCOST=VREC.PCOST*1.1
      WHERE CURRENT OF PROD_CURSOR;
   END LOOP;
   CLOSE PROD_CURSOR;
END;
/
PAUSE Wait for Commit or Rollback
```

Execution and illustration

Concurrent sessions that use the same program in two sessions in parallel are demonstrated in Figure 9.1.

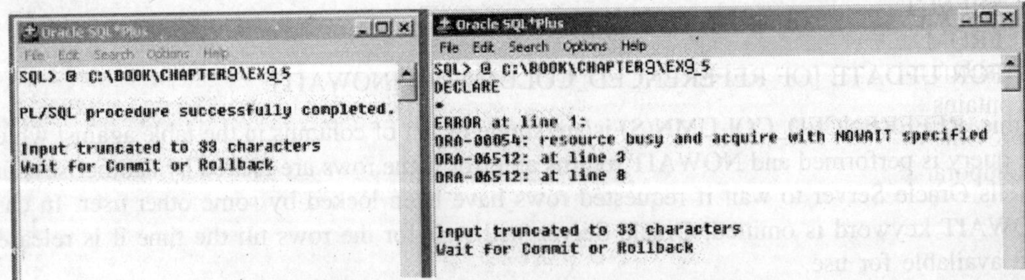

FIGURE 9.1 Concurrent session of a program.

EX9_6 This program demonstrates concurrent use of same program without (i.e. EX9_5) FOR UPDATE/WHERE CURRENT OF clause.

```
SET SERVEROUTPUT ON
SET VERIFY OFF
DECLARE
   VREC PROD%ROWTYPE;
   CURSOR PROD_CURSOR IS SELECT * FROM PROD
   WHERE PID IN ('P1','P3')
   ORDER BY PID;
BEGIN
   OPEN PROD_CURSOR;
   LOOP
      FETCH PROD_CURSOR INTO VREC;
      EXIT WHEN PROD_CURSOR%NOTFOUND;
      UPDATE PROD
      SET PCOST=VREC.PCOST*1.1;
   END LOOP;
   CLOSE PROD_CURSOR;
END;
/
PAUSE Wait for Commit or Rollback
```

Execution and Illustration

Observe the difference between EX9_5 and EX9_6, where FOR UPDATE/ WHERE CURRENT OF clause is used. In this example cursor just waits till the time transaction is complete in the other parallel session (Figure). Note that no message is displayed in the right window of Figure 9.2.

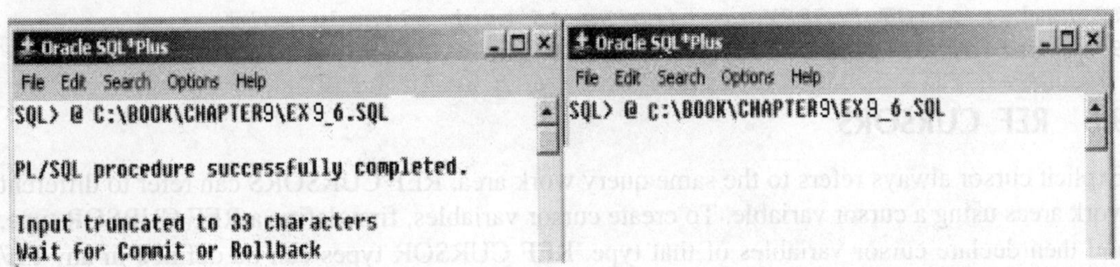

FIGURE 9.2 Concurrent use of a program.

9.5 CURSORS WITH FROM SUBQUERY

A subquery is a query inside a query. A subquery is also called inner query. The query which contains the subquery is called outer query. A subquery is usually enclosed in a parentheses and provides a single or set of values to the outer query. In FROM clause, subquery creates a temporary data source for the outer query.

EX9_7 Write a PL/SQL program to display details of sale of all products which are sold more than 5 are displayed. This example demonstrates use of FOR subqueries in a cursor.

```
SET SERVEROUTPUT ON
SET VERIFY ON
SET ECHO OFF
DECLARE
   CURSOR FORE_CURSOR IS
   SELECT P.PNAME, P.PCOST, SD.ABOVE5
   FROM PROD P,
   (SELECT PID, SUM(SALE) ABOVE5
   FROM SALE_DETAIL
   GROUP BY PID) SD
   WHERE P.PID=SD.PID AND SD.ABOVE5>5;
   VPNAME PROD.PNAME%TYPE;
   VPCOST PROD.PCOST%TYPE;
   VABOVE5 NUMBER(2);
BEGIN
   OPEN FORE_CURSOR;
   LOOP
      FETCH FORE_CURSOR INTO VPNAME,VPCOST,VABOVE5;
      EXIT WHEN FORE_CURSOR%NOTFOUND;
      DBMS_OUTPUT.PUT_LINE(VABOVE5||' number(s) OF '||VPNAME || '
      costing Rs '||VPCOST||' each already sold. ');
   END LOOP;
END;
/

SQL> @ C:\BOOK\CHAPTER9\EX9_7
12 number(s) OF FLOPPY costing Rs 46 each already sold.
8 number(s) OF PEN costing Rs 32.55 each already sold.
```

9.6 REF CURSORS

Explicit cursor always refers to the same query work area. REF CURSORS can refer to different work areas using a cursor variable. To create cursor variables, first define a REF CURSOR type, and then declare cursor variables of that type. REF CURSOR types can be defined in any PL/SQL block, subprogram or package.

EX9_8

```
SET SERVEROUTPUT ON
DECLARE
  TYPE REFCURSOR IS REF CURSOR RETURN CUST%ROWTYPE;
  RC REFCURSOR;
   RREC RC%ROWTYPE;
```

```
BEGIN
   OPEN RC FOR SELECT * FROM CUST;
   LOOP
      FETCH RC INTO RREC;
      EXIT WHEN RC%NOTFOUND;
      DBMS_OUTPUT.PUT_LINE(RREC.CNAME || ' LIVES IN ' || RREC.CCITY);
   END LOOP;
   CLOSE RC;
END;
/
```

Execution

```
SQL> @ C:\BOOK\CHAPTER9\EX9_8
Input truncated to 1 characters
PRADIP LIVES IN MYSORE
AASTIK LIVES IN KOLKATA
TUSHAR LIVES IN PUNE
ARPAN LIVES IN CHENNAI
ANUMITA LIVES IN INDORE
```

EX9_9

```
SET SERVEROUTPUT ON
DECLARE
   TYPE REFCURSOR IS REF CURSOR;
   RC REFCURSOR;
   RREC PROD%ROWTYPE;
   VPCOST NUMBER := &PCOST;
BEGIN
   DBMS_OUTPUT.PUT_LINE('-----------------------------------');
   DBMS_OUTPUT.PUT_LINE('COST DETAILS OF ITEMS ABOVE '|| VPCOST);
   DBMS_OUTPUT.PUT_LINE('-----------------------------------');
   OPEN RC FOR SELECT * FROM PROD WHERE PCOST>VPCOST;
   LOOP
      FETCH RC INTO RREC;
      EXIT WHEN RC%NOTFOUND;
      DBMS_OUTPUT.PUT_LINE('COST OF ' || RREC.PNAME || ' IS '
      || RREC.PCOST);
   END LOOP;
   CLOSE RC;
   DBMS_OUTPUT.PUT_LINE('------------------------------');
   DBMS_OUTPUT.PUT_LINE('COST DETAILS OF ALL THE ITEMS');
   DBMS_OUTPUT.PUT_LINE('------------------------------');
   OPEN RC FOR SELECT * FROM PROD;
   LOOP
      FETCH RC INTO RREC;
```

```
      EXIT WHEN RC%NOTFOUND;
      DBMS_OUTPUT.PUT_LINE('COST OF ' || RREC.PNAME || ' IS'
      || RREC.PCOST);
   END LOOP;
   CLOSE RC;
END;
/
```

Execution

```
SQL>  @ C:\BOOK\CHAPTER9\EX9_9
Input truncated to 1 characters
Enter value for pcost: 10
old   5: VPCOST NUMBER := &PCOST;
new   5: VPCOST NUMBER := 10;
----------------------------------
COST DETAILS OF ITEMS ABOVE 10
----------------------------------
COST OF PEN IS 20.5
COST OF FLOPPY IS 30
----------------------------------
COST DETAILS OF ALL THE ITEMS
----------------------------------
COST OF PEN IS 20.5
COST OF FLOPPY IS 30
COST OF PENCIL IS 5.25

SQL> /
Enter value for pcost: 25
old   5: VPCOST NUMBER := &PCOST;
new   5: VPCOST NUMBER := 25;
----------------------------------
COST DETAILS OF ITEMS ABOVE 25
----------------------------------
COST OF FLOPPY IS 30
----------------------------------
COST DETAILS OF ALL THE ITEMS
----------------------------------
COST OF PEN IS 20.5
COST OF FLOPPY IS 30
COST OF PENCIL IS 5.25
```

9.7 SUMMARY

The major objective of this chapter is to consolidate learning of implicit and explicit cursors in the previous chapter with the parameterized cursors. Sound knowledge of cursors is vital to expertise PL/SQL programming and to achieve the maximum benefit, students are advised to complete all the workouts given in this chapter.

SHORT/OBJECTIVE TYPE QUESTIONS

1. Write short notes on parameterized cursor?
2. Write a program to demonstrate SELECT FOR UPDATE statement.
3. How you can fetch a current row from a cursor?
4. Which data type cannot be used within a RECORD type?
5. What is the difference between CREATE PROCEDURE and CREATE ANY PROCEDURE system privilege?
6. Write a program to pass parameters to a cursor.
7. What is the difference between EXIT WHEN and EXIT statements?
8. What is the difference between LONG and LOB?
9. What is the difference between BLOB and CLOB data types?
10. Can you convert LONG objects to LOB objects?
11. Name two components of LOB data type.
12. Is it possible to use LOB data type as PL/SQL variables?
13. Can you use BFILE for transactions?
14. What is the use of DBMS_LOB package? Does it support concurrency control?
15. Can you use SELECT statement to see the content in BLOB or BFILE data type?
16. Does Oracle implicitly maintain concurrency for LOB data types?
17. Can you generate random numbers in Oracle?
18. How do you manage Oracle locks related services?
19. What happens to the view when a new column is added to the related table?
20. Do you feel the concept of cursors in PL/SQL is similar to that of pointers in C?

WORKOUT SECTION

W9_1 to W9_4 are based on PROJ, EMP, DESGRATE and PROJ_DETAIL tables. All the tables along with data are shown in Figure 5.8.

W9_1 What will be the output of this PL/SQL program? Trace the values corresponding to the cursors as per Table 9.2.

TABLE 9.2 Movement of Pointers

Iteration	Cursor status			Active set and pointer of cursors		
Outer Loop	Inner Loop	DESG_ CURSOR	PROJ_ CURSOR	DESG_CURSOR	PROJ_CURSOR	
				DESGRATE	ENAME	PROJNAME
1st	1st					
	2nd					
	3rd					
2nd	1st					
	2nd					
	3rd					
	4th					
3rd	1st					
	2nd					
	3rd					

```
SET SERVEROUTPUT ON
SET VERIFY OFF
DECLARE
CURSOR DESG_CURSOR IS
SELECT DESG FROM DESGRATE ORDER BY DESG;
CURSOR PROJ_CURSOR(VDESG1 VARCHAR2) IS
SELECT E.ENAME, P.PROJNAME
FROM EMP E, PROJ P, PROJ_DETAIL PD
WHERE E.EMPNO=PD.EMPNO AND P.PROJNO=PD.PROJNO
AND E.DESG=VDESG1;
VDESG  EMP.DESG%TYPE;
VENAME EMP.ENAME%TYPE;
VPROJNAME PROJ.PROJNAME%TYPE;
BEGIN
    OPEN DESG_CURSOR;
    LOOP
        FETCH DESG_CURSOR INTO VDESG;
        EXIT WHEN DESG_CURSOR%NOTFOUND;
        DBMS_OUTPUT.PUT_LINE('_________');
        DBMS_OUTPUT.PUT_LINE(VDESG);
        DBMS_OUTPUT.PUT_LINE('_________');
        OPEN PROJ_CURSOR(VDESG);
        LOOP
            FETCH PROJ_CURSOR INTO VENAME,VPROJNAME;
            EXIT WHEN PROJ_CURSOR%NOTFOUND;
            DBMS_OUTPUT.PUT_LINE(VENAME || ' worked in ' ||
            VPROJNAME || ' project');
        END LOOP;
    END LOOP;
    CLOSE DESG_CURSOR;
END;
/
```

W9_2 Write a procedure which will display all the PROJNAME in which total expenditure (MONEYSPENT) is more than the input value.

SQL> @ C:\BOOK\CHAPTER9\W9_1.SQL

Procedure created.

W9_3 Write a PL/SQL program to call the procedure created in W9_2.

SQL> @ C:\BOOK\CHAPTER9\W9_2

Enter value for moneyspent: 20000
PROJECTS ABOVE EXPENDITURE ARE:
[DATABASE SW] [CODING]

SQL> @ C:\BOOK\CHAPTER9\W9_2

Enter value for moneyspent: 1000
PROJECTS ABOVE EXPENDITURE ARE:
[DATABASE SW] [CODING] [DATA RECOVERY]

W9_4 Write a PL/SQL program using FOR Subquery to display name of all employees worked only on one project. Also display names of employees who worked in more than one project.

SQL> @ C:\BOOK\CHAPTER9\W9_4

NAME OF EMPLOYEE WORKED ONLY IN ONE PROJECT

ANUP
KAUSHIK
AMIT
CHANDRA
NAME OF EMPLOYEE WORKED MORE THAN ONE PROJECT

- *ARUP has worked in 3 projects.*

W9_5 What will be the output of this program?

```
SET SERVEROUTPUT ON
SET VERIFY OFF
DECLARE
   VREC PROD%ROWTYPE;
   CURSOR PROD_CURSOR IS SELECT * FROM PROD;
BEGIN
   OPEN PROD_CURSOR;
   LOOP
      FETCH PROD_CURSOR INTO VREC;
```

```
            EXIT WHEN PROD_CURSOR%NOTFOUND;
            UPDATE PROD
            SET PCOST=VREC.PCOST*1.1
            WHERE CURRENT OF PROD_CURSOR;
        END LOOP;
        CLOSE PROD_CURSOR;
    END;
    /
```

Questione W9_5 to W9_7 are based on PROJ, EMP, DESGRATE and PROJ_DETAIL tables. All the tables along with data are shown in Figure 5.8.

W9_6 Check values of PCOST from PROD table and execute this program. Open a new SQL*Plus session.
Type UPDATE PROD SET PCOST=PCOST*1.2 WHERE PID='P2';
COMMIT;
SELECT * FROM PROD;
What will be the output?

```
SET SERVEROUTPUT ON
SET VERIFY OFF
DECLARE
   VREC PROD%ROWTYPE;
   CURSOR PROD_CURSOR IS SELECT * FROM PROD
   WHERE PID IN ('P1','P3')
   ORDER BY PID
   FOR UPDATE OF PID,PNAME,PCOST NOWAIT;
BEGIN
   OPEN PROD_CURSOR;
   LOOP
      FETCH PROD_CURSOR INTO VREC;
      EXIT WHEN PROD_CURSOR%NOTFOUND;
      UPDATE PROD
      SET PCOST=VREC.PCOST*1.1
      WHERE CURRENT OF PROD_CURSOR;
   END LOOP;
   CLOSE PROD_CURSOR;
END;
/
PAUSE Wait for Commit or Rollback
```

W9_7 Execute this program and all other SQL statements in the same SQL *Plus window.
Press RETURN key.
UPDATE PROD SET PCOST=PCOST+10 WHERE PID IN ('P2','P3');
COMMIT;
SELECT * FROM PROD;

What will be the output?

```
SET SERVEROUTPUT ON
SET VERIFY OFF
DECLARE
   VREC PROD%ROWTYPE;
   CURSOR PROD_CURSOR IS SELECT * FROM PROD
   WHERE PID IN ('P1','P3')
   ORDER BY PID
   FOR UPDATE OF PID,PNAME,PCOST NOWAIT;
BEGIN
   OPEN PROD_CURSOR;
   LOOP
      FETCH PROD_CURSOR INTO VREC;
      EXIT WHEN PROD_CURSOR%NOTFOUND;
      UPDATE PROD
      SET PCOST=VREC.PCOST*1.1
      WHERE CURRENT OF PROD_CURSOR;
   END LOOP;
   CLOSE PROD_CURSOR;
END;
/
PAUSE Wait for Commit or Rollback
```

10

PL/SQL Collections and Records

Learning Objectives

You will learn following key concepts after completion of the chapter:

✓ Use of VARRAYS in PL/SQL
✓ Use of ASSOCIATIVE ARRAYS in PL/SQL
✓ Use of NESTED TABLES in PL/SQL
✓ Use of COLLECTION methods

10.1 INTRODUCTION

Collection in PL/SQL is similar to arrays in other third-generation programming languages. A record is a group of related data fields having a unique name and allowed data types. In this chapter, PL/SQL collections and record are explained in depth. Examples and workouts in this chapter are given assuming that you have access to Oracle 9i, Oracle 10g and Oracle 11g. Collection is considered to be an advanced topic in PL/SQL programming. It helps to execute program faster as all the processing is done in the main memory using arrays and records instead of interacting directly with tables, which is stored in the secondary storage.

10.2 COLLECTION

A collection is an ordered group of similar types of elements. Each element is addressed by a unique subscript. Collection types offered by PL/SQL are Varrays, Associative Arrays and Nested Tables. Arrays in other languages become Varrays in PL/SQL. Sets are equivalent to nested tables in PL/SQL. Associative arrays in PL/SQL is similar to hash tables in other languages.

To create collections, define a collection type and then declare variables of that type. Collections follow the same scoping and instantiation rules as other types and variables in PL/SQL.

10.2.1 Varrays

Varrays hold a fixed number of elements. The number of elements can be altered at run-time. They use sequential numbers as subscripts. It can be defined equivalent to SQL types and can be stored/retrieved through SQL, but with less flexibility.

Syntax to create Varrays

TYPE TYPE_NAME IS {VARRAY | VARYING ARRAY} (SIZE_LIMIT)
OF ELEMENT_TYPE [NOT NULL];

The meanings of TYPE_NAME and ELEMENT_TYPE are same for nested tables. SIZE_LIMIT is a positive integer literal representing the maximum number of elements in the array. When defining a VARRAY type, its maximum size must be specified.

EX10_1 This PL/SQL program demonstrates use of varrays. It stores ZERO to NINE in an array and displays the same along with string digit.

```
SET SERVEROUTPUT ON
DECLARE
SET SERVEROUTPUT ON
DECLARE
   TYPE DIGIT_NAME IS VARRAY(10) OF VARCHAR2(10) NOT NULL;
   DN DIGIT_NAME;
BEGIN
   DN:=DIGIT_NAME ('ZERO', 'ONE', 'TWO', 'THREE', 'FOUR','FIVE',
   'SIX','SEVEN', 'EIGHT', 'NINE');
   FOR I IN 0 .. 9 LOOP
      DBMS_OUTPUT.PUT_LINE(I || ' -> ' ||DN(I+1));
   END LOOP;
END;
/
```

Execution

```
SQL> @ C:\BOOK\CHAPTER10\EX10_1
0 -> ZERO
1 -> ONE
2 -> TWO
3 -> THREE
4 -> FOUR
5 -> FIVE
6 -> SIX
7 -> SEVEN
8 -> EIGHT
9 -> NINE
```

Illustration

In this example, DIGIT_NAME is declared as a variable type to hold arrays of character type data. DN is an instance (or variable) of DIGIT_NAME and cannot be NULL. 'ZERO' to 'NINE' are stored in DN and displayed using FOR Loop.

10.2.2 Associative Arrays

Associative arrays, also known as index-by tables, allow to look up elements using arbitrary numbers and strings for subscript values. There function is similar to hash tables in other programming languages. In associative arrays, elements can be inserted using arbitrary key values. The keys need not have to be consecutive.

Syntax to create an associative array

TYPE TYPE_NAME IS TABLE OF ELEMENT_TYPE [NOT NULL]
INDEX BY [PLS_INTEGER | BINARY_INTEGER | VARCHAR2(SIZE_LIMIT)];
INDEX BY KEY_TYPE;

The KEY_TYPE can be PLS_INTEGER, BINARY_INTEGER, VARCHAR2 or LONG data types. The types RAW, LONG RAW, ROWID, CHAR and CHARACTER are not allowed as keys for an associative array. Associative arrays can store data using a primary key value as the index, where the key values are not sequential.

EX10_2 This PL/SQL program demonstrates use of associative array of different types.

```
SET SERVEROUTPUT ON
DECLARE
   TYPE AS_NUM_TYPE IS TABLE OF NUMBER INDEX BY PLS_INTEGER;
   TYPE AS_STR_TYPE IS TABLE OF VARCHAR(50) INDEX BY PLS_INTEGER;
   TYPE AS_STR_ANOTHERTYPE IS TABLE OF VARCHAR2(50)
   INDEX BY VARCHAR2(50);
   TYPE AS_NUM_ANOTHERTYPE IS TABLE OF NUMBER
   INDEX BY VARCHAR2(20);
   CLASS_STUDENT AS_NUM_TYPE;
   ROLL_NO AS_STR_TYPE;
   STATE_CAPITAL AS_STR_ANOTHERTYPE;
   AVERAGE_MARKS AS_NUM_ANOTHERTYPE;
BEGIN
   DBMS_OUTPUT.PUT_LINE('EXAMPLE OF NUMBER VS NUMBER');
   DBMS_OUTPUT.PUT_LINE('——————————————');
   CLASS_STUDENT(1):=50;
   CLASS_STUDENT(2):=40;
   CLASS_STUDENT(3):=45;
   CLASS_STUDENT(4):=50;
   CLASS_STUDENT(10):=48;
   DBMS_OUTPUT.PUT_LINE('NUMBER OF STUDENTS IN CLASS I IS   ' ||
   CLASS_STUDENT(1));
```

```
    DBMS_OUTPUT.PUT_LINE('NUMBER OF STUDENTS IN CLASS II IS ' ||
    CLASS_STUDENT(2));
    DBMS_OUTPUT.PUT_LINE('NUMBER OF STUDENTS IN CLASS III IS ' ||
    CLASS_STUDENT(3));
    DBMS_OUTPUT.PUT_LINE('NUMBER OF STUDENTS IN CLASS IV IS ' ||
    CLASS_STUDENT(4));
    DBMS_OUTPUT.PUT_LINE('NUMBER OF STUDENTS IN CLASS X IS ' ||
    CLASS_STUDENT(10));
    DBMS_OUTPUT.PUT_LINE('####################################');

    DBMS_OUTPUT.PUT_LINE('EXAMPLE OF NUMBER VS STRING');
    DBMS_OUTPUT.PUT_LINE('---------------------------');
    ROLL_NO(1):='ANUMITA';
    ROLL_NO(20):='AASTIK';
    DBMS_OUTPUT.PUT_LINE('ROLL NUMBER 1 - ' || ROLL_NO(1));
    DBMS_OUTPUT.PUT_LINE('ROLL NUMBER 20 - ' || ROLL_NO(20));
    DBMS_OUTPUT.PUT_LINE('####################################');

    DBMS_OUTPUT.PUT_LINE('EXAMPLE OF STRING VS STRING');
    DBMS_OUTPUT.PUT_LINE('---------------------------');
    STATE_CAPITAL('ORISSA'):='BHUBANESWAR';
    STATE_CAPITAL('WEST BENGAL'):='KOLKATA';
    DBMS_OUTPUT.PUT_LINE('CAPITAL OF WEST BENGAL IS ' ||
    STATE_CAPITAL('WEST BENGAL'));
    DBMS_OUTPUT.PUT_LINE('CAPITAL OF ORISSA IS ' ||
    STATE_CAPITAL('ORISSA'));
    DBMS_OUTPUT.PUT_LINE('####################################');

    DBMS_OUTPUT.PUT_LINE('EXAMPLE OF STRING VS NUMBER');
    DBMS_OUTPUT.PUT_LINE('---------------------------');
    AVERAGE_MARKS('HINDI'):=80;
    AVERAGE_MARKS('ENGLISH'):=75;

    DBMS_OUTPUT.PUT_LINE('AVERAGE MARKS OBTAINED IN HINDI IS ' ||
    AVERAGE_MARKS('HINDI'));
    DBMS_OUTPUT.PUT_LINE('AVERAGE MARKS OBTAINED IN ENGLISH IS '
    || AVERAGE_MARKS('ENGLISH'));
END;
/
```

Execution

```
SQL> @ C:\BOOK\CHAPTER10\EX10_2
EXAMPLE OF NUMBER VS NUMBER
---------------------------
NUMBER OF STUDENTS IN CLASS I IS 50
NUMBER OF STUDENTS IN CLASS II IS 40
```

```
NUMBER OF STUDENTS IN CLASS III IS 45
NUMBER OF STUDENTS IN CLASS IV IS  50
NUMBER OF STUDENTS IN CLASS X IS   48
########################################################
EXAMPLE OF NUMBER VS STRING
----------------------------
ROLL NUMBER 1 - ANUMITA
ROLL NUMBER 20 - AASTIK
########################################################
EXAMPLE OF STRING VS STRING
----------------------------
CAPITAL OF WEST BENGAL IS KOLKATA
CAPITAL OF ORISSA IS BHUBANESWAR
########################################################
EXAMPLE OF STRING VS NUMBER
----------------------------
AVERAGE MARKS OBTAINED IN HINDI IS 80
AVERAGE MARKS OBTAINED IN ENGLISH IS 75
```

Illustration

In this example, different types of key-type is indexed. The following segment of code explains CLASS_STUDENT which is declared as NUM_TYPE.

```
TYPE AS_NUM_TYPE IS TABLE OF NUMBER INDEX BY PLS_INTEGER;
CLASS_STUDENT AS_NUM_TYPE;
CLASS_STUDENT(1):=50;
DBMS_OUTPUT.PUT_LINE('NUMBER OF STUDENTS IN CLASS I IS'||
CLASS_STUDENT(1));
SQL> NUMBER OF STUDENTS IN CLASS I IS 50
```

In the first line, NUM_TYPE is created, which is the table of numbers and its index is represented by an integer. In the second line, CLASS_STUDENT is declared as an instance of NUM_TYPE. In the third line, CLASS_STUDENT(1) is assigned with the number '50'. Note the use of integer in the index. Finally in the last two lines, its value is displayed.

Readers are advised to correlate AS_STR_TYPE with ROLL_NO, AS_STR_ANOTHERTYPE with STATE_CAPITAL and AS_NUM_ANOTHERTYPE with AVERAGE_MARKS in the example.

10.2.3 Nested Tables

Nested tables hold an arbitrary number of elements. They use sequential numbers as subscripts.

Syntax to create Nested Tables

TYPE TYPE_NAME IS TABLE OF ELEMENT_TYPE [NOT NULL];

TYPE_NAME is a type specifier used later to declare collections. For nested tables declared within PL/SQL, ELEMENT_TYPE is any PL/SQL data type except REF CURSOR.

Nested tables declared in SQL using the CREATE TYPE statement have additional restrictions on the element type. They cannot use BINARY_INTEGER, PLS_INTEGER, BOOLEAN , LONG, LONG RAW, NATURAL, NATURALN, POSITIVE, POSITIVEN, REF CURSOR, SIGNTYPE or STRING type elements.

EX10_3 This program demonstrates use of nested tables.

```
SET SERVEROUTPUT ON
DECLARE
   TYPE NESTED_TYPE IS TABLE OF VARCHAR2(10);
   THIS_BOOK NESTED_TYPE;
BEGIN
   THIS_BOOK:=NESTED_TYPE('THIS', 'BOOK', 'COVERS', 'ALL',
   'CONCEPTS','FROM', 'BASICS', 'TO', 'ADVANCE');
   FOR I IN 1 .. 9 LOOP
   DBMS_OUTPUT.PUT_LINE(THIS_BOOK(I));
   END LOOP;
   DBMS_OUTPUT.PUT_LINE('------------------------------');
   DBMS_OUTPUT.PUT_LINE(THIS_BOOK(3)||' '||THIS_BOOK(9)||'
   '||THIS_BOOK(5));
   DBMS_OUTPUT.PUT_LINE('------------------------------');
END;
/
```

Execution

```
SQL> @ C:\BOOK\CHAPTER10\EX10_3
THIS
BOOK
COVERS
ALL
CONCEPTS
FROM
BASICS
TO
ADVANCE
----------------------
COVERS ADVANCE CONCEPTS
----------------------
```

Illustration

In this example, THIS_BOOK is of the type NESTED_TYPE, which can hold an arbitrary number of variables and can be referenced using the index value.

Associative arrays are appropriate for relatively small lookup tables where the collection can be constructed in memory. They are good for collecting information whose volume is not known in advance as there is no fixed limit on their size. Associative array subscripts can be negative, nonsequential or can use string. Varrays are a good choice when the number of elements is known in advance or the elements are usually accessed in sequence.

10.3 COLLECTION METHODS

A collection method is a built-in function or procedure that operates on collections and can be called using dot notation. Collection methods cannot be called from SQL statements.

10.3.1 EXISTS Function

Checks whether a collection element exists.

Description

EXISTS(*n*) returns TRUE if the *n*th element in a collection exists. Otherwise, EXISTS(*n*) returns FALSE.

EX10_4 This example demonstrates use of EXISTS Function in PL/SQL code.

```
SET SERVEROUTPUT ON
SET VERIFY OFF
DECLARE
   TYPE ODDNUM IS TABLE OF INTEGER;
   TYPE EVENNUM IS TABLE OF INTEGER;
   ODD ODDNUM := ODDNUM(1,3,5,7,9);
   EVEN EVENNUM := EVENNUM(2,4,6,8);
BEGIN
   IF ODD.EXISTS(1) = TRUE THEN
      DBMS_OUTPUT.PUT_LINE('THE FIRST ODD NUMBER IS ' || ODD(1));
   END IF;
   IF ODD.EXISTS(6) = FALSE THEN
      DBMS_OUTPUT.PUT_LINE('THE  SIXTH ODD NUMBER DOES NOT
      EXISTS');
   END IF;
   IF EVEN.EXISTS(3) = TRUE THEN
      DBMS_OUTPUT.PUT_LINE('THE THIRD EVEN NUMBER IS ' ||
      EVEN(3));
   END IF;
   IF EVEN.EXISTS(5) = FALSE THEN
      DBMS_OUTPUT.PUT_LINE('THE  FIFTH EVEN NUMBER DOES NOT EXISTS');
   END IF;
END;
/
```

Execution

```
SQL> @ C:\BOOK\CHAPTER10\EX10_4
Input truncated to 1 characters
THE FIRST ODD NUMBER IS 1
THE  SIXTH ODD NUMBER DOES NOT EXISTS
THE THIRD EVEN NUMBER IS 6
THE  FIFTH EVEN NUMBER DOES NOT EXISTS
```

10.3.2 COUNT Function

Counts the elements in a collection.

Description

For varrays, COUNT always equals LAST. For nested tables, COUNT normally equals LAST. But if the elements are deleted from the middle of a nested table, COUNT becomes smaller than LAST.

EX10_5 This example demonstrates use of COUNT Function in PL/SQL code.

```
SET SERVEROUTPUT ON
SET VERIFY OFF
DECLARE
   TYPE ODDNUM IS TABLE OF INTEGER;
   TYPE EVENNUM IS TABLE OF INTEGER;
   ODD ODDNUM := ODDNUM(1,3,5,7,9);
   EVEN EVENNUM := EVENNUM(2,4,6,8);
BEGIN
   DBMS_OUTPUT.PUT_LINE('ODD NUMBERS IN THE LIST IS ' || ODD.COUNT);
   DBMS_OUTPUT.PUT_LINE('EVEN NUMBERS IN THE LIST IS ' || EVEN.COUNT);
END;
/
```

Execution

```
SQL>  @ C:\BOOK\CHAPTER10\EX10_5
ODD NUMBERS IN THE LIST IS 5
EVEN NUMBERS IN THE LIST IS 4
```

10.3.3 LIMIT Function

Checks the maximum size of a collection.

Description

For varrays, LIMIT returns the maximum number of elements that a varray can contain. For nested tables and associative arrays, which have no maximum size, LIMIT returns NULL.

EX10_6 This example demonstrates use of LIMIT Function in PL/SQL code.

```
SET SERVEROUTPUT ON
SET VERIFY OFF
DECLARE
   TYPE ODDNUM IS VARRAY(10) OF INTEGER;
   TYPE EVENNUM IS TABLE OF INTEGER;
   ODD ODDNUM := ODDNUM(1,3,5,7,9);
   EVEN EVENNUM := EVENNUM(2,4,6,8);
```

```
BEGIN
   DBMS_OUTPUT.PUT_LINE('ODD NUMBERS IN THE LIST IS ' || ODD.COUNT);
   DBMS_OUTPUT.PUT_LINE('ODD NUMBERS LIST CAN HOLD ' || ODD.LIMIT || '
   VALUES');
   DBMS_OUTPUT.PUT_LINE('EVEN NUMBERS IN THE LIST IS ' || EVEN.COUNT);
   DBMS_OUTPUT.PUT_LINE('EVEN NUMBERS LIST CAN HOLD ' || EVEN.LIMIT ||
   ' VALUES');
END;
/
```

Execution

```
SQL> @ C:\BOOK\CHAPTER10\EX10_6
ODD NUMBERS IN THE LIST IS 5
ODD NUMBERS LIST CAN HOLD 10 VALUES
EVEN NUMBERS IN THE LIST IS 4
EVEN NUMBERS LIST CAN HOLD VALUES
```

10.3.4 FIRST Function

Finds the first collection element.

Description

For nested tables, FIRST returns 1. If the elements are deleted from the beginning of a nested table, FIRST returns a number larger than 1.

For varrays, FIRST always returns 1.

10.3.5 LAST Function

Finds the last collection element.

Description

For nested tables, LAST equals COUNT. If elements are deleted from the middle of a nested table, LAST becomes larger than COUNT.

For varrays, LAST always equals to COUNT.

EX10_7 This example demonstrates use of FIRST and LAST Functions in PL/SQL code.

```
SET SERVEROUTPUT ON
SET VERIFY OFF
DECLARE
   TYPE ODDNUM IS VARRAY(10) OF INTEGER;
   TYPE EVENNUM IS TABLE OF INTEGER;
   ODD ODDNUM := ODDNUM(1,3,5,7,9);
   EVEN EVENNUM := EVENNUM(2,4,6,8);
BEGIN
   DBMS_OUTPUT.PUT_LINE('FIRST/LAST FUNCTION RETURNS THE FIRST/LAST
   SUBSCRIPT OF THE LIST');
```

```
    DBMS_OUTPUT.PUT_LINE('---------------------------------');
    DBMS_OUTPUT.PUT_LINE('VALUE RETURNED BY EVEN.FIRST IS ' ||
    EVEN.FIRST);
    DBMS_OUTPUT.PUT_LINE('VALUE RETURNED BY EVEN.LAST IS ' ||
    EVEN.LAST);
    DBMS_OUTPUT.PUT_LINE('VALUE RETURNED BY ODD.FIRST IS ' ||
    ODD.FIRST);
    DBMS_OUTPUT.PUT_LINE('VALUE RETURNED BY ODD.FIRST IS ' || ODD.LAST);
END;
/
```

Execution

```
SQL> @ C:\BOOK\CHAPTER10\EX10_7
FIRST/LAST FUNCTION RETURNS THE FIRST/LAST SUBSCRIPT OF THE LIST
-----------------------------------------------------------------
VALUE RETURNED BY EVEN.FIRST IS 1
VALUE RETURNED BY EVEN.LAST IS 4
VALUE RETURNED BY ODD.FIRST IS 1
VALUE RETURNED BY ODD.FIRST IS 5
```

10.3.6 PRIOR Function

Loops through the collection to find previous elements.

Description

PRIOR(*n*) returns the index number that precedes index *n* in a collection. If *n* has no predecessor, PRIOR(*n*) returns NULL.

This method is more reliable than looping through a fixed set of subscript values, because elements might be inserted or deleted from the collection during the loop. This is especially true for associative arrays, where the subscripts might not be in a consecutive order. Use PRIOR to traverse collections indexed by any series of subscripts.

10.3.7 NEXT Function

Loops through the collection to find subsequent elements.

Description

NEXT(*n*) returns the index number that succeeds index *n*. If *n* has no successor, NEXT(*n*) returns NULL. This method is more reliable than looping through a fixed set of subscript values, because elements might be inserted or deleted from the collection during the loop. This is especially true for associative arrays, where the subscripts might not be in a consecutive order. Use NEXT to traverse collections indexed by any series of subscripts.

EX10_8 This example demonstrates use of PRIOR and NEXT Functions in PL/SQL code.

```
SET SERVEROUTPUT ON
SET VERIFY OFF
DECLARE
   TYPE ODDNUM IS VARRAY(10) OF INTEGER;
   TYPE EVENNUM IS TABLE OF INTEGER;
   ODD ODDNUM := ODDNUM(1,3,5,7,9);
   EVEN EVENNUM := EVENNUM(2,4,6,8);
BEGIN
   DBMS_OUTPUT.PUT_LINE('VALUE RETURNED BY ODD.NEXT(3) IS ' ||
   ODD.NEXT(3));
   DBMS_OUTPUT.PUT_LINE('VALUE RETURNED BY ODD.PRIOR(4) IS ' ||
   ODD.PRIOR(4));
   DBMS_OUTPUT.PUT_LINE('VALUE RETURNED BY EVEN.NEXT(4) IS ' ||
   EVEN.NEXT(4));
   DBMS_OUTPUT.PUT_LINE('VALUE RETURNED BY EVEN.PRIOR(4) IS ' ||
   EVEN.PRIOR(4));
END;
/
```

Execution

```
SQL>  @ C:\BOOK\CHAPTER10\EX10_8
Input truncated to 1 characters
VALUE RETURNED BY ODD.NEXT(3) IS 4
VALUE RETURNED BY ODD.PRIOR(4) IS 3
VALUE RETURNED BY EVEN.NEXT(4) IS
VALUE RETURNED BY EVEN.PRIOR(4) IS 3
```

10.3.8 EXTEND Procedure

Increases the size of a collection.

Description

Use EXTEND to increase the size of a nested table or varray. EXTEND cannot be used with index-by tables.

This procedure has three forms, which are discussed next.

10.3.9 TRIM Procedure

Decreases the size of a collection.

Description

This procedure has two forms:

- TRIM removes one element from the end of a collection.
- TRIM(*n*) removes *n* elements from the end of a collection.

TRIM cannot be used with associative arrays.

EX10_9 This example demonstrates use of EXTEND and TRIM Procedures in PL/SQL code.

```
SET SERVEROUTPUT ON
SET VERIFY OFF
DECLARE
   TYPE EVENNUM IS TABLE OF INTEGER;
   EVEN EVENNUM := EVENNUM(2,4,6,8);
BEGIN
   DBMS_OUTPUT.PUT_LINE('EVEN.COUNT = '||EVEN.COUNT);
   EVEN.EXTEND(2);
   DBMS_OUTPUT.PUT_LINE('EVEN.COUNT AFTER EVEN.EXTEND(2)=
   '||EVEN.COUNT);
   EVEN.TRIM(4);
   DBMS_OUTPUT.PUT_LINE('EVEN.COUNT AFTER EVEN.TRIM(4)=
   '||EVEN.COUNT);
END;
/
```

Execution

```
SQL> @ C:\BOOK\CHAPTER10\EX10_9
EVEN.COUNT = 4
EVEN.COUNT AFTER EVEN.EXTEND(2)= 6
EVEN.COUNT AFTER EVEN.TRIM(4)= 2
```

10.3.10 DELETE Procedure

Deletes collection elements.

Description

This procedure has various forms:

- DELETE removes all elements from a collection.
- DELETE(*n*) removes the *n*th element from an associative array with a numeric key or a nested table. If the associative array has a string key, the element corresponding to the key value is deleted. If *n* is null, DELETE(*n*) does nothing.
- DELETE(*m*,*n*) removes all elements in the range *m*,..., *n* from an associative array or nested table. If *m* is larger than *n* or if *m* or *n* is null, DELETE(*m*,*n*) does nothing.
- Varrays always have consecutive subscripts, so you cannot delete individual elements except from the end (by using the TRIM method).
- If an element to be deleted does not exist, DELETE simply skips it; no exception is raised. PL/SQL keeps placeholders for deleted elements, so you can replace a deleted element by assigning it a new value.
- DELETE lets you maintain sparse nested tables. You can store sparse nested tables in the database, just like any other nested tables.

- The amount of memory allocated to a nested table can increase or decrease dynamically. As you delete elements, memory is freed page by page. If you delete the entire table, all the memory is freed.

EX10_10 This example demonstrates use of DELETE Procedure in PL/SQL code.

```
SET SERVEROUTPUT ON
SET VERIFY OFF
DECLARE
   TYPE EVENNUM IS TABLE OF INTEGER;
   EVEN EVENNUM := EVENNUM(2,4,6,8,10,12,14);
BEGIN
   DBMS_OUTPUT.PUT_LINE('EVEN.COUNT BEFORE DELETE =
   '||EVEN.COUNT);
   EVEN.DELETE(3);
   DBMS_OUTPUT.PUT_LINE('EVEN.COUNT AFTER EVEN.DELETE(3) =
   '||EVEN.COUNT);
   EVEN.DELETE(5,6);
   DBMS_OUTPUT.PUT_LINE('EVEN.COUNT AFTER EVEN.DELETE(5,6) =
   '||EVEN.COUNT);
   EVEN.DELETE;
   DBMS_OUTPUT.PUT_LINE('EVEN.COUNT AFTER EVEN.DELETE =
   '||EVEN.COUNT);
END;
/
```

Execution

```
SQL>  @ C:\BOOK\CHAPTER10\EX10_10
Input truncated to 1 characters
EVEN.COUNT BEFORE DELETE = 7
EVEN.COUNT AFTER EVEN.DELETE(3) = 6
EVEN.COUNT AFTER EVEN.DELETE(5,6) = 4
EVEN.COUNT AFTER EVEN.DELETE = 0
```

10.4 PL/SQL RECORDS

A record is a group of related data items stored in columns. Each column of the record has name and data type. A record is similar to a variable that can hold a table row, or some columns from a table row. %ROWTYPE attribute declares a record that represents a row in a database table, without listing all the columns. PL/SQL code keeps working even after columns are added to the table. To represent a subset of columns in a table, or columns from different tables, one can define a view or declare a cursor to select the right columns and then apply %ROWTYPE to the view or cursor. In this section, we will briefly discuss records that can be defined in a PL/SQL program. To create record in a PL/SQL, it needs to be declared in declaration section of PL/SQL program. We will conclude this chapter with a small example to create, assigning values to the columns of the record and finally retrieving the columns.

EX10_11 This example demonstrates application of PL/SQL records in PL/SQL code.

```
SET SERVEROUTPUT ON
DECLARE
   TYPE EMPREC IS RECORD
   (
   EMPID NUMBER(6),
   NAME  VARCHAR2(20),
   AGE   NUMBER
   );
   EREC1 EMPREC;
   EREC2 EMPREC;
BEGIN
   EREC1.EMPID := 1;
   EREC1.NAME  :='PRANAB';
   EREC1.AGE   :=35;
   DBMS_OUTPUT.PUT_LINE('EREC1.EMPID= '||EREC1.EMPID);
   DBMS_OUTPUT.PUT_LINE('EREC1.NAME = '||EREC1.NAME);
   DBMS_OUTPUT.PUT_LINE('EREC1.AGE  = '||EREC1.AGE);
   DBMS_OUTPUT.PUT_LINE('——————————————');
   EREC2.EMPID := 2;
   EREC2.NAME  :='VINOD';
   EREC2.AGE   :=25;
   DBMS_OUTPUT.PUT_LINE('EREC2.EMPID= '||EREC2.EMPID);
   DBMS_OUTPUT.PUT_LINE('EREC2.NAME = '||EREC2.NAME);
   DBMS_OUTPUT.PUT_LINE('EREC2.AGE  = '||EREC2.AGE);
END;
/
```

Execution

```
SQL> @ C:\BOOK\CHAPTER10\EX10_11
EREC1.EMPID= 1
EREC1.NAME = PRANAB
EREC1.AGE  = 35
-------------------------------
EREC2.EMPID= 2
EREC2.NAME = VINOD
EREC2.AGE  = 25
```

Illustration

PL/SQL record is analogous to structures in 'C' programming language. In this example, EMPREC comprises of EMPID, NAME and AGE fields. EREC1 and EREC2 are variables of EMP_REC type. In the body of the code, the association of value and their display is demonstrated.

EX10_12 This example is based on Figure 5.6. In this example, %ROWTYPE is used to declare variables of cursor.

```
SET SERVEROUTPUT ON
DECLARE
CURSOR PURCUR IS
SELECT C.CNAME, C.CCITY,P.PNAME,S.STATE,SD.SALE,SD.SALEDT
FROM CUST C, PROD P, STATE_NAME S, SALE_DETAIL SD
WHERE C.CID=SD.CID AND P.PID=SD.PID AND C.CCITY=S.CCITY
ORDER BY C.CNAME,SD.SALEDT;
PURREC PURCUR%ROWTYPE;
BEGIN
OPEN PURCUR;
LOOP
FETCH PURCUR INTO PURREC;
EXIT WHEN PURCUR%NOTFOUND;
DBMS_OUTPUT.PUT_LINE(PURREC.CNAME || ' OF ' || PURREC.CCITY || ', '||
PURREC.STATE || ' HAS PURCHASED ' ||PURREC.SALE || ' ' ||PURREC.PNAME
|| ' ON ' || PURREC.SALEDT);
END LOOP;
CLOSE PURCUR;
END;
/
```

Execution

```
SQL>  @ C:\BOOK\CHAPTER10\EX10_12
AASTIK OF KOLKATA, WEST BENGAL HAS PURCHASED 10 FLOPPY
ON 15-JUL-13
ANUMITA OF INDORE, MADHYA PRADESH HAS PURCHASED 2 FLOPPY
ON 18-SEP-13
ARPAN OF CHENNAI, TAMILNADU HAS PURCHASED 2 PEN ON 14-NOV-13
PRADIP OF MYSORE, KARNATAKA HAS PURCHASED 2 PEN ON 14-JUL-13
PRADIP OF MYSORE, KARNATAKA HAS PURCHASED 5 PENCIL ON 14-JUL-13
PRADIP OF MYSORE, KARNATAKA HAS PURCHASED 3 PEN ON 20-AUG-13
TUSHAR OF PUNE, MAHARASHTRA HAS PURCHASED 1 PEN ON 14-JUL-13
```

10.5 SUMMARY

PL/SQL provides three ways to handle arrays using varrays, associative arrays and nested tables. Collectively, all these three are called collections. PL/SQL records are mainly used in conjunction with a table and cursors. All the conceptions in this chapter are explained with the help of examples and workouts. A large number of workouts and short objective type questions included in this chapter will be helpful to provide in-depth knowledge on the advanced features of PL/SQL programming.

SHORT/OBJECTIVE TYPE QUESTIONS

1. What do you understand by VARRAYS?
2. Which system table is responsible to store VARRAY definition?
3. What do you understand by NESTED TABLE?
4. Write Syntax with suitable example of NESTED TABLE.
5. Which System table is used to check NESTED TABLE information?
6. Can you store NESTED TABLE as a database column?
7. Can you store ASSOCIATIVE ARRAY as a database column?
8. When you should use VARRAY?
9. Can we delete arbitrary elements from NESTED TABLE?
10. What element types are used in a NESTED TABLE?
11. Name the exception used in collection?
12. Can you compare two COLLECTIONS using the greater than or less than command?
13. Can you create Multilevel COLLECTIONS?
14. What do you understand by COLLECTION METHOD?
15. What COLLECTION METHODS are used in Oracle?
16. Which method is used to increase the size of a COLLECTION?
17. Which method is used to decrease the size of a COLLECTION?
18. Is ASSOCIATED ARRAYS also known as INDEX BY TABLE?
19. Write short notes on RECORD data type.
20. What is the advantage of implicit record?
21. Can you define a NOT NULL field in a record?
22. Can you define a CONSTANT value in a record?
23. Can you copy contents of one record to another record?
24. Do records contain methods?
25. Is it possible to use VARRAY in a record definition?
26. What is the similarity and difference between NESTED TABLES and VARRAYs?
27. Can DELETE method be used in VARRAY?
28. Which method returns the maximum number of elements in the VARRAY?
29. Which method returns NULL for nested tables?
30. Is it possible to use EXISTS method in index-by table?

WORKOUT SECTION

W10_1 Write a PL/SQL program that will accept input string comprising of string digits from ZERO to NINE. The program should separate out each string digit, store all values in an associative array and display each string digit. Store extra blank space in the array.

```
SQL> @ C:\BOOK\CHAPTER10\W10_1
Enter value for input_str: ONE THREE FIVE NINE
DS(1)->ONE
DS(2)->THREE
DS(3)->FIVE
DS(4)->NINE

SQL> /
Enter value for input_str: TWO TWO FIVE ZERO
DS(1)->TWO
DS(2)->TWO
DS(3)->FIVE
DS(4)->ZERO

SQL> /
Enter value for input_str: EIGHT  SIX
DS(1)->EIGHT
DS(2)->
DS(3)->SIX
```

W10_2 Write a PL/SQL program using collections, which will accept input string (ZERO to NINE) and display the corresponding digit.

```
SQL> @ C:\BOOK\CHAPTER10\W10_2
Enter value for input_str: ZERO
0

SQL> /
Enter value for input_str: SIX
6
```

W10_3 Write a PL/SQL program using collections that will accept input string comprising of multiple digit string and display the corresponding number. Assume that there is exactly one blank space among digit strings.

```
SQL>  @ C:\BOOK\CHAPTER10\W10_3
Enter value for input_str: TWO NINE SEVEN EIGHT
TWO NINE SEVEN EIGHT ->2978
SQL> /
Enter value for input_str: ONE ZERO ZERO ZERO FIVE
ONE ZERO ZERO ZERO FIVE ->10005
```

```
SQL> /
Enter value for input_str: ZERO ZERO NINE
ZERO ZERO NINE ->009
```

W10_4 Write a PL/SQL program using collections that will accept a number and print corresponding string digits.

```
SQL> @ C:\BOOK\CHAPTER10\W10_4
Enter value for num: 11897
11897 ->  ONE ONE EIGHT NINE SEVEN

SQL> /
Enter value for num: 10004
10004 ->  ONE ZERO ZERO ZERO FOUR

SQL> /
Enter value for num: 00009
9 ->  NINE
```

W10_5 Modify W10_3 in such a manner as to handle multiple blank space among string digits.

```
SQL> @ C:\BOOK\CHAPTER10\W10_5
Enter value for input_str: ONE       FIVE NINE
ONE        FIVE NINE ->159

SQL> /
Enter value for input_str: TWO ZERO   SEVEN   NINE
TWO ZERO   SEVEN   NINE ->2079
```

W10_6 Minutely study the PL/SQL program and write the output that will be displayed in positions shown in ?.

```
SET SERVEROUTPUT ON
SET ECHO OFF
SET VERIFY OFF
DECLARE
   TYPE CHECK_DIGIT IS VARRAY(10) OF VARCHAR2(10);
   CD CHECK_DIGIT;
   CHK NUMBER(1);
   TYPE LOOKUP_STR IS TABLE OF NUMBER INDEX BY VARCHAR2(10);
   LS LOOKUP_STR;
   INPUT_STR VARCHAR2(200):= '&INPUT_STR';
   TYPE DIGIT_STR IS TABLE OF VARCHAR2(10) INDEX BY PLS_INTEGER;
   DS DIGIT_STR;
   ISTR_LEN NUMBER;
   CS VARCHAR2(10);
```

```
    NUM_STR VARCHAR2(10);
    INPUT_CHAR VARCHAR2(1);
    CNT NUMBER := 0;
BEGIN
    —CREATE AN ARRAY COMPRISING OF ALL POSSIBLE DIGIT STRING FROM
    ZERO TO NINE
    CD:=CHECK_DIGIT('ZERO','ONE','TWO','THREE',
    'FOUR','FIVE','SIX', 'SEVEN','EIGHT', 'NINE');
    LS('ZERO')   :=0;
    LS('ONE')    :=1;
    LS('TWO')    :=2;
    LS('THREE')  :=3;
    LS('FOUR')   :=4;
    LS('FIVE')   :=5;
    LS('SIX')    :=6;
    LS('SEVEN')  :=7;
    LS('EIGHT')  :=8;
    LS('NINE')   :=9;
    —CALCULATE THE LENGTH OF INPUT STRING
    ISTR_LEN := LENGTH(INPUT_STR)+1;
    —ITERATE THROUGH EACH CHARACTER INPUT STRING
    FOR I IN 1..ISTR_LEN LOOP
       INPUT_CHAR := UPPER(SUBSTR(INPUT_STR,I,1));
       —CONCAT IF THE CHARACTER IS NOT NULL
       IF INPUT_CHAR != ' ' THEN
          CS:=CS||INPUT_CHAR;
       ELSE
          —INCREMENT THE COUNTER AND POPULATE DS
          CNT:=CNT+1;
          DS(CNT):=CS;
          —INITIALIZE CHK WITH 0.
          CHK:=0;
          —SET CHK WITH 1, IF CS IS A VALID DIGIT STRING (I.E. ZERO
          TO NINE)
          FOR K IN 0..9 LOOP
          IF CD(K+1)=CS THEN
             CHK:=1;
          END IF;
          END LOOP;
          —IF DS(CNT) IS A BLANK SPACE OR INVALID STRING, DECREMENT
          CNT BY 1
          IF (DS(CNT) IS NULL OR CHK=0) AND CNT>0 THEN
            CNT:=CNT-1;
          END IF;
          —IF CS IS NOT A VALID DIGIT STRING, PRINT THE MESSAGE.
          IF CHK=0  AND CS IS NOT NULL THEN
```

```
            DBMS_OUTPUT.PUT_LINE('WRONG ENTRY -> '|| CS ||'
            - IGNORED');
         END IF;
         CS:='';
      END IF;
END LOOP;
-PRINT THE DIGIT STRING IN NUMERIC FORM
FOR J IN 1..CNT LOOP
   NUM_STR := NUM_STR || LS(DS(J));
END LOOP;
   DBMS_OUTPUT.PUT_LINE(INPUT_STR||' ->'||NUM_STR);
END;
/

SQL> @ C:\BOOK\CHAPTER10\W10_6
Enter value for input_str: ONE TWO THREE
?
SQL> /
Enter value for input_str: ONE TWO THREE
?
SQL> /
Enter value for input_str:                FIVE NINE
?
SQL> /
Enter value for input_str: ZERO   ON   TWO FIVE
?
SQL> /
Enter value for input_str: TEN NINE    FIV    SEVEN
?
SQL> /
Enter value for input_str: THREE SIX ZER SEN SEVEN TEN SIX
?
SQL> /
Enter value for input_str: FIVE        ZERO NINE
?
SQL> /
Enter value for input_str: FOUR SX THREE
?
SQL> /
Enter value for input_str: SEVEN NNE      SEVN   FOUR FIVE
?
SQL> /
Enter value for input_str: THRE FIVE     THREE
?
SQL> /
Enter value for input_str: ON  TW  FIVE   SEVEN   TEN  ZERO IVE
?
```

W10_7 What will be the output of this program?

```
SET SERVEROUTPUT ON
SET VERIFY OFF
DECLARE
   TYPE ODDNUM IS VARRAY(5) OF INTEGER;
   ODD ODDNUM := ODDNUM(1,3,5,7,9);
BEGIN
   DBMS_OUTPUT.PUT_LINE('ODD.COUNT = '||ODD.COUNT);
   ODD.EXTEND(2);
   DBMS_OUTPUT.PUT_LINE('ODD.COUNT AFTER ODD.EXTEND(2)=
   '||ODD.COUNT);
END;
/
```

W10_8 What will be the output of this program?

```
SET SERVEROUTPUT ON
SET VERIFY OFF
DECLARE
   TYPE EVENNUM IS TABLE OF INTEGER;
   EVEN EVENNUM := EVENNUM(2,4,6,8,10,12,14);
BEGIN
   DBMS_OUTPUT.PUT_LINE('EVEN.COUNT BEFORE DELETE =
   '||EVEN.COUNT);
   EVEN.DELETE(3);
   DBMS_OUTPUT.PUT_LINE('EVEN.COUNT AFTER EVEN.DELETE(3) =
   '||EVEN.COUNT);
   EVEN.DELETE(5,6);
   DBMS_OUTPUT.PUT_LINE('EVEN.COUNT AFTER EVEN.DELETE(5,6) =
   '||EVEN.COUNT);
   FOR I IN EVEN.FIRST .. EVEN.LAST LOOP
      IF EVEN.EXISTS(I) THEN
         DBMS_OUTPUT.PUT_LINE(I ||' -> '||EVEN(I));
      ELSE
         DBMS_OUTPUT.PUT_LINE(I ||' DOES NOT EXISTS ');
      END IF;
   END LOOP;
END;
/
```

Oracle Objects and Dynamic SQL

Learning Objectives

You will learn following key concepts after completion of the chapter:

- ✓ Use of objects in PL/SQL
- ✓ Use of dynamic SQL
- ✓ Use of EXECUTE IMMEDIATE
- ✓ Creating dynamic queries

11.1 INTRODUCTION

Oracle provides full support to create object-oriented database. A conceptually pure implementation of object-oriented relational database would restrict all operations on the object's attributes. All operations (whatsoever) related to database must be written by the developer to handle the data. In this chapter, we have introduced the basics related to objects. Dynamic SQL is one which builds up programmatically whose exact statement is not known until run-time. Dynamic SQL allows execution of statements such as CREATE, DROP GRANT and REVOKE in PL/SQL program. It can also be used to build search conditions in WHERE clause of SELECT statement dynamically or to pass the name of an object dynamically. In this chapter, we will learn all the important concepts related to objects and dynamic SQL with the help of examples.

11.2 ORACLE OBJECTS

Oracle object types are user-defined types that make it possible to model real-world entities. An object type is a blueprint or template that defines structure and behaviour. An instantiation of the object type creates an object built according to the template. Object-oriented features can be used while continuing to work with most of the data relationally; alternately, one can go over to an object-oriented approach entirely. PL/SQL has been enhanced to operate on user-defined types seamlessly, allowing application developers to use PL/SQL to implement logic and operations on user-defined types.

11.2.1 Advantages of Objects

Objects make it easier to model complex, real-world business entities and logic. Objects can include the ability to perform operations that are likely to be needed on that data. Reusability of objects makes it possible to develop database applications faster and more efficiently. Object abstraction and the encapsulation of object behaviours also make applications easier to understand and maintain. Oracle enables application developers to directly access the data structures used by their applications using object types. Object types enable you to model the real-world entities. But this is just the first step in exploiting the capabilities of objects. With objects, one can define different specialized types of objects in a type hierarchy under the original type. It consists of a parent base type, called a supertype, and one or more levels of child object types, called subtypes. A subtype becomes a specialized version of the parent type by adding new attributes and method to the set inherited from the parent or by redefining methods. Redefining an inherited method gives a subtype its own way of executing the method. Polymorphism provides a means to the method to execute differently depending on the input.

11.2.2 Object and Member Methods

Object methods are functions or procedures that can be declared in an object type definition. Main use of methods is to provide access to the data of an object. An application calls the methods to invoke the behaviour. Member methods are the means by which an application gains access to an object instance's data. A member method can be defined in the object type for each operation that you want an object of that type to be able to perform.

11.2.3 Object Tables

An object table is a special kind of table in which each row represents an object. By default, every row object in an object table has an associated logical object identifier (OID) that uniquely identifies it in an object table.

An SQL object type can be created with the CREATE TYPE statement. Syntax to create object type specification is as follows:

```
CREATE [OR REPLACE] TYPE OBJECT_TYPE_NAME
AS OBJECT (
ATTRIBUTE_NAME1 DATATYPE,
ATTRIBUTE_NAME2 DATATYPE,
ATTRIBUTE_NAME3 DATATYPE,
...
[MEMBER | PROCEDURE | FUNCTION
PROGRAM SPECIFICATION]
);
```

Syntax to create object body specification is as follows.

```
CREATE [OR REPLACE] TYPE BODY OBJECT_TYPE_NAME
AS OBJECT
```

```
[MEMBER | PROCEDURE | FUNCTION
PROGRAM BODY]
);
```

EX11_1A This example demonstrates declaration of OBJECT SPECIFICATION.

```
CREATE OR REPLACE TYPE FAMILY_V1 AS OBJECT
(
   FAMILY_CODE INTEGER,
   FATHER_NAME VARCHAR2(20),
   MOTHER_NAME VARCHAR2(20),
   MEMBER FUNCTION SET_FAMILY_CODE(NEW_FAMILY_CODE IN INTEGER)
   RETURN FAMILY_V1,
   MEMBER PROCEDURE PRINT_SELF
);
/
```

Execution

```
SQL> @ C:\BOOK\CHAPTER11\EX11_1A
Type created.
```

EX11_1B This example demonstrates declaration of OBJECT BODY.

```
CREATE OR REPLACE TYPE BODY FAMILY_V1 AS
MEMBER FUNCTION SET_FAMILY_CODE(NEW_FAMILY_CODE IN INTEGER)
RETURN FAMILY_V1
IS
THE_FAMILY FAMILY_V1 := SELF;
BEGIN
   THE_FAMILY.FAMILY_CODE := NEW_FAMILY_CODE;
   RETURN THE_FAMILY;
END;


MEMBER PROCEDURE PRINT_SELF
IS
BEGIN
   DBMS_OUTPUT.PUT_LINE('FAMILY CODE : '||FAMILY_CODE);
   DBMS_OUTPUT.PUT_LINE('FATHER      : '||FATHER_NAME);
   DBMS_OUTPUT.PUT_LINE('MOTHER      : '||MOTHER_NAME);
END;
END;
/
```

Execution

```
SQL>  @ C:\BOOK\CHAPTER11\EX11_1B
Type body created.
```

```
SQL> DESC FAMILY_V1
Name                     Type
FAMILY_CODE              NUMBER(38)
FATHER_NAME              VARCHAR2(20)
MOTHER_NAME              VARCHAR2(20)

METHOD
MEMBER FUNCTION SET_FAMILY_CODE RETURNS FAMILY_V1
Argument Name                Type          In/Out Default?
NEW_FAMILY_CODE              NUMBER        IN
MEMBER PROCEDURE             PRINT_SELF
```

EX11_1C This PL/SQL program demonstrates use of FAMILY_V1 object.

```
SET SERVEROUTPUT ON
DECLARE
MY_FAMILY FAMILY_V1;
BEGIN
   MY_FAMILY := FAMILY_V1(101,'PRANAB','ESHA');
   MY_FAMILY.PRINT_SELF();
   DBMS_OUTPUT.PUT_LINE('_____________________');
   DBMS_OUTPUT.PUT_LINE('OUTPUT AFTER INVOKING SET_FAMILY_CODE
   FUNCTION TO CHANGE FAMILY_CODE');
   DBMS_OUTPUT.PUT_LINE('_____________________');
   MY_FAMILY := MY_FAMILY.SET_FAMILY_CODE(999);
   MY_FAMILY.PRINT_SELF();
END;
/
```

Execution

```
SQL> @ C:\BOOK\CHAPTER11\EX11_1C
FAMILY CODE : 101
FATHER      : PRANAB
MOTHER      : ESHA
--------------------------------------------------------------------
OUTPUT AFTER INVOKING SET_FAMILY_CODE FUNCTION TO CHANGE FAMILY_CODE
--------------------------------------------------------------------
FAMILY CODE : 999
FATHER      : PRANAB
MOTHER      : ESHA
```

EX11_1D This example demonstrates creation of table using object.

```
CREATE TABLE FAMILY_TABLE OF FAMILY_V1
(PRIMARY KEY (FAMILY_CODE));
DESC FAMILY_TABLE
```

Execution

```
SQL> @ C:\BOOK\CHAPTER11\EX11_1D
Table created.
Name                        Null?        Type
FAMILY_CODE                 NOT NULL     NUMBER(38)
FATHER_NAME                              VARCHAR2(20)
MOTHER_NAME                              VARCHAR2(20)
```

EX11_1E This example demonstrates insertion of data in an object-based table.

```
INSERT INTO FAMILY_TABLE VALUES (FAMILY_V1(201,'PRAKASH','RITA'));
INSERT INTO FAMILY_TABLE VALUES (FAMILY_V1(301,'RAVI','SEEMA'));
INSERT INTO FAMILY_TABLE VALUES (FAMILY_V1(401,'RANJAN','SRABONI'));
COMMIT;
SELECT * FROM FAMILY_TABLE;
```

Execution

```
SQL> @ C:\BOOK\CHAPTER11\EX11_1E
1 row created.
1 row created.
1 row created.
Commit complete.

FAMILY_CODE      FATHER_NAME      MOTHER_NAME
201              PRAKASH          RITA
301              RAVI             SEEMA
401              RANJAN           SRABONI
```

Illustration

In EX11_1A, FAMILY_V1 object is created with three variables, one function and one procedure. Specifications or function, procedure, as defined in EX11_1A is coded in EX11_1B. Note the description of FAMILY_V1 object on execution using SQL command. For instance, MY_FAMILY based on FAMILY_V1 object is created and populated with the values in EX11_1C. Observe the use of PRINT_SELF procedure and SET_FAMILY_CODE function in EX11_1C. In EX11_1D, an array FAMILY_TABLE FAMILY_V1 object is created. In EX11_1E, FAMILY_TABLE is populated and displayed with multiple sets of values.

11.2.4 Nesting of Objects

Nesting of objects within an object is allowed in Oracle. To nest an object, the object must be created before nesting it in the parent object.

EX11_2A An object named CHILD_V2 is created. It will be nested in FAMILY_V2 object.

```
CREATE OR REPLACE TYPE CHILD_V2 AS OBJECT
(
   CHILD_CODE INTEGER,
```

```
    CHILD_FIRSTNAME VARCHAR2(10),
    CHILD_LASTNAME VARCHAR2(10),
    CHILD_AGE INTEGER
);
/
```

Execution

```
SQL> @ C:\BOOK\CHAPTER11\EX11_2A
Type created.

SQL> DESC CHILD_V2
Name                    Type
CHILD_CODE              NUMBER(38)
CHILD_FIRSTNAME         VARCHAR2(10)
CHILD_LASTNAME          VARCHAR2(10)
CHILD_AGE               NUMBER(38)
```

EX11_2B This example demonstrates nesting of object inside an object.

```
CREATE OR REPLACE TYPE FAMILY_V3 AS OBJECT
(
    FAMILY_CODE INTEGER,
    FATHER_NAME VARCHAR2(20),
    MOTHER_NAME VARCHAR2(20),
    CHILDREN CHILD_V2
);
/
```

Execution

```
SQL> @ C:\BOOK\CHAPTER11\EX11_2B
Type created.

SQL> DESC FAMILY_V3
Name                    Type
FAMILY_CODE             NUMBER(38)
FATHER_NAME             VARCHAR2(20)
MOTHER_NAME             VARCHAR2(20)
CHILDREN                CHILD_V2
```

EX11_2C This example simply demonstrates creation of table using nested object.

```
CREATE TABLE FAMILY_NESTED OF FAMILY_V3;
DESC FAMILY_NESTED
```

Execution

```
SQL> @ C:\BOOK\CHAPTER11\EX11_2C
Table created.
```

```
Name                Type
FAMILY_CODE         NUMBER(38)
FATHER_NAME         VARCHAR2(20)
MOTHER_NAME         VARCHAR2(20)
CHILDREN            CHILD_V2
```

EX11_2D This example demonstrates few DMLs in the table based on nested object.

```
DELETE FROM FAMILY_NESTED;
INSERT INTO FAMILY_NESTED VALUES
(FAMILY_V3(11,'PRANESH','SUDHA',CHILD_V2(1,'PK','SEN',10)));
INSERT INTO FAMILY_NESTED VALUES
(FAMILY_V3(11,'PRANESH','SUDHA',CHILD_V2(2,'SK','SEN',5)));
INSERT INTO FAMILY_NESTED VALUES
(FAMILY_V3(17,'BOSE','MANISHA',CHILD_V2(1,'VAIBHAV','BOSE',1)));
INSERT INTO FAMILY_NESTED VALUES
(FAMILY_V3(17,'BOSE','MANISHA',CHILD_V2(1,'GUNJAN','BOSE',2)));
INSERT INTO FAMILY_NESTED VALUES
(FAMILY_V3(17,'BOSE','MANISHA',CHILD_V2(1,'RIMJHIM','BOSE',5)));
COMMIT;
SELECT FATHER_NAME, CHILDREN FROM FAMILY_NESTED;
```

Execution

```
SQL> @ C:\BOOK\CHAPTER11\EX11_2D
0 rows deleted.
1 row created.
1 row created.
1 row created.
1 row created.
1 row created.
Commit complete.

FATHER_NAME
CHILDREN(CHILD_CODE, CHILD_FIRSTNAME, CHILD_LASTNAME, CHILD_AGE)
PRANESH
CHILD_V2(1, 'PK', 'SEN', 10)
PRANESH
CHILD_V2(2, 'SK', 'SEN', 5)
BOSE
CHILD_V2(1, 'VAIBHAV', 'BOSE', 1)
BOSE
CHILD_V2(1, 'GUNJAN', 'BOSE', 2)
BOSE
CHILD_V2(1, 'RIMJHIM', 'BOSE', 5)
```

Illustration

In EX11_2A, CHILD_V2 object is created with integer and character type variables. In EX11_2B, FAMILY_V3 object is created and variable FAMILY_CODE, FATHER_NAME, MOTHER_NAME and an instance CHILDREN of CHILD_V2 object. EX11_2C creates an array of FAMILY_V3 and DMLs are performed to manipulate FAMILY_NESTED in EX11_2D.

11.2.5 References

A REF is a logical pointer to a row object that is constructed from the object identifier (OID) of the referenced object and is an Oracle built-in data type. REFs are useful to reduce the need for foreign keys. REFs provide an easy mechanism for navigating between objects. Oracle does joins when needed, and in some cases avoids doing joins implicitly. REF can be used to examine or update the object it refers to. REF can also be used to obtain the object it refers to. It is possible for the object identified by a REF to become unavailable through either deletion of the object or a revoking of privileges. Oracle SQL provides a predicate to allow testing REF for dangling condition. Oracle provides the DEREF operator to do this. Dereferencing a dangling REF returns a null object.

A conceptually pure implementation of object-oriented relational database would restrict all operations on the object's attributes. This implies that all DMLs must be done by the developers' defined methods, or in other words SELECT, INSERT, UPDATE, DELETE, etc. commands cannot be used. In case if we use the commands provided by Oracle, the very purpose of object- oriented relational database would be defeated. In actual practice, the minimal privileges assigned to any user are CONNECT and RESOURCE. In case of pure implementation of object-oriented relational database, only EXECUTE privilege is sufficient! All operations (whatsoever) related to database must be written by the developer to handle the data. In this chapter, we have only discussed the basics, as complete treatment of Oracle objects needs altogether a separate book. In case you are interested to develop your application purely using objects, you may refer to books exclusively written for Oracle objects.

11.3 DYNAMIC SQL

Dynamic SQL allows direct execution of any kind of SQL statement. Statements can be build where table names, WHERE clauses and other information are not known in advance. For example, a reporting application might build different SELECT statements for different reports or database management applications might issue DDLs and DCLs that cannot be coded directly in a PL/SQL program.

Dynamic SQL statements built as character strings built at run-time. The strings may contain the text of a SQL statement or a PL/SQL block. They can also have placeholders for bind arguments. Placeholder names are prefixed by a colon, and the names themselves do not matter.

Dynamic SQL can be used for the following purpose.

- Executing Data Definition Language (CREATE, DROP, etc.) in PL/SQL program
- Executing Data Definition Language (GRANT, REVOKE, etc.) in PL/SQL program
- To build search conditions in WHERE clause of SELECT statement dynamically
- Pass the name of an object dynamically

11.3.1 EXECUTE IMMEDIATE Statement

The EXECUTE IMMEDIATE statement immediately executes a dynamic SQL statement or an anonymous PL/SQL block.

The main argument to EXECUTE IMMEDIATE is the string containing the SQL statement to execute. The string can be build using concatenation, or using a predefined string.

The dynamic string can contain any SQL statement or any PL/SQL block except multirow queries. In case of a single SQL statement in a string, do not include any semicolon at the end. Whereas in case of a PL/SQL anonymous block, include the semicolon at the end of each PL/SQL statement and at the end of the anonymous block. The string can also contain placeholders, arbitrary names preceded by a colon, for bind arguments. In this case, PL/SQL variables must correspond to the placeholders with the INTO, USING and RETURNING INTO clauses.

Placeholders can be used in places where variables need to be substituted in the SQL statement, for example, conditional clause in WHERE. Placeholders cannot be used for the names of schema objects.

EXECUTE IMMEDIATE can be used only for DML statements that have a RETURNING clause without a BULK COLLECT clause. The RETURNING INTO clause specifies the variables into which column values are returned. For each value returned by the DML statement, there must be a corresponding variable in the RETURNING INTO clause. During run-time, bind arguments replace corresponding placeholders in the dynamic string.

Dynamic SQL supports all the SQL data types. Dynamic SQL statement can be executed repeatedly using new values for the bind arguments. However, this will incur some overhead because EXECUTE IMMEDIATE re-prepares the dynamic string before every execution.

With the USING clause, the mode defaults to IN for input bind arguments and for the RETURNING INTO clause, the mode is OUT.

Parameter mode must be specified in more complicated cases, for example, to call a procedure from a dynamic PL/SQL block.

EX11_3 This program demonstrates use of EXECUTE IMMEDIATE to create a table at run-time.

```
SET ECHO OFF
SET VERIFY OFF
SET SERVEROUTPUT ON
DROP TABLE EMP_TABLE;
DECLARE
   SQL_STMT VARCHAR2(500);
   VNAME VARCHAR2(20)              := '&NAME';
   VAGE NUMBER(4)                  := &AGE;
   REPEAT NUMBER(4)                := &REPEAT;
   VCNT NUMBER(2);

BEGIN
   EXECUTE IMMEDIATE 'CREATE TABLE EMP_TABLE
   (NAME VARCHAR2(20), AGE NUMBER(3))';
```

```
    IF REPEAT<10 THEN
        FOR I IN 1..REPEAT LOOP
            VNAME := VNAME||I;
            SQL_STMT := 'INSERT INTO EMP_TABLE VALUES (:1,:2)';
            EXECUTE IMMEDIATE SQL_STMT USING VNAME,VAGE;
        END LOOP;
    ELSE
        DBMS_OUTPUT.PUT_LINE('VALUE OF REPEAT MUST BE LESS THAN 10');
    END IF;
END;
/
SELECT * FROM EMP_TABLE;
```

Execution

```
SQL> @ C:\BOOK\CHAPTER11\EX11_3
Enter value for name: NARESH
Enter value for age: 45
Enter value for repeat: 4
PL/SQL procedure successfully completed.

NAME            AGE
------------------------
NARESH1         45
NARESH12        45
NARESH123       45
NARESH1234      45
SQL> @ C:\BOOK\CHAPTER11\EX11_3
Table dropped.

Enter value for name: ANIL
Enter value for age: 20
Enter value for repeat: 15
VALUE OF REPEAT MUST BE LESS THAN 10
PL/SQL procedure successfully completed.
no rows selected
```

Illustration

This example accepts NAME, AGE and REPEAT as inputs. Table is created at run-time and input values are populated, saved and displayed using the PL/SQL code. Observe the use of EXECUTE IMMEDIATE command in the program.

EX11_4A This example simply creates a procedure, which inserts the supplied values in a table. This procedure is called by EX11_4B program.

```
CREATE TABLE EMP_TABLE (NAME VARCHAR2(20), AGE NUMBER(3));

CREATE OR REPLACE PROCEDURE CREATE_EMP
```

```
(NAME IN VARCHAR2,
AGE IN VARCHAR2) AS
BEGIN
   INSERT INTO EMP_TABLE VALUES (NAME, AGE);
END;
/
```

Execution

```
SQL>  @ C:\BOOK\CHAPTER11\EX11_4A
Procedure created.
```

EX11_4B This program demonstrates PL/SQL block dynamically. It calls CREATE_EMP procedure to insert data in the table dynamically.

```
SET ECHO OFF
SET VERIFY OFF
SET SERVEROUTPUT ON
DECLARE
   PLSQL_BLOCK VARCHAR2(1000);
   VNAME VARCHAR2(20)  := 'RAMESH';
   VAGE NUMBER(4)      := 20;
BEGIN
   PLSQL_BLOCK := 'BEGIN CREATE_EMP(:1, :2); END;';
   EXECUTE IMMEDIATE PLSQL_BLOCK USING IN VNAME, VAGE;
END;
/
SELECT * FROM EMP_TABLE;
DROP TABLE EMP_TABLE;
```

Execution

```
SQL> @ C:\BOOK\CHAPTER11\EX11_4B
PL/SQL procedure successfully completed.

NAME                AGE
RAMESH              20
Table dropped.
```

11.3.2 Repetitive and Dynamic Input

Execution of '&' clause in a PL/SQL results into single time execution. It simply ignores the iteration of the loop. There is no way to write a real loop in SQL* Plus. Now the problem is how to input repetitive and dynamic inputs? There is way to simulate a loop using iteration, using SQL* Plus, using recursion, that is, calling the same program till the time user wants to input some data. EX11_5A and EX11_5B demonstrate how to achieve iteration to read input using SQL* Plus.

EX11_5A This SQL* Plus program simply print 'GOOD BYE'.

```
PROMPT
PROMPT GOOD BYE!!!
PROMPT
```

Execution and illustration

This program is used in EX11_5B. Ensure that this program is available in native directory of Oracle. The easiest way to do this is to Invoke SQL Environment → Edit EX11_5A → Press 'Y' → Type the code (Figure 11.1) → File → Save → Exit.

FIGURE 11.1 SQL editor.

EX11_5B This program simulates behaviour of loop using SQL* Plus.

```
SET ECHO OFF
SET VERIFY OFF
INSERT INTO PROD_TABLE VALUES ('&PID','&PNAME');
COMMIT;
PROMPT
ACCEPT I_NEXT_PID PROMPT 'CONTINUE (Y/N) > '
COLUMN NEXT_SCRIPT NOPRINT NEW_VALUE I_NEXT_SCRIPT
SELECT DECODE ('&&I_NEXT_PID',
'N','EX11_5A.SQL',
'EX11_5B') NEXT_SCRIPT
FROM DUAL;
@&&I_NEXT_SCRIPT
```

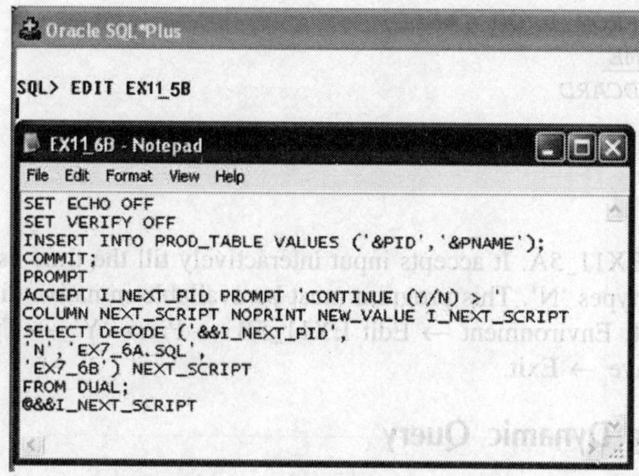
```
SQL> EDIT EX11_5B

SET ECHO OFF
SET VERIFY OFF
INSERT INTO PROD_TABLE VALUES ('&PID','&PNAME');
COMMIT;
PROMPT
ACCEPT I_NEXT_PID PROMPT 'CONTINUE (Y/N) >'
COLUMN NEXT_SCRIPT NOPRINT NEW_VALUE I_NEXT_SCRIPT
SELECT DECODE ('&&I_NEXT_PID',
'N','EX7_6A.SQL',
'EX7_6B') NEXT_SCRIPT
FROM DUAL;
@&&I_NEXT_SCRIPT
```

FIGURE 11.2 Working with SQL editor.

Execution

```
SQL> CREATE TABLE PROD_TABLE
(PID VARCHAR2(10), PNAME VARCHAR2(20));
Table created.

SQL> SELECT * FROM PROD_TABLE;
no rows selected

SQL> @ EX11_5B
Enter value for pid: P1
Enter value for pname: RAIDCARD
1 row created.
Commit complete.

CONTINUE (Y/N) >Y

Enter value for pid: P2
Enter value for pname: SAN
1 row created.
Commit complete.

CONTINUE (Y/N) > Y

Enter value for pid: P3
Enter value for pname: NAS
1 row created.
Commit complete.

CONTINUE (Y/N) > N
GOOD BYE!!!
```

```
SQL> SELECT * FROM PROD_TABLE;
PID          PNAME
P1           RAIDCARD
P2           SAN
P3           NAS
```

Illustration

This program uses EX11_5A. It accepts input interactively till the time user type 'Y' and exits only when the user types 'N'. This program must be available in native directory of Oracle. To do this, Invoke SQL Environment → Edit EX11_5B → Press 'Y' → Type the code (Figure 11.2) → File → Save → Exit.

11.3.3 Creating Dynamic Query

To build a dynamic query with dynamic SQL, three statements are used to process a dynamic multirow query. They are OPEN-FOR, FETCH and CLOSE statements. OPEN a cursor variable FOR a multirow query followed by FETCHing rows from the result set one at a time. Finally, when all the rows are processed, CLOSE the cursor variable.

EX11_6 This example demonstrates creation and execution of dynamic query. Tables used in the program are shown in Figure 5.6.

```
SET SERVEROUTPUT ON
SET VERIFY OFF
DECLARE
   TYPE SALESCURSORTYP IS REF CURSOR;
   SALES_CV SALESCURSORTYP;
   SALES_REC SALE_DETAIL%ROWTYPE;
   SQL_STMT VARCHAR2(200);
   VCID CUST.CID%TYPE := '&CID';
BEGIN
   SQL_STMT := 'SELECT * FROM SALE_DETAIL WHERE CID=:1';
   OPEN SALES_CV FOR SQL_STMT USING VCID;
   LOOP
   FETCH SALES_CV INTO SALES_REC;
   EXIT WHEN SALES_CV%NOTFOUND;
   DBMS_OUTPUT.PUT_LINE(SALES_REC.CID || ' DID SHOPPING ON ' ||
   SALES_REC.SALEDT);
END LOOP;
CLOSE SALES_CV;
END;
/
```

Execution

```
SQL> @ C:\BOOK\CHAPTER11\EX11_6
Enter value for cid: C1
```

```
C1 DID SHOPPING ON 14-JUL-12
C1 DID SHOPPING ON 14-JUL-12
C1 DID SHOPPING ON 20-AUG-12
PL/SQL procedure successfully completed.

SQL> /
Enter value for cid: C2
C2 DID SHOPPING ON 14-JUL-12
PL/SQL procedure successfully completed.

SQL> /
Enter value for cid: C3
C3 DID SHOPPING ON 15-JUL-12
PL/SQL procedure successfully completed.

SQL> /
Enter value for cid: C4
C4 DID SHOPPING ON 14-NOV-12
PL/SQL procedure successfully completed.
```

Illustration

In this example, SALESCURSORTYP is declared as REF_CURSOR and SALES_CV is an instance of the same. SQL_STMT acts as a container for SQL statement at run-time. Observe the use of SQL_STMT in the main body of the PL/SQL code. Rest of the code in the example is handling of explicit cursor.

11.3.4 Using BULK COLLECT Statement

Bulk SQL is used to pass the entire collections back and forth, not just individual elements. This technique improves performance by minimizing the number of transactions between PL/SQL and SQL engines. A single statement is used instead of a loop that issues a SQL statement in every iteration.

Bulk binding lets Oracle bind a variable in a SQL statement to a collection of values. The collection type can be any PL/SQL collection type. The allowed data type in collection elements are CHAR, DATE or NUMBER. The three statements that support dynamic bulk binds are EXECUTE IMMEDIATE, FETCH and FORALL.

BULK COLLECT INTO clause can be used with the EXECUTE IMMEDIATE statement to store values from each column of a query's result set in a separate collection. RETURNING BULK COLLECT INTO clause is used with the EXECUTE IMMEDIATE statement to store the results of an INSERT, UPDATE or DELETE statement in a set of collections.

BULK COLLECT INTO clause is used with the FETCH statement to store values from each column of a cursor in a separate collection.

EXECUTE IMMEDIATE statement can be put with the RETURNING BULK COLLECT INTO inside a FORALL statement. The results of all the INSERT, UPDATE or DELETE statements can be stored in a set of collections.

EX11_7 This program demonstrates use of BULK COLLECT statement. Tables used in the program are shown in Figure 5.6.

```
SET SERVEROUTPUT ON
SET VERIFY OFF
DECLARE
   —TYPE CUSTCURSORTYP IS REF CURSOR;
   TYPE CIDLIST IS TABLE OF CUST.CID%TYPE;
   TYPE CNAMELIST IS TABLE OF CUST.CNAME%TYPE;
   TYPE CCITYLIST IS TABLE OF CUST.CCITY%TYPE;
   —CUST_CV CUSTCURSORTYP;
   VCID CIDLIST;
   VCNAME CNAMELIST;
   VCCITY CCITYLIST;

BEGIN
   EXECUTE IMMEDIATE 'SELECT CID,CNAME,CCITY FROM CUST'
   BULK COLLECT INTO VCID,VCNAME,VCCITY;
   FOR I IN VCID.FIRST..VCID.LAST LOOP
   DBMS_OUTPUT.PUT_LINE(VCID(I)||' '||VCNAME(I)||' '||VCCITY(I));
   END LOOP;
END;
/
```

Execution

```
SQL> @ C:\BOOK\CHAPTER11\EX11_7
Input truncated to 1 characters
C1 PRADIP MYSORE
C3 AASTIK KOLKATA
C2 TUSHAR PUNE
C4 ARPAN CHENNAI
C5 ANUMITA INDORE
PL/SQL procedure successfully completed.
```

Illustration

In this example, all the fields of CUST are transformed into an array. This is done to keep all the transactions in the main memory and commit the transaction in one go. This strategy is extremely useful to make execution of PL/SQL faster and reduce the network traffic.

11.4 SUMMARY

In this chapter, we have discussed Oracle objects and Dynamic SQL with the help of examples. Both the topics are vast and students are advised to refer additional information on the subject from Oracle website.

SHORT/OBJECTIVE TYPE QUESTIONS

1. What are the advantages of Oracle objects?
2. What do you understand by Member methods in Oracle objects?
3. Where you use nested objects? Explain using a suitable example.
4. Where do you use References in objects?
5. When the use of dynamic SQL is advantageous?
6. Explain EXECUTE IMMEDIATE command with the help of a suitable example.
7. How you can handle iteration using dynamic SQL?
8. What do you understand by 'creating dynamic query'? Explain using a suitable example.
9. Write short notes on BULK COLLECT.
10. What are the advantages of using BULK COLLECT statement?
11. What are the major advantages of using VIEWS instead of TABLES?
12. Can you invalidate a table or synonym?
13. What do you understand by granting system privilege WITH ADMIN OPTION?
14. Mention the difference between CLOSE_CONNECTION and CLOSE_ALL_CONNECTIONS.
15. What do you understand by GRANT and REVOKE statements?
16. What is the function of CATPROC.SQL?
17. Is it possible to view compiled object code?
18. Name the privileges required to execute a procedure owned by another user.
19. Write advantage of OTHERS exception handler.
20. What is the difference between privilege and role?
21. Write difference between database trigger and stored procedure.
22. In which schema errors encountered in a trigger is stored?
23. Define the SQLCODE and SQLERRM functions.
24. What is the reason for INVALID_CURSOR exception?
25. How you can improve the performance of a trigger?
26. Can we have a view of mutating?
27. Do you agree that NESTED TABLES use sequential numbers as subscripts?
28. Which collection type should be used if the number of elements is known in advance?
29. Illustrate use of constructor in PL/SQL program. Do you require constructor to add elements to an index by table?
30. Can you access SQL session information?

WORKOUT SECTION

W11_1A Write code to create an object CHILD_V1 as per the details given below.

```
SQL> @ C:\BOOK\CHAPTER11\W11_1A
Type created.

SQL> DESC CHILD_V1
Name                        Type
------------------------------------------
CHILD_CODE                  NUMBER(38)
CHILD_FIRSTNAME             VARCHAR2(10)
CHILD_LASTNAME              VARCHAR2(10)
CHILD_AGE                   NUMBER(38)

METHOD
MEMBER FUNCTION FULL_NAME RETURNS VARCHAR2
MEMBER PROCEDURE PRINT_CHILD
```

W11_1B Write code to create body of the CHILD_V1 object. The PRINT_CHILD procedure should display all columns including FULL_NAME. Sample PL/SQL program along with its output is shown below.

```
SQL>  @ C:\BOOK\CHAPTER11\W11_1B
Type body created.

— W11_1C (Sample PL/SQL program to use CHILD_V1 object)
SET SERVEROUTPUT ON
DECLARE
MY_CHILD CHILD_V1;
BEGIN
MY_CHILD := CHILD_V1(2,'ANUMITA','DASGUPTA',7);
MY_CHILD.PRINT_CHILD();
END;
/

SQL>  @ C :\BOOK\CHAPTER11\W11_1C
CHILD CODE  : 2
FIRST NAME  : ANUMITA
LAST NAME   : DASGUPTA
AGE         : 7
FULL NAME   : ANUMITA DASGUPTA
```

W11_2 What will be the output for the following sequence of commands in Option A, B and C?

Option A

```
SQL> DROP TYPE FAMILY_V3;
SQL> DROP TYPE CHILD_V2;
?
```

Option B

```
SQL> DROP TYPE CHILD_V2;
SQL> DROP TYPE FAMILY_V3;
SQL> SELECT COUNT(*) FROM FAMILY_NESTED;
?
```

Option C

```
SQL> DROP TABLE FAMILY_NESTED;
SQL> DROP TYPE FAMILY_V3;
SQL> DROP TYPE CHILD_V2;
SQL> SELECT COUNT(*) FROM FAMILY_NESTED;
?
```

W11 3A Create EMP_INDEX table, EMP_SEQ sequence and CREATE_EMP_INDEX procedure as per the details shown below.

```
SQL>  @ C:\BOOK\CHAPTER11\W11_2A
Table created.
Sequence created.
Procedure created.

SQL> DESC EMP_INDEX
Name                 Type
EMPID                NUMBER(5)
NAME                 VARCHAR2(10)
AGE                  NUMBER(3)

SQL> SELECT SEQUENCE_NAME, MIN_VALUE, INCREMENT_BY
FROM USER_SEQUENCES
WHERE SEQUENCE_NAME LIKE 'EMP_SEQ';
SEQUENCE_NAME        MIN_VALUE    INCREMENT_BY
EMP_SEQ              1            1

SQL> DESC CREATE_EMP_INDEX
PROCEDURE CREATE_EMP_INDEX
Argument Name        Type         In/Out Default?
EMPID                NUMBER       IN/OUT
NAME                 VARCHAR2     IN
AGE                  VARCHAR2     IN
```

W11 3B Write a program, which uses EMP_INDEX table, EMP_SEQ sequence and CREATE_EMP_INDEX procedure. The program uses EMP_SEQ to assign input to EMPID. Values related to NAME and AGE field is passed from the program to the CREATE_EMP_INDEX procedure.

```
SQL> @ C:\BOOK\CHAPTER11\W11_2B
Enter value for name: VIVEK
```

```
Enter value for age: 35
PL/SQL procedure successfully completed.

EMPID         NAME          AGE
---------------------------------
1             VIVEK         35

SQL> @ C:\BOOK\CHAPTER11\W11_2B
Enter value for name: PUNEET
Enter value for age: 32
PL/SQL procedure successfully completed.

EMPID         NAME          AGE
---------------------------------
1             VIVEK         35
2             PUNEET        32

SQL> @ C:\BOOK\CHAPTER11\W11_2B
Enter value for name: PRANAB
Enter value for age: 38
PL/SQL procedure successfully completed.

EMPID         NAME          AGE
---------------------------------
1             VIVEK         35
2             PUNEET        32
3             PRANAB        38
```

12

PL/SQL Optimization Techniques

Learning Objectives

You will learn following key concepts after completion of the chapter:

- ✓ Performance tuning of PL/SQL code
- ✓ Using FORALL and BULK COLLECT in PL/SQL
- ✓ Using Oracle optimization parameter
- ✓ Oracle cost-based optimizer

12.1 INTRODUCTION

There are situations when a developer needs to modify the code to gain better performance. Poor performance of PL/SQL-based application is often due to badly written SQL statements, poor programming practices and inattention to PL/SQL basics.

Expertise in optimization of PL/SQL code will only come with experience and hard work. There is no ready-made solution to optimize PL/SQL code. In this chapter, we will execute examples in Oracle 9i, Oracle 10g and Oracle 11g to observe the improved performance in new versions. The points discussed are solely based on the theoretical concepts and practical experience of the author and are not exhaustive.

12.2 PL/SQL OPTIMIZATION SITUATIONS

There are primarily four situations which effects execution of PL/SQL code. They are related to excessive computation, excessive use of methods, extensive use of insert, update and delete (DMLs) and use of older version of Oracle. The above-mentioned situations with suggested action are provided in Table 12.1.

Major improvement in optimization took place in Oracle 10g. There is slight improvement in performance in Oracle 11g when compared to Oracle 10g. In Oracle 11g, PL/SQL code can be modified without shutting down the database server, which was not possible in Oracle 10g.

TABLE 12.1 Optimization Situations

Situation	What to do?
Excessive computation	Use data types PLS_INTEGER, BINARY_FLOAT and BINARY_DOUBLE
Excessive methods	Look at all performance features to make the method as efficient as possible
Excessive DMLs	Use FORALL statement for issuing DML, and the BULK COLLECT INTO and RETURNING BULK COLLECT INTO clauses for queries
Old PL/SQL code	Re-execute the codes in Oracle 11g for performance improvements without doing any tuning

12.3 DATA CONVERSION

At run-time, avoid automatic PL/SQL data conversions to improve performance. A lot of time is wasted to do data conversion, leading into overall performance degradation of the program. Oracle 11g optimizes the program at its own; however, in case of lower versions of Oracle, the programmer has to do optimization.

EX12_1A This PL/SQL code demonstrates bad performance due to improper data conversion. In this program, GET_TIME procedure is used to compute time difference. The same program is executed both in Oracle 9i and in Oracle 11g to compare the performance.

```
SET SERVEROUTPUT ON
DECLARE
   N NUMBER;
   T1 INTEGER;
   T2 INTEGER;
   T INTEGER;

   PROCEDURE GET_TIME(T OUT NUMBER) IS
   BEGIN
      T:=DBMS_UTILITY.GET_TIME;
   END;

BEGIN
   GET_TIME(T1);
   N:=1;
   FOR I IN 1..10000000 LOOP
   N := N+'2';
   END LOOP;
   GET_TIME(T2);
   T:=T2-T1;
   DBMS_OUTPUT.PUT_LINE('N = '||N);
   DBMS_OUTPUT.PUT_LINE('T2-T1 = '||T);
END;
/
```

```
Oracle 9i
SQL> @ C:\BOOK\CHAPTER12\EX12_1A
N = 20000001
T2-T1 = 1900
Oracle 11g
SQL> @ C:\BOOK\CHAPTER12\EX12_1A
N = 20000001
T2-T1 = 114
```

EX12_1B This PL/SQL code demonstrates performance improvement due to the input of correct data type. The same program is executed both in Oracle 9i and in Oracle 11g to compare the performance.

```
SET SERVEROUTPUT ON
DECLARE
   N NUMBER;
   T1 INTEGER;
   T2 INTEGER;
   T INTEGER;

   PROCEDURE GET_TIME(T OUT NUMBER) IS
   BEGIN
      T:=DBMS_UTILITY.GET_TIME;
   END;

BEGIN
   GET_TIME(T1);
   N:=1;
   FOR I IN 1..10000000 LOOP
   N := N+2;
   END LOOP;
   GET_TIME(T2);
   T:=T2-T1;
   DBMS_OUTPUT.PUT_LINE('N = '||N);
   DBMS_OUTPUT.PUT_LINE('T2-T1 = '||T);
END;
/
```

```
Oracle 9i
SQL> @ C:\BOOK\CHAPTER12\EX12_1B
N = 20000001
T2-T1 = 1226

Oracle 11g
SQL> @ C:\BOOK\CHAPTER12\EX12_1B
N = 20000001
T2-T1 = 112
```

12.4 OPTIMIZED VARIABLES

Use PLS_INTEGER or BINARY_INTEGER in place of INTEGER or NUMBER data types for Integer Arithmetic. They are the most efficient integer type. They require less storage than INTEGER or NUMBER values and use machine arithmetic. Similarly, use BINARY_FLOAT and BINARY_DOUBLE for floating-point arithmetic. The BINARY_FLOAT and BINARY_DOUBLE types can use native machine arithmetic instructions, are more efficient for number-crunching applications and also require less space in the database.

EX12_1C This program demonstrates improvement in performance in EX12_1B just by changing the type from INTEGER to PLS_INTEGER.

```
SET SERVEROUTPUT ON
DECLARE
   N PLS_INTEGER;
   T1 PLS_INTEGER;
   T2 PLS_INTEGER;
   T PLS_INTEGER;

   PROCEDURE GET_TIME(T OUT NUMBER) IS
   BEGIN
      T:=DBMS_UTILITY.GET_TIME;
   END;

BEGIN
   GET_TIME(T1);
   N:=1;
   FOR I IN 1..10000000 LOOP
   N := N+2;
   END LOOP;
   GET_TIME(T2);
   T:=T2-T1;
   DBMS_OUTPUT.PUT_LINE('N = ' ||N);
   DBMS_OUTPUT.PUT_LINE('T2-T1 = '||T);
END;
/
```

```
Oracle 9i
SQL>  @ C:\BOOK\CHAPTER12\EX12_1C
N = 20000001
T2-T1 = 745

Oracle 11g
SQL> @ C:\BOOK\CHAPTER12\EX12_1C
N = 20000001
T2-T1 = 88
```

Illustration

Execution time in Oracle 9i and Oracle 11g is shown in Table 12.2. Note that hardware configuration was the same for both the versions of Oracle.

TABLE 12.2 Execution Time Comparison

PL/SQL code	Oracle 9i (execution time in ms)	Oracle 11g (execution time in ms)	Remarks
EX12_1A	1900	114	Unoptimized code. Oracle has to convert string to number. NUMBER and INTEGER type variable declarations are also responsible for performance degradation
EX12_1B	1226	112	Performance increase in Oracle 9i is significant, whereas in Oracle 11g it is not. This has happened because Oracle 11g has internally optimized the code
EX12_1C	745	88	Optimized code. Performance gain is because of setting INTEGER data types to PLS_INTEGER data types

12.5 FORALL STATEMENT

FORALL can be used to run multiple DML statements very efficiently. It is usually much faster than an equivalent FOR loop. It improves performance where the index value is used as a subscript.

The FORALL statement issues a series of DML statements. It requires some setup code, because each iteration of the loop must use values from one or more collections in its VALUES or WHERE clauses.

EX12_2A In this example, a table with 10,000 records is created. All records are then deleted using FOR loop and the execution time is computed. The same program is executed both in Oracle 9i and in Oracle 11g to compare the performance.

```
CREATE TABLE EMP_TABLE
(EMPID NUMBER(5), ENAME VARCHAR2(20), EADDRESS VARCHAR2(20));

SET SERVEROUTPUT ON
DECLARE
   N NUMBER;
   T1 INTEGER;
   T2 INTEGER;
   T INTEGER;
   PROCEDURE GET_TIME(T OUT NUMBER) IS
```

```
    BEGIN
       T:=DBMS_UTILITY.GET_TIME;
    END;

BEGIN
    FOR I IN 1..10000 LOOP
       INSERT INTO EMP_TABLE VALUES (I,'NAME'||I,'ADD'||I);
    END LOOP;
    COMMIT;
    GET_TIME(T1);
    FOR I IN 1..10000 LOOP
       DELETE FROM EMP_TABLE WHERE EMPID=I;
    END LOOP;
    COMMIT;
    GET_TIME(T2);
    T:=T2-T1;
    DBMS_OUTPUT.PUT_LINE('TIME ELAPSED USING FOR LOOP');
    DBMS_OUTPUT.PUT_LINE('T2-T1 = '||T);
END;
/
DROP TABLE EMP_TABLE;
```

Oracle 9i

```
SQL> @ C:\BOOK\CHAPTER12\EX12_2A
Table created.

TIME ELAPSED USING FOR LOOP
T2-T1 = 6035

PL/SQL procedure successfully completed.
Table dropped.
```

Oracle 11g

```
SQL>  @ C:\BOOK\CHAPTER12\EX12_2A
Table created.

TIME ELAPSED USING FOR LOOP
T2-T1 = 1046

PL/SQL procedure successfully completed.
Table dropped.
```

EX12_2B EX12_2A is modified to use FORALL statement. This is done to demonstrate the improvement in performance due to the use of FORALL over FOR loop. Refer to Table 12.3 to see the gain in performance.

```
CREATE TABLE EMP_TABLE
(EMPID NUMBER(5), ENAME VARCHAR2(20), EADDRESS VARCHAR2(20));

SET SERVEROUTPUT ON
DECLARE
   N NUMBER;
   TYPE EMPIDTAB IS TABLE OF NUMBER INDEX BY PLS_INTEGER;
   VEMPID EMPIDTAB;
   T1 INTEGER;
   T2 INTEGER;
   T INTEGER;

   PROCEDURE GET_TIME(T OUT NUMBER) IS
   BEGIN
      T:=DBMS_UTILITY.GET_TIME;
   END;

BEGIN
   FOR I IN 1..10000 LOOP
      INSERT INTO EMP_TABLE VALUES (I,'NAME'||I,'ADD'||I);
   END LOOP;
   COMMIT;
   FOR I IN 1..10000 LOOP
      VEMPID(I):=I;
   END LOOP;
   GET_TIME(T1);
   FORALL I IN 1..10000
      DELETE FROM EMP_TABLE WHERE EMPID=VEMPID(I);
   COMMIT;
   GET_TIME(T2);
   T:=T2-T1;
   DBMS_OUTPUT.PUT_LINE('TIME ELAPSED USING FORALL');
   DBMS_OUTPUT.PUT_LINE('T2-T1 = '||T);
END;
/
DROP TABLE EMP_TABLE;
```

Oracle 9i

```
SQL> @ C:\BOOK\CHAPTER12\EX12_2B
Table created.

TIME ELAPSED USING FORALL
T2-T1 = 5496
PL/SQL procedure successfully completed.
Table dropped.
```

```
Oracle 11g

SQL> @ C:\BOOK\CHAPTER12\EX12_2B
Table created.

TIME ELAPSED USING FORALL
T2-T1 = 947

PL/SQL procedure successfully completed.
Table dropped.
```

EX12_2C This program demonstrates that merely changing type from INTEGER to PLS_INTEGER does not guarantee improvement in performance. It is the responsibility of the programmer to see the volume of usage of the changed variables. Refer to Table 12.3 to see the effect.

```
CREATE TABLE EMP_TABLE
(EMPID NUMBER(5), ENAME VARCHAR2(20), EADDRESS VARCHAR2(20));

SET SERVEROUTPUT ON
DECLARE
   N PLS_INTEGER;
   TYPE EMPIDTAB IS TABLE OF NUMBER INDEX BY PLS_INTEGER;
   VEMPID EMPIDTAB;
   T1 PLS_INTEGER;
   T2 PLS_INTEGER;
   T PLS_INTEGER;

   PROCEDURE GET_TIME(T OUT NUMBER) IS
   BEGIN
      T:=DBMS_UTILITY.GET_TIME;
   END;

BEGIN
   FOR I IN 1..10000 LOOP
      INSERT INTO EMP_TABLE VALUES (I,'NAME'||I,'ADD'||I);
   END LOOP;
   COMMIT;
   FOR I IN 1..10000 LOOP
      VEMPID(I):=I;
   END LOOP;
   GET_TIME(T1);
   FORALL I IN 1..10000
      DELETE FROM EMP_TABLE WHERE EMPID=VEMPID(I);
   COMMIT;
```

```
    GET_TIME(T2);
    T:=T2-T1;
    DBMS_OUTPUT.PUT_LINE('TIME ELAPSED USING FORALL');
    DBMS_OUTPUT.PUT_LINE('T2-T1 = '||T);
END;
/
DROP TABLE EMP_TABLE;
```

Oracle 9i

```
SQL> @ C:\BOOK\CHAPTER12\EX12_2C
Table created.

TIME ELAPSED USING FORALL
T2-T1 = 5489
PL/SQL procedure successfully completed.
Table dropped.
```

Oracle 11g

```
SQL>  @ C:\BOOK\CHAPTER12\EX12_2C
Table created.

TIME ELAPSED USING FORALL
T2-T1 = 947

PL/SQL procedure successfully completed.
Table dropped.
```

Illustration

Execution time in Oracle 9i and Oracle 11g is shown in Table 12.3. Note that hardware configuration was the same for both the versions of Oracle.

TABLE 12.3 Execution Time Comparison

PL/SQL code	Oracle 9i (execution time in ms)	Oracle 11g (execution time in ms)	Remarks
EX12_2A	6035	1046	Unoptimized code as FOR loop is used
EX12_2B	5496	947	Optimized because of the use of FORALL construct. Optimization is observed even better in situations where a subset of records are deleted by multiple users
EX12_2C	5489	947	No improvement in execution time. It is therefore not wise to blindly change all INTEGER type data variables to PLS_INTEGER. Note that the converted variables are not a part of records

12.6 BULK COLLECT STATEMENT

BULK COLLECT clause can be used to bring the entire result set into memory in a single operation. This is likely to improve the performance in most cases. To see the dramatic improvement due to BULK COLLECT, refer to the examples and Tables 12.4 and 12.5.

EX12_3A In this program, conventional cursor is used to fetch records. The same program is executed in both Oracle 9i and Oracle 11g to compare the performance.

```
CREATE TABLE EMP_TABLE
(EMPID NUMBER(5), ENAME VARCHAR2(20), EADDRESS VARCHAR2(20));

SET SERVEROUTPUT ON
DECLARE
   T1 PLS_INTEGER;
   T2 PLS_INTEGER;
   T PLS_INTEGER;
   CURSOR EMP_CURSOR IS SELECT * FROM EMP_TABLE;
   EMPREC EMP_CURSOR%ROWTYPE;

   PROCEDURE GET_TIME(T OUT NUMBER) IS
   BEGIN
      T:=DBMS_UTILITY.GET_TIME;
   END;

BEGIN
   FOR I IN 1..10000 LOOP
      INSERT INTO EMP_TABLE VALUES (I,'NAME'||I,'ADD'||I);
   END LOOP;
   COMMIT;
   GET_TIME(T1);
   OPEN EMP_CURSOR;
   LOOP
      FETCH EMP_CURSOR INTO EMPREC;
      EXIT WHEN EMP_CURSOR%NOTFOUND;
   END LOOP;
   CLOSE EMP_CURSOR;
   GET_TIME(T2);
   T:=T2-T1;
   DBMS_OUTPUT.PUT_LINE('TIME ELAPSED USING CURSOR AND SIMPLE LOOP');
   DBMS_OUTPUT.PUT_LINE('T2-T1 = '||T);
END;
/
DROP TABLE EMP_TABLE;
```

```
Oracle 9i
SQL> @ C:\BOOK\CHAPTER12\EX12_3A
Table created.

TIME ELAPSED USING CURSOR AND SIMPLE LOOP
T2-T1 = 70

PL/SQL procedure successfully completed.

Table dropped.
```

```
Oracle 11g

SQL> @ C:\BOOK\CHAPTER12\EX12_3A
Table created.
TIME ELAPSED USING CURSOR AND SIMPLE LOOP
T2-T1 = 15
PL/SQL procedure successfully completed.
Table dropped.
```

EX12_3B In this program, EX12_3A is modified to use BULK COLLECT statement. Note the improvement in performance due to the use of BULK COLLECT statement. Refer to Table 12.4 to see the gain in performance.

```
CREATE TABLE EMP_TABLE
(EMPID NUMBER(5), ENAME VARCHAR2(20), EADDRESS VARCHAR2(20));
SET SERVEROUTPUT ON
DECLARE
   T1 PLS_INTEGER;
   T2 PLS_INTEGER;
   T PLS_INTEGER;
   TYPE EMPIDTAB IS TABLE OF EMP_TABLE.EMPID%TYPE;
   TYPE ENAMETAB IS TABLE OF EMP_TABLE.ENAME%TYPE;
   TYPE EADDRESSTAB IS TABLE OF EMP_TABLE.EADDRESS%TYPE;
   VEMPID EMPIDTAB;
   VENAME ENAMETAB;
   VEADDRESS EADDRESSTAB;

   PROCEDURE GET_TIME(T OUT NUMBER) IS
   BEGIN
      T:=DBMS_UTILITY.GET_TIME;
   END;

BEGIN
   FOR I IN 1..10000 LOOP
      INSERT INTO EMP_TABLE VALUES (I,'NAME'||I,'ADD'||I);
```

```
    END LOOP;
    COMMIT;
    GET_TIME(T1);
    SELECT EMPID,ENAME,EADDRESS
    BULK COLLECT INTO VEMPID, VENAME, VEADDRESS
    FROM EMP_TABLE;
    GET_TIME(T2);
    T:=T2-T1;
    DBMS_OUTPUT.PUT_LINE('TIME ELAPSED USING BULK COLLECT');
    DBMS_OUTPUT.PUT_LINE('T2-T1 = '||T);
END;
/
DROP TABLE EMP_TABLE;
```

Oracle 9i

```
SQL> @ C:\BOOK\CHAPTER12\EX12_3B
Table created.
TIME ELAPSED USING BULK COLLECT
T2-T1 = 11
PL/SQL procedure successfully completed.
Table dropped.
```

Oracle 11g

```
SQL> @ C:\BOOK\CHAPTER12\EX12_3B
Table created.
TIME ELAPSED USING BULK COLLECT
T2-T1 = 3
PL/SQL procedure successfully completed.
Table dropped.
```

Illustration

Execution time in Oracle 9i and Oracle 11g is shown in Table 12.4. Note that hardware configuration was the same for both the versions of Oracle.

TABLE 12.4 Execution Time Comparison

PL/SQL code	Oracle 9i (execution time in ms)	Oracle 11g (execution time in ms)	Remarks
EX12_3A	70	15	Simple Cursor and loop used
EX12_3B	11	3	BULK COLLECT used

EX12_4A This example demonstrates the elapsed time to fetch 50% record using the conventional cursor. The same program is executed in both Oracle 9i and Oracle 11g to compare the performance.

```
CREATE TABLE EMP_TABLE
(EMPID NUMBER(5), ENAME VARCHAR2(20), EADDRESS VARCHAR2(20));

SET SERVEROUTPUT ON
DECLARE
   T1 PLS_INTEGER;
   T2 PLS_INTEGER;
   T PLS_INTEGER;
   CURSOR EMP_CURSOR IS SELECT * FROM EMP_TABLE;
   EMPREC EMP_CURSOR%ROWTYPE;
   N PLS_INTEGER := 0;
   PROCEDURE GET_TIME(T OUT NUMBER) IS
   BEGIN
      T:=DBMS_UTILITY.GET_TIME;
   END;

BEGIN
   FOR I IN 1..10000 LOOP
      INSERT INTO EMP_TABLE VALUES (I,'NAME'||I,'ADD'||I);
   END LOOP;
   COMMIT;
   GET_TIME(T1);
   OPEN EMP_CURSOR;
   LOOP
   FETCH EMP_CURSOR INTO EMPREC;
   EXIT WHEN EMP_CURSOR%NOTFOUND OR N>5000;
   N:=N+1;
   END LOOP;
   CLOSE EMP_CURSOR;
   GET_TIME(T2);
   T:=T2-T1;
   DBMS_OUTPUT.PUT_LINE('TIME ELAPSED USING CURSOR AND SIMPLE LOOP');
   DBMS_OUTPUT.PUT_LINE('T2-T1 = '||T);
END;
/
DROP TABLE EMP_TABLE;
```

Oracle 9i

```
SQL> @ C:\BOOK\CHAPTER12\EX12_4A
Table created.
TIME ELAPSED USING CURSOR AND SIMPLE LOOP
T2-T1 = 35
PL/SQL procedure successfully completed.
Table dropped.
```

```
Oracle 11g
SQL> @ C:\BOOK\CHAPTER12\EX12_4A
Table created.
TIME ELAPSED USING CURSOR AND SIMPLE LOOP
T2-T1 = 11
PL/SQL procedure successfully completed.
Table dropped.
```

EX12_4B This program demonstrates improvement in performance to fetch 50% records using BULK COLLECT. Refer to Table 12.5 to see the gain in performance.

```
CREATE TABLE EMP_TABLE
(EMPID NUMBER(5), ENAME VARCHAR2(20), EADDRESS VARCHAR2(20));

SET SERVEROUTPUT ON
DECLARE
   T1 PLS_INTEGER;
   T2 PLS_INTEGER;
   T PLS_INTEGER;
   TYPE EMPIDTAB IS TABLE OF EMP_TABLE.EMPID%TYPE;
   TYPE ENAMETAB IS TABLE OF EMP_TABLE.ENAME%TYPE;
   TYPE EADDRESSTAB IS TABLE OF EMP_TABLE.EADDRESS%TYPE;
   VEMPID EMPIDTAB;
   VENAME ENAMETAB;
   VEADDRESS EADDRESSTAB;

   PROCEDURE GET_TIME(T OUT NUMBER) IS
   BEGIN
      T:=DBMS_UTILITY.GET_TIME;
   END;

BEGIN
   FOR I IN 1..10000 LOOP
      INSERT INTO EMP_TABLE VALUES (I,'NAME'||I,'ADD'||I);
   END LOOP;
   COMMIT;

   GET_TIME(T1);
   SELECT EMPID,ENAME,EADDRESS
   BULK COLLECT INTO VEMPID, VENAME, VEADDRESS
   FROM EMP_TABLE SAMPLE(50);
   GET_TIME(T2);
   T:=T2-T1;
   DBMS_OUTPUT.PUT_LINE('TIME ELAPSED USING BULK COLLECT');
   DBMS_OUTPUT.PUT_LINE('T2-T1 = '||T);
END;
/
```

```
DROP TABLE EMP_TABLE;
```

Oracle 9i

```
SQL> @ C:\BOOK\CHAPTER12\EX12_4B
Table created.
TIME ELAPSED USING BULK COLLECT
T2-T1 = 15
PL/SQL procedure successfully completed.
Table dropped.
```

Oracle 11g

```
SQL>  @ C:\BOOK\CHAPTER12\EX12_4B
Table created.
TIME ELAPSED USING BULK COLLECT
T2-T1 = 1
PL/SQL procedure successfully completed.
Table dropped.
```

Illustration

Execution time in Oracle 9i and Oracle 11g is shown in Table 12.5. Note that hardware configuration was the same for both the versions of Oracle.

TABLE 12.5 Execution Time Comparison

PL/SQL code	Oracle 9i (execution time in ms)	Oracle 11g (execution time in ms)	Remarks
EX12_4A	35	11	Simple Cursor and loop used for 50% of data
EX12_4B	15	1	BULK COLLECT used for 50% of data

12.7 ORACLE 10G AND 11G OPTIMIZATION PARAMETER

Oracle 11g uses a PL/SQL optimizing compiler to rearrange code for better performance. In Oracle releases prior to 11g, the PL/SQL compiler translated the code to machine code without optimizing for performance. The parameter used to optimize the performance is PLSQL_OPTIMIZE_LEVEL. By default the value of PLSQL_OPTIMIZE_LEVEL is set to the highest value (i.e., 2). With this value, the compiler applies a wide range of modern optimization techniques to optimize the code. It can also be set to 1 or 0. If the value is set to 1, the compiler applies optimization techniques to PL/SQL programs but does not alter the original source order. The use of level 0 will forfeit most of the performance gains of PL/SQL in Oracle Database 11g and therefore should not be set without any reason. In most cases, setting this parameter to 2 ensures the best execution performance. However, if the compiler runs slowly for some code, then setting this parameter to 1 ensures less use of compile-time resources with almost as good a compilation as with parameter set to 2. It is recommended to re-execute the codes written in older version of Oracle in Oracle 11g. In most cases, there will be performance improvements without doing any tuning.

12.8 COST-BASED OPTIMIZER

Query optimization is the process of choosing the most efficient execution plan. The goal is to achieve the result with the least cost in terms of resource usage. Cost-Based Optimizer (CBO) works by gathering statistics on tables and indexes, the order of tables and columns in the SQL statements and available indexes to pick the most efficient way to access them. The different modes of the OPTIMIZER_MODE are as follows:

(i) ALL_ROWS: This is the default mode and it directs Oracle to use the Cost-Based Optimizer, whether there is any statistics on any of the tables in a query or not. Setting the initialization parameter OPTIMIZER_MODE to ALL_ROWS ensures that we can get the complete result set of the query as soon as feasible.

(ii) FIRST_ROWS_*n*: This optimizing mode uses cost optimization regardless of the availability of statistics. The goal is to achieve the fastest response time for the first *n* number of rows of output, where *n* can take the value of 10, 100 or 1000.

(iii) FIRST_ROWS: The FIRST_ROWS mode uses cost optimization and certain rules, regardless of whether there is any statistics or not. This is particularly used for backward compatibility. This is used when the first few rows are fetched quickly so that the response time can be minimized.

CBO evaluates various statistics and chooses the most optimal execution plan. The optimizer works based on certain rules. Hints may be provided to override the CBO execution plan. Hints can alter the join method, join order or access path. These are also provided to parallelize the SQL statement operation. The following hints may be used.

(iv) ALL_ROWS: The ALL_ROWS hint instructs the Oracle to optimize throughput, not optimize the response time of the statement.

(v) FIRST_ROWS (*n*): The FIRST_ROWS (*n*) hint dictates that Oracle returns the first *n* rows quickly. Low response time is the goal of this hint.

(vi) FULL: The FULL hint requires that a full table scan be done on the table, ignoring any index that may be present. Basically to force Oracle to do full table scan, we use FULL hint.

(vii) Ordered: This hint forces the join order for the tables in the query.

(viii) Index: This hint forces the use of an index scan, even if the optimizer ignores the use of existing indexes and does the full table scan.

(ix) Index_FFS: An index fast full scan hint forces a fast full scan of an index, just as full table scan. INDEX_FFS scans all the blocks in an index using multiblock I/O, the size of which is determined by the DB_FILE_MULTIBLOCK_READ_COUNT parameter.

CBO assumes data to uniformly distribute in a table. There are times when data is not distributed uniformly. In case of skewed data distribution in a table, histogram is used to store column statistics. Histograms are buckets to represent distribution of data in a column. There are following two types of histograms:

- Height-based histograms: It divides the column values into bands, with each band containing a roughly equal number of rows. If a table is having 100 rows, a histogram can be created with 10 buckets and each bucket containing 10 rows.
- Frequency-based histogram: It determines the number of buckets based on the distinct values in the column. Each bucket contains all the data having the same value.

Histograms can be created using METHOD_OPT attribute of the DBMS_STATS procedure such as GATHER_TABLE_STATS, GATHER_DATABASE_STATS and so on. The METHOD_OPT attribute is assigned with the values as AUTO, FOR COLUMNS and SKEWONLY. AUTO makes Oracle to decide which columns it should collect histograms for, based on the data distribution and workload. If we choose SKEWONLY, Oracle will base the decision on the data distribution of the columns.

CBO does not use the same execution strategy and varies due to change in version or initialization of parameters. Oracle's plan stability features are used to ensure that the execution plan remains stable regardless of any changes in the database environment. The plan stability feature uses outlines to preserve the current execution plans, even if the statistics and the optimizer mode are changed. Outlines are useful for migrating from one version of Oracle to another. To implement plan stability, we require making the QUERY_REWRITE_ENABLE, STAR_TRANSFORMATION_ENABLE and OPTIMIZER_FEATURES_ENABLE initialization parameters consistent in all environments.

12.9 PERFORMANCE TUNING IN DYNAMIC SQL

When INSERT, UPDATE, DELETE and SELECT statements are directly used in a PL/SQL program, by default PL/SQL converts the variable into bind variables. This is done to make the code efficient to improve the performance. In cases INSERT, UPDATE, DELETE and SELECT statements are used in dynamic SQL, it is better to specify the bind variables in the program itself to get the same improved performance.

EX12_5A This example demonstrates a dynamic SQL code that is not efficient.

```
CREATE OR REPLACE PROCEDURE OUT_OF_STOCK (VPID NUMBER) AS
BEGIN
   EXECUTE IMMEDIATE
   'DELETE FROM CUST WHERE PID = ' || TO_CHAR(VPID);
END;
/
```

EX12_5B This example demonstrates a dynamic SQL code that is efficient in terms of performance.

```
CREATE OR REPLACE PROCEDURE OUT_OF_STOCK (VPID NUMBER) AS
BEGIN
   EXECUTE IMMEDIATE
   'DELETE FROM CUST WHERE PID = :1' || USING VPID;
END;
/
```

In PL/SQL programs, SQL statements do most of the work. Slow SQL statements are the main reason for slow execution. To overcome this problem, it must be ensured that appropriate indexes are created and used. Analyze the execution plans and performance of the SQL statements, using EXPLAIN PLAN statement, SQL Trace facility with TKPROF utility and DBMS_STATS package. For PL/SQL programs that do not depend on OUT parameters, it is wise to declare NOCOPY parameter along with OUT or IN OUT parameters. This technique can give significant speedup, especially if large amounts of data are handled. An effort must be made to make all loops as efficient as possible. To improve the performance, it is important to optimize the loop itself and the code inside the loop. If it is possible, move initializations or computations outside the loop. Intelligent nesting of queries generally results in performance improvement. PL/SQL provides many highly optimized string functions such as REPLACE, TRANSLATE, SUBSTR, INSTR, RPAD and LTRIM. These built-in functions use low-level code and are more efficient than regular PL/SQL.

In PL/SQL, when evaluating multiple conditions separated by AND or OR, put the least expensive ones first and the most expensive last.

Group Related Subprograms into Packages so that when the packaged subprogram is called for the first time, the whole package is loaded into the main memory. Subsequent calls to related subprograms in the package will not require any disk I/O, and the code will execute faster.

As you develop larger and larger PL/SQL applications, it becomes more difficult to isolate performance problems. PL/SQL provides a Profiler API to profile run-time behaviour and Trace API for tracing the execution of programs on the server to identify performance bottlenecks. The Profiler API is implemented as PL/SQL package DBMS_PROFILER that provides run-time statistics in database tables, which can be queried later. These statistics can be used to improve performance.

12.10 SUMMARY

There are few concepts that come under the purview of SQL or DBA are hot topics, which are sometimes asked in interviews. We will briefly introduce some of them to provide an overview.

(i) INLINE VIEW: An inline view is a SELECT statement in the FROM clause of another SELECT statement. Inline views are commonly used to simplify complex queries by removing join operations. This results into condensing several separate queries into a single query.

(ii) CORRELATED SUB-QUERIES: A query which uses values from the outer query is called a correlated subquery. In case of correlated subqueries, subquery is executed once and uses the results for all the evaluations in the outer query.

(iii) LISTAGG: Oracle 11gR2 LISTAGG built-in function allows for many table columns to be displayed within a single row. At times, it is necessary to aggregate data from a number of rows into a single row, giving a list of data associated with a specific value.

(iv) CAST FUNCTION: CAST function is an ANSI standard function that lets you converts one built-in data type into another built-in data type value. You can cast a date or the result set of a subquery, varray or a nested table into a type compatible data type. It may be useful sometimes, but use of TO_CHAR, TO_NUMBER and TO_DATE functions provides more control over the conversions.

(v) MATERIALIZED VIEWS: Oracle provides materialized views to replicate data to the dependent sites in a replication environment and to cache expensive queries in a distributed environment. A materialized view stores both definitions of view plus rows resulting from the execution of the view. It is useful if query involves summaries, multiple joins or both. It is a pre-computed table comprising aggregated or joined data and is mainly used for improving query performance or providing replicated data.

(vi) PIPELINING: A regular table function fetches the entire collection before returning it to the requesting query resulting into delayed response. Performance of table functions can be improved by the implementation of pipelining and parallelization. Pipelining allows tuples to be made available as they are produced. It does not wait for whole collections to be produced before the results are returned. The advantage of using pipelining is reduction in the time taken for the initial rows to be produced and overall reduction in the amount of utilized memory.

(vii) TABLE PARTITIONING: Partitioning addresses key issues in supporting very large tables and indexes. It allows decomposing very large tables and indexes into smaller and more manageable pieces called partitions. One good thing is that SQL queries and DML statements do not need to be modified in order to access partitioned tables. DDL statements access and manipulate individual partitions instead of entire tables or indexes. This is how partitioning can simplify the manageability of large database objects and partitioning is transparent to applications. Partitioning is useful for different types of applications, which manage large volumes of data. OLTP systems benefit from improvements in manageability and availability, whereas data warehousing systems benefit from improved performance.

(viii) DATABASE LINK: A database link enables you to access objects on another database. A database link is basically a pointer that defines a one-way communication path from an Oracle Database server to another database server. The other database may or may not be Oracle Database system. To access non-Oracle systems, you must use Oracle Heterogeneous Services. CREATE DATABASE LINK statement is used to create a database link. Once a database link is created, you can use it to refer to a table or view the other database by appending @dblink to the table or view name with the SELECT and DML statements.

In this chapter, common PL/SQL optimization techniques have been discussed. The developer may follow the simple tips discussed in chapter to achieve big gains in terms of performance. In the concluding section, few currently hot topics are also introduced. The primary objective of this part of the book is to ensure firm grip on PL/SQL programming.

SHORT/OBJECTIVE TYPE QUESTIONS

1. How will you tune a number crunching intrinsic application?

2. How will you improve performance of an application, the large number of methods are used?

3. What are the major steps to handle a large number of DMLs to speed up the processing?
4. Do PL/SQL program running in older version of Oracle (8i or 9i) run faster in Oracle 10g or 11g with the default setting?
5. What do you understand by using optimized variable?
6. What is SQL Plan Management baseline?
7. What do you understand by histogram?
8. What is EXPLAIN PLAN and how it is used to enhance the performance of SQL?
9. What do you mean by AUTOTRACE and how is it used?
10. Write short notes on PL SQL_OPTIMISE_LEVEL.
11. What do you understand by query optimization?
12. What are the different phases the SQL statement goes through?
13. What are the actions performed during the Parse, Optimize and Execute phases?
14. What action is performed in the query rewrite phase?
15. What are the actions performed in the execution plan generation phase?
16. How does Cost-Based Optimizer works?
17. How statistics are provided to the optimizer?
18. What are the different modes of the parameter OPTIMIZER_MODE?
19. What do you understand by SQL transformation?
20. What are the different join methods used by the Cost-Based Optimizer?
21. What is the joining strategy followed by the optimizer?
22. What do you mean by adaptive search strategy?
23. What are the different methods for providing statistics to the Cost-Based Optimizer?
24. When we collect the statistics manually?
25. What is the name of the DBMS_STATS procedure which is used to gather statistics for all objects in the database?
26. Which procedure in DBMS_STATS package is used for gathering statistics for schema?
27. Which procedure in DBMS_STATS package is used for gathering statistics for tables?
28. Which procedure in DBMS_STATS package is used for gathering statistics for index?
29. What are the steps followed to avoid full table scan?
30. How can we avoid applying multiple aggregates from the same table?
31. What should be the design approach to make the subqueries work faster?
32. What is meant by database hint and why it is used?
33. How many types of hints are there and where they are used?
34. What does it mean by Bitmap join indexes and where it is used?
35. How do you stabilize the Cost-Based Optimizer and why it is required?

WORKOUT SECTION

W12_1 Execute EX12_1C in Oracle 9i and Oracle 10g (installed on the same machine) and compare the performance in terms of time.

W12_2 Execute EX12_2B and EX12_2C in Oracle 9i and Oracle 10g (installed on the same machine) and compare the performance in terms of time.

W12_3 Execute EX12_3A and EX12_3B in Oracle 9i and Oracle 10g (installed on the same machine) and compare the performance in terms of time.

W12_4 Execute EX12_4A and EX12_4B in Oracle 9i and Oracle 10g (installed on the same machine) and compare the performance in terms of time.

Part III

Database Management System

Advanced Concepts and Technologies

Query Processing, File Organization, and Distributed Processing

Learning Objectives

You will learn following key concepts after completion of the chapter:

- ✓ Query processing, optimization and execution plan
- ✓ Index file organization, B+ and B- trees
- ✓ Static and dynamic hashing
- ✓ Two and three tier architectures

13.1 INTRODUCTION

Query processing attempts to find the best solution using query parser, query optimizer, query code generation and run-time database processor. Indexing and hashing are the methodologies related to random access of records. Distributed architecture deals with two and three tier based solution. All these important topics will be discussed in this chapter. This chapter will conclude with a brief introduction to data warehousing and data mining.

13.2 QUERY PROCESSING, OPTIMIZATION AND EXECUTION PLAN

For a specific query, there are many alternative solutions that a database management system can follow to process and produce the result. All solutions are equivalent in terms of the final result, but vary in their costs. Primarily the cost is based on time and space needed to execute the query. The cost difference between multiple alternative solutions can be enormous. Ideally the best alternative is the one which needs the least amount of time and space to run the query.

Let us try to understand the concept of query processing, query optimization and execution plans with the help of a realistic example. Figure 13.1 shows various paths to reach from source to destination. It also shows important details related to various paths, railway gate, etc. For example, distance between source and destination via A–D–G–E–C is 10 km (1 + 2 + 2 + 3 + 1 + 1). Similarly, distance between source and destination via A–D–F–E–C and A–B–C is 12 km and 16 km, respectively. The other paths may be via A–D–G–D–F–E–C, A–D–G–A–B–

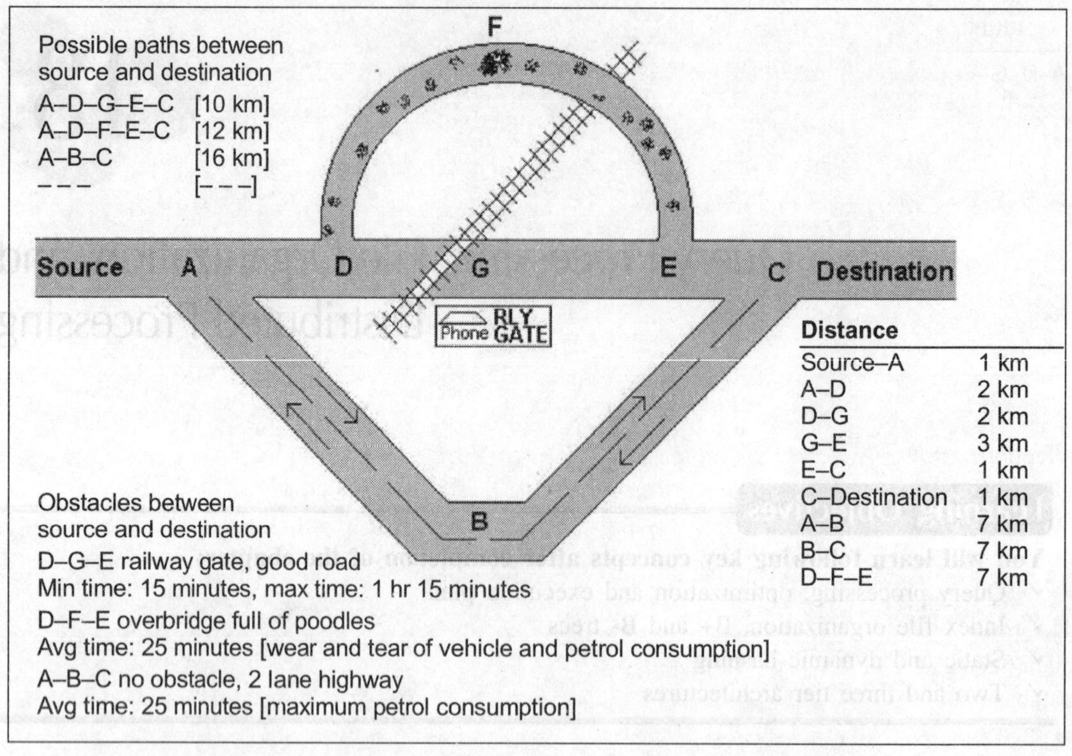

FIGURE 13.1 Various paths to reach from source to destination.

C and so on. In these cases path followed is going up to G (i.e. railway gate) and backtrack in case the railway gate is closed and go via over-bridge (A–D–G–D–F–E–C) or through highway (A–D–G–A–B–C).

The choice of path solely depends on personal preference and type of event at destination. For example, a person, who enjoys driving and not bothered for petrol will always go via highway. Similarly, a person who does not bother for discomfort will prefer the over-bridge route. Similarly if a person is going to meet a friend (at destination) and not in hurry, may follow the railway gate path, as delay due to railway gate will not create any problem. The positive and negative aspects of major paths are briefly described in Figure 13.2. Now, suppose there is an important meeting and a person does not like to take risk because of railway gate and also wants to ensure driving comfort and least distance. What will be the best solution? We will answer this later, first let us corelate this example with respect to query processing, optimization and execution plan.

Reaching from source to destination is analogous to query processing. Final objective to reach destination may be 'going to a friend', 'attending a meeting' and so on. Execution plans are various paths between source and destination like A–D–G–E–C, A–D–F–E–C, A–B–C, etc. Query optimization is to find best alternative, which will ensure driving comfort, least distance and no risk because of railway gate.

Now, let us address the problems to attend the meeting and to reach the destination with maximum comfort, least distance and minimum time. Note that the railway gate is equipped with

Path	Positive aspects	Negative aspects
A–D–G–E–C	• Shortest path • Good road • Driving comfort	• Railway track • Closing of railway gate varies from 15 minutes to 1 hour depending on the type of train
A–D–F–E–C	• Over-bridge • Shortest path after A–D–G–E–C	• Lack of driving comforts and wear and tear of vehicle due to multiple poodles • More petrol consumption as the vehicle has to be driven in low gear
A–B–C	• 2 way highway • Driving comfort	• Longest route • Maximum petrol consumption

FIGURE 13.2 Positive and negative aspects of major paths.

telephone. Hence, the optimal (or may be the best) solution in this case is to call the railway gate (through telephone) before starting, to confirm whether the railway track passage is clear at railway gate or not and decide accordingly.

13.2.1 Query Processing

The four major components of query processing in DBMS are query parser, query optimizer, query code generation and run-time database processor. It is supported by system catalogs, database statistics and main database. Diametrically it is shown in Figure 13.3. The two ways of query processing are dynamic query optimization and static query optimization. In dynamic query optimization, parsing and optimization is performed every time the query is executed. This is suitable for high DML intrinsic database applications. In static query optimization, parsing and optimization is performed only once for the same query. In realistic scenarios, combination of dynamic as well as static query optimization are employed depending on DMLs performed between two queries.

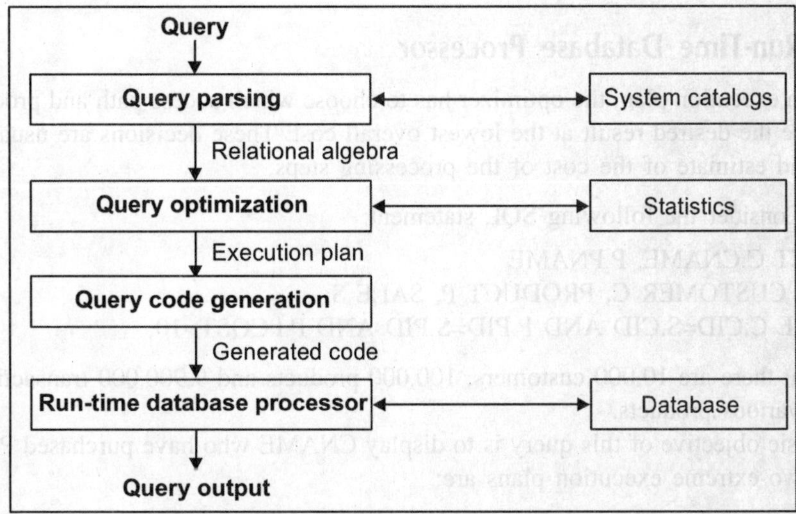

FIGURE 13.3 Query processing.

13.2.2 Query Parsing

The parsing process checks the query for correct syntax and breaks down the syntax into component parts that can be understood by the RDBMS. Different stages of query parsing are: syntax analysis, semantic analysis and query restructuring. In the syntax analysis stage, the query is lexically and syntactically checked. In the semantic analysis, incorrectly formulated queries are rejected. In the query re-structuring, common sub-expressions are eliminated and the query is restructured to provide a better implementation.

13.2.3 Query Optimization

The activities involved in choosing an efficient execution strategy for processing query is termed as query optimization. In query optimization, a query tree is taken from the query parser to decide on the best evaluation of the query in terms of time and/or space. The goal of the query optimization is to produce an efficient execution plan for processing the query. Query optimizer maintains both system performance and throughput of a relational database system. The major components related to query optimization are as under.

Storage cost: This cost is related to access secondary storage for read or write related operations.

Computation cost: This cost is related to perform computation in primary memory.

Communication cost: This cost is related to communicate the query from source to destination and back.

13.2.4 Query Code Generation

A code generation program uses the meta-data and the input query to generate new query. Generated queries share the characteristics of the input query. Code generator can save a lot of coding and testing.

13.2.5 Run-Time Database Processor

To select an execution plan, the optimizer has to choose which access path and processing steps will produce the desired result at the lowest overall cost. These decisions are usually based on statistics and estimate of the cost of the processing steps.

EX13_1 Consider the following SQL statement:

```
SELECT C.CNAME, P.PNAME
FROM CUSTOMER C, PRODUCT P, SALE S
WHERE C.CID=S.CID AND P.PID=S.PID AND P.PCOST>10;
```

Assume that there are 10,000 customers, 100,000 products and 9,900,000 transactions because of sale of various products.

The basic objective of this query is to display CNAME who have purchased PNAME. Out of many, two extreme execution plans are:

(a) Use the indexed/hashed CUSTOMER, PRODUCT and SALE tables. Find PNAME whose cost is greater than 10 and then join the three tables.

(b) Take cross product of tables CUSTOMER, PRODUCT and SALE, which are neither sorted nor hashed. Join rows based on CID and PID and after that find PNAME based on PCOST greater than 10.

In case of (a), execution time will be in terms of few seconds, whereas in case of (b) execution time will be in terms of minutes.

13.2.6 Optimization in Oracle Database Server

Oracle 11g and 10g use a PL/SQL optimizing compiler to rearrange code for optimal performance. In Oracle releases prior to 10g, the PL/SQL compiler used to translate the code to machine code without optimizing. The parameter used in Oracle 10g and 11g to optimize the performance is PLSQL_OPTIMIZE_LEVEL. By default the value of PLSQL_OPTIMIZE_LEVEL is set to the highest value (i.e. 2). With this value, the compiler applies a wide range of optimization techniques to improve the performance of the code. It can also be set to 1 or 0. If the value is set to 1, the compiler applies optimization techniques to PL/SQL programs, but does not alter the original source order. Use of level 0 will forfeit most of the performance gains and therefore, should not be set without any reason. In most cases setting this parameter to 2 ensures best execution performance. However, if the compiler runs slowly for some code, then setting this parameter to 1 ensures less use of compile-time, resources with almost as good a compilation with parameter set to 2. It is always recommended to re-execute the codes written in older version of Oracle in Oracle 10g/11g. In most cases there will be significant performance improvements without doing any tuning.

13.3 INDEX FILE ORGANIZATION

A file organization is a methodology to physically organize the records of a file on secondary storage devices. The primary file organizations are sequential, indexed and hashed. The most important governing factors related to any file organization are as under.

(a) Speed of retrieval and updation of records
(b) Use of storage space
(c) Frequency of re-organization of records
(d) Issues related to security and reliability

In sequential file organization, records are stored in sequence based on primary key value. It is cost effective to archive data in magnetic tape drive as backup. Sequential file organization is not suitable for applications which call for frequent retrieval, re-organization and DMLs as it takes long access time.

Index file organization is mainly designed to reduce the access time. It allows the use of variable length records. An additional file viz. 'index file' is created to store the indexes. Index is basically a pointer to identify the record in the 'data file'. Index is a data structure that allows speeding up of queries by enabling scanning of records. Index file organization does not reduce overall storage requirement of a file.

A primary index is defined as a primary key on which the records in the file are stored. A file can have at most one primary index. Indexes defined on non-prime key attributes are called **secondary indexes**. Dense index has an index record in the index file for all the search key value in the data file. Sparse index, on the other hand, has an index record in the index file only for some of the search key values in the data file. For dense index, the number of index records is equal to the number of records in the data file, whereas in case of sparse index it is less than the number of records in the data file. Index based on primary key can be either sparse or dense. However, index based on non-prime attributes should be dense. An index file is said to be clustered index if the order of the records in the data file is similar to the order of the index records in the index file. An index is said to be composite, if the search key contains more than one attribute.

EX13_2 This example illustrates use of dense and sparse index corresponding to the table named DAILY_ALLOWANCE (DA) as shown in Table 13.1. The table shows the minimum and maximum DA based on the class of the city. For example, for class A1 city, minimum DA is ₹ 1250 and maximum DA is ₹ 6500. In DAILY-ALLOWANCE table, CITY acts as a primary key. Dense index and sparse index corresponding to the prime attribute CITY is shown in Table 13.2 and Table 13.3, respectively. Note that for any non prime attribute, dense index is essentially required to locate the record.

TABLE 13.1 DAILY_ALLOWANCE Table

CITY#	CLASS	MIN_DA	MAX_DA
AGRA	B1	850	4250
AHMEDABAD	A	1000	5250
ALLAHABAD	B1	850	4250
BANGALORE	A	1000	5250
BHOPAL	B1	850	4250
CHENNAI	A1	1250	6500
COIMBATORE	B1	850	4250
DARJEELING	A	1000	5250
DELHI	A1	1250	6500
HYDERABAD	A	1000	5250
INDORE	B1	850	4250
JAIPUR	B1	850	4250
KANPUR	A	1000	5250
KOCHI	B1	850	4250
KOLKATA	A1	1250	6500
LACCADIVE	B1	850	4250
LUCKNOW	B1	850	4250
LUDHIANA	B1	850	4250
MUMBAI	A1	1250	6500
NAGPUR	A	1000	5250
NEW DELHI	A1	1250	6500
PANAJI	A	1000	5250
PATNA	B1	850	4250
PUNE	A	1000	5250
SHIMLA	B1	850	4250
SURAT	B1	850	4250
VADODARA	B1	850	4250
VARANASI	B1	850	4250

TABLE 13.2 DENSE INDEX Corresponding to CITY#

CITY#
AGRA
AHMEDABAD
ALLAHABAD
BANGALORE
BHOPAL
CHENNAI
COIMBATORE
DARJEELING
DELHI
HYDERABAD
INDORE
JAIPUR
KANPUR
KOCHI
KOLKATA
LACCADIVE
LUCKNOW
LUDHIANA
MUMBAI
NAGPUR
NEW DELHI
PANAJI
PATNA
PUNE
SHIMLA
SURAT
VADODARA
VARANASI

TABLE 13.3 SPARSE INDEX Corresponding to CITY#

CITY#
AGRA
CHENNAI
DARJEELING
KANPUR
LACCADIVE
LUDHIANA
MUMBAI
NAGPUR
PANAJI

13.3.1 Index Sequential Access Method

The Index Sequential Access Method (ISAM) is closely related to the physical characteristics of the storage media. It has two parts—Index Part (IP) and Data Part (DP). IP stores pointers to the actual record location on the disk. DP holds actual data records and is made up of two distinct areas. They are prime area and overflow area. The prime area holds records of the file and the overflow area holds records when the prime area overflows. Key searching in ISAM is somewhat similar to searching word in a dictionary, which is combination of random and sequential search.

EX13_3 Assume a file comprising of 10,000 records.
Average comparison is 5000 (half of 10,000) in case of sequential search.
Use of evenly spaced index uniformly distributed with 100 entries, the average number of comparisons is reduced to 500 (half of 10,000/100) in the index file plus 50 (half of 100).
Average comparison time ratio between sequential search and ISAM is approximately 10:1.

13.3.2 Binary Tree

Before discussing binary tree, it is worthwhile to quickly go through the relevant terminologies. A 'node' stores the actual data and links to the other node. The 'parent' of a node is the immediate predecessor of a node. All the immediate successors of a parent node are known as **child**. A 'root' is a specially designated node which has no parent. The node which is at the end and does not have any child is called **leaf node**. 'Level' is the rank in the hierarchy. The maximum number of nodes that are possible in a path starting from the root node to a leaf node is called the **height** of a tree. The maximum number of children that are possible for a node is known as the **degree** of a node. The nodes which have the same parent are called 'siblings'. A binary tree is either empty or it consists of a node (called **root**) together with two binary trees called the **left subtree** and **right subtree** of the root. A binary tree is a full binary tree if it contains the maximum possible number of nodes at all levels.

To construct a binary tree, elements (or nodes) must be sorted in ascending order. The sorted list is roughly divided into half at each stage. An example of creation of binary tree is shown in Figure 13.4.

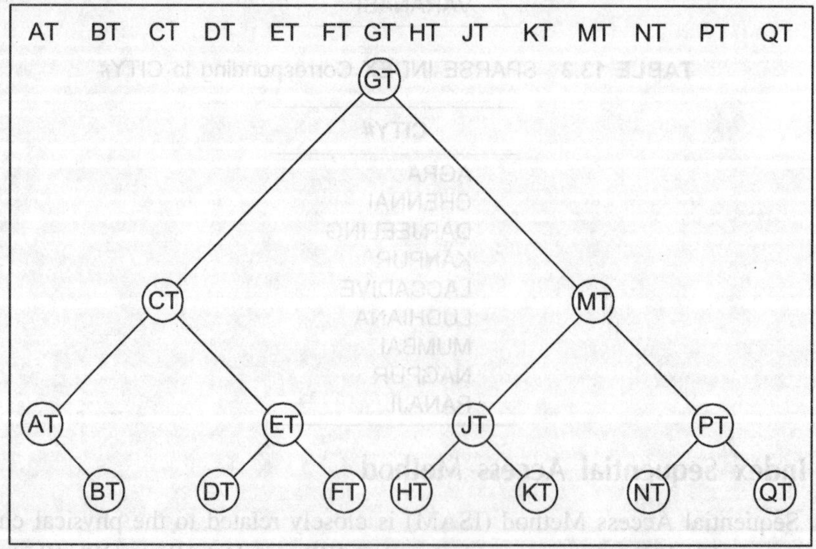

FIGURE 13.4 Binary tree.

Note that GT and HT lies in the middle of the sorted elements. GT is selected as root of the tree at the top level. CT lies in the middle of AT and GT. Similarly MT lies in the middle of GT and QT. Note that all the nodes contain 2, 1 or 0 element(s).

A binary search tree is a binary tree that is either empty or in which each node contains a key that fulfils the conditions as mentioned: (a) all keys in the left subtree of the root precede the key in the root, (b) the key in the root precedes all keys in its right subtree, (c) the left and right subtrees of the root are again search trees.

Searching an element in a binary tree is a trivial process. For example to search DT element in Figure 13.4, following methodology is used:

DT < GT hence, search the element on left side of GT

DT > CT hence, search the element on right side of CT

DT < ET hence, search the element on left side of ET to locate DT

In almost all applications related to binary tree, movement through all the nodes of the binary tree is essentially required. The three methodology to traverse are pre-order, in-order and post-order.

With pre-order traversal the node is visited before the subtree. In other words the sequence of traverse is VLR, where 'V' is the node itself, 'L' is left subtree and 'R' is right subtree. An example of pre-order traverse is shown in Figure 13.5.

With in-order traversal the sequence of traverse is LVR. An example of in-order traverse is shown in Figure 13.6.

With post-order traversal the root is visited after both of the subtrees. In other words, the sequence of traverse is LRV. An example of post-order traverse is shown in Figure 13.7.

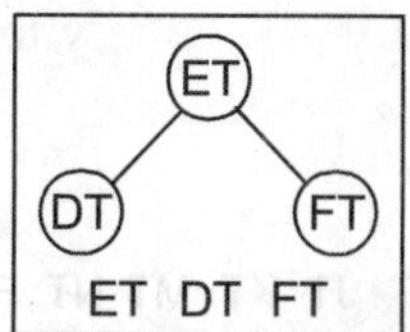

FIGURE 13.5 Pre-order traversal.

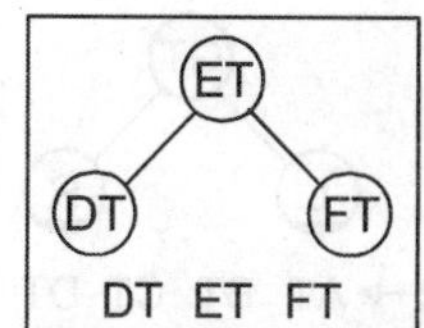

FIGURE 13.6 In-order traversal.

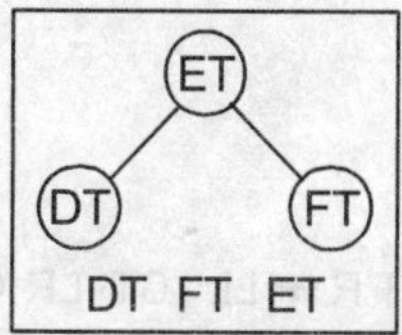

FIGURE 13.7 Post-order traversal.

Traversing in any order is exceptionally simple process. The key to success is to represent the binary tree using three (or two) nodes at all the stages. For example, to traverse the binary tree shown in Figure 13.4 in pre-order, simply represent the left subtree using 'L' and the right subtree using 'R' (Figure 13.8). In the subsequent stages, repeat the same till the time leaf nodes are reached. Convert the leaf nodes using VLR (Like Figure 13.5) and replace the intermediate nodes viz. LL, LR, RL, RR, L and R as shown in Figure 13.8. Same methodology is applicable in case of in-order and post-order traverse.

Pre-order, in-order and post-order traverse corresponding to binary tree shown in Figure 13.4 is illustrated in Figure 13.8, Figure 13.9 and Figure 13.10, respectively.

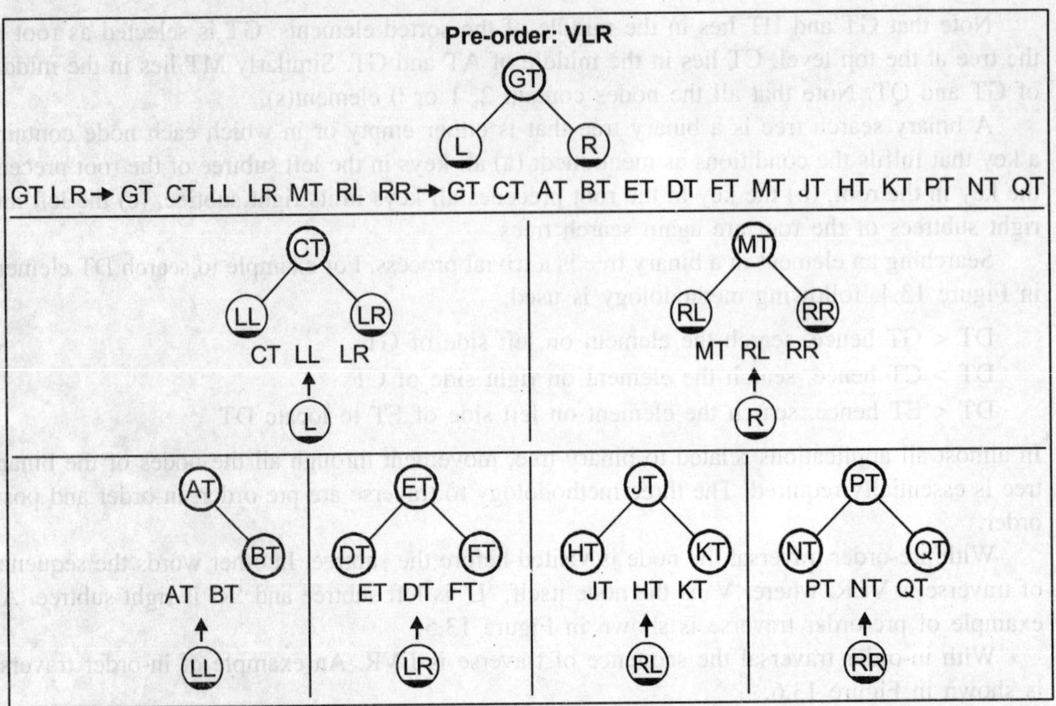

FIGURE 13.8 Pre-order traversal in a binary tree.

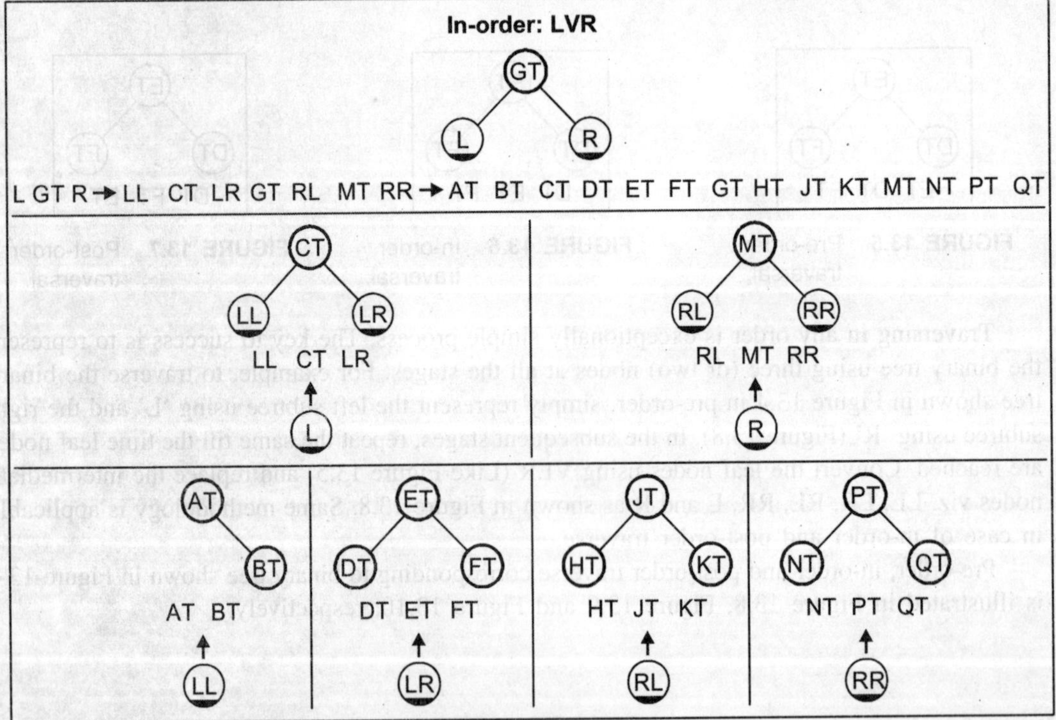

FIGURE 13.9 In-order traversal in a binary tree.

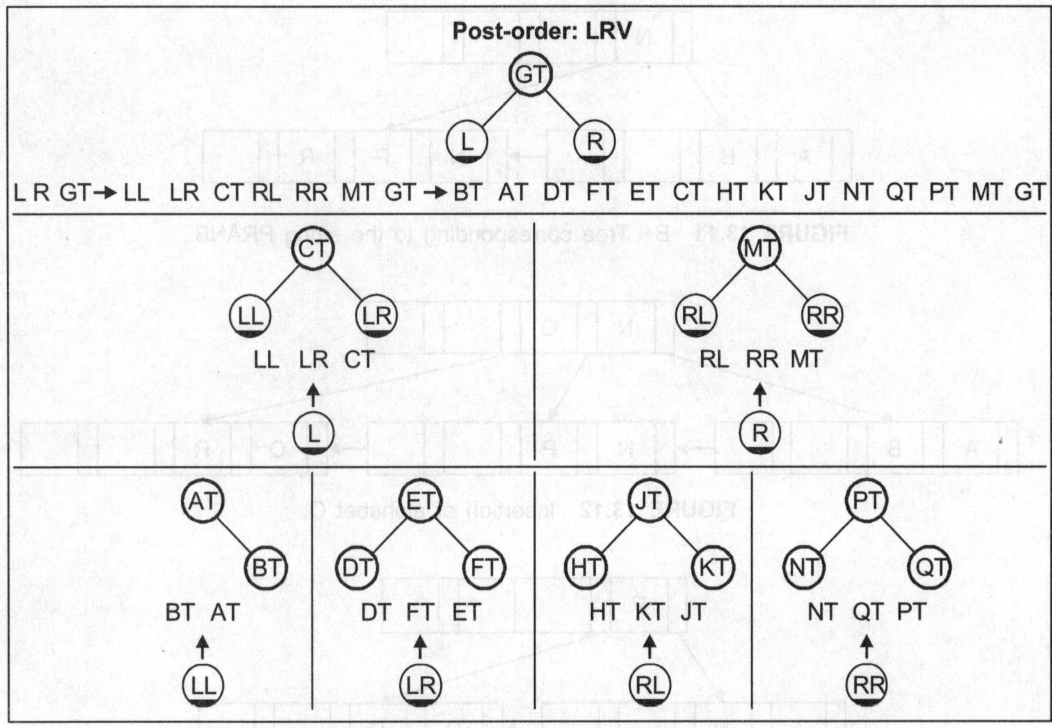

FIGURE 13.10 Post-order traversal in a binary tree.

B+ Tree

Performance of ISAM degrades as the file grows. B+ tree maintain its efficiency even as the file grow/shrink because of insert/delete operations. B+ tree ensures formation of balanced tree where each path from the root to the tree leaf is of same length. B+ tree is the most popular index structure in relational database systems, even though they impose overhead related to space, insertion and deletion. The B+ tree is a form of a balanced tree structure. The leaf nodes contain the data entries and the non-leaf nodes contain entries, which direct the search. A distinction is made in a B+ tree between the entries in leaf nodes and entries in the non-leaf nodes. The entries in the leaf nodes contain pointers to the data records.

Search, insert and delete in B+ trees

Searching of node is trivial in B+ trees because of its organization. The number of node access is equal to the height of the tree. The insertion and deletion of node requires search of the tree. The node is inserted (or deleted) to the desired location to the left or right of the key. The insertion and deletion that violates the key requires re-distribution of keys.

EX13_4 This example demonstrates insertion and deletion of node in a B+ tree. Figure 13.11 shows B+ tree corresponding to a string PRANB. Insertion of alphabet Q is shown in Figure 13.12. Deletion of alphabet B from PRANB (Figure 13.11) and from PRANBQ (Figure 13.12) are demonstrated in Figure 13.13.

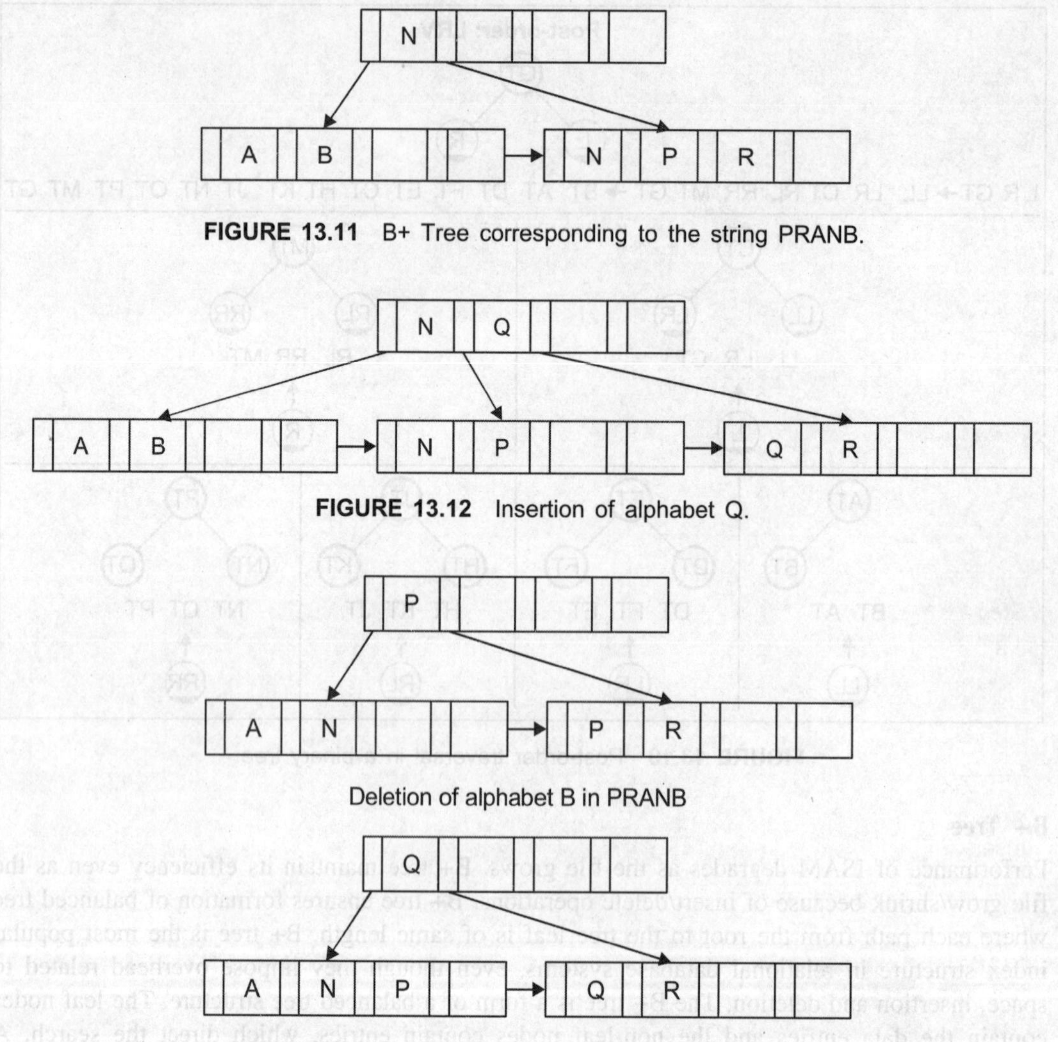

FIGURE 13.11 B+ Tree corresponding to the string PRANB.

FIGURE 13.12 Insertion of alphabet Q.

FIGURE 13.13 Deletion of alphabet B in PRANABQ.

B– Trees

The B– tree is a tree structure similar to the B+ tree, with a difference that the B– tree permits search key values to appear only once in the tree, whereas B+ trees permit redundancy to allow for a dense index at the leaf level. The B– tree is a height balanced tree. By contrast, the leaf level of a B– tree is a sparse index. Because search keys are not duplicated, an extra pointer member must be included in each index entry to reference the target data file page. In practice, few DBMS use B– trees over B+ trees.

EX13_5 This example demonstrates B– tree corresponding to a string CANKHMEGQ (Figure 13.14). Deletion of alphabet M from CANKHMEGQ is shown in Figure 13.15. Insertion of alphabets T, W and Z is shown in Figure 13.16. For better understanding insertion operation is demonstrated in two steps.

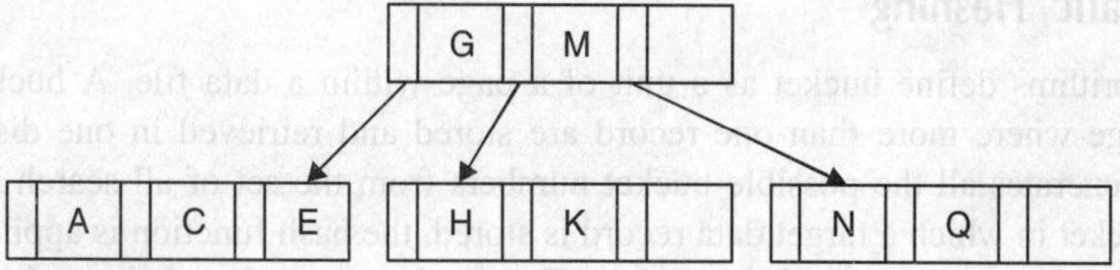

FIGURE 13.14 B–tree corresponding to the string CANKHMEGQ.

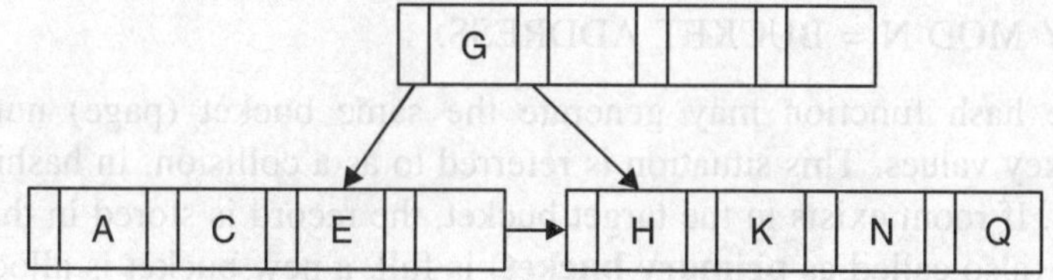

FIGURE 13.15 Delete M from B–tree CANKHMEGQ.

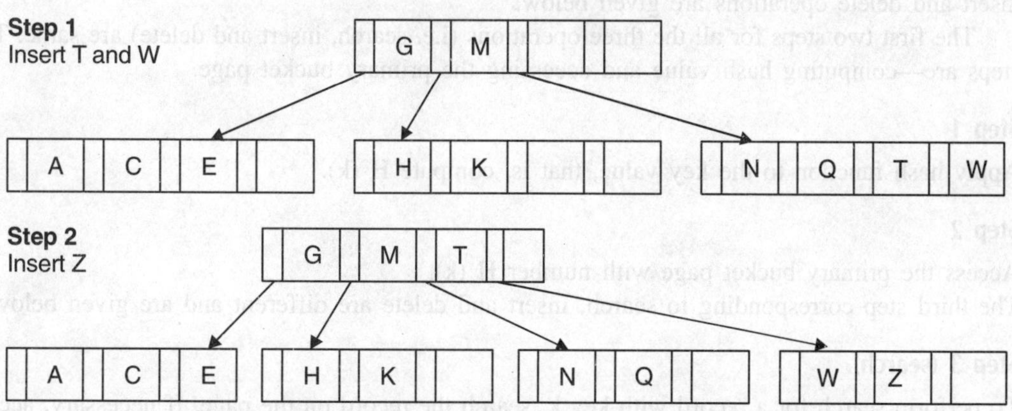

FIGURE 13.16 Insert T, W and Z in B–tree CANKHMEGQ.

13.4 HASHING

Indexing is the most powerful and flexible tools for organizing files. However, indexes take up space, time and I/O to keep them organized. This problem can be addressed with hashing in which the address of the desired record is found directly. This kind of file organization is known as **hash file organization** or direct file organization. Hashing is a technique that provides key-to-address transformation using the function known as **hashing function**. There are two types of hashing viz. static and dynamic. In the static hashing, the address space size is predefined and does not grow or shrink with file. In dynamic hashing the address space size can grow and shrink with file.

13.4.1 Static Hashing

Hashing algorithms define bucket as a unit of a page within a data file. A bucket is a logical unit of storage where more than one record are stored and retrieved in one disk I/O. A hash function H generates all the possible bucket numbers from the set of all search key values. To locate the bucket in which a target data record is stored, the hash function is applied to the target search key resulting into a bucket number. The bucket is retrieved from the data file and searched for the target data record. A well-defined hash function distributes the keys to buckets uniformly. A commonly used hash function is

H(KEY) = KEY MOD N = BUCKET ADDRESS.

Some times, the hash function may generate the same bucket (page) number for several different search key values. This situation is referred to as a collision. In hashing, the collisions must be resolved. If room exists in the target bucket, the record is stored in that bucket. In case the target bucket (also called as **primary bucket**) is full, a new bucket is allocated and chained to the primary bucket set. The new bucket is often referred to as overflow bucket and the chain of overflow buckets with the primary bucket is known as **overflow chain**. The steps for search, insert and delete operations are given below:

The first two steps for all the three operations (i.e. search, insert and delete) are same. The steps are—computing hash value and accessing the primary bucket page.

Step 1

Apply hash function to the key value, that is, compute H (k).

Step 2

Access the primary bucket page with number H (k).
The third step corresponding to search, insert and delete are different and are given below.

Step 3 (search)

To perform search for a record with key k, search the record on the page. If necessary, access the overflow chain H(k).

Step 3 (insert)

To perform insertion of a record with key k, If there is a room in the primary bucket, then insert the record on this page. Otherwise, access the overflow chain of bucket H (k), and insert the record on the free page. If necessary, add a overflow bucket to the chain of bucket H (k).

Step 3 (deletion)

To perform deletion of a record with key k, search the record on this page and delete the record from this page. If necessary, follow the overflow chain of bucket H (k) for searching the record.

Frequent deletion of data entries is also a problem. If new entries do not hash to the same bucket where the free pages exist, space will be wasted. The only solution to this case is to rehash (reorganize) the entire file.

The disadvantage of static hashing is that once buckets start to overflow, performance will degrade. To overcome the problem, if we allocate large number of buckets for the expected size initially to build the database, lot of space will go waste. Periodic reorganization avoids these problems, but is very expensive. Dynamic hashing allows modifying the number of buckets dynamically to minimize the above-mentioned problems.

EX13_6 In this example table comprising of two columns (i.e. NAME and AGE) are used (Table 13.4). H(KEY) for hashing is done on the field AGE with an assumption that all the values are unique. The global depth is defined as 1 (i.e. 0 and 1 in binary number system). Local depth decides number of buckets. In this case, local depth is defined as 1 bit, hence, two buckets viz. Bucket X and Bucket Y. Both the buckets have two pages each. H(KEY) is operated with MOD 2 so that to assign the record (0 or 1) to either Bucket X or Bucket Y. For the first four values of AGE (i.e. 10, 13, 15 and 18), records are equally distributed in two buckets (Table 13.5). Diametrically hashing is shown in Figure 13.17. However, for the last two values age (i.e. 9 and 11), there is an overflow in Bucket Y. Handling such type of situation is shown in Figure 13.18.

TABLE 13.4 Snapshot for Static Hashing

NAME	AGE	Remark
BX1	10	
BY1	13	
BY2	15	
BX2	18	
BY3	9	Overflow
BY4	11	Overflow

TABLE 13.5 Distribution of AGE in Bucket X and Y

H(KEY) (= AGE)	H(KEY) MOD 2	Binary	Local depth	Global depth	Bucket
10	0	00	0	0	X
13	1	01	0	1	Y
15	1	01	0	1	Y
18	0	00	0	0	X
9 [Overflow]	1	01	0	1	Y
11 [Overflow]	1	01	0	1	Y

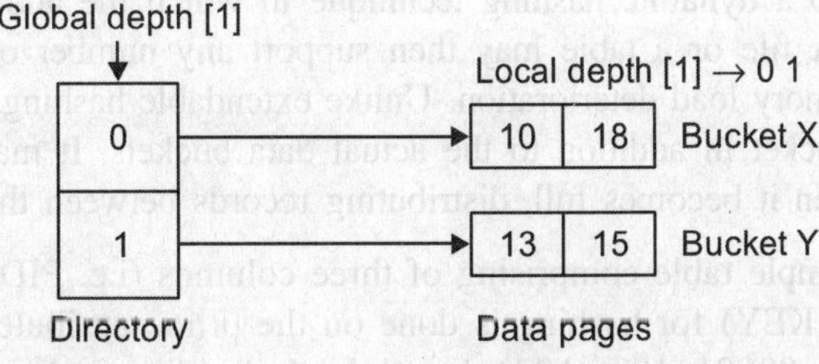

FIGURE 13.17 Global and local depths in hashing.

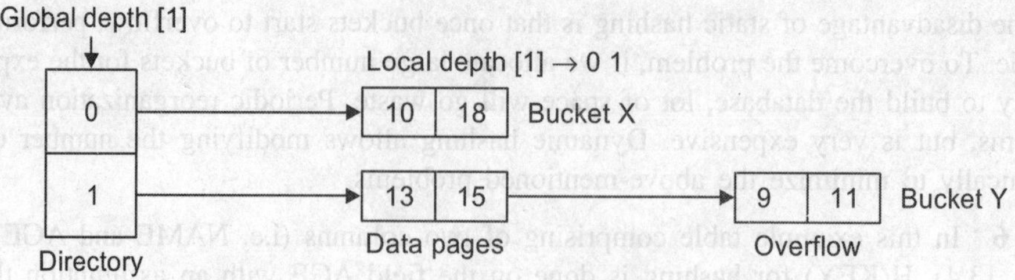

FIGURE 13.18 Handling overflow in static hashing.

13.4.2 Dynamic Hashing

Dynamic hashing methods deal with the problems of overflow that static hashing suffers from. It overcomes this problem by growing or shrinking dynamically when overflow occurs. The two most commonly used forms of dynamic hashing are extendible hashing and linear hashing.

Extendible hashing

Dynamic extendible hashing manages expansion and shrinking by splitting a bucket when it becomes full, distributing records between old and new buckets and coalescing two buckets when one of buckets becomes empty. The number of buckets also changes dynamically due to coalescing and splitting of buckets. When a search key value finds a bucket after hashing, and if it is already full, the bucket will be split into two.

In this type of hashing, a directory of pointers to hash-buckets is maintained. The hash key value is converted into a long bit string and it uses only as many bits as needed. The extendible hashing maintains two parts: bucket directory and data buckets. Each part is associated with a depth. The number of bits that are used for directory access are known as **directory depth** or **global depth**. Similarly, the number of bits that we used for data bucket access are known as **local depth**. The hash values of all data records in a particular data bucket agree on their last local depth bits. The process of splitting and coalescing of buckets take place during insertions and deletions. The directory doubles on growing and halves on shrinking. The advantage of extendable hashing is: it provides performance that does not degrade as the file grows. Minimal space overhead is ensured, as no buckets need to be reserved for future use. The disadvantages of extendable hashing are extra level of indirection in the bucket address table and complexity.

Linear hashing

Linear hashing is also a dynamic hashing technique in which the address space may grow or shrink dynamically. A file or a table may then support any number of insertions or deletions without access or memory load deterioration. Unlike extendable hashing, linear hashing does not require a directory bucket in addition to the actual data buckets. It manages the expansion by splitting a bucket when it becomes full, distributing records between the old and new buckets.

EX13_7 In this example table comprising of three columns (i.e. PID, NAME and AGE) are used (Table 13.6). H(KEY) for hashing is done on the prime attribute PID. The global depth is defined as 2 bit (i.e. 00, 01, 10 and 11). Local depth decides number of buckets. In this case,

TABLE 13.6 Snapshot for Dynamic Hashing

PID#	NAME	AGE
1	BB1	17
4	BA1	15
5	BB2	21
7	BD1	19
10	BC1	23
12	BA2	15
13	BB3	12
15	BD2	14
16	BA3	18
19	BD3	19
21	BB4	18
32	BA4	22
20 [Overflow]	BA5	34
28 [Overflow]	BA6	28

local depth is defined as 2, hence, four buckets viz. Bucket A, Bucket B, Bucket C and Bucket D. All the buckets have four pages each. H(KEY) is operated with MOD 12 so that to assign the record to either Bucket A, Bucket B, Bucket C or Bucket D. For the first twelve values of PID, records are distributed in buckets and there is no overflow (Table 13.7). Diametrically hashing is shown in Figure 13.19. However, for the last two values of PID (i.e. 20 and 28), there is an overflow in Bucket A. Handling such type of situation will be explained in EX13_8.

TABLE 13.7 Distribution of PID in Bucket A, B, C and D

H(KEY) (= PID)	H(KEY) MOD 12	Binary	Local depth	Global depth	Bucket
1	1	0001	00	01	B
4	4	0100	01	00	A
5	5	0101	01	01	B
7	7	0111	01	11	D
10	10	1010	10	10	C
12	0	0000	00	00	A
13	1	0001	00	01	B
15	3	0011	00	11	D
16	4	0100	01	00	A
19	7	0111	01	11	D
21	9	1001	10	01	B
32	8	1000	10	00	A
20	8	Overflow in Bucket A. Handling such type of overflow will be illustrated in the next example.			
28	4				

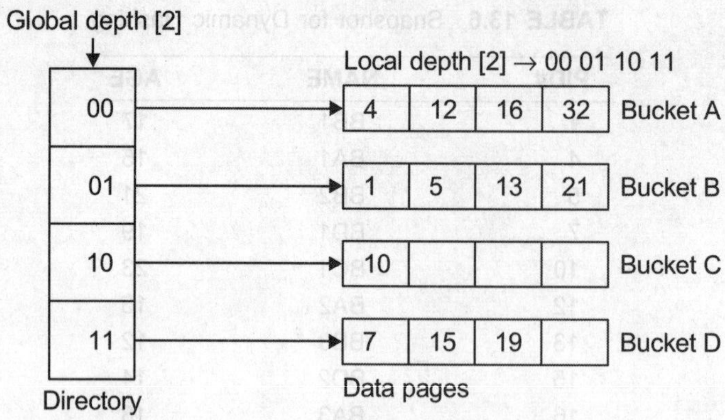

FIGURE 13.19 Local and global depth in dynamic hashing.

EX13_8 This example is the continuation of EX13_7. Here we will demonstrate handling overflow in a dynamic manner. In the previous example there was overflow in Bucket A because of the new entries corresponding to PID (i.e. 20 and 28). To make the things simple, PIDs corresponding to 'A' along with new values are used in this example. To handle the overflow, Bucket A [00] is doubled with Bucket A1 [000] and Bucket A2 [100] as shown in Figure 13.20. Previous values (i.e. 4, 12, 16 and 32) and the new values (i.e. 20 and 28) are

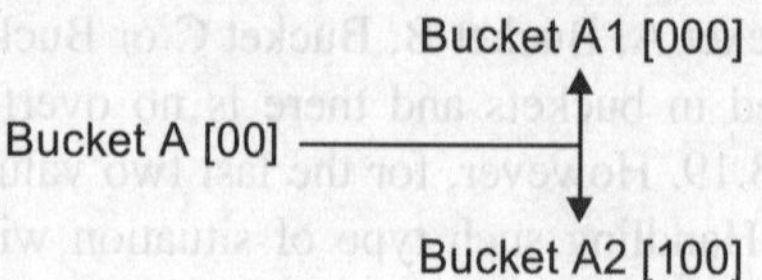

FIGURE 13.20 Handling overflow in dynamic hashing.

recomputed to assign the records to either Bucket A1 or Bucket A2 (Table 13.8). Values corresponding to PID 12, 32 and 20 are assigned to Bucket A1, whereas PID 4, 16 and 28 are assigned to Bucket A2 (Figure 13.21). Graphically hashing is shown in Figure 13.21. Compare Bucket A of Figure 13.19 with Buckets A1 and Bucket A2 of Figure 13.21.

TABLE 13.8 Distribution of New PIDs in Bucket A1 and A2.

H(KEY) (= PID)	H(KEY) MOD 12	Binary	Local depth	Global depth	Bucket
4	4	000100	000	100	A2
12	0	000000	000	000	A1
16	4	000100	000	100	A2
32	8	001000	001	000	A1
20 [New]	8	001000	001	000	A1
28 [New]	4	000100	000	100	A2

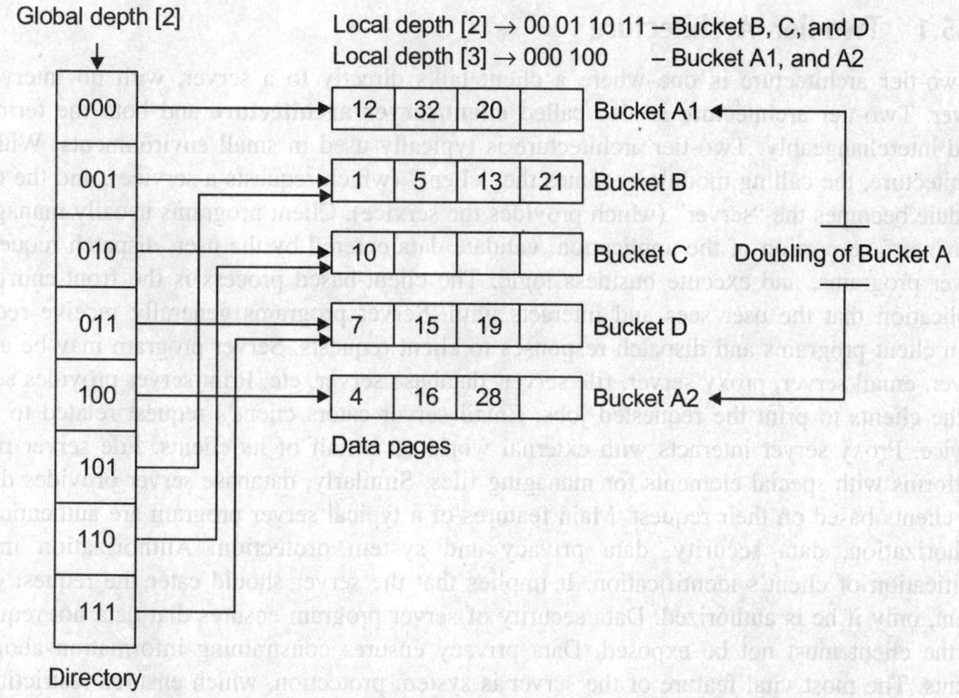

FIGURE 13.21 Global and local depths after handling overflow.

13.5 DISTRIBUTED ARCHITECTURE

Distributed architecture mainly corresponds to two-tier and three-tier architecture. Two-tier architecture (also known as **client/server architecture**) as well as three-tier architecture both are revolutionary development in the field of computer science. Careful selection of architecture is therefore, important to extract best of both worlds. Use of both the architectures for the same software is quite prevalent in the software industries.

In client/server architecture, client program is an application that initiates communication and server program is an application waiting to cater the requests. An important characteristic of client–server architecture is scalability. Horizontal scaling means adding or removing client workstations with only a slight performance impact. Vertical scaling means migrating to a larger and faster server machine, or to a group of multiple servers.

Three-tier architecture has been a technological development because of the increasing performance need in distributed computing. The three-tier software architecture (also known as multi-tier architecture as the middle-tier may consist of several tiers by itself) emerged in early 90s to overcome the limitations of the two-tier architecture. The middle-tier is between the user interface (client) and the data management (server) components. This middle-tier provides process management where business logic and rules are executed and can accommodate hundreds of users by providing functions such as queuing, application execution, and database staging. The three-tier architecture is used when an effective distributed client/server design is needed that provides increased performance, flexibility, maintainability, reusability, and scalability, while hiding the complexity of distributed processing from the user.

13.5.1 Two-tier Architecture

A two-tier architecture is one where a client talks directly to a server, with no intervening server. Two-tier architecture is also called **client/server architecture** and both the terms are used interchangeably. Two-tier architecture is typically used in small environments. With this architecture, the calling module becomes the "client" (which requests a service), and the called module becomes the "server" (which provides the service). Client programs usually manage the user interface portion of the application, validate data entered by the user, dispatch requests to server programs, and execute business logic. The client-based process is the front-end of the application that the user sees and interacts with. Server programs generally receive requests from client programs and dispatch responses to client requests. Server program may be a print server, email server, proxy server, file server, database server, etc. Print server provides service to the clients to print the requested jobs. Email server caters client's request related to email service. Proxy server interacts with external world on behalf of its clients. File server run on platforms with special elements for managing files. Similarly, database server provides data to the clients based on their request. Main features of a typical server program are authentication, authorization, data security, data privacy and system protection. Authorization implies verification of client's identification. It implies that the server should cater the request of the client, only if he is authorized. Data security of server program ensures that data not requested by the client must not be exposed. Data privacy ensures constraining information about the clients. The most vital feature of the server is system protection, which ensures restricting the server's environment to its clients.

EX13_9 Payroll software running on Oracle database server is a typical example of two-tier (or client/server) architecture. In this example payroll application is developed using Visual Basic software and Oracle database server. This type of setup is usually required in application, which is data entry intrinsic and are used by limited number of people. In this example, a total of three computers are used, one for database (server side or back-end) and two for clients (or front-ends). TCP/IP networking protocol is used to establish the network. IP address of server is 192.168.128.100 and its sub-domain is 255.255.255.0 (or 24). In short this is represented with 192.168.128.100/24. Name of server is TestServer. Name of both the clients is TestClient1 and TestClient2 respectively. All the details mentioned are consolidated in Figures 13.22 and Table 13.9.

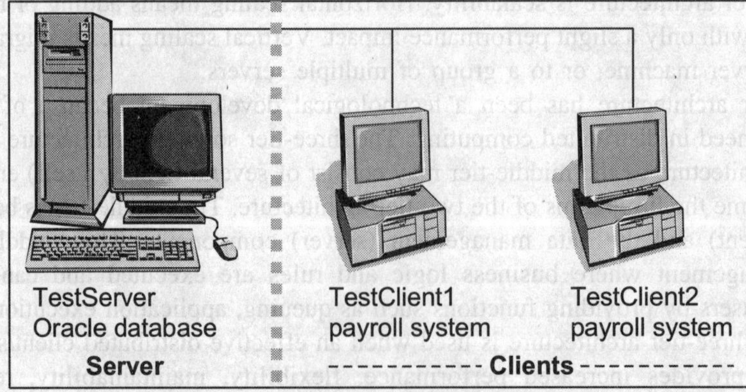

FIGURE 13.22 Two-tier architecture.

TABLE 13.9 Two-tier Architecture—Scenario 1

Features	Server	Clients (2)	
		1	2
Operating system	Windows 2000 server	Windows XP Professional	Windows XP Professional
Network protocol	TCP/IP	TCP/IP	TCP/IP
IP address	192.168.128.100/24	192.168.128.1/24	192.168.128.2/24
Machine name	TestServer	TestClient1	TestClient2
Software	Oracle database	Visual Basic	Visual Basic
Program/tables used	Tables in Oracle for payroll system	Payroll system	Payroll system

EX13_10 There is a misconception that at least two computers are essentially required in client/server architecture. This example demonstrates that client/server architecture can be very well established in one single machine, i.e. TestClientServer. In this example, Oracle database server as well as payroll software (along with Visual Basic) is installed in the same machine. This type of setup is useful in small offices where limited number of computers is used. Important details related to this example are illustrated in Table 13.10.

TABLE 13.10 Two-tier Architecture—Scenario 2

Features	Server	Client
Operating system	Windows XP Professional	Windows XP Professional
Network protocol	TCP/IP	TCP/IP
IP address	192.168.128.200/24	192.168.128.200/24
Machine name	TestClientServer	TestClientServer
Software	Oracle database	Visual Basic
Program/tables used	Tables in Oracle for payroll system	Payroll system

EX13_11 This example demonstrates that the server machine can be used for more than one server program. In this example the server machine is configured with Oracle, MS SQL server and Print server. A total of ten clients are in the network along with the server. In two clients, VC++ is used to develop Meteorology Management System software, which uses Oracle database server to manage its data. In the remaining eight clients, Library Management software is developed using Java, which uses MS SQL server to manage its data. All the ten clients use Print server program. Important details related to this example are consolidated in Table 13.11.

13.5.2 Three-tier Architecture

A three-tier can be divided into three layers: the data-tier (back end), logic-tier (middle-tier) and presentation tier (front-tier). The logic layer differentiates three-tier from "traditional" two-tier client/server architectures. In practice, it means that the fat clients from the traditional client/server model have been broken into two pieces in the logic-tier. The first piece is the thin client, usually a web browser for display and data entry. And the second piece of the logic-tier is the application logic running on a server. Precisely the logic-tier coordinates the application, processes commands, and makes logical decisions and evaluations. It also processes data between the two surrounding layers.

TABLE 13.11 Two-tier Architecture—Scenario 3

Features	Server	Clients (10)	
		1–2	3–10
Operating system	Windows 2003 server	Windows XP Professional	Windows 2000 Professional
Network protocol	TCP/IP	TCP/IP	TCP/IP
IP address	192.168.128.50/24	192.168.128.1/24 to 192.168.128.2/24	192.168.128.3/24 to 192.168.128.10/24
Machine name	OraMSSQLserver	TestClient1–2	TestClient3–10
Software	Oracle database MS SQL server Print server	VC++ printer driver	Java printer driver
Program/tables used	Tables in Oracle and MS SQL for Met Mgt system and Library Mgt system	Met Mgt system (uses Oracle and print server)	Library Mgt system (uses SQL server and Print server)

Three-tier architecture is diversified by the functionality provided to the system by the middle-tier. The most popular are related to transaction processing, messaging, application server and distributed architecture. Each of them are elaborated in brief in succeeding sections.

Transaction processing

The most basic type of three-tier architecture has a middle layer consisting of Transaction Processing (TP) monitor technology. The TP monitor technology is a type of message queuing, transaction scheduling, and prioritization service where the client connects to the TP monitor (middle-tier) instead of the database server. The transaction is accepted by the monitor, which queues it and then takes responsibility for managing it to completion, thus, freeing up the client. TP monitor technology provides the ability to update multiple DBMSs in a single transaction.

Message server

Messaging is yet another way to implement three-tier architectures. Messages are prioritized and processed asynchronously. The message server connects to the relational DBMS and other data sources. The difference between TP monitor technology and message server is that the message server architecture focuses on intelligent messages, whereas the TP Monitor environment has the intelligence in the monitor, and treats transactions as dumb data packets. Messaging systems are generally used for wireless infrastructures.

Application server

The three-tier application server architecture allocates the main body of an application to run on a shared host rather than in the user system interface client environment. The application server does not drive the graphics user interfaces; rather it shares business logic, computations, and a data retrieval engine. Advantages of application server are less software on the client, less security to worry about, and scalable applications. In addition to this, support and installation costs are lower on a single server than maintenance of each installation on a desktop client. The application server designs are used when security, scalability and cost are major considerations.

Distributed architecture

The distributed architecture emerged in mid 90s. This software architecture is based on using shared and reusable business models on an enterprise-wide scale. The benefit of this architectural approach is that standardized business object models and distributed object computing are combined to give an organization flexibility to improve effectiveness organizationally, operationally, and technologically.

The three-tiered client/server architecture provides an environment, which supports all the benefits of both the one-tiered approach and the two-tiered approach, and also supports the goals of a flexible architecture. The application components communicate with each other using an abstract interface that hides the underlying function performed by the component.

The three-tier architecture has some unique advantages, as the deployment is made easier because the client is simple and logic is centralized. Few notable advantages are mentioned below.

- A three-tiered environment extend beyond the life cycle of a single application. In fact, what is being built is not just an application, it is a collection of client and server modules that communicate through standardized and abstract interfaces, and when combined they behave like an integrated application system. Each module is therefore, a shareable, reusable object that can be included in other application systems.
- As application functions are isolated within small granular application objects, application logic can be modified much more easily than ever before.
- The application logic is no longer tied directly to the database structures or a particular DBMS. When application objects communicate, they only need to send the data parameters rather than entire database records, thereby reducing network traffic.
- In the two-tiered methods, each programmer must develop all aspects of an application, including presentation, business, and data access logic. In the three-tiered systems, programmers who have excellent user interface skills can concentrate on developing powerful presentation components, and they do not need to know about the inner workings of the applications business logic or how the data is accessed from a database. Meanwhile database analysts who know the best ways to access data from a database do not need to be concerned with how the data is presented to an end user. Business analysts can concentrate on developing business algorithms.

EX13_12 In this example, we will see functionality and implementation of Message Board—a three-tier architecture based application. Message Board software displays important messages posted by key person in the organization. It also systematically manages the messages in a database. Message Board software uses Oracle database server and Dot Net technology. If we compare with three-tier technology, Oracle database server is used in the data-tier (or back end), and in the logic-tier (or middle-tier). Dot net server is installed and configured to develop message board software ASP.NET. All the logic and business rules are programmed in this tier. Finally, in the presentation tier (or front end), Internet Explorer is used. In this setup one server is used in each data-tier and logic-tier. In the presentation-tier 50 clients are installed along with Internet explorer browser. All the 52 machines are connected with network. Figure 13.23 depicts the setup. All the three-tiers are partitioned using dotted lines. In the top, data-tier is shown, which contains Oracle Database Server. In the centre, logic-tier contains middle-tier, Dot Net server is installed as the Message Board software is developed in ASP.NET. Oracle

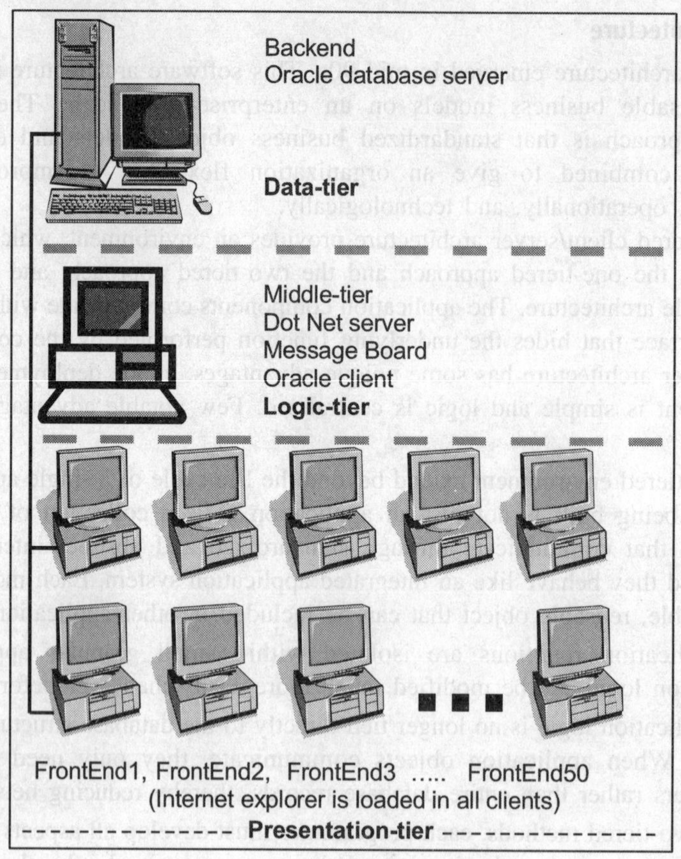

FIGURE 13.23 Three-tier architecture.

client is also installed in the middle-tier so that Message Board software can connect to Oracle database server to manage its data. Dot Net server and Oracle is essentially required to run the Message Board software. In the presentation layer one or all the clients can access Message Board using the IP address 192.168.128.200 of logic-tier server. It is assumed that Message Board software is running in the default HTTP port number. Other important details like the IP addresses, machine names, etc. are illustrated in Table 13.12.

TABLE 13.12 Three-tier Architecture—Scenario 1

Features	Data-tier (Back end)	Logic-tier (Middle-tier)	Presentation-tier (Front end) (50)
Operating system	Windows 2000 server	Windows 2000 server	Windows XP Professional
Network protocol	TCP/IP	TCP/IP	TCP/IP
IP address	192.168.128.100	192.168.128.200	192.168.128.1 to 192.168.128.50
Machine name	BackEnd	MiddleTier	FrontEnd1 to FrontEnd50
Software	Oracle database	Dot Net Oracle Client	Internet Explorer (IE)
Program/tables used	Tables in Oracle for Message Board	Message Board software in ASP.NET	URL in IE http://192.168.128.200

EX13_13 This example demonstrates that three-tier architecture can be established in one machine. In this setup execution of Message Board software developed using ASP.NET is described. Note that the name of machine and its IP address are same in all the tiers, i.e. AllTier and 192.168.128.100, respectively. All the required software—Oracle Database Server, Oracle Client, Dot Net Server, Message Board software and Internet explorer are installed and configured in one machine. Table 13.13 consolidates the above-mentioned details.

TABLE 13.13 Three-tier Architecture—Scenario 2

Features	Data-tier (Back end)	Logic-tier (Middle-tier)	Presentation-tier (Front end)
Operating system	Windows 2000 server	Windows 2000 server	Windows 2000 server
Network protocol	TCP/IP	TCP/IP	TCP/IP
IP address	192.168.128.100	192.168.128.100	192.168.128.100
Machine name	AllTier	AllTier	AllTier
Software	Oracle database	Dot Net Oracle Client	Internet Explorer (IE)
Program/tables used	Tables in Oracle for Message Board	Message Board software in ASP.NET	URL in IE http://192.168.128.200

13.5.3 Appropriate Use of Two-tier and Three-tier Architecture

Two-tier architecture is suitable for specialized type of applications, which is used by few clients (may be up to 10 clients). These applications are mostly data-entry oriented where the data is posted to the target tables after large number of checks and computations. These types of applications usually demand for greater level of security. Two-tier architecture indirectly provides additional security, as the application software must be installed and configured in each of the client machine. In addition to this normal authorization and authentication is also used. It is also suitable for applications, which are graphics intensive. In such type of cases, network congestion is also avoided to a large extent.

Three-tier architecture is most suited for the application software, which is used by large number of clients, and often the number of clients are not known in advance. In such cases maintenance of software is easy for the software professional as the software is present in the middle-tier and any change in the software is immediately reflected in the network. If otherwise, two-tier architecture is used in such cases, maintenance of software will be a nightmare for the software professional as he/she is to go to each client to load the modified software. This situation may further worsen, if the exact number of clients who are using the software is not known. Authentication in three-tier architecture is usually done through conventional user name and password strategy. For sensitive application related to finance, etc. secure channels are used for communication. However, if the username and password is disclosed or known to unauthorized person, protection cannot be ensured.

Precisely two-tier architecture is suited for applications, which are used by less number of people and three-tier architecture is most appropriate where the number of users are large and not known in advance.

13.6 DATA WAREHOUSING AND DATA MINING

The major task of any operational database system is to perform On Line Transactional Processing (OLTP). OLTP deals with insert, update, delete and query related to the database. Extract, Transform and Loading (ETL) is moving data from source to target repositories. In ETL, extraction of data deals with extraction of data from source, cleansing, formatting, and write it to target repository. Transformation of data deals with conversion of source data according to the requirements of the target system. Loading involves putting the transformed data in standard RDBMS preferably with data warehouse and data mining capability. Data warehouse can be defined as a single, complete and consistent source of data obtained from a variety of different sources made for usage in a business context. The four main properties of data warehouse are: data should be subject oriented, integrated, non-volatile and time-variant. Data warehouse is used to support Business Intelligent System (BIS) to allow companies to take faster decisions. A typical example of data warehouse used in BIS is shown in Figure 13.24.

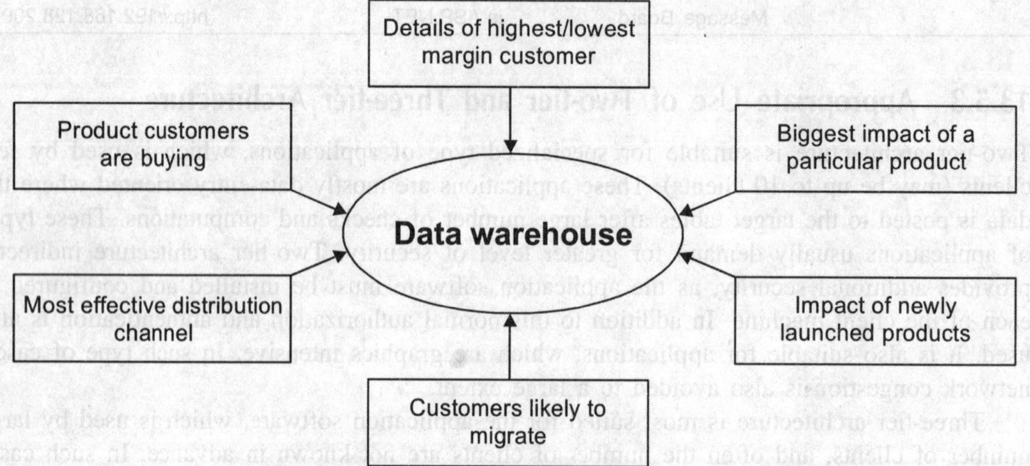

FIGURE 13.24 Data warehouse examples.

Data mining is analogous to excavation in the earth for extracting coal, metal or diamond. Data mining implies extraction of non-trivial, implicit, previously unknown and potentially useful information from a huge database. In case of data mining, we focus to reveal hidden or unexpected information. A few applications of data mining are web data, e-commerce, departmental stores, bank, credit card transactions, scientific simulation, weather prediction, etc.

On Line Analytical Processing (OLAP) helps analyst, managers and executives in Decision Support System (DSS). Data mining concept is used to explore knowledge from the data warehouse using different methods. OLAP and data mining both assume data warehouse is already created and available for use. Few examples where data mining concept can be used are: to find certain surnames that are more prevalent in certain locations, group together similar documents returned by a search engine according to their context and similar to that. Just to clarify further, few examples, which do not fall in the category of data mining are—look up phone number in phone directory or query a web search engine for information about 'data mining'. These examples essentially fall under the category of OLTP/OLAP. Unlike OLAP, data mining output are not exact; rather it returns a 'trend' or 'knowledge'. Data mining is essentially a creative task, which asks for innovativeness in addition to domain and technical knowledge. Major components of data warehouse and data mining are shown in Figure 13.25.

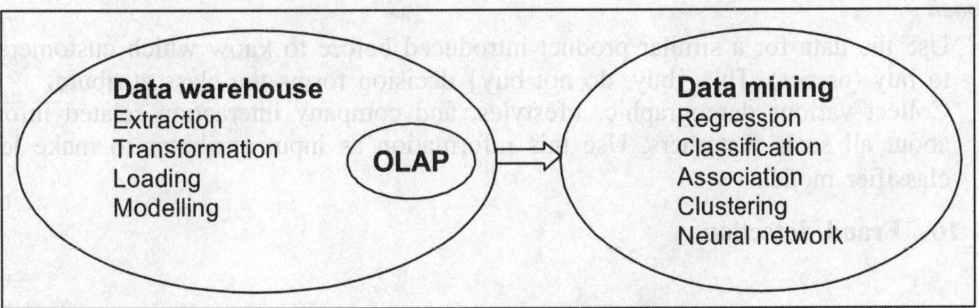

FIGURE 13.25 Link between data warehouse and data mining.

13.6.1 Data Pre-processing

A data miner often comes across huge volume of information from which he wants to draw inferences. Time and cost limitations make it impossible to go through every entry in these enormous datasets. In such cases, the data miners resort to sampling techniques. To handle missing values in the data, he has to process the data before any mining method is applied on it. The user has to detect the missing values in the data and handle them the way he wants, may be, using the mean or median or mode or a value specified by him. All datasets are not perfectly numeric, making it difficult to apply standard procedures on them. Transformations from non-numeric to numerical data are applied to handle such type of data sets.

13.6.2 Regression

In regression analysis, we map a data item to a real-valued prediction variable. In linear regression, the data is modelled to fit a straight line. Multiple regression is an extension of linear regression; it allows responsive (or dependent) variable to be represented as a linear function of independent variables.

EX13_14 Few examples related to regression are:

(i) Prediction of sales of new product based on advertising expenditure.
(ii) Prediction of wind velocities as a function of temperature, humidity, air pressure, etc.
(iii) Time series prediction of stock market indices.

13.6.3 Classification

Classification is finding the description of several predefined classes and classifies data item into one of them. In this process, attempt is made to find a set of models that describe and distinguish classes.

EX13_15 Direct marketing

Goal

Reduction of cost of mailing by targeting a set of potential consumers likely to buy a newly launched cell-phone.

Approach

- Use the data for a similar product introduced before to know which customers intend to buy (or not). This {buy, do not buy} decision forms the class attribute.
- Collect various demographic, lifestyles, and company interaction related information about all such customers. Use this information as input attributes to make learn the classifier model.

EX13_16 Fraud detection

Goal

Predict fraudulent cases in credit card transactions.

Approach

- Use credit card transactions and the information of its account-holder. It may be information like—when does a customer buy?, what does he buy?, how often he pays on time? and so on.
- Label past transactions as fraud or fair transactions. This forms the class attribute.
- Develop a model for the class of the transactions. Use this model to detect fraud by observing credit card transactions on an account.

13.6.4 Association Rules

Association rule is used to find a model, which describes data dependency. Association rule finds interesting associations and/or correlation relationships among large set of data items. Association rules show attribute value conditions that occur frequently together in a given dataset.

EX13_17 Misleading corelation

Broad observation

Increase in sale of washing machine during summer.
No increase in sale of washing powder!

Minute observation

Increase in sale of curd during summer.

Association

Washing machine was used like a mixie to prepare lassi.

Important comments

- Trivial association does not always hold good. Manufacturer of washing powder suffered huge loss due to increase in production because of anticipated increase in consumption.
- 'Out of box' thinking is effective. Use of washing machine as a 'mixer' may sound funny, but the very thinking was proved to be effective, as it served the purpose.
- The milk product-manufacturing firm, who discovered the association between washing machine and curd first, made huge profit.

13.6.5 Cluster Analysis

A cluster is a collection of similar data objects within the same cluster and is dissimilar to the objects in other clusters (Figure 13.26). In cluster analysis, we identify a finite set of categories or clusters to describe the data. It analyzes data objects without consulting a known class label.

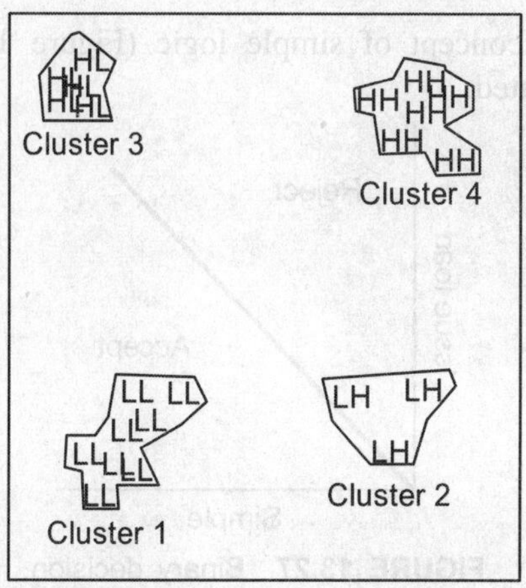

FIGURE 13.26 Cluster example.

EX13_18 Market segmentation

Goal

Subdivide a market into distinct subsets of customers where any subset may conceivably be selected as a market target to be reached with a distinct marketing mix.

Approach

- Collect different attributes of customers based on their geographical and lifestyle related information.
- Find clusters of similar customers. Measure the clustering quality by observing buying patterns of customers in same cluster vs those from different clusters.

EX13_19 Document clustering

Goal

To find groups of documents that are similar to each other based on the important terms appearing in them.

Approach

- To identify frequently occurring terms in each document. Form a similarity measure based on the frequencies of different terms. Use it to cluster.
- Information Retrieval can utilize the clusters to relate a new document or search term to clustered documents.

13.6.6 Neural Networks and Fuzzy Logic

Neural network is a non-linear model. It is similar to a 'brain'. The network is built based on the input of a training set. Model sets run through this network will return accurate results based on the patterns identified in the training set. Fuzzy sets allow tolerance in partitioning a set of values. Both these concepts are used in data mining.

EX13_20 In this example concept of simple logic (Figure 13.27) as well as fuzzy logic (Figure 13.28) are demonstrated.

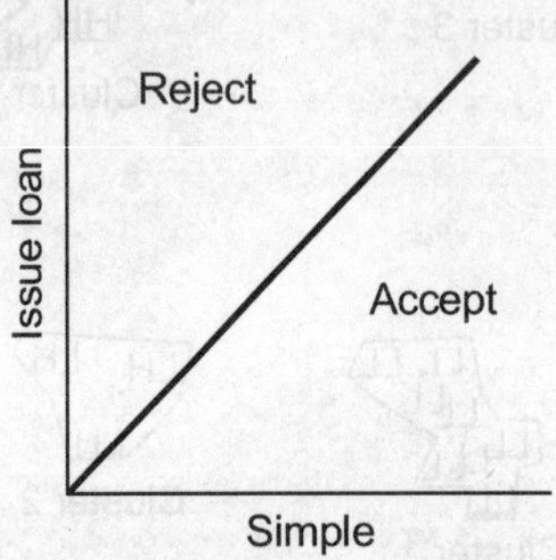

FIGURE 13.27 Binary decision.

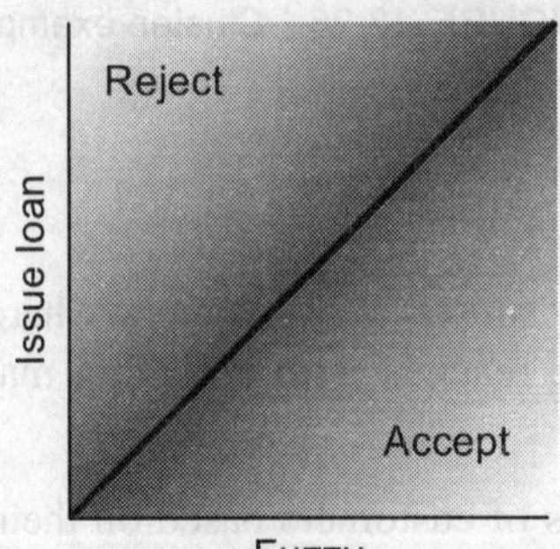

FIGURE 13.28 Fuzzy decision.

In this section, basic concepts related to the data warehouse and data mining have been introduced to generate interest on the subject. In succeeding chapters, data warehouse and data mining will be discussed in detail.

13.7 SUMMARY

In this chapter query processing, index file organization, hashing, two- and three-tier architectures, data warehouse and data mining concepts are elaborated with the help of suitable examples.

SHORT/OBJECTIVE TYPE QUESTIONS

1. What is the corelation between 'execution plan' and 'query optimization' in query processing?
2. Describe optimization technique used in Oracle database server.

3. Briefly describe ISAM.

4. What is the difference between B+ Tree and B– Tree?

5. Illustrate advantages of dynamic hashing over static hashing.

6. Describe advantages of two-tier and three-tier architectures.

7. Describe ETL, OLTP, and OLAP.

8. Describe 'classification' and 'association' in data mining with the help of example.

9. Write two software suitable for middle-tier of three-tier architecture.

10. Elaborate query processing with the help of appropriate diagram.

11. Major components of query processing is/are
(a) Query parser
(b) Query optimizer
(c) Run-time database processor
(d) Query file organizer

12. In dense index, the number of index record is
(a) More than the number of records in the data file
(b) Less than the number of records in the data file
(c) Equal to the number of records in the data file
(d) None of the above

13. Index part and data part are related to
(a) B+ tree
(b) ISAM
(c) B– tree
(d) Hashing

14. B+ tree and B– tree are form of a
(a) Binary tree
(b) Balanced tree
(c) Basic tree
(d) Bi-variant tree

15. The situation when static hash function generates the same bucket number for several search key values is known as
(a) Overflow
(b) Underflow
(c) Collision
(d) Spitting

16. Two-tier architecture is known as
(a) Web-based architecture
(b) Client/server architecture
(c) Multi-tier architecture
(d) Master–slave architecture

17. Example of presentation-tier (or front-tier) in three-tier is/are
(a) Oracle database server
(b) Internet explorer
(c) Mozila firefox
(d) Visual basic

18. Primary job ETL is/are
(a) Finding interesting patterns
(b) Moving data from source to destination repositories
(c) On line transaction processing
(d) On line analytical processing

19. Keyword related to data mining is/are
(a) Extraction of non-trivial information
(b) Data preprocessing
(c) On line analytical processing
(d) Revealing unexpected information

20. Popular data mining technique(s) is/are
(a) Cluster analysis
(b) Association
(c) Missing values analysis
(d) Classification

WORKOUT SECTION

W13_1 Table comprising of two columns PID & AGE are shown in Table 13.14. H(KEY) for hashing is done on the prime attribute PID. The Global Depth and Local Depth is defined as 2 bit each. There are four buckets viz. Bucket A, Bucket B, Bucket C and Bucket D. All the buckets have three pages each. H(KEY) is operated with MOD 4 to assign the record to buckets. For the first twelve values of PID , find distribution of records in buckets. Use the table shown in Table 13.15 for the purpose. Will addition of new record results overflow?

TABLE 13.14 Snapshot for Hashing

PID#	AGE
1	27
2	35
3	21
4	49
5	23
6	25
7	22
8	34
9	28
10	19
11	28
12	22

TABLE 13.15 Skeleton for Hash Table

H(KEY) (= PID)	H(KEY) MOD 4	Binary	Local depth (2 Bits)	Global depth (2 Bits)	Bucket
1					
2					
3					
4					
5					
6					
7					
8					
9					
10					
11					
12					

W13_2 In an organization, pool of servers is configured to provide computing power to the intranet. Details of servers are given in Table 13.16. Data-tier and logic-tier related information is given in Table 13.17 and Table 13.18, respectively. Presentation-tier related details are shown in Table 13.19. Write the correct architecture used in each column in Table 13.19.

TABLE 13.16 Distributed Architecture (Example 1)

Data-tier (4 Servers)	Logic-tier (4 Servers)	Presentation-tier
Oracle database server	Dot Net server	Internet explorer
MySQL database server	Qmail server	
MS SQL server	PHP server	
	Oracle application server	
Ref to Table 13.17 for details	Ref to Table 13.18 for details	Ref to Table 13.19 for details

TABLE 13.17 Distributed Architecture (Example 2)

Features	Data-tier (Back end)			
Operating system	Windows 2003 server	Windows 2003 server	Linux server	Windows 2003 server
Network protocol	TCP/IP	TCP/IP	TCP/IP	TCP/IP
IP address	192.168.128.50	192.168.128.100	192.168.128.150	192.168.128.200
Machine name	OraServer1	OraServer2	MySQLServer	MsSQLServer
Software	Oracle database server	Oracle database server	MySQL database server	MS SQL database server

TABLE 13.18 Distributed Architecture (Example 3)

Features	Logic-tier (Middle-tier)			
Operating system	Windows 2000 server	Red Hat Linux server	Windows 2000 server	Sun Solaris 10
Network protocol	TCP/IP	TCP/IP	TCP/IP	TCP/IP
IP address	192.168.128.25	192.168.128.75	192.168.128.125	192.168.128.175
Machine name	DotNetServer	QmailServer	PhpServer	OraAppServer
Software	Dot Net server (to execute ASP.NET programs)	Qmail server (to create internet accounts)	Php server (to execute programs written in Php)	Oracle App server (to execute programs written in Developer 2000 in three-tier)
Programs	Message board data entry	Internet access	Message board viewing	Library access system

TABLE 13.19 Distributed Architecture (Example 4)

Features	Presentation-tier (Front end)				
Operating system	Windows XP		Windows XP Professional		Windows XP Professional
Network protocol	TCP/IP		TCP/IP		TCP/IP
IP address	192.168.128.1 to 192.168.128.24		192.168.128.26 to 192.168.128.49		192.168.128.51 to 192.168.128.55
Machine name	TestClient1 to TestClient24	TestClient26 To TestClient30	TestClient28 To TestClient45	TestClient45 To TestClient49	TestClient51 to TestClient55
Software	ASP.Net for Message board viewing Php for library access system	Visual basic	Internet explorer	Oracle App server	Developer 2000
Program	Machine are used to access message board, book availability status in library and Internet	Message board data entry (Uses MySQL server)	Machines are used to access message board, book availability status in library and Internet	Library access system (Uses MS SQL server)	Library Mgt system (Uses MS SQL server)
Architecture used	?	?	?	?	?

Transaction Processing, Concurrency Control, Oracle Architecture, Backup and Recovery

Learning Objectives

You will learn following key concepts after completion of the chapter:

✓ Transaction processing concurrency control
✓ Lost update, inconsistent read, phantom phenomena and serializability
✓ Locking schemes
✓ Backup and recovery techniques

14.1 INTRODUCTION

Transaction processing deals with Atomicity, Consistency, Isolation and Durability (ACID). The first two are related to concurrency control. The last two, i.e. isolation and durability are topics of backup and recovery. All these topics are elaborated with the help of numerous examples.

14.2 TRANSACTION PROCESSING

Transaction management is achieved by maintaining its ACID property. These properties are atomicity, consistency, isolation and durability. Atomicity implies either all actions within a transaction occur fully, or none. Consistency ensures that each transaction takes the database from one consistent state to another. Isolation guarantees that events within a transaction must be invisible to other transactions. Durability implies that once a transaction is committed, its results must be preserved even in the case of failures. Atomicity and Consistency of ACID is guaranteed by concurrency control. Maintaining Isolation and Durability of ACID property is the task of database recovery. A transaction is an execution of a series or list of actions. The actions can include reads and writes of database objects. A schedule is a series of overlapping transactions.

14.3 CONCURRENCY CONTROL

Concurrency control is the process of regulating access to the same data by multiple transactions operating in the same database environment. Without regulation, a database could easily become inconsistent or corrupt. Concurrency control deals with the issues involved with allowing multiple people simultaneous access to shared entities. Several transactions execute concurrently in the database, it is therefore, necessary for the system to control the interaction among them. This control is achieved through one of the mechanisms known as **concurrency control schemes**.

EX14_1 In this example concurrency without any problem is illustrated. The transaction $\mathbf{T_1}$ (Table 14.1) uses variable V1, whereas transaction $\mathbf{T_2}$ (Table 14.2) uses variable V2. Two schedules with interleaving transactions are shown in Schedule 1 (Table 14.3) and Schedule 2 (Table 14.4). Both the schedules ensure concurrency without any problem as $\mathbf{T_1}$ and $\mathbf{T_2}$ does not operate on common variable.

TABLE 14.1 Simple Transaction

Transaction T_1
Read(V1)
V1=Func1(V1)
Write(V1)

TABLE 14.2 Simple Transaction

Transaction T_2
Read(V2)
V2=Func2(V2)
Write(V2)

TABLE 14.3 Concurrent Transaction

Schedule 1
Read(V1)
V1=Func1(V1)
Write(V1)
Read(V2)
V2=Func2(V2)
Write(V2)

TABLE 14.4 Concurrent Transaction

Schedule 2
Read(V2)
V2=Func2(V2)
Read(V1)
V1=Func1(V1)
Write(V1)
Write(V2)

There are mainly four problems, which arises due to concurrency. They are the problems associated with deadlock, lost update problem, the inconsistent analysis problem and the phantom read problem.

14.3.1 Deadlock

A deadlock occurs when there exists a cyclic dependency between two or more transactions trying to access the same data in a database. The presence of deadlock in systems is characterized by four necessary conditions. The term necessary means that if there is a deadlock then all the four must be present.

Mutual exclusion

A resource acquired is held exclusively, i.e. it is not shared by other processes.

No preemption

Process resources cannot be taken away from it.

Hold and wait

A process has some resources and is blocked requesting more.

Circular wait

This means that there is a circular chain of two or more processes in which the resources needed by one process are held by the next process.

To prevent the deadlock, at least one of these four conditions must be eliminated.

14.3.2 Lost Update Problem

In lost update problem, two transactions attempt to modify the same data item. Let us assume that two people **A** and **B** are working with some word processing software in a network environment. The word-processing software as well as the network does not support concurrency control. Suppose **A** and **B** starts editing the same document. Both **A** and **B** modifies the document independently and then saves the modified document, thereby overwriting the original document. If **A** saves his changed copy last, he will overwrite changes made by **B** resulting in a loss of work without **B**'s knowledge and vice versa. This type of problem can be resolved if one person is updating the document others can not update it till he finishes. It can be handled using the concept of serializability and precedence graph.

EX14_2 This example demonstrates lost update problem. There are two transactions $\mathbf{T}_1$ (Table 14.5) and $\mathbf{T}_2$, (Table 4.6) and both operate on common variable, V1. Outcome of variable V1 due to Write(V1) operation in $\mathbf{T}_1$ and $\mathbf{T}_2$ is 2100 and 3000, respectively (Table 14.5 and 14.6). Value of V1 for the transaction sequence $\mathbf{T}_1 \rightarrow \mathbf{T}_2$ and $\mathbf{T}_2 \rightarrow \mathbf{T}_1$ is 3150 and 3100 (Table 14.7), respectively. Two schedules comprising of statements related to $\mathbf{T}_1$ and $\mathbf{T}_2$ is shown in Tables 14.8 and 14.9. Note that the final value of V1 corresponding to Schedule 1 (Table 14.8) and Schedule 2 (Table 14.9) is 3000 and 2100, respectively, which is neither 3150 nor 3100. Hence, both the schedule results into lost update problem.

TABLE 14.5 Simple Transaction

Transaction T_1
Read(V1)
V1 = V1 + 100
Write(V1)
V1 = 2100

TABLE 14.6 Simple Transaction

Transaction T_2
Read(V1)
V1 = V1 * 1.5
Write(V1)
V1 = 3000

Initially V1 = 2000

Table 14.7 Serial Transactions

Transaction sequence	Valid V1 values
$T_1 \rightarrow T_2$	3150
$T_2 \rightarrow T_1$	3100

TABLE 14.8 Concurrent Transaction

Schedule 1	Transaction T_1	Transaction T_2	V1	Remark
Read(V1)		Read(V1)	2000	Finally, **V1 = 3000**
V1 = V1 * 1.5		V1 = V1 * 1.5	3000	which is neither
Read(V1)	Read(V1)		2000	3150 nor 3100
V1 = V1 + 100	V1 = V1 + 100		2100	
Write(V1)	**Write(V1)**		**2100**	
Write(V1)		**Write(V1)**	**3000**	

TABLE 14.9 Concurrent Transaction

Schedule 2	Transaction T_1	Transaction T_2	V1	Remark
Read(V1)	Read(V1)		2000	Finally, **V1 = 2100**
V1 = V1+100	V1 = V1 + 100		2100	which is neither
Read(V1)		Read(V1)	2000	3150 nor 3100
V1 = V1 * 1.5		V1 = V1 * 1.5	3000	
Write(V1)		**Write(V1)**	**3000**	
Write(V1)	**Write(V1)**		**2100**	

14.3.3 Inconsistent Read Problem

In this problem, minimum two transactions are involved. One modifies while the other reads. Let us assume that two people **A** and **B** are working with some word processing software in a network environment. The word-processing software as well as the network does not support concurrency control. **A** reads the same document twice, but between each reading, **B** rewrites the document. When **A** reads the document for the second time, it has completely changed. The original read was not repeatable, leading to confusion. This type of problem can be resolved if **A** could read the document only after **B** has completely finished writing it.

EX14_3 This example demonstrates inconsistency read problem. In $\mathbf{T_1}$ value of V1 is decremented by 1000, whereas value of V2 is incremented by 1000 (Table 14.10). 'Sum' is summation of V1 and V2 (Table 4.11). Values corresponding to V1, V2 and Sum for transaction sequence $\mathbf{T_1} \rightarrow \mathbf{T_2}$ and $\mathbf{T_2} \rightarrow \mathbf{T_1}$ is shown in Table 14.12. Schedule of interleaved statements of transactions are shown in Table 14.13. It is basically combination of statements mentioned in $\mathbf{T_1}$ in random order. Note that the final value of 'Sum' is 16,000 (not 15,000), which is not correct (Table 14.13).

TABLE 14.10 Simple Transaction

Transaction T_1
Read(V1)
V1 = V1 – 1000
Write(V1)
Read(V2)
V2 = V2 + 1000
Write(V2)
V1 = 4000 and V2 = 11,000

TABLE 14.11 Simple Transaction

Transaction T_2
Sum = 0
Read(V1)
Sum = Sum + V1
Read(V2)
Sum = Sum + V2
Write(Sum)
Sum = 15,000

TABLE 14.12 Serial Transactions

Initially
V1 = 5000
V2 = 10,000
$T_1 \rightarrow T_2$ or $T_2 \rightarrow T_1$
V1 = 4000
V2 = 11,000
Sum = 15,000

TABLE 14.13 Concurrent Transaction

Schedule	Transaction T_1	Transaction T_2	Value V1	Value V2	Value Sum
Read(V1)	Read(V1)		5000		
Sum = 0		Sum = 0			0
Read (V1)		Read(V1)	5000		
V1 = V1 – 1000	V1 = V1 – 1000		4000		
Write(V1)	**Write(V1)**		**4000**		
Sum = Sum + V1		Sum = Sum + V1			5000
Read(V2)	Read(V2)			10,000	
V2 = V2 + 1000	V2 = V2 + 1000			11,000	
Write(V2)	**Write(V2)**			**11,000**	
Read(V2)		Read(V2)		11,000	
Sum = Sum + V2		Sum = Sum + V2			16,000
Write(Sum)		**Write(Sum)**			**16,000**

14.3.4 Phantom Phenomenon

Let us assume that two people **A** and **B** are working with some word processing software in a network environment. The word-processing software as well as the network does not support concurrency control. **A** reads and edits a document submitted by **B**, but when the editing is being done into the master copy of the document by the production department, they find that new, unedited material has been added to the document. The document contains new material that previously did not exist, leading to confusion and anomalies. It would be better if no one could add new material to the document until A and the production department finish working with the original document.

14.3.5 Serializability

A serializable schedule over a set of transactions is a schedule whose effect on any consistent database instance is identical to that of some complete serial schedule over the set of completed transactions.

Given an interleaved execution of a set of transactions; the following conditions hold for each transaction in the set.

- All transactions are correct in the sense that if any of the transactions is executed by itself on a consistent database, the resulting database will be consistent.
- Any serial execution of the transactions is also correct and preserves the consistency of the database; the results obtained are correct. This implies that the transactions are logically correct and that no two transactions are interdependent.

EX14_4 Serializability is a technique to handle lost update problem. In this example transactions shown in Tables 14.5 and 14.6 of EX14_2 are used. Final value of V1 in Schedule 1 (Table 14.14) and Schedule 2 (Table 14.15) is 3150 and 3100, respectively. It is worthwhile to recall that in EX14_2, valid values of V1 are 3150 and 3100. Hence, the problem faced in EX14_2 due to lost update is resolved.

TABLE 14.14 Serializable Schedule of Transaction

Schedule 1	Transaction T_1	Transaction T_2	Result(V1)	
Read(V1)	Read(V1)		2000	**Initially**
V1 = V1 + 100	V1 = V1 + 100		2100	**V1=2000**
Write(V1)	**Write(V1)**		**2100**	
Read(V1)		Read(V1)	2100	
V1 = V1 * 1.5		V1 = V1 * 1.5	3150	
Write(V1)		**Write(V1)**	**3150**	

TABLE 14.15 Serializable Schedule of Transaction

Schedule 2	Transaction T_1	Transaction T_2	Result(V1)	
Read(V1)		Read(V1)	2000	**Initially**
V1 = V1 * 1.5		V1 = V1 * 1.5	3000	**V1=2000**
Write(V1)		**Write(V1)**	**3000**	
Read(V1)	Read(V1)		3000	
V1 = V1 + 100	V1 = V1 + 100		3100	
Write(V1)	**Write(V1)**		**3100**	

14.3.6 Schedule and Precedence Graph

Graph based protocol impose a partial ordering on the database data items. In graph based protocol only exclusive mode locks are allowed. Precedence graph consists of a set of nodes and a set of directed arcs.

EX14_5 Ensuring acyclic precedence graph is used to handle inconsistency read and lost update problems. Schedule along with precedence graph comprising of three transactions is shown in Tables 14.16 and Figure 14.1 respectively. In this case the precedence graph is non-cyclic, this ensures elimination of inconsistent read and lost update problem.

TABLE 14.16 Non-cyclic Precedence Graph.

Schedule	Transaction T_1	Transaction T_2	Transaction T_3
Read(V1)	Read(V1)		
V1 =Func1(V1)	V1=Func1(V1)		
Write(V1)	Write(V1)		
Read(V1)		Read(V1)	
V1=Func2(V1)		V1=Func2(V1)	
Write(V1)		Write(V1)	
Read(V2)		Read(V2)	
V1=Func3(V2)		V2=Func3(V2)	
Write(V2)		Write(V2)	
Read(V2)			Read(V2)
V1=Func4(V2)			V2=Func4(V2)
Write(V2)			Write(V2)

FIGURE 14.1 Transaction Sequence.

EX14_6 An example of a schedule comprising of two transactions and a cyclic precedence graph is shown in Table 14.17 and Figure 14.2, respectively. This type of schedule/precedence graph leads to inconsistency and/or lost update problem.

TABLE 14.17 Cyclic Precedence Graph

Schedule	Transaction T_1	Transaction T_2
Read(V1)	Read(V1)	
V1=Func1(V1)	V1=Func1(V1)	
Read(V1)		Read(V1)
V1=Func2(V1)		V1=Func2(V1)
Write(V1)		Write(V1)
Write(V1)	Write(V1)	

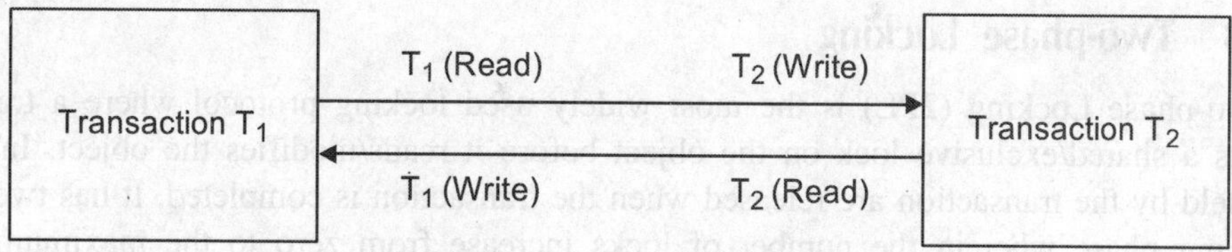

FIGURE 14.2 Transaction sequence.

Concurrency control related issues can be handled in two ways, they are locking and time stamping. In case of locking, If one user is updating the data, all the other users are denied access to the same data. In time stamping, a unique global time stamp is assigned to each transaction.

14.3.7 Locking Scheme

A lock is associated with a data item to describe the status of the item with respect to its possible operations. Locking ensures that all changes to a particular data item will be made in the correct order in a transaction. The amount of data that can be locked with the single instance or groups of instances defines the granularity of the lock. Thus, a lock is a mechanism to control concurrent access to a data item.

Exclusive lock

The exclusive lock is also called an **update** or a **write lock**. The intention of this mode of locking is to provide exclusive use of the data-item to one transaction. If a transaction locks a data-item in an exclusive mode, no other transaction can access or read the data-item until the lock is released by the transaction.

Shared lock

The shared lock is also called a **read lock**. The intention of this mode of locking is to ensure that the data-item does not undergo any modification while it is locked. Any number of transactions can concurrently lock and access a data-item in the shared mode, but none of these transactions can modify the data-item. A data-item locked in a shared mode cannot be locked in the exclusive mode until the shared lock is released by all transactions holding the lock. A data-item locked in the exclusive mode cannot be locked in the shared mode until the exclusive lock on the data-item is released. Compatibility of locking is very important. If current state is 'unlocked', 'shared' as well as 'exclusive' locks can be requested. In case the current state is 'shared', 'shared' lock can be requested, however 'exclusive' lock can not be requested for. If the current state is 'exclusive' neither 'shared' nor 'exclusive' locks can be requested. Compatibility of locking is shown in Table 14.18.

TABLE 14.18 Shared and Exclusive Locks

Compatibility of locking		Current state of lock		
		Unlocked	Shared	Exclusive
Lock requested	Unlock		Yes	Yes
	Shared	Yes	Yes	No
	Exclusive	Yes	No	No

14.3.8 Two-phase Locking

The two-phase Locking (2PL) is the most widely used locking protocol where a transaction requests a shared/exclusive lock on the object before it reads/modifies the object. In 2PL all locks held by the transaction are released when the transaction is completed. It has two phases, a growing phase wherein the number of locks increase from zero to the maximum for the transaction, and a contracting phase wherein the number of locks held decreases from the maximum to zero. Both of these phases are monotonic; the number of locks are only increasing in the first phase and decreasing in the second phase. Once a transaction starts releasing locks, it is not allowed to request any further locks. In this way a transaction is obliged to request all locks it may need during its life before it releases any. In strict 2PL, any locks acquired during the progress of a transaction are held until the transaction commits or aborts.

EX14_7 This example demonstrates a schedule causing an inconsistent read. Two transactions with lock requests are shown in Tables 14.19 and 14.20. Initial values of V1 and V2 are 5000 and 10,000 respectively. Values corresponding to V1 and V2 after transaction sequence $T_1 \rightarrow T_2$ and $T_2 \rightarrow T_1$ are shown in Table 14.21. Schedule causing an inconsistency read is shown in Table 14.22. Note that the values corresponding to V1 is incremented and V2 is decremented correctly. However, value of "sum" is 16,000 instead of 15,000. This is an undesirable condition.

TABLE 14.19 Simple Transaction Using Locks

Transaction T_1
Lockx(V1)
Read(V1)
V1 = V1 – 1000
Write(V1)
Unlock(V1)
Lockx((V2)
Read(V2)
V2 = V2 + 1000
Write(V2)
Unlock(V2)

TABLE 14.20 Simple Transaction Using Locks

Transaction T_2
Lockx(sum)
Sum = 0
Locks(V1)
Read(V1)
Sum = Sum + V1
Unlock(V1)
Locks(V2)
Read(V2)
Sum = Sum + V2
Write(Sum)
Unlock(V2)
Unlock(sum)

TABLE 14.21 Serial Transactions

Initially
V1=5000
V2=10,000
$T_1 \rightarrow T_2$ or $T_2 \rightarrow T_1$
V1 = 4000
V2 = 11,000
Sum = 15,000

TABLE 14.22 Concurrent Transaction

Schedule	Transaction T_1	Transaction T_2	Value		
			V1	V2	Sum
Lockx(Sum)		Lockx(Sum)			
Sum = 0		Sum = 0			0
Locks(V1)		Locks(V1)			
Read(V1)		Read(V1)	5000		
Sum = Sum + V1		Sum = Sum + V1			5000
Unlock(V1)		Unlock(V1)			
Lockx(V1)	Lockx(V1)				
Read(V1)	Read(V1)		5000		
V1 = V1 – 1000	V1 = V1 – 1000		4000		
Write(V1)	**Write(V1)**		**4000**		
Unlock(V1)	Unlock(V1)				
Lockx(V2)	Lockx(V2)				
Read(V2)	Read(V2)			10,000	
V2 = V2 + 1000	V2 = V2 + 1000			11,000	
Write(V2)	**Write(V2)**			**11,000**	
Unlock(V2)	Unlock(V2)				
Locks(V2)		Locks(V2)			
Read(V2)		Read(V2)		11,000	
Sum = Sum + V2		Sum = Sum + V2			16,000
Write(Sum)		**Write(Sum)**			**16,000**
Unlock(V2)		Unlock(V2)			
Unlock(Sum)		Unlock(Sum)			

EX14_8 This example resolves the problem encountered in EX4_7 by locking all the items before unlocking, transaction $\mathbf{T_1}$ and $\mathbf{T_2}$ are shown in Tables 14.23 and 14.24, respectively. Values corresponding to V1, V2 and Sum after $\mathbf{T_1 \rightarrow T_2}$ and $\mathbf{T_2 \rightarrow T_1}$ are shown in Table 14.25. Possible solutions to the inconsistent read problem are shown in Tables 14.26 and 14.27.

TABLE 14.23 Simple Transaction Using Lock

Transaction T_1
Lockx(V1)
Read(V1)
V1 = V1 – 1000
Write(V1)
Lockx(V2)
Unlock(V1)
Read(V2)
V2 = V2 + 1000
Write(V2)
Unlock(V2)

TABLE 14.24 Simple Transaction Using Lock

Transaction T_2
Lockx(sum)
Sum = 0
Locks(V1)
Read(V1)
Sum = Sum + V1
Locks(V2)
Read(V2)
Sum = Sum + V2
Write(Sum)
Unlock(V2)
Unlock(V1)
Unlock(Sum)

TABLE 14.25 Serial Transactions

Initially
V1=5000
V2=10,000
$T_1 \rightarrow T_2$ or $T_2 \rightarrow T_1$
V1 = 4000
V2 = 11,000
Sum = 15,000

TABLE 14.26 Concurrent Transaction

Schedule 1	Transaction T_1	Transaction T_2	Value		
			V1	**V2**	**Sum**
Lockx(Sum)		Lockx(Sum)			
Sum = 0		Sum = 0			0
Locks(V1)		Locks(V1)			
Read(V1)		Read(V1)	5000		
Sum = Sum + V1		Sum = Sum + V1			5000
Locks(V2)		Locks(V2)			
Read(V2)		Read(V2)		10,000	
Sum = Sum + V2		Sum = Sum + V2			15,000
Write(Sum)		**Write(Sum)**			**15,000**
Unlock(V2)		Unlock(V2)			
Unlock(V1)		Unlock(V1)			
Unlock(sum)		Unlock(sum)			
Lockx(V1)	Lockx(V1)				
Read(V1)	Read(V1)		5000		
V1 = V1 -1000	V1 = V1 -1000		4000		
Write(V1)	**Write(V1)**		**4000**		
Lockx(V2)	Lockx(V2)				
Unlock(V1)	Unlock(V1)				
Read(V2)	Read(V2)			10,000	
V2 = V2 +1000	V2 = V2 +1000			11,000	
Write(V2)	**Write(V2)**			**11,000**	
Unlock(V2)	Unlock(V2)				

Another solution to the inconsistent read problem

TABLE 14.27 Serial Transactions

Schedule 2	Transaction T_1	Transaction T_2	Value		
			V1	**V2**	**Sum**
Lockx(V1)	Lockx(V1)				
Read(V1)	Read(V1)		5000		
V1 = V1 – 1000	V1 = V1 – 1000		4000		
Write(V1)	**Write(V1)**		**4000**		
Lockx(V2)	Lockx(V2)				
Unlock(V1)	Unlock(V1)				
Read(V2)	Read(V2)			10,000	
V2 = V2 +100	V2 = V2 +1000			11,000	
Write(V2)	**Write(V2)**			**11,000**	
Unlock(V2)	Unlock(V2)				
Lockx(Sum)		Lockx(sum)			
Sum = 0		Sum = 0			0
Locks(V1)		Locks(V1)			
Read(V1)		Read(V1)	4000		
Sum = Sum + V1		Sum = Sum + V1			4000
Locks(V2)		Locks(V2)			
Read(V2)		Read(V2)		11,000	
Sum = Sum + V2		Sum = Sum + V2			15,000
Write(Sum)		**Write(Sum)**			15,000
Unlock(V2)		Unlock(V2)			
Unlock(V1)		Unlock(V1)			
Unlock(Sum)		Unlock(Sum)			

14.3.9 Timestamp-Based Order

One of the problems of locking mechanisms is the possibility of occurrence of deadlock. Deadlock occurs when two or more transactions are mutually waiting for each other's resources. This problem can be solved using time stamping. Timestamping states that each transaction is assigned a unique timestamp value. Every operation in a transaction also assigned this value.

Timestamp-based protocols provide a mechanism to enforce order. One way to realize this is to use the system clock. The time stamp of the transaction determines the serializability order.

EX14_9 This example demonstrates a schedule based on timestamp scheme. Transactions $\mathbf{T_1}$ and $\mathbf{T_2}$ are shown in Tables 14.28 and 14.29, respectively. Initial values of $\mathbf{T_1}$ and $\mathbf{T_2}$ along with final value of V1 and V2 after $\mathbf{T_1 \rightarrow T_2}$ and $\mathbf{T_2 \rightarrow T_1}$ are shown in Table 14.30. The schedule based on timestamp scheme is shown in Table 14.31. Result shown in last column of Table 14.31 are explained in detail in Table 14.32.

TABLE 14.28 Simple Transaction

Transaction T_1
Sum = 0
Read(V1)
Sum = Sum + V1
Read(V2)
Sum = Sum + V2
Write(Sum)

TABLE 14.29 Simple Transaction

Transaction T_2
Sum = 0
Read(V1)
V1 = V1 – 10
Write(V1)
Sum = Sum + V1
Read(V2)
V2 = V2 + 10
Write(V2)
Sum = Sum + V2
Write(Sum)

TABLE 14.30 Serial Transaction

Initially
V1 = 40
V2 = 50
$T_1 \rightarrow T_2$ or $T_2 \rightarrow T_1$
V1 = 30
V2 = 60
Sum = 90

Initially V1: 40, Wv1, Rv1 & V2: 50, Wv2, Rv2

TABLE 14.31 Concurrent Transaction

Step	Schedule	Transaction T_1	Transaction T_2	Result
1	Sum = 0	Sum = 0		
2	Read(V1)	Read(V1)		V1: 40, Wv1, T_1 V2: 50,Wv2,Rv2
3	Sum = Sum + V1	Sum = Sum + V1		
4	Sum = 0		Sum = 0	
5	Read(V1)		Read(V1)	V1: 40, Wv1, T_2 V2: 50,Wv2,Rv2
6	V1 = V1 – 10		V1 = V1 – 10	
7	Write(V1)		Write(V1)	V1: 30, T_2, T_2 V2: 50,Wv2,Rv2
8	Read(V2)	Read(V2)		V1: 30, T_2, T_2 V2: 50,Wv2, T_1
9	Sum = Sum + V2	Sum = Sum + V2		
10	Write(Sum)	Write(Sum)		Sum = 90
11	Sum = Sum + V1		Sum = Sum + V1	
12	Read(V2)		Read(V2)	V1: 30, T_2, T_2 V2: 50,Wv2, T_2
13	V2 = V2 + 10		V2 = V2 + 10	
14	Write(V2)		Write(V2)	V1: 30, T_2, T_2 V2: 60, T_2, T_2
15	Sum = Sum + V2		Sum = Sum + V2	Align
16	Write(Sum)		Write(Sum)	Sum = 90

Explanation

There are four operations related to the result, where Read or Write operations are involved. They are:

(i) the variable (V1 or V2)
(ii) current value of V1 or V2
(iii) Write operation on V1 (Wv1) or V2 (Wv2) by the transaction
(iv) Read operation on V1 (Rv1) or V2 (Rv2) by the transaction

The values corresponding to the four operations are mentioned in Table 14.32.

TABLE 14.32 Illustration of EX14_9

Step	Result	Explanation
		(i) the variable (V1 or V2) (ii) current value of V1 or V2 (iii) Write operation on V1 (Wv1) or V2 (Wv2) by the transaction (iv) Read operation on V1 (Rv1) or V2 (Rv2) by the transaction
2	V1: 40, Wv1, T_1	(i) V1 (ii) 40 (iii) Wv1 as no Write operation is performed by T_1 or T_2 (iv) T_1 because T_1 has performed a Read operation
	V2: 50,Wv2, Rv2	(i) V2 (ii) 50 (iii) Wv2 as no Write operation is performed by T_1 or T_2 (iv) Wv2 as no Read operation is performed by T_1 or T_2
5	V1: 40, Wv1, T_2	(i) V1 (ii) 40 (iii) Wv1 as no Write operation is performed by T_1 or T_2 (iv) T_2 has performed a Read operation
	V2: 50,Wv2, Rv2	(i) V2 (ii) 50 (iii) Wv2 as no Write operation is performed by T_1 or T_2 (iv) Rv2 as no Read operation is performed by T_1 or T_2
7	V1: 30, T_2, T_2	(i) V1 (ii) 30 as V1 is modified (iii) T_2 has performed a Write operation (iv) T_2 carried from Step 5
	V2: 50,Wv2, Rv2	(i) V2 (ii) 50 (iii) Wv2 as no Write operation is performed by T_1 or T_2 (iv) Rv2 as no Read operation is performed by T_1 or T_2
8	V1: 30, T_2, T_2	Same as Step 7 as no change taken place.
	V2: 50,Wv2, T_1	(i) V2 (ii) 50 (iii) Wv2 as no Write operation is performed by T_1 or T_2 (iv) T_1 has performed a Read operation.
12	V1: 30, T_2, T_2	Same as Step 8 as no change has taken place.
	V2: 50,Wv2, T_2	(i) V2 (ii) 50 (iii) Wv2 as no Write operation is performed by T_1 or T_2 (iv) T_2 has performed a Read operation.
14	V1: 30, T_2, T_2	Same as Step 7 as no change has taken place.
	V2: 60, T_2, T_2	(i) V2 (ii) 60 as V2 is modified (iii) T_2 has performed a Write operation (iv) T_2 is carried from Step 12.

14.4 BACKUP AND RECOVERY TECHNIQUES

The backup is based on periodically making copy of databases. These backups are usually created and stored in multiple secondary backup media. The backup content is also copied in geographically distant locations. This strategy is followed to ensure redundancy in the storage media. Copying the same content in distant geographical locations ensures recovery of data in case of flood, earthquake, avalanche and other natural calamities. In order to perform a data file media recovery two steps are carried out. The first is copy of data file restored from the backup. And second is update all the changes that took after the backup is restored.

The recovery techniques are essentially required as the transactions may fail because of a computer failure, system crash, erroneous parameter values, programming error, system or human error. There are various types of failures, because of which the recovery scheme must be invoked. The common types of failures are logical errors, system errors or system crash. In Logical Errors, the transaction can no longer continue its normal execution due to an error in the logic. In case of system errors, operating system or procedural rules do not recognize a transaction. Media failure may also occur if any of instance components such as data files, redo logs and control files are lost. If a failure occurs, the database is left in an inconsistent and unusable state. This state is usually referred as crash. In case of a crash, it is desirable to move the database back to a consistent and usable state. This is done by rolling back incomplete transactions and completing committed transactions that were still in memory when the crash occurred.

14.4.1 Shadow Paging

Shadow paging is a technique for providing atomicity and durability (as discussed in ACID properties) related to transaction control. A page in this context refers to a unit of physical storage usually on a hard disk. Shadow paging is a copy-on-write technique to avoid in-place updates of pages. Shadow paging is useful if transactions execute serially.

The main idea is to maintain two page tables during the lifetime of a transaction, the current page table and the shadow page table. Shadow page table is stored in non-volatile storage so that state of the database prior to transaction execution may be recovered. Initially, both the page tables are identical. Only current page table is used for data item accesses during execution of the transaction. Whenever any page is about to be written for the first time—a copy of this page is made onto an unused page. The current page table is then made to point to the copy and update is performed on the copy. The positive aspect of shadow paging is: recovery is trivial as new transactions can start right away, using the shadow page table and there is no overhead of writing log records. However, the negative aspect is: copying the entire page table is very expensive, fragmentation and garbage collection.

14.4.2 Write Ahead Logging

Write Ahead Logging (WAL) is also a technique for providing atomicity and durability in transaction control. In case of WAL, all modifications are written to a log before they are applied to the database. Usually both redo and undo information is stored in the log. The basic strategy of WAL is to allow updates of the database to be done in-place.

14.4.3 Algorithms for Recovery and Isolation Exploiting Semantics

The Algorithm for Recovery and Isolation Exploiting Semantics (ARIES) is a popular algorithm in the WAL family. ARIES is a recovery algorithm designed to work with a no-force, steal database approach. Any change to an object is first recorded in the log, and the log must be written to a stable storage before changes to the object. Changes made to the database while undoing transactions are logged to ensure such an action is not repeated in the event of repeated restarts. On restart after a crash, ARIES retraces the actions of a database before the crash and brings the system back to the exact state that it was in before the crash. Then it undoes the transactions still active at crash time. This algorithm is used by majority of the database systems. The actual recovery process consists of three passes. They are Analysis, Redo and Undo. In case of Analysis, the system determines the starting log record from which the next pass must start. It also searches for the log forward from the checkpoint record to construct a snapshot of what the system looked like at the instant of the crash. In case of Redo, data pages are read again and the updates reapplied from the log. In case of Undo, the log is scanned backward and this is continued till all the updates corresponding to loser transactions are undone.

For better understanding, backup and recovery techniques related to Oracle will be revisited later in this chapter.

14.5 ORACLE ARCHITECTURE

The Oracle server is an object relational database management system that provides an open, comprehensive, integrated approach to information management. The Oracle server consists of an Oracle instance and an Oracle database as shown in Figure 14.3. There are several processes, memory structures, and files in an Oracle server. They are used to improve the performance of the database, ensure that the database can be recovered in the event of a software or hardware error, or perform other tasks necessary to maintain the database.

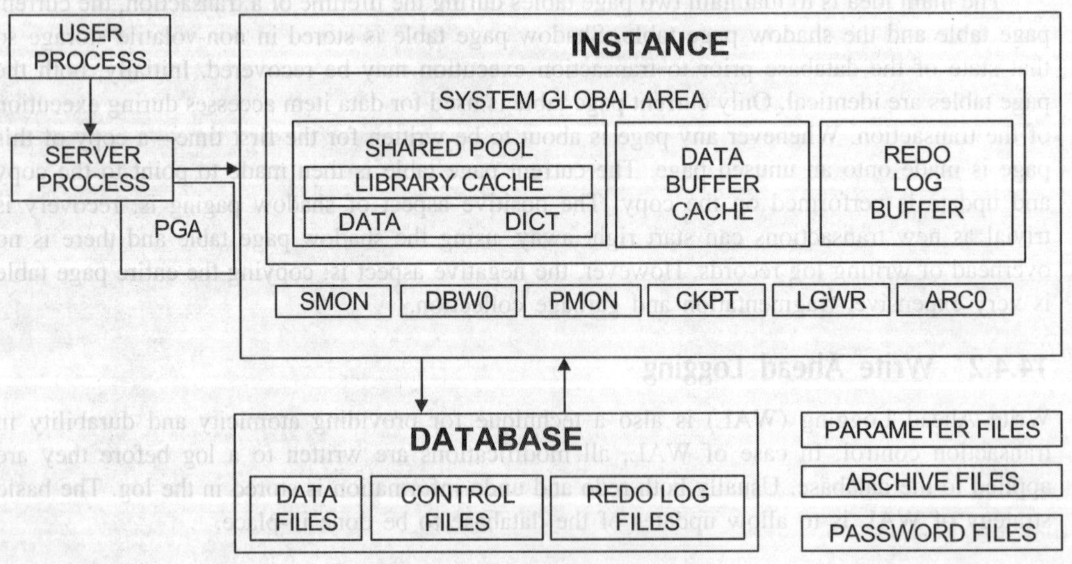

FIGURE 14.3 Oracle architecture.

14.5.1 Program Global Area Components

The Program Global Area or Process Global Area (PGA) is a memory region that contains data and controls information for a single server process or a single background process. In contrast to the System Global Area (SGA), which is shared by several processes, the PGA is an area that is used by only one process. In a dedicated server configuration, the PGA of the server includes these components:

Sort area: Used for any sorts that may be required to process the SQL statement.

Session information: Includes user privileges and performance statistics for the session.

Cursor state: Indicates the stage in the processing of the SQL statements that are currently used by the session.

Stack space: Contains other session variables.

The PGA is allocated when a process is created and de-allocated when the process is terminated.

14.5.2 Oracle Instance

An Oracle instance is the combination of the background processes and memory structures. The instance must be started to access the data in the database. Every time an instance is started, a System Global Area (SGA) is allocated and Oracle background processes are started.

14.5.3 System Global Area

The System Global Area (SGA) is a memory area used to store database information that is shared by database processes. It contains data and control information for the Oracle server. It is allocated in the virtual memory of the computer where the Oracle server resides. The SGA consists of several memory structures:

- The **shared pool** is used to store the most recently executed SQL statements and the most recently used data from the data dictionary. These SQL statements may be submitted by a user process or, in the case of stored procedures, read from the data dictionary.
- The **database buffer** cache is used to store the most recently used data. The data is read from, and written to, the data files.
- The **redo log buffer** is used to track changes made to the database by the server and background processes.
- There are also two optional memory structures in the SGA:

  Java pool: Used to store Java code.

  Large pool: Used to store large memory structures not directly related to SQL statement processing: for example, data blocks copied during backup and restore operations.

14.5.4 Data Dictionary Cache

The data dictionary cache, also known as the **dictionary cache** or **row cache**, is a collection of the most recently used definitions in the database. It includes information about database files, tables, indexes, columns, privileges, and other database objects.

14.5.5 Function of the Database Buffer Cache

When a query is processed, the server process looks in the database buffer cache for any block it needs. If the block is not found in the database buffer cache, the server process reads the block from the data file and places a copy in the buffer cache. Because subsequent requests for the same block may find the block in memory, the request may not require physical reads. The Oracle server uses a Least Recently Used (LRU) algorithm to age out buffers that have not been accessed recently to make room for new blocks in the buffer cache.

14.5.6 Background Processes

The background processes in an instance perform common functions that are needed for service requests from concurrent users without compromising the integrity and performance of the system. They consolidate functions that would otherwise be handled by multiple Oracle programs running for each user. The background processes perform I/O and monitor other Oracle processes to provide increased parallelism for better performance and reliability.

Depending on its configuration, an Oracle instance may include several background processes, but every instance includes the following required background processes:

- **Database Writer** (DBWR) is responsible for writing changed data from the database buffer cache to the data files.
- **Log Writer** (LGWR) writes changes registered in the redo log buffer to the redo log files.
- **System Monitor** (SMON) checks for consistency of the database and, if necessary initiates recovery of the database when the database is opened.
- **Process Monitor** (PMON) cleans up resources if one of the Oracle processes fails.
- The **Checkpoint Process** (CKPT) is responsible for updating database status information in the control files and data files whenever changes in the buffer cache are permanently record in the database.
- The **Archival Process** (ARC0) is crucial for recovering a database after the loss of a disk. This is usually created in a production database.

14.5.7 Oracle Database Files

An Oracle database is a collection of data that is treated as a unit. The general purpose of a database is to store and retrieve related information. The database has a logical structure and a physical structure. The physical structure of the database is the set of operating system files in the database. An Oracle database consists of three file types:

Data files contain the actual data in the database. The data is stored in user-defined tables, but data files also contain the data dictionary, before—images of modified data, indexes, and other types of structures. A database has at least one data file. The characteristics of data files are:

- A data file can be associated with only one database.
- The data files can have certain characteristics set to allow them to automatically extend when the database runs out of space.
- One or more data files from a logical unit of database storage called a **tablespace**.

- **Redo logs** contain a record of changes made to the database to enable recovery of the data in case of failure. A database requires at least two redo log files.
- **Control files** contain information necessary to maintain and verify database integrity. For example, a control file is used to identify the data files and redo log files. A database needs at least one control file.

14.5.8 Other Key Files

The Oracle server also uses other files that are not part of the database:

- The **parameter file** defines the characteristics of an Oracle instance. For example, it contains parameters that size some of the memory structures in the SGA.
- The **password file** authenticates which users are permitted to start up and shut down an Oracle instance.
- **Archived redo log files** are offline copies of the redo log files that may be necessary to recover from media failures.

14.5.9 Creation of Database

Step I

Decide on a unique instance, service and database name

Instance name : test
Service name : test
Database name : test

Step II

Create directory and sub-directories

Directory name : test
Sub-directories in 'test':

- pfile : for parameter file
- database : for database, control and redo files
- udump : for user dump files
- bdump : for background dump files
- archive : for archive files

Step III

Prepare the parameter file (inittest.ora)

db_name=test
service_name=test
instance_name=test
control_files=("c:\test\database\control01.ctl")
db_block_buffers=1000
shared_pool_size=10000000
background_dump_dest=c:\test\bdump
db_block_size=4096
log_archive_start=true
log_archive_dest=c:\test\archive
rollback_segment=(rbs01)

Step IV

Create a service
In the DOS prompt type the following:
set oracle_sid=test
oradim -new -sid test -intpwd -oracle -pfile 'c:\test\pfile\inittest.ora' -startmode manual
start the service "oracleservicetest" from start -> setting -> control panel -> services

Step V

Create the database
In the DOS prompt type
C:\>svrmgrl "connect internal\oracle"
C:\svrmgrl>stratup nomount pfile = c:\test\pfile\inittest.ora

Type following to create database:
create database test
maxinstances 1
maxlogfiles 100
maxloghistory 100
maxlogmembers 4
datafile 'c:\test\database\sys01.dbf' size 100m
logfile 'c:\test\database\redo01.rdo' size 10m, 'c:\test\database\redo02.rdo' size 10m
character set USASCII;

Step VI

Execute following scripts to generate the data dictionary and post creation step:
catalog.sql
catproc.sql
pupbuild.sql

Step VII

Create tablespace, rollback segment and user
create tablespace tbs01 datafile 'c:\test\database\data01.dbf' size 50m;
create rollback segment rbs01 tablespace tbs01;
create user user01 identified by user1 default tablespace tbs01 quota 30m on tbs01;
grant connect, resource to user01;

14.6 COMMON SCENARIOS IN BACKUP AND RECOVERY IN ORACLE

One of a database administrator's major responsibilities is to keep the database available for use. The DBA can take precautions to minimize failure of the system. Inspite of the precautions, failure may occur. In case of failure, it is the responsibility of DBA to make the database operational as early as possible. To protect the data from various types of failure, backup is required to be taken regularly. Without a backup it is not possible to recover the data. Backups are therefore, critical for recovering from different types of failures. Common scenarios related to backup and recovery are briefly illustrated in Table 14.33.

TABLE 14.33 Various Backup/Recovery Scenarios

Backup/Recovery scenario	Description
Cold backup and recovery	• Shutdown the database so that header in all files are synchronized • Create a directory c:\coldbkup and copy all files from c:\test and its subdirectory • Files from cold backup can be used to recover the data
Data file is corrupted and archive mode off	• In this case data can be recovered up to the last cold backup
Data file is corrupted and archive mode on	• All changes made after the last cold backup can not be recovered • Almost all data can be recovered • Shutdown the database • Copy data file Oracle needs for recovery • Start the database • Oracle first applies all archive files • After that it applies redo log files • Header information in all files are synchronized and database is operational
Online redo log file corruption	• Archive mode is ON • Oracle database will give error if redo log file is corrupted • Shutdown database (may be using Abort) • Startup the database • After mount stage, error will be displayed • Alter database clear unachieved logfile <redo log file name> • Startup the database
Hot backup	• Database is ON • Alter tablespace tbs01 begin backup • Create a folder c:\ test\ hotbkup and copy datafile • Transactions continues • Alter tablespace tbs01 end backup • In case of data crash desired file need to be copied and 'recover datafile <filename>'
Cancel based incomplete recovery	• Required when archive files are applied partially • Shutdown database • Exit • Copy all datafiles to c:\test\database from c:\coldbkup • Recover database until cancel • Alter database open resetlogs • Shutdown database and take cold backup
Time based incomplete recovery	• Shutdown database • Exit • Copy all datafiles to c:\test\database from c:\coldbkup • Recover database until time '2007-08-09:100:00:00' • Alter database open resetlogs • Shutdown database and take cold backup
Export/Import	• Logical type of backup/recovery • exp.exe : for export of data • imp.exe : for import of data

14.7 CODD'S RULE

Dr. Codd published a list of 12 rules that precisely define an ideal relational database. It has provided a guideline for the design of all relational databases. This chapter is concluded with a brief discussion related to Codd's rule with respect to Oracle (Table 14.34).

TABLE 14.34 Codd's Rules

Codd's Rule 1	The Information Rule
Meaning	All data should be presented to the user in tabular form
Support in Oracle	Oracle is fully compliant with Rule 1 as all values are stored in a table
Codd's Rule 2	Guaranteed Access Rule
Meaning	All data should be accessible without any ambiguity
Support in Oracle	In Oracle this is accomplished through a combination of the table name, primary key and column name
Codd's Rule 3	Systematic Treatment of Null Values
Meaning	A field should be allowed to remain empty.
Support in Oracle	Oracle provides support of a Null value, which is distinct from an empty string or a number with a value of zero. Null values are not allowed in primary key
Codd's Rule 4	Dynamic On-line Catalog Based on the Relational Model
Meaning	A relational database must provide access to its structure through the same tools that are used to access the data
Support in Oracle	This is accomplished in Oracle by storing the structure definition within system level tables. Structure of any table can be accessed using DESC command
Codd's Rule 5	Comprehensive Data Sublanguage Rule
Meaning	The database must support at least one clearly defined language that includes functionality for data definition, data manipulation, data integrity and database transaction control.
Support in Oracle	Oracle uses SQL for data definition, data manipulation, data integrity and database transaction control
Codd's Rule 6	View Updating Rule
Meaning	Each view should support the same full range of data manipulation whose direct-access to a table is available
Support in Oracle	This rule is partially supported in Oracle
Codd's Rule 7	High Level Insert, Update and Delete
Meaning	This rule states that insert, update and delete operations should be supported for any retrievable set rather than just for a single row in a single table.
Support in Oracle	In Oracle data can be retrieved from a relational database in sets constructed of data from multiple rows and/or multiple tables.
Codd's Rule 8	Physical Data Independence
Meaning	This rule states that user is isolated from the physical method of storage and retrieval of information from a database.
Support in Oracle	This rule is supported in Oracle. User is isolated from the physical method of storage and retrieval of information from a database.
Codd's Rule 9	Logical Data Independence
Meaning	This rule states that the viewing of data by a user should not change when the table structure of database changes.
Support in Oracle	This rule is not supported in Oracle. Oracle relies on strong ties between the user view of the data and the actual structure of the underlying tables.
Codd's Rule 10	Integrity Independence
Meaning	The database language should support constraints on user input that maintain database integrity.
Support in Oracle	This rule is partially supported in Oracle. In Oracle the following constraints can be ensured through SQL. • No component of a primary key can have a Null value. • If a foreign key is defined in one table, any value in it must exist as the primary key in another table.
Codd's Rule 11	Distribution Independence
Meaning	A user should be totally unaware of whether or not the database is distributed.
Support in Oracle	This rule is not supported in Oracle in totality.
Codd's Rule 12	Nonsubversion Rule
Meaning	There should be no way to modify the database structure other than through the multiple row database language.
Support in Oracle	Oracle uses SQL to modify the database structure. However other tools support change of database structure.

14.8 SUMMARY

In this chapter transaction processing, concurrency control, backup and recovery techniques are discussed in detail. Realistic scenarios related to Oracle backup/recovery are also briefly illustrated.

SHORT/OBJECTIVE TYPE QUESTIONS

1. Describe ACID in transaction processing.
2. What are the four necessary conditions for a deadlock occurrence?
3. Describe lost-update and inconsistent read problem in concurrency control.
4. Describe two-phase locking.
5. Describe the role of backup and recovery techniques in DBMS.
6. Describe timestamp-based concurrency control protocol.
7. Describe serializability with the help of an example.
8. Describe the shadow page recovery technique.
9. The concept of locking can be used to solve the problem of
   (a) Lost update
   (b) Phantom's problem
   (c) Inconsistent data
   (d) Deadlock
10. What are the potential problems when a DBMS executes multiple transactions concurrently?
    (a) Unrepeatable read problem
    (b) Phantom problem
    (c) Lost update problem
    (d) None of the above
11. Concurrency control deals with
    (a) Atomicity
    (b) Durability
    (c) Consistency
    (d) Isolation
12. Growing and shrinking of phase is related to
    (a) Serializability
    (b) Two-phase locking
    (c) Precedence graph
    (d) Timestamp-based order

13. Recovery techniques is/are
    (a) Serializability
    (b) Shadow paging
    (c) Write ahead logging
    (d) ARIES
14. Oracle database server consists of
    (a) Oracle instance
    (b) Oracle database server
    (c) Oracle security manager
    (d) Oracle data warehouse
15. Program global area comprise of
    (a) Sort area
    (b) Cursor state
    (c) Stack space
    (d) None of the above
16. Export/import in Oracle is a
    (a) Logical type of backup/recovery technique
    (b) Physical type of backup/recovery technique
    (c) Hot backup/recovery technique
    (d) Time-based incomplete recovery technique
17. Database recovery deals with
    (a) Atomicity
    (b) Durability
    (c) Consistency
    (d) Isolation
18. Oracle instance is combination of
    (a) SGA
    (b) PGA
    (c) User process
    (d) Background processes
19. Total number of rules published by Dr. Codd is
    (a) 10
    (b) 11
    (c) 12
    (d) 13

20. Match the following w.r.t. Codd's rule

1. The information rule	(a) All data should be accessible without any ambiguity
2. Guaranteed access rule	(b) The database language should support constraints on user input that maintain database integrity.
3. Systematic treatment of null values	(c) A user should be totally unaware of whether or not the database is distributed.
4. Dynamic on-line catalog based on the relational model	(d) A relational database must provide access to its structure through the same tools that are used to access the data.
5. View updating rule	(e) This rule states that the viewing of data by a user should not change when the table structure of database changes.
6. Physical data independence	(f) There should be no way to modify the database structure other than through the multiple row database language.
7. Logical data independence	(g) Each view should support the same full range of data manipulation that direct-access to a table is available.
8. Distribution independence	(h) This rule states that user is isolated from the physical method of storage and retrieval of information from a database.
9. Nonsubversion rule	(i) A field should be allowed to remain empty.
10. Integrity independence	(j) All data should be presented to the user in tabular form.

WORKOUT SECTION

W14_1 Two transactions T_1 and T_2, are shown in Tables 14.35 and 14.36. Both operate on common variable V1. Initial value of V1 is 1000.

(a) What will be the value of V1 after the transaction sequence $T_1 \rightarrow T_2$ and $T_2 \rightarrow T_1$?

(b) Schedules comprise statements related to T_1 and T_2 are shown in Table 14.37. What will be the value after the schedule?

(c) Suggest serializable solution corresponding to T_1 and T_2.

TABLE 14.35 Simple Transaction

Transaction T_1
Read(V1)
V1 = V1 * 1.1
Write(V1)

TABLE 14.36 Simple Transaction

Transaction T_2
Read(V1)
V1 = V1 – 100
Write(V1)

TABLE 14.37 Concurrent Transaction

Schedule	Transaction T_1	Transaction T_2
Read(V1)		Read(V1)
V1 = V1 * 1.1		V1 = V1 * 1.1
Read(V1)	Read(V1)	
V1 = V1 – 100	V1 = V1 – 100	
Write(V1)	Write(V1)	
Write(V1)		Write(V1)

15 Data Warehousing

Learning Objectives

You will learn following key concepts after completion of the chapter:

- ✓ Establish the need of Business Intelligence and study its enabling technologies
- ✓ Understand the basic definitions and concepts of data warehouses
- ✓ Learning Data Warehouse characteristics
- ✓ Study different ways of designing a data warehouse
- ✓ Understanding the basic architecture components of a data warehouse
- ✓ Understanding ETL and its processes
- ✓ Able to understand the basic building blocks for dimensional modeling
- ✓ To determine the underlying elements of fact and dimension tables
- ✓ Why relational DBMS support is needed for dimensional modeling

15.1 INTRODUCTION

Data warehousing is a modern paradigm specially intended to provide vital strategic information. It is the process of integrating enterprise-wide data into a single repository. This data originates from a variety of sources, formats, types and is generally consolidated, transformed, loaded into a database. Business organizations began to achieve a competitive advantage by building data warehouse systems. This chapter introduces data warehousing and describes about the need of data warehouse and the approaches adopted to build a data warehouse. ETL (extract, transform and load) and Dimensional Modeling are described in this chapter whereas OLAP (Online Analytical Processing) and data warehousing case studies are discussed in the next chapter.

15.2 BUSINESS INTELLIGENCE OVERVIEW

Traditionally, decision support systems have been used to get information mostly from a small set of data captured from homogeneous data sources for supporting decision-making process. However, due to increased adoption of technologies, large organizations have complex, multiple and heterogeneous data sources. So the existing decision support systems find difficulty when dealing with such data. A rapid growth in online (transactional) data is being made by organizations and the widespread use of databases across the organizations necessitates the development of techniques for efficiently integrating and storing huge amounts of data, for extracting useful knowledge and for facilitating database access.

Data Warehousing and *Knowledge Discovery in Databases (KDD)*, which are often characterized as *Business Intelligence* solutions, are emerging as key technologies for enterprises wishing to improve their data analysis and decision support activities, and the extraction of knowledge from large data. Data warehousing technology provides the solution for decision support process and ad hoc reporting. On the contrary, KDD (or Data Mining) helps in discovering understandable patterns in data and extracts interesting patterns from the enterprise data to achieve business advantage out of it. Developing and deploying data warehousing and knowledge discovery solutions facilitates effective decision-making, and it is true for any organization.

Data Warehousing embraces technology and industrial practice to integrate data from distributed data sources and then aggregates that data to carry out further analysis and support business decision-making. That is, a data warehouse serves as a special kind of database that can be used for deep analysis. Distinct from day-to-day operational databases, which are known as Online Transaction Processing systems (OLTPs), that capture transactional data, for example, point-of-sale data, a data warehouse combines disparate data sources, possibly including external sources such as census data, to provide a centralized view for decision support. The aggregated data provides the consolidated and summary data that facilitates high-level business analysis. Data warehouses along with data mining tools are further useful to discover trends and patterns in the data.

KDD is a broad area that overlaps methods and techniques from various fields such as statistics, databases, AI, machine learning, pattern recognition, uncertainty modeling, data visualization, optimization, high performance computing, management information systems and knowledge-based systems. KDD refers to a multi-step process that can be highly interactive and iterative. It includes selection, preprocessing, transformation, data mining, interpretation/evaluation and deployment. Data mining techniques are used to discover patterns, clusters and models from data, which can be represented graphicaly for easy visualization and understanding. Though there is a difference in the terms KDD and Data Mining, both the terms are usually used synonymously.

Business intelligence solutions helps in understanding and analyzing the data better, discover actionable insights and make informed decisions with a greater speed and accuracy. So, Business Intelligence can be defined as a combination of a set of concepts, methods and processes which improves decision-making process in organizations. An organization has three primary resources: capital, human resources and data. The data sources and information engineering, combined together, supports the human resources to work in an intelligent way. The knowledge environment and business intelligence, joined together, are the key factors to support business strategies. The major source of business intelligence is the business itself. For instance, if banks can look inward into their own business and the huge data generated by their business, they would forecast needs and preferences of customers in relation to their business offerings.

Recently, the value of business intelligence applications has increased significantly. The need for reporting has moved from static reporting to proactive/interactive information discovery and from highly structured data to more unstructured information. The primary purpose of the data warehouse is shifting focus from data transformation into information to—most recently—transformation into intelligence. To better understand this trend, it is useful to look at the graph of value over time for data warehousing. As shown in Figure 15.1, the context of the data warehouse has changed with time, moving from a focus on static reporting to a focus on the business intelligence value chain. This evolution in the data warehousing is discussed next.

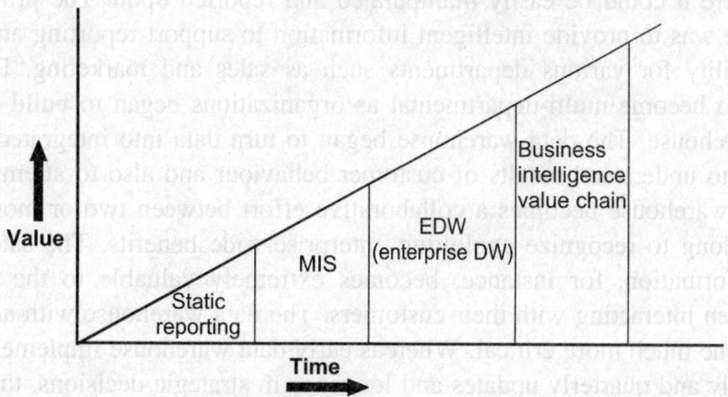

FIGURE 15.1 BI value chain.

Static reporting

The need for information has always been the part of business. There are a variety of systems to get information in (operational systems) to process transactions and manage business operations. Likewise, there are countless systems that are used to get information out (data warehouse) to support business decision-making and reporting across the enterprise. Both these systems can generate static reports. These management reports were extremely costly because stacks and stacks of reports were mailed or delivered to desks across the company, country and even globe. The recipients of the information would have to sift through the reports to find the critical piece(s) of information. Although these reports provided the information needed, they were not well integrated, easy to use or interactive. These frustrations, and the continuing business need for intelligent information, led to the next phase of the business intelligence value curve.

Management Information System (MIS)

Data is used in the raw form and in order to transform data into information, it must be subjected to processing. The information system was designed to collect the data from the source, process it immediately and generate highly accurate information. If the information systems generate information useful for managers for the purpose of planning and control, those systems are known as the Management Information Systems. Management information is reported for the managerial decision-making or action. Business as well as management happened to be simple in yesteryears. As the organizations have grown in different levels of complexity, the amount of data to be processed for the organization has also grown in complexity. Management of such a large amount of data also became complex. Hence, the role of MIS is to process the data and present it in the form of reports (information) at regular intervals.

Enterprise-wide Data Warehouse (EDW)

In the early days of the data warehousing discipline, the data warehouse was often built as a means to make highly structured reporting results available in a more timely fashion. It was not unusual to see early data warehouse deployments justify their development based on cost avoidance of report generation from transaction systems. Such transaction systems were not optimized for ad hoc reporting or historical trend analysis; therefore, data was moved into the warehouse where it could be easily manipulated and reported upon. The primary focus of the data warehouse was to provide intelligent information to support reporting and historical trend analysis capability for various departments such as sales and marketing. Data warehousing efforts began to become multi-departmental as organizations began to build customer profiles in the data warehouse. The data warehouse began to turn data into integrated information that could be used to understand results of customer behaviour and also to attempt to influence it. Once the data warehouse becomes a collaborative effort between two or more departments, it does not take long to recognize exploiting enterprise-wide benefits. The sales and marketing department information, for instance, becomes extremely valuable to the customer service department when interacting with their customers. The data warehouse with an enterprise focus begins to become much more critical. Whereas early data warehouse implementations delivered weekly, monthly and quarterly updates and longer term strategic decisions, the warehouse with enterprise characteristics demands that information be updated with transaction results much more frequently, often daily, in order to present the complete and latest information possible. Static reporting gives way to multidimensional analytics and data mining activities. Organizations recognize the data warehouse as an enabler of their business strategies, and decisions made based on information in the warehouse affect the entire enterprise in terms of increased profits and improved customer satisfaction.

BI value chain (individualized integrated intelligent information)

As business becomes more global in nature with mergers, acquisitions and partnerships, the data warehouse and business intelligence take another step forward in the value added proposition. Emphasis on how to provide better service to existing customers and extend the customer base involves an organization's suppliers, distributors and new sales and marketing channels. The customer profile is extended with psychographic, behavioural and competitive ownership information as organizations attempt to go beyond understanding a customer's preferences. The data warehouse is extended with information such as how a customer is likely to feel about a product or purchase, what competitors' products a customer might own and when the customer is likely to make the next purchasing decision. The data warehouse is used to automate actions based on business intelligence. Examples include extending an offer for insurance when a new automobile is purchased and sending an e-mail product offering to key prospects when the competitors' product they own is nearing the end of its warranty.

Demand for access to the data warehouse evolves to include entities external to the company. Organizations may help their customers make new purchasing decisions by displaying previous purchases and marketing complementary products. Companies may determine that suppliers need access to aggregate demand levels for certain products or product companies in order to support in making effective manufacturing planning decisions. New distributors can benefit from intelligence arrived from the data warehouse about product sales trends or marketing campaigns. As access to external parties increases, the warehouse evolves yet again to increase a company's competitive position by sharing business intelligence across the value chain.

Stages of analytic evolution

The five stages of analytical requirements in an organization are the following:

1. Reporting
   - Describes 'What happened'
   - Primarily focus on canned/batch and few ad hoc reports
   - MIS systems serve the reporting needs
2. Analyzing
   - Describes 'Why did it happen'
   - More focus on ad hoc reports
   - Data Warehouse systems enable analyzing the data and present ad hoc reports
3. Predicting
   - Present 'What will happen'
   - Need development of analytical models
   - Data Mining techniques helps in building analytical models
4. Operationalizing
   - Explores 'What is happening'
   - Need continuous update and time-sensitive queries
5. Activating
   - Perform 'Make it happen'
   - Need to capture events and trigger corresponding actions/procedures
   - Target Complex Event Processing (CEP) based solutions

These analytical requirements heavily depend on the nature of data, size of the data and availability of the data.

15.3 INTRODUCTION TO DATA WAREHOUSE

Decision Support Systems (DSS) have become an integral part of several organizations. As stated in the previous section, DSS help organizations to analyze their current performance as well as build new and effective strategies for achieving higher growths.

Performance of an organization can be analyzed by the data generated from its daily transactions. The organization must have both historical and current data to monitor their performance. This data must be efficiently stored for faster retrieval, report generation and analyses. The organizations use Online Transaction Processing (OLTP) systems for their day-to-day business. Note that these systems are designed to facilitate daily transactions. OLTP systems store only the data generated from the transactions at their end. Over the years, organizations accumulate a huge amount of transactional (operational) data. Operational data can be defined as the data that is used to run business. This data gives only a restricted view of the business and cannot be efficiently used for analysis and reporting. The data used for decision-making should present an overall picture of the performance. This is possible only if a large amount of data collected is used for analysis.

The data used for decision-making should be stored in a very different manner to provide efficient querying. The transactional data need to be translated into informational data and stored in another database so that information can be made available for the purpose of analysis. Data warehouses are large storage systems which support these features. That is, the data generated from different sources are consolidated and aggregated to a single point called Data Warehouse. They help end-users to quickly analyze the data and generate regular (canned) and ad hoc reports. They also help in finding the facts, trends and relationships among the products and services of an organization. So, data warehouse is a process of integrating and managing data from various sources for the purpose of providing a **single view of a business**. Applications of data warehouse for various industries are given in Table 15.1.

TABLE 15.1 Industry-Wide Data Warehouse Usage Areas

Industry	Potential areas
Telecom	Churn analysis, deactivation/trend analysis, geographical analysis, customer and product analysis
CPG	Sales, promotion analysis, vendor analysis, logistics and product finance analysis
Banking	Customer analysis, profit analysis, risk management, assets and liability management
Insurance	Premium analysis, commission analysis, claim analysis, underwriting analysis, expenses analysis
Retail	Sales analysis, revenue analysis, actuals versus budgeted analysis, profit analysis, shrinkage analysis

15.3.1 Data Warehouse Definition

According to Barry Devlin, Data Warehouse is defined as

A Data Warehouse is a single, complete and consistent store of data obtained from a variety of different sources made available to end-users in way they can understand and use in a business context.

Bill Inmon, who is considered as the father of Data Warehouse, defined Data Warehouse as

A Data Warehouse is a ***Subject-oriented***, ***Integrated***, ***Time-variant***, and ***Non-volatile*** collection of data to support management decision-making.

15.3.2 Data Warehouse Characteristics

The following are the characteristics of data warehouse:

(i) *Subject oriented:* Data is organized based on the subject instead of an application. The data organized by subject obtain only the information necessary for decision support processing.

(ii) *Integrated:* When data resides in many separate applications in the operational environment, encoding of data is often inconsistent. When data are moved (or integrated) from operational environment into the data warehouse, they assume a consistent coding convention.

(iii) *Time-variant:* The data warehouse contains place for storing data that are 5–10 years old, or older, to be used for comparisons, trends and forecasting. These data are not updated.

(iv) *Non-volatile:* Data are not updated or changed in any way once they enter the data warehouse, but are only loaded and accessed and used for queries.

These four data warehouse characteristics are elaborated next.

Subject–oriented

OLTP systems are developed according to an application. For example, a bank can develop applications for Loan processing, Internet banking, Credit Cards, Human Resource (HR) application, etc. However, the data in the data warehouse is organized according to a ***subject***. For instance, data warehouse for a bank organized the data by subjects such as Assets and Liability, Profitability, Customer Relationship and Risk Management. A customer and his/her relationship with the bank can be better understood by having data from multiple applications such as loan application, savings application and credit card application and thus the subject 'Customer Relationship' enables analyzing customers. Similarly, analysis of 'Profitability of a bank per employee' can be done by organizing data from both HR application and other applications of the bank. Application orientation with respect to subject orientation in the context of banking industry can be viewed as given in Table 15.2.

TABLE 15.2 Application Orientation versus Subject Orientation

Application orientation	Subject orientation
Deposits and Loans	Customer; Assets and Liability
Investments	Risk management
Products; HR	Sales and marketing; Profitability
Card (credit/debit) management; internet banking	Delivery channel management

So, the data can be organized by *subject* to obtain the information necessary for decision support processing, instead of organizing the data as application oriented. For instance, in the financial industry, customer relationship analysis helps in

- Profiling customer buying patterns
- Analyzing customer needs according to the market, thereby enabling quick product and service customization
- Tracking business trends
- Analyzing customer acquisition and retention strategies to increase profitable customers

Integrated

Enforcing data integrity is essential. Before loading data into data warehouse from multiple heterogeneous source systems (RDBMS, flat files, XML files, etc.), the data must be integrated to have a single view of the data. Different source systems follow different coding schemes while capturing the data and thus leads to inconsistencies when the data is consolidated and loaded into the data warehouse. Some of the commonly occurred integrity problems are as follows:

1. Different product codes entered for the same product; similarly, multiple customer ids for the same customer.
2. Different ways of typing the name of the same person. Examples: Neeharika, Niharika, Niharica.
3. Multiple ways of denoting an organization with different names. Examples: State Bank of India, SBI, Imperial Bank of India.
4. City name changes over a time. Examples: Calcutta to Kolkata, Bombay to Mumbai, Madras to Chennai, Bezwada to Vijayawada.
5. Fields with NULL value contain values; similarly, mandatory fields are left blank.

Rules have to be developed to maintain the integrity of the data in the data warehouse. Usually, the integration tasks are carried out in a separate area (also known as data staging area), rather than at source systems. The data integrity process ensures that the data warehouse data is always in a consistent and correct form.

Time-variant

Data are stored in a data warehouse to provide a historical perspective. Data in a data warehouse contains, implicitly or explicitly, an element of ***time***. Usually, huge amounts of data are needed to carry out analysis such as trends and forecasting. A data warehouse generally contains both historical and current data.

Non-volatile

Once data is populated into a warehouse database, the data should not change. Unlike operational databases, data warehouses primarily support ad hoc reporting. A data warehouse is always a physically separate store of data. Owing to this separation, data warehouses do not require transaction processing, recovery, concurrency control, etc. Data are not updated or changed in any way once they enter the data warehouse, but are only loaded, refreshed and accessed for queries. So, information from a data warehouse is consistent irrespective of its time of access. Moreover, non-volatile property of data warehouse data allows having historical data.

15.3.3 Data Mart

A Data Mart is a data warehouse (that is small in size) specifically designed for the use of a department. The departments that typically have data marts are sales, marketing, accounting and finance. Separate data marts are built because each department looks at data in different ways, such as (i) one department looks at data summarized by the week and another looks at data summarized by the month, (ii) some departments look at customers along the lines of geographical regions and others look at commercial and retail customers and so on. There are fundamentally different ways of looking at customers, products and all other aspects of the corporation for each department. So, *Data Mart is a smaller, but more focused, data warehouse for a department in an organization*. It is useful to create a data mart if a department has a very specific data analysis need. A typical example of a departmental data mart in a bank would be that of a Human Resource Department.

A data mart and a data warehouse can be differentiated based on various perspectives such as Scope, Data, Subjects, Sources and other characteristics.

15.3.4 Data Warehouse Building Approaches

There are five different basic approaches for building a data warehouse along with data marts: (1) Centralized Approach (2) Top-down Approach, (3) Bottom-up Approach, (4) Architected Approach, and (5) Practical Approach.

Centralized approach

In this approach, the data warehouse is situated at the central place and the user querying is carried out on the central data warehouse (Figure 15.2). Here, there are no separate data marts.

This approach can be implemented easily, but the querying and reporting takes a considerable amount of time.

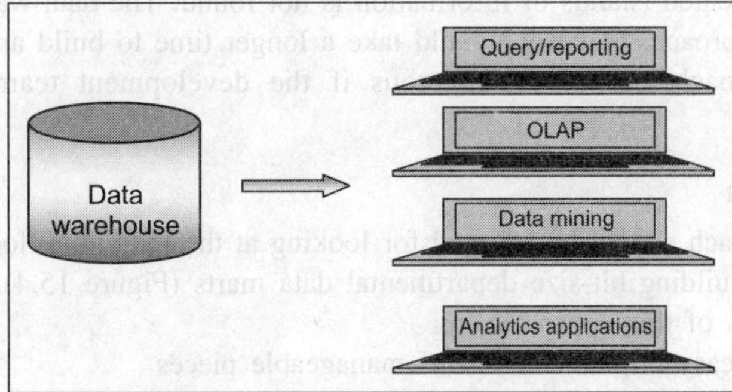

FIGURE 15.2 Centralized approach.

Top-down approach

In the top-down approach, initially a Data Warehouse is built and then according to departmental requirements, a set of data marts (DMs) for different applications are created (Figure 15.3).

The advantages of this approach are:

- Provides an enterprise view of data
- Inherently architect—not a union of disparate data marts
- Single, central storage of data with respect to the content
- Centralized rules and control can be followed
- May see quick results if implemented with iterations

The disadvantages are:

- Takes longer to build even with an iterative method
- High exposure/risk to failure
- Needs high level of cross-functional skills
- High outlay without proof of concept

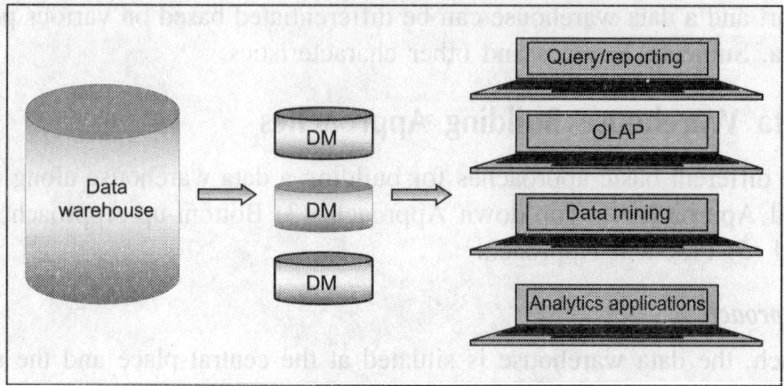

FIGURE 15.3 Top-down approach.

In this approach, the overall big and enterprise-wide data warehouse is build. Here, a collection of fragmented islands of information is not found. The data warehouse is large and integrated. This approach, however, would take a longer time to build and has a high risk of failure. This approach could be dangerous if the development team lacks experienced professionals.

Bottom-up approach

A bottom-up approach should be adopted for looking at the individual local and departmental requirements and building bit-size departmental data marts (Figure 15.4).

The advantages of this approach are:

- Faster and easy implementation of manageable pieces
- Favourable return on investment and proof of concept
- Less risk of failure
- Inherently incremental; can schedule important data marts first
- Allows project team to learn and grow

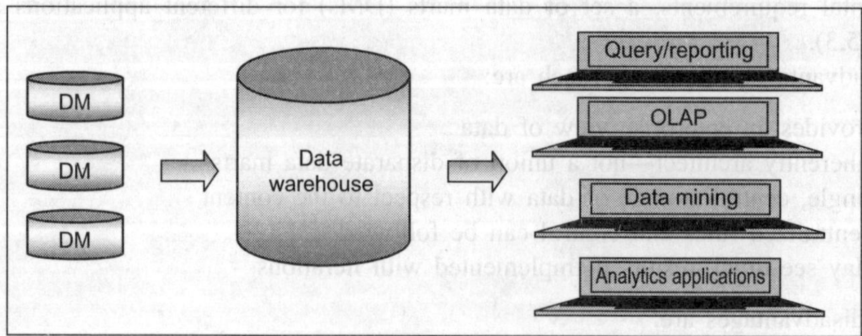

FIGURE 15.4 Bottom-up approach.

The disadvantages are:

- Each data mart has its own narrow view of data
- Permits redundant data in every data mart

- Be responsible for inconsistent and irreconcilable data
- Propagates unmanageable interfaces

In the bottom-up approach, the departmental data marts are built one by one. But a priority scheme should set to determine which data marts must build first. The most severe drawback of this approach is data fragmentation. Each independent data mart will be blind to the overall requirements of the entire organization.

Architected approach

This is a mixed approach where the *logical architecture of the data warehouse* at the enterprise–wide level is developed first. Then the data marts are developed according to requirements, whose design is guided by the enterprise-wide logical structure developed in the beginning (Figure 15.5).

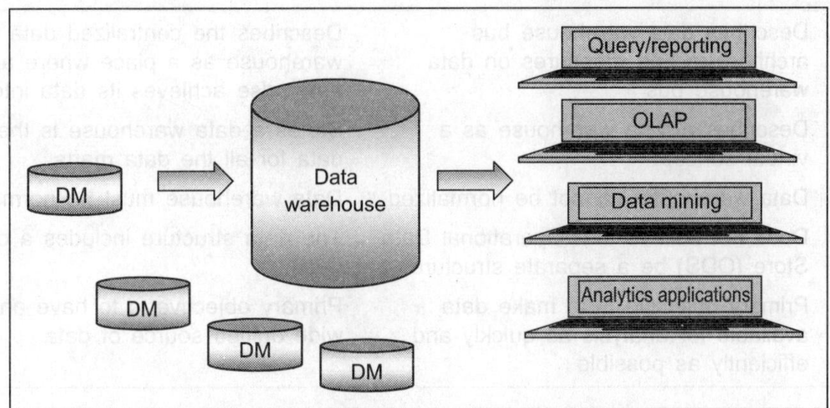

FIGURE 15.5 Architected approach.

Practical approach

To formulate an approach for any organization, there is a need to examine what exactly the organization requires, whether the organization is looking for (i) long-term results, (ii) fast data marts for only a few subjects for now, (ii) quick, proof-of-concept, throwaway implementations, etc. Although both top-down and bottom-up approaches have their own advantages and drawbacks, a compromising approach accommodating both views appears to be practical. The chief promoter of this practical approach is Ralph Kimball, an eminent author and data warehouse expert. The steps in this practical approach are as follows:

1. Plan and define requirements at the overall corporate level
2. Create a surrounding architecture for a complete warehouse
3. Confirm and standardize the data content
4. Implement the data warehouse as a series of data marts, one at a time

This practical approach starts with understanding basics and determining what exactly the organization wants in the long term. The key to this approach is that first plan at the enterprise level and gather requirements at the overall level, and then establish the architecture for the complete warehouse. Next, determine the data content for each data mart. Finally implement these data marts, one at a time. Before implementing each department, the data content among the various data marts should confirm in terms of data types, field lengths, precision and semantics. A certain data element must mean the same thing in every data mart. This will avoid spread of disparate data across several data marts.

A data mart in this practical approach is a logical subset of the complete data warehouse, a sort of pie-wedge of the whole data warehouse. A data warehouse, therefore, is a conformed union of all data marts. Individual data marts are targeted to particular business groups in the enterprise, but the collection of all the data marts form the enterprise-wide data warehouse.

Table 15.3 illustrates the steps followed in the Inmon and Kimball approaches.

TABLE 15.3 Kimball's versus Inmon's Approaches

S.No.	Kimball's appraoch	Inmon's approach
1.	Describes data warehouse bus architecture and measures on data warehouse bus	Describes the centralized data warehouse as a place where an enterprise achieves its data integration
2.	Describes a data warehouse as a virtual concept	States a data warehouse is the source of data for all the data marts
3.	Data warehouse cannot be normalized.	Data warehouse must be normalized
4.	Does not believe that Operational Data Store (ODS) be a separate structure	The data structure includes a component ODS
5.	Primary objective is to make data available for analysis as quickly and efficiently as possible	Primary objective is to have an enterprise-wide unified source of data

15.4 DATA WAREHOUSE ARCHITECTURE

Data Warehouse Architecture represents the structure that brings all components of a data warehouse together. In a data warehouse, architecture includes a number of factors, such as:

- Integrated data that is the centerpiece
- Preparing the data and storing
- The means of delivering information from the data warehouse.

The architecture is further composed of rules, procedures and functions that enable the data warehouse to work and fulfil the business requirements. Finally, the architecture is made up of the technology that empowers the data warehouse.

Figure 15.6 shows the data warehouse architecture. A data warehousing system mainly consists of six components. These includes: *Data Sources*, *ETL (Data Extraction, Transformation and Loading)*, *Data Storage*, *Information Delivery*, *Management and Control* and *Metadata Repository*.

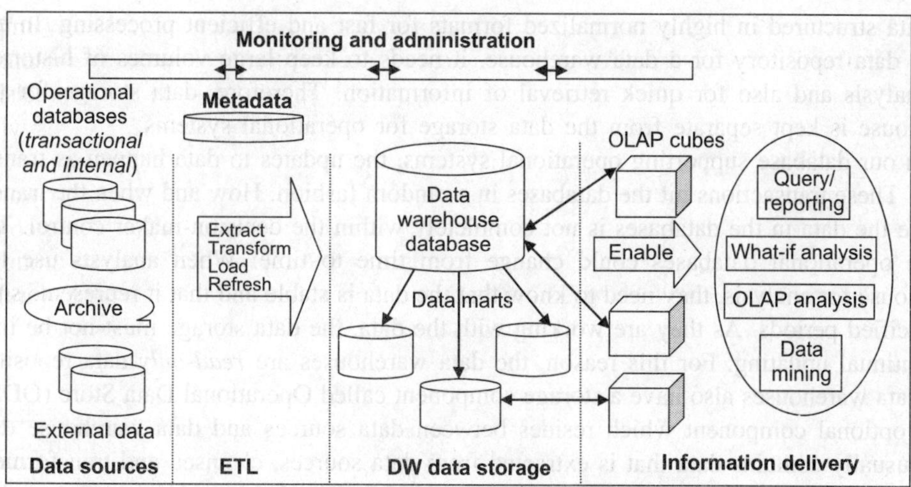

FIGURE 15.6 Data warehouse architecture.

Data sources

The data sources for the data warehouse can be any one or a combination of the following:

1. *Transaction data:* Usually this is the data coming from operational systems.
2. *Internal data:* Private information or sensitive information pertaining to the organization.
3. *Archived data:* Historical data.
4. *External data:* Market analysis data, data from rating agencies, census data, geography data, etc.

Data extraction and transformation and loading

Source (operational) systems data will change daily and hence to keep the Data Warehouse in synchronization with operational system changes, the data (incremental data) needs to be captured and loaded to Data Warehouse at regular intervals.

ETL extracts the data from different sources and populate it into the data warehouse. This component integrates data that has been extracted from the data sources. First, raw data is loaded into this component (*load time*) and then it is cleansed and transformed to achieve data integrity in the data warehouse. ETL is a very time–consuming and resource intensive process. Any erroneous operations at ETL may lead to data warehouse in an unusable form.

Data warehousing implements the process to access heterogeneous data sources; clean, filter, and transform the data; and store the data in a structure that is easy to access, understand and use. Then the data is used for query, reporting and data analysis. As such, the access, use, technology and performance requirements are completely different from those in a transaction-oriented operational environment. For all these reasons, there is poor quality of data in the data warehouse. So, the data should be cleaned and conformed before loading into the warehouse.

Data storage

The data storage for a data warehouse is a separate repository. The data repositories for the operational systems typically contain only the current data. Also, these data repositories contain the data structured in highly normalized formats for fast and efficient processing. In contrast, in the data repository for a data warehouse, it needs to keep large volumes of historical data for analysis and also for quick retrieval of information. Therefore, data storage for the data warehouse is kept separate from the data storage for operational systems.

In our database supporting operational systems, the updates to data happen as transactions occur. These transactions hit the databases in a random fashion. How and when the transactions change the data in the databases is not completely within the decision-maker control. The data in the operational databases could change from time to time. When analysts use the data warehouse for analysis, they need to know that the data is stable and that it represents snapshots at specified periods. As they are working with the data, the data storage must not be in a state of continual updating. For this reason, the data warehouses are *read-only* data repositories.

Data warehouses also have a storage component called Operational Data Store (ODS). This is an optional component which resides between data sources and data warehouse database. ODS usually contains data that is extracted from data sources, cleansed and transformed. This data (also known as detailed data) is then aggregated and loaded into data warehouse database. However, the data in the ODS is retained for short duration only, say 3–6 months, in the data warehouse. The ODS data is also useful to carry out analysis for the (detailed) data that is not available in the data warehouse. Data granularity actually differentiates ODS from the main data warehouse database.

Generally, the database in a data warehouse must be open to different tools. Depending on the user requirements, the analysts are likely to use tools from multiple vendors. Most of the data warehouses employ relational database management systems. Some data warehouses also employ multidimensional database management systems. Data extracted from the data warehouse storage is aggregated in many ways and the summary data is kept in the multidimensional databases (MDDBs). Such multidimensional database systems are usually proprietary products.

Information delivery

This component encompasses all applications and databases that serve as specific user interfaces for exploration of the data. There are different types of users who are in need of information from the data warehouse. The range is fairly comprehensive. The novice user comes to the data warehouse with no training and, therefore, needs make-up reports and preset queries. The casual user needs information once in a while, not regularly. This type of user also needs prepackaged information. The business analyst looks for ability to do complex analysis using the information in the data warehouse. The power user wants to be able to navigate throughout the data warehouse, pick up interesting data, format his/her own queries, drill through the data layers and create custom reports and ad hoc queries. So, the information delivery components encompass query/reporting, what-if analysis, OLAP analysis, data mining and other analytical needs.

Management and control

This component coordinates the services and activates all components within the data warehouse. It also controls the data transformation and data transfer into data warehouse storage, works with the database management systems and enables data to be properly stored in repositories.

The management and control component interacts with the metadata component to perform the management and control functions. As the metadata component contains information about the data warehouse itself, the metadata is the source of information for the management module.

This component is also responsible for managing back-up of significant parts of the data warehouse and recovering from failures. Management services include monitoring the growth and periodically archiving data from the data warehouse governing data security and provide authorized access to the data warehouse, interfacing with the end-user information delivery component to ensure that information delivery is carried out properly.

Metadata repository

Metadata is the data about the data in the data warehouse. It is similar to the data dictionary or the data catalog in a database management system. However, it contains a lot of additional details when compared to traditional database management systems. For instance, all processes and structures within a data warehouse system should be documented. The metadata repository component serves as a storage system for metadata, which describes the data sources of a data element as well as the applied processes and transformations. Usually, the metadata in a data warehouse is classified into two types (i) technical metadata and (ii) business metadata.

Technical metadata consists of data sources and targets registration, objects (table and column names, data types, sizes, constraints, etc.) information, mapping and transformation rules, workflow of the ETL processes, data refreshment scheduling and running statistics (rows processed, updated, rejected, etc.). Business metadata consists of business rules, notation and terminology, domain entities' descriptions and business vocabulary.

Other classifications of metadata include the following:

(i) *Static metadata*: Static metadata is used to document or browse in the system. Metadata of a dimension is an example for this kind of metadata. The content of this metadata is fixed in the data warehouse.

(ii) *Dynamic metadata*: Dynamic metadata is the metadata that can be generated and maintained at run-time. For instance, metadata for a new frequent access query.

(iii) *Build-time metadata*: The metadata generated during the data warehouse build is termed as a build-time metadata. It links various business and technical terminologies used by all types of users and also describes the data's technical architecture. Warehouse designers, developers and administrators mostly use it as it is very detailed in nature and hence serves all their needs.

(iv) *Usage metadata*: Once the data warehouse becomes functional, usage metadata is derived from built-time metadata, which is mainly used by users and administrators.

(v) *Control metadata*: Control metadata is mainly used for information about the timeliness of the warehouse data and helps track the sequence and timing of warehouse events.

Metadata makes the query execution efficient and helps in the designing, developing and maintenance of data warehouse. Query and reporting tools, OLAP tools and data mining tools use the metadata to analyze the data present in the data warehouse. Also, metadata, along with Change Data Capture, is useful during data warehouse refreshment for both initial and incremental loading.

15.5 EXTRACT–TRANSFORM–LOAD

ETL stands for Extract, Transform and Load. At the start of the Data Warehouse, the complete data will be extracted from all the source systems, which is called initial loading of Data Warehouse. This will be a one-time activity. Once the initial data load is done, the changes to data in various operational systems (incremental data) need to be captured and refreshing the Data Warehouse is done at regular intervals. Following are the main processing stages involved in ETL stage (Figure 15.7):

- Extraction of (incremental) data from source systems and loading into staging database
- Transformation, Aggregation, Cleansing and Loading of incremental data into EDW from staging database

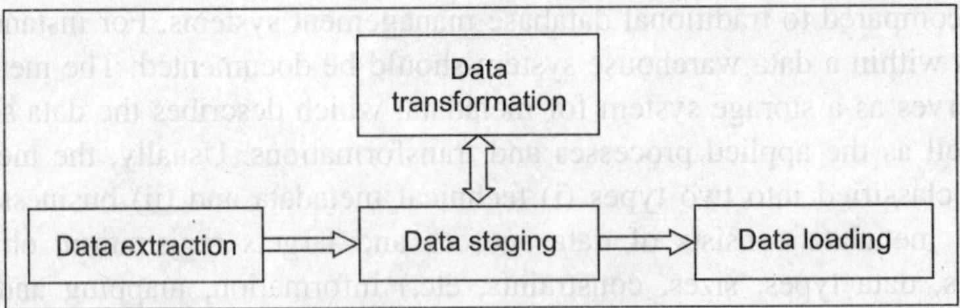

FIGURE 15.7 ETL overview.

After extraction of data from various operational systems and external sources, the next step is to prepare the data for storing in the data warehouse. The extracted data coming from several disparate sources needs to be changed converted, and made ready in a format that is suitable to be stored for querying and analysis. So, the three major functions that need to be performed for getting the data ready are extracting the data, transforming the data and loading the data into the data warehouse storage. These three major functions of extraction, transformation and preparation for loading take place in the staging area.

ETL is an important phase in the data warehousing life cycle. The ETL component should be designed with utmost care. ETL system design functionalities include (i) extracting data from the heterogeneous source systems, (ii) enforcement of data quality and consistency standards, (iii) conforming to data such that separate sources can be used together and (iv) storing the data in a more convenient form so that application developers can build applications and end-users can make decisions.

Data extraction

The first step in ETL process is mapping the data between source systems and target database (data warehouse or data mart). Data Extraction has to deal with numerous data sources and appropriate extraction mechanisms have to be employed for each data source. The extraction step identifies the appropriate data set among the data sources. Source data may be from different source machines in diverse data formats. A part of the source data may be in relational database systems and the other may be in flat files. Sometimes there is a need to include data from spreadsheets and the local departmental data sets. So, the source systems usually span

Transaction processing systems, Legacy systems, Stream Data, Spreadsheets, Web pages, etc. That is, data extraction could be quite complex.

Timeliness of data extraction The timeliness of data extraction refers to the frequency of the data extraction. This determines how current the data will be in the Staging area and in the target data warehouse database. Frequency-based Data Extraction means that the data extraction process would run at specified *intervals*. This process extracts the updated data from the source database and replicates it in the Staging area. Each time the process is run, it must first identify what data has changed on the source database before extracting the data. Frequency of data extraction is based on the frequency of the operational process that generates the data.

For the Data Warehouse refreshment, the data which is different from the one already present in the Data Warehouse (i.e., incremental data) is identified. This process is called ***Change Data Capture (CDC)***. It captures the changes in the data sources and identifies the appropriate updates required to the Data Warehouse. Generally, a snapshot of the source is taken and compared with its previous snapshot to find the updates such as addition, deletion or modify operations.

Data transformation

In every system implementation, data conversion is an important function. As data for a data warehouse comes from disparate sources, data transformation presents even greater challenges than what data extractions for a data warehouse presents. In addition to the initial transformations that has taken place, it is required to perform the transformation periodically for the data that updated base relations after initial transformation.

The transformation operations that are often used are filters and checks. These operations ensure that the data populated into the data warehouse is in accordance with the business rules and integrity constraints.

A number of individual tasks as part of data transformation should be performed. Once the data from operational systems is extracted into staging database, the data needs to be checked whether it is clean. *Data profiling* does this activity by analyzing tables and column attributes and provides the ability to assess quality and patterns in the data. Through the profiling process, database entities and their relationships can be discovered and defects in the data can be determined, as well as what data must be restructured, and corrected. So, the first task in transformation stage is to clean the data extracted from the source. Cleaning could be as simple as correction of misspellings, resolution of conflicts between state codes and zip codes in the source data, dealing with providing default values for missing data elements, or elimination of duplicates when bringing in the same data from multiple source systems, etc. During this step, issues may arise at schema level or record level. At the schema level, naming conflicts arise when similar columns in different source system may have different names and vice versa. At the record level, there may be inconsistent data due to duplicated values or having conflicting values. Furthermore, standardization of data elements forms a large part of data transformation. The data types and field lengths (i.e., domain of an attribute) for same data elements retrieved from various sources have to be standardized. Attributes should also follow business rules that are independent or dependent on other attributes. Any data, which violates business rule, will be flagged as bad data and loaded into exception tables.

Semantic standardization is another major task, that is, resolving synonyms, etc. When a single term means many different things in different source systems, the synonym should be resolved. Tasks such as merge, purge, de-duplication, normalization, pivot, formatting, aggregation and summarization are some of the widely used transformation activities as part of ETL.

Since the source (data sources) and target (data warehouse database) schemas are different, the transformation step also contains schema mapping and transformations.

To perform ETL operations on the data that is captured from various sources and platforms, it is always better to keep the collected data at a single location, which is often referred to as **Data Staging** Component. Staging database contains replica of the tables identified to be captured from the source system, and hence it is useful as the source for providing all business data integrated at one place. This database is an intermediate storage area that would hold the incremental data extracted from the sources systems. Furthermore, data staging provides a place and an area to perform data transformation operations on the data extracted from various source systems. It also facilitates storage of the external data that is to be populated into the data warehouse. So, all the tasks, such as transformation, homogenization and cleansing, take place in data staging area.

After the extraction, cleansing and transformation, data from staging database needs to be loaded into data warehouse database.

Data loading

There are two kinds of data loading: full loading and incremental loading. On completion of the design and construction of the data warehouse, we will perform *Full loading* (also known as *Refresh*) of the data into the data warehouse storage. The initial load moves large volumes of data which takes substantial amount of time. During this step, if any data exists in the data warehouse database, that old data is removed and completely rewritten with the new data. Full loading is usually used to initially populate the data warehouse.

Once the data warehouse starts functioning, extract the changes to the source data, transform the data revisions and feed the incremental data revisions to data warehouse storage on an ongoing basis. So, in addition to the initial loading taken place, it is required to perform the loading periodically for the data that updated base relations after initial loading. This step is known as *incremental loading* (also referred to as *Update*). During this step, the changes to source system after the previous load are added to the data warehouse. However, incremental loading step do not modify or delete the data that already exist in the data warehouse database.

Several optimization techniques such as dropping the indices before loading the data warehouse, Oracle's parallel loading, such as bulk loading option and OS tuning are used to improve the performance of data loading.

15.6 DIMENSIONAL MODELING

Data models are about capturing and presenting information. Every organization has information that is typically either in the operational form or in the informational form. Traditionally, in the relational database management systems, Entity Relationship (ER) diagrams have been used for the data modeling process. Designing data models to support complex analyses requires a different approach than that used for operational systems design.

For a data warehousing system to be useful, reliable, adaptable and economic, it must be based on sound data modeling. Dimensional modeling is an approach that is commonly used for modeling in data warehouses. It gives an improved capability to visualize the very abstract questions that business analysts are required to answer. With dimensional modeling, it is very easy to navigate and fully exploit the data. Although ER and dimensional modeling are related, they are extremely different. Dimensional models are usually denormalized. Table 15.4. shows the differences between ER and dimensional models.

TABLE 15.4 ER Model versus Dimensional Model

S. No.	ER model	Dimensional model
1.	Designed with a focus on insert, update and delete	Designed with a focus on mostly querying
2.	Consists of more tables, less indexes, morejoins	Consists of less tables, more indexes and less joins
3.	ER model is a Conceptual model	Dimensional model is a logical model
4.	Once ER model is developed, it is not easy to incorporate changes later in the design	These models are flexible to accommodate changes in the design
5.	Tables are usually normalized, that is, broken into many small tables	Tables are denormalized
6.	Suitable for OLTP	Suitable for OLAP
7.	No prescribed methods to handle changes in the entities	Prescribed methods available to handle changes in dimensions

A Dimension Model consists of two kinds of tables: **Fact table** and **Dimension table**. Fact table is used to store facts and business information (*measures*) and Dimension table stores the background information for facts. Here, dimensions determine the contextual background for facts. Thus, dimensional modeling uses three basic concepts, namely, *facts*, *measures* and *dimensions*.

Dimension modeling features include the following:

- It is optimized for querying. There would be less tables, more indexes and less joins.
- It is a logical model.
- It is very easy to understand and flexible to accommodate changes in the design.
- Denormalized. Many small tables are combined together.
- Easy to use for OLAP.
- There are prescribed methods to handle changes in dimensions.

Fact table

Fact table contains *facts* and *measures*. It is the central table in the dimensional model, containing the measures of interest. For example, sales amount would be such a measure. This measure is stored in the fact table with the appropriate granularity, mostly in the raw numeric form. Usually fact table contains a less number of attributes when compared to the record count. Fact table is accessed via dimensions around which it has been organized.

The fact table has a *compound primary key* (where each segment corresponds to a primary key of each dimension table) and additional columns of additive and numeric facts.

Granularity of a fact table is the lowest level of information that will be stored in the fact table. Granularity is usually based on (i) which dimensions will be included and (ii) the hierarchy of each dimension the information will be kept.

Dimension table

Dimension tables contain details for each dimension. It contains hierarchies and attributes. Usually these tables are smaller in size when compared to fact table in terms of number of records. Dimension table are joined to fact table by a foreign key. For each dimension table, there is an entry in the fact table as a foreign key. All these foreign keys constitute a composite primary key in the fact table. Null values should not be allowed in these fields.

Each dimension usually contains a hierarchy.

Hierarchy characterizes the specification of levels that represent relationship between different attributes within a dimension. For example, one possible hierarchy in the time dimension is

Year → Quarter → Month → Week → Day → Hour → Minute → Second

Similarly for location,

Continent → Country → State → District → City → Place

For products,

Category → Brand → Item

Surrogate keys are system generated (i.e., artificial) primary key values. These are alternative to the natural or intelligent key values that are often business related.

15.6.1 Schema Design

In designing data models for data warehouses/data marts, the most commonly used schema types are **Star Schema** and **Snowflake Schema**. These schemas contain *one fact table* and *multiple dimensional tables*. The basic difference between these two schemas are that in snowflake schema one or more dimensional tables are in the normalized form, whereas in star schema all the dimensions are in denormalized form. The dimensional modeling for designing data warehouses is often referred to as ***multi-dimensional modeling***. There is another schema type called **Galaxy Schema.**

Star schema

The star schema is sometimes referred to as star join schema. It consists of a single fact table at the center and multiple dimension tables that are directly connected to the fact table. These dimension tables are in the denormalized form (i.e., denormalized dimensions) and these table keys are usually surrogate keys. The name star schema is derived from the fact that the schema diagram is shaped like a **star.** Figure 15.8 shows an example star schema for deposits, which has one central fact table and five dimensional tables. Note that all these tables are in the denormalized form.

Commonly accessed information is often pre-aggregated and summarized to further improve performance. Although the star schema is primarily considered a tool for the database

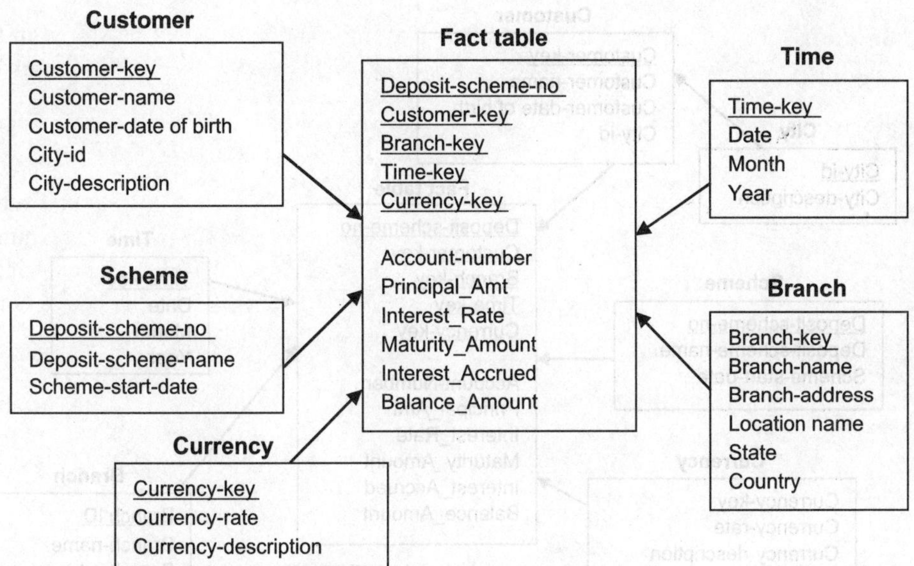

FIGURE 15.8 Star schema example for modeling bank fixed deposits.

administrator to increase performance and simplify data warehouse design, it also represents data warehouse information in a way that makes better sense to end-users.

There are two disadvantages for Star schema:

- De-normalization schema may require too much disk storage
- Very large dimension tables can adversely affect performance, partially offsetting benefits gained through aggregation.

As dimension tables are not normalized in the star schema, joining the fact table with the dimension tables facilitates different views of the data warehouse in an efficient way.

Snowflake schema

Snowflake schema is similar to star schema except that one or more dimension tables are normalized. Figure 15.9 shows a Snowflake schema for a sample Deposit data mart with one fact table and dimension tables representing Customer, Branch, Scheme, Currency and Time, where Customer and Branch dimension tables are normalized, and Scheme, Currency and Time dimensions are not normalized. Note that the dimensions that have hierarchies are candidates for normalizing.

The main disadvantage of the snowflake (versus the star) is the relative complexity of the normalized snowflake data structure. In addition, the overall maintenance becomes more difficult to manage as the data model gets complex.

Galaxy schema

Two or more schemas can be combined to form as galaxy schema, also referred to as *fact constellation*. Galaxy schema can be viewed as a set of star (and snowflake) schemas. For

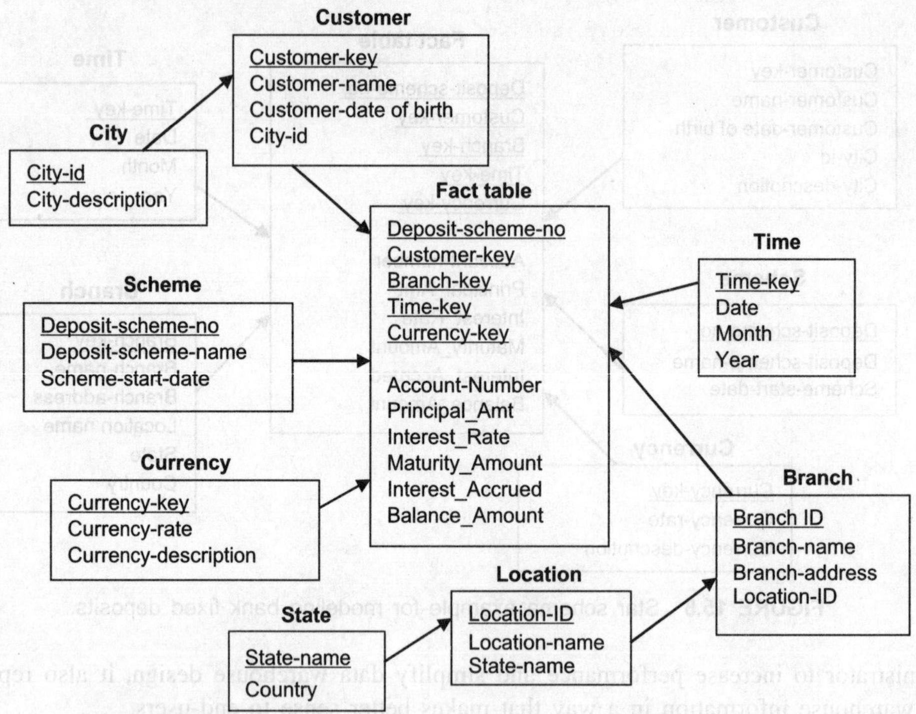

FIGURE 15.9 Snowflake schema example for modeling bank deposits.

example, the loan and deposit departments share customer dimension table for their analysis, although there are some other tables, which are peculiar to credit department only, such as a NPA (Non Performing Asset) status, etc.

A dimension table which is used for more than two fact tables is called the ***conformed dimension***. Consider that there are two data marts, namely, loan data mart and deposit data mart. Here, the Customer dimension table is a common dimension table which is shared between the Loan fact and the Deposit fact. So, the Customer Dimension table is a conformed dimension. A common example of conformed dimension in most data warehouses is the time dimension. Conformed dimension also ensures maintaining data integrity as it provides single version of truth from two or more perspectives.

15.6.2 More on Fact and Dimension Tables

Types of facts

There are three types of facts/measures: fully additive, semi-additive and non-additive measures.

- ***Fully additive:*** Additive facts are facts that can be summed up through all of the dimensions in the fact table. The ideal measure in a star schema should be fully additive. A fully additive measure will aggregate to a correct value no matter what levels and dimensions are queried. At the time of creation of the cube, a fully additive fact is pre-aggregated. With pre-aggregation, rapid browsing for analysis can be achieved.

- ***Semi-additive:*** Semi-additive facts are facts that can be summed up for some of the dimensions in the fact table, but not all dimensions.
- ***Non-additive measures:*** A fact which cannot be aggregated or summed up correctly across any dimension is called a non-additive measure. The example for non-additive fact is '*average values*'.

Factless fact table

A fact table that does not have any measures is known as factless fact table. That is, a fact table contains only foreign keys of dimension tables without any measures (facts). Normally such a fact table is created to enable intersection of dimensions. Furthermore, in a fact table, there may not be corresponding source values to derive a value for measures. Those measures that do not have a value in the source data are called factless facts. Normally these measures have a value of 1. The primary advantage of having factless facts is to design a fact table that acts as an intersection of multiple dimension tables and gets meaningful analysis out of these tables.

Figure 15.10 shows an example for factless fact table. This star schema pertains to students' enrollment into one or more courses. Note that there is no measure in the fact table. This kind of a schema is useful to find the number of students enrolled for a course.

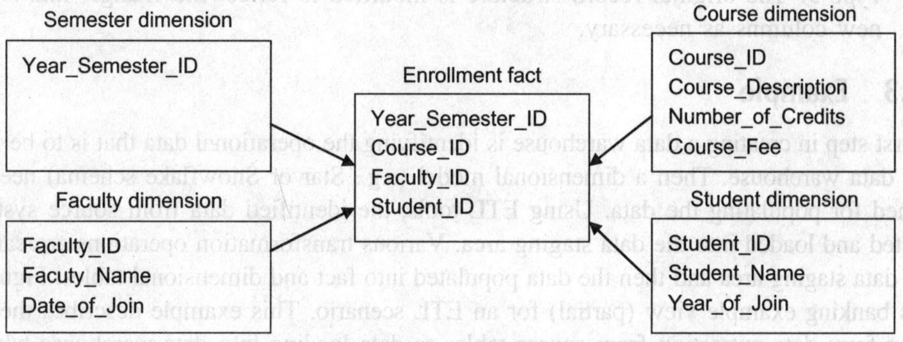

FIGURE 15.10 An example student enrollment dimensional model.

Degenerate dimension

A dimension which has only one attribute is referred to as *degenerate dimension.* This cannot be accommodated with any other dimension. Usually, the degenerate dimension attribute is included as part of fact table itself. In the Figure 15.10, the Semester Dimension is degenerate dimension as it has only one attribute, namely, 'Year_Semester_ID'. If the attribute of this degenerate dimension is included in the fact table itself (as shown in Figure 15.10), a separate dimension table for 'Semester Dimension' is not required and can be removed.

Junk dimensions

A group of attributes which does not belong to any dimension can be merged into one dimension.

There are generally some pieces of data that are left over the fact table and the dimensions tables. These separate pieces of dissimilar information could each be used to create a separate dimension table or they could be left in fact table as degenerated dimensions. But one more possibility is to put these leftovers into their own separate dimension tables. These dimensions created under this strategy are called Junk dimensions. For example, the fields such as Class_Representative, Hostel_Block_Name and Library_Books_issued (not shown in Figure 15.10) can be included in a separate dimension table (Junk dimension) for student enrollment schema.

Slowly changing dimensions

Dimension tables normally do not change. A dimension (such as a customer or product) that evolves slowly is termed as ***slowly changing dimension***. Dimensional modeling provides specific techniques for handling slowly changing dimensions, depending on business requirements. There are three ways to incorporate changes in the dimension table:

- *Type 1:* The new record replaces the original record. No trace of the old record exists.
- *Type 2:* A new record is added into the dimension table. For example, in a customer dimension table, the customer, after change, is treated essentially as two people.
- *Type 3:* The original record structure is modified to reflect the change, that is, adding new columns as necessary.

15.6.3 Example

The first step in creating a data warehouse is identifying the operational data that is to be included in the data warehouse. Then a dimensional model (e.g., Star or Snowflake schema) needs to be designed for populating the data. Using ETL tools, the identified data from source systems are extracted and loaded into the data staging area. Various transformation operations are carried out in the data staging area and then the data populated into fact and dimensional tables. Figure 15.11 shows banking example view (partial) for an ETL scenario. This example describes the process starting from data extraction from source tables to data loading into data warehouse tables. The data warehouse tables are in denormalized form (star schema), where Outstanding fact table is connected directly with four dimension tables, namely Customer, Product, Account and Collateral. Few steps in the data staging area are also shown in the Figure 15.11.

15.6.4 Relational DBMS Support for Dimensional Modeling

Relational DBMS can be used to implement a dimensional model. Other DBMSs that support dimensional modeling are multidimensional databases and object-oriented databases. The design aspects for dimensional modeling in a RDBMS include specifying primary and foreign key relationships, designing surrogate keys, indexes, partitions for fact tables, creating views, etc.

Generally, indexes are created on primary key for a dimension table. These are corresponding to surrogate keys specified in tables. In the case of fact table, a unique index on the primary key will be created. Based on the number of schemas needed to be maintained in the data warehouse, these indexes can be clustered or non-clustered.

For direct access, views can be created in the data warehouse relational database. Indexes can also be created for better performance so that users can query and access the data through these views.

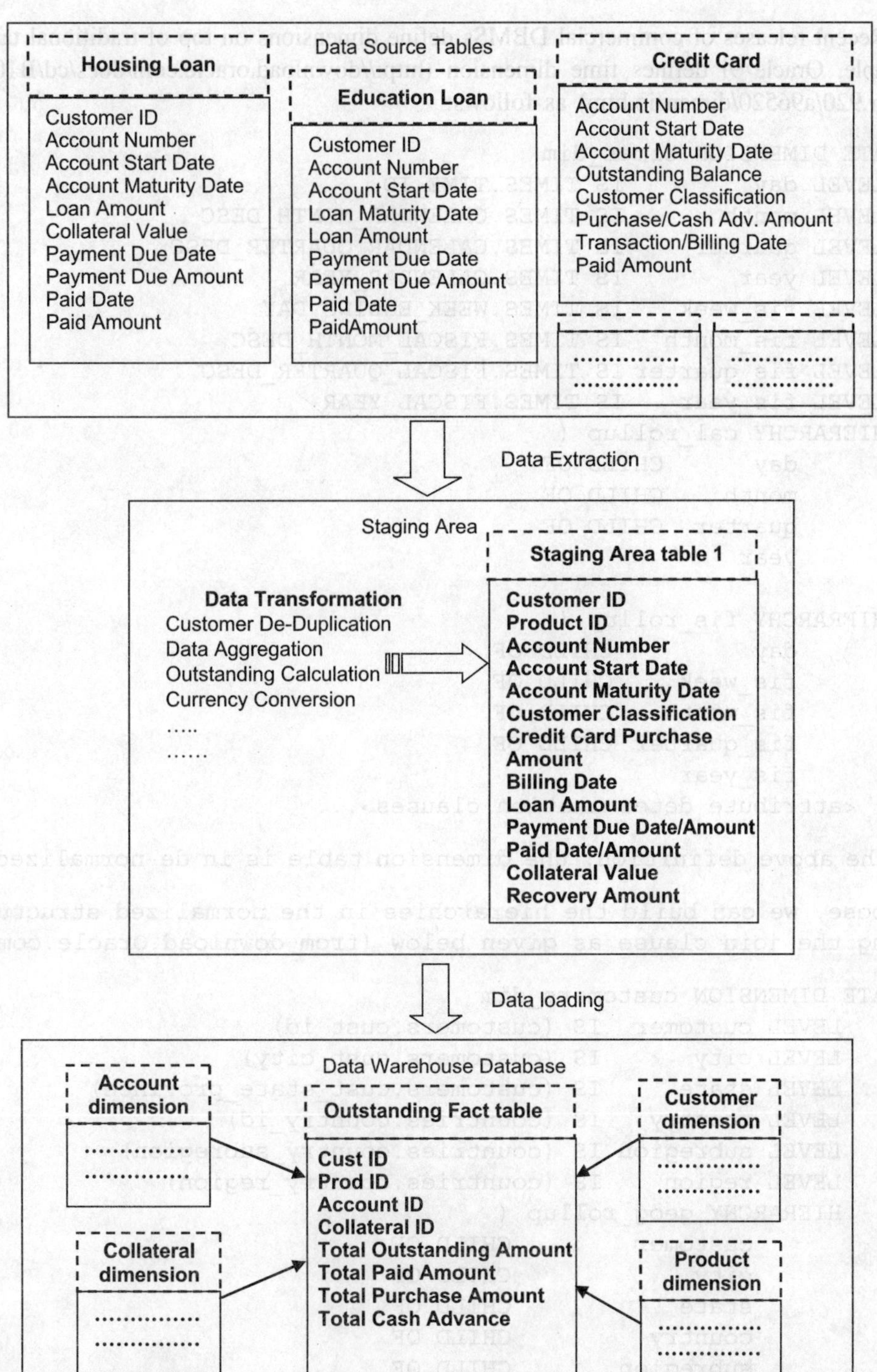

FIGURE 15.11 A banking example on data extraction to data loading.

Recent releases of commercial DBMSs define dimensions on top of traditional tables. For example, Oracle 9i defines time dimension (http://download.oracle.com/docs/cd/B10501_01/server.920/a96520/dimensio.htm) as follows:

```
CREATE DIMENSION times_dim
    LEVEL day         IS TIMES.TIME_ID
    LEVEL month       IS TIMES.CALENDAR_MONTH_DESC
    LEVEL quarter     IS TIMES.CALENDAR_QUARTER_DESC
    LEVEL year        IS TIMES.CALENDAR_YEAR
    LEVEL fis_week    IS TIMES.WEEK_ENDING_DAY
    LEVEL fis_month   IS TIMES.FISCAL_MONTH_DESC
    LEVEL fis_quarter IS TIMES.FISCAL_QUARTER_DESC
    LEVEL fis_year    IS TIMES.FISCAL_YEAR
    HIERARCHY cal_rollup (
            day       CHILD OF
            month     CHILD OF
            quarter   CHILD OF
            year
    )
    HIERARCHY fis_rollup (
            day          CHILD OF
            fis_week     CHILD OF
            fis_month    CHILD OF
            fis_quarter  CHILD OF
            fis_year
    ) <attribute determination clauses>...
```

In the above definition, the dimension table is in de-normalized form.

Suppose, we can build the hierarchies in the normalized structures by using the join clause as given below (from download.Oracle.com):

```
CREATE DIMENSION customers_dim
    LEVEL customer  IS (customers.cust_id)
    LEVEL city      IS (customers.cust_city)
    LEVEL state     IS (customers.cust_state_province)
    LEVEL country   IS (countries.country_id)
    LEVEL subregion IS (countries.country_subregion)
    LEVEL region    IS (countries.country_region)
    HIERARCHY geog_rollup (
        customer       CHILD OF
        city           CHILD OF
        state          CHILD OF
        country        CHILD OF
        subregion      CHILD OF
        region
    JOIN KEY (customers.country_id) REFERENCES country
    ) ...attribute determination clause;
```

Thus, LEVEL and HIERARCHY can be defined in both normalized and denormalized structures. The metadata (relational between columns) is stored in the system tables so that performance of queries will be high. Similar to Oracle DBMS, other RDBMS vendors also facilitate defining dimension structures in their RDBMSs.

15.7 SUMMARY

In this chapter, we introduced the Business Intelligence and its two main components, namely, data warehousing and data mining. Then we presented the basic concepts of data warehousing, which start from the components of data warehouse, ETL functionalities and dimensional modeling. In the next chapter, we discuss the OLAP cube along with its operations and a data warehousing case study.

SHORT/OBJECTIVE TYPE QUESTIONS

1. Which of the following are part of Business Intelligence?
   (a) Data warehouse
   (b) Data mining
   (c) DBMS
   (d) All the above

2. Which is not a characteristic of a Data Warehouse?
   (a) Integrated
   (b) Data Mart
   (c) Non-volatile
   (d) Subject oriented
   (e) Time-variant

3. Data Warehouse is about collecting data from different ___________ data sources.

4. What is a staging area?

5. Fact table contains.
   (a) Keys referenced from dimensional tables
   (b) Measures
   (c) Degenerated Keys
   (d) Only A and B
   (e) All the above

6. Junk Dimension means
   (a) Merging the low cardinality tables into one table
   (b) Merging the high cardinality tables into one table
   (c) Splitting the Dimension table into two tables, one for History Data and another for Current Data
   (d) None of the above

7. Factless fact table
   (a) Contains only Surrogate Keys
   (b) Contains only measures
   (c) Contains keys and measures
   (d) None of the above

8. What is a Data Mart?

9. What is meant by dependant Data Mart?
   (a) Data Mart derived from Enterprise Data Warehouse
   (b) Data Mart sharing the conformed dimensions
   (c) Data Mart derived from another Data Mart
   (d) None of the above

10. If a data warehouse user want to maintain all the changes of a master record, which type of dimensions will suits?
   (a) Type 1
   (b) Type 2
   (c) Type 3
   (d) Any one of the above

WORKOUT SECTION

W15_1 Draw the data warehouse architecture diagram and explain architecture components.

W15_2 What is an ETL? Briefly describe the ETL process.

W15_3 Explain dimensional modeling. Briefly describe Star Schema, Snowflake schema and fact constellation.

W15_4 An organization decided to build data marts for Finance, HR and Sales but some of the master data can be shared between them. What kind of dimensions will you suggest for that and why?

W15_5 Which kind of slowly changing dimension is suitable to track changes for few columns and does not care for other columns.

16

Online Analytical Processing and Materialized Views

Learning Objectives

You will learn following key concepts after completion of the chapter:

- ✓ Understand what is an OLAP
- ✓ Describing the role of multi-dimensional modeling for data analysis
- ✓ Learning OLAP operations
- ✓ Understanding the role of hierarchy in roll-up and drill-down operations
- ✓ Understanding various OLAP models
- ✓ Use of materialized views
- ✓ Demonstrating Oracle data warehouse facilities
- ✓ How to build a prototype data mart

16.1 INTRODUCTION

OLAP is a short form of Online Analytical Processing. It enables data warehouse users to retrieve information from a data warehouse databases in an easy and selective way and present the data that can be viewed from multiple perspectives. On the other hand, materialized views help for fast query response by materializing the frequently accessing of the data. This chapter explains the OLAP concepts, operations on OLAP cubes and materialized views. We also illustrate a data warehousing case study.

Traditional analytical tools (e.g., spreadsheet) do not provide the intelligence required to make informed business decisions. Suppose we want to analyze the *Number of Account Types* along different *Zones*, for which we capture the account type having more number of customers and in which zone it was offered. When considering how to analyze such data using a spreadsheet, as the table is just a two-dimensional spreadsheet, our first requirement is that we want to see not only the number of customers by Account Type and Zone, but also the two kinds of subtotals, number of customers by Account Type and also by City, and the grand total of the number of customers. This means that formulas for producing the (sub)totals must be added to the spreadsheet, each requiring some consideration. It is possible, though cumbersome, to add new data to the spreadsheet, for example, introducing new Account types introduced. Thus, for two dimensions, we can perhaps somehow manage with a spreadsheet. (Note that in the recent releases of Microsoft Excel, new capabilities have been incorporated to carry out advanced data analytics, and several features covered in this section can be performed with Excel.)

Suppose we want to include time. Then we have to consider three dimensions. The obvious solution is to use separate worksheets to handle the extra dimension, with one worksheet for each dimension value. This will work only for a few dimension values and only to some extent. Analysis involving several values of the extra dimension are cumbersome, and with many thousands of, say, time dimension values, the solution becomes infeasible, and the situation becomes even worse if we need to support four or more dimensions, which in any case will require a very complex setup.

Another problem arises if we want to group, for example the Account Types into higher level Account Types such as 'Demand Deposits' and 'Term Deposits.' Then we must duplicate the grouping information across all worksheets, resulting in a system that uses considerable extra space and is very hard to maintain. The essence of the problem is that spreadsheets tie the storage of data too tightly to the presentation—the structure and the desired views of the information are not separated. However, spreadsheets are good for viewing and querying multi-dimensional data, for example, using pivot tables.

A pivot table of MS-Office is a two-dimensional table of data with associated subtotals and totals. For example, if we add subtotals by Zone and Account type and a Zone/Account type grand total to the above table, we will have an example of a pivot table. To support viewing of more complex data, several dimensions may be nested on the *X* or *Y* axis and data may be displayed on multiple pages, for example, one for each Account Type. Pivot tables generally also offer support for interactively selecting subsets of the data and changing the displayed level of details.

With spreadsheets falling short for the management and storage of multidimensional data, we can then consider using a SQL-based, relational system for data storage, as the relational model offers considerable flexibility in the structuring of data. The problem here is that many desirable computations, including cumulative aggregates (the number of customers in year to date), totals and subtotals together and rankings (top three Account Types offered), are hard or impossible to formulate in standard SQL.

The main underlying issue is that inter row computations are difficult to express in SQL, and only inter column computations are easy to specify. Additionally, transpositions of rows and columns are not easily possible, requiring the manual specification and combination of multiple views. Although extensions of SQL will remedy some of the problems, the concept of hierarchical dimensions is still not handled satisfactorily.

As seen above neither spreadsheets nor relational databases fully support the requirements for advanced data analysis. Such technologies may be adequate in more restricted circumstances. For example, if we have only few dimensions that do not need hierarchical dimensions and the data volume is small, spreadsheets could provide adequate support. However, the only robust solution to the above problems is to provide data models and database technology that offer inherent support for the full range of multi-dimensional concepts. The standard data analysis technique used today for analysis of large volumes of data is online analytical processing. OLAP transforms raw data to reflect the real dimensions of the information as understood by the user and provides users with a wide variety of interactive views of the information.

Online Analytical Processing is a term coined by E.F. Codd. OLAP is a category of software technology that is used for decision support. OLAP enables application users (analysts, managers and executives) to quickly analyze information that has been summarized into multi-dimensional views and hierarchies. By summarizing predicted queries into multi-dimensional views prior to run-time, OLAP provides the benefit of increased performance over traditional database access.

OLAP tools provide analysis of data stored in a database. These tools enable users to analyze different dimensions of multi-dimensional data. Data analysis aims at extracting information from data. ***Multi-dimensional data analysis*** is the process of consolidating data with respect to certain *dimensions*. Multi-dimensional information is often described as a *data cube*.

A ***cube*** is a set of data that is organized and structured in a hierarchical, multi-dimensional arrangement. The cube is usually derived from a subset of a data warehouse. Unlike relational databases that use two-dimensional data structures (often in the form of columns and rows in a spreadsheet), OLAP cubes are logical, multi-dimensional models that can have numerous dimensions and levels of data. Also, an organization typically has different cubes for different types of data.

The core component of OLAP is the OLAP server, which sits between a client and a Database Management Systems (DBMS). The OLAP server understands how data is organized in the database and has special functions for analyzing the data. Logical data modeling of data warehouses, that is, multi-dimensional models, is well suited for large and complex data analysis and so form the basis for OLAP systems.

16.2 OLAP CONCEPTS

Data cubes provide true multi-dimensionality. They generalize spreadsheets to any number of dimensions. In addition, hierarchies in dimensions and formulas are built-in concepts, meaning that these are supported without duplicating their definitions. A collection of related cubes is commonly referred to as a multi-dimensional database or a multi-dimensional data warehouse.

Figure 16.1. shows a cube capturing the number of customers of the two cities, with the additional dimension Time. The combinations of dimension values define the ***cells*** of the cube. The actual numbers of customers are stored within the corresponding cells.

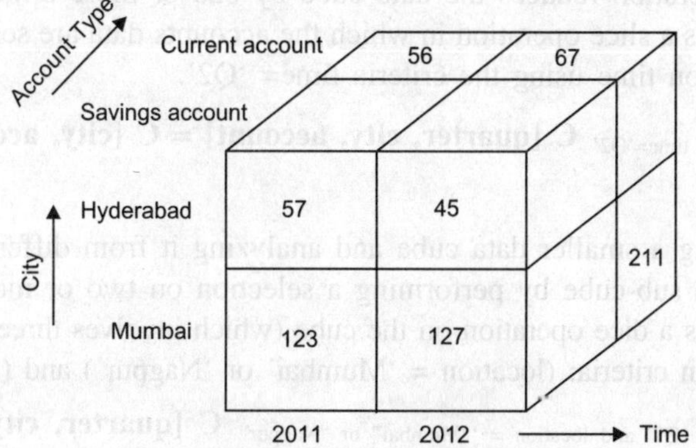

FIGURE 16.1 Account cube.

In a cube, dimensions are associated with *subject* domains and the addition of new dimension values is easily handled. Here, each dimension specifies the context. Although the term 'cube' implies three dimensions, an OLAP cube can have any number of dimensions. To better illustrate the high number of dimensions, the term 'hypercube' is often used instead of 'cube'.

Depending on the specific application, a highly varying percentage of the cells in a cube are non-empty, meaning that cubes range from sparse to dense. Cubes tend to become increasingly sparse with increasing dimensionality and with increasingly finer granularities of the dimension values. A non-empty cell represents a fact. The example has a fact for each combination of Time, Account Type and Zone, where at least one customer had an account. A fact has associated with it a number of measures. These are numerical values that 'live' within the cells. In our case, we have one measure, the number of customers. Generally, only two or three dimensions may be viewed at the same time, although for low-cardinality dimensions, up to four dimensions can be shown by nesting one dimension within another on the axes. Thus, the dimensionality of a cube is reduced, at query time, by projecting it down to 2D or 3D via aggregation of the measure values in the projected-out dimensions, resulting in higher level measure values for the desired view of data. For example, if we want to view only the number of customers by City and Time, we aggregate over the entire Account Type dimension for each combination of City and Time. In the example, we get the total number of customers for Mumbai in 2012 by adding 127 and 211.

16.2.1 OLAP Operations

The basic OLAP operations on a Cube are Slicing, Dicing, Roll-up, Drill-down, Drill-within Drill-across and Pivot.

For reducing the data cube by one or more dimensions, slicing and dicing operations are useful. Drilling operations, such as Roll-up and Drill-down, allow for moving up and down along classification hierarchies. The Pivot operation enables rotation of the cube to perform a different view of the data.

Slicing

The slice operation results in a sub-cube by performing a selection on one dimension of the given cube. Slice operation reduces the data cube by one or more dimensions.

Figure 16.2 shows a slice operation in which the accounts data are selected from the central cube for the dimension time using the criteria time= 'Q2'.

$$\textbf{Slice}_{\text{time='Q2'}}\ \textbf{C [quarter, city, account] = C [city, account]}$$

Dicing

Dicing is for selecting a smaller data cube and analyzing it from different perspectives. This operation results in a sub-cube by performing a selection on two or more dimensions.

Figure 16.3 shows a dice operation on the cube (which involves three dimensions) based on the following selection criteria: (location = 'Mumbai' or 'Nagpur') and (time = 'Q1' or 'Q2').

$$\textbf{Dice}_{\text{time = 'Q1' or 'Q2' and location = "Mumbai" or "Nagpur"}}\ \textbf{C [quarter, city, product]}$$

$$\textbf{= C [quarter, city, account].}$$

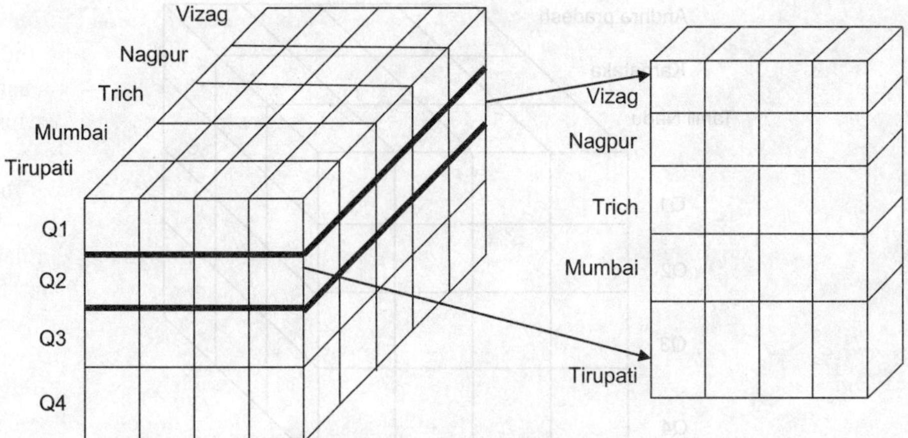

FIGURE 16.2 Slice operation.

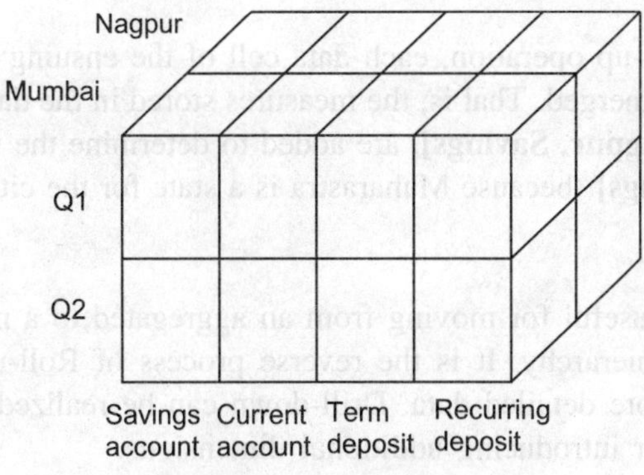

FIGURE 16.3 Dice operation.

where **quarter and city** have truncated domains such as {Q1, Q2} and {Mumbai, Nagpur}, respectively.

Roll-up

Within the same classification hierarchy, this operation deals with switching from a detailed to an aggregated level. The Roll-up operation is also called **drill-up** operation. Roll-up performs aggregation on a data cube, either by climbing up a dimension hierarchy or by dimension reduction.

Figure 16.4 shows how the Roll-up operation is performed on the central cube by climbing up the dimension hierarchy for the *location*. The roll-up operation aggregates the data by climbing the location hierarchy from the level of the city to the level of province, that is, the grouping of data is done by the *province*, instead of city.

Roll-up $_{\text{time}}$ C [quarter, city, account] = C [quarter, province, account]

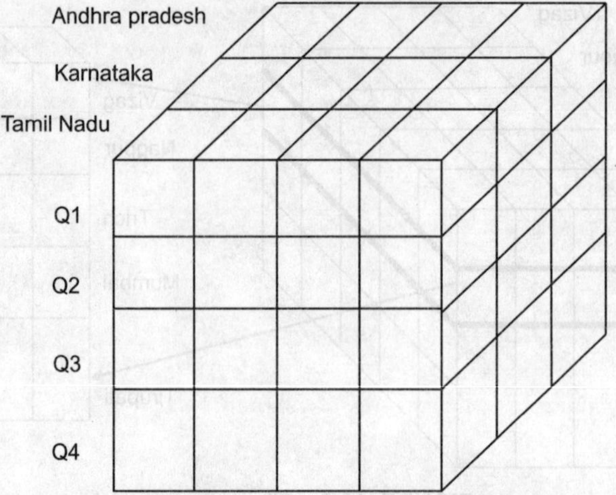

FIGURE 16.4 Roll-up operation.

Here, due to the roll-up operation, each data cell of the ensuing cuboid is the aggregation of the data cells that are merged. That is, the measures stored in the data cells, **C [Q1, Mumbai, Savings]** and **C [Q1, Nagpur, Savings]**, are added to determine the measure to be stored at **C [Q1, Maharastra, Savings]** (because Maharastra is a state for the cities Mumbai and Nagpur).

Drill-down

Drill-down operation is useful for moving from an aggregated to a more detailed level within the same classification hierarchy. It is the reverse process of Roll-up operation. It navigates from detailed data to more detailed data. Drill-down can be realized by either stepping down a dimension hierarchy or introducing additional dimensions.

Figure 16.5 explains the operation of Drill-down. The drilling occurs in the time hierarchy from the level of a quarter to the level of a month.

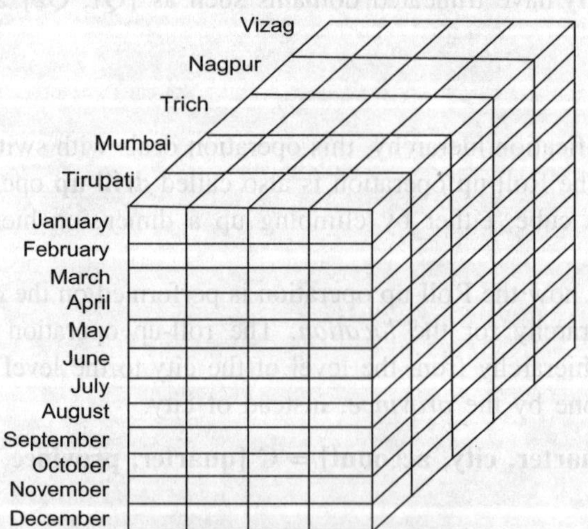

FIGURE 16.5 Drill-down operation.

The resulting data cube also is performed by adding new dimensions to the cube. For example, a drill-down on the given cube can occur by introducing an additional dimension, such as *customer-type*.

Drill-within

Drill-within operation is used within the same dimension for switching from one classification to a different one.

Drill-across

Drill-across operation switches from a classification in one dimension to a different classification in another dimension.

Pivot (rotate)

Pivot means rotate. It is a visualization operation. This rotates the data axes for providing an alternative presentation of the same data. Rotating the axes in a 3D cube and transforming a 3D cube into a series of 2D planes are the other examples for Pivot operations.

16.2.2 OLAP Models

There are three types of OLAP models: ROLAP, MOLAP and HOLAP.

ROLAP (relational OLAP)

ROLAP (relational online analytical processing) is a form of OLAP that performs dynamic multi-dimensional analysis of *data stored in a relational database* rather than in a multi-dimensional database. Since ROLAP uses a relational database, it requires more processing time and disk space to perform some of the tasks that multi-dimensional databases are designed for. However, ROLAP supports larger user groups and greater amounts of data and is often used when these capacities are crucial, such as in a large and complex department of an enterprise.

MOLAP (multi-dimensional OLAP)

MOLAP (multi-dimensional online analytical processing) is a form of OLAP that indexes directly into a multi-dimensional database. In general, an OLAP application treats data multi-dimensionality; the user is able to view different aspects of data aggregates, such as number of saving accounts by time, by region, etc. If the data is stored in a relational database, it can be viewed multidimensionally, but only by successively accessing and processing a table for each dimension. MOLAP processes data that is already stored in a *multi-dimensional array* in which all possible combinations of data are reflected, each in a cell that can be accessed directly. For this reason, MOLAP is, for most uses, faster and more user responsive than ROLAP.

HOLAP (hybrid OLAP)

HOLAP (Hybrid Online Analytical Processing) is a combination of ROLAP and MOLAP. HOLAP was developed to combine the greater data capacity of ROLAP with the superior processing capability of MOLAP. HOLAP can use varying combinations of ROLAP and MOLAP technologies. Typically, it stores data in both a relational database and a multi-dimensional database (MDDB) and uses whichever is best suited to the type of processing desired. The databases are used to store data in the most functional way. For data-heavy processing, the data is more efficiently stored in a relational database, while for speculative processing, the data is more effectively stored in an MDDB.

16.3 MATERIALIZED VIEWS

A data warehouse serves as a decision support system and supports ad hoc analysis. Large data volumes are extracted and summarized for Online Analytical Processing. To reduce the cost of executing aggregate queries in a data warehousing environment, frequently used aggregates are often *pre-computed* and *materialized* in the form of summary views. Since the data is computed and stored in aggregated form (after computing joins, etc., if required), the future queries can utilize them directly. The tables from which the materialized view is created are referred to as *base tables*.

The difference between normal views (i.e., virtual views) and materialized views is that the virtual views are logical and a query on a view needs to access the base tables on which the view is created. On the other hand, materialized view exists along with the data, and hence there is no need to access base tables to query the data existing in the materialized view. However, a query can be accessed by both materialized views and base tables based on the availability of the data. Virtual views are useful when the information sources are changing frequently, whereas the materialized views are useful when the information sources are changing infrequently and a quick query response time is required. There is always a trade-off between time (taken for query processing) and space (occupied by materialized views) for choosing materialized views. The tasks involved in building materialized views are as follows:

- *Materialized view selection:* Identify the views to materialize for the queries that are frequently accessing data warehouse
- Use the materialized views to answer queries
- *Materialized views maintenance:* Efficiently update the materialized views during load and refresh

Materialized views are important in data warehouses for fast retrieval of derived data regardless of the access paths and complexity of view definitions. These materialized views avoid scanning the large data sets for the queries that occur frequently. For a given set of base relations and frequent queries, the materialized view selection process selects a smallest set of views to materialize so that it minimizes the cost of responding to queries and the maintenance cost of view. When the underlying database relations are updated by insertion and deletion of tuples, a materialized view must also be updated (i.e., maintenance) to ensure the correctness of answers to queries against it. Updating the materialized view by full re-computation is often expensive. Maintaining materialized views incrementally facilitates updation of only the portions of the view that are affected by the changes in the relevant sources. That is, a new view is computed from the existing view as and when there are changes to the base relations. On the other hand, additional views (often called auxiliary relations) are stored at the data warehouse to ensure enough information to maintain the views without accessing the base relations.

16.4 ORACLE FEATURES FOR DATA WAREHOUSING

Oracle provides the following DML features that support loading data from source systems into data warehouse:

- External table—Allows querying data from external tables
- Multitable INSERT statement—Allows inserting data into multiple tables simultaneously
- Merge statement—Allows combining data from multiple tables into one table simultaneously. Enables conditionally update or insert new data

External tables

External tables are created outside the database. These kinds of tables are useful to load data from external sources. External tables can be created using CREATE TABLE statement with the clause ORGANIZATION EXTERNAL.

```
The syntax is
CREATE TABLE ……. ORGANIZATION EXTERNAL.
```

Like views, the metadata is only stored in the Oracle data dictionary when an external table is created. This is because the external tables are located outside the database. The actual data is placed in the form of flat files, where the record and column values are separated by a user-specified delimiter. So, the syntax of external table creation contains the directory path, where the file exists, and delimiter information.

The data in these tables are read-only. That is, external tables are useful only to query the data (using normal SELECT statement), but they do not permit INSERT, UPDATE, DELETE and MERGE statements. Moreover, indexes also cannot be created on external tables.

The external tables can be queried along with the normal database tables. That is, WHERE clause of SELECT statement can have database tables and external tables.

Multitable INSERT statement

This statement allows transferring data from one or more source tables to a set of target tables in a single statement. This statement is useful to refresh materialized views.

Multitable INSERT statement has two forms: unconditional and conditional. Syntax of unconditional form is

```
INSERT INTO tablename1 [VALUES (…..)]
                         INTO tablename2 [VALUES (…. )]
                         …….
               SELECT ……
```

Here, multiple INTO clauses can have the same table. Also, for each row of subquery result, the INTO clause list is executed once. The VALUES clause is optional and its list must refer to the columns of the select list in the subquery. In the case of no VALUES clause, the subquery must return all the column values that the corresponding (target) table has.

There is an additional WHEN clause present for the conditional form of multitable INSERT statement. The syntax of conditional form is

```
INSERT {ALL | FIRST}
    WHEN condition1 THEN INTO tablename1 [VALUES (.....)]
    WHEN condition2 THEN INTO tablename2 [VALUES (.....)]
    ........
    [ ELSE INTO tablenameN [VALUES (.....)] ]
    SELECT .....
```

Here, the condition can have an expression or another SELECT statement like WHEN departnumber in {SELECT departmentnumber FROM payroll}. ALL indicates that the rows are inserted in all the tables, which satisfies the conditions specified in the WHEN clause. That is, rows are inserted into zero or more tables, based on satisfying the condition by the query result. On the other hand, FIRST indicates that rows are inserted into the first matching INTO clause. That means, the order to the WHEN … INTO plays a role while inserting the rows in a specific table. The optional ELSE INTO clause allows to insert rows into the specified table when no WHEN condition is satisfied.

Note that INSERT ALL statement without any WHEN clause is equal to an unconditional multitable INSERT statement.

Merge statement

MERGE statements enable a single SQL statement to carry out an UPDATE and INSERT (commonly known as UPSERT referring to UPDATE or INSERT). The MERGE statement updates if the row exists, otherwise it inserts the new row. Using this statement, data from multiple tables can be loaded into a single table.

Oracle also provides features that support query and reporting of data warehouse. Oracle extends the GROUP BY clause to improve the aggregation performance by introducing ROLLUP, CUBE and GROUPING SETS. The output for these three statements is a single result set, which is equivalent to the result of UNION ALL of differently grouped rows. These three extensions perform groupings that are needed in the GROUP BY clause of normal SQL statement.

ROLLUP

ROLLUP performs aggregate functions such as SUM, COUNT, MAX, MIN and AVG. These aggregations are carried out in increased hierarchy levels, that is, starting from the detailed to highest aggregated level. The syntax is

```
SELECT..... GROUP BY ROLLUP(grouping column reference list).
```

ROLLUP is very useful in computing aggregations along a hierarchical dimension (e.g., time or location). It creates subtotals that roll up from the most detailed level to a grand total, following a grouping list specified in the ROLLUP clause.

CUBE

CUBE is similar to ROLLUP. It computes all possible combinations of aggregations in a single statement. CUBE also produces information needed in cross-tabulation reports in a single statement. The syntax is

```
SELECT..... GROUP BY CUBE(grouping column reference list).
```

This operation avoids repetitive aggregations.

With regard to performance, CUBE is more suitable to queries that involve columns from multiple dimensions, but not the columns that represent different levels of a single dimension. In the later case, ROLLUP is more suitable.

GROUPING SETS

A grouping set represents a set of groupings that have to be performed to get the aggregation on those groupings. GROUPING SETS clause also identifies the exact groupings out of overall groups. That is, using this clause, it is possible to get a fewer groups computation instead of all the groups computation. So, precise specification across multiple dimensions can be allowed by using GROUPING SETS without computing the whole CUBE.

This clause allows analyzing the data in a dimension without completely rolling it up. Similarly, it allows analysis of data across multiple dimensions without whole cube computation and permits multiple arbitrary groupings according to the user needs.

Syntax of grouping sets is

```
GROUP BY [GROUPING sets(dimension column).. ]
```

GROUPING SETS can be treated as a superset of ROLLUP and CUBE operations. The ROLLUP and CUBE are introduced as the part of GROUP BY in the Oracle 8i release, whereas GROUPING SETS is introduced in Oracle 9i in order to have more flexibility in handling GROUP BY. Unlike ROLLUP and CUBE, GROUPING SETS does not require explicit specification of UNION ALL in order to combine multiple queries. Moreover, GROUPING SETS require only one pass over base tables. However, a CUBE operation exhibits huge processing load when compared to GROUPINGS SETS.

Materialized view

Materialized views can be created using CREATE MATERIALIZED VIEW statement. Its syntax is

```
CREATE MATERIALIZED VIEW [schema.]mv_view
    Mv_view_Options
        [USING INDEX storage_options]
            [{REFRESH [refresh_options] | NEVER REFRESH]
                [FOR UPDATE] [{ENABLE|DISABLE} QUERY REWRITE]
                    AS query;
```

In addition to table names and views, the FROM clause of the SQL query can have other materialized views.

16.5 DEPOSIT DATA MART—A CASE STUDY

This section illustrates a simple case study on building a deposit data mart for a bank. Figure 16.6 represents extracting data from heterogeneous source system into data mart. This component was scheduled to extract data from source systems in periodic times.

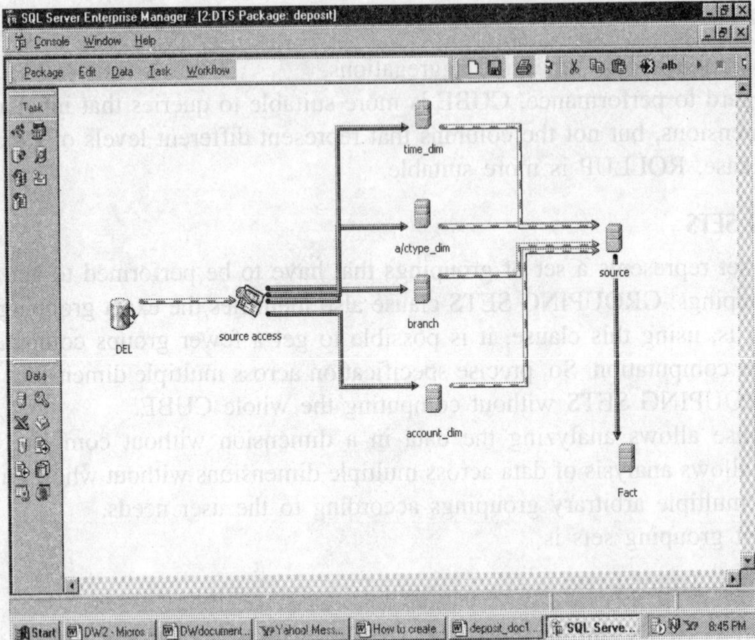

FIGURE 16.6 ETL process for creating Deposit Data Mart.

Figure 16.7 represents Deposit cube data in the cube browser to browse the cube. Here, the data is shown with respect to Time dimension, whereas Debit, Credit and Balance are measures of the fact table. User can drag the Dimensions, which appear as buttons on the upper half of

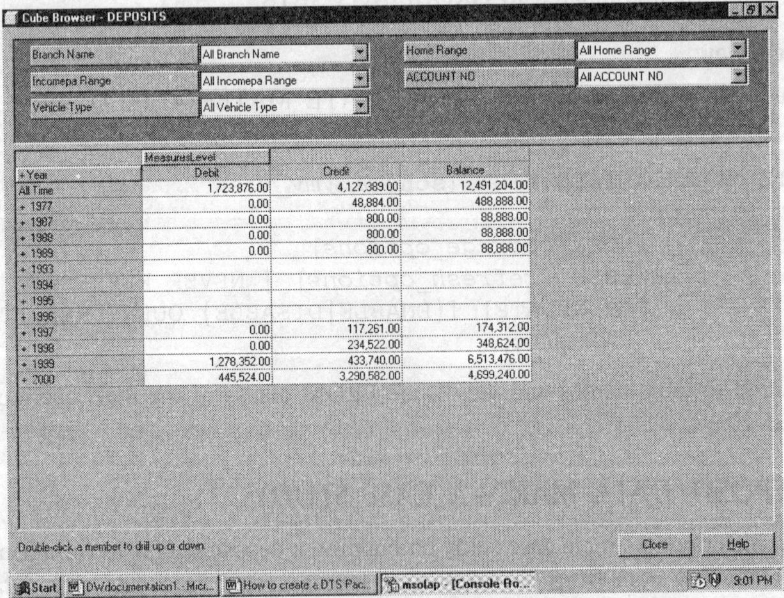

+ Year	Debit	Credit	Balance
All Time	1,723,876.00	4,127,389.00	12,491,204.00
+ 1977	0.00	48,884.00	488,888.00
+ 1987	0.00	800.00	88,888.00
+ 1988	0.00	800.00	88,888.00
+ 1989	0.00	800.00	88,888.00
+ 1993			
+ 1994			
+ 1995			
+ 1996			
+ 1997	0.00	117,261.00	174,312.00
+ 1998	0.00	234,522.00	348,624.00
+ 1999	1,278,352.00	433,740.00	6,513,476.00
+ 2000	445,524.00	3,290,582.00	4,699,240.00

FIGURE 16.7 Deposit Cube with time dimension.

the Cube browser. Note that one can drag the desired dimension and drop on *X*-axis of the cube grid. The screen shown in Figure 16.7 represents deposits data with respect to Time. The + sign on the time Dimension indicates that it is a hierarchical Dimension. Hierarchical Dimensions have two or more levels. By clicking on the plus sign of year 2000 (i.e., drill-down operation on the cube), user can get the detailed data with respect to month of the year 2000. Then the screen will appear as shown in Figure 16.8. By clicking on the + sign of month hierarchy, Deposit data can be analyzed up to day level (Figure 16.9).

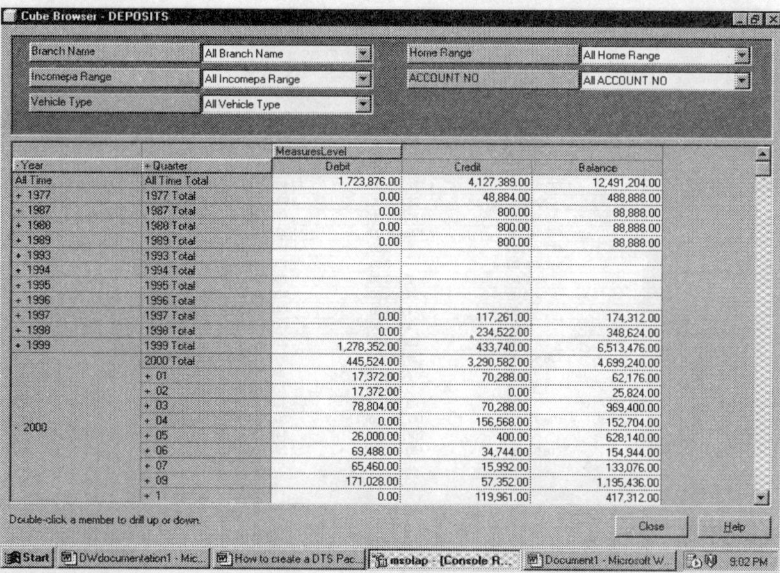

FIGURE 16.8 Drill-down (Month) operation Deposit Cube.

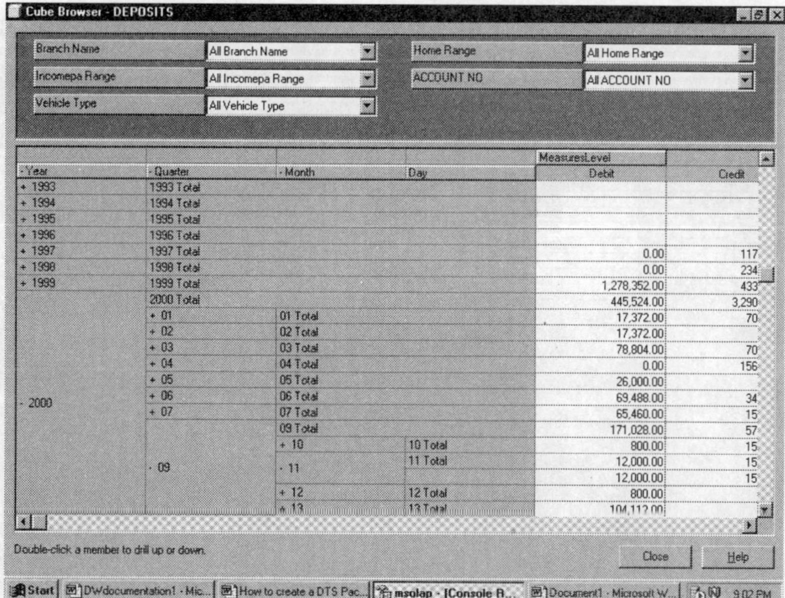

FIGURE 16.9 Drill-down (Day) operation Deposit Cube.

Figure 16.10 represents Deposits data with respect to Account Dimension and Measures of the cube. This screen can be obtained by dragging Account Dimension from Dimension Pane in the cube browser to the Cube grid's *X*-axis. Figure 16.11 represents deposits Cube data with respect to Branch Dimension and Measures of the cube. To get this combination, drag the Branch Name Dimension from Dimension pane to the Cube grid's *X*-axis. The + sign on the Branch Name Dimension indicates that it is a Hierarchical Dimension. By clicking on the + sign, the user can get the detailed level up to Branch Level.

Cube Browser - DEPOSITS

Branch Name	All Branch Name	Home Range	All Home Range
Incomepa Range	All Incomepa Range	Time	All Time
Vehicle Type	All Vehicle Type		

	MeasuresLevel		
A c No	Debit	Credit	Balance
All ACCOUNT NO	1,723,876.00	4,127,389.00	12,491,204.00
1	3,200.00	26,100.00	2,637,000.00
10	18,172.00	170,177.00	421,608.00
11	467,460.00	2,405,106.00	1,327,756.00
12	467,460.00	0.00	1,150,528.00
13	467,460.00	0.00	1,150,528.00
14	0.00	2,400.00	266,664.00
15	0.00	39,996.00	400,000.00
16	0.00	4,444.00	44,444.00
17	0.00	4,444.00	44,444.00
2	0.00	63,968.00	320,000.00
3	138,976.00	234,522.00	555,216.00
4	0.00	518,374.00	268,096.00
5	3,200.00	5,400.00	774,000.00
6	0.00	63,968.00	320,000.00
7	138,976.00	117,261.00	380,904.00
8	0.00	281,152.00	145,408.00
9	18,972.00	190,077.00	2,284,608.00

Double-click a member to drill up or down.

Close Help

Start | DWdocumentation1 - Mic... | How to create a DTS Pac... | msolap - [Console R... | Document1 - Microsoft W... | 9:03 PM

FIGURE 16.10 Deposit Cube with Account Dimension.

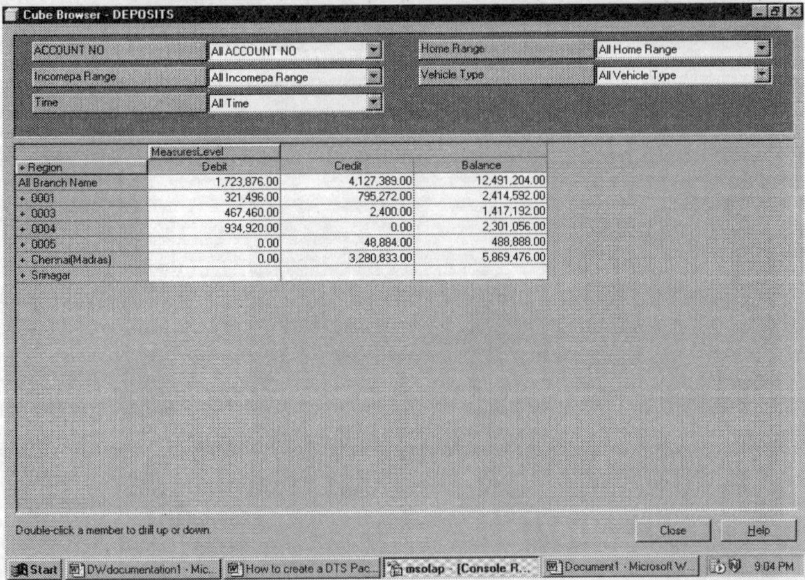

	MeasuresLevel		
+ Region	Debit	Credit	Balance
All Branch Name	1,723,876.00	4,127,389.00	12,491,204.00
+ 0001	321,496.00	795,272.00	2,414,592.00
+ 0003	467,460.00	2,400.00	1,417,192.00
+ 0004	934,920.00	0.00	2,301,056.00
+ 0005	0.00	48,884.00	488,888.00
+ Chennai(Madras)	0.00	3,280,833.00	5,869,476.00
+ Srinagar			

FIGURE 16.11 Deposit Cube with Branch Dimension.

Figure 16.12 represents the cube presented in MS Excel. Users can interactively change the Dimensions and Measures by dragging and Dropping the dimensions and Measures from pivot table to the layout. User can remove the Dimensions and Measures by dragging from layout and dropping back to the pivot table. Figure 16.13 shows the graphical representation of data shown in Figure 16.12. User can change the Dimensions and Measures by dragging and dropping Dimension from pivot table to the graph area. User can change his view by removing Dimensions from graph and drop it back to the pivot table. Figures 16.14 and 16.15 represent the drill-down information.

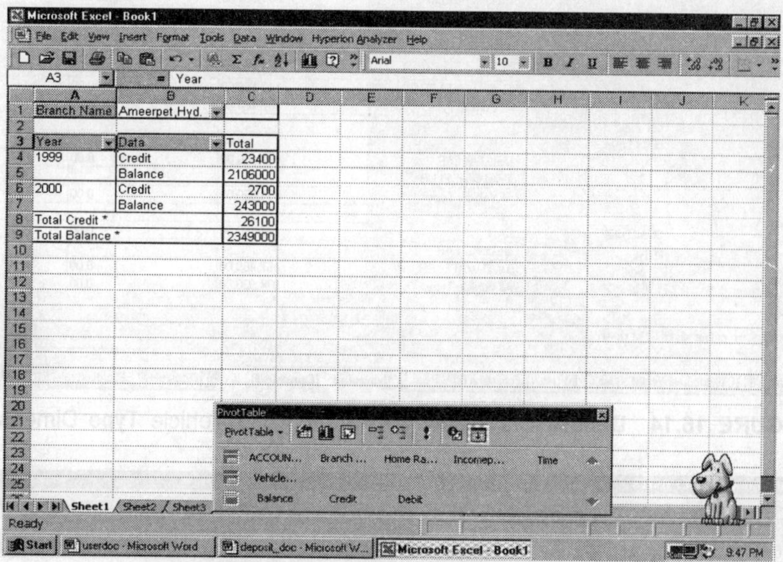

FIGURE 16.12 Deposit Cube view in Excel.

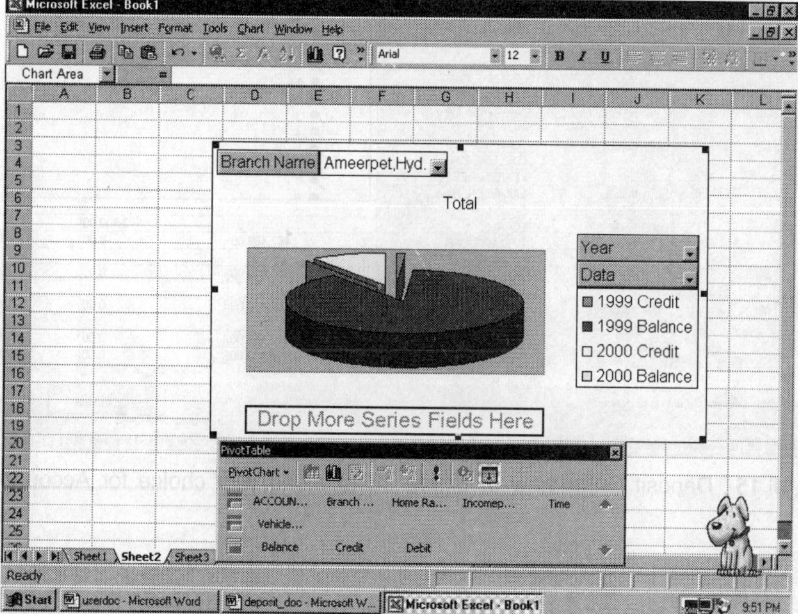

FIGURE 16.13 Deposit Cube view in Excel.

Cube Browser - DEPOSITS

Home Range	All Home Range	Incomepa Range	All Incomepa Range
Time	All Time	ACCOUNT NO	All ACCOUNT NO

Region	Branch	Vehicle Type	Debit	Credit	Balance
			MeasuresLevel		
All Branch Name	All Branch Name Total	All Vehicle Type	1,723,876.00	4,127,389.00	12,491
			0.00	39,996.00	400
		CAR	606,436.00	473,669.00	2,352
		DELUXE CAR	507,804.00	2,791,460.00	6,670
		TWO WHEELER	609,636.00	822,264.00	3,067
+ 0001	0001 Total	All Vehicle Type	321,496.00	795,272.00	2,414
		CAR	138,976.00	345,120.00	672
		DELUXE CAR	40,344.00	105,032.00	782
		TWO WHEELER	142,176.00	345,120.00	960
+ 0003	0003 Total	All Vehicle Type	467,460.00	2,400.00	1,417
		CAR	0.00	2,400.00	266
		DELUXE CAR	467,460.00	0.00	1,150
		TWO WHEELER			
+ 0004	0004 Total	All Vehicle Type	934,920.00	0.00	2,301
		CAR	467,460.00	0.00	1,150
		DELUXE CAR			
		TWO WHEELER	467,460.00	0.00	1,150
- 0004		All Vehicle Type	934,920.00	0.00	2,301

Double-click a member to drill up or down.

Close Help

Start | DWdocumentation1 - Mic... | How to create a DTS Pac... | msolap - [Console R... | Document1 - Microsoft W... | 9:05 PM

FIGURE 16.14 Deposit Cube view with Branch and Vehicle Type Dimensions.

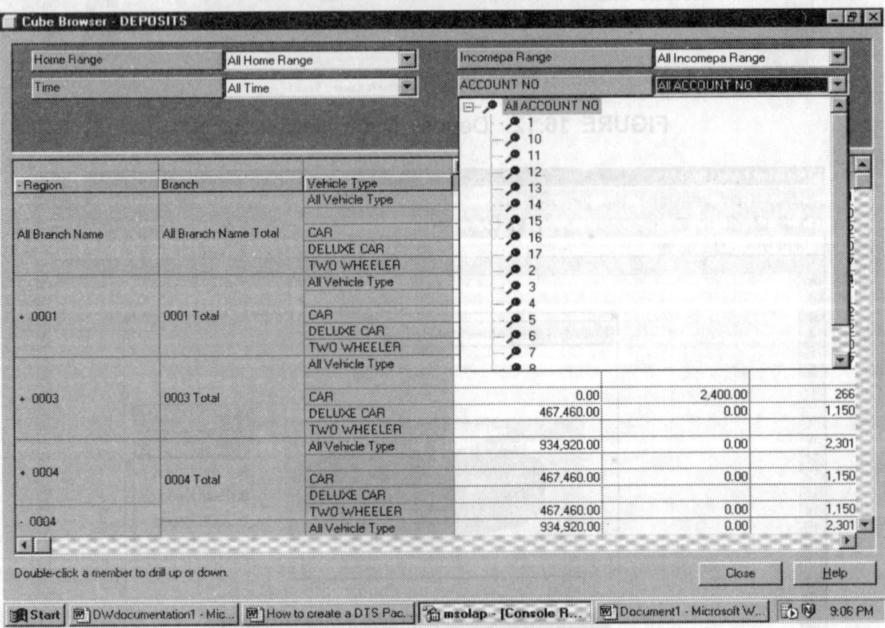

FIGURE 16.15 Deposit Cube view of Figure 16.14 along with choice for Account Dimension.

16.6 SUMMARY

In this chapter, we described OLAP that is useful to carry out analysis of the data present in the data warehouse. OLAP operations such as Slicing, Dicing, Roll-up, Drill-down and Pivoting are explained. We also discussed the advantages of materialized views, besides highlighting materialized view selection and maintenance issues. ORACLE support for building and accessing data warehousing is also covered in this chapter. Finally, we presented a case study on building Deposit data mart.

SHORT/OBJECTIVE TYPE QUESTIONS

1. What is a cube concept in Data Warehouses?
2. ______allows to model and view data in multi-dimensional form.
3. Operational databases support OLAP.

   True/False
4. Data warehouses support OLAP.

   True/False
5. In OLAP, a query is viewed as ________ transaction.
   (a) Read-only
   (b) Write-only
   (c) Read and Write
   (d) None of the above
6. Distinguish between OLTP and OLAP.
7. OLAP tools have slice-and-dice techniques to view multi-dimensional information from different perspectives

   True/False
8. List the OLAP operations in multi-dimensional data model?
9. What is the role of hierarchy with respect to OLAP operations?
10. Explain the purpose of External table in Oracle.

WORKOUT SECTION

W16_1 What is OLAP? Explain the use of dimensional modeling in OLAP.

W16_2 Describe common OLAP operations with examples.

W16_3 What are the differences between ROLAP and MOLAP?

W16_4 Explain the difference between Views in DBMS and Materialized Views in Data Warehouse.

W16_5 Describe the additional features of Oracle that supports data warehousing.

Data Mining Overview

Learning Objectives

You will learn following key concepts after completion of the chapter:

- ✓ Identifying the key processes of knowledge discovery and data mining
- ✓ Understanding the basic definitions and concepts of data mining
- ✓ Understanding different purposes and applications of data mining
- ✓ Learning different methods of data mining and their benefits
- ✓ Defining predictive and descriptive data mining tasks
- ✓ Learning basic principles of association rules, classification and clustering
- ✓ Understand how support and confidence are used for association rule discovery
- ✓ Understand the difference between clustering and classification
- ✓ Study various measures to ascertain data mining techniques
- ✓ Exploring advanced data mining techniques and their objectives

17.1 INTRODUCTION

Data mining deals with the problem of extracting useful information from large data. Enterprises are applying data mining techniques that provide data-driven intelligence in order to address various business problems such as determining high-value customers, personalization by customizing product offerings and reducing frauds by providing early warnings. Thus, understanding the data mining approaches and methods is becoming increasingly important to achieve improved decision-making. This chapter introduces data mining tasks that are useful to extract intelligence from business data.

In today's businesses, data mining is essential as there are tremendous amounts of data generation for business transactions. This data could be useful in deriving insights that in turn help in improving businesses. Advanced database technologies available today facilitate collection of such large data and their analysis.

Data mining is a class of advanced analytical methods that have the ability to automatically (or semi-automatically) assist humans in analyzing the huge data for nuggets of useful knowledge. The knowledge could be represented in the form of rules, regularities, relationships, constraints, etc., which are often referred to as ***Patterns***.

Data mining can simply be defined as follows: Data mining is the process of extracting hidden patterns from large databases.

The notable definitions of data mining are:

- Data mining is the *nontrivial extraction of implicit, previously unknown, and potentially useful information from data.*
- Data mining is a process of semi-automatically analyzing large databases to find patterns that are *valid*, *novel*, *useful* and *understandable*.
- Data mining is the process of extracting *valid, previously unknown, comprehensible* and *actionable* information from large databases and using it to make crucial business decisions.

The patterns (or information) extracted by data mining techniques should possess the following characteristics:

- Implicit—should inherent within the data
- Previously unknown—new knowledge that was not discovered earlier
- Valid—knowledge obtained from historical data should also hold on the new data with some confidence
- Novel—non-obvious to the system
- Potentially useful—should be possible to act on the pattern/knowledge
- Comprehensible/Understandable—humans should be able to interpret the pattern
- Actionable—discovered patterns should lead to business benefit

So, the focus of data mining is to divulge information which is hidden or unexpected, and the patterns and relationships are identified by examining the underlying rules and features of the data. The major goal of data mining is to extract knowledge from large databases and interpret the derived patterns/knowledge in human-understandable form so that decision-makers can use the knowledge and take right decision to improve their businesses. According to Aristotle Onassis, the key to data mining in business is *to know something that nobody else knows.*

Data mining techniques have modulation of manifold disciplines such as Database Management Systems, Machine Learning, Pattern Recognition, Artificial Intelligence, Information Sciences, Computational Statistics, Mathematical Modeling and Visualization.

The application of data mining is emerging as a powerful technology for improving business strategies and designing new products with high quality. It complements and can often replace other business analytics tools, such as reporting and querying and statistical analysis.

17.2 DATA MINING—BUSINESS APPLICATION AREAS

Data mining techniques are useful in taking business decisions in almost all business verticals, such as Banking, Finance, Insurance, Healthcare, Manufacturing and Life Sciences. Potential areas of data mining include Direct Marketing, Fraud detection, churn modeling, cross-sell and up-sell, stock market prediction and sales forecasting. A few application areas are described next.

Target marketing

Target marketing actions such as direct mail campaigns are more expensive to execute, and hence it is necessary to target those individuals which are most likely to buy. Generating business models under various conditions is very difficult and complex. The function of target marketing can be achieved by data mining applications. A lot of business groups in India and abroad, from various business areas, are utilizing these applications for attracting customers on a suit promotion.

Fraud detection

Credit card frauds are the most frequently occurring frauds in banking industry. The fraudulent behaviour may happen when a card is used by a dishonest person. Similarly, in telecommunications, fraudulent behaviour may result when there is a drastic change from normal calling pattern of a customer. In healthcare industry, frauds may occur due to the overbilled medical test and treatments. Most of the fraud detection models analyze the abnormal transactions behaviour by determining the deviation from normal patterns.

Given historical data, the analysts can develop fraud models with a number of attributes describing fraudulent characteristics. Data mining examines all records in a database and detects fraudulent instances according to the fraud models. Data mining can help in early detection of fraudulent behaviour so that frauds can be avoided by taking necessary steps proactively. From the result of the data mining, potential fraud can be prevented.

Risk management

Risk management has been a major concern for investment and insurance industries. In investment industry, such as stock market, the investors often worry about the accuracy of the forecasting rate of return of investment (ROI) in the long run. Data mining is able to identify the best combination of profitable stocks and investment strategies and analyzes the developing market trends. In insurance industry, the policymakers want to know the competitive premium that would attract more customers. Here, data mining technology can cluster the source of customers into the individual, group, and corporate policies. In each group, the premium varies with certain insured items, such as age and health conditions for health insurance.

Other applications of data mining include manufacturing (fault analysis, quality control, preventive maintenance scheduling, automated systems) and Medicine (epidemiological studies, drug discovery, medical diagnosis, risk analysis, clinical trials).

17.3 KDD AND DATA MINING PROCESS

The overall process starting from identifying raw data, pre-processing the data, discovering knowledge from that data to interpreting the knowledge is often referred to as *Knowledge Discovery in Databases* (*KDD*). Figure 17.1 shows the KDD process that involves multiple steps, in which data mining is one. In the data mining step of KDD, one or more data mining methods (or algorithms) are applied on the preprocessed data in order to derive knowledge out of the data. Usually, data mining is an iterative process to extract interesting and useful knowledge from large databases. However, the two terms KDD and Data Mining are synonymously used in real-world applications. The KDD process is described next.

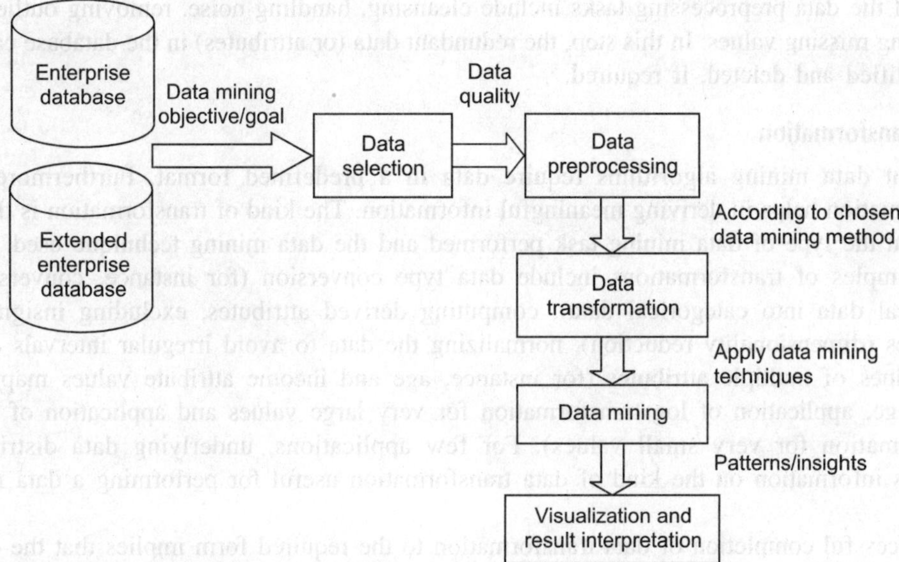

FIGURE 17.1 KDD process.

Determine business objectives

To start creating any data mining solution, first the business objectives must be determined appropriately. A domain expert who is well versed with the business can help in understanding the business objectives whereas a data analyst can map those objectives, in terms of data mining application. Very often the end outcome of data mining application could be initially vaguely known. However, it will be clear over a period of time as the discovery process is going on.

Examples of business objectives for data mining applications are:

- Trend discovery for fast and slow moving products
- Discover purchasing patterns of high-value customers
- Identify fraudulent patterns from credit card transactions

Select the data

Based on the high-level business objectives, the next step is to select the data from which the desired objectives can be met. Usually, an enterprise database consists of data for the entire organization. The key aspect here is to understand the relationships between different data entities in order to discover the useful information. For instance, to recommend items to a customer, data pertaining to customer demographic data, past purchase data and customer feedback data is needed. Some applications may require extended enterprise data such as geographic data, census data and social media data.

The selected data that might have nuggets of information can be moved to a separate set of tables for easy processing of data mining methods.

Data preprocessing

Data preprocessing is needed to improve the data quality in order to analyze the data effectively.

Some of the data preprocessing tasks include cleansing, handling noise, removing outliers and projecting missing values. In this step, the redundant data (or attributes) in the database can also be identified and deleted, if required.

Data transformation

Different data mining algorithms require data in a predefined format. Furthermore, data transformation helps in deriving meaningful information. The kind of transformation is decided based on the type of data mining task performed and the data mining technique used.

Examples of transformations include data type conversion (for instance, conversion of numerical data into categorical data), computing derived attributes, excluding insignificant attributes (dimensionality reduction), normalizing the data to avoid irregular intervals among data values of multiple attributes (for instance, age and income attribute values mapped to 0–1 range, application of log transformation for very large values and application of square transformation for very small values). For few applications, underlying data distribution provides information on the kind of data transformation useful for performing a data mining task.

Successful completion of data transformation to the required form implies that the data is now ready to apply data mining techniques.

Applying data mining techniques

Here, the actual data mining process starts. One or more data mining techniques are used to mine the data in order to extract the patterns. Selection of an appropriate data mining technique to meet the desired business objective is an important activity. Once one or more techniques are chosen, a model is built on the available data (often referred to as historical data). For example, a decision tree model can be constructed to classify whether a loan applicant repays the loan or not, if the loan is sanctioned. Model building is a key step in this overall process. The constructed model is evaluated based on various measures such as accuracy. In case the constructed model is not providing the satisfactory results, it is required to revise the data mining technique and repeat the process. If it is required, additional data need to be considered to meet the data mining goal.

Visualization and result interpretation

The data mining results exhibit the patterns that facilitate business insights. These results are presented in a more sophisticated form so that the decision-maker can easily interpret and use that information for decision-making purpose. Often the results are shown in the visual/graphical forms, such as graphs, charts and histograms. Patterns that are not useful to the businesses can be filtered. A better visualization of insights enables quick and comprehensive view of entire results.

17.4 DATA MINING TASKS

Data mining tasks can be broadly divided into two (Figure 17.2) types: *prediction methods* and *description methods*:

- **Prediction** involves predicting an unknown value (or future values) that is of interest for decision-making using available variables.

- **Description** aims at describing the data using the patterns derived (e.g., rules) and present them in a human–understandable form.

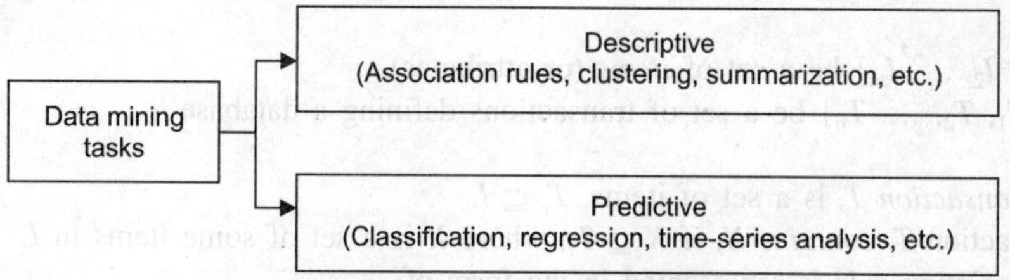

FIGURE 17.2 Data mining tasks.

Recent advances in data mining exhibit *prescriptive results* that facilitate actionable insights as an outcome of data mining. That is, data mining (or analytics) landscape can be treated as ***Descriptive → Predictive → Prescriptive.***

The well-known data mining tasks are given in Table 17.1.

TABLE 17.1 Data Mining Tasks

Task	**Description**
Association rule	Describe dependencies among the data elements (attributes). This type of modeling is also termed as dependency modeling
Classification	Build a model that describes predefined classes and classify (or categorize) an unseen data item (new record) into one of those classes
Clustering	Categorize the given data set into a finite set of classes (or clusters) that describe the data. Unlike classification, in clustering the number of classes is not predefined
Regression	Predict a value of an unknown dependent variable based on the given independent variables
Deviation detection	Discover the abnormal changes that are most significant from normal behaviour in the data
Summarization	Describe summarized (or aggregated) information about the data or subset of the data

A detailed description and algorithms for major data mining tasks, namely, association rules, classification and clustering, is given in the following sections.

17.4.1 Association Rule Mining

Association Rule Mining technique is a quite popular data mining technique to analyze ***market basket data***, where each customer transaction consists of a set of items (or products) purchased by that customer. Customers pick the items from the shelf and place them into their baskets, and hence the name *market basket data.*

The basic idea of Association rules is to discover important associations between sets of attribute values in such a way that the presence of any value of some set in a database record implies the presence of another value belonging to another set. A set of items that occurs together is called as ***Itemset***.

A formal definition of the association rule mining problem can be stated as follows:

Let

$I = \{I_1, I_2, \ldots, I_m\}$ be a set of *items* (or attributes)

$D = \{T_1, T_2, \ldots, T_n\}$ be a set of transactions defining a database

Here,

Each *transaction* T_i is a set of items, $T_i \subseteq I$.

A transaction T_i *contains* X, if $X \subseteq T_i$, where X is a set of some items in I.

An ***association*** *rule* is represented in the form of

$$X \Rightarrow Y,$$

where $X, Y \subseteq I$, and $X \cap Y = \phi$ (i.e., X and Y are two disjoint sets). Here, X is called *antecedent* and B is called *consequent.* X and Y are known as itemsets.

An association rule $X \Rightarrow Y$ means that if X holds in D, then one should expect that Y also holds in D with some probability.

The two commonly used measures for association rules are *support* and *confidence*.

The number of transactions containing X in the database D is called the *frequency* of X, also termed as **support of** X, and can be simply represented as Support (X).

The rule $X \Rightarrow Y$ has ***Support*** S in the database D if the number of transactions in D that contain $X \cup Y$ is at least S. That is, the *support* is the ratio of transactions (records) that contain $X \cup Y$ to the total number of records in the database:

$$\textit{Support} = \textit{prob}\ (X, Y).$$

Alternatively, the support of the association rule $X \Rightarrow Y$ can be represented as

$$\text{Support } (X \Rightarrow Y) = \text{Support } (X \cup Y).$$

The rule holds for the database D with ***Confidence*** C if the number of transactions containing X that also contain Y is at least C. That is, *Confidence* is the ratio of the number of records that contain $X \cup Y$ to the number of records that contain X:

$$\textit{Confidence} = \frac{\text{prob}\ (X, Y)}{\text{prob}\ (X)}$$

Alternatively, the above equation can be represented as

$$\textit{Confidence}\ (X \Rightarrow Y) = \frac{\text{Support } (X \cup Y)}{\text{Support } (X)}$$

The confidence factor indicates the strength of the affinity between the two patterns whereas the support factor indicates the relative frequency with which the rule occurs in the data. For example, consider a sales database in a supermarket. If an item "Coffee" occurs in 20% of the transactions and 15% of the total transactions contain another item "Sugar" and 10% of the transactions contain both these items, then the support for "Coffee" and "Sugar" is said to be 10%, whereas the confidence for "Coffee" ⇒ "Sugar" is 50% because 50% of the transactions that contain "Coffee" also contain "Sugar" and the confidence for "Sugar" ⇒ "Coffee" is 75% because 75% of the transactions containing "Sugar" contain "Coffee".

Consider the following item data:

A	B	C	D	E	F	G
1	1	0	1	1	1	0
0	1	1	0	0	1	1
1	0	0	1	1	0	0
1	0	1	1	1	1	0
1	1	0	1	1	1	1

One of the association rules could be:

A, D, E ⇒ B, F

Support(A, D, E) = (4/5) × 100 = 80%

Support(B, F) = (3/5) × 100 = 60%

Support(A, D, E ⇒ B, F) = (2/5) × 100 = 40%

Confidence(A, D, E ⇒ B, F) = (40/80) × 100 = 50%

The confidence of the rule is 50% and support of the rule is 40%. Hence, one can devise that 50% of total customers who buy products A, D and E also buy products B and F.

Suppose for the association rule B, F ⇒ A, D, E on the same data set, the support is the same as the previous rule (i.e., 40%). However, the confidence is 66.6%.

Confidence (B, F ⇒ A, D, E) = (40/60) × 100 = 66.6%.

An association rule is said to be meaningful if its support and confidence exceed certain **minimum support** (*s*) and **minimum confidence** (*c*) values, respectively.

An itemset is said to be a ***frequent itemset*** if the support of that itemset meets the minimum support criteria.

The minimum support and minimum confidence parameters are user-defined parameters. These parameters are set depending on both application and data set chosen.

Association rules are useful to find the items that are purchased together, promoting items and cross-sell the items. Consider the association rule

{Coffee, … } ⇒ {Sugar}

The following insights/actions can be drawn:

(i) ***Sugar in the consequent:*** Place the items coffee powder and sugar close to each other to increase sugar sales.

(ii) ***Coffee in the antecedent:*** If the supermarket stops selling Coffee powder, one can determine the sales of other items/products that would affect.

(iii) ***Coffee in antecedent and sugar in consequent:*** Which items (for instance, Tea powder) have to be placed near to Coffee to improve sales of Sugar (cross-sell).

A few important factors that should be considered in the context of association rules are as follows:

- Support can be computed for an itemset or an association rule. In the case of association rule, the support is simply the support of antecedent and consequent itemsets together.
- The support measure is associated with an itemset, but whereas the confidence is associated with the association rule. That is, confidence measure cannot be attributed to an itemset, but it is only for a association rule.
- The confidence of an association rule depends on its direction. That is, the confidence of $X \Rightarrow Y$ might be quite different from confidence of $Y \Rightarrow X$. However, the support of an association rule does not depend on the direction of the association rule.

Most of the association rule mining algorithms start with searching for itemsets that satisfy minimum support criteria for a given database and then derive association rules that satisfy minimum confidence.

Association rules can be categorized into multiple ways. One kind of categorization is based on itemsets of interest that indicate positive or negative. Positive association rules ($X \Rightarrow Y$), simply called association rules, describe interestingness and usefulness of a rule. Negative association rules are of the forms $X \Rightarrow \neg B$. These association rules are also useful in some cases where infrequent itemsets of interest are more.

Other classifications of association rules are Boolean and Quantitative. Boolean Association Rules are used to find associations among attributes in a data set, which have values 0 or 1. For instance, market-based data contain only information that indicates whether an item is purchased or not. In general, all data sets contain quantitative attributes rather than Boolean attributes. An example is the market basket data that contains the number of pieces (quantity) for each item purchased in place of simply whether purchased that item or not. Quantitative and Categorical attributes define the quantitative association rules. Mining quantitative association rules discretize the quantitative attributes domain into different intervals. Discovered rules from these intervals are mostly not informative for domain experts as the intervals were not concise and meaningful.

Additional measures for association rules

In addition to support and confidence, there are several measures to exploit association rules. Some of these measures are *Any confidence*, *All confidence, Collective strength*, *Interest* and *Conviction*.

Any confidence is defined as the *confidence* of the rule with the largest *confidence* which can be generated from an itemset. Note that since confidence is not *downward-closed closure property*, *any confidence* cannot be used efficiently as a measure of interestingness. However, finding all itemsets with a set *any confidence* would enable users to find all rules with a given minimum confidence.

All confidence is defined as the smallest *confidence* of all rules, which can be produced from an itemset. That is, all rules produced from an itemset will have a *confidence* greater than or equal to its all-*confidence* value.

Collective strength is a measure to find correlation among itemsets. This measure give results in

- **0** for perfectly negative correlated items,
- ***infinity*** for perfectly positive correlated items and
- **1** if the items co-occur as expected under independence.

For itemsets, collective strength produces values close to 1, even if the itemset appears several times more often than expected together.

Interest (also known as *Lift*) measure finds the dependency among itemsets. This is defined as a factor by which probability of B can be enhanced given A.

A statistical definition of dependence for the sets X and Y is

$$\text{Interest}(X, Y) = \frac{p(X \cup Y)}{p(X)\,p(Y)}$$

Interest of Y given X is one of the main measurements of uncertainty of association rules.

1. If $\frac{p(X \cup Y)}{p(X)\,p(Y)} = 1$, then $p(X \cup Y) = p(X)\,p(Y)$, or Y and X are independent;

2. If $\frac{p(X \cup Y)}{p(X)\,p(Y)} > 1$, then $p(X \cup Y) > p(X)\,p(Y)$, or Y is positively dependent on X; and

3. If $\frac{p(X \cup Y)}{p(X)\,p(Y)} < 1$, then $p(X \cup Y) < p(X)\,p(Y)$, or Y is negatively dependent on X.

Interest measures how many times more often X and Y occur together than expected, with the assumption that both X and Y are statistically independent.

Conviction measure is defined as the reciprocal of the factor by which *probability* of NOT Y can be enhanced given X. This measure is used for finding strength of directed associations. Conviction is defined as follows:

$$\text{conv}(X \to Y) = \frac{(1 - \text{support}(Y))}{(1 - \text{confidence}(X \to Y))}$$

where

(i) $0 < \text{conv}(X \to Y) < \infty$

(ii) X and Y are independent if $\text{conv}(X \to Y) = 1$

(iii) $0 < \text{conv}(X \to Y) < 1$ if and only if Y is negatively correlated with X

(iv) $1 < \text{conv}(X \to Y) < \infty$ if and only if Y is positively correlated with X

17.4.2 Classification

Consider a bank that seeks to minimize loan defaults by identifying potential credit risks during the loan approval cycle. Here, the problem is to predict whether an applicant will be a good or poor debtor. This is an example of classification problem and there are two classes (often referred to as *class label*): Good and Poor. So, the aim of classification is to group the records into a set of predefined classes.

Figure 17.3 illustrates the classification process. Given a set of objects, the classification process identifies each object class it belongs to. In Figure 17.3, there are four predefined classes, namely, Square, Circle, Rectangle and Triangle. The figure shows all the objects in one bucket initially and placed into four different buckets after the classification process. Note that this figure is for understanding the process; however, each object corresponds to one record in a database, and classification approach follows specific procedures to carry out classification.

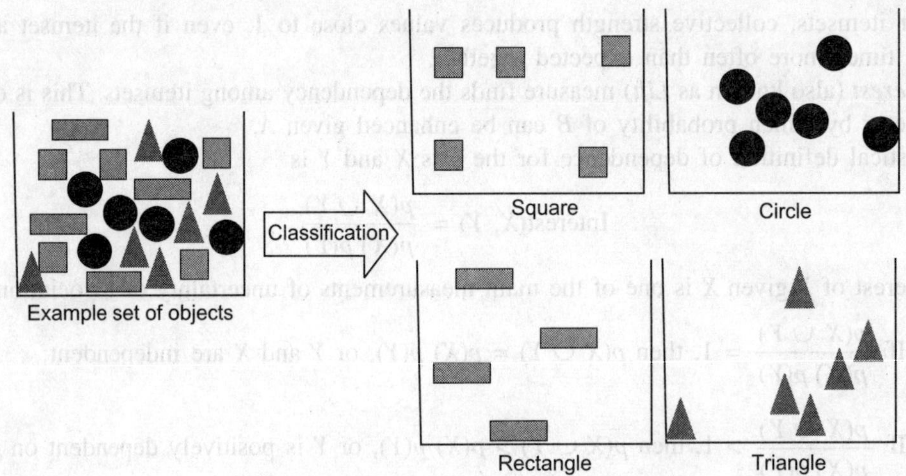

FIGURE 17.3 Classification—example.

Classification task divides the given data into disjoint groups (also known as classes). It involves finding models (or rules) that partition the data into classes for future prediction. So, the goal of classification is to build a concise model that can be used to predict the class label of future unlabelled records.

For performing classification, the data (historical data) is usually divided into two sets: training data and test data. The data contains multiple attributes or features, out of which there is one distinguished attribute called the *class label*. Training data is used to build the classification model and the test data is used to evaluate the model.

Classification is also known as *supervised learning* because the class labels are already known previously and a model is built based on the class labels of training data. Class label attribute is called dependent attribute and the other attributes are often called independent attributes.

There are several well-known classification techniques, including decision tree, *k*-nearest neighbour, Bayes classification, neural networks and genetic algorithms.

Classification model evaluation

The classifier outcomes, which are required to evaluate the performance of a classifier, can be represented in the form of a confusion matrix (Table 17.2). A ***confusion matrix*** contains information about actual and predicted classifications done by a classification system. The confusion matrix lists the correct classification against the predicted classification for each class.

Table 17.2 derives the following measures (baselines) to facilitate the classifier performance:

- True positive rate (TP rate) is the percentage of correctly classified positive samples.
- True negative rate (TN rate) is the percentage of correctly classified negative samples.
- False positive rate (FP rate) is the percentage of negative samples predicted as positives.
- False negative rate (FN rate) is the percentage of positive samples predicted as negative.

TABLE 17.2 Confusion Matrix

	Predicted negative	Predicted positive
Actual Negative	TN	FP
Actual Positive	FN	TP

The goal of any ideal classifier is to maximize TP and TN rates. The accuracy, precision and recall values for model evaluation are calculated from the confusion matrix as follows:

$$\text{Accuracy} = \frac{(\text{TP} + \text{TN})}{(\text{TP} + \text{FP} + \text{TN} + \text{FN})}$$

$$\text{TP}_{\text{rate}} = \text{Recall} = \frac{\text{TP}}{(\text{TP} + \text{FN})}$$

$$\text{Precision} = \frac{\text{TP}}{(\text{TP} + \text{FP})}$$

$$\text{F–measure} = \frac{2 \times \text{Recall} \times \text{Precision}}{\text{Recall} + \text{Precision}}$$

Here, recall measure shows the ability of correctly predicting positive samples from all (actual) positive samples in a given data set. Precision measure indicates the accuracy provided that a specific class has been correctly predicted.

Classifiers are also validated by drawing ***ROC*** (Receiver Operating Characteristics) ***curves***. A ROC curve is a graphical plot of the *sensitivity* versus *1 – specificity* for a binary classifier system as its discrimination threshold is varied. This plot is equivalent to draw between TP rate and FP rate. Sensitivity and Specificity can be calculated from confusion matrix as

$$\text{Sensitivity} = \text{TP}/(\text{TP} + \text{FN})$$
$$\text{Specificity} = \text{TN}/(\text{FP} + \text{TN})$$

ROC curves provide a visual tool for examining the trade-off between the ability of a classifier to correctly identify positive cases and the number of negative cases that are incorrectly classified. Discrete classifiers, such as decision trees or rule sets, are designed to produce a discrete class value for each instance. This results in the single pair of TP and FP values, which in turn generate single point on the curve. The discrete classifier can be used with a threshold to produce a curve. If the classifier output is above the threshold, the instance is classified as positive else negative.

Given a particular threshold value, a confusion matrix is obtained when the classifier is applied to a data set. With a set of threshold values, a set of confusion matrices is obtained, and hence a set of (false positives rate, true positive rate) pairs is obtained. These points when plotted on Cartesian space results in ROC curve. Each point on the curve corresponds to classifier's performance at a particular cut-off. The ROC curve can also be used to select a threshold value, trading off between the true positive rate and the false positive rate.

ROC curves are extensively used to compare the performance of two or more classification models and select the best model. Figure 17.4 shows ROC curves for two typical classification models. The more the ROC curve of a model is towards northwest, the better is the model performance. This is because a higher true positive rate can be achieved with a lesser false positive rate as the curve is more towards northwest. In Figure 17.4, the classification performance of model 1 is better than that of model 2.

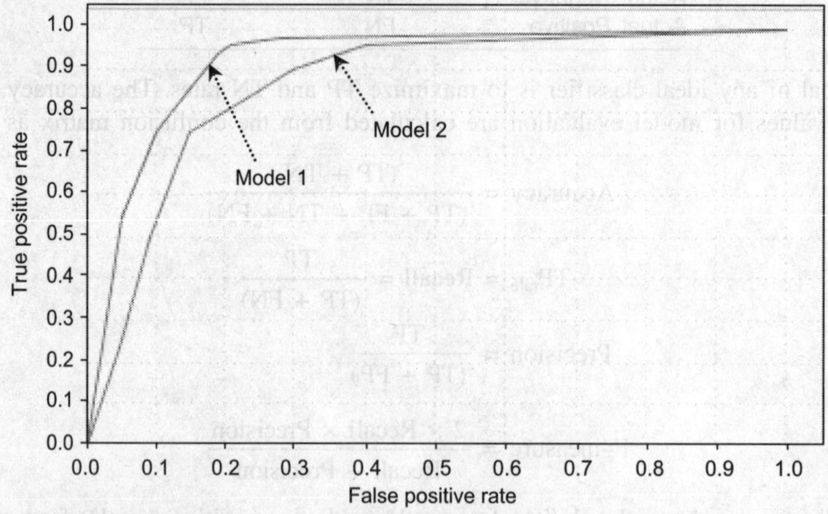

FIGURE 17.4 ROC curves of two typical classification models.

However, plotting the ROC curves of different models may not directly show which model is better in performance. This is because the curves may overlap and it may become difficult to choose the best model. To address this problem, the **Area Under ROC curve** (AUC) is used as a measure to evaluate the classification model's performance. The higher the AUC value, the better the performance of the classification model.

Another approach to determine the performance of a classifier is ***k-fold Cross-Validation***. Cross-validation is a resampling technique. Usually, to build a classification model, the historical data set is divided into two sets: training data and testing data. The model is built using the training data and validated using test data. In *k*-fold cross-validation, the entire data is divided into *k* partitions of an equal size and one partition out of *k* is chosen for testing and rest *k*–1 partitions for training. This process is repeated *k* times and in each run a new partition is chosen for testing and others for training so that each partition is participated in the testing exactly once. Average of all the *k* iteration measure values is considered for the final value. The commonly used *k*-fold cross-validation is the 10-fold cross-validation.

17.4.3 Clustering

Clustering is a very fundamental and starting step for most of the data analysis. Clustering task categorizes the given data into groups (classes), where similar data together form each group. That is, members of each cluster share a number of common properties. Clustering results in understandable groups so that one can label each group. In clustering, the number of classes/ groups is not known previously, and hence the clustering process is often referred to as

Unsupervised classification. Suppose there are objects with different shapes (namely, square, circle and triangle) as shown in Figure 17.5. Clustering process will group all the similar objects into one class as shown in Figure 17.6. After formation of the groups, each group can be assigned a class label based on the characteristic nature of that group (such as Square, Circle and Triangle in Figure 17.6). Note that, unlike classification, the total number of classes is not known before the clustering process. However, an intuitive number on the number of classes will help in applying some of the clustering methods.

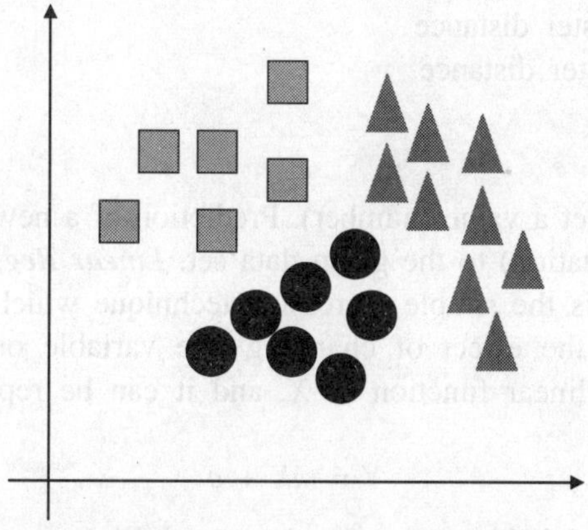

FIGURE 17.5 Example set of objects.

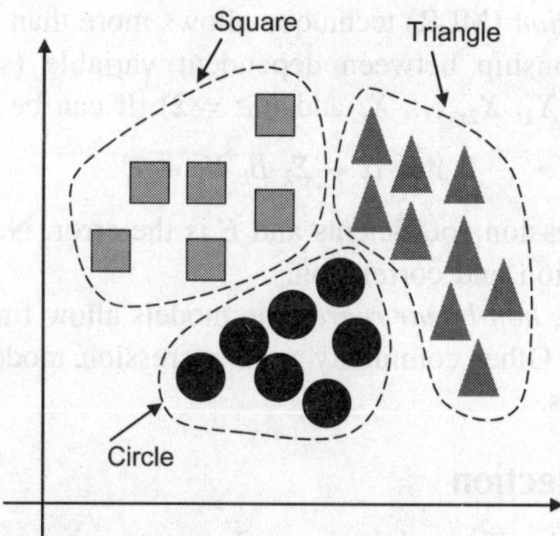

FIGURE 17.6 Grouping the objects of Figure 17.5 based on the shape.

Since there are no class labels for data to be clustered, there is no distinction between dependent and independent attributes in the clustering task.

Clustering algorithms find a partition that optimizes the chosen partitioning criterion. Since the number of possible partitions is large, certain heuristics are used to find a near-optimal solution. Clustering algorithms partition the data set into different groups or clusters on the basis of similarity or distance among records. The quality of the cluster formed is dependent on the different similarity measures chosen. The goal of clustering is to group a set of patterns into a number of more or less homogeneous clusters with respect to a suitable similarity measure. Patterns that are similar are allocated to the same cluster, while the patterns that differ significantly are put in different clusters. So, the clustering process can be defined as follows: Given a set of records where each record has a set of attributes, find clusters such that the records in one cluster are more similar to one another and the records in different clusters are dissimilar to one another. The two important properties of clustering are:

- Maximize inter-cluster distance
- Minimize intra-cluster distance

17.4.4 Regression

Regression is used to predict a value (number). Prediction of a new value is done by fitting a predefined function (or equation) to the given data set. *Linear Regression* (also referred to as *Straight Line Regression*) is the simple regression technique which fits the given data into a straight line. It estimates the effect of changing one variable on another variable. Linear regression models Y as a linear function of X, and it can be represented as a straight line equation as shown below:

$$Y = mX + c$$

Linear regression finds suitable values for slope m and intercept c, and predicts the y value for a given x value. Here, m and c are known as regression coefficients. Regression model finds the best values for function parameters so that they minimize the error (e.g., sum of squared error).

Multiple Linear Regression (MLR) technique allows more than one input variable. MLR is useful to study the relationship between dependent variable (say, Y) and two or more independent variables (say, X_1, X_2, ..., X_k and $k \geq = 2$). It can be represented as

$$Y = \alpha + \Sigma_k \beta_k X_k + E$$

Here, α and β_k are the regression coefficients and E is the error. Note that MLR combines the ideas of both linear regression and correlation.

Unlike linear regression, *non-linear regression* models allow fitting of higher order models such as quadratic or cubic. Other commonly used regression models are *Logistic regression*, *Logit* and *Probit* regressions.

17.4.5 Deviation Detection

Deviation detection is to identify outlying records (or transactions, events) in a given data set and derive the cause for deviation. Deviations may arise due to (i) noise, (ii) outliers, (iii) impurities present in the data and (iv) trivial reasons. So, ***deviation detection** is the process of determining the objects that are different from other objects.*

Data segmentation is useful to discover useful patterns pertaining to each segment and analyze further any deviation (or exception) from previously derived patterns for new samples. The deviations can be obtained by calculating the values of measures of current data and then comparing them with the previous data as well as with the normal data.

Deviation detection approaches are useful to predict misuse detection and abnormality detection. Moreover, these techniques are also useful to find both new phenomenon and unusual behaviour.

There are three kinds of approaches for deviation detection: *model based*, *proximity based* and *density based*. In the model-based approach, first a model is build (using some data mining techniques such as clustering) on a data set and then an object (or a new object) is determined that do not fit into the model as an exception. Consider a clustering example where the clusters are formed for a given data set. If an object does not belong to any cluster, it can be treated as an abnormal object. In the proximity-based approach, a proximity measure to compute among the objects is defined and an object is found out that is distant from most of the objects using that measure. An example of proximity measure is threshold distance. In the case of density-based approach, density of the objects is estimated, and regions that have low density are determined. The objects that are in low density are potential candidates for abnormal objects. An example of determining low density objects is that of objects which have less number of neighbours in a certain radius.

Application of deviation detection are fraud detection, customer retention, intrusion detection (for Networks), rare symptom detection (for health care), natural disasters (such as floods, tsunamis, hurricanes), etc.

17.4.6 Summarization

Summarization provides a concise view of the given data or subset of the data. It could be a more generalization or high-level abstraction of the data. So, ***summarization** is the process of reducing the data in a meaningful and intelligent manner so that it exhibits important and relevant features of the data.*

Often the data is aggregated and presented in tabular reports during data analysis. Another example of summarization is Text summarization, where useful information is extracted for large sets of documents and presented in a summarized form. The goal of summarization is to condense a given set of transactions into a smaller set such that (i) there is no loss of important and useful information and (ii) maximum possible information is retained.

17.5 ADVANCED DATA MINING AREAS

Owing to increase in capturing data in various forms, data mining has become a common approach for analyzing the data. Data sources are very diverse and appear in varied forms. Based on the kind of data, there are advanced data mining techniques which are mainly based on the data they employ.

Web mining

World Wide Web (WWW) has become a ubiquitous tool, used in day-to-day work, to find information and conduct business over Internet. Navigation is one of the main activities of users interacting with the web, where users follow the link and browse the destination web pages. Web mining is the process of discovering hidden patterns from web data. Web data mining is mainly categorized into three types: Web content mining, Web structure mining and Web usage mining.

- *Web content mining* discovers the useful information from data collected by search engines and web spiders.
- *Web structure mining* tries to discover the structure of a particular website. The model is based on the topology of hyperlinks with or without the description of links.
- *Web usage mining* tries to make sense of the data gathered by the web surfers' behaviours.

While the web content and structure mining utilize the real or primary data on the web, web usage mining uses the secondary data derived from the interactions of users while interacting with the web. Web usage data includes the data from web server access logs, proxy server logs, user profiles, registration data, user sessions or transactions, cookies, user queries, bookmark data, mouse clicks, scrolls and any other data resulting from the interaction.

An example of web usage mining is clickstream data mining. Clickstream is a sequence of URLs browsed by a user within a particular website in one session. A user session is the clickstream of page views for a single user in the website. Finding the pattern of groups of users with similar interest and motivation for visiting that particular website can be done by clustering users' clickstream on a particular website.

Sequence mining

Sequence mining involves mining sequence data. Sequential data may arise from diverse application domains which may have time stamp associated with it or not. That is, sequential data can be temporal or non-temporal. Temporal data are those data which have time stamp attached to them. Non-temporal data are those which are ordered with respect to some dimension other than time such as space.

Examples of sequence data include music files, system calls, transaction records, web logs, genomic data and so on. In these data, there are hidden relations that should be explored to find interesting information. For example, from web logs one can extract the information regarding the most frequent access path, from genomic data one can extract letter or motif (the sequence of letters) frequencies, from music files one can discover harmonies, etc. One can extract features from sequential data, represent them as vectors and classify (supervised or unsupervised) the data using existing clustering/classification techniques.

Sequence pattern mining is a branch of sequence mining where sequence association rules are generated. In the discovery of association rules, we are interested in finding associations between items irrespective of their order of occurrence. But it is more relevant to identify whether there is some pattern in the occurrence of all these items. Then it is more likely to conclude that the items are not just associated, but one is influencing the occurrence of another. Thus, the discovery of temporal sequences of events concerns casual relationships among the events in a sequence.

Data stream mining

Data stream mining is concerned with extraction of knowledge represented in the form of models and patterns from non-stopping streams of data. Advances in hardware, software and sensor technology in the recent years have enabled the capture of different measurements of continuously generated and highly fluctuating data in a wide range of fields, including sensor networks and computer network traffic. The storage, querying and mining of such data sets are highly computationally intensive. Therefore, many data mining operations such as classification, clustering and frequent pattern mining become significantly more challenging in this context.

Other advanced data mining techniques include text mining, image mining, spatial data mining, social network data mining, big data mining, etc.

17.6 SUMMARY

Data Mining or Knowledge Discovery in Databases (KDD) is a rapidly emerging field. Business competition requires timely and sophisticated analysis on the data and data mining techniques act as an aid to these decision support tools for making a timely and effective decision. Companies have deployed a wide range of successful applications of data mining systems to get insights into their data. Since the applications of data mining are broad and diverse, it is expected that various kinds of data mining techniques have to be explored. Commercial databases often contain critical business information concerning past performance which could be used to predict the future. This chapter provided an overview of data mining and its applications. Data mining tasks such as association rules, classification and clustering are described in this chapter.

SHORT/OBJECTIVE TYPE QUESTIONS

1. The goal of data mining is
   (a) To confirm on existence of the data
   (b) To discover some interesting patterns
   (c) To retrieve the data for some expected query
   (d) To create a data warehouse

2. Define Data Mining.

3. Which of the following is used to generate class labels?
   (a) Classification
   (b) Clustering
   (c) Association Rules
   (d) Deviation Detection

4. The best example of association rule mining is ____________________.

5. ____________________ is used to generate frequently occurring patterns from large databases.

6. __________and ________ are two measures used to generate association rules.

7. Which of the following is a measure to compare Classification algorithms?
   (a) Accuracy
   (b) F-measure
   (c) RoC curve
   (d) All the above

8. In ________ technique, the class labels are not known and the number of classes may not be known in advance for learning.

9. What is Regression?

10. Web Mining is not one of the following:
(a) Web Structure
(b) Web Service
(c) Web Content
(d) Web Usage

WORKOUT SECTION

W17_1 Explain and distinguish predictive and descriptive data mining tasks.

W17_2 Describe various applications of Data Mining.

W17_3 Explain the process of KDD and describe its steps.

W17_4 Describe evaluation measures/approaches for classification methods.

W17_5 The transaction database is shown in the following table:

	Items				
Transaction ID	**A**	**B**	**C**	**D**	**E**
T_1	1	1	1	0	0
T_2	1	1	1	1	1
T_3	0	0	1	1	0
T_4	1	0	1	1	1
T_5	1	1	0	1	0

Find Support (A); Support (E), Support (A, C), Support (B, D, E), Confidence (A $\rightarrow$ C), Confidence (A, D $\rightarrow$ B, E).

18

Data Mining Techniques

Learning Objectives

You will learn following key concepts after completion of the chapter:

- ✓ Describing the basic data mining algorithms and understand their strengths and weaknesses
- ✓ Understand how to choose algorithms for different data mining tasks
- ✓ Study the Apriori algorithm and demonstrate the impact of Apriori principle for association rule generation
- ✓ Able to apply basic algorithms for supervised and unsupervised classifications
- ✓ Study *k*-NN and Naïve Bayes classification
- ✓ How to construct decision trees
- ✓ Understand the algorithmic details of *k*-Means and its extension
- ✓ Learning the underlying ideas of agglomerative hierarchical clustering
- ✓ Learning practical use of data mining techniques through case studies

18.1 INTRODUCTION

The general problem one encounters during mining the data is that of finding effective methodologies and algorithms which produce models to represent the patterns, regularities or trends in business data. This chapter presents algorithms and methods for association rule mining, classification and clustering. We also illustrate data mining case studies for industrial applications.

18.2 ASSOCIATION RULES

The process of generating association rules involves identifying the frequent itemsets using the parameters ***confidence*** and ***support***. Association rules are typically mined by following a two-phase strategy as follows:

1. Finding frequent itemsets for a given minimum support (i.e., support of frequent itemset ≥ minimum support)

2. Generating association rules from the frequent itemsets resulted from step 1 that satisfies minimum confidence (i.e., confidence of association rule ≥ minimum confidence)

Finding frequent itemsets from a given database is a computation intensive task. Various approaches have been proposed to minimize the computational efforts.

The second step of generating association rules from frequent itemsets is relatively straightforward and does not require to access the database. For each frequent itemset F, output all rules:

Rule $(F, a) : a \Rightarrow F - a$

where a is subset of F and Confidence of Rule(F, a) ≥ minimum-confidence.

Consider a frequent itemset $F = \{a, b, c\}$. The possible rules are:

$\{a\} \Rightarrow \{b, c\}$

$\{b\} \Rightarrow \{a, c\}$

$\{c\} \Rightarrow \{a, b\}$

$\{a, b\} \Rightarrow \{c\}$

$\{a, c\} \Rightarrow \{b\}$

$\{b, c\} \Rightarrow \{a\}$

From the above rules, the rules that have confidence more than or equal to minimum confidence will qualify as association rules.

To optimize the search for the frequent itemsets, the algorithms use two closure properties (known as Apriori principles):

1. ***Property 1:*** If an itemset is infrequent, all its supersets must be infrequent and they need not be examined further.
2. ***Property 2:*** If an itemset is frequent, all its subsets must be frequent and they need not be examined further.

The two approaches for generating association rules based on the two above properties are bottom-up and top-down approaches, respectively.

18.2.1 Apriori Algorithm

Apriori algorithm is the first and popular association rule mining algorithm that discovers frequent itemsets in a database. This algorithm was developed by Agrawal and Srikant in 1994. Apriori algorithm is a levelwise ***algorithm***. That is, it considers itemsets with different cardinality at each step.

The Apriori algorithm starts by counting the single itemsets by scanning the database. Here, 1-itemset, referred to as F_1, is the frequent itemset that has only one item and satisfies the minimum support criteria. In the second step, we consider 2-itemsets for counting. We count those 2-itemsets (F_2) that contain only 1-itemsets as subsets, and all other 2-itemsets are pruned. In the third step, the algorithm proceeds with the 3-itemsets (F_3) that contain only frequent 2-itemsets as subsets. Continuing in this way, at step k, we get frequent k-itemsets, F_k.

At each step, first *potential (k)-itemsets* are generated from elements in F_{k-1}. Then their support is computed by scanning the database, discarding those itemsets whose support is below the minimum support. The result is the list of frequent itemsets F_k.

The iterations continue until no more itemsets can be generated. So, the algorithm stops when F_k is empty or when k reaches the maximum itemset length (l_m). Frequent itemsets are obtained by merging frequent itemsets at all levels ($F_1 \cup F_2 \cup \ldots \cup F_k$; $k = 1$ to l_m).

The two terms, namely, *Frequent itemsets* and *Large itemsets,* are used synonymously to refer to itemsets that qualify minimum support criteria.

The Apriori algorithm is given below. It calls two functions: AprioriGen and Prune.

```
APRIORI Algorithm
procedure AprioriAlgorithm()
begin
   F1 := {frequent 1-itemsets};
   for ( k := 2; Fk-1 ≠ Ø; k++ ) do
   {
      Ck= AprioriGen(Fk-1); // generating potential candidates at level k.

      Prune(Ck) // Prune the candidates whose subsets are not frequent.

      for all transactions T in the dataset do //scan the database and count the
                                                // remaining candidate itemsets.
      {
         for all candidates c ∈ Ck contained in T do
         c:count++
      }
      Fk = { c ∈ Ck | c:count >= min-support}
   }
   Answer := ∪ Fk
end

AprioriGen(Fk-1)
begin
   Ck = Ø
      //self-joining
   For all itemsets l1 ∈ Fk-1 do
      For all itemsets l2 ∈ Fk-1 do
         If l1[1] = l2[1] ∧ l1[2] = l2[2] ∧ … ∧ l1[k-1] = l2[k-1]
            Then c = l1[1], l1[2],…. l1[k-1], l2[k-1]
      Ck= Ck ∪ {c}
End

prune (Ck)
begin
   for all itemsets c ∈ Ck
      for all (k-1)-subsets d of c do
         if d ∉ Fk-1
            then delete c from Ck
end
```

The **AprioriGen** function takes as argument F_{k-1}, the set of all frequent (k–1)-itemsets. It returns a superset of the set of all candidate frequent k-itemsets, say C_k. The **Prune** function takes C_k as argument and deletes all itemsets $c \in C_k$ for those any (k–1)-subset of c is not frequent (i.e. not existing in F_{k-1}).

Consider the following sample database

Transaction Id	Tea	Beans	Oil	Potato	Chocos	Lime
1	1	0	1	1	0	0
2	0	0	0	1	1	0
3	1	0	1	1	1	0
4	1	0	0	0	0	1

Here, there are six items T, B, O, P, C, L. Let the minimum support is 2.

Step 1:

Candidate ItemSet C_1		Frequent ItemSet F_1	
Itemset	Support	Itemset	Support
{T}	3	{T}	3
{B}	0	{0}	2
{0}	2	{P}	3
{P}	3	{C}	2
{C}	2		
{L}	1		

Step 2:

Candidate ItemSet C_2		Frequent ItemSet F_2	
Itemset	Support	Itemset	Support
{T, O}	2	{T, O}	2
{T, P}	2	{T, P}	3
{T, C}	1	{O, P}	2
{O, P}	2	{P, C}	2
{O, C}	1		
{P, C}	2		

Step 3:

Candidate ItemSet C_2		Frequent ItemSet F_3	
Itemset	Support	Itemset	Support
{T, O, P}	2	{T, O, P}	2

The process stops as there is no 4-itemset generation from the 3-itemset. Note that in step 3 the itemsets {T, P, C} and {O, P, C} are eliminated by the pruning step. These two itemsets are not generated as part of the candidate itemsets C_3. This is because all subsets of these itemsets are not frequent. Here, the subsets for {T, P, C} are {T, P}, {P, C}, {T, C}, {T}, {P} and {C}. Out of these subsets, {T, C} is not having minimum support. According to the Apriori principle, if an itemset is frequent, all its subsets must be frequent. Hence, the itemset {T, P, C} is an infrequent itemset. Similarly, the subset {O, C} is infrequent (see step 2), and thus {O, P, C} is also infrequent.

Several extensions to the Apriori algorithm, as well as new algorithms, have been developed to discover association rules. In addition to Apriori algorithm, well-known algorithms for association rule mining include Dynamic Itemset Counting (DIC) algorithm, Pincer Search algorithm, Frequent Pattern (FP)–Tree Growth algorithm and Partition algorithm. Some other area of work in this direction includes mining generalized and multi-level association rules by progressive deepening, meta-rule guided mining of association rules in relational databases and interesting measurement for association rules. Also, several techniques have been incorporated that improve the efficiency of mining association rules using database scan reduction, sampling, incremental updating of discovered association rules and parallel and distributed data mining.

18.3 DISTANCE/SIMILARITY MEASURES

Several classification and clustering algorithms require finding distance (or similarity) between objects or records. A brief description of commonly used distance/similarity measures is given in this section.

The distance between objects is measured based on the distance metric. The distance metric to be considered is dependent on the type of attributes considered for analyzing. Each distance metric should satisfy the following conditions:

1. *Distance (x, y) >= 0*: non-negativity
2. *Distance (x, y) = 0*, if and only if *x = y*: distance of an object to itself is zero
3. *Distance (x, y) = Distance (y, x)*: symmetry
4. *Distance (x, z) <= Distance (x, y) + Distance (y, z)*: triangle inequality

Some of the distance metrics for different types of attributes are explained next..

Euclidean distance

Euclidean distance is a widely used distance measure for vector spaces to find the distance between two points. For two vectors X (X_1, X_2, …., X_n) and Y (Y_1, Y_2, …, Y_n) in an n-dimensional Euclidean space, it is defined as the square root of the sum of difference of the corresponding dimensions of the vector. Mathematically, it is given as

$$D(X, Y) = \left[\sum_{s=1}^{n}(X_s - Y_s)^2\right]^{1/2}$$

Note that the size of the two vectors (the number of attributes in the case of database) must be the same to compute the Euclidean distance. Moreover, the data must be in numeric form. Normalizing the data may be needed if ranges of different attribute values are diverse.

Jaccard similarity

Jaccard similarity function is used for measuring similarity between binary values. It is defined as the degree of commonality between two sets. It is measured as a ratio of the number of common attributes of *X* AND *Y* to the number of elements possessed by *X* OR *Y*. If *X* and *Y* are two distinct sets then the similarity between *X* and *Y* is:

$$S(X, Y) = \frac{|X \cap Y|}{|X \cup Y|}$$

Consider two sets $X = \langle M, N, P, Q, R, M, S, Q\rangle$ and $Y = \langle P, M, N, Q, M, P, P\rangle$. $X \cap Y$ is given as $\langle M, N, P, Q\rangle$ and $X \cup Y$ is $\langle M, N, P, Q, R, S\rangle$. Thus, the similarity between *X* and *Y* is 0.66.

Cosine similarity

Cosine similarity is a widely used vector–based similarity measure. Cosine similarity metric calculates the angle of difference in the direction of two vectors, irrespective of their lengths. Cosine similarity between two vectors *X* and *Y* is given by

$$S(X, Y) = \frac{|X \bullet Y|}{|X|\,|Y|}$$

Here, $X \bullet Y$ is the dot product of *X* and *Y* vectors.

If the data is in the form of sets, first they need to be converted into *n*-dimensional vector space. This is because direct application of Cosine similarity measure is not possible across sets. Cosine similarity measure is applied over the transformed vectors to find the angular similarity. For two sets $X = \langle M, N, P, Q, R, M, S, Q\rangle$ and $Y = \langle P, M, N, Q, M, P, P\rangle$, the equivalent transformed frequency vector is $X' = <2, 1, 1, 2, 1, 1>$ and $Y' = <2, 1, 3, 1, 0, 0>$. The Cosine similarity of the transformed vector is 0.745.

18.4 CLASSIFICATION

18.4.1 *k*-NN Classifier

The *k*-nearest neighbour (*k*-NN) classifier is a simple classifier and it is based on learning by analogy. *k*-Nearest neighbour is a predictive technique suitable for classification models. Unlike other predictive algorithms, the training data is not scanned or processed to create the model. Instead, the training data itself is the model. When a new case is presented to the model, the algorithm looks at all the data to find a subset of cases that are most similar to it and uses them to predict the outcome. That is, in *k*-nearest neighbour classification, the *k* closest patterns are found and a voting scheme is used to determine the outcome.

The *k*-NN classification algorithm assumes that all instances correspond to points in an *n*-dimensional space. Nearest neighbours of an instance are described by a distance/similarity measure. When a new unknown sample comes, a *k*-NN classifier searches the pattern space for the *k* training samples closest to the unknown samples using distance or similarity measure for building the training data set. These *k* training samples are the *k*-nearest neighbours of the new sample. The new unknown sample is assigned the most common class among its *k*-nearest neighbours. Nearest neighbour algorithm can be summarized as follows:

```
Algorithm: k-NN

Input:
  D →Training Data
  k →Number of nearest neighbours
  s →new unknown sample
Output:
  c →class label assigned to new sample s

Begin
  Let I1.. Ik denote the k instances from training set T that are nearest
    to new unknown sample s
  C = the class from k nearest neighbor samples with maximum count.
    Return (c).
End
```

Consider the training data set shown in Table 18.1 to predict the credit risk. Each row corresponds to a case. Here, Debt, Income and Marital status are independent attributes. Credit risk is the dependent attribute. The goal is to predict whether an applicant will have a *Good* or a *Poor* Credit Risk. The same records as shown in Table 18.1 are used for prediction in this example.

TABLE 18.1 Credit Risk Training Data Set

Name	Debt	Income	Marital status	Risk
Raman	High	High	Married	Good
Anil	Low	High	Married	Good
Sharma	Low	High	Unmarried	Poor
Suma	High	Low	Married	Poor
Rao	Low	Low	Married	Poor

Let $k = 3$, that is 3-NN. The distance measure used is a simple metric that is computed by summing scores for each of the three independent columns, where the score for a column is 0 if the values in the two instances are the same and 1 if they differ. For example, the distance between Anil and Sharma is 1, since the three column scores for them are 0, 0 and 1 as they have a different value is only "Marital Status". For simplicity, equal weights are assigned to the attributes *Debt*, *Income* and *Marital Status*. Table 18.2 shows all the distances between all the records in the training data set.

TABLE 18.2 Distances between Cases

	Raman	Anil	Sharma	Suma	Rao
Raman	0	1	2	1	2
Anil		0	1	2	1
Sharma			0	3	2
Suma				0	1
Rao					0

The three nearest neighbours to Raman are Raman (self), Anil and Suma because they have the lowest distance scores. Here, Raman is considered to be nearer to Raman himself, because the test data and training data are the same in this case. The Risk values for Raman's three nearest neighbours (Raman himself, Anil and Suma) are *Good*, *Good* and *Poor,* respectively. Now, the predicted Risk for Raman is the value that is most frequent among the three neighbours, that is, *Good*, in this case.

In cases when more than three neighbours have the same distance, one can include all of them, exclude all of them or include all of them with a proportionate vote. For example, to compute Anil's nearest three neighbours, other than Anil himself, there are three neighbours, namely, Raman, Sharma and Rao, having the same distance, that is, 1. Thus, Anil is very near to Anil himself (with distance 0), and we have to select next nearest 2 cases out of 3, that is, from Raman, Sharma and Rao. If we consider the proportionate vote option to decide, we get 2/3 vote each for this example, resulting in votes of *Good* (Anil himself), 2/3 *Good*, 2/3 *Poor* and 2/3 *Poor*, for a consensus of *Good*. However, the decision of selecting one among the three options is entirely dependent on the implementation of the algorithm.

The *k*-NN technique does not classify a case if there is no majority outcome out of *k* neighbours. For example, consider the three nearest neighbours of Sharma: Sharma himself (with distance 0), Anil (with distance 1) and Raman and Rao, both having the same distance, that is, 2. Again, if we consider the proportionate vote option to decide one from neighbours Raman and Rao, we get 1/2 vote for each. Thus, we have the resulting votes of *Poor* (Sharma himself), *Good* (Anil with distance 1), 1/2 *Good* (Raman with distance 2) and 1/2 *Poor* (Rao with distance 2). Here, half of the nearest neighbours are Good and other half of the nearest neighbours are Poor, and hence there is no consensus on the outcome and the case Sharma is Unclassified (see Table 18.3). To avoid these circumstances, another value of *k* can be selected with the help of an expert by iteratively testing with different *k* values. Table 18.3 shows the predictions from the 3-NN algorithm for the present sample training data.

TABLE 18.3 Predicted Risks Based on 3-NN

Name	Debt	Income	Married?	Actual risk	Predicted risk
Raman	High	High	Married	Good	Good
Anil	Low	High	Married	Good	Good
Sharma	Low	High	Unmarried	Poor	Unclassified
Suma	High	Low	Married	Poor	Poor
Rao	Low	Low	Married	Poor	Poor

In *k*-NN model, the choice of a suitable distance function and the number of nearest neighbours (*k*) are very crucial. The parameter *k* represents the complexity of nearest neighbour model.

The chosen distance measure is important because the choice of a measure greatly affects the predictions. Different measures, used on the same training data, can result in completely different predictions. In *k*-NN classification, each new case being predicted requires a complete pass through the training data to compute the distance between the target instance and each instance in the training set. The algorithm keeps track of *k* nearest instances as it proceeds through the training set, predicting an outcome when the pass is complete.

18.4.2 Naïve Bayes Classification

Naïve Bayes classifier is one of the simplest probabilistic classifiers that works well for many applications. This technique is fast to classify the categorical data. Naïve Bayes classification applies Bayes' theorem with strong (naïve) independence assumptions. The classifier is called naïve as the classes defined are mutually exclusive and independent. The attributes are defined independently from the class.

Naïve Bayes technique is based on the concept of conditional probabilities derived from observed frequencies in the training data. Bayes' theorem finds the probability of an event occurring given the probability of another event that has already occurred. If an event B represents the dependent event and the event A represents the prior event, Bayes' theorem can be stated as follows:

$$P(B|A) = \frac{P(A \mid B) \times P(B)}{P(A)}$$

Here,

$P(B|A)$ is the ***conditional probability*** of B given evidence A. Conditional property is also referred to as *posterior probability*.

$P(A|B)$ is the ***conditional probability*** of A given B.

$P(B)$ is the ***prior probability*** (also known as *marginal probability*) of B. This is called *prior* because this is calculated without incorporating the information available in A.

$P(A)$ is the *priori probability* of A.

The ratio $P(B|A)/P(A)$ is called Standardized likelihood function.

Given a set of attributes $(A_1, A_2, \ldots, A_n)$, the goal is to predict class C. That is, find the value of C that maximizes $P(C|A_1, A_2, \ldots, A_n)$.

$$P(C \mid A_1, A_2, \ldots, A_n) = \frac{P(A_1, A_2, \ldots, A_n \mid C) \times P(C)}{P(A_1, A_2, \ldots, A_n)}$$

Here, $P(A_1, A_2, \ldots, A_n|C)$ is the joint probability distribution function, which is equivalent to the product of individual conditional probabilities (also known as likelihood function) as given below.

$$P(A_1, A_2, \ldots, A_n \mid C) = \prod_{i=1}^{n} P(A_i \mid C)$$

The training data is assumed to fit a certain probability distribution in terms of values of the features for different classes. This is used to estimate the parameters of this probability distribution. For a given test data, the features in it are used to determine its class label. To simplify the process of model building, it is often assumed that the features are statistically independent of one another.

Naïve Bayes classification technique analyzes the relationship between each independent attribute and the dependent attribute to derive a *conditional probability* for each relationship. A prediction is made by combining the effects of the independent variables on the dependent variable (the outcome that is predicted) to classify a new record.

The procedure for classification using Naïve Bayes technique is as follows: During training phase of classification, the ***prior probability*** of each outcome is determined by counting the number of times it occurs in the training data set. For example, out of 5 cases, if one outcome occurs 2 times, then the prior probability for that outcome is 0.4. In addition to the prior probabilities, Naïve Bayes technique also computes how frequently each independent attribute value occurs in combination with each dependent attribute value. These frequencies are then used to compute ***conditional probabilities*** that are combined with the prior probability to make the predictions. In essence, Naïve Bayes uses the conditional probabilities to modify the prior probabilities.

Now, the probability of dependent attribute is to be computed based on the conditional probabilities of independent attributes. This is nothing but computing a score for each possible value (posterior probability) of the dependent attribute simply by multiplying the prior probability for the dependent attribute times all the conditional probabilities for the independent attributes. The highest scoring value becomes the predicted value.

One significant advantage of Naïve Bayes technique is that it also allows us to make predictions from partial information. For example, in the absence of known values for all the independent variables, prediction can be made using just the prior probability. Also, if we know only the value for income, we can use the conditional probabilities associated with Income to modify the prior probabilities and make a prediction. Another advantage of this technique is that it requires only one pass through the training set to generate a classification model. This makes it the most efficient data mining technique. However, Naïve Bayes does not handle numerical data, and so any independent or dependent variable that contains numerical values must be grouped/discretized.

18.4.3 Decision Trees

One of the widely used technique for classification is "decision trees". Decision trees are powerful models produced by a class of techniques such as CART, CHAID, ID3 and C4.5.

Unlike *k*-NN and Bayes classifiers, Decision trees generate rules. A rule is a conditional statement (e.g., IF..THEN...ELSE...) that is easily understood and used within a database to identify a set of records. Decision Tree Classification generates the output as a tree-like structure, which gives fairly easy interpretation for people to understand. All leaf nodes represent class labels. On the other hand, internal nodes of a decision tree represent simple decision rules on attributes.

Figure 18.1 illustrates one of the possible decision tree for the data given in Table 18.4. A path from root node to each leaf node will form a rule. There are six rules in Figure 18.1 corresponding to the six paths existing from root node to leaf nodes.

A decision tree model contains rules to predict the target variable. The goal is to set up a model that gives prediction of a value based on multiple input values.

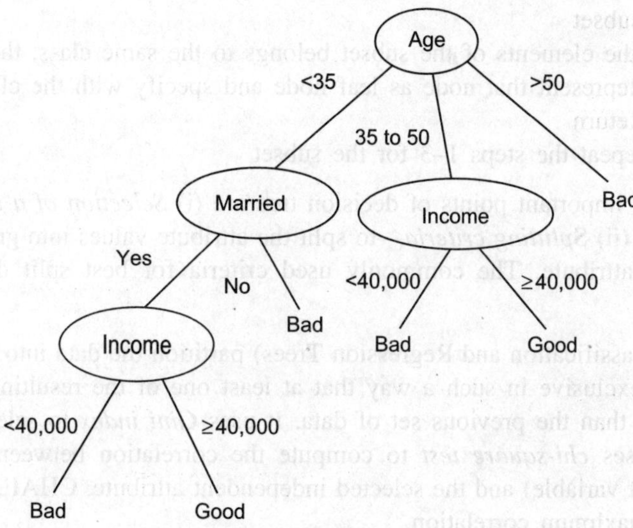

FIGURE 18.1 Decision tree.

TABLE 18.4 Sample Training Data

S. No.	Age	Income	Married	Loan class
1	36	30,000	Yes	Bad
2	26	35,000	Yes	Bad
3	45	48,000	Yes	Good
4	28	45,000	No	Good
5	25	32,000	Yes	Good
6	56	62,000	Yes	Bad
7	30	42,000	Yes	Good
8	52	37,000	Yes	Bad
9	49	33,000	Yes	Bad
10	33	50,000	No	Bad

A decision tree (also known as classification tree) is constructed using the training data set. Decision tree construction starts by identifying a root node (variable) and recursively adding child nodes until the complete training data fits perfectly. The selection of root variable is based on the highest importance among all the variables in determining the classification and also represents all the records in the training data set. Then recursively the records are partitioned into each node of a tree and for each partition, a child is created to represent it. The split into partitions is determined by the values of the given attributes. This recursive process is stopped when all the records of each partition belong to one class. The steps in building a decision tree are as follows:

1. Select an attribute
2. Partition the attribute values into subsets

3. For each subset
   (a) If all the elements of the subset belongs to the same class, then
      (i) Represent that node as leaf node and specify with the class label
      (ii) Return
   (b) Else repeat the steps 1–3 for the subset

The two most important points of decision tree are (i) *Selection of a node* for partition at each iteration and (ii) *Splitting criteria*—to split the attribute values into groups which form as branches to that attribute. The commonly used criteria for best split during decision tree construction are:

- CART (Classification and Regression Trees) partition the data into two subsets that are mutually exclusive in such a way that at least one of the resulting subsets has lower dispersion than the previous set of data. It uses *Gini index* to select an attribute.
- CHAID uses *chi-square test* to compute the correlation between the *class* attribute (dependent variable) and the selected independent attribute. CHAID selects an attribute that has maximum correlation.
- C4.5 uses *entropy* measure to partition the data into mutually exclusive subsets. These methods select an attribute that minimizes the entropy. C4.5 is an extension of ID3 (Iterative Dichotomizer 3).

The computation of splitting indices are discussed next.
Assume that T is a set of records that are divided into classes $C_1, C_2, \ldots, C_n$ (class labels).

- Entropy
  $\text{Entropy}(P) = -p_1 \log(p_1) - p_2 \log(p_2) - \ldots - p_n \log(p_n)$
  where $P = (p_1, p_2, \ldots, p_n)$ is the probability distribution of an attribute (with respect to n classes). If the probability distribution is more uniform, then the information content is higher.
- Information Gain
  Let X is an independent attribute and T is partitioned into $T_1, T_2, \ldots, T_n$ based on the values of X.
  $\text{Gain}(X, T) = \text{Info}(T) - \text{Info}(X, T)$
  where Info(T) represents the class of an element of T which is equivalent to Entropy(P) (i.e., Info(T) = Entropy(P))
  and

  $$\text{Info}(X, T) = \Sigma_{i=1}^{n} \frac{|T_i|}{|T|} \, Info(T_i)$$

- gini Index

  $$\text{gini}(T) = 1 - \Sigma_{k=1}^{n} p_k^2$$

  where p_k is the relative frequency of class k in T.

The step by step process of CART algorithm is as follows:

Step 1: Get a data set (set of records) from the database.

Step 2: The set of records is divided into two disjoint sets: training set and test set.

Step 3: Place the record-id of all the records from the training set **T** in the root node of a binary tree.
Number the root node as $L = 1$

Step 4: For each *non-class* attribute in ***T***,

(a) Create an attribute list which is a table with three columns. The columns correspond to *attribute value, class label* (a distinguished attribute*), record_id(rid)* of the record of **T** from which the values are obtained. The number of rows in the attribute list is same as the number of tuples in **T**.

(b) Calculate distinct values of the *attribute* and distinct values of the *class label.*

Step 5: Create *record list* which is a table consisting of two columns. First column contains the *record_id(rid)* and the second column contains the *node number* of the tree to which the record is currently allocated.

Step 6: Initialize the record list,
The second column of the record list is initialized to L since all the records are in the root node.

Step 7: For each attribute list,

(a) Create a *count matrix* ($n \times k$), where n corresponds to the number of distinct values of the attribute and k corresponds to the number of the distinct values of the class label.

The (i, j) entry in the count matrix represents the number of records having attribute value i and class label j.

(b) Calculate *gini index* of **T** which is defined as

$$\text{gini(T)} = 1 - \Sigma P_i^2$$

where P_i is the relative frequency of the class j in **T**.

(c) Calculate gini index for all the non-class attributes of **T**.

(d) Calculate information *gain* for each attribute which is the difference between gini index of **T** and the gini index of attribute.

(e) Select the attribute with the maximum gain as the *splitting attribute* at the root node.

Step 8: For the attribute selected for splitting,

(a) Create intermediate matrix $2 \times k$, where *2 rows* correspond to the left child and the right child of the node and *k columns* correspond to number of distinct values of the class label.

a1	a2
b1	b2

Here, $k = 2$.

(b) Initialize the intermediate matrix.

(i) Initialize the *first row* of the matrix to *zero.*

(ii) Initialize the *second row* to the number of records falling in the distinct values of the class label.

(c) Calculate *gini index* for the intermediate matrix created in **step 8(b).** The gini index is given as follows:

$$\text{Gini index} = \frac{(a1+a2)}{n}\left(1-\left(\frac{a1}{a1+a2}\right)^2-\left(\frac{a2}{a1+a2}\right)^2\right)+\frac{(b1+b2)}{n}\left(1-\left(\frac{b1}{b1+b2}\right)^2-\left(\frac{b2}{b1+b2}\right)^2\right)$$

Step 9: For all the subsets of distinct values of the splitting attribute.

(a) Create intermediate matrix from the matrix created in **step 8(a).**

(b) Calculate the gini index for the matrix formed above.

(c) Compare the gini index of each subset of distinct values of the attribute with the gini index calculated in the step 8(c) and find the subset whose gini index decreases the index value to the maximum.

Step 10: Select the subset found in the **step 9(c)** as the *splitting criteria* and split the root node with the records satisfying the criteria in *left child node* and remaining records in *right child node.*

Step 11: Update the record list.

The second column of the record list is updated to the *node number* of the node into which the records are currently allocated.

Step 12: For each *subtree,* repeat **steps 7–11** until there are no possible splits.

CHAID method to construct a decision tree is described next.

Chaid (chi-square automatic interaction detector)

In CHAID, like other decision tree algorithms, the tree is constructed by partitioning the data set into two or more subsets, based on the values of one of the attribute (belonging to non-class attributes). The maximum number of partitions for an attribute for its splitting can be the number of distinct values of that attribute. (Note that in the CART classification, each node is always split into two.)

Choosing a splitting attribute:

The splitting attribute is chosen according to a chi-square test (χ^2) of independence in a contingency table (i.e., a cross-tabulation of the non-class and class attribute). The main stopping criterion used by such method is the *p*-value from this chi-square test. Here, the first step is to merge any categories of predictor variable that correspond to the same value of the class label.

χ^2 test

The χ^2 test is a test to determine statistical significance of an attribute. χ^2 is defined as the sum of the squares of the standardized differences between the expected and observed frequencies of some occurrence in each data set. The χ^2 test measures the probability of evidence that is due to a chance. In the CHAID algorithm, the χ^2 test is used to decide whether two predictors should be merged or not. In CHAID, the tree keeps growing until no more splits are available, leading to statistically significant differences in classification.

18.5 CLUSTERING

Clustering aims at grouping the given objects into a set of clusters (classes). Unlike classification, the class labels are not known a priori in clustering. So, the clustering approaches are concerned with

- Choosing the number of clusters
- Assigning each object to a cluster
- Defining the criteria to establish the goodness of clusters and
- Labelling the cluster based on characteristics of each group.

The two criteria that should be satisfied by the clusters are:

- Maximizing the inter-cluster distance, that is, objects from different clusters should be dissimilar
- Minimizing the intra-cluster distance, that is, objects within a cluster should be similar

The distance/similarity metric chosen in deriving clusters plays a major role in the formation of clusters.

There are two major clustering techniques: *partition clustering* and *hierarchical clustering.*

- Partitioning clustering approaches partition the data set into a predefined number of clusters (say, *k*) and then evaluate the obtained clusters by some criterion
- Hierarchical clustering approaches construct the clusters in a hierarchical form by either merging two small clusters into one cluster (agglomerative) or dividing a cluster into two small clusters (divisive), using some criterion

18.5.1 Partitioning Algorithms

Partitioning algorithms divide the database *D* of *n* objects into a set of *k* clusters. The partitioning algorithm typically starts with initial *k* partitions of *D* and then uses an iterative control strategy to optimize an objective function. Choosing the value of *k*, that is, the number of clusters, needs some domain knowledge. The partition clustering techniques can be divided into three types based on the centroid chosen for the cluster representative:

- ***k-means clustering:*** Each cluster is represented by the centre of gravity of the cluster.
- ***k-medoid clustering:*** Each cluster is represented by one of the objects of the cluster located near the centre.
- ***k-mode clustering:*** Each cluster is represented by the mode of the cluster

k-means and *k*-medoids are the frequently used clustering techniques. The *k*-medoid is preferred over *k*-means for most of the clustering algorithms designed for the real-life business cases as the mean of a cluster may not represent a real object, whereas the medoid of a cluster is the actual object in that cluster. The well-known algorithm of *k*-medoid is the Partition Around Medoid (PAM). Below we describe the *k*-means clustering algorithm.

k-means clustering

In the *k*-means clustering, one should specify the number of desired clusters (say, *k*) initially. Figure 18.2 shows an example of *k*-means clustering process, where $k = 2$. There are 13 objects (Figure 18.2a).

In the first step, the entire data is divided randomly into k nonempty partitions (Figure 18.2b), and the centre for each partition is computed (Figure 18.2c). Then, the distance from each data point to each of the k centres is computed (Figure 18.2d) and assigned that point to the nearest centre forming new clusters (Figure 18.2e). Note that the partition boundaries will change due to new assignments. Now, again k centres for the new k-clusters are computed (Figure 18.2f). This process is repeated till there is no updation of cluster centres.

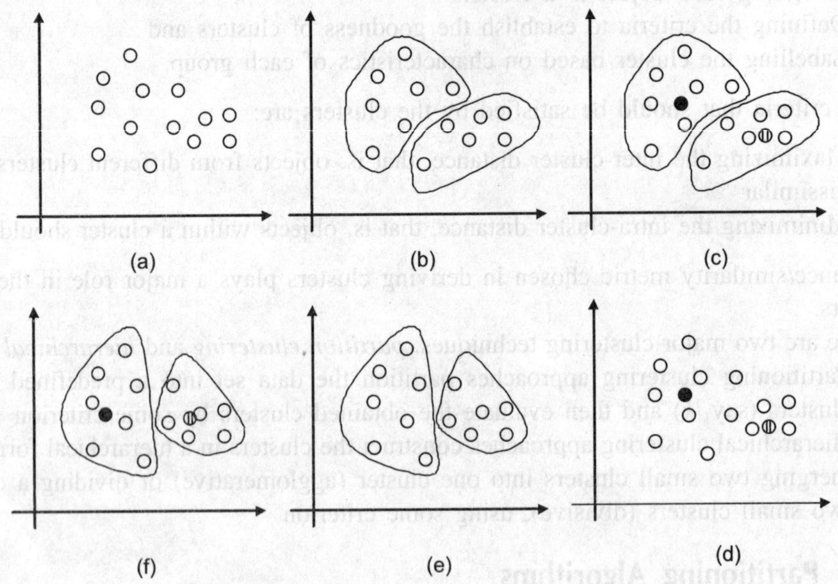

FIGURE 18.2 *k*-means clustering example.

```
Algorithm: k-means
  Input:   k-Number of desired clusters
  Output:  k clusters

  1. Partition the data into k nonempty subsets arbitrarily
  2. Determine k centroids, one for each cluster (that is, cluster
     seeds) The centroid is the centre (mean) of the cluster.
  3. Repeat
     (a) Assign (or re-assign) each data point to the nearest centroid
     (b) Determine the new centroids
  4. Until there is no change in the position of cluster centroids.
```

Similar to k-means, PAM algorithm partitions the data into specified k clusters with the exception that instead of mean, PAM computes medoid of the cluster elements, which is one of the real-object of the cluster.

```
Algorithm: PAM
  Input:   k-Number of desired clusters
  Output:  k clusters
```

```
1. Partition the data into k nonempty subsets arbitrarily
2. Select k representative objects as medoids for each partition
3. Repeat
   (a) For each pair of chosen object Om (selected in step 2) and non-
       selected object On
       i. Compute the total swapping cost (Costmn)
   (b) For each pair of m and n,
       i. If Costmn < 0 then replace n with m. // candidate for
          a new medoid
       ii.Assign (or re-assign) each non-selected object to the
          nearest representative object.
  Until there is no change in the representative objects.
```

In step 3 of the PAM algorithm, the cost of swapping is computed between each of the current representative object and non-representative objects. The cost is negative, meaning that it is a potential candidate to specify as a new medoid in place of the current representative object and can be swapped. Once swapping is done, all the remaining objected (non-selected in this iteration) are assigned to the nearest selected representative object.

18.5.2 Hierarchical Algorithms

Hierarchical algorithms create a hierarchical decomposition of *D*. They can be agglomerative (top-down) or divisive (bottom-up).

Agglomerative algorithm

Agglomerative hierarchical clustering algorithms begin with each object as a separate group. These groups are successively combined based on distance (or similarity) till there is only one group remaining or a specified termination condition is satisfied. AGNES algorithm is an example of agglomerative hierarchical clustering algorithm. Figure 18.3 shows the agglomerative clustering of sample data that consists of six objects O_1 to O_6.

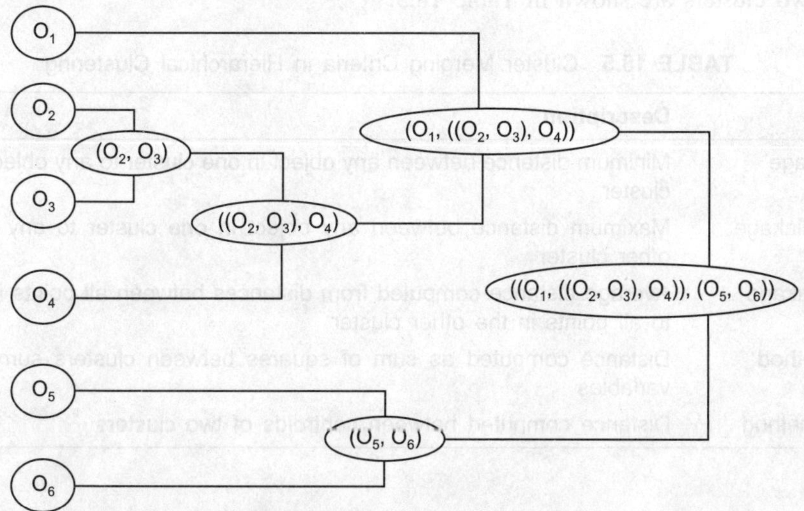

FIGURE 18.3 Divisive clustering example.

Divisive algorithms

Divisive algorithms follow the opposite strategy. They start with one group of all objects and successively split groups into smaller ones, until each object falls in one cluster, or as desired. DIANA algorithm is an example of divisive clustering approach. Figure 18.4 shows the divisive clustering process on the sample data. Note that in both agglomerative and divisive clustering approaches, the process can be visually represented as a *dendrogram*.

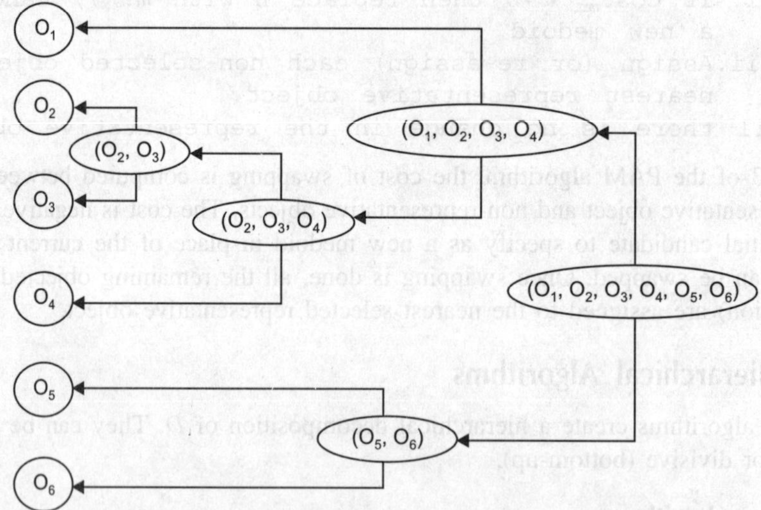

FIGURE 18.4 Agglomerative clustering example.

One of the important aspects of hierarchical clustering is how to find distance between two clusters. When there is only one element in each cluster, the distance between the two clusters is straightforward way of applying a specific distance (or similarity) measure. However, the problem arises when each consists of more than one object. Few approaches to find the distance between two clusters are shown in Table 18.5.

TABLE 18.5 Cluster Merging Criteria in Hierarchical Clustering

Approach	Description
Single linkage	Minimum distance between any object in one cluster to any object in the other cluster
Complete linkage	Maximum distance between any object in one cluster to any object in the other cluster
Average linkage	Average distance computed from distances between all points in one cluster to all points in the other cluster
Ward's method	Distance computed as sum of squares between clusters summed over all variables
Centroid method	Distance computed between centroids of two clusters

As in partitioning algorithm, we do not require k as an input for hierarchical algorithm. However, a termination condition has to be defined, indicating when the merger or division process should be terminated. It is interesting to note that in partition clustering any error in the initial partition would be rectified in the iterations, whereas any erroneously merging (or division) of clusters at any one iteration cannot be rectified in the later iterations.

18.6 CASE STUDY: CREDIT ANALYSIS OF BANK CUSTOMERS

In the current market scenario where competition is at peak, it is important for banks to introduce new products and schemes in the market for survival. For assessing the customer creditworthiness in relation to new products/schemes introduced by the bank, bank may not have the past data and it becomes difficult to address the problem and assess the customer. Since classification algorithms require training data set for credit scoring, clustering techniques are helpful for scoring customers of these new volatile products. In this section, a prototype for scoring a customer using k-means clustering algorithm is described.

18.6.1 Problem Formulation

The quantitative credit scoring models assign credit applicants to one of the two groups: *good creditor* and *bad creditor*. A good creditor group comprises of those creditors that are likely to repay the financial obligations, whereas bad creditor group comprises of creditors whose likelihood of defaulting on the financial obligation is high. Thus, a creditor from a bad creditor group should be denied a credit by financial institutions.

With the proliferation of large loan portfolios and credit industry, the process of developing more accurate credit scoring models has become more active for the credit assessment problem. Even a minor increase in the credit scoring accuracy is a significant accomplishment.

Credit scoring problems are generally a classification problem that classifies credit customers into different groups. Credit scoring is based on the assumption that past experience can be used as a guide in predicting credit worthiness. With the availability of a large amount of training data sets, classification algorithms have found major application in credit scoring. Training data set is associated with class attribute, that is, creditor's quantitative measurement is available to the model that supervises the banks/financial institution to score new creditors. Increasing competition in the market has resulted in the launch of new products by banks/ financial institutions. In practice, banks/financial institution may not have the training data set or past behaviour of the customer for new products. Hence, models based on classification techniques may fail, resulting in a need of an unsupervised-based system.

Clustering is an unsupervised technique of partitioning the database into groups such that objects within a group are quite similar to each other and object from two groups are quite dissimilar. In this section, we provide a credit scoring model that uses a well-known partitioning clustering technique, k-means algorithm to partitions the creditors into various groups. These clusters are ranked as *good* or *bad* using well-known *voting* technique. To find the accuracy of our model, we classified the creditors with their known classes (expected class) and found their new class (observed class). Class label is used to find only the misclassification ratio and hence higher accuracy of the system.

18.6.2 Credit Scoring Using *k*-means

Partitioning clustering algorithms tries to partition the database D into k partitions ($k \leq n$) where n is the number of records in the database. One of the most popular and efficient partitioning clustering algorithms is k-means algorithm. In the k-means approach, randomly selected k objects are used as the initial centroids of clusters. Remaining $(D - k)$ objects are assigned to different clusters based on their distance from the centroids. As k-means works well over data assumed to be spread in a Euclidean space, Euclidean distance measure is used to compute the distance among the pair of objects. After assigning all the objects to the clusters, a new set of clusters are formed. From these new set of clusters, new centroids are computed. The process is continued until the cluster stabilizes or there is no change in centroids.

First, training data set is divided into k clusters using k-means clustering algorithm. Then, a prototype vector consisting of k cluster mean elements is derived. The prototype vector (PV) can be represented as

$$\text{PV} = \langle m_1, m_2, \ldots, m_k \rangle$$

where m_i is the ith cluster mean.

For ranking the clusters, the percentage composition of a class is seen. For a cluster, class which has the value greater than or equal to the distribution in the original data set is assigned to that cluster. For example, let us assume that for a two-class problem in a training data set, the distribution of class is 60:40%, that is, 60% of the data in the training data set belong to class A and 40% of the data belong to class B. While ranking the cluster C, if the contribution of class A objects are greater than 60%, then we rank the cluster C as class A, else it is ranked as class B.

Once the ranking of clusters is completed, it is required to validate the model. To validate the model, objects from test data set are used. Object O is assigned to a class that has a minimum distance from its cluster mean to the object O. This class is known as *expected class*. As it is an object of test data set, we have a class label associated with it. The associated class label to the object is called *desired class*. If the expected class and the desired class do not match each other, it is known as misclassification. Thus, misclassification of the model with the help of test data set is carried out. Figure 18.5 shows the prototype model for classifying a test data.

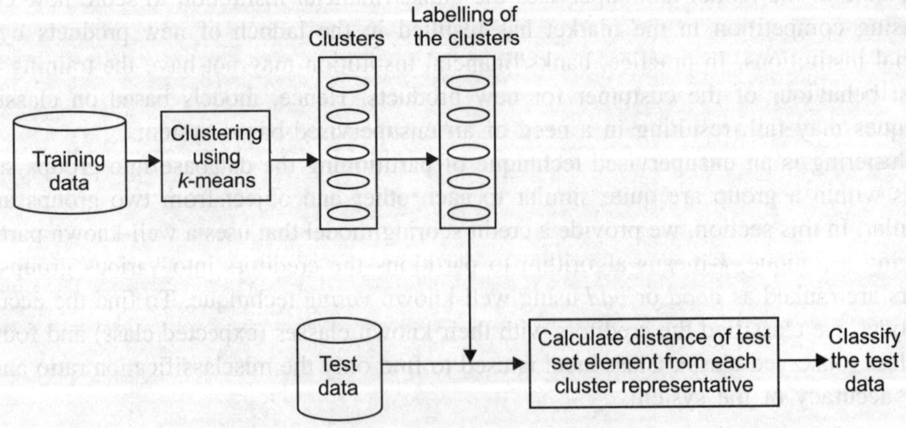

FIGURE 18.5 Classification of test data.

18.6.3 Experimental Results

Experiments were conducted on Australian credit data set, which is downloaded from ftp://ftp.ics.uci.edu/pub/machine-learning-databases/statlog/australian. This credit data set consists of 690 records. Each record has 15 attributes consisting of 8 nominal, 6 continuous and 1 as a class variable. The six continuous attributes and the class variable are considered for the experiments.

There are two types of class labels, namely, 0 and 1 with a distribution of 55.5% and 45.5%, respectively. Training data set and testing data set are built as 70:30, that is, training and testing data sets consist of 483 and 207 records, respectively. In the training set, out of 483 records 268 records are from class 0 and 215 records are from class 1. Similarly, in the test set, out of 207 records, 115 records are from class 0 and 92 records are from class 1.

TABLE 18.6 Classification Table for Australian Credit Data Set (Testing Data Set) (%)

Number of clusters	0–0	0–1	1–0	1–1
2	98.26	1.74	78.26	21.74
3	98.26	1.74	78.26	21.74
4	90.43	9.57	65.22	34.78
5	5.22	94.78	7.61	92.39
6	90.43	9.57	61.96	38.04
7	53.91	46.09	26.09	73.91
8	60.0	40.0	31.52	68.48
9	18.26	81.74	25.0	75.0
10	12.17	87.83	18.48	81.52
11	22.61	77.39	27.17	72.83
12	23.48	76.52	27.17	72.83
13	35.65	64.35	32.61	67.39
14	46.10	53.90	36.96	63.04
15	45.22	54.78	36.96	63.04

Figure 18.6 shows the misclassification rate for the training data set of Australian credit data. Table 18.6 shows the classification and the misclassification ratio for various values of k (the number of clusters). For security reasons, the meanings of 0 and 1 are not given for the downloaded data set. In general, the objective of any classification algorithm is to maintain balance between false positive and false negative. False positive means the bad creditors are being labelled as good, whereas false negative means good creditors are labelled as bad. If 0 is assumed as label for good creditors, and 1 is the label for bad creditors, then the objective is achieved for $k = 8$. Also, we analyzed using cluster validation index the *sum of squared error* and for $k = 8$, it was minimum.

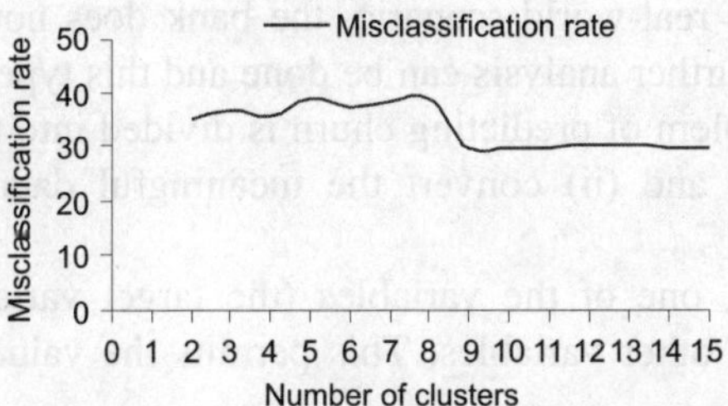

FIGURE 18.6 Misclassification rate for training.

18.6.4 Discussion

Scoring a new customer is the necessity of every bank/financial institution in today's rapidly growing volatile economic environment. Existing credit scoring models are based on classification techniques. These techniques require training data set that may not be available for newly launched product. Also, newly launched product may have a small lifespan. Thus, a technique based on clustering is required for credit scoring. In this case study, a prototype for credit scoring using *k*-means clustering algorithm is designed. To validate the model, Australian credit data set is used. Misclassification rate of both testing and training data set is reported. At $k = 8$, a low misclassification rate is observed where the sum of squared error is minimum.

18.7 CASE STUDY: MODELING CHURN BEHAVIOUR

Acquiring new customers is a costlier process than retaining existing customers. Therefore, maintaining relationship with customers is vital in improving the overall profitability of a company. Churn is defined as the propensity of a customer to cease doing business with a company in a given period. In this case study, modeling churn behaviour for a bank is described. Ideally, many characteristics of customers, such as demographic details, transactional details and customer perception details, are vital in modeling the churn behaviour of bank customers. This case study provides a detailed guideline to preprocess customer data that suits modeling churn behaviour. We built models with three decision tree algorithms, namely, CART, TreeNet and C5.0.

18.7.1 Problem Formulation

High cost of customer acquisition and customer education requires companies to make large upfront investments on customers. However, due to easy access to information and a wide range of offerings, it is easier than ever before for customers to switch between service providers. Therefore, customer churn has become a significant problem and is one of the prime challenges for financial institutions. Studies reveal that customer churn is a costly affair. Identifying the churn beforehand and taking necessary steps to retain them (customer retention) would increase the overall profitability of the company.

In banking domain, we define a churn customer as one who closes all his/her accounts and stops doing business with the bank. There are many reasons for a customer to close the account(s). For example, a person creates an account for a specific purpose and closes it immediately after the purpose is solved, a person is relocated and has to move to another place and hence closes all the accounts or a customer may stop transacting with the bank just because of the unavailability of bank's ATMs in important places and hence closes his/her accounts. The problem here is that in the real-world scenario, the bank does not always capture this kind of feedback data. Hence, no further analysis can be done and this type of churning behaviour could not be stopped. So the problem of predicting churn is divided into two steps: (i) convert the raw data into meaningful data and (ii) convert the meaningful data into knowledge using data mining techniques.

In a predictive model, one of the variables (the target variable or response variable) is expressed as a function of other variables. This permits the value of the response variable to be predicted from given values of the other variables (the explanatory or predictor variables). In the churn prediction problem, the response variable, that is, the future status of customers, can take two values, namely, *Active* or *Churn*, and it can be treated as a classification problem.

18.7.2 Churn Modeling

Decision tree classification technique is used for churn modeling in this case study. Decision tree based algorithms are commonly used to examine the data and to induce a tree and its rules that will be used to make predictions. By observing the number of cases and the class they belong to, in the leaf nodes, the corresponding rules can be generated. For the purpose of this study, CART, TreeNet and C5.0 are employed in order to build the churn model to help one identify sub-segments of the customer base that is likely to churn away, providing a well-identified segment to target with retention programs.

Data preparation

Data plays a vital role in building data-driven models and data–preparation is an important step in churn prediction, which takes almost 60–70% of total time. Building a model for churn prediction implicitly means that we are trying to model the behaviour of customers before churning out. For this to be successful, the customer transaction activities should be analyzed in a particular period. Hence, taking a snapshot of data would never suffice the requirement. On the other hand, considering the transaction activities in a fixed time period would also not suffice the requirement. The reason would be best explained by an example. Say, for example, a model is built using data of 1000 customers, of which 700 are active and 300 are known to be churned out and their 3 months activities are analyzed (say, Jan. 2012 to March 2012). Here, the timeline is fixed and the activities done during this period by all the 1000 customers are only analyzed. Now, out of 300 churn customers, say 50% of them have churned away in January. This means, the model will not be fully trained with the behaviour of churn customers before churning as only 1 month's activity is analyzed. This problem occurred because of fixing the timeline before hand. In this case study, a dynamic timeline is considered, which varies for each customer. This concept would be better explained by continuing the above example. If a customer has churned away in January 2012, from that point of time, the past 3 months activity is considered, that is, transaction activities done in November, December 2011 and January 2012 are considered. And if another customer churns away in February, transaction activity of December 2011 and January and February 2012 should be considered. This way, we adapt a dynamic timeline for each customer and hence avoid the problem of not training the model properly. This concept applies to only churn records. For active records, we considered the behaviour of last 3 months before last transaction date of the active customers. Though this study considers 3 months, actually the number of months of data to be considered for churn analysis is a business problem.

The details of the data set obtained from a bank are shown in Table 18.7. The Customer table contains customer details such as customer number, name, address, date of birth, education and status. There are 40,880 customers in total. The general ledger table contains the account numbers, account types, date of opening and description of accounts held by each customer. There are 108,029 accounts in all for the above specified numbers of customers. The Dormant

TABLE 18.7 Details of Customer Data

Table name	Attributes	No. of records
Customer	Custno, Name1, Name2, Address, Status, DoB (Date of birth), Edn	40,880
General ledger	Custno, AcNo, Descr, DOP (Date of a/c opening)	108,029
Dormant	Acno, Descr, Dormant	18,002
Master	Acno, Balance, Dormant flag.	31,022
Txn	Acno, Trntype, Date, Amount	3,139,020
Ttype	Ttype#, Typecode, Descr	93

table contains all the account numbers that are flagged as inactive (dormant) for a while. The Master table contains account numbers and latest balances of all the accounts. The Txn table contains the previous 5 years transactional details of all the accounts. Finally Ttype table contains description for various transaction types. There are in total 93 transaction types defined.

The final data set prepared from the available data contains the following attributes: Customer number, Duration (Dur), number of Credit transactions in 3 months (CRTxns), number of Debit transactions in 3 months (DRTxns), Average credit amount in 3 months (AvgCrAmt), Average debit amount in 3 months (AvgDrAmt), total number of other accounts (NumOtherAccs), percentage of accounts closed in 3 months (PercClosedRecently) and Status (Status). The Duration attribute contains the number of months that a customer has transacted with the bank. In this study, the behaviour of savings account customers is analyzed. Out of 108,029 total accounts, the number of savings accounts is 22,165. In this, 6643 accounts are found to be dormant from Dormant table. In this analysis, these accounts are removed from our target customer base. Also, filtered those transaction records that have duration less than 6 months and transaction count less than 50. After applying the filtering steps, the target customer base size is reduced to 1494 accounts with 1173 active records and 321 churn records.

The transactional behaviour of these 1494 customers is analyzed by extracting the right kind of data from the available raw data. The recent behaviour is extracted from the Txn table which contains the transactional details of all the accounts. Each record in the Txn table contains the Trntype field which indicates the type of the transaction (credit voucher, inward cheque clearing, cash deposit are some of the values the Trntype field can take). There are 93 distinct transaction types and each can be identified as either a credit type of transaction or a debit type of transaction. We segregated the transactions done by customers into credit transaction or a debit transaction and eventually calculated the number of credit transactions (CRTxns) and the number of debit transactions (DRTxns) for all the 1494 customers. The average amount of money transacted by customers in the considered period may also help in training the model better. Hence, two more attributes, namely, the average amount involved in credit transactions (AvgCrAmt) and the average amount involved in debit transactions (AvgDrAmt), were calculated for 1494 customers. The number of accounts (other than savings account) and the percentage of accounts closed in the considered period are also useful for the study. Hence, two more attributes, namely, the number of other accounts (NumOtherAccs), and the percentage of other accounts closed in the considered time period of 3 months (PercClosedRecently), were calculated for all the 1494 customers.

Data mining model building and experimental results

Three classification tree algorithms, namely, CART, C5.0 and TreeNet, are used for building models. The data set is split into training data set and testing data set in 80 : 20 ratio in building the three classification trees.

CART CART does binary splitting. It produces rules for the target variable as a function of other fields in the data set that are previously identified as explanatory variables. Gini concentration coefficient is used to summarize power curves of prediction. Customer Duration, CRTxns, DRTxns, AvgCrAmt, AvgDrAmt and PercClosedRecently are used as explanatory variables and Status is taken as target variable. 80% of the data set, that is 1192 samples containing 929 active customer records and 263 churned customer records, are considered as training data set. The remaining 20% of the data set, that is, 299 samples containing 244 active customer records and 58 churned customer records, are considered as test data set. The confusion matrix and classification success rate of training data set and test data set are shown in Tables 18.8 and 18.9, respectively.

TABLE 18.8 Confusion Matrix and Prediction Success Rate for Training Data

True class	Total # samples	Predicted active	Predicted churn	Success %
Active	929	800	129	**86.11**
Churn	263	13	250	**95.05**

TABLE 18.9 Confusion Matrix and Prediction Success Rate for Test Dataset

True class	Total # samples	Predicted active	Predicted churn	Success %
Active	244	210	34	**86.06**
Churn	58	5	53	**91.37**

The success rate of active customers is relatively less. This is because some of the customers, although their status is marked as active, showed churn characteristics. It reveals that to this segment of customers the bank has to concentrate on and apply churn prevention methodologies. There are 17 leaf nodes in the tree generated using CART, and hence 17 decision rules can be drawn from it. Table 18.10 shows 17 decision rules.

Out of the 17 rules generated by CART, 12 rules (shown in bold) have sufficient number of cases and these rules can be used by the manager for predicting probable churn customers.

TreeNet TreeNet uses stochastic gradient boosting algorithm as a technique for improving the accuracy of a predictive function by applying the function repeatedly in a series and combining the output of each function with weighting so that the total error in the prediction is minimized. In many cases, the predictive accuracy of such a series greatly exceeds the accuracy of the base function used alone. The stochastic gradient boosting algorithm used by TreeNet is optimized for improving the accuracy of models built on decision trees.

TABLE 18.10 Decision Rules Generated by Cart

Rule No.	Rule	Predicted class	No. of cases
1	AvgDrAmt <= 608 and AvgCrAmt <= 37.5	Churn	93
2	AvgDrAmt <= 608 and AvgCrAmt > 37.5 and AvgCrAmt <= 1655.5 and Duration > 18	Active	61
3	AvgCrAmt <= 1655.5 and AvgDrAmt > 608	Churn	102
4	AvgCrAmt > 1655.5 and Duration <= 23.5 and AvgDrAmt <= 1300.5	Active	20
5	AvgCrAmt > 1655.5 and Duration <= 23.5 and AvgDrAmt > 1300.5 and PercClosedRecently > 0.0416667	Churn	26
6	AvgCrAmt > 1655.5 and Duration > 23.5 and Duration <= 27.5	Active	615
7	Duration > 27.5 and Duration <= 68.5 and AvgDrAmt <= 3421.5 and AvgCrAmt > 1655.5 and AvgCrAmt <= 3674	Churn	16
8	Duration > 27.5 and Duration <= 68.5 and AvgDrAmt <= 3421.5 and AvgCrAmt > 3674	Active	18
9	AvgCrAmt > 1655.5 and Duration > 27.5 and Duration <= 68.5 and AvgDrAmt > 3421.5	Churn	38
10	AvgCrAmt > 1655.5 and Duration > 68.5	Active	43
11	AvgDrAmt > 1300.5 and PercClosedRecently <= 0.04 and AvgCrAmt > 1655.5 and AvgCrAmt <= 17894.5 and Duration <= 17.5	Churn	70
12	PercClosedRecently <= 0.04 and Duration > 17.5 and Duration <= 23.5 and AvgDrAmt > 1300.5 and AvgDrAmt <= 7449 and AvgCrAmt > 3527 and AvgCrAmt <= 17894.5	Active	32
13	PercClosedRecently <= 0.04 and Duration > 17.5 and Duration <= 23.5 and AvgDrAmt > 1300.5 and AvgDrAmt <= 7449 and AvgCrAmt > 1655.5 and AvgCrAmt <= 3527	Churn	10
14	AvgDrAmt <= 608 and AvgCrAmt > 37.5 and AvgCrAmt <= 1655.5 and Duration <= 18	Churn	4
15	PercClosedRecently <= 0.04 and AvgCrAmt > 1655.5 and AvgCrAmt <= 17894.5 and Duration > 17.5 and Duration <= 23.5 and AvgDrAmt > 7449	Churn	10
16	Duration <= 23.5 and PercClosedRecently <= 0.04 and AvgCrAmt > 17894.5 and AvgDrAmt > 1300.5 and AvgDrAmt <= 14238.5	Active	10
17	Duration <= 23.5 and PercClosedRecently <= 0.04 and AvgCrAmt > 17894.5 and AvgDrAmt > 14238.5	Churn	10

The number of trees formed by TreeNet was set to 200 and the regression loss criterion used was Huber-M. The confusion matrix and classification success rate of training data set and testing data set are shown in Tables 18.11 and 18.12, respectively.

TABLE 18.11 Confusion Matrix and Prediction Success Rate for Training Data

True class	Total # samples	Predicted active	Predicted churn	Success %
Active	929	809	120	**87.08**
Churn	263	24	239	**90.87**

TABLE 18.12 Confusion Matrix and Prediction Success Rate for Test Data

True class	Total # samples	Predicted active	Predicted churn	Success %
Active	244	218	26	**89.34**
Churn	58	6	52	**89.65**

C5.0 Unlike CART, C5.0 algorithm produces trees with variable branches per node. Customer Duration, CRTxns, DRTxns, AvgCrAmt, AvgDrAmt and PercClosedRecently are used as explanatory variables and Status is taken as target variable. 80% of the data set, that is, 1192 samples containing 929 active customer records and 263 churned customer records, are taken in training data set. The remaining 20% of the data set, that is, 299 samples containing 244 active customer records and 58 churned customer records, are taken in testing data set. The confusion matrix and classification success rate of training data set and testing data set are shown in Tables 18.13 and 18.14, respectively.

TABLE 18.13 Confusion Matrix and Prediction Success Rate for Training Data

True class	Total # samples	Predicted active	Predicted churn	Success %
Active	929	883	46	**95.04**
Churn	263	61	182	**69.2**

TABLE 18.14 Confusion Matrix and Prediction Success Rate for Test Data

True class	Total # samples	Predicted active	Predicted churn	Success %
Active	244	234	10	**95.9**
Churn	58	18	40	**68.9**

18.7.3 Discussion

The prediction success rate of Churn class by CART and TreeNet are quite high, but C5.0 had shown poor results in predicting churn customers. However, the prediction success rate of Active class by C5.0 is more than the other two techniques. But for reaping significant benefits, the model should be able to predict the churn behaviour better. Hence, a model with higher prediction success rate of Churn class has to be chosen for reaping higher benefits. In all the decision tree models, all the explanatory attributes were found to be influencing the target variable, that is status of the customer.

While CART yielded 95.05% classification rate on training data and 91.37% on test data, TreeNet yielded 90.87% classification rate on training data and 89.65% on test data and C5.0 yielded 69.2% classification rate on training data and 68.9% on test data.

CART yielded better classification rate in predicting the churn behaviour and C5.0 yielded better classification rate in predicting the non-churn (active) behaviour of customers. As predicting churn is more important for a bank, it can be said that CART yielded a better overall classification rate. The 17 decision rules generated by CART can be useful in predicting probable churners.

18.8 SUMMARY

Each data mining technique has its own merits and demerits, besides underlying assumptions. This chapter covers few data mining algorithms for Association Rule mining, Classification and Clustering. Apriori algorithm is based on the Apriori principle. It finds frequent itemsets from a given market basket data that are useful to discover association rules. Most of the classification and clustering techniques require distance/similarity measure. The commonly used distance and similarity measures are also described in this chapter, along with various classification and clustering methods. Data Mining algorithms are mostly data driven, and they are very sensitive to updations in the data. So, the models built using data mining algorithms should be remodeled (or re-learned) periodically when a new data is added and it influences the results. This chapter also described two case studies namely Credit Assessment and Modeling Churn behaviour using data mining techniques.

SHORT/OBJECTIVE TYPE QUESTIONS

1. _____ and ______ are the two steps for frequent itemset generation in Apriori algorithm.
2. Decision Tree classifier model can be easily formed as___________ Rules.
   (a) GROUP BY
   (b) IF-THEN-ELSE
   (c) NESTED IF
   (d) None of the above
3. In *k*-NN algorithm, what is *k* stands for
   (a) Number of rules
   (b) Number of classes
   (c) Number of neighbours
   (d) Number of training samples
4. Which of the following is not a classification method?
   (a) *k*-NN
   (b) *k*-Means
   (c) Decision tree
   (d) All the above
5. Classification models are built using ______ data set and validated using _____ data set.

6. What is the basic assumption of Naïve Bayes classifier?
7. C4.5 decision tree algorithm uses __________ measure to select an attribute.
8. In CART, how many splits an attribute is split into?
   (a) Two
   (b) Three
   (c) Five
   (d) No limit
9. CHAID algorithm performs __________ test for splitting next attribute
10. What is a dependent attribute?

WORKOUT SECTION

W18_1 Assume that the user-specified minimum support is 50%. Then generate all frequent itemsets of below transaction database.

	Items				
Transaction ID	**A**	**B**	**C**	**D**	**E**
T_1	1	1	1	0	0
T_2	1	1	1	1	1
T_3	0	0	1	1	0
T_4	1	0	1	1	1
T_5	1	1	0	1	0

W18_2 State Bayes' theorem. Distinguish between prior probability and conditional probability.

W18_3 What are decision trees? How are the splits determined in the CART, CHAID and ID3 algorithms?

W18_4 Elucidate the main difference between hierarchical clustering and partitioning clustering.

W18_5 State the process of agglomerative and divisive clustering approaches

Advanced Databases

A.1 INTRODUCTION

The traditional relational DBMSs (RDBMSs) represent data in the form of rows and columns of tables. They allow basic data types such as number, character and string. Further, SQL (Structured Query Language) is the de-facto standard query language for storing and accessing the data in RDBMSs. Typically, RDBMSs do not allow extending the data types that they support or add new data types to store complex data structures. With the increase in variety of data and evolution of new architectures, new database technologies are emerging to support advanced features of information systems. In this we present well-known advanced database management systems that have emerged in the recent past.

A.2 OBJECT-ORIENTED DATABASES

Object-oriented programming (OOP) treats the data as objects. For example, all the attribute values of an employee can be treated as an employee object. That is, an employee's attributes such as employee number, name, date of joining and salary constitute one object. The object data can be persisted by storing these objects in a database. Such databases are often referred to as object-oriented databases. Thus, object-oriented databases add a new dimension to object-oriented programming languages by way of enabling ***persistence of objects.***

Object-oriented database management system (OODBMS) is a database management system that represents data in the form of objects.

Unlike traditional relational databases where the data is stored in the form of tables consisting of rows and attributes, object-oriented databases store the data as objects. So, all the values of an object constitute a single unit, and the relationships in object-oriented databases exist among objects. That is, OODBMS facilitate relations between data as relations between objects and their attributes, but not between individual attributes.

RDBMSs support normalization of tables and the basic normal form is *first normal form* (1NF). INF ensures that each column value is atomic. That is, RDBMSs do not allow complex data structures such as lists, sets and bags (also nested tables, that is tables within a table) as a column value. OODBMS stores objects and thus the data structures such as lists, sets, bags and embedded objects can be stored as objects. Moreover, objects can be nested. So, the major advantage of OODBMS is that one can store complex data structures as well as the relationships between them as objects in the database. This feature of storing complex data as objects also allows incorporating any changes to objects easily at a later point of time when new business requirements arise.

Object-oriented programming languages such as Python, Perl, Java, Ruby and Smalltalk are useful to interact (i.e., storage and retrieval of objects) with OODBMS. Some commercial OODBMSs have their own query languages, referred to as *object query languages* (OQL). Note that the objects that are created by object-oriented programming language can be stored exactly in the same way in OODBMS. That is, the schema of a database can be defined in the same manner for both OOP language and OODBMS.

OODBMS have features of both DBMS and OOP constructs (Figure A.1). It consists of the DBMS features such as persistence, concurrency, recovery, storage management and retrieval, as well as the OOP features such as complex objects, object identity, encapsulation, inheritance, polymorphism and extensibility. Like RDBMSs, each instance of object in OODBMS must be identified uniquely (i.e., object identity). This unique identifier distinguishes an object from other objects. Note that object identity is independent of object's value.

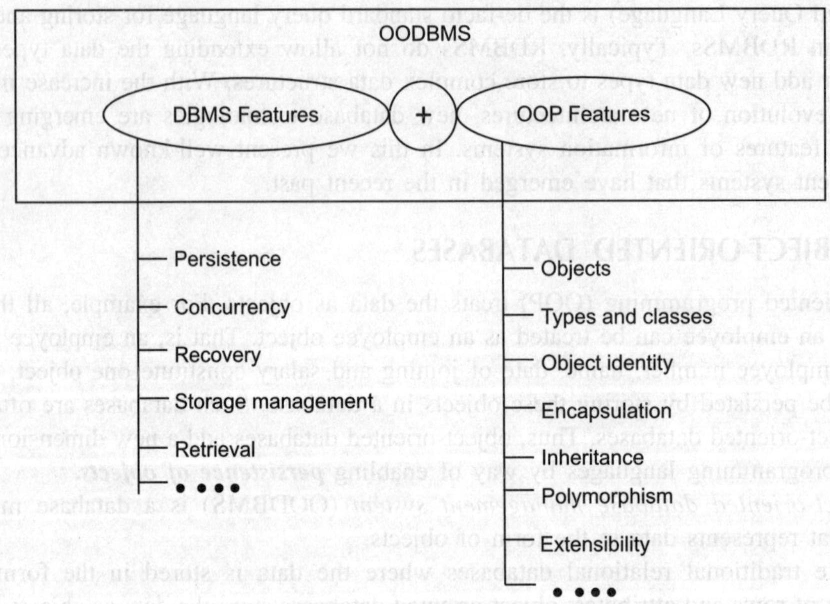

FIGURE A.1 OODBMS features.

In relational DBMS, joins are considered as costly operations, and thus accessing relational data is slower when joins are involved. In OODBMS, joins are not needed to access the data (i.e., objects) and thereby provides faster data access. Note that in OODBMS, relationships between objects are established by pointers, and hence the objects are retrieved by using pointers.

Object-relational database management systems (ORDBMSs) are hybrid of object-oriented databases and relational databases. ORDBMS allows storage of data as a combination of both relational tables and objects, thereby providing benefits of both relational and object-oriented database systems. Most of the commercial RDBMSs available today support ORDBMS features.

A.3 DISTRIBUTED DATABASES

A *distributed database* is a database in which the data and the DBMS are present in two or more computers.

In a distributed database system, data is physically stored across several systems, and each system has a DBMS and is capable of running it independently. However, the data distribution and its access are transparent to the database user. Moreover, the user can access the database without knowing the exact location of the system on which the data is stored. Figure A.2 shows a high-level view of distributed DBMS, consisting of *n* nodes (systems). Typically, one node among the existing nodes will act as a ***coordinator***, which distributes the work and aggregates the query results.

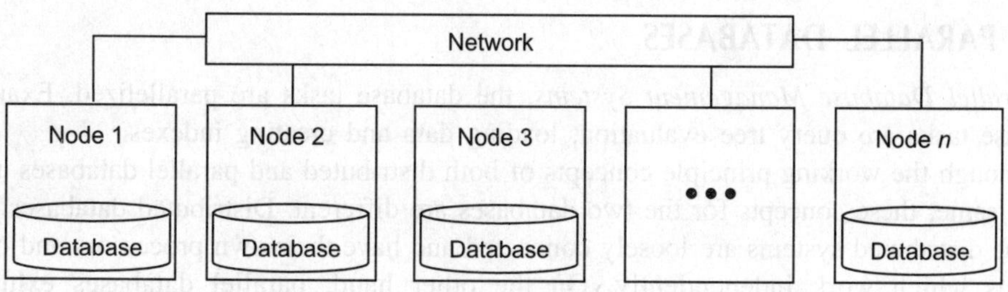

FIGURE A.2 Distributed DBMS—high-level view.

There are two ways to store the data in distributed databases (also referred to as fragmentation): horizontal partition and vertical partition. In horizontal partition, subsets of records pertaining to some group (or criteria) are stored in one system. Whereas in vertical partition, few attributes of a table are stored in one system, few on second system, and so on. The fragments may be replicated to support data availability when a node fails.

Since the data is distributed in the distributed databases, there is a need of sophisticated mechanisms such as distributed locking and distributed transaction models. Distributed database transactions typically follow two-phase commitment (2PC) protocol in order to satisfy ACID (Atomicity, Consistency, Isolation and Durability) properties of databases. 2PC consists of two phases: preparation phase and commit/abort phase.

- ***Phase 1 (preparation):*** Coordinator sends a request for commit to all participants and waits until it receives response from them.
- ***Phase 2 (commit/abort):*** Coordinator decides to commit the transaction, if it receives YES from all participants; it decides to abort if it receives NO from any of the participants.

Figure A.3 shows 2PC protocol between the coordinator and two participants (two nodes). 2PC guarantees atomicity in a distributed environment. It involves message communications for Request for vote, voting and decision, and so the delay is large. Moreover, 2PC is a blocking protocol. That is, all participants who voted YES block if the coordinator fails before sending the decision in phase 2. There are several variations of 2PC such as three-phase commit (3PC) and volatile 2PC to support distributed transactions for distributed database management systems.

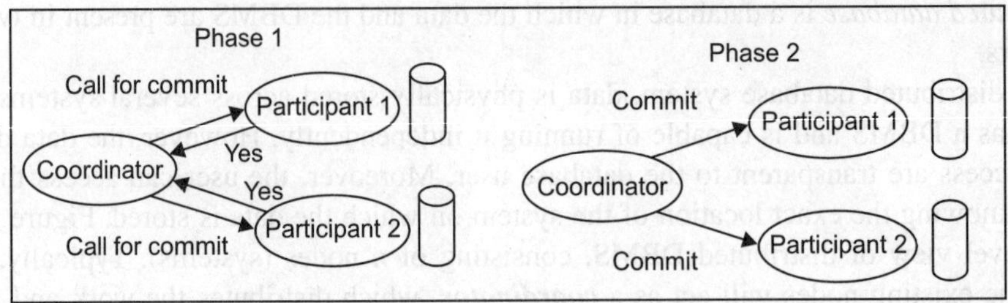

FIGURE A.3 Two-phase commit protocol.

A.4 PARALLEL DATABASES

In *Parallel Database Management Systems*, the database tasks are parallelized. Examples of database tasks are query tree evaluation, loading data and creating indexes.

Though the working principle concepts of both distributed and parallel databases appear to be the same, these concepts for the two databases are different. Distributed databases presume that the distributed systems are loosely connected and have their own processors and operating systems which work independently. On the other hand, parallel databases exhibit high performance and high availability and operate on multiprocessor computer architecture systems. The high performance in parallel databases is achieved through parallel task/command execution. Note that the data in parallel databases is also stored in a distributed manner; however, this distribution is meant only for performance increase.

There are three major parallel DBMS architectures that are distinguished based on their hardware architecture: (i) Shared memory architecture, (ii) Shared disk architecture and (iii) Shared nothing architecture. Their characteristics are as follows:

- *Shared memory*—The main memory and disk storage are shared among multiple processors, and the data is accessed through high-speed interconnect bus (Figure A.4). This kind of architecture facilitates load balancing. However, it allows high availability and scalability.

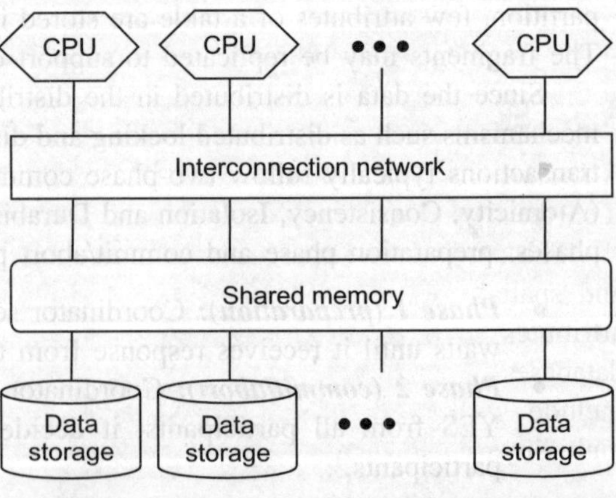

FIGURE A.4 Shared memory architecture.

- *Shared disk*—Here, the system consists of multiple CPUs and each CPU is associated with its own main memory. However, all these processors share common disk storage (see Figure A.5). This architecture faces system failures when the shared disk fails, thereby limiting the availability.
- *Shared nothing*—In this case, each processor has its own main memory and disk storage (Figure A.6). The communication among these units happens through a network connection. This architecture exhibits high availability and reliability, however, is suffers from load balance issue.

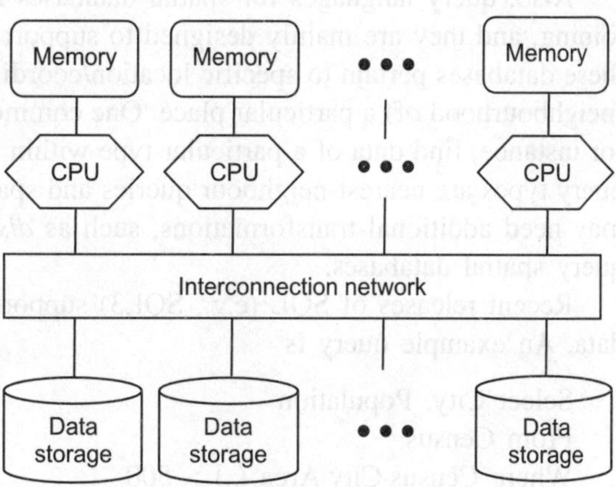

FIGURE A.5 Shared disk architecture.

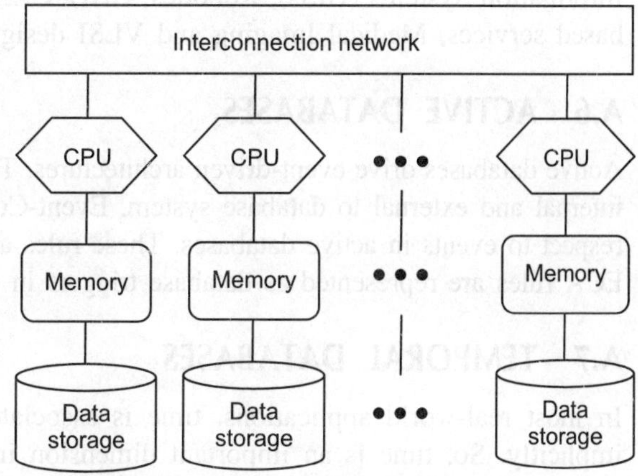

FIGURE A.6 Shared nothing architecture.

Parallel databases typically follow two different dataflow parallelism approaches to process a query: (a) pipelined parallelism and (b) partition parallelism.

- *Pipelined parallelism*—In this approach, a task execution is divided into multiple sub-tasks and each task is run on a separate processor.
- *Partition parallelism*—The data is partitioned in this approach. Each partitioned data serves as an input to a processor and its associated memory, and the task is executed on that partition. Finally, the outputs from all the processors are merged.

A.5 SPATIAL DATABASES

A *spatial database* is a database that is designed to store and query spatially referenced data (i.e., the data related to objects in space).

The data in spatial databases corresponds to various fields such as geometry, geographic and spatial data. Spatial database management systems are concerned with storing spatial attributes such as location, points, lines and polygons, besides regular attributes. These databases support *spatial data types* as part of their data model. Examples of spatial operations include *distance*, *nearest neighbour* and *overlap*. In general, spatial databases are multidimensional databases.

Also, query languages for spatial databases have methods for spatial indexing and spatial joining, and they are mainly designed to support querying spatial data. Most of the queries on these databases pertain to specific location/coordinates (geometrical properties) or are closest to (neighbourhood of) a particular place. One commonly posed query type is *Spatial Range Query*, for instance, find data of a particular type within a specified distance from a given point. Other query types are nearest-neighbour queries and spatial join queries. To support such queries, one may need additional transformations, such as *distance-preserving transformations,* in order to query spatial databases.

Recent releases of SQL (e.g., SQL3) support some of the spatial functions to retrieve the data. An example query is

```
Select City, Population
From Census
Where Census·City·Area ( ) > 500
```

Example application areas where spatial databases are very useful include Geographical Information Systems (GISs), Robotics, CAD–CAM, vehicle autonomous navigation, Location-based services, Medical Imaging and VLSI design.

A.6 ACTIVE DATABASES

Active databases drive event-driven architectures. These databases respond to events that are both internal and external to database system. Event-Condition-Action (ECA) rules are defined with respect to events in active databases. These rules are executed when corresponding event arises. ECA rules are represented as database triggers in most active database management systems.

A.7 TEMPORAL DATABASES

In most real-world applications, time is associated with each transaction/event explicitly or implicitly. So, time is an important dimension in such applications. Temporal databases are concerned with storing time-related data explicitly. These databases have built-in time provisions and addresses queries related to past, present and future aspects.

The time maintained in applications built over temporal databases is based on the granularity such as 1 day, 1 h, 1 min, 1 s, 1 ms, etc. as required by the application.

A.8 NoSQL DATABASES

NoSQL means not only SQL. NoSQL databases are designed to provide horizontal scalability, and the data is stored in distributed nodes. Also, the data is replicated on multiple nodes to provide availability. NoSQL databases are mainly intended to store big data (i.e., data volume is in the order of petabytes, exabytes, zettabyte, yottabyte, etc.).

NoSQL Databases do not have a fixed schema. That is, they allow modifying schema as and when required. Further, join operations are not needed as these databases store the data in a more denormalized form. Other advantages of NoSQL databases include (i) storing the data in a more compressed form and (ii) no indexing is required. These databases are well suited for read-*intensive* applications.

There are several kinds of NoSQL Databases based on the formats they follow. These include key-value store, document based and graph based.

NoSQL databases follow *eventual consistency*, meaning that all the replicas are consistent at a later point of time, thereby relaxing the consistency of ACID properties. More particularly, NoSQL databases follow **CAP** (Consistency, Availability and Partition) **theorem** which states that a distributed system can satisfy any two of these three (namely, Consistency, Availability and Partition) at the same time, but not all of them. Since NoSQL databases are distributed in nature, it should guarantee the Partition. So, they have to relax consistency or availability. The database which relaxes availability usually follows eventual consistency.

A.9 UNSTRUCTURED DATABASES

An unstructured database is intended to store unstructured data such as text, audio, image and video. Working with such data is becoming most essential as there is an unprecedented pace of various technology adoptions such as social networks in businesses. Metadata plays a major role while working with unstructured databases.

One of the frequently used operations over text databases is the *Search*. For example, in text databases, a search is carried out using one or more keywords to retrieve the documents that contain keywords. Note that both *syntactic search* and *semantic search* are of great value in the real-world applications.

Image databases are useful to efficiently store Images. The data model for image databases should have functionalities to represent images in databases. Examples of operations on such data model could be crop and resize. CBIR (Content-Based Image Retrieval) is the commonly used technique to retrieve similar images of a given query image. Here, the search is carried out by analyzing actual content of the image. The features such as colour, texture and shape are derived from the image content.

Most of the available commercial DBMSs support storing of unstructured data in a limited way. Due to the special features of unstructured data such as variable length records and non-atomic values, relational DBMSs are difficult to support unstructured databases. New database technologies (for instance, video indexing) are yet to emerge to fully develop unstructured databases and support data operations and query languages on those databases.

A.10 SUMMARY

This appendix discusses some of the popular and matured DBMSs that are part of several information systems. There are several factors that distinguish these databases, including the type of data that a database supports, the operations that can be supported or the underlying hardware/DBMS software concerns.

Answers

CHAPTER 1

Short/Objective Type Questions

1. Refer to Section 1.3

2. Refer to Section 1.2

3. Refer to Section 1.5

4. Refer to Section 1.8

5. Refer to Section 1.8

6. Refer to Section 1.8

7. Refer to Section 1.9

8. Refer to Section 1.7

9. Refer to Section 1.7

10. (a)

11. (b)

12. (c)

13. (a), (b), (c)

14. (b)

15. (a)—(b)
(b)—(a)
(c)—(c)

16. (b) (c)

17. (c)

18. (b)

19. (c)

20. (b)

Workout Section

1. and 2.

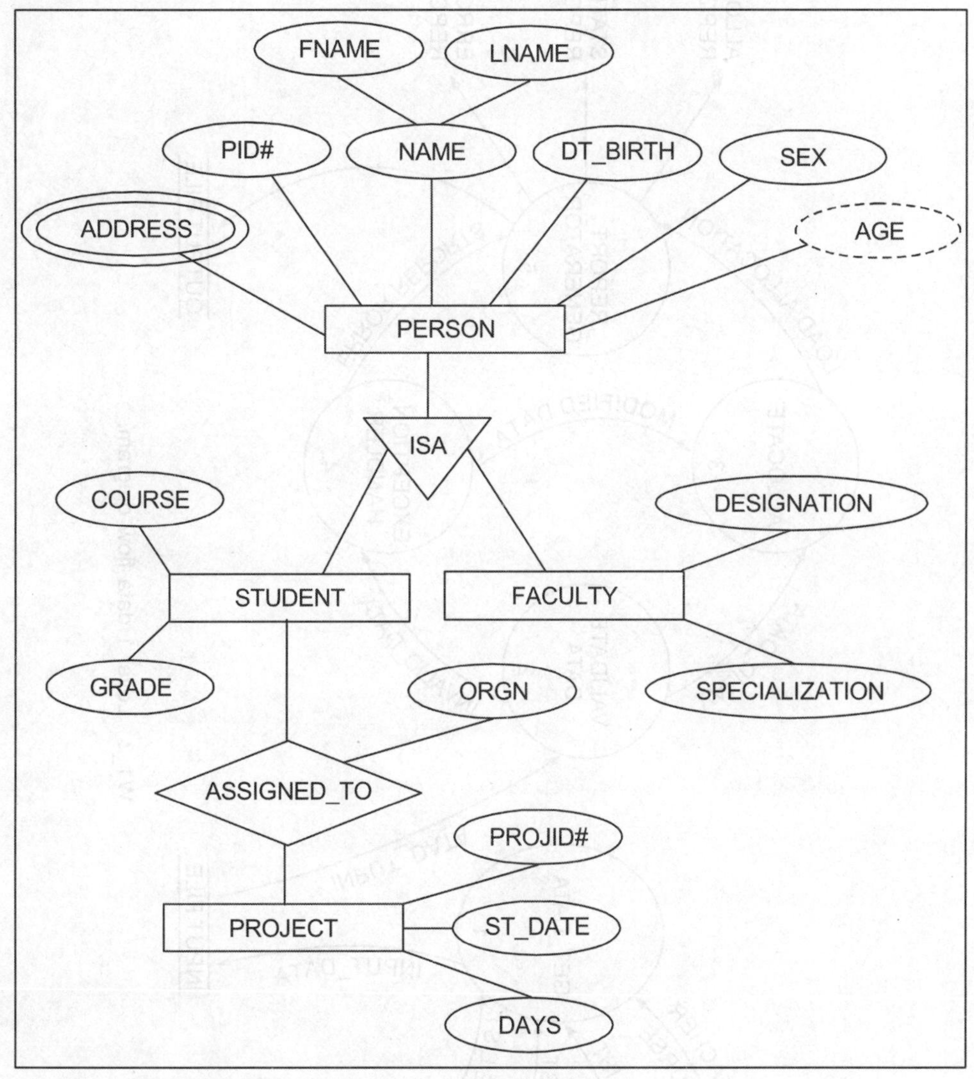

WL_1

PERSON(PID#, FNAME, LNAME, ADDRESS_ID, DT_BIRTH, SEX)
ADDRESS(ADDRESS_ID#, DETAILS#)
STUDENT(PID#, COURSE, GRADE)
FACULTY(PID#,DESIGNATION, SPECIALIZATION)
ASSIGNED_TO(PID#, PROJID#, ORGN)
PROJECT(PROJID#, ST_DATE, DAYS)

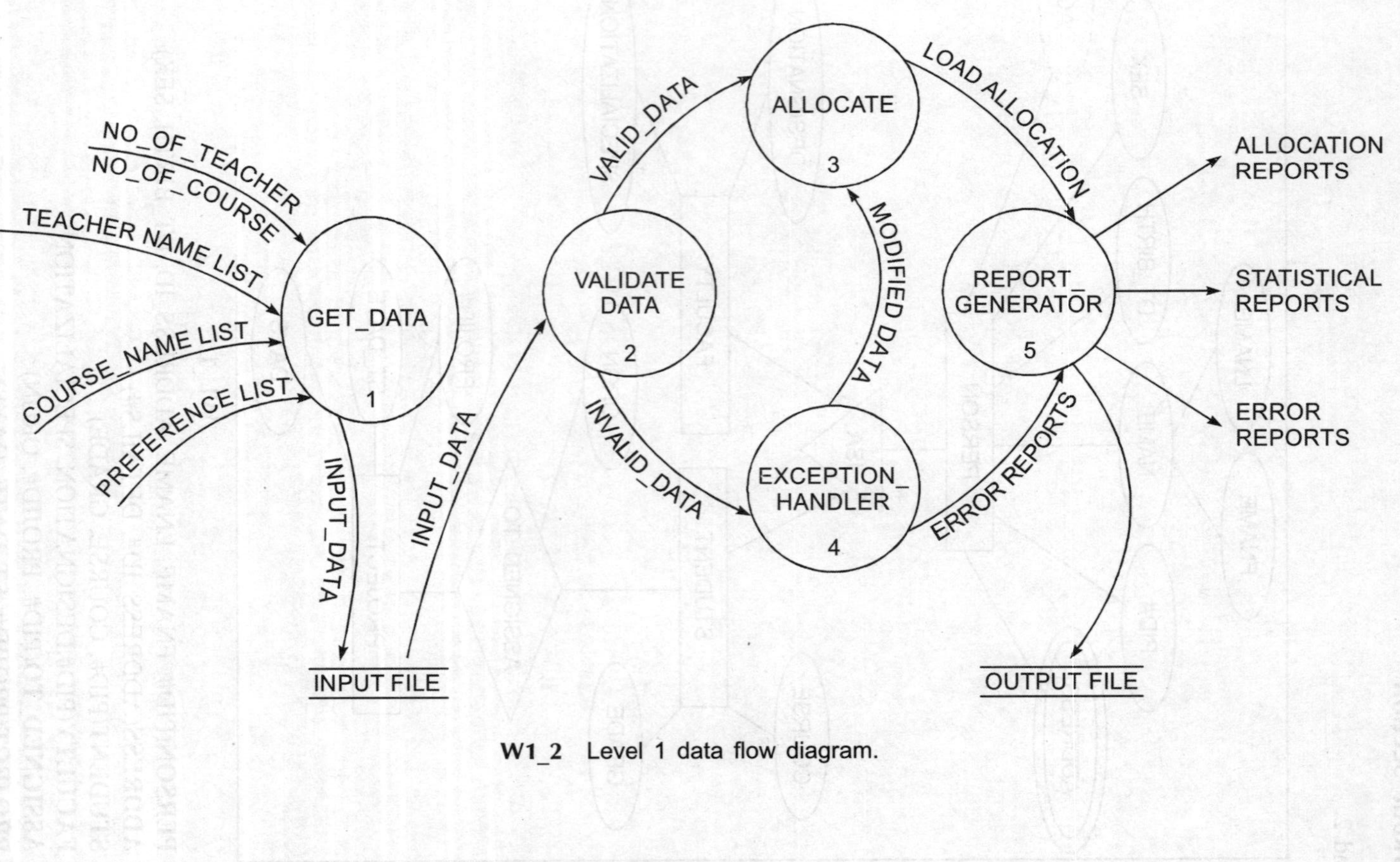

W1_2 Level 1 data flow diagram.

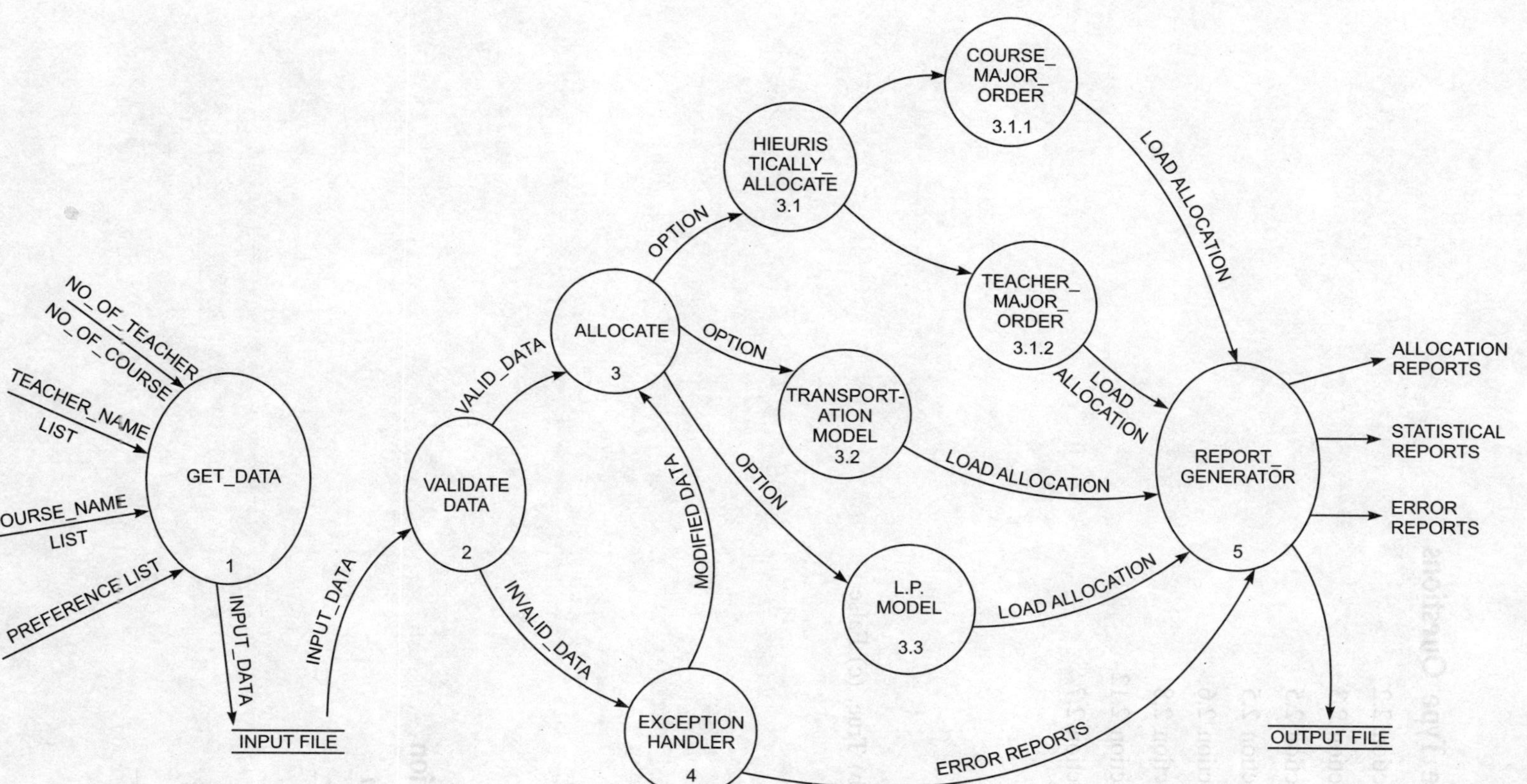

W1_3 Level 2 data flow diagram.

CHAPTER 2

Short/Objective Type Questions

1. Refer to Section 2.2
2. Refer to Section 2.3
3. Refer to Section 2.5
4. Refer to Section 2.5
5. Refer to Section 2.6
6. Refer to Section 2.8
7. Refer to Section 2.12
8. Refer to Section 2.7
9. (a)
10. (b)
11. (d)
12. (b)
13. (a) False, (b) True, (c) False
14. (d)
15. (a), (b)
16. (a)—(b)
(b)—(a)
(c)—(c)
17. (a) (b)
18. (a), (b), (c)
19. (b)
20. (c)

Workout Section

W2_1 (i) **P ÷ Q1**

X
x1
x2
x3
x5
x6

(ii) $P \div Q2$

X
x1
x2
x3
x4
x5
x6

W2_2 (i) $\Pi_{EMP\#}(\sigma_{PRJ\# = 'P6'}(ALLOTTED))$

EMP#
6
7
9

(ii) $EMPLOYEE \bowtie \Pi_{EMP\#}(ALLOTTED \bowtie \Pi_{PRJ\#}(\sigma_{PRJ\_NAME='RDBMS'}(PROJECT)))$

EMP#	ENAME
1	DEVASIA
6	DARSHAN
7	JAWAHAR
9	MINI

(iii) $EMPLOYEE \bowtie (ALLOTTED \div \Pi_{PRJ\#}(\sigma_{(PRJ\# = 'P6' \vee PRJ\# = 'P2')}(ALLOTTED)))$

EMP#	ENAME
6	DARSHAN
9	MINI

(iv) $ALLOTTED \div \Pi_{PRJ\#}(PROJECT)$

EMP#
6

(v) $\Pi_{EMP\#}$ (ASSIGNED_ TO) $\bowtie$ $\Pi_{PRJ\#}(\sigma_{EMP\# = 7}$ (ASSIGNED_ TO)) − 7

EMP#
6
9

W2_3 (i) CCODE+PCODE is primary key in DAILY_ALLOWANCE.

(ii) No, it is not possible to insert data in CCODE, CNAME, etc. without inserting data in PCODE, which is part of primary key.

(iii) If MUMBAI is changed to BOMBAY and it is correctly changed in 3 places and not changed in 2 place it will lead to non-synchronization. A1 will be MUMBAI as well as BOMBAY, which is not intended.

(iv) CCODE → CNAME
PCODE → LOSAL, HISAL
CCODE, PCODE → HOTELRATE, ORDYRATE

(v) Draw ER model yourself.

(vi) CITY(CCODE#, CNAME)
PAY(PCODE#, LOSAL, HISAL)
DARATE(CCODE#, PCODE#, HOTELRATE, ORDYRATE)

(vii) There is no transitive dependency.

W2_4 (i) EMPNO+PROJNO

(ii) No, it is not possible to enter data in EMPNO, ENAME, DESG, etc. without inserting data in PROJNO, which is part of primary key.

(iii) No, it is not possible to enter data in PROJNO, PROJNAME, etc. without inserting data in EMPNO, which is part of primary key.

(iv) ARUP is the only DBA in the company. If all relevant records are deleted HRRATE of DBA will also be lost. Also P3 related information will also be lost as only ARUP was associated with that project.

(v) EMPNO → ENAME, DESG, HRRATE
PROJNO → PROJNAME
EMPNO, PROJNO → HRWORKED

(vi) Draw ER model yourself.

(vii) PROJ(PROJNO#, PROJNAME)
EMP(EMPNO#, ENAME, DESG, HRRATE)
PROJ_DETAIL(EMPNO#, PROJNO#, HRWORKED)

(viii) EMPNO → DESG → HRRATE ==> EMPNO → HRRATE

(ix) PROJ(PROJNO#, PROJNAME)
EMP(EMPNO#, ENAME, DESG)
DESGRATE(DESG#, HRRATE)
PROJ_DETAIL(EMPNO#, PROJNO#, HRWORKED)

CHAPTER 3

Short/Objective Type Questions

1. Refer to Section 3.1
2. Refer to Section 3.5
3. Refer to Section 3.8
4. | | |
   |---|---|
   | DDL | Create Table |
   | DML | Insert, Update, Delete |
   | DCL | Grant, Revoke |
   | Transaction | Commit |
   | Data Retrieval | Select |

VARCHAR2(10)	'Allahabad'
NUMBER(4)	1947
Arithmetic Operators	+, –, *
Relational Operator	>, like, =
NUMBER(4,2)	15.35

5. It is not possible to insert the record as ENAME is defined to be primary key and RAVI already exists.

6. Do it yourself

7. SQL> DROP TABLE EMPLOYEE;
SQL> DESC EMPLOYEE
ERROR:
ORA-04043: object EMPLOYEE does not exist

8. SQL> DROP USER EMP;
DROP USER EMP
*
ERROR at line 1:
ORA-01031: insufficient privileges

9. SQL> CONNECT SYSTEM/MANAGER@MKGCONNECT
SQL> DROP USER EMP;
User dropped.

10. SQL> CONNECT EMP/MKG@MKGCONNECT
ERROR:
ORA-01017: invalid username/password; logon denied
Warning: You are no longer connected to ORACLE.

Workout Section

W3_1 (i) SQL> SELECT C.CNAME, SN.STATE FROM CUST C,STATE_NAME SN WHERE C.CCITY=SN.CCITY ORDER BY C.CNAME;

(ii) SQL> SELECT CID, SALEDT FROM SALE_DETAIL;

(iii) SQL> SELECT S.CID, P.PNAME, S.SALE*P.PCOST
FROM SALE_DETAIL S, PROD P
WHERE S.PID=P.PID AND P.PNAME LIKE 'F%';

(iv) SQL> SELECT DISTINCT C.CNAME
FROM CUST C,PROD P, SALE_DETAIL SD,STATE_NAME SN
WHERE C.CID=SD.CID AND P.PID=SD.PID AND C.CCITY=SN.CCITY
AND SN.STATE='KARNATAKA' AND P.PNAME='PEN';

(v) It cannot be inserted because CID is prime attribute and it cannot be empty. No, It is not possible to insert.

W3_2 (i) No solution to this question.

(ii) SQL> SELECT HOTELRATE,ORDYRATE FROM DARATE WHERE CCODE= 'A1';

(iii) SQL> SELECT PCODE FROM PAY WHERE LOSAL<10000 AND HISAL>10000;
SQL> SELECT PCODE FROM PAY WHERE 10000 BETWEEN LOSAL AND HISAL;

(iv) SQL> SELECT CNAME FROM CITY WHERE CCODE='A1';

(v) SQL> SELECT DARATE.HOTELRATE FROM DARATE,CITY,PAY
WHERE DARATE.PCODE=PAY.PCODE AND DARATE.CCODE=CITY.CCODE
AND CITY.CCODE='A' AND LOSAL<20000 AND HISAL>20000;

W3_3 (i) No solution for this question.

(ii) SQL> SELECT E.ENAME, E.DESG,D.HRRATE,P.PROJNAME,PD.HRWORKED
FROM EMP E, DESGRATE D, PROJ P, PROJ_DETAIL PD
WHERE E.EMPNO=PD.EMPNO AND P.PROJNO=PD.PROJNO AND E.DESG = D.DESG;

(iii) SQL> SELECT E.ENAME, PD.HRWORKED
FROM EMP E, DESGRATE D, PROJ P, PROJ_DETAIL PD
WHERE E.EMPNO=PD.EMPNO AND P.PROJNO=PD.PROJNO AND E.DESG= D.DESG
AND D.DESG='DBA' AND P.PROJNAME='CODING';

(iv) SQL> SELECT E.ENAME, P.PROJNAME
FROM EMP E, PROJ P, PROJ_DETAIL PD
WHERE E.EMPNO=PD.EMPNO AND P.PROJNO=PD.PROJNO
ORDER BY E.ENAME DESC, P.PROJNAME ASC;

(v) For all the records, HRWORKED will be printed in the next line.

(vi)

Emp No	*Name*	*Designation*	*HR Rate*	*Proj No*	*Project*	*HR Worked*
E1	*ANUP*	*ANALYST*	*800*	*P2*	*CODING*	*15*
E3	*KAUSHIK*	*ANALYST*	*800*	*P1*	*DATABASE SW*	*20*
E2	*ARUP*	*DBA*	*1000*	*P1*	*DATABASE SW*	*40*
E2	*ARUP*	*DBA*	*1000*	*P3*	*DATA RECOVERY*	*10*
E2	*ARUP*	*DBA*	*1000*	*P2*	*CODING*	*10*
E4	*AMIT*	*PROGRAMMER*	*500*	*P2*	*CODING*	*40*
E5	*CHANDRA*	*PROGRAMMER*	*500*	*P1*	*DATABASE SW*	*30*

(vii)

Name	*Project*
ANUP	*CODING*
KAUSHIK	*DATABASE SW*
ARUP	*DATABASE SW*
ARUP	*DATA RECOVERY*
ARUP	*CODING*
AMIT	*CODING*
CHANDRA	*DATABASE SW*

W3_4 (i) SQL> SELECT SALEDT,PID,SUM(SALE) FROM SALE_DETAIL GROUP BY SALEDT,PID;

(ii) SQL> SELECT MAX(PCOST) || ' ' || MIN(PCOST) "Max and Min Cost Product" FROM PROD;

(iii) SQL> SELECT C.CNAME || 'HAS' || 'PURCHASED' || P.PNAME || 'AT THE COST OF' || P.PCOST || 'ON' || S.SALEDT FROM CUST C, PROD P, SALE_DETAIL S WHERE C.CID=S.CID AND P.PID=S.PID;

(iv) SQL> SELECT PNAME, ROUND (PCOST*(1-NVL(PCOST,0)/100)) ACTUAL _COST
FROM PROD;

(v) SQL> SELECT C.CNAME,C.CCITY,SUBSTR(S.STATE,1,5) STATE FROM CUST C, STATE_NAME S WHERE C.CCITY=S.CCITY;

W3_5 (i) SQL> SELECT DISTINCT C1.CNAME,C1.CCITY FROM CUST C1,CUST C2 WHERE SUBSTR (C1.CNAME,1,1)<SUBSTR(C2.CCITY,1,1);

(ii) SQL> SELECT C.CNAME,P.PNAME FROM CUST C, PROD P, SALE_DETAIL S WHERE S.CID=C.CID AND S.PID=P.PID AND P.PID IN (SELECT S.PID FROM CUST C,SALE_DETAIL S WHERE S.CID=C.CID AND C.CNAME='ANUMITA');

(iii) SQL> SELECT * FROM CUST,PROD;

(iv) SQL> SELECT C.CNAME, P.PNAME, S.SALE FROM CUST C, PROD P, SALE _DETAIL S WHERE P.PID=S.PID AND C.CID=S.CID AND (C.CID, P.PID) IN (SELECT S.CID, S.PID FROM SALE_DETAIL S, PROD P WHERE P.PID=S.PID AND P.PNAME LIKE '%F%');

(v) SQL> SELECT C.CNAME,P.PNAME FROM CUST C, PROD P, SALE_DETAIL S WHERE C.CID=S.CID AND P.PID=S.PID
MINUS
SELECT C.CNAME,P.PNAME FROM CUST C, PROD P, SALE_DETAIL S WHERE C.CID=S.CID AND P.PID=S.PID AND C.CNAME LIKE 'A%';

(vi) Result of inner query and outer query when 'P3' is passed in the inner query
Result of inner query and outer query when 'P2' is passed in the inner query
Result of inner query and outer query when 'P1' is passed in the inner query

AVG(SALE)

5

no rows selected

PID	*SALE*
P3	*1*
P2	*2*

W3_6 (i) COUNT(*)

21

(ii) SQL> SELECT E.ENAME,P.PROJNAME
FROM EMP E, PROJ P,PROJ_DETAIL PD
WHERE E.EMPNO=PD.EMPNO AND P.PROJNO=PD.PROJNO
AND E.ENAME LIKE 'A%P';

(iii) SQL> SELECT P.PROJNAME,SUM(PD.HRWORKED*D.HRRATE)*0.20 PROFIT
FROM PROJ P, DESGRATE D, PROJ_DETAIL PD, EMP E
WHERE P.PROJNO=PD.PROJNO AND E.DESG=D.DESG AND E.EMPNO =PD.EMPNO
GROUP BY P.PROJNAME;

(iv) SQL> SELECT DESG,HRRATE
FROM DESGRATE
WHERE HRRATE !=(SELECT MAX(HRRATE) FROM DESGRATE)
AND HRRATE !=(SELECT MIN(HRRATE) FROM DESGRATE);

(v) SQL> SELECT E.ENAME,SUM(D.HRRATE*P.HRWORKED) EARNED
FROM EMP E, DESGRATE D, PROJ_DETAIL P
WHERE E.EMPNO=P.EMPNO AND E.DESG=D.DESG
GROUP BY E.ENAME
HAVING SUM(D.HRRATE*P.HRWORKED)<
(SELECT AVG(D.HRRATE*P.HRWORKED)
FROM EMP E, DESGRATE D, PROJ_DETAIL P
WHERE E.EMPNO=P.EMPNO AND E.DESG=D.DESG)
ORDER BY E.ENAME;

CHAPTER 4

Short/Objective Type Questions

1. Refer to Section 4.6
2. Refer to Section 4.8
3. Refer to Section 4.7
4. Refer to Section 4.9
5. Refer to Section 4.10
6. Refer to Section 4.11, 4.12
7. Do it yourself.
8. Do it yourself.
9. Do it yourself.
10. (i) SQL> CREATE VIEW CUST_PROD_VIEW1 AS
SELECT C.CNAME, C.CCITY, S.STATE, P.PNAME, P.PCOST*SD.SALE SPENT, SD.SALEDT FROM PROD P, CUST C, STATE_NAME S, SALE_DETAIL SD
WHERE P.PID=SD.PID AND C.CID=SD.CID AND C.CCITY=S.CCITY;

(ii) SQL> SELECT * FROM CUST_PROD_VIEW1
WHERE PNAME='PEN';

Workout Section

W4_1 SQL> CREATE SEQUENCE QUES_SEQ
INCREMENT BY -1
MINVALUE 5
MAXVALUE 10
NOCACHE
CYCLE;

SQL> SELECT SEQUENCE_NAME, MIN_VALUE, MAX_VALUE, INCREMENT_BY
FROM USER_SEQUENCES
WHERE SEQUENCE_NAME LIKE 'Q%';

W4_2 (i) Do it yourself.

(ii) Do it yourself.

(iii) Do it yourself.

(iv) Do it yourself.

(v) Do it yourself.

(vi) Do it yourself.

(vii) Do it yourself.

(viii) Do it yourself.

(ix) SQL>CREATE TABLE PROJ_DETAIL
(EMPNO VARCHAR2(5) REFERENCES EMP(EMPNO),
PROJNO VARCHAR2(5) REFERENCES PROJ(PROJNO),
HRWORKED NUMBER(3) NOT NULL,
CONSTRAINT PD_CHECK CHECK (HRWORKED BETWEEN 10 AND 100));

(x) Do it yourself

(xi) Do it yourself.

(xii) Do it yourself.

(xiii) Check it.

(xiv) Check it.

(xv) Check it.

(xvi) Do it yourself.

(xvii) Do it yourself.

W4_3 (i) Do it yourself.

(ii) Do it yourself.

(iii) SQL> GRANT CONNECT, RESOURCE TO MYUSER
WITH ADMIN OPTION;
SQL> CONNECT MYUSER/USER123;

(iv) Do it yourself.

(v) SQL> CONNECT MYUSER/USER123
SQL> GRANT SELECT,INSERT,UPDATE
ON STATE_NAME
TO USER1;
SQL> GRANT SELECT, INSERT, UPDATE
ON CUST
TO USER1;

(vi) SQL> CONNECT SYSTEM/MANAGER
SQL> SELECT GRANTEE,GRANTED_ROLE,ADMIN_OPTION
FROM DBA_ROLE_PRIVS
WHERE GRANTEE='MYUSER';
SQL> SELECT GRANTEE, GRANTED_ROLE,ADMIN_OPTION
FROM DBA_ROLE_PRIVS
WHERE GRANTEE='USER1';

(vii) Do it yourself.

(viii) SQL> SELECT C.CNAME, C.CCITY, S.STATE
FROM MYUSER.CUST C, MYUSER.STATE_NAME S
WHERE C.CCITY=S.CCITY;

(ix) Do it yourself.

(x) SQL> SELECT C.CNAME,C.CCITY,S.STATE
FROM MYUSER.CUST C, MYUSER.STATE_NAME S
WHERE C.CCITY=S.CCITY;

(xi) Do it yourself.

(xii) SQL> CONNECT MYUSER/USER123;
SQL> SELECT * FROM STATE_NAME;
SQL> SELECT * FROM CUST;

W4_4 SQL>CONNECT SYSTEM/MANAGER
SQL> CREATE PROFILE MY_PROFILE LIMIT
FAILED_LOGIN_ATTEMPTS 2
PASSWORD_LOCK_TIME 1/2
PASSWORD_LIFE_TIME 60
PASSWORD_GRACE_TIME 10;
SQL> COLUMN LIMIT FORMAT A10
SQL> SELECT RESOURCE_NAME NAME, LIMIT
FROM DBA_PROFILES
WHERE RESOURCE_TYPE='PASSWORD'
AND PROFILE='MY_PROFILE' ;

CHAPTER 5

Short/Objective Type Questions

7. SQL is a fourth-generation language and suitable for non-programmers. It does not provide conditional statement and looping constructs. PL/SQL exploits the power of SQL along with the constructs relevant to third-generation language. It seamlessly integrate with database and provides better performance, higher productivity and portability.

8. The major advantage of using the %ROWTYPE is to retrieve an entire row from a table, without declaring variables for each column separately. It also ensures that the data type of the variable changes dynamically whenever the associated table is changed.

10. No.

12. DECODE function cannot be used. If … Then… Else… statement is equivalent to DECODE function in PL/SQL within the procedural statements.

13. PL/SQL blocks that are not assigned any name are called anonymous block. It cannot be stored in the database. Anonymous block can call other blocks but they cannot be called by other blocks as they are not assigned any name.

14. Bind variable is a variable within a PL/SQL Select statement that is replaced by a valid value on successful execution of the 'Select' statement. It is always preceded by a ':' in a 'Select' statement.

15. Any variable declared inside a nested block is local to the nested block and is unknown to the outer blocks. Variable declared within a block is local to the block and global to the nested blocks.

16. NVL function is used to replace the NULL values within a PL/SQL statement.

17. Transaction control language comprises two commands, namely, COMMIT and ROLLBACK. Both the commands terminate the active transaction. COMMIT command makes the changes permanent to the database, whereas ROLLBACK command cancels any changes that were made to the database. SAVEPOINT TO clause is associated with ROLLBACK command through which a transaction can be revoked in designated parts rather than rolling back the entire transaction.

18. CREATE ANY TABLE grants privilege to create any table owned by any other schema in addition to its own schema. CREATE TABLE privilege grants permission only to its own schema to create tables.

20. Yes. SQL session information can be accessed using DBMS_SESSION package.

Workout Section

W5_1

```
SET SERVEROUTPUT ON
DECLARE
    A NUMBER := &A;
    B NUMBER := &B;
    C NUMBER := &C;
```

```
BEGIN
    IF A<=B THEN
        IF A<=C THEN
            DBMS_OUTPUT.PUT_LINE('Smallest Number is ' || A);
        ELSE
            DBMS_OUTPUT.PUT_LINE('Smallest Number is ' || C);
        END IF;
    ELSE
        IF B<=C THEN
            DBMS_OUTPUT.PUT_LINE('Smallest Number is ' || B);
        ELSE
            DBMS_OUTPUT.PUT_LINE('Smallest Number is ' || C);
        END IF;
END IF;
END;
/
```

W5_2 LOOP … END LOOP

```
SET VERIFY OFF
SET SERVEROUTPUT ON
DECLARE
    I_NUM NUMBER;
    F_NUM NUMBER;
    FACT_NUM NUMBER;
BEGIN
    I_NUM := &I_NUM;
    FACT_NUM := 1;
    F_NUM := I_NUM;
    IF I_NUM >0 AND I_NUM < 11 THEN
        LOOP
            FACT_NUM := FACT_NUM*I_NUM;
            I_NUM := I_NUM-1;
            EXIT WHEN I_NUM=0;
        END LOOP;
        DBMS_OUTPUT.PUT_LINE('FACTORIAL OF ' || F_NUM || 'IS ' ||
        FACT_NUM);
    ELSE
    DBMS_OUTPUT.PUT_LINE('Input Number Range is from 1 to
    10');
  END IF;
END;
/
```

W5_3

```
SET VERIFY OFF
SET SERVEROUTPUT ON
```

```
DECLARE
   I_NUM NUMBER;
   FACT_NUM NUMBER;
BEGIN
   I_NUM := &I_NUM;
   FACT_NUM := 1;
   IF I_NUM >0 AND I_NUM < 11 THEN
      FOR I IN 1..I_NUM LOOP
         FACT_NUM := FACT_NUM*I;
      END LOOP;
      DBMS_OUTPUT.PUT_LINE('FACTORIAL OF ' || I_NUM || ' IS ' ||
      FACT_NUM);
   ELSE
      DBMS_OUTPUT.PUT_LINE('Input Number Range is from 1 to 10');
   END IF;
END;
/
```

W5_4

```
SET VERIFY OFF
SET SERVEROUTPUT ON
DECLARE
   I_NUM NUMBER;
   F_NUM NUMBER;
   FACT_NUM NUMBER;
BEGIN
   I_NUM := &I_NUM;
   FACT_NUM := 1;
   F_NUM := I_NUM;
   IF I_NUM >0 AND I_NUM < 11 THEN
      WHILE I_NUM > 0 LOOP
            FACT_NUM := FACT_NUM*I_NUM;
            I_NUM := I_NUM-1;
      END LOOP;
      DBMS_OUTPUT.PUT_LINE('FACTORIAL OF ' || F_NUM || ' IS ' ||
      FACT_NUM);
   ELSE
      DBMS_OUTPUT.PUT_LINE('Input Number Range is from 1 to 10');
   END IF;
END;
/
```

W5_5

```
SET VERIFY OFF
SET SERVEROUTPUT ON
DECLARE
   I_NUM NUMBER;
   B_SPACE VARCHAR2(100);
```

```
BEGIN
   I_NUM := &I_NUM;
   IF I_NUM >0 AND I_NUM < 21 THEN
      FOR I IN 1..I_NUM LOOP
         B_SPACE := '';
         FOR J IN 1..I LOOP
            B_SPACE := B_SPACE || '-';
         END LOOP;
         DBMS_OUTPUT.PUT_LINE(B_SPACE || ' *');
      END LOOP;
   ELSE
      DBMS_OUTPUT.PUT_LINE('Input Number Range is from 1 to 20');
   END IF;
END;
/
```

W5_6

```
SET VERIFY OFF
SET ECHO OFF
SET SERVEROUTPUT ON
DECLARE
   VDESG     DESGRATE.DESG%TYPE;
   VHRRATE   DESGRATE.HRRATE%TYPE;
   VCNT      NUMBER(2);
BEGIN
   VDESG := '&DESG';
   SELECT COUNT(*) INTO VCNT
   FROM DESGRATE
   WHERE DESG=VDESG;
   IF VCNT=0 THEN
      DBMS_OUTPUT.PUT_LINE(VDESG || ' DOES NOT EXISTS, PLEASE TRY
      AGAIN');
   END IF;
   IF VCNT=1 THEN
      SELECT HRRATE INTO VHRRATE FROM DESGRATE WHERE DESG=VDESG;
      SELECT COUNT(*) INTO VCNT FROM EMP WHERE DESG=VDESG;
      IF VCNT>1 THEN
         DBMS_OUTPUT.PUT_LINE('THERE ARE '|| VCNT || ' ' || VDESG
         || ' AND THE SERVICE CHARGE IS Rs ' || VHRRATE || ' PER
         HOUR.');
   ELSE
      DBMS_OUTPUT.PUT_LINE('THERE IS ONLY 1 ' || VDESG || '
      AND THE SERVICE CHARGE IS Rs ' || VHRRATE|| ' PER HOUR.');
   END IF;
  END IF;
END;
/
```

W5_7

```
SET VERIFY OFF
SET ECHO OFF
SET SERVEROUTPUT ON
DECLARE
   VCNT           NUMBER(2);
   VPROJNO        PROJ.PROJNO%TYPE;
   VPROJNAME      PROJ.PROJNAME%TYPE;
   VEXPENDITURE   NUMBER(8);
BEGIN
   VPROJNO := '&PROJNO';
   SELECT COUNT(*) INTO VCNT
   FROM PROJ_DETAIL
   WHERE PROJNO=VPROJNO;
   IF VCNT=0 THEN
      DBMS_OUTPUT.PUT_LINE(VPROJNO || ' PROJECT NUMBER DOES NOT
      EXISTS, PLEASE TRY AGAIN');
ELSE
   SELECT PROJNAME INTO VPROJNAME
   FROM PROJ
   WHERE PROJNO=VPROJNO;
   SELECT SUM(PROJ_DETAIL.HRWORKED*DESGRATE.HRRATE)
   INTO VEXPENDITURE
   FROM EMP, DESGRATE,PROJ_DETAIL,PROJ
   WHERE EMP.EMPNO=PROJ_DETAIL.EMPNO AND
   EMP.DESG=DESGRATE.DESG AND EMP.EMPNO=PROJ_DETAIL.EMPNO
   AND PROJ_DETAIL.PROJNO=VPROJNO;
   DBMS_OUTPUT.PUT_LINE('TOTAL EXPENDITURE ON ' || VPROJNAME
   || ' IS ' || VEXPENDITURE);
END IF;
END;
/
```

W5_8

```
SET VERIFY OFF
SET ECHO OFF
SET SERVEROUTPUT ON
DECLARE
   VEMPNO      EMP.EMPNO%TYPE;
   VENAME      EMP.ENAME%TYPE;
   VPROJNO     PROJ.PROJNO%TYPE;
   VPROJNAME   PROJ.PROJNAME%TYPE;
   VCNT        NUMBER(2);
   VCNT1       NUMBER(2);
   VCNT2       NUMBER(2);
BEGIN
   —READ EMPNO AND PROJNO
   VEMPNO := '&EMPNO';
```

```
    VPROJNO:= '&PROJNO';
    —CHECK IF ANY ROW EXISTS WITH VEMPNO AND VPROJNO
    SELECT COUNT(*) INTO VCNT
    FROM PROJ_DETAIL
    WHERE EMPNO=VEMPNO AND PROJNO=VPROJNO;
    IF VCNT>0 THEN
        —FIND ENAME CORRESPONDING TO VEMPNO
        SELECT ENAME INTO VENAME
        FROM EMP
        WHERE EMPNO=VEMPNO;
        —FIND PROJNAME CORRESPONDING TO VPROJNO
        SELECT PROJNAME INTO VPROJNAME
        FROM PROJ
        WHERE PROJNO=VPROJNO;
        —PRINT MESSAGE
        DBMS_OUTPUT.PUT_LINE('YES, ' || VENAME || ' WORKED ON ' ||
        VPROJNAME || ' PROJECT.');
    END IF;
    /*
    IF VCNT CAN BE 0 IN FOLLOWING CONDITIONS
    A. EITHER EMPNO OR PROJNO IS NOT PRESENT IN PROJ_DETAIL TABLE
    B. BOTH EMPNO AND PROJNO ARE NOT PRESENT IN PROJ_DETAIL TABLE
    CHECK WHAT IS THE EXACT REASON FOR VCNT=0 AND PRINT APPROPRIATE
    MESSAGE
    */
    SELECT COUNT(*) INTO VCNT1
    FROM EMP
    WHERE EMPNO=VEMPNO;
    IF VCNT1=0 THEN
    DBMS_OUTPUT.PUT_LINE(VEMPNO || ' IS NOT PRESENT IN EMP
    TABLE');
END IF;
SELECT COUNT(*) INTO VCNT2
FROM PROJ
WHERE PROJNO=VPROJNO;
IF VCNT2=0 THEN
    DBMS_OUTPUT.PUT_LINE(VPROJNO || ' IS NOT PRESENT IN PROJ
    TABLE');
END IF;
/*
    IF VCNT1 AND VCNT2 BOTH ARE 1, THEN FIND ENAME AND PROJNAME
    AND PRINT APPROPRIATE MESSAGE
*/

IF VCNT=0 AND (VCNT1=1 AND VCNT2=1) THEN
    — FIND ENAME CORRESPONDING TO VEMPNO
```

```
        SELECT ENAME INTO VENAME
        FROM EMP
        WHERE EMPNO=VEMPNO;
        – FIND PROJNAME CORRESPONDING TO VPROJNO
        SELECT PROJNAME INTO VPROJNAME
        FROM PROJ
        WHERE PROJNO=VPROJNO;
        DBMS_OUTPUT.PUT_LINE('NO, ' || VENAME || ' HAS NOT WORKED
        ON ' || VPROJNAME || ' PROJECT.');
    END IF;
END;
/
```

W5_9

```
SET SERVEROUTPUT ON
SET VERIFY OFF
SET ECHO OFF
DECLARE
   VENAME EMP.ENAME%TYPE;
   VHRWORKED   PROJ_DETAIL.HRWORKED%TYPE;
   VCNT      NUMBER(2);
BEGIN
   – READ ENAME
   VENAME := '&ENAME';
   – CHECK WHETHER VENAME IS PRESENT IN EMP TABLE
   SELECT COUNT(*) INTO VCNT
   FROM PROJ_DETAIL,EMP
   WHERE EMP.EMPNO=PROJ_DETAIL.EMPNO
   AND EMP.ENAME=VENAME;
   –IF VENAME IS PRESENT THEN FIND THE TOTAL HRWORKED AND PRINT
   APPROPRIATE MESSAGE
   IF VCNT>0 THEN
      SELECT SUM(HRWORKED) INTO VHRWORKED
      FROM PROJ_DETAIL,EMP
      WHERE EMP.EMPNO=PROJ_DETAIL.EMPNO AND EMP.ENAME=VENAME;
      DBMS_OUTPUT.PUT_LINE(VENAME || ' HAS WORKED ON ' || VCNT ||
      ' PROJECT(S) ' || ' FOR A TOTAL OF ' || VHRWORKED || ' HOURS');
   ELSE
      DBMS_OUTPUT.PUT_LINE(VENAME || ' IS NOT PRESENT IN EMP
      TABLE');
   END IF;
END;
/
```

W5_10

```
SET SERVEROUTPUT ON
SET VERIFY OFF
```

```
DECLARE
   VPROJNO  PROJ_DETAIL.PROJNO%TYPE;
   VCNT_BEFORE NUMBER(2);
   VCNT_AFTER  NUMBER(2);
   VCNT_DELETED          NUMBER(2);
BEGIN
   VPROJNO:='&PROJNO';
   SELECT COUNT(*) INTO VCNT_BEFORE
   FROM PROJ_DETAIL;
   DELETE FROM PROJ_DETAIL
   WHERE PROJNO=VPROJNO;
   SELECT COUNT(*) INTO VCNT_AFTER
   FROM PROJ_DETAIL;
   VCNT_DELETED := VCNT_BEFORE-VCNT_AFTER;
   DBMS_OUTPUT.PUT_LINE(VCNT_DELETED || ' ROWS DELETED FROM
   PROJ_DETAIL TABLE');
   IF VCNT_DELETED>0 THEN
      DBMS_OUTPUT.PUT_LINE('INVOKE COMMIT OR ROLLBACK TO MAKE THE
      CHANGES PERMANENT');
   END IF;
END;
/
```

W5_11 In this program there is no INTO clause which is not allowed in a PL/SQL program.

W5_12 This program will fetch more than one row and the container VEMPREC can store one record at a time. This type of requirement where more than one row is in fetched can be handled using explicit cursors. Explicit cursor will be discussed in detail in later chapter.

CHAPTER 6

Short/Objective Type Questions

1. Subprograms are modular, reusable and performance intrinsic. It is also easy to maintain and ensure data integrity and security.
2. There are two different types of subprograms in PL/SQL. They are procedures and functions.
3. Yes.
4. No.
5. The primary advantages of using packages are encapsulation, superior application design, information hiding and better performance.
6. DROP PACKAGE

7. DROP PACKAGE BODY
8. You should use procedure when there are more than one return values.
9. Yes.
10. Oracle supplied packages allow PL/SQL programs to access features of SQL (that are not available in PL/SQL) to extend the functionality of the database.
11. The signature of a procedure comprises its name, data type, modes and the number of parameters.
12. Package can be stored either on the server side in the database or on the client side in the form of Oracle Forms, Oracle Reports or PL/SQL library.
13. A procedure can return none, one or more values, whereas a function returns a single value to the calling environment.
14. Yes.
15. The option REPLACE recreates a procedure if it already exists.
16. Formal parameters are the variables declared as the parameter list in the subprogram specification.
17. Actual parameter values are passed to the subprogram from the calling environment.
18. IN, OUT and IN OUT.
19. No.
20. Yes.
21. Positional and/or Named.
22. This is required whenever any changes are made in the package specification. However, any change in the package body does not require compilation.
23. No.
24. No.
25. No.
26. Yes.
27. Yes.
28. ORA-06575
29. Yes. However, only one is executed.
31. No. Explicit privileges are essentially required in the user to access another schema in methods.
32. USER_ERRORS
33. USER_SOURCE
34. No.
35. Yes.

36. Yes. However, only package subprograms can be overloaded.

37. Yes. The package can include subprograms having the same name as long as they have different formal parameters.

38. Using the SHOW_ERROR or DBMS_OUTPUT command.

39. Using the RAISE_APPLICATION_ERROR.

40. No.

Workout Section

W6_1

```
CREATE OR REPLACE FUNCTION FLEAP(A NUMBER) RETURN VARCHAR2
IS C VARCHAR2(50);
BEGIN
   IF MOD(A,100)=0 THEN
      IF MOD(A,400)=0 THEN
         C:=TO_CHAR(A)||' IS A LEAP YEAR';
      ELSE
         C:=TO_CHAR(A)||' IS NOT A LEAP YEAR';
      END IF;
   ELSE
      IF MOD(A,4)=0 THEN
         C:=TO_CHAR(A)||' IS A LEAP YEAR';
   ELSE
         C:=TO_CHAR(A)||' IS NOT A LEAP YEAR';
   END IF;
   END IF;
  RETURN C;
END;
/
```

W6_2

```
CREATE OR REPLACE FUNCTION FAREA(A NUMBER,B CHAR) RETURN
VARCHAR2 IS C VARCHAR2(50);
BEGIN
   IF B='C' THEN
      C:=TO_CHAR(3.14*A*A);
      C:= 'AREA OF CIRCLE IS '||C;
   ELSE
      C:=TO_CHAR(A*A);
      C:='AREA OF SQUARE IS '||C;
   END IF;
   RETURN C;
END;
/
```

W6_3

```
CREATE OR REPLACE FUNCTION FQ23(VCID VARCHAR2) RETURN VARCHAR2 IS
   VCDETAIL VARCHAR2(100);
   VCNT     NUMBER(2);
```

```
    VCNAME   CUST.CNAME%TYPE;
    VCITY    CUST.CCITY%TYPE;
BEGIN
    SELECT COUNT(*) INTO VCNT FROM CUST WHERE CID=VCID;
    IF VCNT=1 THEN
       SELECT CNAME,CCITY INTO VCNAME,VCITY FROM CUST
       WHERE CID=VCID;
       VCDETAIL := VCID || ' - '||VCNAME||' LIVES IN '||VCITY;
    ELSE
       VCDETAIL := VCID || ' - '||' INVALID CUSTOMER ID';
    END IF;
    RETURN VCDETAIL;
END;
```

W6_4

```
SET SERVEROUTPUT ON
CREATE OR REPLACE PROCEDURE PALL(A NUMBER,B NUMBER) IS
        C NUMBER;
        D NUMBER;
        E NUMBER;
        F NUMBER;
BEGIN
    C:=A+B;
    DBMS_OUTPUT.PUT_LINE('SUM OF '|| A || ' & '|| B || ' IS '
    || C);
    D:=A-B;
    DBMS_OUTPUT.PUT_LINE('DIFF OF ' || A || ' & '|| B || ' IS '
    || D);
    E:=A*B;
    DBMS_OUTPUT.PUT_LINE('MULT OF '|| A || ' & '|| B || ' IS '
    || E);
    F:=A/B;
    DBMS_OUTPUT.PUT_LINE('DIV OF '|| A ||' & '|| B || ' IS '
    || F);
END PALL;
```

W6_5

```
CREATE OR REPLACE PROCEDURE PALL_OUT(A NUMBER,B NUMBER,C OUT
NUMBER, D OUT NUMBER, E OUT NUMBER, F OUT NUMBER) IS
BEGIN
        C:=A+B;
        D:=A-B;
        E:=A*B;
        F:=A/B;
END PALL_OUT;
/

— W6_5_CALL.SQL This program calls W6_5
```

```
SET SERVEROUTPUT ON
SET VERIFY OFF
DECLARE
   A  NUMBER := &A;
   B  NUMBER := &B;
   C  NUMBER;
   D  NUMBER;
   E  NUMBER;
   F  NUMBER;
BEGIN
      PALL_OUT(A,B,C,D,E,F);
      DBMS_OUTPUT.PUT_LINE('SUM OF ' || A || ' & ' || B || ' IS '
      || C);
      DBMS_OUTPUT.PUT_LINE('DIFF OF ' || A || ' & ' || B || ' IS '
      || D);
      DBMS_OUTPUT.PUT_LINE('MULT OF ' || A || ' & ' || B || ' IS '
      || E);
      DBMS_OUTPUT.PUT_LINE('DIV OF ' || A || ' & ' || B || ' IS '
      || F);
END;
/
```

W6_6

```
SET SERVEROUTPUT ON
SET VERIFY OFF
CREATE OR REPLACE PROCEDURE PQ26(VSALEDT DATE) IS
   VSALE NUMBER(10,2);
   VCNT  NUMBER(2);
BEGIN
   SELECT COUNT(*) INTO VCNT FROM SALE_DETAIL
   WHERE SALEDT=VSALEDT;
   IF VCNT>0 THEN
      SELECT SUM(P.PCOST*S.SALE) INTO VSALE
      FROM PROD P, SALE_DETAIL S
      WHERE P.PID=S.PID AND SALEDT=VSALEDT;
      DBMS_OUTPUT.PUT_LINE('TOTAL SALE ON ' || VSALEDT || '
      IS Rs' || VSALE);
   ELSE
      DBMS_OUTPUT.PUT_LINE('NO SALE ON ' || VSALEDT);
   END IF;
END PQ26;
```

W6_7 <u>PROCEDURE</u>

```
CREATE OR REPLACE PROCEDURE FIND_EMPPRJ(VEMPNO IN VARCHAR2,
VPROJNO IN VARCHAR2, VMSG OUT VARCHAR2) IS
VENAME        EMP.ENAME%TYPE;
VPROJNAME     PROJ.PROJNAME%TYPE;
VCNT          NUMBER(2);
```

```
VCNT1      NUMBER(2);
VCNT2      NUMBER(2);
BEGIN
   — CHECK IF ANY ROW EXISTS WITH VEMPNO AND VPROJNO
   SELECT COUNT(*) INTO VCNT FROM PROJ_DETAIL
   WHERE EMPNO=VEMPNO AND PROJNO=VPROJNO;
   IF VCNT>0 THEN
      —FIND ENAME CORRESPONDING TO VEMPNO
      SELECT ENAME INTO VENAME FROM EMP WHERE EMPNO=VEMPNO;
      —FIND PROJNAME CORRESPONDING TO VPROJNO
      SELECT PROJNAME INTO VPROJNAME FROM PROJ
      WHERE PROJNO=VPROJNO;
      —COMPOSE MESSAGE
      VMSG := 'YES, ' || VENAME || ' WORKED ON ' || VPROJNAME
      || ' PROJECT.';
   END IF;

   /*
   IF VCNT CAN BE 0 IN FOLLOWING CONDITIONS
   A. EITHER EMPNO OR PROJNO IS NOT PRESENT IN PROJ_DETAIL TABLE
   B. BOTH EMPNO AND PROJNO ARE NOT PRESENT IN PROJ_DETAIL TABLE
   CHECK WHAT IS THE EXACT REASON FOR VCNT=0 AND PRINT
   APPROPRIATE MESSAGE
   */
   SELECT COUNT(*) INTO VCNT1 FROM EMP WHERE EMPNO=VEMPNO;
   IF VCNT1=0 THEN
      VMSG :=VEMPNO || ' IS NOT PRESENT IN EMP TABLE';
   END IF;
   SELECT COUNT(*) INTO VCNT2 FROM PROJ WHERE PROJNO=VPROJNO;
   IF VCNT2=0 THEN
      VMSG := VMSG || ' ' || VPROJNO || ' IS NOT PRESENT IN PROJ
      TABLE';
   END IF;
   /*
   IF VCNT1 AND VCNT2 BOTH ARE 1, THEN FIND ENAME AND PROJNAME
   AND PRINT APPROPRIATE MESSAGE
   */
   IF VCNT=0 AND (VCNT1=1 AND VCNT2=1) THEN
      —FIND ENAME CORRESPONDING TO VEMPNO
      SELECT ENAME INTO VENAME FROM EMP WHERE EMPNO=VEMPNO;
      —FIND PROJNAME CORRESPONDING TO VPROJNO
      SELECT PROJNAME INTO VPROJNAME FROM PROJ
      WHERE PROJNO=VPROJNO;
      VMSG :='NO, ' || VENAME || ' HAS NOT WORKED ON '
      || VPROJNAME          || ' PROJECT.';
   END IF;
END;
/
```

PROGRAM TO CALL PROCEDURE FIND_EMPPRJ (W6_7_CALL.SQL)

```
SET SERVEROUTPUT ON
SET VERIFY OFF
DECLARE
VEMPNO VARCHAR2(5):='&V1';
VPROJNO VARCHAR2(5) := '&V2';
VMSG VARCHAR2(100);
BEGIN
   FIND_EMPPRJ(VEMPNO,VPROJNO,VMSG);
   DBMS_OUTPUT.PUT_LINE(VMSG);
END;
/
```

W6_8 FUNCTION

```
CREATE OR REPLACE FUNCTION DISP_INFO(VENAME VARCHAR2)
RETURN VARCHAR2 IS DISP_MSG VARCHAR2(100);
   VHRWORKED  PROJ_DETAIL.HRWORKED%TYPE;
   VCNT  NUMBER(2);
BEGIN
   — CHECK WHETHER VENAME IS PRESENT IN EMP TABLE
   SELECT COUNT(*) INTO VCNT FROM PROJ_DETAIL,EMP
   WHERE EMP.EMPNO=PROJ_DETAIL.EMPNO AND EMP.ENAME=VENAME;
   — IF VENAME IS PRESENT THEN FIND THE TOTAL HRWORKED AND PRINT
   APPROPRITE MESSAGE
   IF VCNT>0 THEN
      SELECT SUM(HRWORKED) INTO VHRWORKED
      FROM PROJ_DETAIL,EMP
      WHERE EMP.EMPNO=PROJ_DETAIL.EMPNO AND EMP.ENAME=VENAME;
      DISP_MSG := VENAME || ' HAS WORKED ON ' || VCNT || '
      PROJECT(S) ' || ' FOR A TOTAL OF ' || VHRWORKED || '
HOURS';
   ELSE
      DISP_MSG := VENAME || ' IS NOT PRESENT IN EMP TABLE';
   END IF;
   RETURN DISP_MSG;
END;
/
```

W6_9 PACKAGE SPECIFICATION(PACKSPN_PROJECT.SQL)

```
CREATE OR REPLACE PACKAGE PACK_PROJECT AS
PROCEDURE FIND_EMPPRJ(VEMPNO IN VARCHAR2, VPROJNO IN VARCHAR2,
VMSG OUT VARCHAR2);
FUNCTION DISP_INFO(VENAME VARCHAR2) RETURN VARCHAR2;
END PACK_PROJECT; /
```

PACKAGE BODYPACKBODY_PROJECT.SQL)

```
SET SERVEROUTPUT ON
CREATE OR REPLACE PACKAGE BODY PACK_PROJECT AS
PROCEDURE FIND_EMPPRJ(VEMPNO IN VARCHAR2, VPROJNO IN VARCHAR2,
VMSG OUT VARCHAR2) IS
   VENAME       EMP.ENAME%TYPE;
   VPROJNAME    PROJ.PROJNAME%TYPE;
   VCNT         NUMBER(2);
   VCNT1        NUMBER(2);
   VCNT2        NUMBER(2);
BEGIN
   —CHECK IF ANY ROW EXISTS WITH VEMPNO AND VPROJNO
   SELECT COUNT(*) INTO VCNT FROM PROJ_DETAIL
   WHERE EMPNO=VEMPNO AND PROJNO=VPROJNO;
   IF VCNT>0 THEN
      —FIND ENAME CORRESPONDING TO VEMPNO
      SELECT ENAME INTO VENAME FROM EMP
      WHERE EMPNO=VEMPNO;
      — FIND PROJNAME CORRESPONDING TO VPROJNO
      SELECT PROJNAME INTO VPROJNAME FROM PROJ
      WHERE PROJNO=VPROJNO;
      —COMPOSE MESSAGE
      VMSG := 'YES, ' || VENAME || ' WORKED ON ' || VPROJNAME ||
'     PROJECT.';
   END IF;
   /*
   IF VCNT CAN BE 0 IN FOLLOWING CONDITIONS
   A. EITHER EMPNO OR PROJNO IS NOT PRESENT IN PROJ_DETAIL TABLE
   B. BOTH EMPNO AND PROJNO ARE NOT PRESENT IN PROJ_DETAIL TABLE
   CHECK WHAT IS THE EXACT REASON FOR VCNT=0 AND PRINT APPROPRIATE
   MESSAGE
   */
   SELECT COUNT(*) INTO VCNT1 FROM EMP WHERE EMPNO=VEMPNO;
   IF VCNT1=0 THEN
      VMSG :=VEMPNO || ' IS NOT PRESENT IN EMP TABLE';
   END IF;
   SELECT COUNT(*) INTO VCNT2 FROM PROJ
   WHERE PROJNO=VPROJNO;
   IF VCNT2=0 THEN
      VMSG := VMSG || '  ' || VPROJNO || ' IS NOT PRESENT IN PROJ
      TABLE';
   END IF;
   /*
   IF VCNT1 AND VCNT2 BOTH ARE 1, THEN FIND ENAME AND PROJNAME
   AND PRINT APPROPRIATE MESSAGE
   */
```

```
    IF VCNT=0 AND (VCNT1=1 AND VCNT2=1) THEN
       — FIND ENAME CORRESPONDING TO VEMPNO
       SELECT ENAME INTO VENAME FROM EMP WHERE EMPNO=VEMPNO;
       — FIND PROJNAME CORRESPONDING TO VPROJNO
       SELECT PROJNAME INTO VPROJNAME FROM PROJ
       WHERE PROJNO=VPROJNO;
       VMSG :='NO, ' || VENAME|| ' HAS NOT WORKED ON ' ||
       VPROJNAME || ' PROJECT.';
    END IF;
 END;

 FUNCTION DISP_INFO(VENAME VARCHAR2) RETURN VARCHAR2
 IS DISP_MSG VARCHAR2(100);
    VHRWORKED   PROJ_DETAIL.HRWORKED%TYPE;
    VCNT        NUMBER(2);
    BEGIN
       —CHECK WHETHER VENAME IS PRESENT IN EMP TABLE
       SELECT COUNT(*) INTO VCNT FROM PROJ_DETAIL,EMP
       WHERE EMP.EMPNO=PROJ_DETAIL.EMPNO AND EMP.ENAME=VENAME;
       — IF VENAME IS PRESENT THEN FIND THE TOTAL HRWORKED AND
    PRINT APPROPRITE MESSAGE
       IF VCNT>0 THEN
       SELECT SUM(HRWORKED) INTO VHRWORKED FROM PROJ_DETAIL,EMP
       WHERE EMP.EMPNO=PROJ_DETAIL.EMPNO AND EMP.ENAME=VENAME;
       DISP_MSG := VENAME || ' HAS WORKED ON ' || VCNT|| '
          PROJECT(S) ' || ' FOR A TOTAL OF ' || VHRWORKED || '
          HOURS';
       ELSE
          DISP_MSG := VENAME || ' IS NOT PRESENT IN EMP TABLE';
       END IF;
       RETURN DISP_MSG;
    END;
 END PACK_PROJECT;
 /
```

CALL_PACK_PROJECT.SQL

```
 SET SERVEROUTPUT ON
 SET VERIFY OFF
 DECLARE
    VEMPNO VARCHAR2(5):='&V1';
    VPROJNO VARCHAR2(5) := '&V2';
    VMSG VARCHAR2(100);
 BEGIN
    PACK_PROJECT.FIND_EMPPRJ(VEMPNO,VPROJNO,VMSG);
    DBMS_OUTPUT.PUT_LINE(VMSG);
 END;
 /
```

CHAPTER 7

Short/Objective Type Questions

3. INSERT, UPDATE and DELETE.
4. It is used to disable, enable or recompile a trigger.
5. It is used to remove the trigger from the database.
6. No. None of the data types are allowed inside a trigger.
7. Three different types of exceptions are Predefined Oracle error, Non-Predefined Oracle Error and User-Defined Error.
8. Yes.
9. User-defined exceptions are raised explicitly, whereas Oracle defined exceptions are implicitly raised.
10. ALTER ANY TABLE and CREATE ANY TRIGGER system privileges are essentially required by a user to create a trigger.
11. Database triggers and application triggers. Database triggers are implicitly executed whenever DML or DDL statement is executed. Application triggers, on the other hand, implicitly execute whenever a DML statement is executed within an application like Oracle Developer Forms.
12. Yes, subject to grant of privileges required to reference other tables.
13. Row-level triggers are invoked once for each row, which is altered by a DML statement. Statement-level triggers, on the other hand, are executed only once for each DML statement. Row-level triggers are usually written for data auditing applications. Statement-level triggers, on the other hand, are used to enforce security feature in the application.
14. Yes.
15. Triggers can be written to track DML operations on tables, which can be later used for auditing.
16. By using WHEN clause in the trigger to limit the action of the trigger only to those rows which satisfy the desired condition.
17. Schema-level triggers prevent DDL statements and provide security.
18. Database event triggers can be used for system maintenance immediately after the database start-up. This type of triggers is executed when a database event such as start-up or shut-down occurs.
19. Disabling of a trigger is advantages during load operations to improve the performance of the data loading activities.
20. Yes.
21. No, neither COMMIT nor ROLLBACK is permitted inside a trigger.
22. Yes.

23. Yes.

24. Inclusion of an INSERT statement on the same table to which the trigger is assigned will give rise to a mutating table, as it is not possible to change the same table that is already in the process of update.

25. In such situation, the controller is passed back to the calling environment. Any insert, update and the delete statements are rolled back.

26. No.

27. No.

28. User-defined exceptions are essentially defined in the declarative section and explicitly raised using the RAISE statement.

29. It is built-in procedure that is used to raise an exception to assign an error number associated with custom message to the user-defined errors.

30. If an exception is not trapped in a subblock, it propagates to the enclosing blocks until the associated handler is found. If there is no block to trap the exception, an unhandled exception is passed to the host environment.

31. No. Even after the exception is handled, processing cannot be resumed in the executable section of the current block.

32. The PRAGMA keyword is a compiler directive that is not processed when a PL/SQL code is executed. It basically tells the compiler to interpret all the occurrences of the exception name within the block with the associated Oracle Server number.

33. NSTEAD OF triggers are used with views. It can be defined only as row-level triggers.

34. Mutating table is a state of transition of a table which is being updated at the time of triggering action. This results into viewing of inconsistent data.

35. Trigger information is available in data dictionary views USER_OBJECTS, USER_ERRORS, USER_TRIGGERS and USER_TRIGGERS_COLS.

36. No, we cannot pass parameters to triggers.

37. No. Only INSERT, UPDATE and DELETE statements can cause triggers to fire.

38. The REFERENCING is used in the declarative section of a trigger. It is used to give names to the :old and :new qualifiers, which is useful to refer :old and :new qualifiers using the assigned names.

39. No. It can be used only for each row on a view.

Workout Section

W7_1A
```
/*
A/B - NO EXCEPTION HANDLE FOR B = 0
*/
SET SERVEROUTPUT ON
SET VERIFY OFF
SET ECHO OFF
```

```
DECLARE
   A  NUMBER(2)  := &A;
   B  NUMBER(2)  := &B;
   C  NUMBER(4,2);
BEGIN
   C := A/B;
   DBMS_OUTPUT.PUT_LINE(A||'/'||B||' = '||C);
END;
/
```

W7_1B

```
/*
 A/B - EXCEPTION HANDLE ZERO_DIVIDE USED
*/
SET SERVEROUTPUT ON
SET VERIFY OFF
SET ECHO OFF
DECLARE
   A  NUMBER(2)  := &A;
   B  NUMBER(2)  := &B;
   C  NUMBER(4,2);
BEGIN
   C := A/B;
   DBMS_OUTPUT.PUT_LINE(A||'/'||B||' = '||C);
EXCEPTION
   WHEN ZERO_DIVIDE THEN

   DBMS_OUTPUT.PUT_LINE('*****************************');
       DBMS_OUTPUT.PUT_LINE(A||'/'||B|| ' is invalid operation -
Divide by 0');
END;
/
```

W7_1C

```
/*
A/B - EXCEPTION HANDLER USED EFFECTIVELY
*/
SET SERVEROUTPUT ON
SET VERIFY OFF
SET ECHO OFF
DECLARE
   A  NUMBER(2);
   B  NUMBER(2);
   C  NUMBER(4,2);
BEGIN
   A := &A;
   B := &B;
   IF B=0 THEN
      DBMS_OUTPUT.PUT_LINE(A||'/'||B||' is invalid operation');
```

```
   ELSE
      C := A/B;
      DBMS_OUTPUT.PUT_LINE(A||'/'||B||' = '||C);
   END IF;
EXCEPTION
   WHEN OTHERS THEN
      DBMS_OUTPUT.PUT_LINE('');
END;
/
```

W7_2 *SQL> @ C:\BOOK\CHAPTER11#\W7_2*
ORA-02292: integrity constraint (TEST.SYS_C005403) violated - child record found

Note that the Error Number mentioned in the program is 2200, which is not correct.

W7_3

```
/*
CREATE TABLE EMP_TRIG (ENAME VARCHAR2(20), SAL NUMBER(8));
*/
CREATE OR REPLACE TRIGGER UPPER_CASE BEFORE INSERT ON EMP_TRIG FOR
EACH ROW
BEGIN
   :NEW.ENAME:=UPPER(:NEW.ENAME);
END;
/
```

W7_4 Write a trigger which will not allow to DELETE records of EMP_BKUP.

```
/*
CREATE TABLE EMP_TRIG (ENAME VARCHAR2(20), SAL NUMBER(8));
*/
CREATE OR REPLACE TRIGGER NO_DELETE BEFORE DELETE ON EMP_BKUP FOR
EACH ROW
BEGIN
   RAISE_APPLICATION_ERROR(-20000,'Delete not allowed');
END;
/
```

W7_5

```
/*
CREATE TABLE EMP_TRIG (ENAME VARCHAR2(20), SAL NUMBER(8));
*/
CREATE OR REPLACE TRIGGER MAX_SAL_CHK BEFORE INSERT OR UPDATE ON
EMP_TRIG FOR EACH ROW
WHEN (NEW.SAL>50001)
BEGIN
   RAISE_APPLICATION_ERROR(-20000,'SAL must be below 50000');
END;
/
```

CHAPTER 8

Short/Objective Type Questions

1. Cursor is basically a SQL memory work area. Implicit cursor is defined by Oracle automatically for the select statement which retrieves exactly one row or any DML statement. For fetching multiple rows, explicit cursor must be defined by the programmer in the PL/SQL program.
3. OPEN, CLOSE and FETCH are the essential explicit cursor commands. OPEN command makes the explicit cursors active. FETCH command retrieves the rows from the active cursor, and the cursor is closed using the CLOSE command.
4. Cursor variables act as a container that can hold different values returned by explicit cursors at run-time.
5. %NOTFOUND attribute is used to exit from a loop. This attribute is usually put inside the loop and when it returns TRUE, the controller exits from the loop.
6. Yes. In this, the values of the row are loaded into the fields of the record.
7. Yes. FOR loop is a shortcut of explicit cursor with limited flexibility. It does not require explicit opening of the cursor, fetching of records and closing the cursor.
8. % ROWTYPE attribute can be used to define implicit record, which can have the same structure as the database record.
9. The current status of a cursor can be determined by checking the %FOUND, %NOTFOUND, %ISOPEN and %ROWCOUNT attributes of that cursor.
10. SQL%ISOPEN is opened whenever the Oracle executes any SQL statement. SQL%ISOPEN always returns the false value as Oracle closes the implicit cursor immediately after the query is executed.
11. This can be done using SQL%NOTFOUND. If it returns TRUE, this implies that the update statement has been successfully executed.
12. The sequence of events on execution of OPEN cursor command includes allocation of memory area, parsing of select statement, loading of records in the memory area and placement of pointer just before the first row of the loaded records.
13. In addition to the constructs of WHILE LOOP and FOR LOOP, the major difference is in the iteration process. In case of WHILE LOOP the number of iterations is not known in advance and is purely based on the condition defined in the beginning of the loop. In case of FOR LOOP, the number of iterations is defined before the execution.
14. No. Counter value is a constant variable and it cannot be reassigned inside a FOR LOOP.
15. Yes. It can be done using EXIT statement inside a FOR LOOP.
16. No.
17. NULL.
18. TRUE.
19. NULL.
20. The value of %NOTFOUND attribute can be TRUE or FALSE after the FETCH statement.

Workout Section

W8_1

```
SQL> @ C:\BOOK\CHAPTER8\W8_1
DECLARE
*
ERROR at line 1:
ORA-01422: exact fetch returns more than requested number of rows
ORA-06512: at line 6
```

W8_2

```
SET SERVEROUTPUT ON
SET VERIFY OFF
DECLARE
    VCNT  NUMBER(4);
BEGIN
    —DML statement
    INSERT INTO PROD VALUES ('P10','CD',20,10);
    DELETE FROM PROD;
    —Check effect of %ROWCOUNT attribute
    DBMS_OUTPUT.PUT_LINE('SQL%ROWCOUNT VALUE');
    VCNT := SQL%ROWCOUNT;
    IF SQL%ROWCOUNT>0 THEN
        DBMS_OUTPUT.PUT_LINE(VCNT);
    ELSE
        DBMS_OUTPUT.PUT_LINE('No Row found');
    END IF;
    ROLLBACK;
END;
/
```

W8_3

```
SQL> @ C:\BOOK\CHAPTER8\W8_3
PRADIP
AASTIK
TUSHAR
ARPAN
ANUMITA
ANUMITA
```

W8_4

```
SQL> @ C:\BOOK\CHAPTER8\W8_4
PRADIP
AASTIK
TUSHAR
ARPAN
ANUMITA
ANUMITA
```

```
ANUMITA
ANUMITA
......
____
infinite loop
```

W8_5

```
SQL> @ C:\BOOK\CHAPTER8\W8_5
PRADIP
DECLARE
*
ERROR at line 1:
ORA-01001: invalid cursor
ORA-06512: at line 7
```

W8_6

```
SQL> @ C:\BOOK\CHAPTER8\W8_6
PRADIP
PRADIP
PRADIP
PRADIP
_
infinite loop
```

W8_7

```
SQL> @ C:\BOOK\CHAPTER8\W8_7
AASTIK
ARPAN
```

W8_8

```
—PL/SQL code using Simple Loop
SET SERVEROUTPUT ON
DECLARE
   VTOTALEARN NUMBER;
   VENAME EMP.ENAME%TYPE;
   VDESG DESGRATE.DESG%TYPE;
   CURSOR EMPEARN IS SELECT E.ENAME,D.DESG
   FROM EMP E,DESGRATE D
   WHERE E.DESG=D.DESG AND D.DESG IN ('ANALYST','DBA');
   BEGIN
   OPEN EMPEARN;
   LOOP
      FETCH EMPEARN INTO VENAME,VDESG;
      EXIT WHEN EMPEARN%NOTFOUND;
      SELECT SUM(D.HRRATE*P.HRWORKED) INTO VTOTALEARN
      FROM EMP E,DESGRATE D,PROJ_DETAIL P
      WHERE E.EMPNO=P.EMPNO AND E.DESG=D.DESG
      AND E.ENAME=VENAME;
      DBMS_OUTPUT.PUT_LINE(VENAME||', '||VDESG||'—earned—
      >'||VTOTALEARN);
```

```
   END LOOP;
  CLOSE EMPEARN;
END;
/

—PL/SQL code using For Loop
SET SERVEROUTPUT ON
DECLARE
   VTOTALEARN NUMBER;
   CURSOR EMPEARN IS SELECT E.ENAME,D.DESG
   FROM EMP E, DESGRATE D
   WHERE E.DESG=D.DESG AND D.DESG IN ('ANALYST','DBA');
BEGIN
   FOR VEMPEARN IN EMPEARN LOOP
   SELECT SUM(D.HRRATE*P.HRWORKED) INTO VTOTALEARN
   FROM EMP E,DESGRATE D,PROJ_DETAIL P
   WHERE E.EMPNO=P.EMPNO AND E.DESG=D.DESG
   AND E.ENAME=VEMPEARN.ENAME;
   DBMS_OUTPUT.PUT_LINE(VEMPEARN.ENAME||', '||VEMPEARN.DESG ||
   '—earned —>'||VTOTALEARN);
   END LOOP;
END;
/
```

W8_9

```
—PL/SQL code using Simple Loop
SET SERVEROUTPUT ON
DECLARE
   VHIGH NUMBER;
   VLOW NUMBER;
   VPROJ NUMBER;
   VHIGHPROJ PROJ.PROJNAME%TYPE;
   VLOWPROJ PROJ.PROJNAME%TYPE;
   VPROJNAME PROJ.PROJNAME%TYPE;
   CURSOR PROJ_CURSOR IS SELECT PROJNAME FROM PROJ;
BEGIN
   OPEN PROJ_CURSOR;
   VHIGH:=0;
   VLOW:=99999;
   LOOP
      FETCH PROJ_CURSOR INTO VPROJNAME;
      EXIT WHEN PROJ_CURSOR%NOTFOUND;
      SELECT SUM(PD.HRWORKED*D.HRRATE) INTO VPROJ
      FROM PROJ P,DESGRATE D,PROJ_DETAIL PD,EMP E
      WHERE P.PROJNO=PD.PROJNO AND E.DESG=D.DESG AND
      E.EMPNO=PD.EMPNO AND P.PROJNAME = VPROJNAME;
      IF VPROJ>VHIGH THEN
         VHIGH:=VPROJ;
```

```
            VHIGHPROJ:=VPROJNAME;
         END IF;
         IF VPROJ<VLOW THEN
            VLOW:=VPROJ;
            VLOWPROJ:=VPROJNAME;
      END IF;
      END LOOP;
      CLOSE PROJ_CURSOR;
      DBMS_OUTPUT.PUT_LINE('Highest value project is
      '||VHIGHPROJ||' with a value of'||VHIGH );
      DBMS_OUTPUT.PUT_LINE('Lowest value project is '||VLOWPROJ||'
      with a value of '||VLOW );
   END;
   /

   —PL/SQL code using For Loop
   SET SERVEROUTPUT ON
   DECLARE
      VHIGH NUMBER;
      VLOW NUMBER;
      VPROJ NUMBER;
      VHIGHPROJ PROJ.PROJNAME%TYPE;
      VLOWPROJ PROJ.PROJNAME%TYPE;
      CURSOR PROJ_CURSOR IS SELECT PROJNAME FROM PROJ;
   BEGIN
      VHIGH:=0;
      VLOW:=99999;
      FOR VREC IN PROJ_CURSOR LOOP
      SELECT SUM(PD.HRWORKED*D.HRRATE) INTO VPROJ
      FROM PROJ P,DESGRATE D,PROJ_DETAIL PD,EMP E
      WHERE P.PROJNO=PD.PROJNO AND E.DESG=D.DESG AND
      E.EMPNO=PD.EMPNO AND P.PROJNAME=VREC.PROJNAME;
      IF VPROJ>VHIGH THEN
      VHIGH:=VPROJ;
      VHIGHPROJ:=VREC.PROJNAME;
      END IF;
      IF VPROJ<VLOW THEN
         VLOW:=VPROJ;
         VLOWPROJ:=VREC.PROJNAME;
      END IF;
      END LOOP;
      DBMS_OUTPUT.PUT_LINE('Highest value project is
      '||VHIGHPROJ||'              with a value of '||VHIGH );
      DBMS OUTPUT.PUT LINE('Lowest value project is '||VLOWPROJ||'
      with a value of '||VLOW );
   END;
   /
```

W8_10

```
SET SERVEROUTPUT ON
DECLARE
   VANALYST NUMBER;
   VPROGRAMMER NUMBER;
BEGIN
   SELECT SUM(PD.HRWORKED*D.HRRATE) INTO VANALYST
   FROM DESGRATE D,PROJ_DETAIL PD,EMP E
   WHERE E.DESG=D.DESG AND E.EMPNO=PD.EMPNO
   AND D.DESG='ANALYST';
   DBMS_OUTPUT.PUT_LINE('Total earnings of ANALYST is
   '||VANALYST);
   SELECT SUM(PD.HRWORKED*D.HRRATE) INTO VPROGRAMMER
   FROM DESGRATE D,PROJ_DETAIL PD,EMP E
   WHERE E.DESG=D.DESG AND E.EMPNO=PD.EMPNO
   AND D.DESG='PROGRAMMER';
   DBMS_OUTPUT.PUT_LINE('Total earnings of PROGRAMMER is '||
   VPROGRAMMER);
END;
/
```

W8_11

```
SET SERVEROUTPUT ON
DECLARE
   VTOTALEARN NUMBER;
   VBONUS NUMBER;
   VENAME EMP.ENAME%TYPE;
   VDESG DESGRATE.DESG%TYPE;
   CURSOR EMPEARN IS SELECT E.ENAME,D.DESG
   FROM EMP E,DESGRATE D WHERE E.DESG=D.DESG;
BEGIN
   OPEN EMPEARN;
   LOOP
   FETCH EMPEARN INTO VENAME,VDESG;
   EXIT WHEN EMPEARN%NOTFOUND;
   SELECT SUM(D.HRRATE*P.HRWORKED) INTO VTOTALEARN
   FROM EMP E,DESGRATE D,PROJ_DETAIL P
   WHERE E.EMPNO=P.EMPNO AND E.DESG=D.DESG
   AND E.ENAME=VENAME;
   IF VDESG='ANALYST' THEN
   VBONUS:=LEAST(VTOTALEARN*0.25,3000);
   DBMS_OUTPUT.PUT_LINE('Bonus given to '||VENAME||',
         '||VDESG||' is '||VBONUS);
   END IF;
   IF VDESG='DBA' THEN
   VBONUS:=LEAST(VTOTALEARN*0.1,5000);
   DBMS_OUTPUT.PUT_LINE('Bonus given to '||VENAME||',
         '||VDESG||' is '||VBONUS);
```

```
    END IF;
    IF VDESG='PROGRAMMER' THEN
    VBONUS:=LEAST(VTOTALEARN*0.15,2500);
    DBMS_OUTPUT.PUT_LINE('Bonus given to '||VENAME||',
    '||VDESG||' is '||VBONUS);
    END IF;
    END LOOP;
    CLOSE EMPEARN;
END;
/

-PL/SQL code using For Loop
SET SERVEROUTPUT ON
DECLARE
    VTOTALEARN NUMBER;
    VBONUS NUMBER;
    CURSOR EMPEARN IS SELECT E.ENAME,D.DESG
    FROM EMP E,DESGRATE D WHERE E.DESG=D.DESG;
BEGIN
    FOR VREC IN EMPEARN LOOP
    -Calculate total earnings based on current VNAME
    SELECT SUM(D.HRRATE*P.HRWORKED) INTO VTOTALEARN
    FROM EMP E,DESGRATE D,PROJ_DETAIL P
    WHERE E.EMPNO=P.EMPNO AND E.DESG=D.DESG
    AND E.ENAME=VREC.ENAME;
    -Apply rule to calculate bonus for ANALYST, DBA AND
          PROGRAMMER
    IF VREC.DESG='ANALYST' THEN
    VBONUS:=LEAST(VTOTALEARN*0.25,3000);
    DBMS_OUTPUT.PUT_LINE('Bonus given to '||VREC.ENAME||',
       '||VREC.DESG||' is '||VBONUS);
    END IF;
    IF VREC.DESG='DBA' THEN
    VBONUS:=LEAST(VTOTALEARN*0.1,5000);
    DBMS_OUTPUT.PUT_LINE('Bonus given to '||VREC.ENAME||',
       '||VREC.DESG||' is '||VBONUS);
    END IF;
    IF VREC.DESG='PROGRAMMER' THEN
    VBONUS:=LEAST(VTOTALEARN*0.15,2500);
    DBMS_OUTPUT.PUT_LINE('Bonus given to '||VREC.ENAME||',
       '||VREC.DESG||' is '||VBONUS);
    END IF;
    END LOOP;
END;
/
```

CHAPTER 9

Short/Objective Type Questions

3. ROWID or WHERE CURRENT OF clause can be used to fetch the current row from a cursor.
4. REF CURSOR cannot be used within a record type.
5. CREATE ANY PROCEDURE allows the schema to create any package, procedure or function within its schema or owned by any other schema. CREATE PROCEDURE allows the schema to create package procedure or function within its schema only.
7. The EXIT WHEN statement terminates the new when the given condition is met. The EXIT statement forces the loop to terminate unconditionally.
8. LONG data type can store up to 2 GB of data, whereas LOB data type can store up to 4 GB of data. A SELECT query will return data in case of LONG data type, whereas it will return the location in case of LOB data type. LOB supports random access and LONG supports only sequential access of objects.
9. BLOB data type is used to store in binary large object such as video image file, whereas CLOB data type is used to store a character such as large object.
10. Yes. Using TO_LOB function.
11. LOB locator and LOB value.
12. Yes.
13. No.
14. It is used by PL/SQL to access and manipulate LOB objects. It does support concurrency control.
15. No. BLOB or BFILE can be seen using Oracle Forms or Oracle Reports.
16. Yes.
17. Yes. Using DBMS_RANDOM package.
18. Using DBMS_LOCK package.
19. View is not effected.
20. Yes.

Workout Section

W9_1

Iteration		Cursor Status		Active Set and Pointer of Cursors		
Outer Loop	**Inner Loop**	**DESG_ CURSOR**	**PROJ_ CURSOR**	**DESG_CURSOR**	*PROJ_CURSOR*	
				DESGRATE	ENAME	PROJNAME
1st	1st	Open	Open	**ANALYST** DBA PROGRAMMER	**ANUP** KAUSHIK	**CODING** DATABASE
	2nd	Open	Open		ANUP **KAUSHIK**	CODING **DATABASE**
	3rd	Open	Exit Close			
2nd	1st	Open	Open	ANALYST **DBA** PROGRAMMER	**ARUP** ARUP ARUP	**DATARECOVERY** DATABASE SW CODING
	2nd	Open	Open	ARUP	**ARUP** ARUP	DATA RECOVERY **DATABASE SW** CODING
	3rd	Open	Open		ARUP ARUP **ARUP**	DATA RECOVERY DATABASE SW **CODING**
	4th	Open	Exit Close			
3rd	1st	Open	Open	ANALYST DBA **PROGRAMMER**	**AMIT** CHANDRA	**CODING** DATABASE WS
	2nd	Open	Open		AMIT **CHANDRA**	CODING **DATABASE WS**
	3rd	Open	Exit Close			
4th		Exit Close				

W9_2

```
CREATE OR REPLACE PROCEDURE PROC_PROJ(MONEYSPENT IN
NUMBER,PROJNAME OUT VARCHAR2) IS
CURSOR CURS_PROJ IS SELECT * FROM PROJ ORDER BY PROJNO;
CURSOR CURS_EMP(VPROJNO PROJ.PROJNO%TYPE) IS
SELECT PJ.HRWORKED,E.DESG FROM PROJ_DETAIL  PJ,EMP E
WHERE PJ.EMPNO=E.EMPNO AND PJ.PROJNO=VPROJNO;
E_PROJ CURS_PROJ%ROWTYPE;
E_EMP  CURS_EMP%ROWTYPE;
VHRRATE  DESGRATE.HRRATE%TYPE;
VPAY NUMBER :=0;
VPROJTOTAL NUMBER;
VPROJNAME VARCHAR2(100):='';
```

```
BEGIN
   OPEN CURS_PROJ;
   LOOP
      FETCH CURS_PROJ INTO E_PROJ;
      EXIT WHEN CURS_PROJ%NOTFOUND;
      OPEN CURS_EMP(E_PROJ.PROJNO);
      VPROJTOTAL:=0;
      LOOP
         FETCH CURS_EMP INTO E_EMP;
         EXIT WHEN CURS_EMP%NOTFOUND;
         SELECT  HRRATE INTO VHRRATE FROM DESGRATE
         WHERE DESG=E_EMP.DESG;
         VPAY:=E_EMP.HRWORKED*VHRRATE;
         VPROJTOTAL:=VPROJTOTAL+VPAY;
      END LOOP;
      CLOSE CURS_EMP;
      IF VPROJTOTAL > MONEYSPENT THEN
         VPROJNAME:=VPROJNAME||'  [ '||E_PROJ.PROJNAME||'] ';
      END IF;
   END LOOP;
   CLOSE CURS_PROJ;
   PROJNAME:=VPROJNAME;
END PROC_PROJ;
/
```

W9_3

```
/*CALLING PROGRAM FOR PROC_PROJ*/
SET SERVEROUTPUT ON
SET VERIFY OFF
DECLARE
   MONEYSPENT NUMBER;
   PROJNAME VARCHAR2(100);
BEGIN
   MONEYSPENT:=&MONEYSPENT;
   PROC_PROJ(MONEYSPENT,PROJNAME);
   DBMS_OUTPUT.PUT_LINE('PROJECTS ABOVE EXPENDITURE ARE :');
   DBMS_OUTPUT.PUT_LINE(PROJNAME);
END;
/
```

W9_4

```
SET SERVEROUTPUT ON
SET VERIFY ON
SET ECHO OFF
DECLARE
   CURSOR ONLYONE_CURSOR IS
   SELECT E.ENAME
   FROM EMP E,
   (SELECT EMPNO, COUNT(*) ONLY1
   FROM PROJ_DETAIL
```

```
    GROUP BY EMPNO) PD
    WHERE E.EMPNO=PD.EMPNO
    AND PD.ONLY1=1;
    CURSOR MORETHANONE_CURSOR IS
    SELECT E.ENAME,PD.MORETHAN1
    FROM EMP E,
    (SELECT EMPNO, COUNT(*) MORETHAN1
    FROM PROJ_DETAIL
    GROUP BY EMPNO) PD
    WHERE E.EMPNO=PD.EMPNO
    AND PD.MORETHAN1>1;
    VENAME EMP.ENAME%TYPE;
    VMORETHAN1 NUMBER(2);
BEGIN
    OPEN ONLYONE_CURSOR;
    DBMS_OUTPUT.PUT_LINE('NAME OF EMPLOYEE WORKED ONLY IN ONE
       PROJECT');
    DBMS_OUTPUT.PUT_LINE('———————————————————————');
    LOOP
       FETCH ONLYONE_CURSOR INTO VENAME;
       EXIT WHEN ONLYONE_CURSOR%NOTFOUND;
       DBMS_OUTPUT.PUT_LINE(VENAME);
    END LOOP;
    CLOSE ONLYONE_CURSOR;
    OPEN MORETHANONE_CURSOR;
    DBMS_OUTPUT.PUT_LINE('NAME OF EMPLOYEE WORKED MORE
    THAN ONE PROJECT');
    DBMS_OUTPUT.PUT_LINE('——————————————————');
    LOOP
       FETCH MORETHANONE_CURSOR INTO VENAME,VMORETHAN1;
       EXIT WHEN MORETHANONE_CURSOR%NOTFOUND;
       DBMS_OUTPUT.PUT_LINE(VENAME||' has worked in
       '||VMORETHAN1||' Projects.');
    END LOOP;
    CLOSE MORETHANONE_CURSOR;
END;
/
```

W9_5

```
SQL> CONNECT BOOK/BOOK@CONNECT_STRING
Connected.
SQL> @ C:\BOOK\CHAPTER9\W9_5
DECLARE
*
ERROR at line 1:
ORA-06550: line 12, column 20:
PLS-00404: cursor 'PROD_CURSOR' must be declared with FOR UPDATE
to use with CURRENT OF
```

27. Yes.

28. LIMIT method

29. LIMIT method.

30. Yes.

Workout Section

W10.1
```
SET SERVEROUTPUT ON
SET ECHO OFF
SET VERIFY OFF
DECLARE
  INPUT_STR VARCHAR2(200):= '&INPUT_STR';
  TYPE DIGIT_STR IS TABLE OF VARCHAR2(10) INDEX BY PLS_INTEGER;
  DS DIGIT_STR;
  ISTR_LEN NUMBER;
  CS VARCHAR2(10);
  NUM_STR VARCHAR2(10);
  INPUT_CHAR VARCHAR2(1);
  CNT NUMBER := 0;
BEGIN
  ISTR_LEN := LENGTH(INPUT_STR)+1;
  FOR I IN 1..ISTR_LEN LOOP
    INPUT_CHAR := SUBSTR(INPUT_STR,I,1);
    IF INPUT_CHAR != ' ' THEN
      CS:=CS||INPUT_CHAR;
    ELSE
      CNT:=CNT+1;
      DS(CNT):=CS;
      CS:='';
    END IF;
END LOOP;
FOR J IN 1..CNT LOOP
  DBMS_OUTPUT.PUT_LINE('DS('||J||')-->'||DS(J));
END LOOP;
END;
/
```

W10.2
```
SET SERVEROUTPUT ON
SET ECHO OFF
SET VERIFY OFF
DECLARE
  TYPE LOOKUP_STR IS TABLE OF NUMBER INDEX BY VARCHAR2(20);
  INPUT_STR VARCHAR2(10):='&INPUT_STR';
LS LOOKUP_STR;
```

27. Yes.

28. LIMIT method.

29. LIMIT method.

30. Yes.

Workout Section

W10_1

```
SET SERVEROUTPUT ON
SET ECHO OFF
SET VERIFY OFF
DECLARE
   INPUT_STR VARCHAR2(200):= '&INPUT_STR';
   TYPE DIGIT_STR IS TABLE OF VARCHAR2(10) INDEX BY PLS_INTEGER;
   DS DIGIT_STR;
   ISTR_LEN NUMBER;
   CS VARCHAR2(10);
   NUM_STR VARCHAR2(10);
   INPUT_CHAR VARCHAR2(1);
   CNT NUMBER := 0;
BEGIN
   ISTR_LEN := LENGTH(INPUT_STR)+1;
   FOR I IN 1..ISTR_LEN LOOP
      INPUT_CHAR := SUBSTR(INPUT_STR,I,1);
      IF INPUT_CHAR != ' ' THEN
      CS:=CS||INPUT_CHAR;
      ELSE
      CNT:=CNT+1;
      DS(CNT):=CS;
      CS:='';
      END IF;
END LOOP;
FOR J IN 1..CNT LOOP
      DBMS_OUTPUT.PUT_LINE('DS('||J||')->'||DS(J));
END LOOP;
END;
/
```

W10_2

```
SET SERVEROUTPUT ON
SET ECHO OFF
SET VERIFY OFF
DECLARE
   TYPE LOOKUP_STR IS TABLE OF NUMBER INDEX BY VARCHAR2(20);
   INPUT_STR VARCHAR2(10):='&INPUT_STR';
LS LOOKUP_STR;
```

```
BEGIN
    LS('ZERO')   :=0;
    LS('ONE')    :=1;
    LS('TWO')    :=2;
    LS('THREE')  :=3;
    LS('FOUR')   :=4;
    LS('FIVE')   :=5;
    LS('SIX')    :=6;
    LS('SEVEN')  :=7;
    LS('EIGHT')  :=8;
    LS('NINE')   :=9;
    DBMS_OUTPUT.PUT_LINE(LS(INPUT_STR));
END;
/
```

W10_3

```
SET SERVEROUTPUT ON
SET ECHO OFF
SET VERIFY OFF
DECLARE
    TYPE LOOKUP_STR IS TABLE OF NUMBER INDEX BY VARCHAR2(10);
    LS LOOKUP_STR;
    INPUT_STR VARCHAR2(200):= '&INPUT_STR';
    TYPE DIGIT_STR IS TABLE OF VARCHAR2(10) INDEX BY PLS_INTEGER;
    DS DIGIT_STR;
    ISTR_LEN NUMBER;
    CS VARCHAR2(10);
    NUM_STR VARCHAR2(10);
    INPUT_CHAR VARCHAR2(1);
    CNT NUMBER := 0;
BEGIN
    LS('ZERO')      :=0;
    LS('ONE')       :=1;
    LS('TWO')       :=2;
    LS('THREE')     :=3;
    LS('FOUR')      :=4;
    LS('FIVE')      :=5;
    LS('SIX')       :=6;
    LS('SEVEN')     :=7;
    LS('EIGHT')     :=8;
    LS('NINE')      :=9;
    ISTR_LEN := LENGTH(INPUT_STR)+1;
    FOR I IN 1..ISTR_LEN LOOP
    INPUT_CHAR := upper(SUBSTR(INPUT_STR,I,1));
    IF INPUT_CHAR != ' ' THEN
       CS:=CS||INPUT_CHAR;
```

```
SQL> /
Enter value for input_str: ZERO   ON   TWO FIVE
Wrong entry -> ON - Ignored
ZERO   ON   TWO FIVE ->025
SQL> /
Enter value for input_str: TEN NINE    FIV SEVEN
Wrong entry -> TEN - Ignored
Wrong entry -> FIV - Ignored
TEN NINE    FIV    SEVEN ->97

SQL> /
Enter value for input_str: THREE SIX ZER SEN SEVEN TEN SIX
Wrong entry -> ZER - Ignored
Wrong entry -> SEN - Ignored
Wrong entry -> TEN - Ignored
THREE SIX ZER SEN SEVEN TEN SIX ->3676

SQL> /
Enter value for input_str: FIVE        ZERO NINE
FIVE        ZERO NINE ->509

SQL> /
Enter value for input_str: FOUR SX THREE
Wrong entry -> SX - Ignored
FOUR SX THREE ->43

SQL> /
Enter value for input_str: SEVEN NNE      SEVN   FOUR FIVE
Wrong entry -> NNE - Ignored
Wrong entry -> SEVN - Ignored
SEVEN NNE      SEVN    FOUR FIVE ->745

SQL> /
Enter value for input_str: THRE FIVE     THREE
Wrong entry -> THRE - Ignored
THRE FIVE     THREE ->53
SQL> /
Enter value for input_str: ON  TW  FIVE   SEVEN   TEN  ZERO IVE
Wrong entry -> ON - Ignored
Wrong entry -> TW - Ignored
Wrong entry -> TEN - Ignored
Wrong entry -> IVE - Ignored
ON  TW  FIVE   SEVEN   TEN  ZERO IVE ->570
```

W10.7
```
SQL> @ C:/BOOK/CHAPTER12#/W10_7
Input truncated to 1 characters
ODD_COUNT = 5
DECLARE
*
```

```
SQL> /
Enter value for input_str: ZERO   ON    TWO FIVE
Wrong entry -> ON - Ignored
ZERO   ON    TWO FIVE ->025
SQL> /
Enter value for input_str: TEN NINE     FIV SEVEN
Wrong entry -> TEN - Ignored
Wrong entry -> FIV - Ignored
TEN NINE     FIV     SEVEN  ->97

SQL> /
Enter value for input_str: THREE SIX ZER SEN SEVEN TEN SIX
Wrong entry -> ZER - Ignored
Wrong entry -> SEN - Ignored
Wrong entry -> TEN - Ignored
THREE SIX ZER SEN SEVEN TEN SIX ->3676

SQL> /
Enter value for input_str: FIVE        ZERO NINE
FIVE       ZERO NINE ->509

SQL> /
Enter value for input_str: FOUR SX THREE
Wrong entry -> SX - Ignored
FOUR SX THREE  ->43

SQL> /
Enter value for input_str: SEVEN NNE      SEVN   FOUR FIVE
Wrong entry -> NNE - Ignored
Wrong entry -> SEVN - Ignored
SEVEN NNE     SEVN   FOUR FIVE ->745

SQL> /
Enter value for input_str: THRE FIVE     THREE
Wrong entry -> THRE - Ignored
THRE FIVE    THREE  ->53
SQL> /
Enter value for input_str: ON  TW  FIVE   SEVEN   TEN  ZERO IVE
Wrong entry -> ON - Ignored
Wrong entry -> TW - Ignored
Wrong entry -> TEN - Ignored
Wrong entry -> IVE - Ignored
ON  TW  FIVE   SEVEN   TEN  ZERO IVE ->570
```

W10_7

```
SQL> @ C:\BOOK\CHAPTER12#\W10_7
Input truncated to 1 characters
ODD.COUNT = 5
DECLARE
*
```

```
ERROR at line 1:
ORA-06532: Subscript outside of limit
ORA-06512: at line 6
```

W10_8
```
SQL> @ C:\BOOK\CHAPTER12#\W10_8
Input truncated to 1 characters
EVEN.COUNT BEFORE DELETE = 7
EVEN.COUNT AFTER EVEN.DELETE(3) = 6
EVEN.COUNT AFTER EVEN.DELETE(5,6) = 4
1 -> 2
2 -> 4
3 DOES NOT EXISTS
4 -> 8
5 DOES NOT EXISTS
6 DOES NOT EXISTS
7 -> 14
```

CHAPTER 11

Short/Objective Type Questions

12. No. Only dependent objects are invalidated.

13. It means that the schema in turn can grant the same privilege to any other schema.

16. This is a SQL file which contains the script to create packages in the database.

17. No.

18. To execute a procedure owned by another user, the user should be granted EXECUTE ANY PROCEDURE or EXECUTE privilege on the procedure.

19. It ensures that no exception goes unhandled.

21. The primary difference between database trigger and stored procedure is: Trigger is invoked implicitly and stored procedure is invoked explicitly. Also COMMIT, ROLLBACK and SAVEPOINT are not allowed inside a trigger, however, the same may be included in a stored procedure.

22. USER_ERRORS store the errors that occur in a trigger during the compilation.

23. The SQLCODE function returns the Oracle error number, which can be passed to the SQLERRM function to associate the message with the error number. The former returns the value, whereas the later returns the user-defined exception message.

24. INVALID_CURSOR exception is raised whenever a program attempts to perform an illegal operation.

25. Performance of a trigger can be improved by providing explicit column names with the UPDATE clause inside the trigger.

26. No, there is nothing like view mutating.

27. Yes.

28. VARRAY.

29. Constructor is used to initialize NESTED TABLES and VAARAYs. No constructor is required to initialize an index by table. Index by table is initialized automatically.

30. Yes. SQL session information can be accessed using DBMS_SESSION package.

Workout Section

W11_1A

```
CREATE OR REPLACE TYPE CHILD_V1 AS OBJECT
(
   CHILD_CODE INTEGER,
   CHILD_FIRSTNAME VARCHAR2(10),
   CHILD_LASTNAME VARCHAR2(10),
   CHILD_AGE INTEGER,
   MEMBER FUNCTION FULL_NAME RETURN VARCHAR2,
   MEMBER PROCEDURE PRINT_CHILD
);
/
```

W11_1B

```
CREATE OR REPLACE TYPE BODY CHILD_V1
AS
MEMBER FUNCTION FULL_NAME RETURN VARCHAR2
IS
BEGIN
   RETURN CHILD_FIRSTNAME || ' ' || CHILD_LASTNAME;
END;
MEMBER PROCEDURE PRINT_CHILD
IS
BEGIN
   DBMS_OUTPUT.PUT_LINE('CHILD CODE : '||CHILD_CODE);
   DBMS_OUTPUT.PUT_LINE('FIRST NAME : '||CHILD_FIRSTNAME);
   DBMS_OUTPUT.PUT_LINE('LAST NAME : '||CHILD_LASTNAME);
   DBMS_OUTPUT.PUT_LINE('AGE : '||CHILD_AGE);
   DBMS_OUTPUT.PUT_LINE('FULL NAME : '||FULL_NAME);
END;
END;
/
```

W11_2 Option A

```
SQL> DROP TYPE FAMILY_V3;
DROP TYPE FAMILY_V3
ORA-02303: cannot drop or replace a type with type or table
dependents

SQL> DROP TYPE CHILD_V2;
```

```
DROP TYPE CHILD_V2
ORA-02303: cannot drop or replace a type with type or table
dependents
```

Option B

```
SQL> DROP TYPE CHILD_V2;
DROP TYPE CHILD_V2
ORA-02303: cannot drop or replace a type with type or table
dependents

SQL> DROP TYPE FAMILY_V3;
DROP TYPE FAMILY_V3
ORA-02303: cannot drop or replace a type with type or table
dependents

SQL> SELECT COUNT(*) FROM FAMILY_NESTED;
COUNT(*)
5
```

Option C

```
SQL> SELECT COUNT(*) FROM FAMILY_NESTED;
SQL> DROP TABLE FAMILY_NESTED;
Table dropped.

SQL> DROP TYPE FAMILY_V3;
Type dropped.

SQL> DROP TYPE CHILD_V2;
Type dropped.
SQL> SELECT COUNT(*) FROM FAMILY_NESTED;
SELECT COUNT(*) FROM FAMILY_NESTED
ORA-00942: table or view does not exist
```

W11 3A

```
CREATE TABLE EMP_INDEX
(EMPID NUMBER(5), NAME VARCHAR2(10), AGE NUMBER(3));
CREATE SEQUENCE EMP_SEQ INCREMENT BY 1 START WITH 1;

CREATE OR REPLACE PROCEDURE CREATE_EMP_INDEX
(EMPID IN OUT NUMBER,
NAME IN VARCHAR2,
AGE IN VARCHAR2) AS
BEGIN
SELECT EMP_SEQ.NEXTVAL INTO EMPID FROM DUAL;
INSERT INTO EMP_INDEX VALUES (EMPID,NAME, AGE);
END;
/
```

W11_3B
```
SET ECHO OFF
SET VERIFY OFF
SET SERVEROUTPUT ON
DECLARE
    PLSQL_BLOCK VARCHAR2(1000);
    VEMPID NUMBER(4);
    VNAME VARCHAR2(20) := '&NAME';
    VAGE NUMBER(4) := &AGE;
BEGIN
    PLSQL_BLOCK := 'BEGIN CREATE_EMP_INDEX(:1, :2, :3); END;';
    EXECUTE IMMEDIATE PLSQL_BLOCK USING IN OUT VEMPID,
    VNAME, VAGE;
END;
/
```

CHAPTER 12

Short/Objective Type Questions

6. On upgradation from Oracle 10g to Oracle 11g, SQL Plan Management collects the SQL Plans and stores them as SQL Plan baseline. We can switch to next higher version by setting the OPTIMIZER_FEATURES_ENABLE to 11.1 to exploit new capabilities of 11g without compromising SQL performance. The SQL Plan Management is used to preserve SQL execution plans to prevent performance deterioration when the database undergoes major changes such as database upgrade. SQL Plan management preserves the database performance under the following types of system changes:
   - Database upgrades
   - New optimizer Version
   - Changes in the Optimizer parameters
   - Changes in the system settings
   - Changes in schema and metadata definitions
   - Deployment of a new application module
7. Histograms are buckets to represent distribution of data in a column. There are two types of histograms: Height-based histograms and Frequency-based histogram.
8. The EXPLAIN PLAN facility helps to tune the SQL by allowing us to see the execution plan which is selected by the Oracle optimizer. It is great experiment too as it immediately allows us know how the query will perform with change in the code. The output of the EXPLAIN PLAN tool goes into a table called PLAN_TABLE, where it can be queried to determine the execution plan statements. The EXPLAIN PLAN tool indicates whether the optimizer is using an index. It also tells us the order in which tables are being used and helps us understand the query performance.
9. The AUTOTRACE facility enables you to produce EXPLAIN PLANs automatically when we execute a SQL statement. We automatically have the privilege to use the AUTOTRACE facility when we log in as SYS and SYSTEM.

11. Query optimization is the process of choosing the most efficient execution plan to achieve the result with the least resource usage.

12. Parse, Optimize and Execute.

13. Parse checks syntax and semantics to generate parse tree. Optimize chooses the best access method to retrieve data from the table. In case of Execute, queries generated by the above phases are executed in the execution phase.

14. In query rewrite phase, the parse tree is converted into an abstract logical query plan. The various nodes and branches of the parse tree are replaced by operators of the relational algebra.

15. The logical query is transformed into the physical query plan. The optimizer chooses the most feasible algorithm on the cost of resources such as I/O, memory and CPU.

16. Cost-based Optimizer works by gathering statistics on tables and indexes, the order of tables and columns in the SQL statements, available indexes and any user supplied access hints to pick the most efficient way to access them.

17. By default, the database automatically collects the necessary optimizer statistics using GATHER_STATS_JOB

18. ALL_ROWS, ALL_ROWS, FIRST_ROWS_n and FIRST_ROWS

19. Oracle usually never executes query in its original form. If the Cost-based Optimizer determines that a different SQL formulation will achieve the same result more efficiently, it transforms the statement before executing it. Some common transformations are as follows:

- Transform IN into OR statements
- Transforms OR into UNION or UNION ALL statements
- Transforms non-correlated nested select statements into more efficient joins
- Transforms outer joins into more efficient inner joins
- Transforms complex subqueries into joins and semi-joins

20. Nested loop join, Hash join and Sort merge join.

21. The optimizer joins tables in such a way that the driving table eliminates the largest number of rows.

22. The adaptive search strategy is to limit the time it takes to find the best execution plan. An adaptive search strategy means that the time taken for optimization is always a small percentage of the total time that is taken for execution of query itself.

23. Oracle database (10g onwards) can automatically collect and provide statistics to the optimizer. This is known as Automatic Optimizer Statistics. We can manually provide statistics to the optimizer using DBMS_STATS package.

24. External tables or bulk load.

25. GATHER_DATABASE_STATISTICS

26. GATHER_SCHEMA_STATISTICS

27. GATHER_TABLE_STATS

28. GATHER_INDEX_STATISTICS

29. Check should be performed to make sure that the execution plan shows only the correct indexes that are being used. If huge data is there in the table, histogram is used to provide Oracle with a more accurate representation of the data distribution in the table. The Cost-based Optimizer assumes a uniform distribution of column data. In case Oracle still refuses to use the index, it is forcibly made to use index hint.

30. We can use CASE statement in this case as it enables to compute multiple aggregates from the table with just a read from the database.

31. Subqueries work better when IN clause is used rather than EXISTS. Oracle recommends using the IN clause if the subquery has the selective WHERE clause. But if the parent query contains the selective WHERE clause, it is advisable to use EXISTS rather than IN. It is always good to use WHERE clause instead of HAVING. The WHERE clause restricts the number of rows retrieved at the result set, whereas HAVING forces the retrieval of a lot more rows than necessary.

32. The Cost-based Optimizer evaluates various statistics and come out with choosing the most optimal execution plan. The optimizer works based on certain rules. Hints can be provided to override the Cost-based Optimizer's execution plan. Hints can alter the join method, join order or access path. These are also provided to parallelize the SQL statement operation.

33. ALL_ROWS, FIRST_ROWS (N), FULL, ORDERED, INDEX and INDEX_FFS

34. Bitmap Join Indexes (BJIs) restore the results of a join between two tables in an index and thus do away with the need for an expensive run-time join operations. BJIs are specially designed for data warehouse star schemas, but any application can use them as long as there is a primary key/foreign key relationship between the two tables. The table having the primary key is called the dimension table and the table referencing this table, that is, the table having the foreign key, is called the fact table.

35. The Cost-based Optimizer does not use the same execution strategy. It varies due to change in version or initialization of parameters. Oracle's plan stability features are used to ensure that the execution plan remains stable regardless of any changes in the database environment. The plan stability feature uses outlines to preserve the current execution plans, even if the statistics and the optimizer mode are changed. Outlines are useful for migrating from one version of Oracle to another. To implement plan stability, we require to make the following initialization parameters consistent in all environments.

- QUERY_REWRITE_ENABLE
- STAR_TRANSFORMATION_ENABLE
- OPTIMIZER_FEATURES_ENABLE

Workout Section

Do it yourself.

CHAPTER 13

Short/Objective Type Questions

1. Refer to Section 13.2
2. Refer to Section 13.2
3. Refer to Section 13.3
4. Refer to Section 13.3
5. Refer to Section 13.4
6. Refer to Section 13.5
7. Refer to Section 13.6
8. Refer to Section 13.6
9. Refer to Section 13.5
10. Refer to Section 13.2
11. (a), (b), (c)
12. (c)
13. (b)
14. (b)
15. (c)
16. (b)
17. (b), (c)
18. (b)
19. (a), (d)
20. (a), (b), (d)

Workout Section

W13_1 4, 8, 12 → BUCKET A
1, 5, 9 → BUCKET B
2, 6, 10 → BUCKET C
3, 7, 11 → BUCKET D
Yes. As 3 pages of all the buckets are filled.

W13_2 Architecture used	Three-tier	Two-tier	Three-tier	Two-tier

CHAPTER 14

Short/Objective Type Questions

1. Refer to Section 14.2
2. Refer to Section 14.3

3. Refer to Section 14.4
4. Refer to Section 14.4
5. Refer to Section 14.5
6. Refer to Section 14.4
7. Refer to Section 14.4
8. Refer to Section 14.5
9. (a), (b), (c)
10. (a), (b), (c)
11. (a), (c)
12. (b)
13. (b), (c), (d)
14. (a), (b)
15. (a), (b), (c)
16. (a)
17. (b), (d)
18. (a), (d)
19. (c)
20. Do it yourself

Workout Section

W14_1 (a) $T_1 \rightarrow T_2$ V1 = 1100
$T_2 \rightarrow T_1$ V1 = 990
(b) Value of V1 after the schedule = 1100
(c) Do it yourself

CHAPTER 15

Short/Objective Type Questions

1. (d)
2. (b)
3. Heterogeneous
4. A staging area in a data warehouse is an intermediate stage where data is placed before it is populated into the data warehouse database. This area is also used to carry out some of the Extract–Transform–Load (ETL) processes.
5. (e)
6. (a)
7. (a)

8. A data mart is a subset of a data warehouse that deals with single subject area of data. It usually contains the summarized data. Data Mart is organized in such a way that it provides quick access.

9. (b)

10. (b)

Workout Solution

W15_1 See Section 15.4.

W15_2 See Section 15.5.

W15_3 A schema in a dimensional modeling consists of fact and dimension tables. Star schema is in denormalized form, that is, it allows redundancies. In snowflake schema, one or more dimensions are normalized. Fact constellation allows combining two or more schemas through a shared dimension.

Also see Section 15.6.

W15_4 Confirmed Dimension.

A dimensional table which can be shared between multiple data marts and multiple facts is called a confirmed dimension.

Characteristics of Confirmed Dimensions:

- Should have the same number of columns, data types and size
- All columns should have the same label
- Data should be in the same granular level

Advantages:

- Independent data marts become part of a fully integrated data warehouse.
- The development time for a data warehouse is reduced because each dimension is analyzed, designed and created only once.
- Conformed dimensions deliver a consistent view of a business, allowing you to drill from one area of the business to another.

W15_5 A hybrid of both type 1 and type 2 is suitable for such scenarios, that is Hybrid SCDs of both type 1 and type 2. Type 2 captures the historical data and allows to track changes, whereas type 1 is appropriate for the columns which do not care even if the data changes.

CHAPTER 16

Short/Objective Type Questions

1. Cubes are logical representation of multidimensional data. Each axis corresponds to one dimension.

2. Cube

3. False

4. True
5. (a)
6. OLTP systems are characterized by online transactions that facilitate INSERT, UPDATE and DELETE operations, whereas OLAP systems are characterized to support ad hoc queries and provide faster response as they store aggregated data based on multidimensional schema.
7. True
8. Slicing, Dicing, Roll-up, Drill-down, Drill-across, Drill-within, Pivoting.
9. Hierarchy in a dimension table helps in performing roll-up or drill-down operations. For instance, the roll-up operation performs aggregation over a cube either by climbing up in a dimension hierarchy or by one or more dimension reductions.
10. External table concept is useful to read data from flat files, which is very much similar to reading a data from a relational table. These flat files are external to the database and make it convenient to load the data in the flat files into relational tables.

Workouts Section

W16_1 OLAP is the short name for Online Analytical Processing. It supports retrieving the information efficiently from data warehouse databases. So, OLAP comprises a set of tools and algorithms that allow efficiently querying large amounts of data stored in the data warehouse in the form of multidimensional databases.

In multidimensional modeling, the data warehouse schema contains fact and dimensional tables. An OLAP is built over a multidimensional database where the data is organized as a set of dimensions and fact tables. In this multidimensional model, data can be perceived as a data cube, where each axis corresponds to each dimension table and cell that is intersection of multiple dimensions contains measures of interest (measures from fact table). OLAP dimensions are further organized in hierarchies that support the data aggregation process and carry out Roll-up and Drill-down OLAP operations.

In OLAP, data are organized as a set of dimensions and fact tables.

W16_2 See Section 16.2.1.

W16_3 The main difference between ROLAP and MOALP is the trade-off between speed and flexibility. MOLAP uses array kind of data structures to store the data. It contains a pre-calculated data (i.e., cubes) and hence provides quick response to the data warehouse queries. However, these OALPs have limited scalability.

ROLAP does not use pre-calculated data, rather it responds to a query by accessing the relational database tables. The advantage of ROLAP is that it can respond to a query that drill down to the lowest level of details in the database. However, ROLAP tools have slow response compared to MOLAP.

W16_4 Views in DBMs are build using SQL statements which join single or multiple tables and allow to use the data. However, these views are logical views and do not have the data themselves but point to the data of base tables. Thus, these views do not require (i) any additional storage and (ii) maintenance of views.

Materialized view in Data Warehouses contain the data (materialized) itself. These materialized views are useful for easier/faster access to the data. However, materialized views occupy space to store its data. The two issues that should be handled are materialized view selection and materialized view maintenance.

W16_5 See Section 16.4.

CHAPTER 17

Short/Objective Type Questions

1. (b)
2. Data Mining is the process of extracting hidden information from large databases.
3. (a)
4. Market Basket Analysis
5. Association Rule Mining
6. Support and Confidence are two measures that are used to generate association rules.
7. (d)
8. Clustering
9. Regression is a data mining technique that predicts a number. This technique fits an equation to a given data set.
   Linear regression technique uses straight line equation to fit a line for a given data point. Multiple regression allows more than one variable as input. Non-linear regression allows fitting complex models such as quadratic equation.
10. (b)

Workout Section

W17_1 Descriptive data mining tasks observe the data, analyze the data for patterns/events and provide insights into how to approach the future. These tasks describe a data set in a more concise form and presents interesting patterns from the data without considering any predefined target. Examples of descriptive data mining techniques are association rule mining, Clustering and Summarization.

Predictive data mining tasks use the data to find the potential outcome of an attribute/event in future. Usually, these tasks predict an (dependent) attribute value based on other (independent) attribute values. Examples of predictive data mining techniques are Classification and Regression.

Predictive and descriptive data mining techniques complement each other. Predictive techniques determine the goals for descriptive modeling. On the other hand, the results of descriptive techniques guide the predictive modeling. It is interesting to note this between descriptive and predictive techniques.

Also see Section 17.4.

W17_2 See Section 17.2.

W17_3 See Section 17.3.

W17_4 The measures to evaluate the performance of classification methods are: Confusion Matrix, Accuracy, F-measure, RoC curve and Cross-validation.

See Section 17.4.2.

W17_5 Support (A) = 4 (80%)

Support (E) = 2 (40%)

Support (A, C) = 3 (60%)

Support (B, D, E) = 1 (20%)

Confidence (A $\rightarrow$ C) = Support (A, C)/Support (A) = (3/4) $\times$ 100 = 75%

Confidence (A, D $\rightarrow$ B, E) = Support (A, B, D, E)/Support (A, D) = (1/3) $\times$ 100 = 33%

CHAPTER 18

Short/Objective Type Questions

1. Self-join and Pruning
2. (b)
3. (c)
4. (b)
5. Training, Testing
6. Naïve Bayes classifier is a probabilistic classifier and it assumes that there is no relationship exists among independent attributes.
7. Entropy
8. (a)
9. Chi-square (χ^2)
10. In a classification problem, the class attribute, usually the last attribute in the training table, is a dependent attribute.

Workout Section

W18_1 Given minimum support is 50%, that is, the minimum support count is 3.

Step 1:

Candidate ItemSet C_1	
Itemset	Support
{A}	4
{B}	3
{C}	4
{D}	4
{E}	2

Frequent ItemSet F_1	
Itemset	Support
{A}	4
{B}	3
{C}	4
{D}	4

Step 2:

Candidate ItemSet C_2	
Itemset	Support
{A, B}	3
{A, C}	3
{A, D}	3
{B, C}	2
{B, D}	2
{C, D}	3

Frequent ItemSet F_2	
Itemset	Support
{A, B}	3
{A, C}	3
{A, D}	3
{C, D}	3

Step 3:

Candidate ItemSet C_2	
Itemset	Support
{A, C, D}	2

Here, the pruning step eliminates {A, B, C} and {A, B, D} as candidate 3-itemsets. This is because {B, C}, which is the subset of {A, B, C}, is not frequent itemset in F_2. Similarly, {B, D}, which is a subset of {A, B, D}, is infrequent itemset.

The 3-itemset does not have minimum support, and hence there is no 3-itemset that is frequent.

So, the frequent itemsets for the given dataset are {F_1 U F_2 }, that is, {A}. {B}, {C}, {D}, {A, B}, {A, C}, {A, D} and {C, D}.

W18_2 See Section 18.4.2.

W18_3 See Section 18.4.3.

W18_4 Hierarchical clustering is a process of hierarchical decomposition of data, whereas portioning clustering is a process of portioning the data. The differences are as follows:

Hierarchical clustering	Partitioning clustering
Sequential partitioning process	Iterative portioning process
Results into a hierarchical nested cluster structures	Results into mutually exclusive cluster structures
Once membership of an object is fixed at any stage, it cannot be modified in the later stages	Membership of an object can change during next iterations
Does not require prior knowledge on the number of clusters, but termination criteria are required to obtain the desired number of clusters	The number of clusters must be specified in advance

W18_5 The two approaches of hierarchical clustering are agglomerative and divisive clustering methods:

1. *Agglomerative clustering:* Initially, all objects in a data set are clusters with one element in each cluster. Then two nearest clusters are merged based on the distance/similarity measure. This merging process continues till a termination condition is reached or the desired number of clusters formed.
2. *Divisive clustering:* Initially, all objects in a data set are in one cluster. Then the cluster is divided into two smaller clusters. The division of each cluster is repeated till a termination condition is reached or the desired number of clusters formed.

The hierarchical clustering process is shown visually in the form of a tree-like structure known as dendrogram.

Index